MARKETING GOVERNMENT AND SOCIAL SERVICES

WILEY SERIES ON MARKETING MANAGEMENT

Series Editor: FREDERICK E. WEBSTER, Jr.
The Amos Tuck School
of Business Administration
Dartmouth College

JEAN-MARIE CHOFFRAY and GARY LILIEN, *Market Planning for New Industrial Products*
EUGENE J. CAFARELLI, *Developing New Products and Repositioning Mature Brands: A Risk-Reduction System that Produces Investment Alternatives*
GARY M. GRIKSCHEIT, HAROLD C. CASH, and W.J.E. CRISSY, *Handbook of Selling: Psychological, Managerial, and Marketing Basis*
MELVIN PRINCE, *Consumer Research for Management Decisions*
WILLIAM H. DAVIDSON, *Global Strategic Management*
FREDERICK E. WEBSTER, Jr., *Field Sales Management*
DAN AILLONI-CHARAS, *Promotion: A Guide to Effective Promotional Planning, Strategies, and Executions*
DAVID A. AAKER, *Developing Business Strategies*
FREDERICK E. WEBSTER, Jr., *Industrial Marketing Strategy*, Second Edition
JOHN M. KEIL, *The Creative Mystique: How to Manage It, Nurture It, and Make It Pay*
RUSSELL I. HALEY, *Developing Effective Communications Strategies: A Benefit Segmentation Approach*
JOHN F. MAGEE, WILLIAM C. COPACINO, and DONALD B. ROSENFIELD, *Modern Logistics Management: Integrating Marketing, Manufacturing, and Physical Distribution*
JOHN L. CROMPTON and CHARLES W. LAMB, Jr., *Marketing Government and Social Services*

Marketing Government and Social Services

JOHN L. CROMPTON
CHARLES W. LAMB, Jr.

JOHN WILEY & SONS
New York • Chichester • Brisbane • Toronto • Singapore

Library of Congress Cataloging in Publication Data:

Crompton, John L.
Marketing government and social services.

(Wiley series on marketing management,)
ISSN 0275-875X)
Includes index.
1. Marketing—Management. 2. Government publicity. 3. Social service—Marketing.
I. Lamb, Charles W. II. Title. III. Series.

HF5415.13.L32 1986 658.8 85-12459
ISBN 0-471-09365-3

Printed in the United States of America

10 9 8 7 6 5 4 3 2

To Liz and Sharon

Preface

This is the first comprehensive book to focus exclusively upon the marketing activities performed by government and social service agencies. Its purpose is to demonstrate how the concepts and techniques of marketing relate to the delivery of government and social services.

The authors brought complementary backgrounds and perspectives to the preparation of this book. John Crompton brought knowledge of government and social service agencies gleaned from 20 years of work experience and academic interest in that arena. Charles Lamb is the M.J. Neeley Professor of Marketing at Texas Christian University. His expertise in marketing for non-profit organizations is widely recognized.

It is normal practice when two people collaborate on a book for them to divide the work so that each takes primary responsibility for a predetermined number of chapters. Because of the different perspectives of its authors, this book did not develop in that way. Each chapter was a source of creative conflict and went through a series of iterations. The debate, argument, and long gestation period facilitated the development of insight. As a result, the five-year period during which the book was written has been a time of intellectual adventure and an exciting learning experience for both of us.

In the past seven years, more than 10,000 practitioners have participated in over 100 workshops which the authors have conducted either independently or together. We are pleased with whatever benefit they may have derived from exposure to the developing ideas for this book, but we are most grateful to them for their feedback and input. They have been tolerant of our occasional naivete, forthright in their criticism, and generous in sharing their ideas and illustrations. Hence the content of this book has been repeatedly revised and thoroughly tested. We are convinced that its conceptual foundations are well-rooted, but believe its major contribution is its pragmatic approach. The book is intended to be primarily a "hands-on" reference guide for administrators. It has also been well-received by students in our university classes who have also provided us with useful feedback.

Given the eclectic nature of government and social services, it is not possible to tailor each example to the reader's particular type of agency. The examples should be regarded as being generic, rather than being illustrative only of the service and situation cited. The reader has to make the transition from cited illustrations to the context of his or her own agency.

We anticipate managers will receive three major benefits from reading this book:

1. *A general orientation to the field of marketing.* Few public sector managers have received any formal training in marketing because marketing's relevance to government and social service agencies has been recognized only recently.
2. *New ideas for solving problems.* The marketing perspective used here is likely to be new to many. Management in many public services has historically been inbred. The majority of police, recreation, and library managers, for example, have spent their entire working lives in a single area. Such narrow exposure restricts a manager from sharing the experience of his or her peers in other service areas who may have faced similar situations. In this "hands-on" book, concepts are explained; but the emphasis is on application of these concepts in a large number of practical illustrations and case studies from a variety of services.
3. *A frame of reference within which to view all service delivery decisions.* Marketing doesn't consist of isolated activities, but rather of orchestrated efforts that integrate a number of related activities. Managers will recognize seemingly independent decisions are related when seen in the context of the total set of marketing activities.

Often the biggest obstacle to introducing marketing into an agency is the word "marketing" itself, which can carry negative connotations associated with hucksterism. Though a gross misrepresentation, the semantic problem cannot be ignored. We suggest that ideas from the book be introduced gradually without any reference to marketing. In this way techniques can be implemented quickly without resistance from personnel who would react negatively or feel overwhelmed by "marketing." Once the innovations are successful, you can announce that marketing is in fact being practiced and practiced well.

The cost of government in the United States has become the biggest single item in the family budget—more than housing, food, or health care. The consistent increase in the size of government between 1949 and 1982 is shown in Figure 1. Together federal, state, and local governments collect revenues that amount to more than one-third of the U.S. gross national product and employ nearly one out of five nonagricultural civilian workers. As the size of government has increased, so has the public's criticism of its efficiency, effectiveness, and equity. Marketing is not a panacea for all the financial, service delivery, and accountability problems confronting agencies, but it can definitely help alleviate those problems.

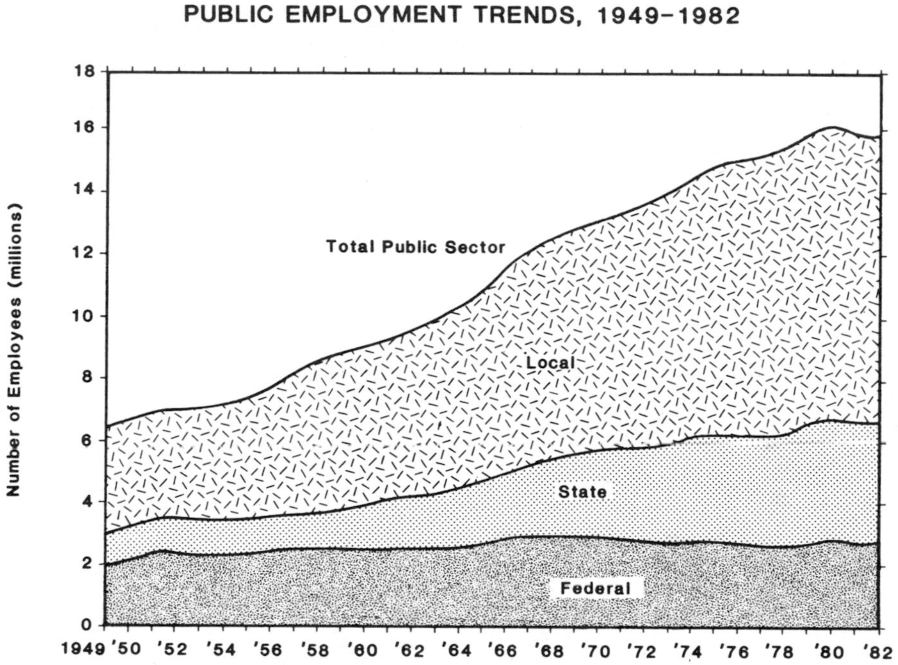

Figure 1. Public Employment Trends, 1949–1982. (*Source:* Bureau of the Census, U.S. Department of Commerce. Government Employment G.E. 82. No. 1 Public Employment.)

This book is directed to managers at all levels of government with responsibility for all sizes of jurisdictions. Government and social services are not part of a homogeneous sector. Instead the sector delivers a myriad of diverse services. Although there are differences in the environments within which each manager operates, the principles discussed in this book are broadly applicable across the public sector spectrum. Most agencies identify the client groups whom they serve; develop and eliminate services; decide upon the appropriate prices to charge; schedule and locate their programs and services at several locations; and promote or communicate their availability through brochures, announcements, or public contact. The large number of application examples from many different service areas will assist readers in making the transition from principle to application in their own field.

JOHN L. CROMPTON
CHARLES W. LAMB

College Station, Texas
Fort Worth, Texas
December 1985

Acknowledgments

Many academic and professional colleagues, friends, and predecessors have directly and indirectly contributed to the development of this book. While it is not possible to recognize most of the contributions, we would like to acknowledge the comments, criticisms, suggestions, and examples provided by our colleagues at Texas A&M University and Texas Christian University. We would particularly like to thank Leslie Reid, former Head of the Department of Recreation and Parks at Texas A&M and Edward A. Johnson, Dean of the M.J. Neeley School of Business at TCU for their encouragement and support.

Our work has also been influenced by many professional managers and university students who have participated in our workshops and classes during the years since this project began in 1980. Their insight and feedback have stimulated us to reexamine, reorganize, revise, and clarify many of our ideas, illustrations, and examples. Former graduate assistants Cheryl Black, Elizabeth Sypien, Cindy Kennedy, Donna Legg, Kathy Rubin, Renuka Arunkumar, Sheila Backman, and Kari Knox were particularly helpful in gathering reference materials, proofreading, and copyediting.

We are grateful to many people whose contributions are referenced throughout the book. We would particularly like to recognize Professor Philip Kotler of Northwestern University whose work has substantially influenced our thinking.

Special thanks are due Nancy Robbins and Pat Townsend for their diligent work in preparing the manuscript, keeping track of countless details, and helping out in various other aspects of the project.

Finally, our deepest thanks go to our wives Liz and Sharon, and our daughters Christine and Joanne Crompton and Christine and Jennifer Lamb. Without their support, encouragement, sacrifices, and tolerance the book could not have been written.

JOHN L. CROMPTON
CHARLES W. LAMB

Contents

MARKETING GOVERNMENT
AND SOCIAL SERVICES

ONE

What Is Marketing?

Many people think the term *marketing* connotes an activity that is only appropriate in commercial profit-seeking enterprises. They do not distinguish marketing from hard selling and envision both as crass exploitation, the foisting of unwanted goods and services on unsuspecting people, the superficial glitter of billboards and neon signs, commercials on television, and aggressive high-pressure sales people. Seen in this light, marketing is considered unprofessional and unethical for government and social service agencies (see Figure 1.1).

Such negative associations reflect an inaccurate view of marketing. Marketing is two things. First, it is a philosophy, an attitude, and a perspective. Second, it is the set of activities used to implement that philosophy. Acceptance of the philosophy is a prerequisite for successful implementation of the activities.

This chapter is intended to remove any misunderstanding of the nature of marketing and to explain why marketing is relevant to government and social service agency administrators. First is an exploration of the philosophy of marketing in which the so-called marketing concept is introduced and its evolution traced. Because of its importance to all government and social service agency marketing efforts, the basics of a marketing orientation are outlined and then contrasted with an alternative orientation that agencies often adopt. Next, we define the term *marketing* and explore the concept of exchange that underlies all marketing actions. Following that is an introduction to the set of activities that comprise marketing. Relationships between these activities are illustrated by a family planning service example. The final section of the chapter briefly reviews the use of marketing to discourage, rather than encourage, service usage.

EVOLUTION OF THE MARKETING CONCEPT

The philosophy of marketing is simple and intuitively appealing: the social and economic justification for an organization's existence is the satisfaction of cus-

Dear Editor:

This letter is in reference to the statements in the September 21 edition of this newspaper attributed to Dr. John Crompton, the visiting American "expert" on parks and recreation. The very thought of marketing leisure facilities in parks and other recreation areas is repugnant. I found Dr. Crompton's crass commercial ideas totally lacking in imagination and creativity. I suppose that he will next recommend the erection of five-story concrete kangaroos in all of our national parks.

Figure 1.1. An Example of the Popular Misconception of Marketing. (*Source:* Based upon a letter that appeared in the *West Australian*, September 27, 1982.)

tomer wants. Marketing entails establishing a way for the organization to learn about customer wants and use that information internally to create programs that will satisfy targeted clientele.

This philosophy has evolved as marketing thinking passed through stages, the three most important of which have been labeled the product era, the sales era, and the marketing era. The differences among these three eras can most vividly be illustrated by reviewing the way in which the philosophy of marketing (often called the marketing concept) emerged in the business world.

Product Era

Development of the assembly line in the early decades of the twentieth century made it possible for the first time in history to produce large quantities of relatively inexpensive products. Customers, many of whom could not previously afford to buy, readily absorbed these products as fast as they were offered for sale. Demand exceeded supply, so business people concentrated their efforts on their products. They were primarily concerned with producing more of what they produced, rather than with selling what they had produced, or trying to learn what customers wanted them to produce.

Sales Era

The sales volume in the 1920s, however, was no longer sufficient to keep all businesses at full capacity. Supply exceeded demand and companies recognized a need to stimulate and arouse demand for their products. There was a growing awareness of the need for firms to go out and persuade customers to buy their products. Consequently, sales departments were established to sell products aggressively. At this point businesses moved from a product orientation to a selling orientation. Their main concern, however, remained the product being sold rather than the benefits that customers wanted or received.

Marketing Era

In the 1950s some companies began to realize that a sale was not predominantly dependent on an aggressive sales force, but rather on a customer's decision to purchase a product. What a business thinks it produces, they realized, is not of primary importance to its success. Instead what a customer thinks he or she is buying—the perceived value—determines what a business is, what it produces, and whether or not it will prosper.

Central to the concept of marketing is the attitude, "produce what you should sell" rather than "sell what you can produce." Thus a company is more likely to succeed if it tries to look through its customers' eyes, identify what they want, and then provide it. According to a well-known marketing aphorism, "To sell Jack Jones what Jack Jones buys, you have to see Jack Jones through Jack Jones' eyes." This increased responsiveness to the customer has led to the emergence of the marketing or customer service orientation, which is the basis of contemporary marketing philosophy. This philosophy, popularly known as the marketing concept, *holds that the social and economic justification for an organization's existence is the satisfaction of customer wants*.

The evolutionary sequence in the private sector of product, sales, and marketing orientations has been mirrored in the public sector. Before the mid-1970s most government and social service agencies practiced minimal marketing. They did not consciously perform marketing functions and assumed that demand for a service would grow simply because they performed it well. Seeing no need to sell a worthwhile service, the agencies concentrated on producing the services.

In the late 1970s, when resources were no longer as plentiful, a number of agencies adopted a more aggressive posture and started to promote their services vigorously in order to increase usage and provide better justification for their budget levels. This selling orientation is now prevalent in the public sector marketplace. In addition, some agencies have recognized the limitations of selling and have moved one step beyond to embrace a marketing orientation.

Thus, although the product, sales, and marketing eras evolved sequentially, all three orientations exist today both among business organizations and among government and social service agencies. Some government and social service agency personnel regard their primary task as providing the facilities, services, and programs which they consider to be the most appropriate, as efficiently as they are able, within the resources that they have available. The extent to which the service meets people's needs is not carefully considered. These agencies feel that they have fulfilled their obligation by providing a product:

> The elderly, for example, may be defined as "needing" homemaker services, "meals on wheels," or institutional care. The mentally retarded may "require" institutional care, special education, or training. . . . Too often services initially introduced (or conceived) as possible mechanisms to assist people in need quickly

> become the only way to do things. Services, once seen as potentially beneficial for certain people with particular needs, become solutions whose benefit is rarely questioned.[1]

Such an orientation is inward looking, dominated by programs, presumptions and processes. "Our agency" is the focus, rather than the residents the agency serves. A product-oriented agency decides what it thinks that it can do best, or what it wants to do, and then offers internally designed programs and services to the public. The agency hopes that the public accepts the programs and services and uses them. If there is no response to an offering, agency personnel are likely to rationalize that they did the best they could. If, for example, students won't come to school, there must be something wrong with the students. It might make more sense to wonder if there is something wrong with the school.[2]

Some government and social service agencies that have moved out of a product orientation seek to aggressively sell and promote their programs to potential users. Instead of merely offering programs and services on a take-it-or-leave-it basis, they attempt to convince prospective clients that they should participate in the program or use the service. This selling orientation, however, causes agencies to ask the wrong questions. The obvious answer to "How do you get street kids into establishment programs?" is, "You don't; you get street kids into *street* programs."

The third approach is more promising, particularly in a period of scarce resources. The marketing orientation attempts first to determine what client groups want and then provide services that meet those needs. Whereas selling focuses on the needs of the seller, marketing focuses on the needs of the buyer. As Peter Drucker has noted:

> The aim of marketing is to make selling superfluous. The aim of marketing is to know and understand the consumer so well that the product or service fits him and sells itself. Ideally, marketing should result in a customer who is ready to buy. All that should be needed then is to make the product available, i.e., logistics rather than salesmanship, and statistical distribution rather than promotion.[3]

The fundamental difference between a selling and a marketing orientation is illustrated in Figure 1.2. A selling orientation starts with a program developed by agency personnel who have not carefully studied their potential clientele. The result is often that the intended clientele do not participate. In contrast, a marketing orientation starts by identifying the benefits particular clientele seek and develops programs on that basis. This approach has a mugh higher probability of eliciting support and participation from targeted clientele.

Two key questions help reveal an agency's orientation. First, to the question "Why do we do what we do today?" the answer should be, "Because our clients want these services and regard them as high priorities." Unfortunately, the answer from a product-oriented agency would be that it has always offered certain services, which the staff have been trained to provide and are com-

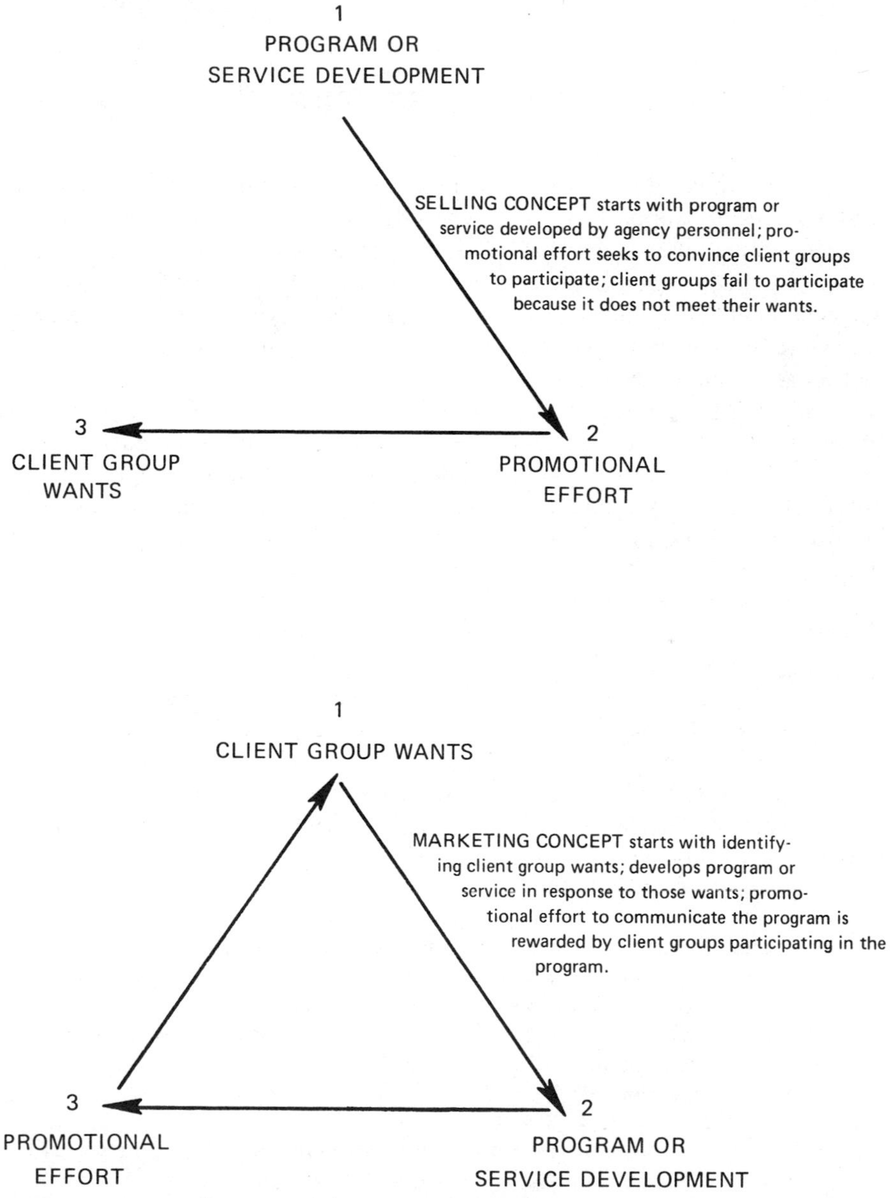
1
PROGRAM OR
SERVICE DEVELOPMENT
SELLING CONCEPT starts with program or service developed by agency personnel; promotional effort seeks to convince client groups to participate; client groups fail to participate because it does not meet their wants.
3
CLIENT GROUP
WANTS
2
PROMOTIONAL
EFFORT
1
CLIENT GROUP WANTS
MARKETING CONCEPT starts with identifying client group wants; develops program or service in response to those wants; promotional effort to communicate the program is rewarded by client groups participating in the program.
3
PROMOTIONAL
EFFORT
2
PROGRAM OR
SERVICE DEVELOPMENT

Figure 1.2. Differences in the Focus of a Marketing and a Selling Orientation.

fortable performing. The second question is: "What are we doing different from five years ago?" If the answer is "not much," then the agency is probably product or selling oriented. Citizen need priorities have probably changed in the last five years.

FUNDAMENTALS OF A MARKETING ORIENTATION

Marketing involves delivering programs and services that people want and that they will readily support, as opposed to delivering the services or programs that the agency deems appropriate. A marketing orientation accepts the centrality of the consumer to the agency's operations. It requires focusing on the wants of potential clients of government and social services whenever decisions regarding an agency's services, their prices, location, scheduling, and promotion are being considered.

A marketing orientation is a state of mind appropriate for all public and social service agencies regardless of size or the particular emphasis of their programs. It is often expressed in such phrases as "We are not in charge, the potential user is"; "We look at the agency through the potential user's eyes"; "We don't promote programs, we solve problems"; "The public proposes and the agency disposes" (see Figure 1.3). The critical question is, "What do potential client groups want or desire?" rather than "What do we want to offer that we must convince them that they need?" Marketing is more than a set of activities; it is a philosophy describing an agency's attitude toward its various publics and its goals.

A public agency may find it difficult to think in terms of the wants, perceptions, or preferences of its markets or publics because it assumes it knows what the public wants. Professionals often see themselves as "taste-setters" or feel that they are technically competent to make decisions about what services the public wants. There is

> a proclivity among public employees to become more elitist in terms of values and actions. This is a message that comes through loudly and clearly in communities throughout the nation. One increasingly encounters experts and professionals whose attitude toward citizen involvement in governmental administration is, "Citizens can't tell me what to do. I know what is best for the community. How can they come in and tell me what to do when they have no idea of what is going on in government?"[4]

Similarly, it is easy for elected representatives who formulate policy and legislation to assume that they know what the public wants.

The time, money, and personnel required to find out what the clientele wants make a marketing approach seem expensive. In the long term, however,

A Client
is the most important person in any agency.
A Client
is not dependent on us—we are dependent on him or her.
A Client
is not an interruption of our work—he or she is the purpose of it.
A Client
does us a favor when he or she participates—we are not doing him or her a favor by serving him or her.
A Client
is a "guest" whose presence is a compliment to the agency.
A Client
is a person who brings us his or her wants—it is our job to fill these wants.
A Client
is not a cold statistic—he or she is a flesh and blood human being with feelings and emotions like our own.
A Client
is deserving of the most courteous and attentive treatment we can give him or her.
A Client
is the life blood of this and every other organization.

Figure 1.3. Our Client: The Real Boss in Any Agency.

an agency that acts responsively and minimizes ineffective allocations of resources will spend less money than one that concentrates on their product or on how to sell it. As Aldous Huxley supposedly pointed out, it is not very difficult to persuade people to do what they are all longing to do. A marketing orientation is more troublesome and more difficult, but it is also more rewarding because it is more successful.

The failures of an agency often can be traced to its neglect of the wants and desires of its potential consumers.[5] Consider the letter shown in Figure 1.4 that was written to the *New York Times* by a frustrated city bus passenger. It illustrates how preoccupation with the development of a product can prevent that product from being tailored to meet the customers' needs.

CONTRASTING SELLING AND MARKETING ORIENTATIONS

As we noted previously, many people confuse the terms selling and marketing. These people believe that a marketing orientation means aggressive advertising and/or personal selling. This is inaccurate. Figure 1.5 contrasts selling and marketing orientations under five headings. Each of these contrasts is discussed in this section.

Dear Editor:

Like many New York citizens, I have finally had an opportunity to ride one of the new Japanese Hano buses that city officials have been bragging about for the past year. Unlike many of our old buses, the air conditioning and fluorescent lights worked well, and the ride was not even too hard or bouncy. My only concern, admittedly a minor issue, is that the buses were not designed for Americans!

Why do we have to have seats that are too low and too narrow, aisles that are too narrow, and ceilings so low that an average size man has to stoop to avoid bumping his head? The buses are probably fine for smaller Japanese people, but why weren't they modified to allow average size Americans to walk and sit comfortably. I noticed one pregnant lady having a terrible time navigating the isle. Fortunately no one on my bus was carrying a shopping bag.

I'm told that the New York police use "C.S.D." (common sense dictates) when faced with a difficult decision. It seems to me that the M.T.A. should consider C.S.D. when acquiring new buses. Why don't they ask riders what they like and dislike about the old buses and the Hanos? Since neither designers nor M.T.A. officials ride the bus, how would they know what we need?

We are all grateful about the possibility of having new buses. But please, let's make them usable.

Figure 1.4. Great Bus for Everyone but the Rider. (*Source:* Based upon a letter that appeared in the *New York Times*, October 13, 1981.)

	THE ORGANIZATION'S FOCUS IS:	WHAT BUSINESS ARE YOU IN?	TO WHOM IS THE SERVICE DIRECTED?	WHAT IS YOUR PRIMARY GOAL?	HOW DO YOU SEEK TO ACHIEVE YOUR GOAL?
SELLING ORIENTATION	Inward Upon the Organization's Needs	Delivering Programs and Services	Everybody	Maximum Numbers through the Door	Primarily through Intensive Promotion
MARKETING ORIENTATION	Outward Upon the Wants and Preferences of Client Groups.	Satisfying Consumer Wants	Specific Groups of People	Customer Satisfaction	Through Coordinated Use of the Set of Marketing Activities

Figure 1.5. Contrasting Marketing and Selling Orientations.

Organization's Focus

Selling-oriented agencies are normally characterized as being highly bureaucratic. Divisions function as separate entities more concerned with defending their status, budget allocation, or role within the agency than with how to best serve potential client groups. Personnel tend to be "inward-looking," concerned with employment security and conditions, and satisfying their own short-term needs rather than the concerns of the people they serve:

> Bureaucrats are not concerned with innovation, with problems outside their specific authority, or with qualifying human factors. They will serve people as long as their problems fall within the limits of their jurisdiction. People's problems are defined in terms of how the bureaucratic organization is set up rather than having the organization set up to respond to people's problems.[6]

Marketing-oriented agencies recognize that client groups direct the activities of the agency, and their internal organization and coordination efforts reflect this awareness. The delivery of services to satisfy wants means that all departments in the agency must be integrated, client-oriented, and outward-looking. In other words, there must be selfless coordination within an agency and a willingness to cooperate rather than to compete with other personnel and/or departments.

The attitude and actions of each employee must also be client-oriented. An employee may be the only contact a particular client has with the agency. Hence, in that client's mind, the employee *is* the agency. Any person, division, or department that is not client-oriented weakens the positive contribution of the entire agency. For example, if the person answering the telephone is abrupt or discourteous, the potential client may assume that attitude is representative of the agency. Consider the lifeguard's action described in a letter to the *Miami Herald* (Figure 1.6), on page 10. The lifeguard was intent upon enforcing an ordinance that prohibited excavation of county property. He interpreted this ordinance as forbidding sandcastles at the water's edge. Clearly, the lifeguard was more concerned with enforcing regulations than with sensitively responding to a client's needs.

The most difficult marketing task is to establish a mentality in an agency in which all personnel focus their efforts on satisfying the wants of actual or potential clientele, rather than on actual or potential programs, rules and regulations, or their own immediate well-being. *For this outward-looking approach to be successfully implemented, it has to be enthusiastically embraced by senior managers, who have the critical task of encouraging its dissemination throughout the organization.*

What Business Are You In?

As Figure 1.5 illustrates, a selling-oriented agency defines its business in terms of programs and services, while a marketing-oriented agency defines its business in terms of benefits its client groups want. The most important question a manager has to ask is, "What business are we in?" The answer to this question guides all marketing actions.

It was a Saturday afternoon on the beach in Larry and Penny Thompson Recreational Park. My wife, my daughter, my toys, and my sunburn were on the sand amid a crowd of children and parents.

First came the lifeguard—you always feel the presence of a lifeguard there because every 10 seconds you hear his whistle or megaphone making the beach sound like Victoria Station in England. But people do not mind; they seem to like being bossed around on the beach.

The lifeguard asked me to destroy the sand castle that my daughter and I were building: "It is not allowed on this beach," he said seriously. My sand castle was nowhere near or in front of a lifeguard station.

Then two park rangers came and again asked me to destroy my sand castle. I told the rangers that I didn't believe there was such a rule. If there is such a rule, no sign said anything about it; therefore the public has not been properly warned. They threatened to put me under arrest.

Imagine the headlines: "Man Arrested for Building Sandcastle." The tourists will eat it up, one wonderful season after another.

So I asked the rangers to destroy the sand castle themselves—if they really believed in the rule. Without really knowing it, I challenged them to make absolute jackasses out of themselves, and they did. Yes, one ranger destroyed my sand castle in front of my daughter.

After a confused conversation with the rangers, the manager of the place, and others, no one has succeeded in giving me a rational reason why sand castles are not allowed on the beach. I detected a fear of possible legal problems, but not a word of reason.

The saddest part of this already-sad story was the apathy of the public around me. It was the look of giving up, the expression of silent fear, fear to say "no" to authority, to say "enough."

This is a rule that is ridiculously stupid, yet you have hundreds of people lying there, taking it quietly, defenseless, beaten.

Figure 1.6. Destroying Castles in the Sand. (*Source:* Letter to *The Miami Herald,* June 30, 1983.)

People spend their money, time, and energy resources with the expectation of receiving benefits, not for the delivery of services themselves. *Citizens don't buy programs or services; they buy the expectation of benefits*. Programs themselves are not marketable. Only their benefits have a value to client groups. A service or program is simply a vehicle for the user benefits that it conveys. This distinction has enormous implications for the way in which agencies define their business.

If an agency defines its business in terms of specific services, it will probably miss opportunities to serve its clientele, whose wants can often be met through a very wide range of programs. Instead of specific programs, an agency should start with meeting client group wants. For example, one of the primary benefits people seek from libraries is to broaden their general knowledge. This benefit can be achieved through a wide variety of programs and services, including books, movies, lectures, discussion groups, trips, and many other "benefit vehicles." Books alone are not what consumers seek; instead, they want the general knowledge benefit derived from learning. By offering other services in addition to books, libraries can reach more clientele and better satisfy their existing clientele.

Those agencies and personnel who think of their jobs in program rather than benefit terms are vulnerable to what is sometimes called marketing myopia.[7]

In this context, myopia means narrow, short-term thinking. Such a mind set can threaten an agency's survival. The results of marketing myopia can best be shown by illustrations taken from the private sector:

> In the early 1900s, horse and carriage companies failed to recognize that people did not want to ride in a carriage; rather, they wanted efficient transportation. The carriage companies failed to apply their skills in efficient transportation to the new automobile. Hence, they went out of business.
>
> Similarly, passenger railroads are in financial difficulty today because they assumed they were in the railroad rather than the transportation business. Other products, such as cars, trucks, airplanes, or even telephones, meet transportation demands more effectively than do railroads. The railroads failed to incorporate these more effective modes of transportation into their own organizations. Their business was defined too narrowly because they were product- rather than customer-oriented.[8]
>
> Some large luxury passenger ships have survived, in spite of competition from the airlines, because they have recognized they are in the floating hotel business, not the transportation business.
>
> In the 1950s tin cans began to be replaced (for some uses) by other types of packaging. Many of the tin-can companies that survived did so because they recognized they were in the packaging not the tin-can business. Their customers sought the best packaging and were not interested in the material from which the packaging was made.[9]

Each of these examples demonstrates how products or services emerged that better delivered the benefits consumers sought. The fundamental importance of accurately defining what business you are in has long been recognized in the private sector. For example, in 1904 Mary Parker Follett, a management consultant, persuaded a window shade company client that they were really in the light control business.[10] That realization expanded the company's opportunities enormously.

In defining an agency's business, the key question is not "What is the best way that benefits can be facilitated *through the traditional services we have offered* given the resources available?" That would be a myopic approach. Rather the appropriate question to ask is "What is the best way that sought benefits can be facilitated, given the resources available?"

In asking "What's our business?" agencies also need to add "And what *will* it be, given the changes in the environment we can presently discern?" Answering the question "What business are you in?" in terms of the benefits client groups seek has at least four important advantages compared to answering it in terms of programs or services:

> It ensures that an agency retains its focus on client groups and does not become preoccupied with programs, services, or the agency's internal needs.

It encourages innovation and creativity of programs and services by suggesting that there are many ways to service similar client group wants.

It stimulates an awareness of changes in client group wants as they occur, and hence services are more likely to remain relevant.

It will probably lead to a broader definition of the role of the agency and thus contribute toward keeping its services abreast of society's wants.

While the definition of an agency's business should be sufficiently broad to provide room for growth in a changing environment, at the same time it should be narrow enough to give specific direction to the agency. A common thread must link existing offerings and proposed new services. A definition that is too broad may not be useful for giving direction. For example, little useful guidance is likely to be gained by a manufacturer of lead pencils defining his or her company as being in the "communications business." Expansion into service areas for which an agency has no "feel" and no management expertise is unlikely to lead to client satisfaction or to enhance the agency's reputation.

Interpreting and Mediating Clientele Preferences. The answer to "What business are you in?" will *not* necessarily result in client groups receiving the specific services that they request. Obviously, the cost of offering a service is a concern. This issue is discussed later under target market criteria in Chapters 5 and 6. Two additional reasons, however, may cause a marketing-oriented agency to amend or reject client group requests.

First, preferences articulated by client groups must be mediated by sound professional judgment as to how sought benefits may be facilitated. We are all prisoners of our experiences, and, as one adage suggests, "People don't know what they want—they only want what they know." Consumers have a limited set of experiences and are unlikely to request anything beyond those experiences because they are not aware of benefits that may accrue from other potential offerings. For example, before the automobile was invented people knew they wanted transportation but could not articulate that sought benefit in terms of a motorized vehicle. The introduction of various outreach programs such as meals-on-wheels and home health services probably resulted from client groups identifying needs and professionals developing the services that met those needs.

Consider the following examples:

Many undergraduate students are vocationally oriented. They want curricula that emphasize hands-on job skills or job-oriented facts. Others argue that higher education should be concerned primarily with teaching students how to think, not with training them for specific jobs. This longer-term perspective suggests that students are best served by developing literate, numerical, and computational skills; by being challenged so they are forced to learn more about their own capabilities; and by developing self-confidence.

This type of educational experience better equips students to respond to a future environment in which getting a job will depend on an individual having the intellectual ability, mastery of basic skills, and self-confidence to continually develop new job skills.

If symphony orchestras always played what a majority of audiences requested, then Beethoven's Fifth Symphony and Tchaikovsky's 1812 Overture could well be played every week! Giving such exclusive decision rights to the audience could endanger the classical music repertoire, which would become relatively narrow and sterile. Perhaps "all of us need to be pulled, pushed, even thrown into new artistic experiences."[11] Otherwise there would be no opportunities for our tastes to develop.

Complete disregard of professional insight as a means of improving service delivery options means ignoring a very substantial resource in which the public have invested. The distinction is subtle between being product oriented and discounting overt popular preference in favor of professional judgment. The latter approach focuses on the long-term needs of the consumer, while the former makes no genuine effort to be responsive to consumers' behavior or needs. The challenge lies in studying client groups, listening to them, and then intelligently interpreting their input and behavior. A literal implementation of what consumers ask for, without the input of professional expertise, would probably be inappropriate.

The second reason why a marketing-oriented agency may amend or reject a client group request is because the request is perceived as not being in the long-term interests of the community. Government and social service agencies have a responsibility to consider the impact a service may have on nonusers. This important refinement of the marketing concept has been termed the *societal marketing concept*. It states, "The justification for an agency's existence is the satisfaction of clients' wants *and the preservation or enhancement of the community's well-being*."[12]

Zoning illustrates the implementation of the societal marketing concept. If individuals were permitted to pursue their own preferences and build what they like, where they like, presumably they would be well satisfied. However, their satisfaction and benefits would be acquired at the expense of the rest of the community. Zoning is intended to safeguard the interests of all citizens in the community.

Consider the following issues:

Should smoking be permitted in public buildings?
Should nude bathing be permitted at public beaches?
Should video games be made available in public facilities?
Should beer be offered for sale at public facilities?

In each of these instances the benefits sought by a client group could be well satisfied. However, since it is owned by, and responsible to, all citizens, an agency has to decide whether these actions would meet with the approval of a majority while enhancing the community's well-being.

To Whom Is the Service Directed?

A selling-oriented agency targets each of its services at "everybody" or "the average user," while a marketing-oriented agency aims at "specific somebodies," that is, targeted groups of people (Figure 1.5). Historically, many agencies have offered their constituents standardized services. This has been termed the "lowest common denominator" approach to service delivery. Such a service seeks to satisfy the maximum number of people at some minimal level.

The fallacy of developing services which are directed at the average user is that relatively few average users actually exist. Typically, populations are characterized by their diversity. An average simply represents a mid-point in some set of characteristics. Most of a potential clientele consists of groups on either side of the mid-point who have very little in common. These very different client groups are unlikely to be interested in an average offering.

A marketing-oriented agency recognizes that different client groups have different wants which may justify the development of different services and/or marketing programs to expedite the agency's exchanges with them. Thus efforts are made to group together those people whose desires are similar and to develop unique offerings for each group. In effect, a number of smaller markets emerge instead of one large market. The only difference—and it is a crucial difference—is that, whereas the total market is a heterogeneous conglomeration of subgroups, each of the smaller markets constitutes a relatively homogeneous group.

Consider, for example, the market for programs and services offered by community colleges. A selling-oriented administration may well adopt the lowest common denominator approach and aim at "everybody" in its efforts to stimulate enrollment. A marketing-oriented administration will recognize that its market is composed of full-time and part-time students, academic and vocationally oriented individuals, recent high school graduates, and people who have been out of high school for several years (the so-called adult market). One study of the adult market for community college services concluded that it consisted of the following subgroups: (1) social improvement learners, (2) career learners, (3) leisure learners, (4) submissive learners, and (5) ambivalent learners. Each group sought different benefits that required different programs, scheduling, pricing and promotional appeals to attract them to the campus.[13]

What Is Your Primary Goal?

The ultimate goal of a marketing-oriented agency is to satisfy client group wants (Figure 1-5). This is a qualitative rather than a quantitative goal. The emphasis is not on how many are served, but rather on providing those who are served with a satisfying experience. This difference substantially influences an agency's organization, business definition, target clientele, and the means employed to achieve the primary goal.

A primary goal of numbers through the door will likely lead to an inward-looking bureaucratic organization that focuses on programs and services targeted at the average user, as well as one that relies heavily on promotion to convince people to participate. Alternatively, a primary goal of customer satisfaction tends to lead to an integrated, outward-looking organization that focuses on the wants and preferences of selected groups and a coordinated marketing strategy to produce that customer satisfaction.

Numbers per se are not only incompatible with a marketing orientation but they are also likely to lead to erroneous conclusions if the numbers are interpreted as being synonymous with satisfaction. Client satisfaction is likely to result in large attendance, but large attendance is not necessarily an indication that a service is providing high levels of client satisfaction.

Some agency managers may contend that quantity of participation is synonymous with a satisfactory experience, arguing that participants would not return or encourage their friends to participate if it were not. Two factors, however, frequently disprove this comforting contention. First, if no similar service is conveniently available elsewhere then the agency is a monopolist. A typical interchange from the field of further education illustrates the point.

> "I must be doing something right, I'm packing them in semester after semester."
>
> "How do you know you're doing something right?"
>
> "Well, the numbers show it."
>
> "What the numbers indicate is that there are some people out there who are anxious to learn something about that subject area. It doesn't necessarily indicate you're doing a good job. They come because that's all that's available on that subject."[14]

If the public recreation and park agency owns the only swimming pool in a community, then on a 95° day in the summer, a large attendance is likely, no matter how poorly the pool is operated. People will participate even though the experience may be considered less than satisfactory because it is the only offering available. Similarly, if a hospital is the only one in an area, then patients, physicians, and employees don't have much choice. Because it is "the only game in town," it is likely to generate substantial throughput regardless of the quality of service it offers.

A second major fallacy follows from the heavy subsidization of many government and social service programs. Any service, no matter how inadequate or inappropriate, will attract clients if it is subsidized deeply enough. At some level of subsidy, benefits accruing to an individual are likely to exceed the costs of dissatisfaction. This point is developed further in the discussion of pricing in Chapter 13, but at this stage a brief example will illuminate the point:

> If the primary goal is to get 300,000 attendance at the public swimming pool for the year, the easiest course is to heavily subsidize. Offer the service free. If numbers are still insufficient, then spend substantial dollars on advertising in the print and broadcast media, hire a pop group to perform at the pool, and provide a frequent, free bus service from all neighborhoods to the pool. If these actions still don't generate the necessary numbers, then offer $5 to each individual who comes to the pool.

Obviously this example is hyperbolic. The point is that no matter how inadequate a service may be, if it is subsidized heavily enough then it will generate clients. The numbers, however, do not reflect satisfaction with the basic service. Rather they result from the substantial subsidy that accompanies it.

What Tools Do You Use to Achieve Your Goal?

Agencies with a selling orientation seek to generate maximum use primarily through intensive promotion activities. In contrast, agencies with a marketing approach recognize that promotion is only one of four marketing tools which together comprise the marketing program or mix (Figure 1.5). The other three elements are program, pricing, and distribution decisions, which are discussed in more detail in the remainder of this chapter. The important distinction to be noted here is that a marketing-oriented agency recognizes each of the four components of the marketing program as being of equal importance, while the selling-oriented agency views promotion as being the primary means of achieving its ends.

A DEFINITION OF MARKETING

Marketing is a set of activities aimed at facilitating and expediting exchanges. It entails:

Gathering information about the environment
Finding out what benefits or wants people desire the agency to deliver
Setting marketing objectives
Deciding exactly which wants, and which sections of the community possessing those wants, it is going to serve
Developing and implementing the appropriate mix of marketing activities
Evaluating marketing efforts

These activities and their relationships are charted in Figure 1.7. Adherence to the marketing concept is implicit in our definition of marketing. Failure to

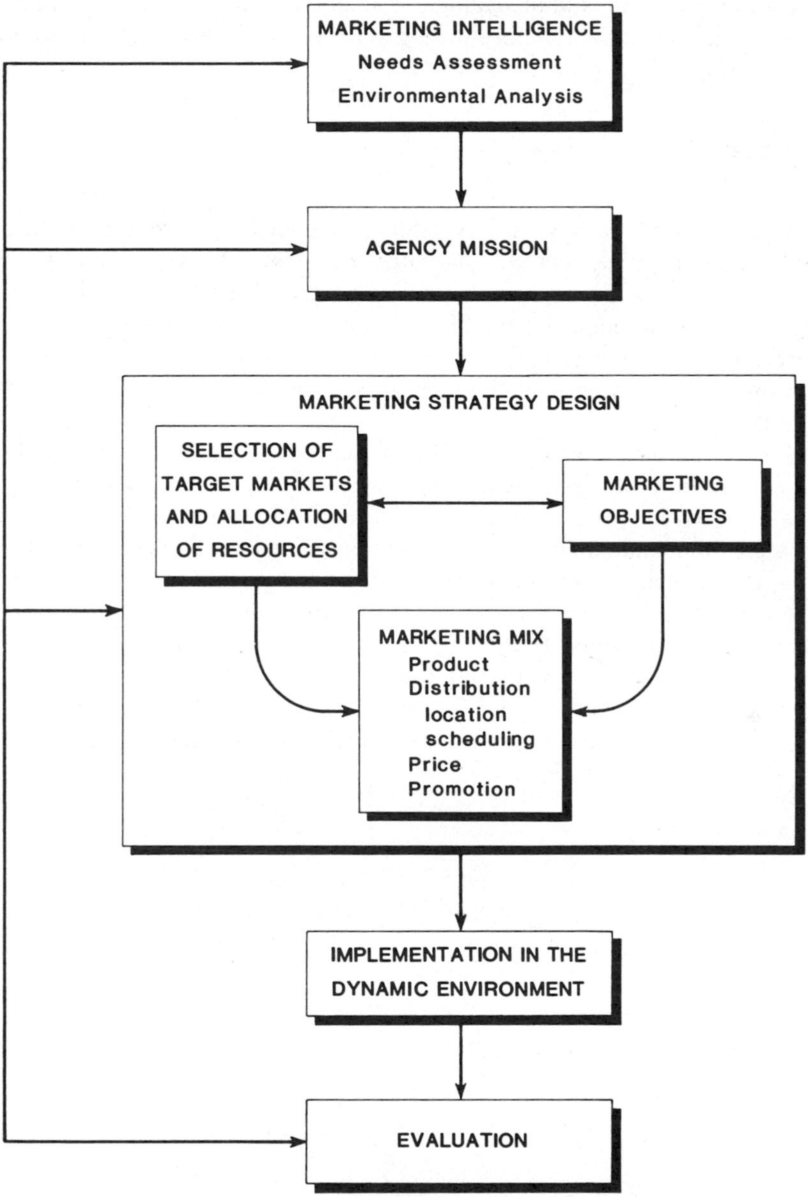

Figure 1.7. The Set of Marketing Activities. (This conceptualization of the marketing process was influenced by D.W. Cravens, G.E. Hills, and R.B. Woodruff. *Marketing Decision Making* (2nd ed.). Homewood, Illinois: R.D. Irvin, Inc., 1980, p. 14.)

adopt a client orientation makes it less likely that these activities will produce mutually satisfying exchanges between an agency and its clientele. Since understanding, planning, and managing exchanges are the essence of marketing,[15] we shall address this issue before discussing the set of marketing activities and their interrelationships.

Nature of Exchange

The nature of the exchange relationship is shown in Figure 1.8. An agency delivers want-satisfying services that citizens perceive to be of value. Citizens provide support to the agency through their payments of tax dollars, direct charges paid by participants, travel costs for such items as transportation, the opportunity cost of not engaging in another activity during the time that they spend utilizing a service, and the personal energy and effort expended to use the service.

Voluntary exchange calls for offering something of value to someone in exchange for something else of value. Before clients use an agency's service they ask two questions, "What's in it for me?" and "How much will it cost me?" They weigh the trade-off between what they will gain and what they will have to give up. As Adam Smith observed, "It is not from the benevolence of the butcher, the brewer, or the baker, that we expect our dinner, but from their regard to their own self-interest."[16]

In the past citizens were too often required to take (or leave) the services offered by a government or social service agency, rather than being offered the services they want. This situation has changed in many public service fields.

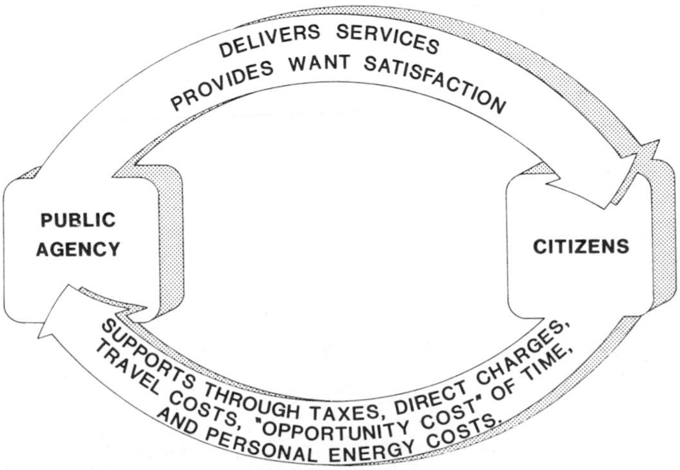

Figure 1.8. Exchange Transaction That Takes Place Between a Public Agency and Its Citizens.

The adoption of the client-oriented marketing concept is a natural response to the present environment and the recognition that voluntary exchange is the essence of marketing.

Some agencies have attempted to implement the marketing concept without recognizing that costs, as well as benefits, are important considerations in any voluntary exchange relationship. Clients are just as interested in the "real" cost of a service as they are in the benefits that it offers. Even if an agency is totally subsidized and no direct fees are charged, for example, users may still be required to expend substantial resources for the service. Travel costs for local services may include such items as automobile expenses, parking fees, or public transportation charges; while the costs associated with using nonlocal services may involve purchasing meals and accommodations.

Personal energy costs may also be involved. For example, the greatest cost a middle-class consumer incurs for an evening adult education class may be the mental and physical effort required to go. At the end of a strenuous workday it may take substantial willpower to overcome feelings of fatigue, ignore the temptation of a comfortable armchair, change clothes, gather the necessary books and supplies together, and face yet another drive to attend the class. These personal energy costs are likely to be a much more decisive factor in deciding whether or not to attend the class than whether the price of the class is $3, $4, or $5.

Opportunity cost of time refers to the benefit that is foregone by choosing one alternative rather than another. The trade-off cost of giving up an evening's interaction with the family or just relaxing may be of much greater concern in the above example than the direct price of the class. Even if the class is free, some will be reluctant to participate because the perceived benefits are not as great as those thought to accrue from spending that time engaging in another activity.

Some agencies have traditionally relied on a strategy of keeping direct prices low in order to attract or retain potential clients. This strategy may not be successful because of all the other costs involved. Direct prices must be viewed in the context of all resources expended. Reducing the costs related to equipment, travel, personal energy, or other opportunities, if possible, may be more effective than reducing direct charges. This realization has led marketing-oriented agencies to recognize that *the problem is never to get people to programs, the problem is always to get programs to people*. This latter approach helps reduce travel, personal energy, and opportunity costs and thus is more likely to consummate an exchange.

The trade-off between different types of costs is vividly illustrated in health care services, where some patients prefer to pay a fee instead of using free hospital services. Consider the following example, set in a Latin American country:

> While there is no charge at the free hospital, there is a substantial cost to the patient in terms of energy and psychological abuse. When he arrives at the hospital, he goes up to see a social worker. When he is finally interviewed, the

social worker asks a lot of questions about his income to determine whether he is really indigent (Do you have a TV set? How much do you get paid? and so on). Then he sees a number of other hospital staff members for various tests, some of them bringing up the question of his income again. Finally, he sees the doctor who discovers that he really needs to see a specialist who will not be available for a few weeks. Throughout the experience, the person is made to feel inferior and a nuisance. It is no wonder that he wishes to avoid these energy and psychological costs even if it means paying for the services.[17]

THE SET OF MARKETING ACTIVITIES

The set of marketing activities used to facilitate and expedite exchanges are interrelated components of a system that together represent the underpinning and operationalization of the marketing concept. These activities, shown in Figure 1.7, form the foundation around which most of our discussion of marketing in government and social service agencies will be focused. Each of these components, though only briefly reviewed at this point, is discussed in greater detail in subsequent chapters. The Louisiana Family Planning Program[18] is used to illustrate the various activities and their interrelationships.

Marketing Intelligence

Marketing intelligence is the gathering and then the evaluation of information. These inputs are necessary to develop a mission statement and design the agency's marketing strategy. Marketing intelligence consists of two principal components, needs assessment and environmental analysis.

Client Wants—The Starting Point. Marketing starts with understanding potential customers, what they want the agency to be, and what services they want it to deliver. The Louisiana Family Planning Program was conceived because it was suspected that some segments of the population residing in the state desired assistance in alleviating problems associated with large family size. A statewide needs assessment supported this notion and revealed that large families with low incomes wanted to curtail family size in order to reduce the financial strain on the existing family unit. Other potential clientele wished to establish a lifestyle that could not be achieved with a large number of children. The needs assessment also investigated the types of services potential clientele sought, their reasons for accepting or rejecting specific services, and their locational preferences for facilities.

Environmental Analysis. Marketing decisions are influenced and often shaped by dynamic, uncontrollable forces that are external to the agency. These macroenvironmental forces must be acknowledged and their potential influences considered. The social environment, for example, must be carefully analyzed by a family planning agency. If segments of the population such as churches or antiabortion groups are strongly opposed to family planning organizations, their community influence must be considered.

The technological environment has produced a variety of birth control methods, such as sterilization, birth control pills, IUDs, and condoms. The availability and reliability of these alternatives affects the variety and types of services that might be offered.

The legal-political environment affects what services can be offered, to whom, and when and how they can be promoted. Until recently, for example, birth control products could not be promoted in broadcast media.

Agency Mission

As noted earlier in this chapter, an agency's mission answers the question "What business are we in?" It is based on a careful analysis of the benefits sought by potential clientele as well as existing and anticipated environmental conditions. This long-term vision of what the agency is or is striving to become establishes the boundaries within which objectives, strategies, and actions must be developed. Based on its needs assessment and environmental analysis, the Louisiana Family Planning Program defined its mission as "encouraging the use of family planning methods to alleviate problems associated with large family size and overpopulation."

Targeting

The needs assessment process will probably reveal a wide range of benefits potential users want. Since resources are limited and the agency will not be able to meet everyone's wants, priorities have to be established. The agency has to identify exactly which wants, and which sections of the community possessing those wants, it is going to serve. This process is termed the selection of client groups, or *targeting*. It is a critical decision because it guides all of the subsequent marketing decisions that the agency must make.

The selection of target markets is influenced by the agency's mission and objectives, which guide the resource allocation decisions that determine who gets what. *Herein lies a fundamental distinction between marketing in the public and private sectors. Government and social service agencies are required to allocate resources equitably, whereas private sector organizations direct resources only at the most responsive target markets.* Determining what constitutes a fair and equitable allocation of resources is a complex issue that we shall address in detail in Chapter 7. Regardless of the allocation model selected, citizens' perspectives should be a starting point for defining what is fair.

The Louisiana Family Planning Program defined its primary target market as low-income, underprivileged, fecund females between the ages of 15 and

44. Management also stipulated that the target market would be expanded when and if the resources allocated to the program increased.

Objectives

Objectives allow an agency to look ahead and describe the desired future of the organization. They translate the mission statement into operational terms that specify what the agency hopes to accomplish. Citizens, as well as an agency's potential client groups, provide the input and direction that enable the agency to define its objectives. Clearly, if agency personnel adopt an inward-looking product-oriented attitude toward establishing objectives, the agency is likely to be unresponsive to its constituents no matter how marketing oriented its staff members try to be in service delivery. All other marketing activities are influenced by these objectives.

On the basis of cost-benefit studies and the needs assessment, the Louisiana Family Planning Program determined that its primary objective should be to reach as many of the target population as possible using a cost-per-active-client ratio of $69.

Marketing Mix

Product, distribution, price, and promotion decisions comprise what is commonly termed the marketing mix (Figure 1.7). These four components can be visualized as parts of an organism that grow together in response to the wants of a target market and the agency's marketing objectives. The marketing mix, together with the selection of client groups to be served, represents the combination of variables that an agency can control and manipulate to achieve desired outcomes. Once these decisions have been made, the service is offered in the dynamic environment of the community, which is comprised of a host of variables that the agency cannot control and to which it must therefore adapt. The following is a brief description of the four marketing mix components.

A *product* may be defined as a bundle of want-satisfying attributes. It is comprised of facilities and/or services that have been carefully designed to deliver benefits which targeted client groups seek. In designing an offering, agencies should consider the "total product," which includes an assortment of auxiliary services as well as the core offering. The total product of a retailer, for example, is more than the merchandise in the store. He or she must also consider parking facilities, proper display of merchandise, charge account services, sales clerks, delivery services, and so on. In the context of adult education, components of the total service include the learning environment, the timeliness of the offering, the ease of registration, the type of participants assembled, and the friendly assistance of the coordinator.[19]

The Louisiana Family Planning Program's product was conceived as a bundle of satisfactions or benefits to be derived from participation in the program. Concern centered on the total product. The services offered were designed not only in terms of medical and human issues, but also in terms of creating a physically pleasant, friendly atmosphere in the clinic that was compatible with the medical services rendered.

Distribution is how services get to client groups where and when they want them. Only in a few instances is an agency likely to be able to deliver a service at exactly the location and time each potential client prefers. Such a level of personalized service would be extraordinarily expensive. In most situations these costs are reduced by offering a service less frequently or at fewer locations. This policy somewhat inhibits exchange with clients because of the inconvenience and the rise in price (in terms of opportunity and time costs to an individual) that the agency is asking in exchange for the service. However, this strategy frees resources so that an agency can provide more and/or different services to its potential client groups.

The distribution element of the Louisiana Family Planning Program involved clinic site selection and service level determination. Service level was measured in terms of (1) time elapsed between initial home visit and delivery of family planning services, (2) the time spent per visit in transportation to the clinic, and (3) the time spent per visit waiting for service delivery at the clinic. To reduce travel time, strategic locations were selected for the program's clinic satellites. Also, clinic layout was planned to reduce the time consumed in information and physical flows. The areas assigned for waiting rooms were limited to force faster customer flows. Bottlenecks in the system were identified and eliminated. Improvements in service were accepted as a means not only to achieve a higher percentage of kept appointments and active customers, but also to better utilize the physical facilities and human resources.

Price is what a user must give up in order to obtain the services offered. Many government and social services are subsidized through the tax system, so service users often do not pay the full price needed to cover the cost of a service. The subsidy encourages use and helps facilitate an exchange. Price is usually expressed in dollar terms such as, "How much money must I pay in order to use that service?" As noted earlier in this chapter, however, money is only the direct cost of a service. Indirect costs are also part of the price. In family planning such costs might include travel expense in getting to a location, waiting time, foregone opportunities for spending that time, the expenditure of personal energy, and psychological concerns aroused by using birth control methods.

Communication facilitates exchanges by transmitting pertinent information about a product, its price, and distribution to the selected client groups. The marketing term used to describe these activities is *promotion*. Promotion consists of four major activities:

Personal selling is probably the form of promotion most commonly used by public agencies. Every time personnel interact in a professional capacity with members of the public they are involved in either directly or indirectly communicating something about the agency's services.

Publicity is any unpaid form of nonpersonal communication, where the agency is not identified as being the direct sponsor of the communication.

Advertising is also a form of nonpersonal communication. It differs from publicity in that it must be paid for and the sponsor of the communication is identified.

Incentives such as free offers, promotional prices, and prizes may be used in an effort to reach more of the client groups.

The Louisiana Family Planning Program's organization included a communication division that handled all matters relating to program presentations in the mass media. The sensitive nature of the services rendered along with concern for the feelings of the participants meant that great care had to be exercised in using the mass media for active program promotion. The personal selling function performed by family planning counselors was managed in a separate division with effective coordination maintained between the directors of the two divisions. When use of mass media communication became more feasible, the two divisions were planned to merge.

Future proposals for mass media and direct promotion included (1) securing public service time from radio stations to announce family planning–oriented messages and (2) a family planning wall calendar for each client on which counselors could mark the appointment day and time as a reminder for the recruited client, and as encouragement to plan for the future.

Evaluation

A service's success in providing satisfaction to client groups in the community should be carefully monitored. Feedback may be obtained from a variety of sources ranging from agency personnel working directly with the service to sophisticated consumer surveys. Constant feedback reduces the chances of institutional needs becoming paramount over client needs. This feedback serves as market intelligence information with which the service's success in satisfying wants may be assessed. If service performance is not considered optimal, then one or more of the controllable variables—that is, the selected client group or one or more elements of the marketing program—should be adjusted in order to deliver a better level of service.

The failure of a particular service to elicit the anticipated amount of support or enthusiasm does not necessarily mean that the targeted client group is disinterested. Rather it may mean that the service is being poorly communicated, presented in the wrong way or place, or offered at the wrong time or price. The service product may not be the problem, as is often assumed. Instead the problem may lie with one of the other variables under the manager's control.

Adjustments to any one or more of these variables may lead to increased success. The four components of the marketing mix can be combined in a multitude of ways: With just four variations in each of these four components, 256 possible combinations result. Refining the marketing mix is analogous to fine-tuning an automobile engine. All of its components need to be tested and adjusted before it functions optimally.

The Louisiana Family Planning Program adopted a continuous research program to test the effects of selected variables on customer continuation as active family planners. In addition, several surveys were conducted to determine reasons for participation or nonparticipation, as well as for keeping or not keeping appointments. The effect of counselor-customer interaction was also studied. Younger customers were found to respond to older counselors and vice versa.

The initial home visit with a customer involved obtaining demographic information to formulate profiles of adopters and nonadopters. These files were complemented with information obtained at the clinic visit, and cross-classification then determined the profiles of adopters of different family planning methods. All the necessary information was stored in computer memory, where it could be easily retrieved.

A management information system was also designed. An integral part of this system was a marketing information system designed to collect information about customer characteristics, customer behavior, and other marketing participant characteristics and attitudes. This information served as a basis for designing future marketing strategy and allowed the Program to monitor the extent to which it was achieving its objective of a cost-per-active client ratio of $69.

DEMARKETING

It is important to recognize that marketing can be used as a means of discouraging as well as of encouraging service usage. This process has been termed demarketing to emphasize that marketing activities may be used to decrease the numbers that the activity is intended to serve.[20] Consider the problem confronting many community health agencies. They have limited resources that are intended to provide relatively inexpensive services for lower socioeconomic groups. Because of the low prices charged they could be overwhelmed with clientele. The potential demand for these services is likely to far exceed the available resources. Accordingly, these agencies sometimes practice demarketing with the following methods:

Promotion. Services are not publicized, so word-of-mouth is the only way a potential client can find the service. Alternative private physician services are suggested for those clients who would prefer or could afford them.

Distribution. Clinics are often located in poor neighborhoods. Their location lets them serve those who are identified as their target markets well, *but* it also discourages middle-class clientele who don't like to visit those neighborhoods.

Price. With a sliding scale, the poor use the services free but others pay the same price as they would to a private physician. It is unlikely that middle-class individuals will pay for community care when they could use a personally selected physician for the same price.

Product. Clinics usually offer only a generic product. That is, a patient sees whatever medical staff are available and is given no choice.

Demarketing is *not* a negative concept. It is a technique for matching client demand with an agency's resources. In the health clinic example, those who are serviced are likely to receive a greater standard of care as a result of demarketing. A decrease in numbers can lead to an increase in clientele satisfaction through preserving a higher-quality experience. If demarketing alleviates overcrowding at a park, those using the facility will probably enjoy themselves more.

Demarketing has to be subtly and gradually introduced in order not to lose public support. Skill in implementing the demarketing mix is the key to its success. The nature of that mix is guided by an agency's policies, goals, and objectives.

Sometimes an agency may be engaged in marketing and demarketing activities at the same time. Some periods or some services may be overstressed by demand, while other periods of time or other services may be underused. The term *synchromarketing* has been used to describe the balance of encouraging people to use a service, but at another time, rather than persuading them not to use the service at all.[21] This practice is common in businesses such as airlines, hotels, and other service-oriented businesses. Telephone rates are probably the best example of pricing at different levels to encourage long distance calling at off-peak times.

SUMMARY

The marketing concept is a philosophy that states that the social and economic justification for an organization's existence is the satisfaction of client group wants. This philosophy has evolved through three major stages: the product era, the sales era, and the marketing era. Although the three orientations associated with these eras developed sequentially, they all exist today.

A product-oriented agency decides what it can do best, or what it wants to do, and then offers internally designed services to the public. A selling-oriented agency goes further and, after deciding what services should be offered, seeks to aggressively sell and promote them to potential users. A marketing orientation, on the other hand, is based on acceptance of the client as central to the agency's operations. Its focus remains on the wants of potential clients whenever decisions about an agency's services, their prices, location, scheduling, and promotion are made.

Personnel in selling-oriented agencies tend to be inward-looking, concerned with building their own empires, and serving their own short-term needs, whereas in marketing-oriented agencies individuals are client-oriented, outward-looking, and work together as a team.

The most important question a manager has to ask is, "What business are we in?" An agency should define its business in terms of the benefits its clients seek, not in terms of providing particular facilities, services, or programs. Focusing on customary programs may cause agencies to define their roles too narrowly and miss good opportunities for supplying those same benefits through nontraditional offerings.

Program preferences articulated by client groups should be mediated by sound professional judgment as to how sought benefits may be best facilitated. Client groups may be unaware that a better service vehicle is available to deliver the benefits than the program they suggest. Also the programs sought by client groups have to meet with the approval of a majority of citizens in the community.

A selling-oriented agency targets each of its services at "everybody" or "the average user," while a marketing-oriented agency aims at "specific somebodies," that is, targeted groups of people. The fallacy of developing services directed at the average user is that there are actually relatively few "average" users.

The goal of a marketing-oriented agency is to satisfy client group wants, whereas selling-oriented agencies are primarily concerned with numbers of users. Equating numbers with client satisfaction can lead to erroneous conclusions. Large numbers of users may reflect the absence of alternative suppliers of a service or a heavy subsidy rather than client satisfaction with the service.

A selling-oriented agency seeks to generate maximum use primarily through intensive promotion activities. In contrast, a marketing orientation recognizes that promotion is only one of four marketing tools that comprise the marketing mix. The other three elements are program, pricing, and distribution decisions.

Marketing is a set of activities aimed at facilitating and expediting exchanges. Voluntary exchange is the essence of marketing. An agency offers want-satisfying services that citizens perceive to be of value. In exchange for those services, citizens support the agency through their tax payments, direct charges, and expenditures on related equipment if necessary. Travel and personal energy costs are incurred by participation, as well as the opportunity cost of the clients' time.

The set of marketing activities is a system of interacting elements. The starting point is identifying what potential client groups want. This needs assessment, or marketing intelligence, provides the basic information for selecting client groups or target markets. The selection of target markets is strongly influenced by resource allocation decisions that determine which markets receive priority in resource allocation. Citizens and an agency's potential client groups provide input and direction for formulating an agency's objectives.

The four marketing activities of product, distribution, price, and promotion decisions comprise the marketing mix. The identification of client groups and the marketing mix results in a combination of variables that an agency can manipulate to achieve desired outcomes. The success of a service offering in providing satisfaction to client groups should be carefully monitored. If it is not satisfactory, then one or more of the marketing activities should be adjusted in order to deliver a more acceptable level of service.

Although marketing mix activities usually are directed to encourage client use, sometimes demarketing may be required to discourage demand for a service. Demarketing allows client demand to be better matched with an agency's resources.

NOTES

1. Anderson, W.F., Freeden, B.J., and Murphy, M.J., *Managing Human Services*. Chicago: International City Managers Association, 1977, p. 131.
2. Rados, D.L., *Marketing for Non-Profit Organizations*. Boston: Auburn House, 1981, p. 257.
3. Drucker, P.F., *Management: Tasks, Responsibilities, Practices*. New York: Harper & Row, p. 64.
4. Herbert, A.W., "Does Decentralization Mean a Change in Managerial Philosophy?" In L.E. Grosenick (ed.), *The Administration of New Federalism: Objectives and Issues*. Washington, DC: American Society for Public Administration, 1973, p. 86.
5. Perlman R., *Consumers and Social Services*. New York: Wiley, 1975, p. vi.
6. Kotler, P., *Marketing for Nonprofit Organizations* (2nd ed.). Englewood Cliffs, NJ: Prentice-Hall, 1982, p. 63.
7. Reprinted by permission of the *Harvard Business Review*. Excerpt from "Marketing Myopia," Levitt, T.N., July-August 1960, pp. 45–56. Copyright © 1960 by the President and Fellows of Harvard College; all rights reserved.
8. Ibid.
9. Tilles, S., "Making Strategy Explicit." In I. Ansoff (ed.), *Business Strategy*. New York: Penguin, 1969, p. 184.
10. Naisbitt, J., *Megatrends*. New York: Warner, 1982, p. 85.
11. Searles, P.D. "Marketing Principles and the Arts." In M.P. Mokwa, W.M. Dawson, and E.A. Prieve (eds.), *Marketing the Arts*. New York: Praeger, 1980, p. 69.
12. Adapted from Kotler, *Marketing*, p. 23.
13. Goodnow, W.E., "Benefit Segmentation: A Technique for Developing Program and Promotional Strategies for Adults in a Community College." Unpublished Ph.D. dissertation, Northern Illinois University, DeKalb, IL, May 1980.
14. Adapted from Grobowski, S., "Marketing and Promotion Strategies and Techniques." In S.G. Bowes (ed.), *Distinguished Adult Educators Explore Issues, Trends, and Strategies in Adult and Continuing Education*. Department of Secondary and Adult Teacher Education, University of New Mexico, 1979, p. 27.
15. Kotler, *Marketing*, p. 37.

16. Quoted by James M. Buchanan in foreword to Tullock, G., *The Politics of Bureaucracy*. Washington, DC: Public Affairs Press, 1965, p. 1.

17. Kotler, P., and Zaltman, G., "Social Marketing: An Approach to Planned Social Change," *Journal of Marketing*. vol. 35, No. 3, July 1971, p. 9.

18. Based on El-Ansary, A.I., and Kramer, Jr., O.E., "Social Marketing the Family Planning Experience," *Journal of Marketing*. vol. 37, No. 3, July 1973, pp. 3–4, 7.

19. Philips, M., *The Marketing Process: A Handbook to Guide the Continuing Higher Education Administrator*. Memphis, TN: Memphis State University, 1977, p. 24.

20. Kotler, P., "The Major Tasks of Marketing," *Journal of Marketing*, vol. 37, No. 4, October 1973, pp. 42–49.

21. Kotler, *Marketing*, p. 25.

TWO

Relevance of Marketing to Government and Social Service Agencies

Although marketing concepts and techniques have been widely used in the commercial sector for many years, marked interest in marketing among government and social service agencies emerged only in the late 1970s. The stimulus to move away from "business as usual" was a series of dramatic shifts in the social and financial environments within which agencies operate. As these factors became more threatening, government and social service agencies began to turn to marketing.

The new environments were characterized by reduced availability of financial resources from traditional tax and philanthropic sources, decreasing client satisfaction and participation, increasing competition from both public and private organizations, and vocal criticism from taxpayers, lawmakers, bureaucrats, employees, clients, consumerists, and other interested groups.

This chapter focuses on how interest in marketing was stimulated in the public sector and its relevance to government and social service agencies. Since such agencies must service not only client groups but also many other publics, what publics are and the implications of serving multiple publics are the next concern. Differences between public and private sector marketing are also explored in terms of environment and organization differences, profit versus nonprofit orientations, and distinctions between the marketing of goods and services.

GROWTH OF AGENCY INTEREST IN MARKETING

Although marketing is appropriate for all government and social service agencies, it becomes increasingly important as more of an agency's financial costs are shifted directly onto clients and personnel start to recognize that clients have gained control of at least some of the resources that the agency needs to survive. Reduced tax support, increased reliance on revenues derived from direct user pricing, and increased critical scrutiny by citizens caused many agencies to conclude in the early 1980s that they were in a state of crisis. Their traditional ways of operating were no longer receiving the necessary level of support from appointed or elected officials, or from citizen taxpayers. It became clear that agencies and professional helpers who could not attract satisfied users or clients were unlikely to survive. This feeling of crisis provoked agency personnel to explore marketing concepts and techniques and to accept them as a promising framework for planning and implementing service delivery.

Crises force reappraisal of existing operating methods and persuade managers that yesterday's formulas for success are often neither effective nor efficient in meeting the needs and wants of today's clientele. As Kevin White, former mayor of Boston, once observed, "I hate these constant crises, but without them would we ever get anything done?" The Chinese explain the potential that a crisis offers for improvement through their written symbol for the word. This symbol is composed of two characters, one indicating danger and the other

Figure 2.1. Chinese Symbol for Crisis.

opportunity (Figure 2.1). Danger is an effective stimulus for action and change. It has forced many agencies to examine the opportunities offered by marketing concepts and techniques.

Now that agencies are experimenting with marketing, the remaining challenge, to which this book is intended to make a contribution, has been expressed as follows:

> To further increase acceptance of marketing tools and concepts among public and nonprofit managers will require the *marketing of marketing itself*. The task is two-fold. First, it must be demonstrated that marketing is applicable to their specific situations. Second, nonbusiness managers (like their business counterparts) must be educated to recognize the scope and complexity of marketing.[1]

RELEVANCE OF MARKETING FOR GOVERNMENT AND SOCIAL SERVICE AGENCIES

Marketing does not require government and social service agencies to implement a series of highly sophisticated new activities or assign substantial new responsibilities. Indeed, it is sometimes argued that agency personnel are already marketers because they perform at least some marketing activities. For this reason, the appropriate question is not whether an organization should practice marketing or not, but rather how thoughtful it should be about it, and whether it will practice it well or poorly.

A commitment to marketing offers public sector agencies three major benefits. First, because marketing is a systematic process and offers a framework for decision making, relationships between actions previously regarded as independent are likely to become more apparent. Marketing activities are coordinated to achieve goals that otherwise might not be attained if they were pursued in an uncoordinated fashion. If, for example, a marketing problem or opportunity is seen only in information terms, or program terms, or distribution terms, it is unlikely to be optimally resolved. Optimal marketing decisions require that all marketing activities and their interactions be reviewed simultaneously and integrated action taken.

The second major benefit is that some of the concepts and techniques used by marketers in their decision processes are often unfamiliar to public sector managers because they have not been exposed to these tools in their formal training. Familiarity with these marketing tools is likely to lead to improvements in decision making.

Finally, a commitment to marketing is likely to result in more popular and legislative support. To the extent that marketing improves the satisfaction levels of client groups, an agency is likely to receive improved support for its activities from legislators.

CONCEPT OF PUBLICS

A public may be defined as a distinct group of people and/or organizations that have an actual or a potential interest in, or impact upon, an agency.[2] To this point, our discussion has focused upon the exchange relationship between an agency and its potential client groups. Government and social service agencies, however, have to interact with publics other than their direct clients. These other publics influence an agency's operations by supporting or criticizing it. Each of these publics is likely to answer the question "What's in it for me?" differently. An agency must identify the benefits each of these publics is seeking and develop a marketing mix that will best expedite an exchange with that public. In that way it will garner the group's valued resources and support.

Figure 2.2 identifies many of the publics with which government and social service agencies interact. Designating them as primary, secondary, and tertiary suggests their relative importance but is not absolute. Each of these publics can be further subdivided into smaller groups of constituents, and for any agency additional publics that impact it uniquely can probably be identified. The configuration of publics is what makes each individual agency's environment unique.

Not all of the publics will be equally as important to the agency in every project. In some instances a particular public may be disinterested, while in other instances it may be concerned and involved. The level of interest will influence the amount of marketing effort that needs to be directed to each of the publics.

In Figure 2.3 a high school is used to illustrate the differing concerns of the major publics and to suggest how they might answer the question "What is in it for me?" The importance of developing a separate marketing strategy for

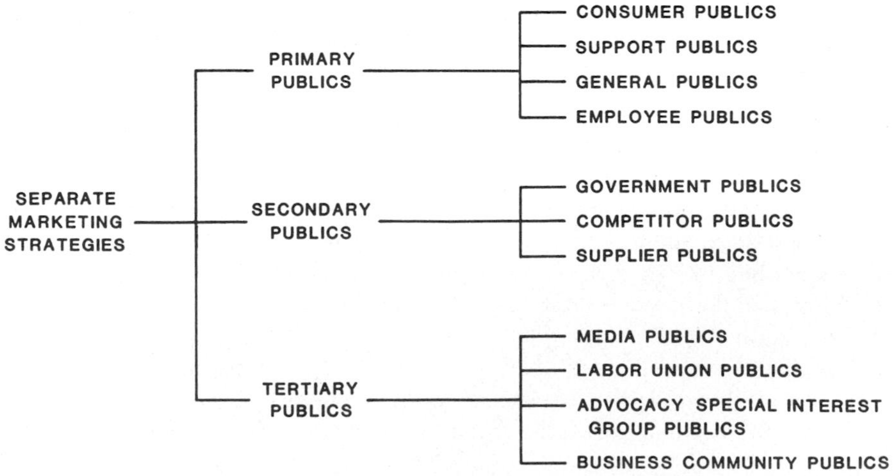

Figure 2.2. Major Publics.

PRIMARY PUBLICS

Consumer Publics–Those who directly benefit from the services, i.e., students and parents.

Benefits they seek could include:
- Vocationally relevant skills
- Development of self-confidence and self-esteem
- Knowledge necessary to be an informed citizen
- Preparation for college

Support Publics–Those who provide funds for the school, i.e., school board, foundations, civic groups, parent-teacher organizations, alumni associations.

Benefits they seek could include:
- Evidence that resources are efficiently and effectively utilized
- Increase in personal stature and reputation in the community
- Meeting commitments that they made to constituents when they were placed in the role of resource provider
- The satisfaction of contributing to students' educational process through allocation of resources

General Public–Consists of nonusers as well as users. They provide the tax support base either directly through their vote in bond referendums (in which case they should be viewed as a Support Public) or through more indirect influence on their elected representatives.

Benefits they seek could include:
- Satisfaction of contributing to the education of young people
- Evidence that resources are being efficiently and effectively used
- Evidence that the curriculum is consistent with the citizen's perception of educational priorities
- Increase in property values because the community is recognized as having an excellent school system

Employee Publics–Those who work for the school. If their needs are well served, they will be inclined to serve the students' needs well. The commitment, skill, and enthusiasm of groups such as teachers, administrators, janitors, and health and safety personnel will ultimately affect how the school is judged.

Benefits they seek could include:
- Recognition of their contribution
- An equitable work load that is challenging but not onerous
- Good renumeration and security
- Opportunities for personal growth, training, and advancement
- Pleasant working environment

SECONDARY PUBLICS

Government Publics–Legislatures, aid-granting agencies, licensing and accreditation agencies.

Benefits they seek could include:
- Evidence of a superior system and staff
- Evidence that resources are being efficiently and effectively allocated
- Noncontroversial programs that are unlikely to arouse public criticism

Competitor Publics–Alternative private schools in the area; other school systems; other public service agencies. Emphasis here is likely to be on securing passive acceptance rather than on active support.

Benefits they seek could include:
- Compatibility of the services offered with their own operations, emphasizing complementary rather than competitive dimensions of the services
- If competitors are seeking only passive acceptance, the agency need only emphasize how it will not hurt them rather than what benefits it will bring to them.

Figure 2.3. "What's in It for Me?"—The Benefits Sought by the Major Publics of a High School.

Supplier Publics–Textbook publishers, equipment and furnishing suppliers, contractors.
Benefits they seek could include:
Opportunities to sell their products and services

TERTIARY PUBLICS

Media Publics–Broadcast and print media.
Benefits they seek could include:
News item that will be of interest to their publics
Feature and human interest stories
Sports activities

Labor Unions–For professional and janitorial staff.
Benefits they seek could include:
Improved working conditions for their members
Clearly defined job responsibilities
Higher salaries
A voice in administering the school

Advocacy and Special Interest Group Publics–Examples include handicapped groups, advocates of specific subject areas, athletic booster groups, groups concerned with raising academic standards, advocates for gifted and talented students.
Benefits they seek will vary according to their mission. A handicapped group, for example, may seek:
Mainstreaming, which ensures that the handicapped will be integrated with other children in classes
Particular physical design features incorporated in the school to accommodate the handicapped
Sports programs for the handicapped

Business Community Publics–Future employers in the community and establishments of further education.
Benefits they seek could include:
Cooperation with school classes to offer "live" project experiences
Students with the basic skills required to function effectively in the workforce (or in further education)
Students with positive attitudes toward work (or further education)

Figure 2.3. (Continued)

each of these publics lies in the impact that a public's lack of support could have on an agency's offering.

DIFFERENCES BETWEEN PUBLIC AND PRIVATE SECTOR MARKETING

Our proposition, and the premise upon which this book is developed, is that private sector marketing knowledge is transferable, with important modifications, to government and social service agencies. Marketing is as relevant to government and social service agencies as it is to profit-seeking organizations in the private sector.

Initially, the claim that marketing concepts and techniques were appropriate for nonprofit and public organizations generated considerable controversy.[3] Critics argued that marketing should be confined to transactions for the sale and purchase of goods and services by private sector firms.[4] However, the goal of government and social service agencies is to provide satisfaction to their client groups, which is exactly the same goal pursued by private sector organizations.

All marketing activities are directed by an agency's mission and its objectives (see Figure 1.7). *The set of marketing activities are neutral tools that can be used to assist an agency in achieving whatever objectives it establishes. This definition makes their application as appropriate for humanistic, social service organizations as for capitalist, commercial organizations*. Marketing is a process concerned with maximizing the use of scarce resources to achieve whatever objectives the community seeks.

Now that marketing is becoming recognized as an appropriate activity for government and social service managers, the new challenge is to examine the marketing skills, techniques, and concepts that have been developed in the private sector. Agencies need to identify what they can transfer into the public sector and determine what modifications are needed for the different environment within which government and social service agencies operate. Some marketing ideas may not be directly transferable from the private to the public sector, but then some marketing ideas are not directly transferable between private sector firms either.

Successful transfer depends on understanding the different contexts within which people in private and public sector organizations operate. Differences that influence the transferability of private sector marketing knowledge into the public sector include (1) environmental and organizational differences, (2) profit and nonprofit orientations, and (3) distinctions between goods and services.

Environmental and Organizational Differences

Differences in the environments and organizational structures of public and private sector organizations may be categorized under three broad headings: environmental forces, organization–general public interrelationships, and internal structures and processes.[5]

Environmental Forces. Marketing decisions and activities do not occur in a vacuum. They are influenced by many events, including social, economic, legal, technological, and competitive forces that are external to the agency and frequently beyond the control of agency personnel. There are three environmental factors that are perhaps not as widely recognized but that are of particular relevance in this context because of their differential impact on public and private sector organizations. They are autonomy and flexibility, degree of market exposure, and political influences.

Public sector organizations have less autonomy and flexibility than private firms. These limitations affect the extent and speed with which they are able to implement marketing activities such as introducing and withdrawing programs, changing price structures, advertising, opening or closing facilities, or focusing attention on the most responsive segments of the market. This description is not intended to imply that public organizations cannot effectively engage in marketing. It simply acknowledges that they often do not have as much flexibility as private firms in this regard.

Degree of market exposure refers to the extent to which an organization is subject to the forces of supply, demand, and competition for revenues. Public organizations have less market exposure than private firms because they obtain some, most, or all of their revenues from political appropriations instead of directly from clients who purchase their services. Because they experience less market pressure, government and social service agencies are generally believed to have less incentive for reducing costs, improving efficiency, or generally improving performance than their private sector counterparts. It is frequently argued that "managers of organizations financed by appropriations will seek organizational growth and personal aggrandizement by maximizing appropriations and thus tend to deemphasize operating efficiency."[6]

Political forces have a much greater impact on public sector organizations than on private organizations. Popular elections, political appointments, interest group demands, lobbying efforts, and the political agendas of elected and appointed officials tend to have a destabilizing effect on many government and social service organizations because political consensus and program and resource priorities change frequently. This adversely affects the implementation of marketing activities such as mission and objective specification, long-range planning, budgeting, pricing, program prioritizing, and general operating procedures. Private organizations are not nearly as impacted by the destabilizing events that regularly occur in the political arena because, in the private sector, professional managers control resource allocations and tend to be guided by consistent long-term objectives.

Organization–General Public Interrelationships. Government and social service agencies have a much more comprehensive interrelationship with the general public than their private sector counterparts. These interrelationships provide both marketing opportunities and constraints that do not exist in the private sector. For example, individuals cannot avoid participating in the financing of most government activities. They pay for them indirectly with their taxes regardless of whether or not they use the services offered. Furthermore, individuals cannot avoid using many of the services of government organizations either because no alternative service suppliers exist or because citizens are required by law to use them. Examples include municipal water, sewerage, police, and fire services.

Government entities exist to serve the citizens in their jurisdiction. Thus the citizens as a whole establish government entities through the constitutional and charter process. Business enterprises, in contrast, are created by, and are responsible to, only a limited number of individuals. Since government agencies are essentially owned by citizens, potential clientele often have performance expectations beyond those that they have for private organizations. These may include higher levels of integrity, fairness, responsiveness, and accountability. This proprietary interest of citizens means that government and social service agencies are subject to much greater public scrutiny, outside monitoring, and are able to keep fewer secrets than businesses. Citizens desire openness in government and make efforts to reduce or eliminate abuses of government power.

Internal Structures and Processes. Internal structure and process differences between public and private organizations include the nature and complexity of objectives, decision making, individual authority, and motivation. The objectives of government and social service agencies, for example, are normally more complex, diverse, vague, and intangible than the objectives of private organizations. Sales and profit goals are much easier to specify and evaluate than most public organization objectives. Furthermore, many public organization objectives are contradictory and involve intricate tradeoff regarding who gets what. These complex issues are explored in Chapters 3 and 7.

Line authority and decision-making responsibilities are normally more clearly defined in private organizations. In public agencies the political process, bureaucratic procedures, and multiple hierarchies often create uncertainty regarding authority and responsibility for decisions and subsequent actions.

Incentives and rewards for performance tend to be greater in private than in public organizations. Civil service regulations, government employee unions, and rigid pay and promotion guidelines are a few of the factors that limit an agency's ability to motivate and reward public employees.

Profit and Nonprofit Orientations

The distinction between profit and nonprofit orientations is often cited as a major difference between private and public sector organizations and their abilities to engage in marketing activities.[7] Two primary implications stem from this difference. First, the public sector focuses on service rather than profit objectives, which can create difficulties in measuring performance. Second, private enterprises use direct client pricing to raise revenue, whereas government and social service organizations typically rely upon taxation or philanthropy for at least some of their revenues.

Profit and Service Objectives. In the private sector the profit motive provides both a consistent objective that guides decisions and a criterion for evaluating results. However, most government and social service agencies are expected to provide equitable, effective, and efficient services that are responsive to the wants and preferences of their clientele, elected and appointed officials, and the general public. The complexity and intangibility of public organization objectives make performance evaluation difficult. Cost-benefit analysis and similar methods of performance assessment used in the public sector are less objective and precise than the bottom line profit figure used by private organizations for measuring performance and assessing opportunities.

The emphasis on service rather than on profit creates dilemmas for public sector marketers that do not exist in the private sector. A business organization will seek to make profit by directing its offerings exclusively at responsive client groups and it is likely to ignore others who may be less responsive. In contrast, the most critical question facing many public agencies is not how to service relatively responsive target markets, but rather what strategies may be most useful for attracting those who are apathetic, disinterested, or reluctant to use a service. Public agencies frequently are mandated to give highest priority in marketing services to those who are least likely to respond, for example, antismoking, vaccination, family planning, wellness, or fitness programs. This issue is discussed in detail in Chapters 6 and 7.

Pricing. The primary function of pricing in the private sector is to raise revenue. However, in public organizations the income redistribution, equity, and efficiency functions of price are generally of more concern than raising revenues. Herein lies a fundamental distinction between marketing in the public and private sectors. Public agencies are required to allocate resources and distribute services equitably, whereas private sector organizations direct resources only at the most responsive market segments. All organizations strive to be efficient, effective, and accountable, but in addition public agencies have to be equitable. Because equity is such a complex and pervasive issue in the public sector, intruding into every marketing mix decision, a detailed discussion of its role is provided in Chapter 7.

Other dimensions of pricing that are different in the public sector include indirect payment through taxes for "free" services, separation between those who pay for and those who use services, and below-cost pricing. These issues are addressed in Chapters 13 and 14.

Distinctions Between Goods and Services

Traditional marketing concepts and tools were developed primarily by businesses concerned with producing goods rather than services, but most government and social service agencies are responsible for the delivery of services rather than physical goods. By the end of the 1980s, however, services could account for more than half of the nation's economic activity.[8] Thus even the private sector has shown considerable interest in adapting traditional techniques to the marketing of services.

The key distinction between goods and services is that services are intangible.[9] They cannot be seen, heard, smelled, tasted, or felt in the same manner as goods. Whereas goods may be produced, stored, sold, and then delivered at some later date, services are produced and consumed simultaneously.

Service quality is more difficult to assess and control than that of tangible goods. Services cannot be inspected and tested as they move along a production line. Service quality may vary based upon the individual providing or receiving the service. Even the quality of service provided by a particular individual may vary from day to day.

Furthermore, it is more difficult for clients to evaluate a service than a tangible good. Most goods have characteristics that can be evaluated prior to purchase (e.g., the color of an appliance) and during usage (e.g., whether or not a deodorant is "runny"). The benefits of a physical fitness program or an educational experience, on the other hand, are more difficult to assess objectively.

SUMMARY

Although marketing concepts and techniques have been widely used in the commercial sector for many years, marked interest among government and social service agencies emerged only in the late 1970s as the result of dramatic shifts in the environment within which agencies operated. A feeling of crisis grew from the realization that traditional ways of operating were no longer receiving the customary level of support from decision makers or citizens. This necessary stimulus forced managers to explore the opportunities offered by marketing.

Commitment to marketing offers public sector agencies three major benefits. First, because marketing is a systematic process and offers a framework for decision making, relationships between actions previously regarded as independent are likely to become apparent. Second, some of the concepts and techniques used by marketers in their decision processes are often unfamiliar to public sector managers because they have not been exposed to these tools in their formal training. Familiarity with these marketing tools is likely to lead to improvements in decision making. Finally, a commitment to marketing is likely to result in more citizen and legislative support.

Government and social service agencies have to interact with publics other than their direct clients. Each of these publics is likely to answer the question "What's in it for me?" differently, so different marketing programs will be required to expedite exchanges with each of them.

Private sector marketing knowledge is transferable to government and social agencies, but it has to be adopted and modified for the public sector context. Three broad differences influence the extent of transferability of private sector marketing knowledge into the public sector: (1) environmental and organizational differences, (2) profit and nonprofit orientations, and (3) distinctions between goods and services.

The most important environmental and organizational differences can be categorized under three headings: environmental forces, organization–general public interrelationships, and internal structures and processes. The two primary implications stemming from differences in profit and nonprofit orientations are (1) the public sector focuses on service rather than profit objectives, which creates subsequent difficulties in measuring performance, and (2) private enterprises use direct client pricing to raise revenue, whereas government and social service organizations typically rely on taxation or philanthropy for at least some of their revenues. The key distinction between goods and services is that services are intangible. Quality control and evaluation thus become more difficult.

NOTES

1. Lovelock, C.H., and Weinberg, C.B., "Public and Non-Profit Marketing Comes of Age," in G. Zaltman and T.V. Bonoma, *Review of Marketing*. Chicago: American Marketing Association, 1978, p. 449.
2. Kotler, P. *Marketing For Nonprofit Organizations* (2nd ed.). Englewood Cliffs, NJ: Prentice-Hall, 1982, p. 63.
3. Kotler, P., and Levy, S., "Broadening the Concept of Marketing," *Journal of Marketing*, vol. 33, January 1969, pp. 10–15.
4. See, for example, Luck, D.J. "Broadening the Concept of Marketing Too Far," *Journal of Marketing*, vol. 33, July 1969, pp. 53–55.
5. This section draws extensively from the comprehensive literature review undertaken by Rainey, H.G., Backoff, R.W., and Levine, C.H., "Comparing Public and Private Organizations," *Public Administration Review*, March/April 1976, pp. 234–239.
6. Ibid., p. 235.
7. See, for example, Lovelock, C.H., and Weinberg, C.B., "Contrasting Private and Public Sector Marketing." Chicago: In R.C. Curhan (ed.), *Proceedings of the 1974 American Marketing Association Educator Conference*, 1974, pp. 242–247.
8. "Service Industries: Growth Field of '80's," *U.S. News and World Report*, March 17, 1980, pp. 80–84.
9. Bateson, J.E.G., Langeard, P.E., and Lovelock, C.H., *Testing a Conceptual Framework for Consumer Service Marketing*. Cambridge, MA: Marketing Science Institute, 1978, p. 11.

THREE

Developing a Marketing Plan

A key requirement for good marketing is good marketing planning. This chapter focuses on formulating and implementing a plan. (Chapter 4 addresses evaluation, the final step in the planning process.) The business community has long recognized the importance of a formalized marketing plan for successful management. Planning is the key to survival because it is the road map or blueprint that guides all marketing endeavors.

> In today's complex world of business, strategic planning is indispensable to effective management. Ever since the mid-1950's, when American companies began to develop formal long-range planning systems, wise managers have understood the importance of knowing where their firm was headed and how it intended to get there. To function effectively in a modern, planned operation, *every* manager must have a practical understanding of how the planning process works.[1]

Foresight is an essential part of marketing. To foresee, in this context, means both to assess the future and to make provision for it. Some people believe that planning is merely deciding what to do in the future. A better description of planning, however, may be deciding what you have to do in order to *have* a future!

EMERGENCE OF MARKETING PLANNING

In government and social service agencies, the term *planning* traditionally has been used to refer to infrastructure or facility planning, and its use has revolved around construction of new facilities. This limited view of planning is no longer appropriate. Planning must incorporate anticipation of change and the development of appropriate strategies to deal with change. Such planning is concerned with identifying environmental impacts and making appropriate adjustments in *all* aspects of an agency's service delivery efforts. Physical planning is only one small part of an agency's operations.

In an era of retrenchment, physical planning gives place to the much more substantial concern of formulating directions and realigning resources to facilitate effective total service delivery efforts in the future. The marketing plan embodies, in capsule form, an agency's realistic intentions for competing successfully in the marketplace.[2] As Figure 3.1 illustrates, strategic marketing planning is a continuous process concerned with:

1. Analyzing the macro environment
2. Undertaking needs assessments to analyze performance and identify future opportunities and threats
3. Determining agency mission
4. Specifying objectives

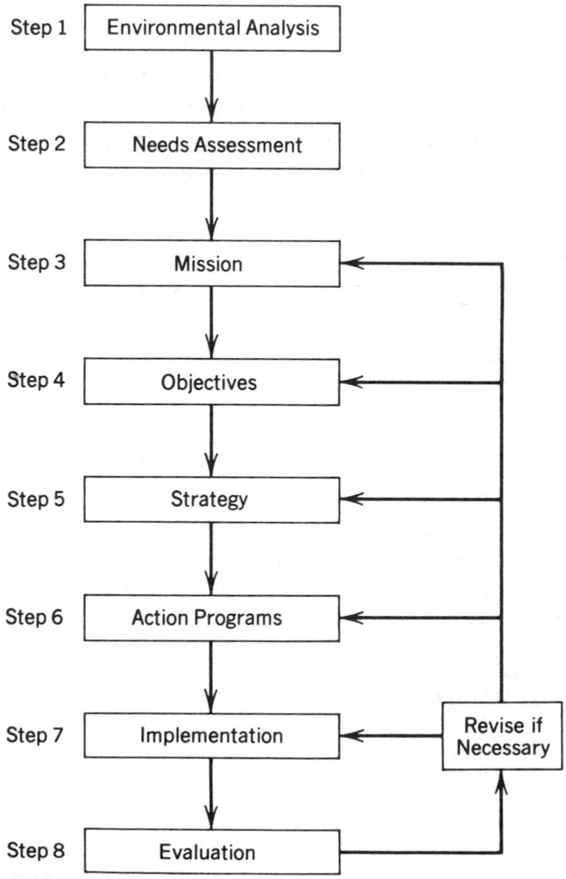

Figure 3.1. Steps in the Marketing Planning Process.

5. Selecting strategies to achieve specified objectives
6. Developing action programs
7. Implementation
8. Evaluating performance

The emergence among public agencies of interest in strategic marketing planning is not accidental. The increasingly complex environmental pressures to which agencies are exposed has intensified the search for a more effective process for guiding agency decisions. The predictable pattern of expanded services, increasing budgets, and new facility developments that provided some logic for the preoccupation with physical planning in the past has been replaced by a much less predictable environment in which primary planning concerns relate to the impact of competitive forces, reduced public support, accountability demands, and increased regulatory and legislative requirements.

It is an unfortunate trait of human nature that we rarely engage in any action until under pressure to do so. Perhaps the major reason for lack of effective marketing planning in public agencies has been the lack of a catalyzing crisis. Growth can be managed on an ad hoc basis; retrenchment cannot. With growth it was possible for agencies to prosper with little strategic planning. Citizen demands could be met by raising taxes and an agency's leaders could "let a thousand flowers" bloom. In an era of decline, they are required to decide consciously not only what to plant, cultivate, and nourish but also what to plow under.[3] This radical change in environmental conditions is encouraging a shift in government and social service agencies from facility-oriented physical planning to market-oriented strategic planning.

> Three forces have pushed strategic planning to the center of executive attention. The first, and most important, reason is *survival*. . . . Strategic marketing planning is a necessary requirement for . . . success in these turbulent times. Second is the recognition by many chief executive officers of the central role of markets and marketing strategies in shaping strategic plans. The third force is the need to track the rapidly changing . . . environment in order to anticipate change and to develop strategies to take advantage of new opportunities.[4]

Strategic marketing planning aids management in two primary ways:

It focuses attention on long-term objectives rather than on short-term expediencies, thus providing direction for action and a guiding perspective in times of crisis.

It forces management to continually realign its resources with the changing external environment and changing clientele want priorities.

Marketing planning, or its lack, is a concrete expression of the way in which an agency, through its management, has decided to live. Many agency managers are too preoccupied with immediate issues to think about what the agency will be doing in the future. Yet these same managers make frequent decisions with long-term implications. A typical comment is, "The pressures of the moment prevent me from giving any attention to the future of the agency." Other managers are action-minded and decision-oriented. They enjoy and derive great satisfaction from "doing things." Instead of engaging in strategic planning they settle for "muddling through."

"Do you want me to plan it or do it?" is not a legitimate question. Planning and doing are separate parts of the same job; they are not separate jobs. The real payoff of a marketing plan is the help it gives management in making better decisions. It enables managers to act today with increased skill, speed, and confidence in order to produce desired results tomorrow. Even those who have no responsibility for the overall direction of the agency can use the marketing planning process to guide departments and subdivisions within the organization.

IMPORTANCE OF PLANNING

Techniques of strategic marketing planning are important, but its success or failure in an agency is likely to depend less on techniques and more on the commitment and participation of senior management. Strategic decisions do not make an automatic claim on top management's attention. Unless actively pursued, planning may be neglected in favor of the on-going urgency of immediate operational problems:

> To illustrate the importance of strategic planning consider the plight of a private university that is experiencing a rapidly deteriorating financial climate. The university begins to suffer financial reverses because of a decrease in the student body and its only recourse is to increase tuition. An increase in tuition will eventually lead to a further deterioration in the number of students enrolled and so a vicious circle begins. In order to justify a higher tuition the private university must achieve a level of greater excellence than the public university. To reduce costs, university managers reduce the salary increases paid to faculty and reduce the number of outstanding new faculty hired. Then, gradually, the university's excellence will deteriorate and it will no longer be in the position to justify the higher tuition cost.
>
> If the university continues to operate in its traditional way, its demise is probably inevitable. To break this vicious circle, the university's leaders need to define an equilibrium position at a smaller size and plan how to get (and stop) there. A strategic marketing plan aims at uncovering such a situation and developing alternatives. Generally, while an organization is contracting and reallocating its resources to a new mix of services and/or target markets, a need will emerge that will allow the organization to remain viable. It may be possible to eliminate some of the educational areas in which the university is losing money or in which there is declining student demand. Resources can be focused into other areas in which the organization has expertise and where demand is relatively high. Perhaps

> reducing the emphasis on producing educational services and increasing the emphasis on research services is in order. Thus students would become less important and outside research contracts and grants more important.[5]

The word "strategy" is derived from a Greek root meaning generalship. Strategic planning is the process during which the really fundamental and fateful decisions that are within the agency's control are made. The resources available to an agency are usually less than the opportunities for service delivery. Hence the importance of planned decision making. It is here that the agency seeks to realign its activities and redirect its efforts to ensure that they are the best fit for the current and predicted future environment.

> Strategic planning looks objectively at where the organization is now, at where it has been in the past, at where it is headed in the future, and how it is going to get there. Strategic planning assumes that change is inevitable: change brings with it risk but strategic planning can chart a course so that an organization minimizes risks while maximizing opportunities.[6]

Good planning takes time and resources. If procrastination prevails and the process described in this section of the book is delayed until a severe crisis, then the necessary resources to undertake the job may become more difficult to obtain. The end result is likely to be less than optimum.

OBJECTIVES OF THE PLANNING PROCESS

The strategic planning process has six key objectives:

1. Challenge the prevailing assumptions about the role and purpose of the agency. All too often agency marketing plans tend merely to project the present offerings and methods of delivery into the future. What is lacking is the challenge of prevailing service delivery efforts implicit in strategic planning.
2. Identify needs in the service area that are not adequately met.
3. Develop a plan that recognizes both external and internal realities.
4. Achieve consensus among key organization members on a common direction and future strategies.
5. Link strategic planning to action and implementation.
6. Educate key people concerning the external and internal realities as well as the values and aspirations of key groups.[7]

Many managers have ideas about what they want to achieve in the future and in this sense they have a plan. However, a formal marketing plan, developed in the form of a written document, is essential for purposeful management since it guides the future operation of marketing functions. Without a written plan, it is likely that short-term decisions will be made to achieve short-term objectives that may be inconsistent with the agency's best long-term interests. "If it isn't on paper, you haven't got a plan. Talking about what you want to do is like a New Year's resolution. It's all verbal, makes you feel good, and nothing ever happens. Put it on paper."[8]

TIMEFRAME OF PLANS

The development of a marketing plan involves both long-term and short-term planning. Long-term plans, often called strategic plans, are prepared for three- to five-year time horizons and focus on broad strategic issues that affect the overall agency. Five years appears to be the appropriate long-term planning timeframe for most agencies, but in a particularly dynamic environment four or even three years may be more appropriate. Generally a period shorter than five years relates too closely to immediate operating problems and discourages the consideration of longer-term planning opportunities and considerations. A planning timeframe of longer than five years is probably too long because, in this very dynamic environment, too much uncertainty exists to allow relatively specific strategic plans to be developed.

Short-term plans, often called action programs, are developed for time periods of one year or less. They normally focus on specific programs. When the actions defined in an action program have been achieved, they should contribute toward achievement of the longer-term strategy plan.

STEPS IN PREPARING A MARKETING PLAN

Figure 3.1 illustrates the steps in developing and evaluating a marketing plan. The sequence is important. Traditionally, many government and social service agencies have started with mission statements and objectives. Such an approach starts from the inside and works out to the consumer. A marketing approach starts from the outside and works inward. That is, it starts with an analysis of the macroenvironment and the consumer and, after identifying consumers' wants and needs, uses them as the basis for formulating the agency's mission and objectives and for guiding its marketing strategy and action programs.

Environmental Analysis

Marketing decisions are influenced, and often shaped, by dynamic, uncontrollable forces that are external to the agency. An understanding of these environmental forces enables an agency to anticipate shifts and formulate adaptive strategies instead of being constantly forced to react to crises. An assessment of the impact of these forces on the agency's mission statement, selection of target markets, and marketing mix decisions should be the starting point in the planning process.

Peter Drucker has said, "A time of turbulence is a dangerous time but its greatest danger is a temptation to ignore reality."[9] It is becoming increasingly apparent that the major opportunities for an agency, and the most dangerous threats that it will face in the future, lie in the environment rather than within the organization. It is a truism that nothing is permanent but change. In the past, many agencies have only paid lip service to the impact of environmental forces. They took no action because crises or changes in needs could frequently be resolved by directing additional resources to them as they emerged. Thus agencies could survive or flourish by concerning themselves only with the microenvironment. Resolving problems or addressing opportunities with new resources, however, is no longer a feasible option for many agencies.

Ecologists suggest that those animals which are best able to adapt to changes in their environment are most likely to survive. This tenet is equally applicable to government and social service agencies, which are clearly not immune to the massive changes taking place in today's society.

Consideration of environmental forces is important because they determine many of the "sideboards" or parameters within which the agency must function. They impact and mold the marketplace. This means that they impact directly on marketing decisions made in the microenvironment. The future influences the present as much or more than does the past. Effective marketing planning requires a systematic analysis of the impact of these influences on the agency.

Agencies will always be confronted with crises created by unpredictable environmental forces that require short-term reaction. While recognizing that, however, an examination of environmental forces enhances an agency's ability to be proactive by looking beyond the short-term horizon and considering the impact of changing demographic and economic conditions, political and legal trends, actions of competitors, unfolding technology, and availability of natural resources. Without an understanding of the potential impact of these forces, an agency is constantly forced to react to crises instead of anticipating shifts and formulating strategies to adapt to them. Good planning has been described as a two-step process: first figure out what is inevitable, then find a way to take advantage of it.

Often managers have a general awareness of environmental trends from reports in the popular media or articles in professional journals, but they don't seem to relate these trends to the daily operation of their agency. They continue to react only to short-term developments and, as a result, are surprised and unprepared for the ultimate impact of changes in the macroenvironment. Many environmental changes may appear to be slow. However, they frequently creep up on us unexpectedly:

> Twenty years seems a vast distance to travel, yet in fact it is a very short distance and one that is traversed quickly by local governments. It takes five to seven

> years to plan, design and build a city hall; a major water system cannot be built in less than twelve years; and major transit systems such as those in San Francisco, Atlanta and Washington, D.C., can take a full twenty years to complete. These services are provided by local governments.[10]

Some government and social service managers regard environmental changes as sources of problems. Service offerings that were once appropriate and successful have to be changed because of fluidity in the external environment. This attitude reveals a product orientation. The marketing-oriented manager, on the other hand, perceives environmental changes as offering new opportunities, not problems. He or she recognizes that client needs have changed because of changes in the environment and is excited by the challenge of adapting services to meet these new needs. Anticipation of environmental changes can transform crisis and disaster into opportunity and success.

Recognizing environmental forces is of no real value to an agency unless the operating implications of these forces are identified. The manager must ask the question, "What *specifically* does this mean to my agency in terms of its operations?"

A myriad of uncontrollable forces influence an agency's marketing decisions. Some of the major trends are briefly noted in the following paragraphs, but these trends are general and must be appropriately amended and interpreted in the unique context of an agency's particular jurisdiction. For example, while there is a declining school population nationally, a number of states and cities are experiencing increases in the number of school-age young people they must serve.

Since marketing efforts are guided by citizens' needs and since many of these needs are related to demographic characteristics, changing demographics are perhaps the most important environmental influence on marketing decisions. Four major changes in population structure are noteworthy.

First, substantial changes are taking place in the composition of the family unit. The key concepts for understanding current family structures are diversity and transitions. The stereotypical family life cycle pattern is likely to be a relevant model for only a minority of citizens. More individuals will be in some stage of fundamental transition than ever before. Families are becoming smaller and periods of being single are becoming more common for all ages.

Second, radical changes are taking place in the age structure of the U.S. population. These changes are emerging as a result of very different fertility rates during three recent time periods. The babies born in these time periods have been called the depression cohort, the baby boom cohort, and the baby bust cohort. As these cohorts pass through life, they disrupt the "normal" pyramidical pattern of a stable population. These disturbances will continue to have a tremendous impact on society. Every government and social service agency will be affected. Responding to the needs of older citizens will become a growing priority.

Third, much of the transition in the lives of women is associated with changes in their employment patterns. Women's employment has surged, particularly among groups who were the least likely to work in the past—married mothers and especially mothers of preschool children. This trend suggests that many women will have less discretionary time in the future. It means they will have less time for activities such as child care, chauffeuring their children, volunteer leadership, and personal leisure.

Fourth, urban communities are likely to continue to become more ethnically diverse, forcing agencies to re-evaluate traditional services and to further expand their range of specialized offerings. Because of their different cultural origins and background, for example, white ethnic groups, blacks, Asians, and Hispanics each express unique lifestyles, interests, and needs.

Two major geographical shifts have occurred: intraregional and interregional. Intraregional transitions reflect the processes of urbanization and suburbanization. The population leaving the large urban centers are mostly younger, better educated, and richer than those that remain in the cities. Interregional transitions have been dominated by a substantial migration to the Sunbelt. These movements bring with them increased demand for agency services in those areas, which must be reconciled with demands for lower tax burdens.

The economic environment has changed drastically from the highly stable, predictable growth pattern that characterized government funding until the mid-1970s. The passing of the Proposition 13 tax limitation measure in California in June 1978 was a watershed that symbolized a dramatic retrenchment in the public attitude toward government spending. Reductions are occurring in both local property taxes and federal aid to local jurisdictions. The situation has been worsened because those most able to pay property taxes and least in need of social services are leaving the older cities, thus eroding the tax base, while socially dependent people tend to concentrate in the central cities. It is clear that, in terms of real dollars, all levels of government will have reduced fiscal resources to allocate for the delivery of services in the future.

Although policy making has classically been perceived as the prerogative of elected officials, managers cannot avoid becoming policy initiators or advocates because they are required to recommend courses of action. Effective marketing can only take place if its outputs are consistent with prevailing laws, mandates, public opinion, and the political climate. This environment has become increasingly dynamic in recent years as more groups have sought to influence the political process.

All government and social service agencies face increased competitive pressures. In recent years the number and range of offerings available from other public and from private sector organizations have proliferated.

The impact of technology on government and social services is both direct and indirect. Technology affects agencies directly by enabling them to perform their functions more efficiently and effectively. Indirectly it influences the lives and the lifestyles of clientele groups. Much of the potential of new technology lies in the opportunities that it offers for improved communications and decentralized service delivery.

The supply of two major natural resources, energy and water, is particularly uncertain. Agencies need to consider the impact of this reduced supply and to develop contingency plans. Certainly higher prices and better conservation procedures for energy services and water will become increasingly pressing concerns.

Needs Assessment

Needs assessments and program evaluations together form an agency's marketing intelligence system. Needs assessment is designed to identify and analyze market opportunities, while program evaluation assesses on-going services. Thus needs assessments are conducted *before* services are introduced or modified, while program evaluations are used to assess services *after* they have been implemented or modified. Both of these assessment tasks frequently use similar techniques for gathering information, so a single data collection effort is sufficient.

The primary role of needs assessments is to "take the pulse" of an agency's constituents and to identify the desires, preferences, and priorities of target markets. In this way, an agency's publics provide the input necessary to develop a mission statement and long-term objectives. Needs assessment, together with analysis of an agency's environments, is the scouting phase of marketing planning. These phases identify needs, opportunities, and threats that provide the basis for setting mission and objective statements.

There are three general qualitative approaches to needs assessment: citizen advisory committees, public meetings/workshops, and unstructured approaches/structured exploratory interviews. In contrast, the survey is a quantitative approach that takes a synthesis of this information and determines how these viewpoints and issues are distributed in the total population. On occasion, secondary data that provide the desired information are already available. By definition, those data were collected from either within or outside the agency for some purpose other than the immediate issues of concern.

The citizen involvement pyramid shown in Figure 3.2 shows that the citizen advisory committee involves the least number of citizens in a needs assessment, while more people are likely to be involved in the decision-making process through surveys than by any of the three nonsurvey approaches. (Secondary sources are omitted from this figure since these indirect methods do not require citizen involvement).

Information gleaned from any or all of the three nonsurvey citizen involvement approaches is not likely to mirror accurately the priorities of all members of the community. The people providing input through these approaches cannot be expected to express the priorities or weighting of specific needs of all citizens in the community.

However, each of these different needs assessment approaches has a complementary role to play, and by using a variety of methods an agency can sense the needs of its constituents and begin to create the political will to do something

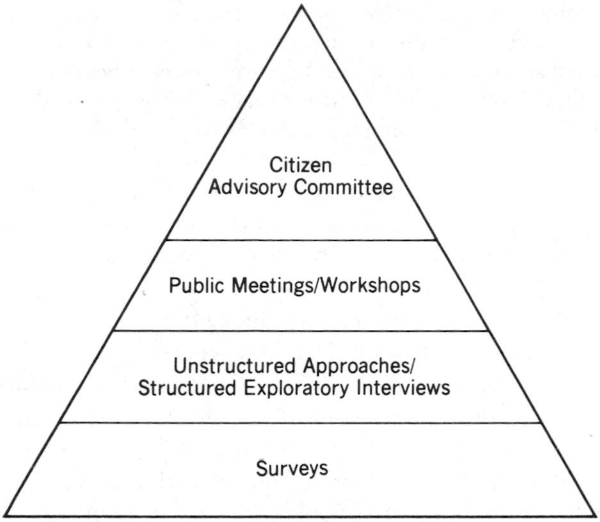

Figure 3.2. Citizen Involvement Pyramid.

about them. The qualitative role of the citizen advisory committee, public meetings/workshops, and unstructured approaches/structured exploratory interviews is to make sure that an issue is fully defined and that all needs and viewpoints are brought to the agency's attention.

This type of citizen input expands an agency's understanding of the problem. Citizens often have different perspectives of needs than do agency personnel. Without citizen input some dimensions of the needs assessment will probably be omitted from the survey, and thus from the analysis, final recommendations, and program actions. Hence the survey's results will be inherently biased.

Mission

One of the most important responsibilities of top management is to formulate the basic purposes and mission of the agency. An agency's mission statement is a long-term vision of what the agency is or is striving to become. It establishes the boundaries within which objectives, strategies, and actions must be developed. Ideally, mission statements are couched in terms narrow enough to provide practical guidance, yet broad enough to stimulate imaginative thinking.[11] The importance of carefully defining an agency's mission should not be underestimated. This point has been addressed by Thomas Watson, Jr., former chairman of the board of IBM.

> This then is my thesis: I firmly believe that any organization, in order to survive and achieve success, must have a sound set of beliefs on which it premises all its policies and actions. . . . Next, I believe that the most important single factor in corporate success is faithful adherence to those beliefs. . . . In other words, the

> basic philosophy, spirit, and drive of an organization have far more to do with its relative achievements than do technological or economic resources, organization structure, innovation, and timing. All these things weigh heavily on success. But they are, I think, transcended by how strongly the people in the organization believe in its basic precepts and how faithfully they carry them out.[12]

Many formerly successful organizations have suffered substantially because management did not heed this advice and properly define their missions. They failed because they did not correctly answer the questions "What is our business?" and "What should it be?"

Where would the Lung Association be today if it had not revised its mission from the eradication of tuberculosis to the control and prevention of lung disease? What would have happened to the National Foundation–March of Dimes had it not changed its mission from the treatment and care of polio victims to treatment and prevention of birth defects? What would be the current status of the YMCA if it had not broadened its original mission of improving the social conditions of lower-class people through religious indoctrination and educational activities, to include all-purpose service activities aimed at middle- as well as lower-class people? Clearly the continued success of these organizations can be largely attributed to the insight of their top management in redefining the missions of their agencies.

A definition of an agency's mission is unlikely to be appropriate for more than 10 years. At its inception an agency usually has a clear mission definition. However, as it grows and accomplishes many things and the environment changes and presents new challenges, management must review and reassess its mission.[13] No phase of the marketing planning process is more important, or deserves more clear and deliberate thinking, than specification of the agency's mission.

It is imperative that senior management be involved in the process of developing the marketing plan. Indeed such planning is perhaps the most important task of senior managers. Their intimate involvement is particularly essential in formulating the mission statement: Without their input, endorsement, and commitment in this initial stage, all subsequent efforts in developing a marketing plan are likely to be futile. At the same time

> Such ideas should not be conceived on Olympus and declared via the agency policy manual. Instead, they should be conceived broadly throughout the organization, summarized in writing, and promulgated in every word and action of all employees.[14]

Establishing Objectives

Objectives involve looking ahead and describing the desired future of an organization. They translate the mission statement into operational terms. The mission statement establishes broad parameters and provides the rationale for initiating a specific program, while objectives specify what that program is meant to accomplish. Careful specification of objectives offers two major benefits.

First, when objectives are attainable and challenging, they offer a potential incentive for improvement *if* they are effectively communicated and related by each employee to his or her job assignment. They can serve as performance standards by which both the agency and the individual gauge progress.

Second, if they are put in writing and are specific, objectives force crystallization of executive thinking. Thus the existence of formal, written objectives and conscientious adherence to them increases the confidence of both agency personnel and taxpayers that management knows what it is doing. Written objectives enable efforts in developing, implementing, and evaluating a marketing plan to be integrated and pointed in the same direction. It is dangerous for an administrator to assume that all staff members understand the objectives of the agency if those objectives have not been articulated and discussed. Probably members of that agency have many different ideas about what is best for the organization. It is quite possible that different divisions may inadvertently be operating at cross-purposes to one another.

An old fable tells of a traveller who saw a group of workmen busy on a building site. To his question of what they were doing, each workman gave a different answer. One said, "Cutting this stone" and another, "Building this wall." A third said, "Working for five pence a day." None of those replies really explained what they were doing—building a cathedral.[15] Organization must be purposeful to be effective. Developing objectives to ensure that all parties work toward the same end is critical.

Some agency managers regard establishing objectives as a rather meaningless academic task—something professors talk about that has little relevance to the realities of managing an agency. As a result, many government and social service agencies operate in ways analogous to a rudderless ship, swept along by the currents of events from one crisis to another without any clear direction. Failure to formulate written objective statements leaves an agency in the uncomfortable position described by the Caterpillar when he told Alice, "If you don't know where you're going, it really doesn't matter which road you take." Without direction, an agency will travel down many roads, some of which lead to dead ends.

Characteristics of Sound Objectives. Government and social service agencies are not guided by the profit motive that predominantly directs decision making in the private sector. They have to use different criteria to focus their marketing efforts and measure their success. These criteria are defined by the agency's objectives. Thus objectives establish a bottom line in lieu of the profit criterion. Without this bottom line orientation, marketing efforts are unlikely to realize their full potential. Objectives provide the evaluative yardstick for making decisions on changes in target markets or changes in particular components of the marketing mix. To be sound, objectives should possess certain characteristics. They should be appropriate, unambiguous and prioritized, specific, attainable, and in some instances, benefit-oriented.

Objectives Should Be Appropriate. Their appropriateness is dependent on the agency accurately defining the problem that a service is designed to resolve. If the problem is incorrectly defined, then the objective will be inappropriate. Consider, for example, this situation related by the legislative auditor in Hawaii.

> We recently audited the . . . program whereby all dogs and cats brought into the State are automatically quarantined for a period of 120 days. The program objectives seem to be reasonable enough: to prevent the introduction of rabies. . . . Hawaii is indeed free of rabies. The department . . . pointed to this condition as "proof positive" that the quarantine program is effective. Our audit used a different criterion. . . . What we wanted to know was how many cases of rabies are actually intercepted. . . . Using this measurement, the outcome was rather startling. Not in 60 years had the quarantine program intercepted a single case of rabies.[16]

This illustration may be a little extreme, but it does emphasize that objectives should be based on an appropriate definition of the problem. If no problem exists, no solution is needed.

Objectives Should Be Unambiguous and Prioritized. Most government and social service agencies are expected to achieve several objectives simultaneously. Unfortunately, these objectives are sometimes in disagreement and/or not ranked in importance.

> A federal program usually has multiple objectives, many of which are never clearly stated. Moreover, which objective, or set of objectives, is paramount is seldom clear. It may in fact differ among various policy spokesmen, individual members of Congress, the President, and the public at large. Further, two or more objectives may be incommensurate—i.e., the attainment of one may be directly counter to the attainment of another.[17]

Ambiguity as to which objectives are paramount frequently results from one of four situations. First, an agency may have accumulated new objectives from new pieces of legislation or from new mandates set by elected officials. These often accrue over a period of years and they may never have been rationalized or prioritized. Second, a program may be designed to achieve different ends with different publics. For example, a criminal justice program may be intended to punish some and to rehabilitate others. Third, there may be such fundamental disagreement among constituents that the agency has never been willing to address and resolve conflicting objectives directly. This situation is exemplified by federal welfare policy: No consensus has been reached on whether the major objectives should be to provide income support or decrease dependency. Since neither side can prevail, the requirement to prioritize the two objectives is ignored.[18] Fourth, some administrators wish to keep objectives ambiguous and in general terms because they believe this increases their ability to maneuver, and perhaps even to survive.

Ambiguous objectives that are not prioritized breed frustration. Peter Drucker states that a "strategy guaranteed to produce non-performance is to try to do several things at once. It is to refuse to establish priorities and to stick to them."[19] He goes on to suggest that the Tennessee Valley Authority (TVA) offers an impressive example of what can be achieved when objectives are prioritized:

> Despite tremendous opposition, the bill establishing the TVA passed Congress because its backers promised a dozen different and mutually antagonistic constituencies: cheap power, cheap fertilizer, flood control, irrigation, navigation, community development and whatnot. TVA's first administrator, Arthur Morgan, a great engineer, then attempted to live up to these promises and to satisfy every one of his constituencies. The only result was an uncontrollably growing bureaucracy, uncontrollaby growing expenditures, and a total lack of any performance. Indeed, the TVA in its early years resembled nothing as much as one of those "messes" which we now attack in Washington. Then President Roosevelt removed Morgan and put in a totally unknown young Wisconsin utilities lawyer, David Lilienthal, who immediately—against all advice from all the "pros"—announced his priority: power production. Within a year, the TVA produced results. Lilienthal, by the way, met no opposition, but was universally acclaimed as a savior.[20]

It is foolhardy for management to believe that they can produce the most possible benefits at the least possible cost. Simultaneously maximizing service and minimizing costs are contradictory objectives. An agency must first determine which objective is most important and then determine the relative emphasis to be placed on others.

Stating objectives in descending order of importance provides a priority structure that identifies what top management wants.[21] It also places subordinate objectives in proper perspective. Philip Kotler, for example, notes that:

> A hospital's basic objective is to deliver medical care to the community. Because it cannot be good at all things, it must set more specific objectives for various services to offer. These in turn suggest subsidiary objectives with respect to facilities, doctors, nurses, and so on, all hierarchically related to the more basic objective of the organization.[22]

Objectives Should Be Specific. There should be no question regarding the desired outcome stated in an objective. Unfortunately,

> Examination of program legislation, regulations, policy manuals, plans, and budgets to determine what a program seeks to achieve can be very deceptive. What at first seems clear, often evaporates when the test of measurability is applied. The language used turns out to be ambiguous.[23]

Objectives should be stated in quantifiable terms. Consider the following objectives established some years ago (subsequently revised) by the Los Angeles County Park System:

1. Provide a comprehensive regional recreation area system and regional recreation programs to service specialized leisure needs of the residents of Los Angeles County.

2. To guide and direct the provision of adequate local recreation programs, facilities, and beautification projects to service residents of unincorporated territories of Los Angeles County.
3. To provide specialized services to all communities within Los Angeles County which will augment or improve the standards of service in the total park and recreation field.
4. To provide specialized services within the particular expertise of personnel and physical resources of the department to other agencies as required.[24]

Are these objectives specific? Are they stated in quantitative terms? Are they measurable? The answer, of course, to each of these is no. Although these objective statements indicate what the County Board of Supervisors would like for the system to accomplish, they do not specify direction for management decisions or offer a means for objectively measuring what progress has been made toward their accomplishment. To use nonmeasurable objectives or very general statements may be worse than having no objectives at all: It conveys the illusion of a commitment when none has been made. These types of objectives have been termed "vaporous wishes" because they are hazy and insubstantial. Examples abound:

> Exactly what are the "unemployability," "alienation," "dependency," and "community tensions" some federal programs desire to reduce? How would one know when a program crossed the line, successfully converting "poor quality of life" into "adequate quality of life"? Would anyone recognize "improved mental health," "improved local capability," or "revitalized institutions"? The problems addressed by social programs are almost never stated so that institutions, people, or the relevant socioeconomic conditions could be classified according to the degree to which they are afflicted with a problem. It is very hard to propose a solution to a problem that is ill-defined or undefined.[25]

The objective of many hospitals in the British National Health System is "to provide the best medical care for the sick." This is not operational. It is much more meaningful to say, "It is our objective to make sure that no patient coming into emergency will go for more than three minutes without being seen by a qualified trained nurse," or to say "By January 1988, our maternity ward is going to be run on a 'zero defects' basis, which means that there will be no 'surprises' in the delivery room and there will not be one case of postpartum puerperal fever in maternity."[26]

Objectives Should Be Attainable. Statements of hopes or desires are not true objectives on which to base strategies and develop programs. Objectives must be realistic. They must reflect the opportunities available to the agency and the constraints imposed on it that are identified by a marketing audit (see Chapter 4). It is probably unrealistic, for example, for a small regional university to cite attainment of national prominence within the next five years as an objective. This goal is expensive and normally takes many years to achieve.

The agency's or department's resources should be considered prior to establishing objectives. If there is no money available with which to pay additional employees, an objective of increasing the number of programs offered by 20 percent is probably inappropriate.

Objectives Should Specify Timing. Objectives are quantified goals related to a specific point in time.[27] Unless the timeframe in which an objective is to be achieved is specified, it is difficult to measure results. Consider the following objectives:

1. To raise $200,000 in contributions from local businesses
2. To reduce the number of customer complaints by 20 percent
3. To increase the number of program participants by 50 percent
4. To develop a formal volunteer recruiting program

Each of these objectives suffers a common limitation. Without a specific time schedule, there is little motivation to push for its accomplishment.

Effectiveness Objectives Should Be Stated in Benefit Terms. In addition to the characteristics just discussed for *all* objectives, objectives that are concerned with effectiveness should be benefit-oriented. A major priority in setting objectives is conceptual clarity about what needs the agency's services are intended to satisfy. We saw in Chapter 1 that the primary focus should be on the end results that programs facilitate rather than on specific programs or services. People seek programs with the expectation of receiving benefits. Services have no value; only their benefits have value to client groups. A program is simply a means to an end.

Evaluating performance and allocating resources should be predicated on the following three propositions:

1. The objective of government and social service agencies is to satisfy client group wants.
2. By translating client group wants into benefits sought, the agency defines its objectives in terms of benefits.
3. Programs and services are the means to achieve ends and are not ends themselves.

If the agency accepts these propositions, some agency objectives will then be stated in terms of the *specific* benefits it intends to provide selected client groups. For example:

1. The proportion of households in neighborhood *X* that report on a citizen survey a "reasonable feeling of security" in walking the neighborhood at night will be increased from 50 percent to 75 percent in the next two years.

2. The proportion of public transit users reporting that they are satisfied with (1) the promptness, (2) the scheduling, and (3) the helpfulness of staff members will be raised to at least 90 percent in the next year.

Writing objectives in benefit terms that also include the other characteristics of good objectives discussed earlier in this section is difficult: Benefits are usually qualitative rather than quantitative. But it is essential if the agency is committed to adopting a marketing orientation.

Strategy

A strategy operates as the connecting link between objectives and detailed action programs.[28] It indicates where major efforts should be directed in order to attain the stated objectives.[29] A strategic plan is similar to a house plan. It shows what the house (agency) will be like at the end of the time period. House plans do not reveal the steps in building the house; likewise, strategic plans do not explain how to reach objectives. How to build the house (or how to achieve the strategic plan) is the task of subsequent operational or action plans.[30]

Strategic decisions deal with the selection of resource commitments. At any given time, a substantial number of strategic alternatives are available to an agency or department. The specific questions an agency addresses in selecting strategic alternatives include:

1. Should the agency seek to expand, contract, or change the emphasis of the range of its offerings or selected target markets?
2. If so, in which service areas and target markets, and how vigorously?

The traditional approach to identifying and assessing strategic marketing options has been revised in recent years and several new methods of strategic analysis have been developed. One particularly useful strategic analysis tool is called *program portfolio analysis*. In this section, we first discuss the traditional approach and then explain program portfolio analysis. Both approaches offer frameworks that may be used by top management to determine which service areas should be emphasized or de-emphasized during the planning period. Similarly, they may also be used by managers in charge of individual service areas to determine which individual programs within the confines of their service area should be emphasized or de-emphasized.

Traditional Approach to Strategic Marketing Planning. Figure 3.3 exhibits a continuum of strategic program options* ranging from developing new pro-

*In this strategic planning context, the term *programs* is used generically to embrace a wide and diverse set of activities that include not only program offerings but also the other components of the marketing mix (pricing, distribution, and promotion) and marketing administration tasks.

Programs or Services / Markets	New Programs or Services	Modifications of Existing Programs and/or Services	Existing Programs or Services	Reduction of Existing Programs or Services	Termination of Existing Programs or Services
Existing	Replacement and Extension Strategies	Reformulation Strategies	Market Penetration Strategies	Reduction Strategies	Termination Strategies
New	Diversification Strategies	Market Extension Strategies	Market Development Strategies		

Figure 3.3. Basic Strategic Marketing Alternatives.

grams to terminating existing programs, with retention of existing programs without change being the mid-point of the continuum.[31] Each of the selected program options can be targeted either at existing markets or at new markets. Two cells are incompatible since it is not possible to retrench or terminate programs in new markets where they have not been offered! By placing each of an agency's program options into one of these eight cells, management makes a commitment that will guide agency resource decisions over the planning period.

Market penetration strategies are efforts to achieve greater clientele support with present programs in existing markets. Typically this entails improving the efficiency and/or effectiveness of prevailing service delivery efforts.

Market development strategies are efforts to develop new target markets for existing programs or services. A community center offering dance lessons to teenagers might, for example, begin offering the same program to adults.

Reformulation strategies are efforts that seek to improve the programs for existing customers. A program may be provided with new leadership, may change its level of sophistication, or be distributed differently. For example, family and welfare counscling services might be provided to citizens in the privacy of their homes. Families would not then be required to come to inconveniently located offices. Reformulation may be achieved by developing a more effective communication program that more successfully communicates the benefits a service offers.

Market extension strategies are efforts designed to reach new markets through modification of the agency's existing programs or services. For example, community colleges have been quite successful in modifying some of their educational courses to appeal to the vocational and hobby interests of citizens who would not otherwise enroll in courses.

Replacement and extension strategies are aimed at increasing the satisfaction provided to existing target markets either by replacing existing programs with improved versions of the same program, or by increasing the range of programs or services offered. Candidates for replacement can be identified by seeking recommendations from present and previous program participants. The proliferation of courses offered by many community education programs is a good example of organizations engaging in extension strategies.

Diversification strategies are characterized by organizations offering new programs or services to new target markets. This strategy is probably the most complex and difficult of the growth strategies. It is most commonly used when an agency redefines its mission or assumes functions previously performed by another agency. For example, several cities have consolidated all social service agencies into one community/human services department. The intent of this consolidation of recreation departments, health departments, counseling and youth agencies, family rehabilitation, and in some cases protective services has been to enhance the coordination and effectiveness of a city's traditionally independent and fragmented social service programs. These new departments often offer a wide array of new programs and services to new target markets.

Reduction strategies are concerned with deploying fewer resources to an existing service. This effort involves either reducing the quantity of an offering to all target markets or reducing the number of target markets to which it is currently offered. Reduction may be expedited by using the marketing mix variables in a subtle way to demarket. Use by the clientele in general can be discouraged, or by certain target groups in particular, on either a temporary or a permanent basis.[32] For example, a health clinic may reduce operating hours, reduce promotional effort, increase the waiting time, or reduce the number of clientele who qualify for the services offered.

The value of strategic planning is by no means limited to an expansion situation. In the military sphere, for example, plans for retreat are as vital as those for attack; they are the difference between retreat and defeat. Reduction strategies are not attractive but they are needed. Reducing efforts in particular service areas frees resources that can be better used elsewhere. In more extreme cases in which an agency is faced with reductions in the real dollar value of available resources, a coherent strategy plan for contraction of efforts is essential. In such situations, the range of strategy options is typically narrower, employee morale is vulnerable, and muddling through will not help to restore confidence. A longer-range strategic view is a fundamental requirement for extricating the agency from prolonged, short-term, reactive crisis management.

Termination strategies are adopted when all resources allocated to a service are withdrawn. Termination is the most difficult of all strategies for a public agency to implement. It is likely to stimulate opposition from the constituency that is adversely affected but little support from other constituencies that are not affected. Typically, when an agency develops a strategy plan, this strategy is ignored because of its potential for arousing opposition and controversy. Nevertheless, in the prevailing financial climate in which few new dollars are available, if new services are to be offered then resources for them can be obtained only by retrenchment or termination of existing services. We address this difficult strategy in detail in Chapter 12.

Program Portfolio Analysis. Program portfolio analysis has become an increasingly popular tool for strategic marketing planning in the private sector during the past decade. Most government and social service agencies are multiprogram organizations. That is, they provide an array of distinctively different services to targeted client groups. Furthermore, these services vary in terms of importance, size, growth rate, quality, image, life cycle stage, and so on. Together they make up an agency's portfolio of services. Like an investor's portfolio of stocks and bonds, an agency's portfolio of programs usually includes some that should be given additional support, some that should be maintained at their present level of support, some that should be retrenched, and some that should be terminated. Program portfolio analysis is a useful method for diagnosing the strengths and weaknesses of an agency's programs, prescribing actions for improving performance, and allocating scarce resources among programs.

The concept employs a simple matrix representation that is easy to communicate and to comprehend. Perhaps the best-known portfolio analysis model is the Boston Consulting Group's (BCG) Model. In this discussion we have adapted the BCG model for use by government and social service agencies. Programs are classified as stars, problem children, plain Janes, or dogs (see Figure 3.4) on the basis of two criteria: (1) growth in the total citizen demand for a service, and (2) magnitude of an agency's existing role or market share in supplying the service.

Suggested strategies for programs in each of the four quadrants might be as follows:

> *Stars*. Support these programs aggressively by expanding the resources allocated to them because demand is growing quickly and the agency is the dominant service supplier. A real opportunity to expand the agency's citizen support base.
>
> *Problem Children* (also called question marks). There is rapid growth in total market demand for this type of program, but the agency only plays a minor role in supplying it. The agency potentially can fill a substantial niche; but

		Agency's Market Share in Supplying a Service	
		High	Low
Growth in Total Citizen Demand for a Service	High	Stars	Problem Children
	Low	Plain Janes	Dogs

Figure 3.4. Program Portfolio Analysis.

in order to do so, a significant investment of resources is required. If this investment is made the problem child is likely to grow into a star. If the investment is not made, it is likely to become a dog.

Plain Janes. The agency plays a leading role in supplying this service, but there is little or no prospect of future growth in demand for it. More of an agency's programs will probably be assigned to this category than any other. It accounts for most existing citizen support because it contains the traditional core programs that remain viable and that citizens expect it to provide. The strategy here is to maintain resource allocations at existing levels.

Dogs. These programs have low opportunity for growth and the agency has no substantial unique target market that others are not serving. The resources used to offer the service could provide greater benefits if they were reallocated to another program. These programs should be retrenched or terminated.

This technique has been applied to a limited extent in the public sector. One study, for example, that used portfolio analysis to analyze the masters degree programs of three Midwestern universities illustrated that the technique "offers a sound, and particularly relevant framework for the difficult decision making that lies before the senior managers of U.S. universities and colleges."[33]

Another portfolio analysis model has been developed by General Electric (GE). The GE model is similar to the BCG model in that is uses a two-dimensional matrix to array an organization's offerings. The dimensions are organizational strength and market attractiveness. It is based on a philosophy of ensuring sustained performance in the short term while guiding the organization's resources to future growth opportunities. This is accomplished by focusing on programs that rate high in terms of both organizational strength and market attractiveness. Figure 3.5 illustrates the GE model.

Programs enjoying a medium-to-strong position in a medium-to-highly-attractive market fall into the invest/grow category. That is, the agency should invest human and financial resources in these programs and grow with them. Programs with low organization strength in medium-to-unattractive markets should be retrenched or terminated. Programs in the remaining cells should be maintained at their present levels.

The key to successfully employing the GE portfolio model is selecting the factors to represent organization strength and market attractiveness. Factors such as program quality, market knowledge, expertise, market share, and participation trends are illustrative organization strength measures. Market attractiveness might be determined on the basis of market size and growth rate, cyclicality and seasonality, and so on.

Action Programs

As previously noted, strategy decisions provide general guidelines that describe how an agency intends to achieve its stated objectives. Sometimes agencies

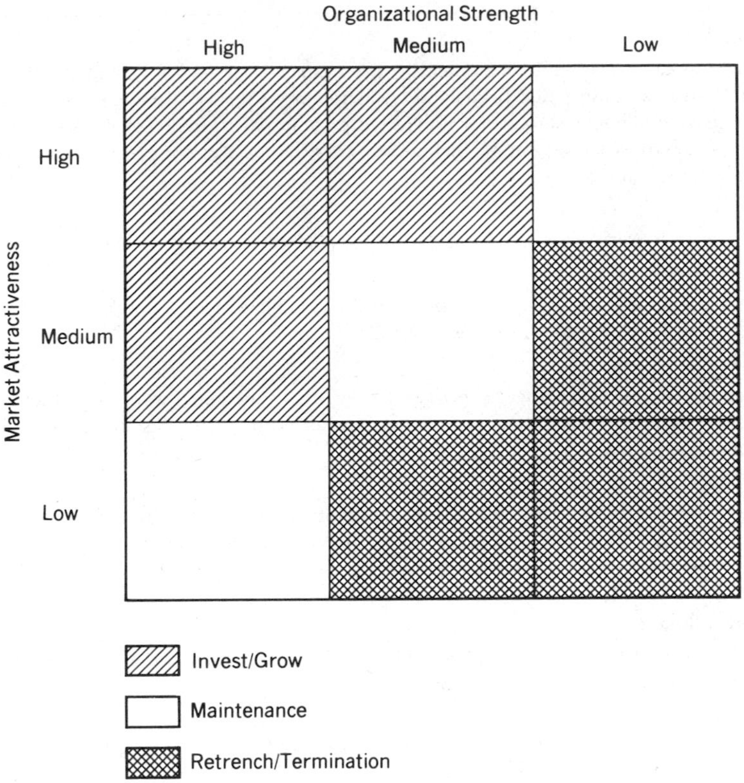

Figure 3.5. General Electric Portfolio Approach.

develop strategic plans but then let daily work pressures keep them from implementing action plans that move personnel out of old habits toward future objectives. It is easier to continue doing things the same old way.

Action programs are typically prepared annually for each program or unit within the agency. They address the question "How do we get there?" and describe the specific actions that are to be taken during this specified portion of the total planning period.

An action program is composed of two separate but interrelated components: action program guidelines and action program responsibilities. As Figure 3.6 illustrates, action program guidelines provide a written description of each target market and program, the needs of each target market that will be fulfilled by each program, specific objectives for each target market and for each program, the marketing plan, performance standards, and key elements of success. This component of the action program addresses the question "What is to be done?" and provides the basis for the action program responsibilities component.

The action program responsibilities component focuses on directing the personnel resources of an agency toward the achievement of planned results. It should contain "a detailed breakdown of the activities that achieve each of the

---

Target Market

Define the target market demographically (key characteristics only), geographically (if appropriate) and in attitudinal and behavioral terms relevant to plans. If common programs are to be targeted at different markets, or if different programs are targeted at the same or different markets, describe each separately. Include secondary targets if appropriate (for additional detail see Chapters 5 and 6).

Programs

Describe each program to be offered during the planning period and justify its existence.

Needs Fulfilled

State the needs of each target market that are/will be fulfilled by each program. Include relative emphasis that will be put on various programs.

Objectives

Specify objectives for each target market and for each program. Target market and program objectives should be appropriate, unambiguous and prioritized, specific, attainable, and benefit-oriented if appropriate.

Price Strategy

State overall policy (i.e., free, subsidized, competitive, etc.), discuss price/value relationships (i.e., as good or better value than competition) and identify relevant legal/regulatory and cost/profit considerations in pricing. This should be done for each program (for additional detail see Chapters 13 and 14).

Distribution Strategy

Describe quantitative and qualitative aspects of the distribution system for each program or service (for additional detail see Chapters 7 and 8).

Promotion

Describe and justify the promotional strategies for each target market and each program (for additional details see Chapters 15–18).

Service Quality Standards

What elements of service are most important? What performance standards are established? How are they monitored?

Key Elements of Success

Highlight those elements of strategy or execution that are critical for success.

Figure 3.6. Action Program Guidelines. (Based on "Instructions for the Marketing Section of a Consumer Services Business Plan-Citibank, N.A." cited in D.S. Hopkins, *The Marketing Plan*. New York: Conference Board, 1981, p. 78.)

objectives and strategies and an assignment of responsibilities by name of individual or office."[34] The following series of headings suggests a framework and format for writing a logical step-by-step flow assignment of responsibilities.

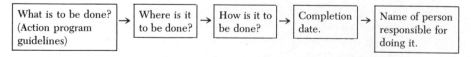

What is to be done? (Action program guidelines) → Where is it to be done? → How is it to be done? → Completion date. → Name of person responsible for doing it.

The program should be result-oriented and it must be personally interpretable and meaningful to the individual if it is to be viewed as something more than an intellectual exercise. Rewards to personnel in the agency should reflect their success in achieving the objectives for which they were responsible. Indeed, the action program forms the basis for implementing a management-by-objectives system. Failure to operate in this mode indicates a failure of the planning process, no matter how impressive the one- or five-year plans appear on paper.

Implementation

Designation of responsibilities for implementation should involve all key decision makers in the agency. "Planning is a process of negotiating and developing institutional consensus as to future courses of action."[35] If key operating managers are not supportive of the plan, they may only give it lip service and block its effective implementation. An involvement and consensus-building approach will optimize acceptance and commitment: People who make decisions are more likely to be enthusiastic about carrying them out.

Although the systematic data-based approach to marketing planning advocated in this chapter is essential for effective planning, at the same time there must be a willingness to recognize that political realities sometimes require compromising:

> Implementation requires gaining acceptance of the plan by both internal and external constituencies. Seeking to modify the perspectives of key publics, or their representatives, must be seen as a legitimate function of strategic planning.[36]

Getting a Marketing Plan Off the Ground.[37] If an agency with no previous experience in developing a marketing plan suddenly commits itself to a comprehensive effort, it may find itself facing considerable frustration. First, planning in government and social service agencies has traditionally been viewed as independent of, and even remote from, the managing process. Hence managers often have to be convinced of the usefulness of marketing planning. Second, marketing planning will impose competing demands on managers who are preoccupied with responding to demands and requirements that may currently be overwhelming. This may foster resentment and a negative attitude toward the process. Third, errors and inefficiencies are inevitable in early efforts as managers struggle to identify the best approaches for developing a plan.

To reduce the likelihood of negative and demoralizing repercussions surfacing, an incremental, developmental approach is recommended for introducing marketing planning into an agency. Instead of a comprehensive strategic plan, it may be better to begin by developing a plan to accomplish immediate and urgent, but relatively simple, objectives. The skills and confidence in the process developed by these early small-scale projects can subsequently be exploited to tackle the more complex long-range objectives and plan. In these pilot exercises it should be possible to get the "feel" of the complete cycle from objective setting to planning, action, accomplishment, and evaluation, within a matter of weeks or months.

These initial projects should be designed and carried out in ways that help managers to develop new competence and confidence in using the process. For instance, each project's objective should be carefully spelled out. The steps to reach a goal should be thought through to the point where they can be stated in the form of rigorous, disciplined, written plans, including managerial responsibilities, timing, subprojects, and related information. Methods for measuring and for reviewing progress should also be incorporated into the plan. Consequently, each project parallels, in miniature, the steps of the marketing planning procedure. The aim is to move from the identification of an objective to its accomplishment in a short time, and then to progress to more ambitious planning efforts.

Once some tangible results have been produced in the initial projects, managers are likely to be more enthusiastic about broadening and extending the process. They will have more confidence in selecting and defining objectives, laying out plans to reach them, generating action to fulfill the plans, and coordinating different elements of an action program.

This developmental approach enables the scope of marketing planning to expand in harmony with the growth in managers' ability to plan well. By contrast, if a major strategic planning effort is launched without any prior experience, objectives are frequently not attained because of overoptimism or lack of ability to develop meaningful plans, thus producing a sense of frustration and inadequacy.

Evaluation

Evaluation addresses the question "Where are we now compared to where we wanted to be?" An agencywide marketing audit is normally conducted at the end of each long-term planning period. Program evaluations are used to judge how successful each of the agency's offerings has been. They are normally conducted at the end of each short-term planning period. Because of the importance and scope of evaluation, we have devoted Chapter 4 to this topic.

SUMMARY

Strategic planning should be part of the basic management process of the agency. It is the road map or blueprint that guides all marketing endeavors. Strategic marketing planning is a continuous process concerned with (1) analyzing the macro environment, (2) undertaking needs assessments to analyze performance and identify future opportunities and threats, (3) determining agency mission, (4) specifying objectives, (5) selecting strategies to achieve specific objectives, (6) developing action programs, (7) implementation, and (8) evaluating performance.

The agency's mission is derived from inputs received from an analysis of the macroenvironment and a comprehensive needs assessment. This initial task requires management to address the question "What business are we in?" This statement establishes the boundaries within which objectives, strategies, and action programs are developed.

Marketing objectives address the question "Where do we want to be at the end of the planning period?" These objectives should be appropriate, unambigious and prioritized, specific, attainable, and should specify the timeframe within which they are to be achieved. In addition, those objectives that are concerned with effectiveness should be benefit-oriented.

The development of a marketing plan involves both long-term and short-term planning. Long-term plans, often called strategic plans, are prepared for three- to five-year time horizons and focus on broad strategic issues that affect the overall agency. The strategy plan seeks to answer the question "How are we going to get to where we want to be at the end of the planning period?" It seeks to modify the agency's present offerings if necessary and to create new ones that will contribute to achievement of objectives. The traditional approach to assessing strategic marketing options recognizes eight major marketing strategy alternatives: market penetration, market development, reformulation, market extension, replacement and extension, diversification, reduction, and termination. In recent years, this traditional approach has been refined and new strategic analysis tools such as program portfolio analysis have been developed. The best-known portfolio analysis models are those developed by the Boston Consulting Group (BCG) and General Electric (GE).

Short-term plans, often called action programs, are developed for time periods of one year or less. They normally focus on specific programs. Action programs contain a detailed breakdown of the activities necessary to implement the strategy and achieve stated objectives. Figure 3.7 illustrates the primary similarities and differences between strategy plans and action programs. The differences reflect the scope and magnitude of effort and the level of specificity included in the plan.

The initial success of strategic marketing planning is likely to depend on the commitment and participation of senior management. However, attainment of strategic planning objectives is dependent on operating managers being supportive of the action programs. If they only give such programs lip service, there is little likelihood of effectively implementing a marketing plan. The involvement and consensus-building approach will optimize acceptance. Plans should be implemented incrementally while skills and confidence in the process are being developed.

Evaluation addresses the question "Where are we now compared to where we wanted to be?" This is the topic of the following chapter.

Activity	Long-Term Strategy Plan	Short-Term Action Program
Needs Assessment	Agency-wide, comprehensive.	Less comprehensive, program specific.
Mission Statement	Essential component of long-term plan. Establishes the boundaries within which objectives, strategies, and programs are developed.	Not a component of short-term plans; however, mission statement establishes the boundaries within which short-term objectives, strategies, and programs are developed.
Objectives	Agency objectives for the coming 3–5 year period. Long-term vision of what the agency hopes to achieve.	Usually program specific. More precise. Achievement assures that gradual, incremental progress is made toward achievement of long-term objectives.
Plan Content	Major decision regarding long-term resource commitments. Addresses which target markets and programs shall be emphasized and de-emphasized. States how objectives will be met.	Steps by which strategies will be implemented to reach long-term objectives. Detailed program activities necessary to implement short-term strategy and achieve short-term objectives. Statement of what is to be done, where, how, when, and by whom.
Implementation	Senior management commitment and involvement is essential. Should be incrementally developed.	Operating managers must be supportive. Involvement and consensus-building approach is required to serve their commitment. Should be incrementally developed.
Evaluation	Agency-wide marketing audit that addresses all of the agency's marketing activities.	Program evaluation that addresses how well each of the agency's offerings is doing in meeting its specified objectives.

Figure 3.7. Differences Between Long-Term Strategy Plans and Short-Term Action Programs.

NOTES

1. Steiner, G.A., *Strategic Planning*. New York: Free Press, 1979, cover jacket.
2. Hopkins, D.S., *The Marketing Plan*. New York: Conference Board, 1981, p. 5.
3. Behn, R.D., "Leadership For Cut-Back Management: The Use of Corporate Strategy," *Public Administration Review,* Vol. 40 No. 6, November/December 1980, pp. 613–620.
4. Cravens, D.W., and Lamb, Jr., C.W., *Strategic Marketing Cases and Applications*. Homewood, IL: Irwin, 1983, pp. 6–7.
5. Adapted from Cyert, R.M., "The Management of Universities of Constant or Decreasing Size," *Public Administration Review,* Vol. 38 No. 4, July/August 1978, pp. 344–349.
6. Ford, R.C., and Neiman, J., "Planning Process a Powerful Tool," *Hospitals: Journal of the American Hospital Association,* Reprinted by permission from *Hospitals* Vol. 53 No. 21, October 16, 1979, p. 70. Copyright 1979, American Hospital Association.
7. Adapted from Thieme, C.W., Wilson, T.E., and Long, D.M., "Strategic Planning Market Orientation," *Hospitals: Journal of the American Hospital Association,* Reprinted by permission from *Hospitals* Vol. 53 No 23, December 1, 1979, p. 57. Copyright 1979, American Hospital Association.

8. Redhead, H., cited in *Bryan College Station Eagle,* Bryan, Texas, January 3, 1982, p. 10.
9. Drucker, P.F., *Managing in Turbulent Times*. London: Heinneman, 1980, p. 10.
10. Rutter, L., *The Essential Community: Local Government in the Year 2000*. Washington, DC: International City Management Association, 1981, p. 6.
11. Hopkins, *Marketing,* p. 21.
12. Watson, Jr., T.J., *A Business and Its Beliefs*. New York: McGraw-Hill, 1963, p. 3.
13. Kotler, P., *Marketing for Nonprofit Organization* (2nd ed.). Englewood Cliffs, NJ: Prentice-Hall, 1982, p. 90.
14. Christopher, W.F., "Marketing Planning That Gets Things Done," *Harvard Business Review,* September/October 1970, p. 6.
15. Littener, J.A., *The Analysis of Organizations* (2nd ed.). New York: Wiley, 1973, p. 44.
16. Brown, R., and Pethtel, R.D., "A Matter of Facts: State Legislative Performance Auditing," *Public Administration Review*. Vol. 34 No. 4, July/August 1974, p. 318.
17. Lewis, F.L., and Zarb, F.C., "Federal Program Evaluation from the OMB Perspective," *Public Administration Review*. Vol. 34 No. 4, July/August 1974, p. 309.
18. Lipsky, M., *Street Level Bureaucracy*. New York: Russell Sage Foundation, 1980, p. 40.
19. Drucker, P.F., "The Deadly Sins in Public Administration," *Public Administration Review*. vol. 4, No. 2, March/April 1980, p. 103.
20. Ibid., pp. 103–104.
21. Granger, C.H., "The Hierarchy of Objectives," *Harvard Business Review,* May/June 1964, pp. 63–74.
22. Kotler, *Marketing for Nonprofit,* p. 92.
23. Horst, P., Nay, J.N., Scandeon, J.W., and Wholey, J.S., "Program Management and the Federal Evaluator," *Public Administration Review,* Vol. 34 No. 4, July/August 1974, p. 302.
24. Murphy, J.F., Williams, J.G., Niepoth, W.E., and Brown, P.D., *Leisure Service Delivery System: A Modern Perspective*. Philadelphia: Lea and Febiger, 1973, p. 109.
25. Horst et al., "Program Management," p. 302.
26. This paragraph is adapted from Drucker, "Deadly Sins," p. 103.
27. Hopkins, D.S., *The Short-Term Marketing Plan*. New York: Conference Board, 1972, p. 63.
28. Hopkins, *Marketing,* p. 25.
29. Kotler, P., *Marketing Management*. Englewood Cliffs, NJ: Prentice-Hall, 1984, p. 68.
30. Hulett, D.G., "Strategic Planning: Important for the 1980's," *Management Strategy,* Vol. 6 No. 4, (Winter) 1982 p. 1.
31. This model represents an extension and modification of that suggested by Kollat, D.T., Blackwell, R.D., and Robeson, J.F., *Strategic Marketing*. New York: Holt, Rinehart & Winston, 1972, p. 22.
32. Kotler, *Marketing Management,* p. 419.
33. Newbould, G.D., "Product Portfolio Diagnosis for U.S. Universities," *Akron Business and Economic Review,* Spring 1980, p. 45.
34. Weinberg, C.B., "Marketing Planning for the Arts Organization." In M.P. Mokwa, W.M. Dawson, and E.A. Price (eds.), *Marketing the Arts*. New York: Praeger, 1980, p. 116.
35. Thieme et al., "Strategic Planning," p. 59.
36. Ibid., p. 58.
37. This section is adapted from Schaffer, R.H., "Putting Action Into Planning," *Harvard Business Review,* November/December 1967, pp. 175–181.

FOUR

Evaluating Marketing Efforts

Chapter 3 discussed the development of a marketing plan. The final stage in strategic planning is to assess the agency's marketing activities after a plan has been implemented. Results are the bottom line of the marketing effort. Hence this final stage of monitoring and evaluation, which identifies where the plan is working and where and why it is not working, is most important. Evaluation answers the question "Where are we now in relation to where we said we wanted to be in our objectives?" The marketing audit and program evaluation are the dimensions of evaluation of primary interest to marketers.

Evaluation of individual services is continuous. However, at the end of the five-year long-term planning period the routine, on-going evaluation process is supplemented by a major state-of-the-organization evaluation. This agency-wide evaluation assesses the overall status of all of the agency's services and marketing activities. Sometimes referred to as a *situation analysis* or a *current assessment*, the evaluation is conducted by means of a marketing audit.

The focus of the annual plan, or *program evaluation*, is more limited in scope. Its purpose is to evaluate the relative success or failure of selected agency programs during a one-year period. Program evaluations provide early warning signals that a program is not adequately meeting the needs and desires of its targeted clientele. The system monitors whether the organization is implementing the plan in the desired manner and whether the specified milestones and objectives are being achieved. The goal of program evaluation is to discover and act on, if necessary, deviations from anticipated happenings and recognize unanticipated new opportunities and problems.

If unsatisfactory results emerge from the evaluation, then it is necessary to explore the situation further. Failure may result from changed environmental conditions, incorrect initial definition of the clientele's wants and needs, or inadequacies in the selected marketing mix. When the cause of the problem has been identified, appropriate actions can be taken to rectify it. Conceptually, the five-year marketing audit emerges from a summation, synthesis, and integration of the annual evaluations of each program.

MARKETING AUDIT

The marketing audit is "an attempt to describe the current marketing situation, to speculate about the relevant future, and to analyze the organization's marketing performance and potential."[1] It operationalizes Abraham Lincoln's advice: "If we could first know where we are, and whither we are tending, we could better judge what to do and how to do it."[2] Thus the audit not only looks back over the past, but forward to speculate about likely changes in the internal and external environments and search for new potential market opportunities. More specifically, a marketing audit has been defined as:

> A systematic, critical, and impartial review and appraisal of the total marketing operation: of the basic objectives and policies and the assumptions which underlie them as well as the methods, procedures, personnel, and organization employed to implement the policies and achieve the objectives.[3]

Although the primary purposes of the audit are to develop a comprehensive profile of an agency's total marketing effort and to provide a basis for developing and revising a strategic marketing plan, the audit is also an excellent mechanism for improving communication and raising marketing consciousness within the agency. That is, it is a useful vehicle for marketing the philosophy and techniques of marketing.

Marketing Audit Procedure

Administration of an audit follows three important and related decisions.[4] First, the scope of the audit must be determined. Second, methods by which data are to be collected must be delineated. Third, an auditor must be selected. Each of these decisions is discussed in the following paragraphs.

Scope of the Audit. The audit is an information-gathering process and, like many new tasks, the first attempt at an agencywide audit is likely to be more costly in effort and resources than the following ones. Ideally, in order to fully evaluate the agency's current overall marketing operation, the audit will be comprehensive.[5] No virtue however, lies in collecting detailed and refined information unless the agency has sufficient resources to use it.

Conducting an audit can take a considerable amount of effort, and each organization must decide how detailed and complex its audit should be and the amount of resources to commit to it. The level of detail may vary considerably. For the small agency, an audit might be more useful if conducted at a rather limited level, since the agency may lack the resources both to collect detailed information and to implement the large number of detailed suggestions that may emerge.

Although no common format is appropriate for all agencies, the major areas usually addressed in an audit are identified in the outline presented in Appendix A. This outline includes a large number of specific questions that may serve as a checklist. The marketing audit outline follows the format of this text and its questions are addressed here as well. After completing the book, the reader should be sufficiently familiar with the philosophy and terminology of marketing to appreciate the significance of each of the questions included in Appendix A.

Initially the scope of this outline may seem overwhelming. An agency, though, is not intended to evaluate every question in depth. Rather, it should select from this list those questions that are deemed to be most pertinent in the development of its own strategic marketing plan and examine those in detail. Other issues may be addressed more casually and in less detail as they are peripheral to the agency's effectiveness and efficiency.

Data Collection. Data are compiled for analysis and evaluation from three main sources: internal interviews, external interviews, and secondary documentary sources. A good audit integrates objective analysis of an agency's marketing practices and performance with subjective probing and appraisal of basic management assumptions, philosophies, and expectations. Internal interviews with key individuals in the agency seek to draw on their knowledge of all aspects of the agency's operations, competencies, and constraints. Interviews are guided by questions selected from the audit outline in Appendix A, and answers to them will generally reveal a level of agreement. When key individuals disagree, the audit has identified a problem area that should be subjected to closer scrutiny.

The internal interviews should be supplemented by a series of extended interviews with key members of the agency's publics, such as elected officials, suppliers, competitors, and customers. On some issues these publics' representatives will have nothing to add, but on other issues their perceptions of the agency's current efforts may be incisive.

In addition to personal interviews, the audit should review all secondary data sources available in agency files or literature searches that pertain to the issues of interest. Secondary sources best provide reliable information on which to base evaluations if they have been developed with this intent in mind. If evaluation capability is not deliberately built into the administrative machinery, then later retrieval of the data becomes a more complicated affair.[6]

Together these three sources of information offer a broad-based approach for assessing an agency's current marketing operations. Again, the extent of the data collection will be governed by the scope of the audit to which the agency is committed. Smaller agencies, for example, may use only one or two sources.

Choice of an Auditor. Marketing audits may be conducted by someone either within or outside the organization. Given severely limited resources, a high-ranking staff member or an agencywide auditing committee may conduct the audit. Self-audits, however, lack the objectivity of independent audits by outside persons or organizations. Self-audits are less likely to get at "sacred cows" for it is difficult for individuals to critique decisions objectively that they themselves or their close colleagues have made or influenced.

Postaudit Tasks

After the audit, three tasks remain for ensuring accrual of full benefits from the process. First, when the data have been assembled, their usefulness will depend on the skill of the auditor in interpreting and successfully presenting these data so that the major points can be grasped quickly by decision makers. The presentation should address results of the appraisal in each of the seven areas of marketing operations (Appendix A) and from these points evaluate the overall performance of marketing operations. The audit should provide a profile that identifies not only existing weaknesses and inhibiting factors, but also the agency's strengths and new opportunities available to it. Recommendations have to be judged and prioritized so that those which contribute most to improving marketing performance are implemented first.

The second task is to ensure that the role of the audit has been clearly communicated. It is unlikely that suggestions will emerge that require radical changes in the way the agency operates. The audit's main role is to address the question "Where are we now?" and to make some tentative suggestions about ways of improving what the organization already does. Kotler and his colleagues note that

> One of the biggest problems in marketing auditing is that the executive who brings in the auditor, or the people in the business being audited, may have higher expectations about what the audit will do for the company than the actual report seems to offer. In only the most extreme circumstances will the auditor develop surprising panaceas or propose startling new opportunities for the company.[7]

Any radical changes in direction that do emerge from the auditing process will probably be concerned with defining the agency's mission, formulating objectives to guide its future actions, developing strategy, and implementing an action plan:

> The marketing audit is not a marketing plan but rather it is an independent appraisal by an inside or outside auditor of the main problems and opportunities facing the agency and what it can do about them.[8]

The final postaudit task is to make someone accountable for implementing the recommendations. We are all familiar with reports that have been prepared, presented, applauded, and filed away to gather dust. The person made accountable should be committed to the project and have the political clout and leverage to make things happen.

PROGRAM EVALUATION

Program evaluation entails assessing the impact of particular programs. Thus it is concerned with evaluation at the microlevel—the individual program—in contrast to the marketing audit, which focuses on evaluation at the macrolevel, or the total set of agency programs. Like the marketing audit, it looks to the past to provide a guide for the future. Program evaluations are intended to determine whether stated program objectives are being met. They also assess whether these stated objectives are in fact appropriate. Program evaluation has been defined as "the systematic examination of specific agency activities to provide information on the full range of the program's short and long-term effects on citizens."[9]

Reasons for the Growth of Program Evaluation

Program evaluation is not a new subject to government and social service agency managers. Efforts to identify means for monitoring and controlling performance have been documented since at least 1900.[10] However, serious efforts to systematically monitor program performance are a relatively recent development. This new emphasis emerged initially at the federal level, where it was closely linked with the flood of new programs in social policy enacted during the Johnson Administration:

> Many of these programs lacked the long gestation period associated with most important legislation and were, in the broad sense, experimental. In some areas parallel programs were started, each dealing with the same problem. We hoped to learn from these; choose the most effective; downgrade or phase out the least effective. Evaluation was frequently linked with these experimental and new programs, and with social policy.[11]

Federal legislation in this period began to mandate program evaluation. A typical mandate was included in the Crime Control Act of 1973, which directed the Law Enforcement Administration's National Institute of Law Enforcement and Criminal Justice:

> To evaluate the various programs and projects carried out under this title (Training, Education, Research, Demonstration, and Special Grants) to determine their impact upon the quality of law enforcement and criminal justice and the extent to which they have met or failed to meet the purposes and policies of this title.[12]

Now when Congress authorizes new social programs, it routinely requires evaluation and provides funds for it. This emphasis on evaluation of programs at the federal level has been increasingly replicated at state and local levels.

It is primarily the result of four factors, first of which is a growing concern with keeping government accountable. Accountability is the link between bureaucracy and democracy.[13] Modern democracy depends on bureaucracies being accountable for carrying out declared policy and delivering authorized services.

Second, after the Johnson Administration, more conservative administrations challenged the success of many social programs and used program evaluation to determine, "Do these new programs work in the desired way?" The current interest in program evaluation may very well be rooted in the practical realization that many "human resource, health improvement, and social development programs have been misguided, misconceived, badly implemented and ineffective."[14] The standard apology for program failure used to be that not enough money was allocated to the program to make it a success. However, "enough" was never defined and this nebulous rationalization is no longer acceptable. If sensible decisions are to be made on altering, terminating, or expanding programs, some evidence must be presented on how effective and efficient these programs are from the viewpoint of the clientele or beneficiaries.

Third is the realization that programs can sometimes have unanticipated harmful effects, not only on the beneficiaries but also on the larger society. A frequently cited example is public assistance programs that have caused family disintegration. The desire to detect and forestall such consequences has contributed to pressures for evaluation.[15]

Fourth, the prevailing mood of retrenchment provoked by citizen discontent with government, high taxes and inflation, together with the introduction of the tools of zero-based budgeting and "sunset" legislation, have stimulated the use of program evaluation to guide in prioritizing reduction and abolition of programs. The public expenditures for social programs are so large that their continuation without evaluation has become a political impossibility. These conditions have forced administrations to more vigorously justify their requests for public funds:

> There seems little doubt that evaluation is the wave of the future. Powerful forces inside and outside government are no longer content to take argument, exhortation, and anecdotes as the main basis for deciding how billions of dollars should be spent. They have been told by social scientists and others that a more scientific and objective basis for making decisions is possible and they are demanding that it be used.[16]

Scope of a Program Evaluation

As in the marketing audit, each agency must decide for each program the data required and the analytical methods to be used in interpretation. The following set of questions provides only a general framework that can be used to evaluate specific programs. The depth in which these questions should be addressed is dictated by the magnitude of the program: "Little projects do not deserve massive evaluations and extensive efforts call for more than a fast eyeball job."[17]

Program Planning Questions

What is the extent and distribution of the target populations?

Is the program designed in conformity with its intended goals and are chances of successful implementation maximized?

Are the original program objectives still valid, necessary, relevant, and appropriate in the light of implementation experience?

Program Monitoring Questions

Is the program reaching the persons, households, or other target units to which it is addressed?

Is the program providing the resources, services, or other benefits that were intended in the project design?

Impact Assessment Questions

Is the program effective in achieving its intended objectives?

To what extent—and why—are program recipients better off, worse off, or unchanged as a result of the program activity?

Can the results of the program be explained by some alternative process that does not include the program?

Is the program having some effects that were not intended?

Economic Efficiency Questions

What are the actual costs (hidden and obvious) of delivering services and benefits to program participants?

What spillover effects does the program involve to other levels of government, the relevant private sector, and the taxpayers?

Is the program an efficient use of resources compared with alternative possible uses of the resources?[18]

Evaluations can be either summative or formative. *Summative* evaluation is the final judgment of merit or worth of a program. Since it is made after the program has been completed, it offers no potential for improving the program during its operation. The evaluation results are used for deciding whether or not to renew a program in the future and for suggesting appropriate modifications.

Formative evaluation is less common but more desirable. It does not make a final determination about a program's merit. Rather, it requires assessments during the course of the program so that decision makers can make improvements while the program is in operation. Formative evaluations are frequently more acceptable to decision makers than the go/no-go decisions offered by summative evaluations: Decision makers are frequently reluctant to terminate programs but may be responsive to suggestions for improving them.

Defining What to Evaluate

Government and social service agencies evaluate their services against three broad criteria:

Effectiveness—end results and the impacts of a service on a clientele
Efficiency—the relationship between inputs and outputs and the amount of effort, expense or waste involved in delivering a service
Equity—fairness of delivery ("Who gets what?")

In this chapter, we focus only on the effectiveness and efficiency issues. Equity is discussed in detail in Chapter 7.

A primary concern in evaluation is defining what should be measured. Budgetary constraints have forced public agency managers to increasingly direct their attention to measuring efficiency. *Too much* emphasis, in fact, is often placed on evaluating a program in terms of its *efficiency*, and insufficient attention is given to evaluating the *effectiveness* of a program's impact on clients.

The average citizen evaluates government and social services on the basis of results. Citizens want their garbage collected on time and without a mess being made. They want good schools, minimal losses from fire, and a sewage system that doesn't back up. These services all result from programs. Evaluation of police services could focus on dollars spent, miles covered patrolling, or arrests made. The local citizen, however, would probably be more interested in crime rate statistics than any of these data. In other words his or her chief concern is with results:[19]

> In the final analysis, achievement of program goals must be measured by whether program recipients are in fact better off, worse off, or unchanged as a result of the program. Without such information, cost factors have little meaning. Counting hospital beds or the frequency of their use tells nothing about the effects of that institution's services on patient clientele.[20]

If objectives have been established in terms of the benefits a program is intended to provide to a clientele, there should be a willingness and an ability to measure performance in terms of users' (and perhaps nonusers') evaluations of the extent to which they received specific benefits from a program.

Hence the first question to ask in evaluating the success of a program is "Does the program offer the benefits that it was intended to deliver to clients?"

Only when this question has been addressed is it appropriate to assess efficiency and ask, "Is the program being delivered in the least costly way?"

Because efficiency and effectiveness measure very different criteria, programs may rate high on one criterion and low on the other. For example, streets may be kept extraordinarily clean, but the street cleaning program may require an inordinate allocation of resources to achieve its results. In contrast, social workers may be very efficient in processing large numbers of clients, but they may be processed with a minimal degree of care and attention to their circumstances.

Efficiency has frequently dominated as the main evaluation criterion because effectiveness and equity are much more difficult to measure. Its validity as an evaluation criterion, however, can only be judged by its relationship to effectiveness.

Measuring Effectiveness. Measuring effectiveness involves finding out if relevant publics are satisfied with the benefits that a program offers. Four main approaches can be used to measure client satisfaction:[21] (1) unsolicited client response, (2) observation, (3) one-dimensional survey measures, and (4) two-dimensional survey saliency measures.

The *unsolicited client response* technique is the least rigorous of the four. This technique simply requires establishing a mechanism for clients to comment on their level of satisfaction if they so desire. Suggestion or comment boxes are commonly used. This approach has two important limitations. First, neither positive nor negative comments can be generalized to all publics, since the views of those who comment may be very different from the views of those who do not. Second, the absence of a large number of complaints cannot be interpreted as demonstrating a high degree of satisfaction because, as long as the service does not deteriorate below some minimal satisfaction level, many people may not make an effort to comment.

The *observation approach* represents an attempt to be a little more representative by directly observing and interacting with clients. A manager may visit a park, library, or neighborhood and talk to participants or residents about their likes, dislikes, and suggestions for improvement of the program. This technique allows a manager to seek input from whomever he or she chooses, but again there is no guarantee that these people are representative of all members in each relevant public.

Both the third and fourth approaches to measuring satisfaction use a survey that potentially is more representative. Figure 4.1 shows a typical set of questions used in a *one-dimensional survey approach*. Directly asking people in this way what they think of the quality of particular services is, however, unlikely to be very helpful. As long as their level of satisfaction is within some adequate range, most will answer positively. A high percentage of favorable evaluations or satisfied responses does not necessarily reflect a high level of satisfaction; it merely reflects a lack of dissatisfaction. Indeed, it has been shown that a program's clients almost always report high satisfaction levels and predominantly

How would you rate the services provided here in the neighborhood:

Service	Very Good	Good	No Opinion	Poor	Very Poor
Garbage collection	—	—	—	—	—
Trash collection	—	—	—	—	—
Street repair	—	—	—	—	—
Recreational facilities	—	—	—	—	—
Police protection	—	—	—	—	—
Lighting of streets	—	—	—	—	—
Water pressure	—	—	—	—	—
Drainage	—	—	—	—	—

Figure 4.1. A One-Dimensional Survey Approach to Measuring Satisfaction.

favorable evaluations, even for programs that are not effective.[22] Only if the service becomes excessively bad are citizens likely to respond negatively to generalized questions. For example:

> Citizens may have little interest in a service like street repair, paying little attention to service performance if quality is above a minimum level. However, if large potholes in the streets make driving difficult and unpleasant, the low quality of streets may become conspicuous enough to affect the evaluation of street repair obtained by citizen surveys.[23]

Hence responses to such questions will often suggest satisfaction, but this approach is too generalized to offer any useful insights for improving the effectiveness of services.

The fourth approach, *two-dimensional saliency measurement,* also uses surveys, but it addresses the measurement of satisfaction differently. First, it attempts to break down and operationalize the concept "satisfaction" into a series of constituent parts. Each of the benefits that are perceived to accrue from a particular program and that when aggregated constitute "satisfaction" are identified. Respondents are asked to evaluate each of them on a scale (1 to 7, for example) ranging from extremely satisfactory to extremely unsatisfactory (Figure 4-2 *a*).

This information alone is of limited value because it gives no indication of the relative importance that clients attach to each of the particular benefits that the program facilitates. For example, if the two scale items shown in Figure 4.2*a* are among those used to measure sociability and prestige benefits facilitated by a recreation program, both may receive a score of 4 on a 7-point scale (neither satisfactory nor unsatisfactory). However, sociability may be a very important benefit to participants in the program, while prestige may be of very little importance to them.

The necessary complement to the benefit evaluation is the second differentiating characteristic of two-dimensional saliency measurement, which is

	Extremely Unsatisfactory	Very Unsatisfactory	Slightly Unsatisfactory	Neither Unsatisfactory nor Satisfactory	Slightly Satisfactory	Very Satisfactory	Extremely Satisfactory
Opportunity to interact with others in this program is	1	2	3	(4)	5	6	7
Discussion generated among my friends by my participation in this program is	1	2	3	(4)	5	6	7

(a)

	Extremely Unimportant	Very Unimportant	Slightly Unimportant	Neither Unimportant nor Important	Slightly Important	Very Important	Extremely Important
Opportunity to interact with others in this program is	1	2	3	4	5	6	(7)
Discussion generated among my friends by my participation in this program is	1	(2)	3	4	5	6	7

(b)

Figure 4.2. A Two-Dimensional Survey Approach to Measuring Satisfaction that Operationalizes Service Satisfaction by Identifying Individual Benefit Components: *(a)* Satisfaction dimension of individual benefits and *(b)* Importance dimension of individual benefits.

shown in Figure 4.2*b*. The second series of questions seek to rate the salient benefit attributes sought by clients from a program. These measures are most useful for determining whether or not more effort should be given to improving dimensions of the service.

If clients rate the sociability and prestige benefits 7 and 2 respectively on this importance scale, then the previous satisfaction score of 4 for the prestige benefit may be considered adequate because a score of 2 shows clients consider it very unimportant. Thus it is of little concern that the program is not facilitating this benefit particularly well. In contrast, sociability is rated extremely important (a score of 7), so the agency should be greatly concerned if the program is not successfully facilitating this benefit. Unless the program is restructured in some way to increase its potential for encouraging interaction with others, client support is likely to diminish.

This approach can be presented very effectively in the form of a graphic action grid, shown in Figure 4.3. The importance and satisfaction scores for each benefit attribute can be spatially located at a single point on the grid which specifies the marketing implications. In this way, a manager can quickly see those attributes of an offering that require remedial attention and those to which it may be possible to devote less effort.

A partial two-dimensional survey approach is shown in Figure 4.4. It includes both the satisfaction and saliency dimensions but the questions are asked only at the general level of the total service. Each service is not broken down into its individual benefit attributes. The information received from this approach is useful only for comparing the effectiveness and importance of one service to another. These data suggest which services should make special efforts to improve their effectiveness. However, the data offer no insights to managers of these services regarding on which aspect of their particular service they should concentrate those efforts.

Agency effectiveness in delivering programs cannot always be evaluated in the same way or with the same ease. Some agencies are much more able to do what is expected of them than others. For example, a sewage treatment plant has much more control over the quality of effluence than a police department has over the level of crime in its jurisdiction.[24] Hence it is more difficult to evaluate the police department. If the department is not effective, it may be because relevant variables are beyond its control, which is less likely for a sewage treatment plant.

Measuring Efficiency.[25] Efficiency is a relation of outputs to inputs. It is concerned with the question "To what degree does the agency produce the output as inexpensively as it could?" Regular measurement of various aspects of efficiency should provide a picture of how service delivery efficiency is changing over time for individual services. Two main types of efficiency measures have been developed. Examples of each type for a number of government services are shown in Figure 4.5.

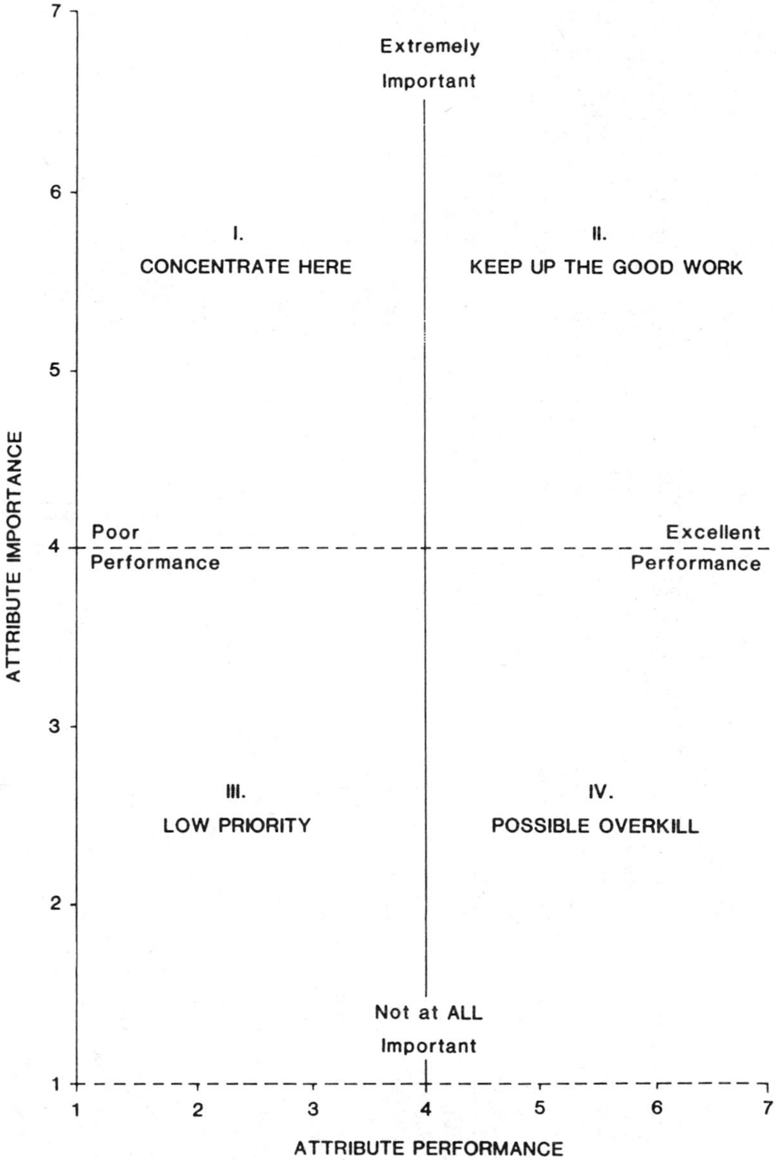

Figure 4.3. Action Grid

A. First of all, I'm going to ask you about several city services, and I would like you to use this plus-and-minus card (SHOW CARD) to tell me how high or how low you would rate the *quality* of each service. Notice that the ratings go from a high of plus 3, the highest or best rating you can give, down to minus 3, the lowest or worst rating you can give. Of course, you can give a rating anywhere in between, depending on how you feel. The first service I want you to rate is *fire protection*—how high or how low would you rate the quality of the fire protection provided by the City of Dallas?

	Ask for each service separately	Ratings						No Rating
a.	Fire protection	+3	+2	+1	−1	−2	−3	9
b.	Police protection	+3	+2	+1	−1	−2	−3	9
c.	Neighborhood parks and playgrounds	+3	+2	+1	−1	−2	−3	9
d.	Recreation centers, swimming pools, lakes and other recreation facilities	+3	+2	+1	−1	−2	−3	9
e.	Garbage collection	+3	+2	+1	−1	−2	−3	9
f.	Collection of branches, leaves and large items	+3	+2	+1	−1	−2	−3	9
g.	Sidewalks	+3	+2	+1	−1	−2	−3	9
h.	Street cleaning	+3	+2	+1	−1	−2	−3	9
i.	Traffic signs and signals *in your neighborhood*	+3	+2	+1	−1	−2	−3	9
j.	Street maintenance and repairs	+3	+2	+1	−1	−2	−3	9
k.	Beautification with trees, flowers and shrubs on public land	+3	+2	+1	−1	−2	−3	9
l.	Library services	+3	+2	+1	−1	−2	−3	9
m.	Bus service	+3	+2	+1	−1	−2	−3	9

B. Finally, the last question about these services is how important you feel each one is for you, here in your neighborhood. Use this plus-and-minus card again (SHOW CARD) to tell me how important or how unimportant each one is. Remember, a rating of plus 3 would mean that you feel the service is *very* important for your neighborhood, and a rating of minus 3 would mean that you feel it is *not* very important—or you can give a rating anywhere in between. How high or how low would you rate the importance of fire protection here in your neighborhood?

	Ask for each service separately			Ratings				No Rating
a.	Fire protection	+3	+2	+1	−1	−2	−3	9
b.	Police protection	+3	+2	+1	−1	−2	−3	9
c.	Neighborhood parks and playgrounds	+3	+2	+1	−1	−2	−3	9
d.	Recreation centers, swimming pools, lakes and other recreation facilities	+3	+2	+1	−1	−2	−3	9
e.	Garbage collection	+3	+2	+1	−1	−2	−3	9
f.	Collection of branches, leaves and large items	+3	+2	+1	−1	−2	−3	9
g.	Sidewalks	+3	+2	+1	−1	−2	−3	9
h.	Street cleaning	+3	+2	+1	−1	−2	−3	9
i.	Traffic signs and signals *in your neighborhood*	+3	+2	+1	−1	−2	−3	9
j.	Street maintenance and repairs	+3	+2	+1	−1	−2	−3	9
k.	Beautification with trees, flowers and shrubs on public land	+3	+2	+1	−1	−2	−3	9
l.	Library services	+3	+2	+1	−1	−2	−3	9
m.	Bus service	+3	+2	+1	−1	−2	−3	9

Figure 4.4. A Two-Dimensional Survey Approach to Measuring Satisfaction Without Identification of Individual Benefit Components. These questions are taken from the Dallas City Profile Survey, which is intended "to measure citizen satisfaction with the quality and effectiveness of city services." The survey uses a random sample of dwelling units, is conducted by personal interviews, and is repeated on a regular basis.

Service	Output in Units of Workload ÷ Input	Output in Units of Effectiveness ÷ Input
Solid Waste Collection	Tons collected per dollar Number of curb-miles of streets cleaned per dollar Number of residential (or commercial) customers served per dollar	Estimated number of total households and commercial customers satisfied with their collection services (as estimated from responses to a citizen survey and survey of businesses) per dollar
Recreation Services	Acres (or square feet of facility) maintained (mowed, cleaned, etc.) per dollar, for various types of facilities Number of hours of operation per dollar, for individual programs or facilities	Attendance (or visit) days per dollar, perhaps for individual programs or facilities Estimated number of different households using recreation services (at least once a year) per dollar Estimated number of total households satisfied with recreation services (as estimated by data from the annual citizen survey) per dollar
Library Services	Number of items circulated (books, records, and other items) per dollar, perhaps including in-library circulation Number of items cataloged per employee-hour Number of items shelved per employee-hour Number of hours of operation per dollar	Number of individual uses of library (including attendance counts plus telephone requests for information) per dollar Estimated number of different households (or persons) using library services at least once (as estimated from an annual citizen survey) per dollar Estimated number of households satisfied with library services (as estimated from the citizen survey) per dollar
Crime Control	Number of service calls responded to per hour of police-officer time—by type of case	Number of felony arrests that pass preliminary hearing per police officer-hour—overall and by type of category

Figure 4.5. Examples of Efficiency Measures. (These examples are taken from Hatry et al., *How Effective Are Your Community Services? Procedures for Monitoring the Effectiveness of Municipal Services* Washington DC: The Urban Institute, 1977, pp. 241–244. More complete descriptions of each of these measures are provided in the original reference.)

Service	Output in Units of Workload ÷ Input	Output in Units of Effectiveness ÷ Input
Crime Control—cont'd	Number of arrests per hour of police officer time	Estimated number of households reporting a reasonable feeling of security in walking their neighborhood at night (as estimated from citizen survey findings) per dollar Estimated number of nonvictimized households and commercial establishments per dollar (the citizen survey could be used to provide estimates of the number of crime incidents not reported)
Fire Protection	Number of households and business establishments "protected" per dollar Number of fire prevention inspections per dollar—perhaps categorized as to whether inspections and costs are residential or commercial	Number of fires fought for which less than a target amount of spread occurred per suppression dollar spent
Street Maintenance	Number of miles (or lane-miles) of street maintained per dollar Number of repairs made (or number of square yards of repairs made) per employee-hour Number of square yards of street surface constructed per dollar	Number of streets maintained in rideability-condition "x" or better per dollar Number of repairs made satisfactorily (for example, "patches lasting at least 'x' months after repair") per dollar
Traffic Signs	Number of signs installed per dollar Number of signals installed per dollar Number of feet of street markings laid per dollar Number of signs or signals repaired per dollar	Number of signs or signals maintained in acceptable operating condition per dollar
Public Transit	Number of vehicle-miles per dollar	Number of passenger-trips per dollar

Figure 4.5. *(Continued)*

Service	Output in Units of Workload ÷ Input	Output in Units of Effectiveness ÷ Input
Public Transit—cont'd	Number of transit vehicle-hours of operation per dollar	Number of passenger-miles per dollar Estimated number of "satisfied" users (perhaps as estimated from an annual citizen survey) per dollar
Water Supply	Number of gallons distributed per dollar Number of gallons treated per dollar Number of customers served per dollar (perhaps divided by residential and commercial customers) Number of repairs completed per employee-hour, by type and size of repair Number of meters read per employee-hour Number of meters inspected per employee-hour Number of meters repaired per employee-hour	Estimated number of customers indicating satisfaction with their water (as obtained from the annual citizen survey) per dollar

Figure 4.5. *(Continued)*

The most common efficiency measures are *output-input ratios, which use workload accomplished as the measure of output*. Examples of outputs are

Tons of refuse collected
Miles of street repaired
Acres of grass mowed
Number of park trees trimmed
Number of complaints or requests handled

These outputs are related to the input resources used in producing them in terms of dollars or employee hours. Thus they can be expressed as ratios such as "the number of tons collected per dollar or per employee hour" (if dollars are used they should be adjusted annually so that they reflect real dollar costs and not inflated dollar costs). The employee hour measure produces major insights regarding personnel, which is likely to be the principal agency input.

Dollar costs represent all inputs and thus, in effect, permit simultaneous consideration of the efficiency of use of all resources, not only personnel. The major weakness in this first method is that improvement in the ratio of work accomplished per unit of input may be attributed to an improvement in efficiency when, in fact, it may more accurately reflect a deterioration in the level of service offered.

To rectify this problem, a second and more sophisticated type of measure has been suggested. This method adopts *output-input ratio measures using effectiveness data as the measure of output*. With this type of measure the proportion or number of households, citizens, or clients *satisfied* with the service per dollar or per employee hour is assessed. It combines the conventional number-of-persons-served rules with a measure of the percentage of citizens satisfied with the service. Using this measure thus ensures that gains in efficiency are not taking place at the expense of effectiveness.

Whenever efficiency measures concentrate on one dimension of a service, agency personnel correctly interpret this imbalance as a signal of management priority and concentrate on the activities measured.[26] For example, if police officers are evaluated on traffic ticketing or vice arrests, efficiency in these areas will increase. Other examples include the following:

> If welfare workers are assessed on their error rate, the error rate will go down because workers pay more attention to it. If teachers are assessed or even remotely evaluated on the proportion of their charges who pass year-end examinations, more will pass because teachers will "teach the test." This is neither surprising nor in itself deplorable, but simply highly probable.[27]

Clearly, whatever efficiency measures are selected should reflect those benefits that the agency's publics perceive as the most important. Otherwise, agency personnel could receive the wrong message, as did the employment counselors who, when assessed in terms of successful placement ratios, concentrated on easy-to-place clients at the expense of more difficult cases.[28]

Three other problems may emerge when government and social service agencies undertake to measure efficiency. First, there is some danger of encouraging excessive concern with current performance at the expense of future performance. If too much emphasis is placed on current efficiency, efforts aimed at improving future performance may be neglected. This may result in much higher expenditures in future years to rectify problems, because the cost of decay is invariably greater than that required to provide timely maintenance.

Second, changes in the results obtained from efficiency measures must be interpreted carefully:

> Substantial increases or decreases in the incoming workload can by themselves significantly affect efficiency values. The type of service offered may change. In addition, differing external characteristics of neighborhoods (such as the terrain or resident population) make it difficult to compare various facilities or different units of workers in different areas.[29]

Third, at a certain level of detail concern for efficiency becomes self-defeating. Excessive efficiency measurement should be avoided. Local governments, for example, have been known to engage in such very detailed efficiency measurement efforts that they were unable to survive their own tests of cost-effectiveness.[30]

Why Evaluation Findings Are Not Used

Within the context of marketing planning, evaluation efforts are an integral part of a total system (see Figure 3.1). The findings are used to fine tune the Action Plan and improve the agency's offerings. However, program evaluations are often ignored by decision makers. "The single most disappointing aspect of the history of evaluation during the last ten or fifteen years has been the generally dismal record concerning the utilization of evaluation research."[31]

A number of factors contribute to this underutilization.[32] First, government agencies function in a political environment and other factors must be considered besides research evidence. At times negative evaluation findings have been ignored because of the adverse effect withdrawal or modification of the program would have had on the clienteles served, other support publics, and the agency's prestige.

At other times, the issues and goals pursued and measured by evaluations are often not the issues or goals in which program managers are interested, so the findings are ignored. In addition, many evaluations fail to offer recommendations as to how the service can be improved. Consequently, the evaluation results are greeted with indifference or hostility.

Still other agency administrators practice "pseudomanagement."[33] They do not support unambiguous statements of objectives or seek tangible evidence of an offering's success or failure. Their attitude develops from inertia and lack of genuine commitment, or because they feel vagueness gives them more room to maneuver. Finally, a major factor in determining the extent to which evaluation findings will be used is the set of motives that initially stimulated the evaluation.

Motives for Undertaking a Program Evaluation

The ideal program evaluation involves three characters: (1) a top executive who supports and uses the results of evaluations to make important decisions, (2) a program manager who encourages and supports the evaluation of his or her program, and (3) an evaluator whose insightful recommendations produce "slam bang" changes in the efficiency and effectiveness of the program.

The reality of program evaluation frequently contrasts markedly with the ideal. Instead we find (1) a top executive who distrusts or ignores any evaluation done by anyone else, (2) a program manager who uses subversive tactics to thwart, mislead, and discredit evaluations and evaluators, and (3) evaluators whose efforts are equally divided between survival and the advocacy of personal agendas with little time left for unbiased, independent assessment.[34]

Obviously, this characterization is a cynical one, but unfortunately it is not uncommon. The underlying reasons stimulating the program evaluation strongly influence the attitudes of all personnel toward the process. In turn, their attitudes create either a sympathetic or an unsympathetic internal climate within which evaluations are conducted and, therefore, influence the usefulness of the results that will emerge from the evaluations. The motives for program evaluation in government and social service agencies fall into three classes: compulsory, defense or attack, and voluntary.[35]

Compulsory. This type of program evaluation motive is imposed by authority from above. This authority might be a higher level of government or it may be senior management within the agency.

Since the late 1960s federal programs typically have required that somewhere between 1 and 3 percent of allocated funds be budgeted for evaluation purposes.[36] Although this mandatory requirement has been an important stimulant, imposing program evaluation on local recipients of federal funds has often caused resentment. Evaluation has often been perfunctory and concerned only with minimally meeting a legislative requirement, rather than with meaningful assessment of program performance.

Similarly, its imposition by senior management within an agency may be perceived as threatening, leading to noncooperation and efforts by personnel to undermine the process rather than to support it. To make evaluation work, the demand for it must emanate from top policy and decision levels, but support from the personnel directly involved with the program being evaluated is equally important. Without their commitment, it is unlikely that evaluation results will be meaningful or that any subsequent improvement in service delivery will be implemented.

To create the right environment, evaluation must be presented positively as a tool to improve service delivery rather than as an attempt to discredit current performance. Unfortunately, evaluations often have given more attention to failures than successes and, as a result, they create negative and inhibiting responses in personnel.

Defense or Attack. Program evaluation is often motivated by a desire to prove the worth or lack of worth of a program. As government and social service agencies confront demands for personnel cuts, demonstratable accountability gains urgency. If agencies cannot demonstrate the effectiveness and efficiency of their programs, they are likely to experience cuts. Hence evaluation may be used as a defense mechanism by agencies or as an attack tool by those seeking the demise of certain programs. In such instances the motivation for its employment can foster a strong research bias in an evaluation. "Evaluations can be scientifically or politically designed and carried out. They can be an effective form of accountability or they can be used to further the ambitions of those who initiate the evaluations."[37]

Sometimes the program administrator is thrust into the role of program advocate. For example, the typical process that takes place annually within federal government agencies preparing for Congressional hearings

> Is not one of developing an even handed presentation of the successes and advantages vs. the failures and difficulties of a program, but rather one of collecting and displaying those things (with limited scrutiny of their validity) which show the program and its accomplishments in a favorable light. This is a situation and a process for which program administrators are not to blame. They know full well from past experience—or at least they believe it to be the case—that if they go before Congress with a report that their program is not working they can expect a cry to go up for their scalp. An admission of program failure will be taken as an admission of personal failure.[38]

Voluntary. The most desirable, but perhaps least common, stimulus for program evaluation is a desire to discover the truth about a program's effectiveness, efficiency, and equity. It is in this environment that the ideal set of circumstances, described at the start of this section, can flourish. An awareness of the potential of evaluation for improving service delivery and of its proper role appears to be growing. It is accompanied by more willingness to accept distasteful judgments about favorite programs if the judgments are based on sound evaluation.

Problem of Resources

Ironically the scarcity of resources, which has been a prime stimulus for program evaluation, also contributes to reducing its potential.[39] Evaluation is not free. Even a relatively sketchy and incomplete assessment involves an expenditure of time. Scarce resources demand that critical decisions be made regarding improvement of effectiveness and efficiency of service delivery. Yet the very data-gathering and analysis activities that can provide needed input for these decisions are often considered too costly to be regular program features. Thus the most pervasive problem surrounding program evaluation is scarcity of resources.

The imperatives of day-to-day operations often push evaluation aside. Agencies face continuing dilemmas of denying services to clients or reducing their own administrative costs. The latter are the first to be reduced, which further de-emphasizes the resources available for program evaluation. It is probably unrealistic for some agencies to evaluate all of their programs on an ongoing or annual basis. In these circumstances the programs that the agency deems most important to its mission or those to which the most resources have been allocated should be selected.

SUMMARY

Evaluation is the final stage in strategic planning. It answers the question "Where are we now in relation to where we said we wanted to be in our objectives?" Its purposes are to review and evaluate current marketing activities. Given the pressures confronting agencies for alternative use of their resources, it is unlikely that sufficient resources will be made available to generate perfect information. Obviously incomplete information may be misleading, but as a general rule incomplete information and imperfect analysis are better than none at all, which is sometimes the only alternative. The task of evaluation is to provide the best possible information at the time when it is needed.

A marketing audit takes place at the end of a long-term planning period and assesses the overall status of all of the agency's services and marketing activities. Conducting a marketing audit requires making three related decisions. First, the scope of the audit must be determined. Ideally, it should be comprehensive. However, if the agency lacks the resources to collect detailed information or to implement a large number of relatively detailed suggestions that may emerge from an in-depth effort, a more limited audit providing generalized rather than detailed information may be more appropriate. Second, sources from which data will be compiled need to be identified. These will usually include internal interviews, external interviews, and secondary documentary sources. Third, an auditor or auditing committee has to be selected either from within or from outside the organization.

Program evaluations are associated with the annual plan and are more limited in scope. They evaluate the individual programs at the microlevel, in contrast to the marketing audit, which focuses on evaluating the total set of agency programs at the macrolevel.

Now that program evaluation has been a mandatory requirement of most federal programs since the mid-1960s, interest in it has trickled down to state and local government and social service agencies. They are increasingly concerned with accountability and prioritizing projects to guide reduction and termination decisions. The appropriate scope of a program evaluation is dictated by its importance to achieving the agency's mission and by the resources it consumes.

Government and social service agencies evaluate their services against three broad criteria: effectiveness, efficiency, and equity. The first question to ask in evaluating the success of a program addresses effectiveness, "Does the program offer the benefits that it was intended to deliver to clients?" Only when this question has been addressed is it appropriate to assess efficiency and ask, "Is the program being delivered in the least costly way?"

Four approaches can be used to measure effectiveness, which is defined as client satisfaction with the benefits delivered. They are (1) unsolicited client response, (2) observation, (3) one-dimensional survey measures, and (4) two-dimensional survey saliency measures. Their utility increases sequentially, with the first approach being the least useful and the fourth the most useful.

Efficiency is a relation of outputs to inputs. It is measured in two primary ways. Most common are output-input ratio measures that use workload accomplished as the measure of output. Their major weakness is that an improvement in this ratio may be attributed to an improvement in efficiency, when in fact it may more accurately reflect a deterioration in the level of service offered. The second type of efficiency measure seeks to rectify this problem. It uses output-input ratio measures with effectiveness data as the measure of output.

Despite their potential for improving client satisfaction, evaluation findings are often ignored by decision makers. An important factor in determining the extent to which they will be used is the underlying motives that initially stimulated the evaluation. The motives for undertaking a program evaluation fall into the three classes of compulsory, defense or attack, and voluntary. The underlying motive frequently determines the legitimacy of the information that the evaluation yields.

Evaluation is an essential management tool. It not only measures the results of marketing efforts but also assists in the specification of appropriate program objectives, supports basic management decisions, and assists public managers in implementing difficult decisions by providing an empirical rationale for them.

NOTES

1. Mokwa, M.P., "Marketing Control and Evaluation: A Framework for Strategic Arts Administration." In M.P. Mokwa, W.M. Dawson, and E.A. Prieve (eds.), *Marketing the Arts*. New York: Praeger, 1980, p. 272.
2. Cited in Stanley, D.T., "How Safe the Streets, How Good the Grant?" *Public Administration Review*, vol. 34, No. 4, July/August 1974, p. 381.
3. Shuschman, A. "The Marketing Audit: Its Nature, Purposes and Problems," *Analyzing and Improving Marketing Performance*, Report No. 32. New York: American Management Association, 1959, p. 13.
4. Mokwa, "Marketing Control," p. 273.
5. Ibid., p. 272.
6. Scioli, Jr., F.P., "Problems and Prospects for Policy Evaluation," *Public Administration Review*, vol. 39, No. 1, January/February 1979, p. 41.
7. Kotler, P., Gregor, W., and Rodgers, W., "The Marketing Audit Comes of Age," *Sloan Management Review*, Winter 1977, p. 37.
8. Kotler, P., *Principles of Marketing*. Englewood Cliffs, NJ: Prentice-Hall, 1980, p. 125.
9. Hatry, H.P., Winnie, R.E., and Fisk, D.M. *Practical Program Evaluation for State and Local Government Officials*. Washington, DC: Urban Institute, 1973, p. 8.
10. Rossi, P.H., Freeman, H.E., and Wright, S.R. *Evaluation: A Systematic Approach*. Beverly Hills, CA: Sage Publications, 1979, p. 21.
11. Poland, O.F., "Program Evaluation and Administrative Theory," *Public Administrative Review*. vol. 34, No. 4, July/August 1974, p. 385.
12. Stanley, "How Safe," p. 385.
13. Lipsky, M., *Street Level Bureaucracy*. New York: Russell Sage Foundation, 1980, p. 160.
14. Freeman, H.J., "The Present Status of Evaluation Research." In M. Guttentag, S. Saar (eds.),

Evaluation Studies Review Annual, Volume 2. Beverly Hills, CA: Sage Publications, 1977, p. 18.

15. Nigro, F.A., and Nigro, L.G., *Modern Public Administration* (5th ed.) New York: Harper & Row, 1980, p. 250.
16. Evans, J.W., "Evaluating Social Action Programs," *Social Science Quarterly*, University of Texas, vol. 50, No. 3, December 1969, p. 570.
17. Stanley, "How Safe," p. 385.
18. Adapted from Rossi et al., *Evaluation*, p. 33.
19. Adapted from Gilbert, D., "A Methodological Framework for Assessing the Possible Effect of Metropolitan Government Reorganization." Unpublished Ph.D. diss., Syracuse University, 1975, p. 54.
20. Seidman, E., "Why Not Qualitative Analysis?" *Public Administration Review*, vol. 37, No. 4, July/August 1977, p. 417.
21. Adapted from Kotler, P., *Marketing for Non-Profit Organizations*. Englewood Cliffs, NJ: Prentice-Hall, 1982, pp. 66–71.
22. Scheirer, M.A. "Program Participants' Positive Perceptions: Psychological Conflicts of Interest in Program Evaluation," *Evaluation Quarterly*. vol. 2, February 1978, p. 55.
23. Stipak, B., "Citizen Satisfaction with Urban Services: Potential Misuse as a Performance Indicator," *Public Administration Review*, January/February 1979, vol. 39, No. 1, p. 48.
24. Gilbert, "Methodological Framework," p. 58.
25. Much of this section is adapted from Hatry, H.P., Blair, L.H., Fisk, D.M., et al., *How Effective Are Your Community Services?* Washington, DC: Urban Institute, 1977, pp. 223–243.
26. Lipsky, *Street Level*, p. 166.
27. Ibid.
28. Blau, P., *The Dynamics of Bureaucracy*. Chicago: University of Chicago Press, 1964, pp. 36–56.
29. Hatry et al., *Practical Evaluation*, p. 239.
30. Ibid.
31. Rocheleau, B., and MacKesey, T., "Utilization-Focused Evaluation: A Case Study from the Human Services Area." In Palumbo, D.J., Fawcett, S.B., and Wright, S. (eds.), *Evaluating and Optimising Public Policy*. Lexington, MA: Heath, 1981, p. 187.
32. Ibid.
33. Nigro and Nigro, *Public Administration*, p. 256.
34. Barkdoll, G.L., "Type III Evaluations: Consultation and Consensus," *Public Administration Review*, vol. 40, No. 2, March/April 1980, p. 174.
35. White, K.R., "What a Small Boy and a Hammer Have to Do with Evaluative Research," *Research, Camping and Environmental Education*, No. 11. State College Pennsylvania, The Pennsylvania State University HPHER Series, 1975, pp. 197–217.
36. Hatry et al., *Practical Evaluation*, p. 19.
37. Mead, B., "Uses and Abuses of Evaluation," *Journal of Physical Education and Recreation*, October 1980, p. 35.
38. Evans, "Evaluating Programs," p. 569.
39. Scioli, "Problems and Prospects," p. 41.

APPENDIX: A MARKETING AUDIT OUTLINE

Orientation

1. Has the agency established a marketing orientation? That is, has the agency identified the benefits particular clientele seek and developed programs based upon this input?
2. Are personnel efforts focused on satisfying the wants of actual potential clientele, rather than on actual or potential programs, rules and regulations, or their own immediate personal well-being?
3. Does the agency define its business in terms of benefits its client groups want rather than in terms of programs and services?
4. Does the agency try to direct its services only to specific groups of people or to everybody?
5. Is the agency's primary goal to maximize customer satisfaction or to get as many people through the door as possible?
6. Does the agency seek to achieve its goal primarily through a coordinated use of the set of marketing activities (i.e., promotion, program, pricing, and distribution) or only through intensive promotion?
7. Does the agency have a mission statement and is it translated into operational terms regarding the objectives of the agency?

Marketing Planning

A. *External Environment*

1. *Social*. What major social and lifestyle developments and trends will have an impact on the agency? What actions has the agency been taking in response to these developments and trends?
2. *Demographics*. What impact will forecasted trends in the size, age, profile, and distribution of population have on the agency? How will the changing nature of the family, increase in the proportion of females in the work force, and changes in ethnic composition of the population affect the agency? What actions has the agency been taking in response to these developments and trends? Has the agency reevaluated traditional services and expanded the range of specialized offerings to respond to these changes?
3. *Economic*. What major developments and trends in taxation and other

income sources will have an impact on the agency? What actions has the agency been taking in response to these developments and trends?

4. *Political, Legal, and Financial.* What financing laws are now being proposed at federal, state, and local levels that could affect marketing strategy and tactics? What changes in regulations and court decisions have occurred that impact the agency? What political changes at each government level are taking place? What actions has the agency been taking in response to these legal and political changes?
5. *Competition.* Which organizations are competing with us directly by offering a similar service? Which organizations are competing with us indirectly by securing our prime prospects' time, money, energy, or commitment? What new competitive trends seem likely to emerge? How effective is the competition? What benefits do our competitors offer that we do not? Is it appropriate for us to compete? Could we more usefully withdraw from some areas where there are alternative suppliers and use our resources to better service new unserved client groups?
6. *Technological.* What major technological changes are occurring which impact the agency?
7. *Ecological.* What is the outlook for the cost and availability of natural resources and energy needed by the agency?

B. Needs Assessments

1. Are needs assessments undertaken?
2. Have secondary data been used in the needs assessment? If so, is the information current? Classified in a useful manner? Impartial? Reliable? Valid?
3. What does the agency want to learn from the needs assessment survey?
4. Are surveys used in the needs assessment process? If so, is each and every question necessary? Can the agency determine what will be done with the information from every question? Do the respondents have the ability to answer the questions accurately? Will respondents provide the information? Are the questions threatening or too personal? Are the questions worded simply so as to be understood by individuals with a low education level? Is the sample size appropriate?
5. How have agency personnel used the information which they have generated about the agency's markets and other publics to improve services?
6. What are the evolving needs and satisfactions being sought by the agency's client groups?
7. Who uses the agency's services? How does a potential user find out about the organization? When and how does a nonuser become a user?

8. What are the major objections given by consumers as to why they do not use the agency's services?
9. How do users find out about and decide to try and/or use the organization's services? When and where?
10. Has an evaluative report on needs assessment been written? If so, is the needs assessment report too long or too technical? Does it provide a summary of the high points of most interest to the reader?

C. *Objectives and Mission*

1. What is the mission of the agency? What business is it in? How well is its mission understood throughout the organization? What business does it wish to be in five years from now?
2. What are the stated objectives of the organization? Are they formally written down? Do they lead logically to clearly stated marketing objectives?
3. Are the organization's marketing objectives stated in hierarchical order? Are they specific so that progress toward achievement can be measured? Are the objectives reasonable in light of the organization's resources? Are the objectives ambiguous? Do the objectives specify a timeframe? Are the objectives that are concerned with effectiveness benefit-oriented?
4. Does the agency have both long-term and short-term plans? Do the short-term plans contribute toward the achievement of the long-term plan?
5. Are the objectives and roles of each element of the marketing mix clearly specified?
6. What policies inhibit the achievement of objectives with respect to organization, allocation of resources, operations, hiring and training, products, pricing and promotion?
7. Should the agency seek to expand, contract, or change the emphasis on the range of its offerings or selected target markets? If so, in which service areas and target markets, and how vigorously?

D. *Marketing Planning and Evaluation*

1. Does the organization have a marketing planning and evaluation system?
2. Does the marketing planning and evaluation system include an annual program evaluation as well as a longer-term agencywide evaluation?
3. Is this agencywide evaluation (marketing audit) conducted every five

years to assess the overall status of all the agency's services and marketing activities? Does the audit describe the current marketing situation as well as speculate about the relevant future?

4. Is someone in the agency held accountable for ensuring that the recommendations of the marketing audit are implemented?
5. Are annual marketing plans developed, implemented, and used as the basis for evaluation?
6. Does the organization carry out periodic reviews of its programs and evaluations of its resource allocation decisions? How and with what results?
7. Is the five-year marketing audit a summation, synthesis and integration of annual evaluations?
8. Are the short-term evaluation procedures (monthly, quarterly, etc.) adequate to ensure that the long-term plan objectives are being achieved?
9. Should the organization enter, expand, contract, or withdraw from any existing segments?
10. What should be the short- and long-term cost and revenue consequences of these changes?
11. Does it seem that the agency is trying to do too much or not enough?
12. What are the core marketing strategies for achieving the agreed objectives? Are they sound?
13. Are the stated objectives being met, and are these objectives indeed the appropriate objectives?
14. Are enough resources (or too many resources) budgeted to accomplish the marketing objectives?
15. Are the marketing resources allocated optimally to prime market segments and products of the organization?
16. Does the program offer the benefits that it is intended to deliver to clients? Are the relevant publics satisfied with these benefits?
17. In which particular service areas should the agency make special efforts to improve effectiveness?
18. Do any programs seem to have excessive costs? Are these costs valid? Can cost-reducing steps be taken?
19. Do registration forms make it hard or easy for someone to sign up? Is more information asked for than is necessary? How are the data used?
20. What is done with negative feedback from consumers about agency staff? How are complaints handled?
21. What is the agency's reputation among its various publics?
22. What are the organization's major strengths and weaknesses?

Target Market Strategies

A. *Target Markets*

1. Are the members of the target market homogeneous or heterogeneous with respect to geographic, sociodemographic, and behavioral characteristics?
2. Describe the size, growth rate, national and regional trends for each of the organization's market segments.
3. Is the size of the market segment sufficiently large or important to develop a unique marketing mix to service it?
4. Are the market segments measurable and accessible? That is, are the market segments accessible to distribution and communication efforts?
5. Which are the high opportunity and low opportunity segments?
6. What are the evolving needs and satisfactions being sought by constituent publics?
7. What benefits does the organization offer to each segment? How does this compare to the benefits offered by competitors?
8. Is the agency offering services to individuals who are not adequately serviced by other organizations?
9. Is the agency positioning itself with a unique service, and is it needed?
10. Is the agency targeting any unresponsive markets? If so, what particular constraints contribute to the underutilizers' unresponsiveness?
11. How much of the program use is repeat versus new business? What percent of the public can be classified as nonusers, light users, and heavy users?
12. How do current prospective client groups rate the agency and its competitors, particularly with respect to reputation, program quality, and price?
13. What is the agency's image with respect to the specific market segments it seeks to serve?
14. Has the agency been efficient and effective in meeting the clientele's needs?

B. *Other Publics*

1. What publics other than direct client groups (financial, media, government, citizen, local, general, and internal) represent particular opportunities or problems for the agency?
2. What steps has the agency taken to deal effectively with key publics?
3. What does each public seek from the agency? (i.e., what's in it for them?)

Distribution Decisions

A. The Equity Issue

1. Is there general understanding of and commitment among all agency personnel to the equity standard under which the agency is seeking to operate?
2. Has the agreed standard of equity been articulated?
3. Is it used as the guideline for the distribution of all agency services and facilities?

B. Strategic Distribution Decisions

1. Has there been a recent evaluation of the agency's existing distribution pattern of both facilities and services?
2. Is there a written statement of distribution objectives?
3. In which areas is it appropriate for the agency to be a direct provider? Facilitator? Engage in outreach efforts?
4. Should the agency attempt to deliver its offerings directly to consumers, or can they better deliver selected offerings by involving other agencies or organizations?
5. Are members of the target market willing and able to travel some distance to use the facility or receive the service?
6. How good is public transportation access to facilities? Can it be improved? How good is parking for bicycles and cars? How good is the access for physically handicapped? Which facilities need priority attention in these areas?
7. How are facility locations selected? Is the site accessible to the target markets? Is it visible to the target markets?
8. When are services made available to users? (a) season of year; (b) day of week; (c) time of day? Are these most appropriate?
9. How frequently are services offered? Are there multiple offerings?
10. Are the timing decisions made in the two previous questions based on analysis of users' preferences? To what extent do the choices reflect staff and/or volunteer convenience? Inertia from the past?

Program Strategies

A. Program Management

1. What are the major services offered by the agency? Do they complement each other or is there unnecessary duplication?

2. Where is (a) the agency and (b) each major service in its life cycle? Calculate by using market share or participation.
3. Is the development of new programs, termination of old programs and allocation of resources correctly prioritized according to each program's life cycle?
4. Is the appropriate type of management used at each stage of the life cycle?
5. What are the pressures among various publics to increase or to decrease the (a) range of services and (b) quality of services?
6. What are the major weaknesses in each program area? What are the major complaints? What goes wrong most often?
7. Does the physical appearance of the facility create an environment that complements and enhances the program itself? Does it aid in the client's participation? Is the environment relaxing and comfortable?
8. Is the program name easy to pronounce? Spell? Recall? Is it descriptive and does it communicate the benefits that the service offers? Does the name distinguish the agency or program from all others?

B. *New Program Development*

1. Have new program committees been established? Do they keep senior management involved and/or informed?
2. What major new programs are in the planning stages?
3. Is the agency well organized to gather, generate, and screen new program ideas?
4. Has a feasibility analysis been conducted to examine the costs and benefits of the proposal? Has the agency established criteria regarding what constitutes feasibility?
5. Does the agency carry out small-scale pilot tests with major new programs before launching them?
6. Are there sufficient personnel resources to effectively evaluate and launch new programs? Do the agency's personnel have the appropriate expertise?
7. Are the promotional efforts for new programs adequate?

C. *Diffusion of New Services*

1. Has the agency identified opinion leaders in order to help speed the rate of diffusion of services?
2. Are the opinion leaders also facilitating the extent of diffusion?

D. Program Retrenchment

1. Are the agency's managerial resources spread too thin?
2. What can the agency do to manage effectively with reduced resources?
3. What programs and services are being, or should be, phased out?
4. How does the organization determine which services are to be terminated?
5. Is there a regular review process to identify candidates for termination?
6. Could the resources allocated to a particular program generate greater total satisfaction to the community if they were reallocated?
7. Is the agency assigning the highest caliber people to the highest priority services in the agency?
8. What strategies are used for terminating services so customer dissatisfaction and internal opposition are minimized?
9. Is retrenchment being implemented as part of an agency's overall plan so all concerned personnel know why it is taking place and are aware of its implications?

Pricing Strategies

A. Pricing Objectives and Policies

1. What are the agency's objectives in pricing each program?
2. Is there a current written pricing policy statement?
3. Is it sufficiently specific to give definitive guidance to pricing decisions?
4. Does the pricing policy address all four functions or objectives of price: revenue production, equity, efficiency, and income redistribution?
5. What mechanisms does the agency have to ensure that disadvantaged groups are not excluded from participating by prices charged?
6. Has the agency used price to improve efficiency? That is, do user prices serve as demand priority indicators? Do they alleviate congestion? Do they require agencies to be more accountable to citizens for the quality of services delivered? Does charging a direct price lead to more responsible use by client groups? Do user prices encourage competitive services from the private sector?
7. If a proposed price increase or decrease is implemented, by how many will the number of users go down or up? What will happen to the total revenue produced, will it increase or decrease?

B. Establishing a Price

1. What are the procedures for establishing and reviewing pricing policy?
2. Are prices reviewed at least annually?
3. Which method(s) is used for establishing a price? (cost-based, going rate, or differential)
4. What discounts to the basic fee structure are offered and with what rationale?
5. Can the agency identify, classify, and equitably allocate the costs associated with each service?
6. What proportion of the costs incurred in delivering the service should be recovered from direct pricing?
7. What is the going rate of similar services?
8. Has the agency considered psychological dimensions of price (e.g., self-esteem) in their initial price decisions as well as price revision decisions?
9. Are there occasions when offering variations of the average price to particular groups may achieve more equitable and efficient service delivery?
10. Are price increases keeping pace with cost increases or general inflation levels?
11. Does the agency use price promotions effectively?
12. Are there any opportunities for interested prospects to sample services at an introductory price?
13. What methods of payment are accepted (i.e., credit cards, check, credit accounts)? Is it in the agency's best interest to use these various payment methods?

Promotion Strategies

A. Strategic Promotion Decisions

1. Are there clear objectives for each element of the communication mix? How are the promotion activities related to these objectives?
2. How does a typical client find out about the agency's services? Word of mouth? Personal selling? Advertising? Publicity?
3. Does the message the agency delivers gain the attention of the intended target audience? Does it address the wants of the potential client group and does it suggest a means for satisfying these wants? Is the message appropriately positioned?
4. Is the agency receiving adequate feedback from its promotional efforts?

5. Is the agency's promotion effort effectively informing, persuading, educating, and reminding clientele about its services? How is this determined?
6. On what basis does the organization measure the effectiveness of its various communication programs (i.e., number of people aware of its services, knowledge about the services, attitudes toward the organization, program enrollment, financial contributions)?
7. Does the agency have a tendency to overpromise?
8. How is the budget for each element determined? Does it appear to be at the appropriate level? How does the organization decide on which programs or markets to concentrate promotion?
9. Is promotion expenditure regarded as a cost or as an investment?

B. *Advertising and Publicity*

1. Is there a well-conceived publicity program?
2. How is the public relations normally done by the agency? By whom?
3. Is the publicity effort directed at all the agency's key publics or restricted only to the potential user public?
4. Are there agency policies restricting some public relations activities?
5. What does the advertising-publicity budget permit? If a significantly greater amount were spent on this activity, would there probably be a proportionately greater benefit to the agency and its clients?
6. Have close working relationships been established and nurtured between individuals in the agency responsible for publicity and reporters and editors in each of the media outlets serving the jurisdiction?
7. Is an effort made to understand the needs of each of the sought publicity outlets and to provide them with the types of stories which will appeal to their audiences in a form that they can readily use?
8. What media are currently being used?
   a. Daily newspapers, articles and letters to the editor
   b. Weekly newspapers
   c. Weekly news magazines
   d. Monthly magazines
   e. Telephone directories
   f. Television, news and talk shows
   g. Radio spots, guest appearances
   h. Exhibitions
   i. Billboards
   j. Catalogs

k. Posters
l. Fliers
m. Newsletters

9. Has the agency selected the type of media that will best reach the selected target markets?
10. Are the types of media used the most cost-effective and do they contribute positively to the agency's image?
11. Are the dates and times the advertisements will appear the most appropriate?
12. Does the organization have a paid or volunteer advertising agency? What functions does the ad agency perform for the organization?
13. Is the agency utilizing public service announcements?
14. Has the agency prepared several versions of its PSAs?
15. What system is used to handle consumer inquiries resulting from advertising and promotion? What follow-up is done?
16. Are news clippings or records kept to evaluate the agency's ability to get accurate and favorable media coverage?
17. How are the advertising and public relations programs evaluated? How often?
18. What does the annual report say about the agency and its services? Who is being effectively reached by this vehicle? Does the benefit of this publication justify the costs?

C. *Personal Selling*

1. How much of a typical program director's time is spent soliciting new clients as compared to serving those already being served?
2. How is it determined which prospect will be called on and by whom? How is the frequency of contacts determined?
3. What incentive does the staff have to encourage more people to use the services offered?
4. Is there a paid or volunteer personal selling force for either fund-raising or increasing service utilization? If so, how is this force organized and managed?
5. Has the agency prepared an approach tailored to each prospect? Does this approach emphasize benefits to potential donors rather than benefits to the agency? Does the agency address the question, "What's in it for them?"
6. Has the agency matched its personnel with the type of people characteristic of the target market?

7. Does the agency's representative generate enthusiasm with respect to the agency's services?
8. Is there appropriate follow-up to the initial personal selling effort? Are donors kept informed and provided with periodic progress reports on the status of projects or services? Are donors made to feel appreciated and part of the team?

D. *Incentives*

1. What is the specific purpose of each incentive? Why is it offered? What does it attempt to achieve?
2. What categories of incentives are being used? Promotional pricing? Free offers? Prizes? Celebrities?
3. How is their effectiveness evaluated?

FIVE

Identifying Potential Target Markets

In Chapter 1 marketing was defined as "a set of activities aimed at facilitating and expediting exchanges with target markets for the purpose of achieving agency objectives." The first task in planning and implementing marketing efforts is to identify potential target markets, which is discussed in this chapter. Every agency must first decide *whose* needs to serve before deciding *what* needs to serve.

As noted earlier, an agency has many publics and has to develop marketing efforts that facilitate exchange not only with direct client groups, but also with other relevant publics such as taxpayers, elected officials, other agencies, and donors. Here the focus is limited to consumer publics in order to illustrate clearly the principles involved. These principles, however, are equally applicable for marketing efforts directed at facilitating exchanges with other publics.

WHAT IS A TARGET MARKET?

The term *market* means different things to different people. We often hear people talk about supermarkets, stock markets, labor markets, flea markets, or black markets. These markets have several characteristics in common. First, they are composed of people and/or organizations. Second, these parties have wants and needs for particular goods and services. Third, they have the ability to exchange resources for sought goods and services. Finally, they have the willingness to exchange.

Markets for public services may include all members of a community or society or only a portion of the members. The markets for water, electricity, sewage, police and fire protection are relatively large. Markets for day care services, marriage counseling, physical rehabilitation, and mental health treatment are likely to be small in comparison. Furthermore, a market may be relatively homogeneous or it may be heterogeneous. That is, the desires of the people or organizations that make up a market may be similar or dissimilar. For example, the market for drinking water is fairly homogeneous, but the market for leisure services is likely to be quite heterogeneous.

Heterogeneous markets may usefully be subdivided into a number of separate, smaller markets termed *segments*. Each of these segments constitutes a potential target market that the agency may elect to service. *A target market is a relatively homogeneous group of people or organizations that have relatively similar service preferences with whom the agency seeks to exchange*.

Selecting the target markets to which a service should be offered is a two-stage process. The first stage, which is addressed in this chapter, is concerned with identifying all of the heterogeneous groups in a market, each of which may be a potential target market. The second stage is to select which of these potential client groups the agency intends to serve with a particular offering. The process by which target markets are selected is discussed in Chapter 6.

The identification and selection of target market groups influences and often directly determines all of the ensuing decisions that must be made regarding types of services, their distribution, pricing, and communication. Once target markets have been identified, everything the agency does must be tailored to the wants of people in these groups.

RATIONALE FOR DELINEATING POTENTIAL TARGET MARKETS

Historically, many public agencies have offered their constituents standardized programs that they have attempted to distribute equally. Often these programs have been homogeneously promoted and offered at a single uniform price (often at no direct cost to the user). With this so-called lowest common denominator approach to service delivery, agencies may recognize that people have diverse desires but do not attempt to maximize customer satisfaction by developing marketing mixes geared to what different groups want. Rather, the lowest common denominator approach seeks to satisfy the maximum number of people at some minimal level by providing an "average" offering.

The problem with developing services that are targeted at the average user is so few average users actually need them. As Figure 5.1 shows, an average simply represents a midpoint. Most of the potential clientele may consist of groups on either side of the midpoint who have very little in common. These very different client groups are unlikely to be interested in an average offering.

In recent years some agencies have begun to realize that reliance on this approach to service is frequently inappropriate. Citizens have become more discriminating and more demanding. Failure to identify and respond to differ-

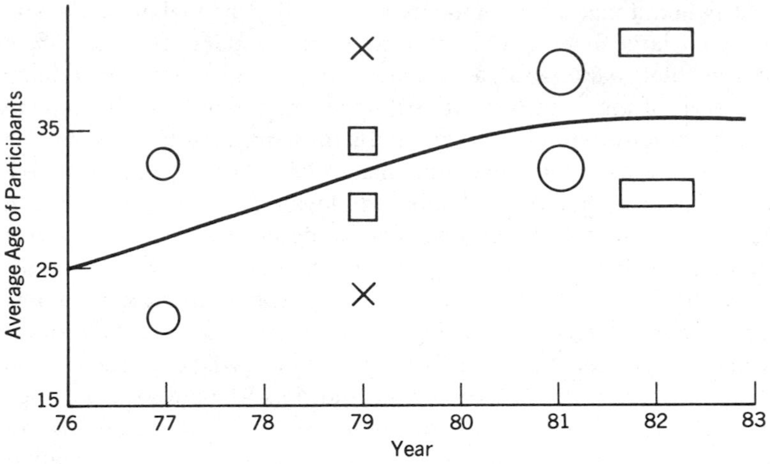

Figure 5.1. Spread of Potential Clients on Either Side of the Midpoint.

ences between client groups has led to widespread dissatisfaction with agencies and their service offerings. In some instances, the catalyst has been the expanding demands of specific, newly energized client groups such as ethnic minorities, women, the handicapped, and the elderly. For marketing to be effective it is essential to think of differences not sameness, and to segment rather than standardize.

The needs of each individual potential client are likely to be uniquely different. Economic feasibility however, generally does not allow an agency to develop services tailored to meet each individual's desires. Some compromise is necessary. The most effective way to compromise is to group together those people whose desires are similar.

This strategy recognizes that, although the service preferences of individuals differ, some individuals have preferences that are relatively similar to those of others, so groups may be satisfied with a common marketing mix. For example, a teenager has a unique set of counseling needs that are likely to be different in some ways from those of other teenagers. All of the teenagers' needs, however, are more similar to each other than to those of persons in different age categories.

This process of dividing a market into potential client groups or segments is known as market segmentation. It recognizes that different client groups seek different wants, which may justify the development of different services and/or marketing mixes to expedite the agency's exchange with them. Marketing segmentation may be defined as

> The process of dividing a total clientele into groups consisting of people who have relatively similar service needs, for the purpose of designing a marketing mix (or mixes) that more precisely matches the needs of individuals in a selected segment (or segments).[1]

In effect, when a market is segmented, a number of smaller markets emerge instead of one large market. The only difference—and it is a crucial difference—is that the total market was a heterogeneous conglomeration of subgroups, whereas each of the subgroups constitutes a relatively homogeneous market. Likewise product-oriented managers think of their markets in terms of "everybody" or the average user while target marketers aim at "specific somebodies."[2] Stated another way, target marketing employs a rifle approach (separate services, pinpointed targets) in contrast to the shotgun approach (common services, general targets) characteristic of a product orientation.

One of the reasons for the interest in segmentation emerging among government and social service agencies is their increased concern with accountability and the greater use that is being made of needs assessments. Research efforts are also suggesting that markets traditionally viewed as homogeneous are frequently composed of a heterogeneous set of client groups. Such results emphasize how unrealistic an agency would be to expect all members of a potential market to respond similarly to a service offering. Typically, populations are characterized by their diversity and plurality. Some client groups will always be more exposed to communication efforts and more likely and able to use a particular service than are other client groups. A government or social service agency may attempt to treat all of its potential markets as if they were homogeneous, but in its daily operations it will inevitably favor some groups over others.[3] Thus research efforts may reveal that an agency that has directed its service efforts at the average user has actually been delivering services that appeal only to the very small, narrow market segment that comprises the average user. All other segments remain unserved.

For example, a large leisure services agency was surprised to find that only one third of the adult residents within its jurisdiction used any of the recreation facilities that it operated. The agency was even more surprised that this one third was comprised predominantly of relatively young, high-income white males even though 38 percent of the city's population was Hispanic and 28 percent was black. Clearly the agency had unintentionally targeted its marketing efforts toward servicing a small number of its potential target clients.

Although its effective target markets were narrowly defined, this agency's pricing, distribution, and promotion policies had been developed on the assumption that all segments were being served. Hence the agency was suffering the disadvantage of a limited market size, while incurring the losses inflicted by low pricing policies and the expense of promoting services that they mistakenly thought had general appeal. The other side of the coin is that the agency was not taking advantage of the potential benefits and economies of a specialized marketing mix developed for a specific homogeneous market.

In summary, agencies should segment and delineate potential target markets because[4]

1. Clientele in many markets are heterogeneous
2. Market segments respond differently to different marketing mixes

3. Market segmentation is consistent with the marketing concept (i.e., it recognizes that people have different wants and needs)

These advantages have long been recognized by politicians, most of whom are very pragmatic marketers. Indeed it has been suggested that target marketing was invented by politicians!

> They do not use the word, to be sure, but when politicians gather to talk the idea is there without question. They do not, in their serious moments, talk about the voter, or even the average voter; they talk instead about the vote—the Polish vote, the Irish vote, the black vote, and the Italian vote; the aged vote and the youth vote; the farm vote, the right wing vote, the labor vote; the Catholic vote and the Jewish vote. They study voting patterns and divide areas into three segments: safe for the other party, safe for my party, and safe for neither. Then they slight the first, continue to persuade voters to turn out on election day in the second, and concentrate most of their resources and oratory on the third, where there are swing voters who are not committed to either party.[5]

REQUIREMENTS FOR EFFECTIVE SEGMENTATION

Three criteria must be met if meaningful market segments are to be developed.[6] First, each segment should be *sufficiently large* (and/or sufficiently important) to be worth considering for the development of separate distinctive programs or services, communication, distribution, and/or pricing strategies. Every service has a market, but the key question is, "Is it large enough to be worthwhile servicing?" The criterion for minimum size is economic practicality.

Potential client groups should be *measurable;* that is, it should be possible to quantify their size. Data regarding the population of a city, the number of persons in different age groups, or other sociodemographic characteristics are easily obtainable and may provide fairly concrete measures. Alternatively, an agency may wish to identify groups based on their stage of readiness for adopting a particular program. Unless the agency is able to measure how many persons are at each stage of readiness, it is difficult to gauge whether there are enough people to justify the development of unique marketing mixes to service those at each stage of readiness.

Much less obvious, but of extreme importance, is that each potential target market should be *accessible*. If, for example, an agency wanted to develop a program for introverted males or females suffering from hypertension between the ages of 20 and 30, it would be very difficult to communicate with or distribute services directly to these groups. Senior citizen groups, particularly those with reading and hearing disabilities, minority groups who do not speak English, and illiterate persons are also difficult to reach. These may be important market segments requiring social services tailored to their needs, but effective communication with such groups may require very imaginative and unique efforts.

TWO ALTERNATIVE APPROACHES TO SEGMENTATION

Benefits sought is the key ingredient in effective segmentation, because the benefits that client groups seek from using a service are the fundamental reason for the existence of that service.[7] Figure 5.2 illustrates the two alternative approaches to segmentation. Both of these approaches are concerned with identifying the principal benefits potential clients seek, but they suggest different paths for achieving that end.

The first approach initially delineates market segments in terms of the principal benefits that potential clients seek from an agency's offerings. Once people have been classified by the benefits they seek and receive, their distinctive characteristics can be outlined by using appropriate geographic, sociodemographic, or behavioral descriptors, which ensure the segments meet the criteria of being measurable and accessible.

This process is shown in Figure 5.3, which suggests that the particular benefits sought by clients are mutually exclusive. This oversimplification is used only to make clear the basic concept and principles of the approach. In reality, potential target markets are often likely to be interested in combinations of benefits rather than a single benefit. An agency may then have to divide and classify its clientele in terms of configurations of benefits rather than individual ones.

An example of this approach is provided by Alan Graefe's study of people who took float trips on rafts down the Rio Grande River through Big Bend National Park.[8] The range of benefits they sought included

Learning about nature
Enjoyment of solitude and freedom from stress
A challenge or adventure
Increased self-awareness, to learn more about themselves
Sociability or companionship with other people
Enjoyment and having a good time
Autonomy, feeling independent and doing things on their own

Some of these benefits were incompatible. For example, floaters seeking enjoyment and having a good time were inhibited from pursuing this benefit by those seeking solitude and a challenge or adventure. The two groups wanted to indulge in different types of behavior on the float trip to maximize the benefits they were seeking. The sociodemographic and behavioral characteristics of the two groups suggested that they were relatively distinctive segments for which unique marketing mixes could be developed. To expect one type of float trip to provide this diverse range of benefits seems unreasonable. The "one raft for all" approach represents the lowest common denominator strategy, which compromises client satisfaction levels by providing an average type of experience. Instead of sending both groups down the Rio Grande in one raft, the rafting organizations should have segmented their market on the basis of benefits

Identify the benefits sought by the total potential clientele	⟶	Define the groups of people who seek each set of benefits using some combination of geographic, sociodemographic, and/or behavioral descriptor
	(a)	
Define the groups of people, using geographic, sociodemographic, and/or behavioral descriptors	⟶	Identify the benefits sought by each of these defined groups
	(b)	

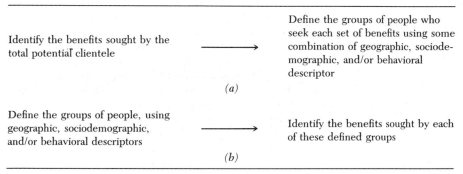

Figure 5.2. Alternative Approaches to Segmentation.

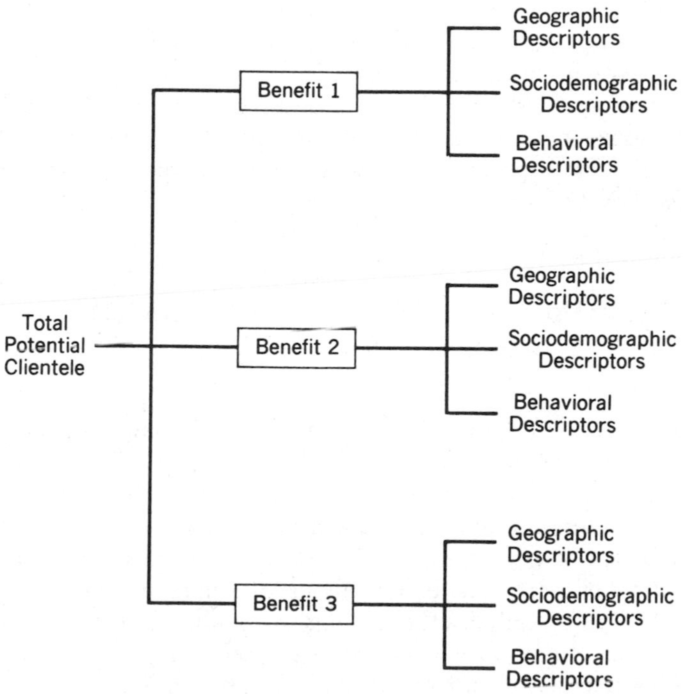

Figure 5.3. Stages in Benefit Segmentation.

sought, encouraged each group to go in a different raft, and developed a unique marketing mix for each group.

On occasion, this first approach has been used to segment markets on the basis of different product dimensions desired from a generic product offering rather than on the basis of benefits sought. Preferences selected from a wide range of product offerings are assumed to reflect the benefits that individuals seek from that generic product category. This approach has been adopted with some success in the performing arts field.

> For example, one study identified five performing arts segments. They were classical, country/folk, theater, pop, and recital. When these dimensions of the performing arts product had been identified, descriptions of the people who comprised each of the five segments were developed. The three most contrasting profiles were: *the classical segment* consisting of somewhat older, better educated, higher income, homeowning households who were more likely to be employed in professional, managerial, or technical occupations. Further, the heavier classical performance attenders were more likely to be in the later stages of the life cycle. In contrast, *the country/folk segment* was younger, in the early stages of the life cycle, nonhomeowners, who were employed as craftsmen or laborers, clerical, and sales, or students. *The pop segment* was very diverse. This music appealed to a broad range of demographic segments and hence was not restricted to any particular demographic composition.[9]

The second approach to segmentation is more frequently used and is easier to implement without sophisticated research and analysis. It attempts to delineate market segments by using appropriate geographic, sociodemographic, or behavioral descriptors first, and then to identify the benefits that each of these market segments seek (Figure 5.2*b*). In essence, this reverses the sequence adopted in the first approach. Examples of this approach are given in the following section.

SOME COMMON DESCRIPTORS USED TO DELINEATE SEGMENTS

A large number of descriptors can be used to segment a heterogeneous market into relatively homogeneous subgroups. They can be grouped, however, into three major categories: (1) geographic, (2) sociodemographic, and (3) behavioral. Examples of descriptors from each category are shown in Figure 5.4.

It is important to emphasize that the descriptors shown in Figure 5.4 are only illustrative of those most commonly used. The actual number of possible descriptors is limited only by the imagination of the marketer and his or her judgment of the extent to which selected descriptors successfully delineate potential client groups for which unique marketing mixes can most fruitfully be developed.

In some instances particular variables are uniquely suited to a specific field.

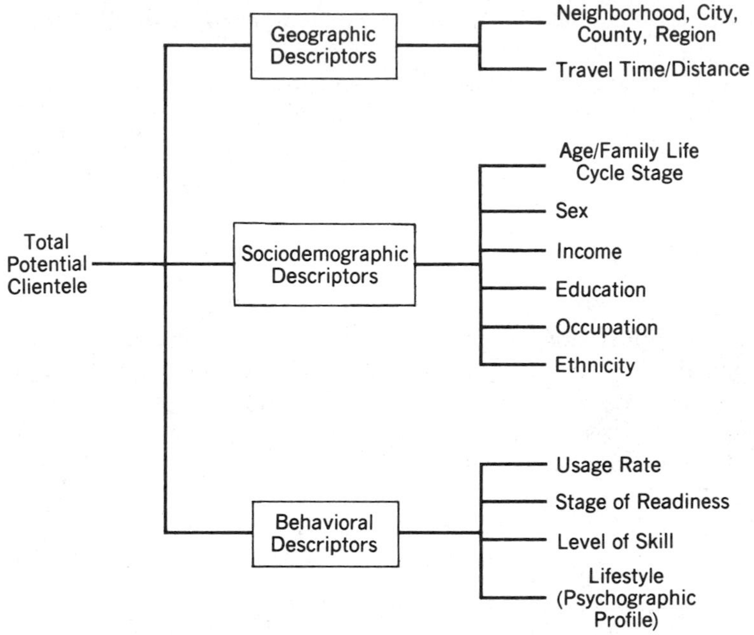

Figure 5.4. Some Common Descriptors.

For example, a blood bank may segment its clientele by blood type or RH factor; a health organization may segment on the basis of degree of patient risk or the method by which individuals came in contact with the agency;[10] a planning agency may segment a city into residential, commercial, and light and heavy industrial zones; and a fire department may segment on the basis of risk by developing fire prevention and fire safety programs tailored to the needs of specific target markets such as high-risk buildings and industrial areas.

A clientele, moreover, often is likely to be most effectively subdivided by several descriptors in combination rather than one alone. Although single-descriptor segmentation is easier than using multiple descriptors, it sacrifices precision for simplicity. For example, the clientele for library services may be subdivided on the basis of age, frequency of library use, and neighborhood of residence, thus using a sociodemographic, a behavioral, and a geographic descriptor in concert. This approach better enables the agency to develop marketing mixes precisely tailored to the needs of particular segments. In the past such combinations of descriptors have had to be developed intuitively and, for some government and social service agency managers, logic and judgment will remain the primary approach. Others may seek, however, to take advantage of the sophisticated methods of research and data analysis now available. A series of quantitative clustering techniques, the most popular of which is probably factor analysis, are being used with increasing frequency. They mechanically process empirical data and produce configurations of benefits and/or market descriptors.

No foolproof formulas can determine which descriptors are likely to be most useful for segmenting a particular market. The process can be aided by research information, but selecting appropriate descriptors is still more art than science. Management experience and judgment will remain the most useful tools for making the selection decision. The following examples, which use some of the more common descriptors, are intended to show their appropriate application.

Geographic Descriptors

As Figure 5.4 illustrates, neighborhood, city, county, and region boundaries are commonly used as segmentation descriptors. There are limits on how far different client groups will travel for particular kinds of services. Consequently travel time and geographical distance can serve as useful variables for identifying potential client groups. Sometimes zip codes may be used rather than a physical boundary. The 36,000 zip codes in the United States each contain approximately 2,000 households.

For several years, large downtown hospitals in many U.S. cities have been experiencing a decline in the number of patients who are able to pay their bill either out of their own pocket or through their private insurance coverage. An increasing number of patients using these hospitals are relatively poor people, often unemployed, who do not have private medical insurance. Their bills are paid by the government's Medicare and Medicaid insurance programs, but these programs do not reimburse the full costs incurred by a hospital in treating patients. This means that the revenues received by such downtown hospitals have been steadily decreasing and their viability is sometimes threatened.

St. Joseph's Hospital is located in downtown Houston. It is administered by the Roman Catholic Church. A layperson management team is governed by nuns who provide an oversight function. In an effort to combat the decreasing revenues resulting from servicing an increased proportion of Medicare and Medicaid patients, St. Joseph's management decided to diversify the patient mix. They sought to identify persons who could use other sources than Medicare and Medicaid to pay their bills.

After a series of studies, they decided to target their services at upper-income persons who visited the Houston area to shop or for other reasons. Because of the hospital's association with the Roman Catholic Church, and because of its existing ties with the Latin American Community, higher-income persons from Mexico and Central America were identified as the specific new target market at which the hospital would direct its marketing efforts.

Institutional changes were initiated, which were designed to make the hospital more attractive to foreign Spanish-speaking patients. Language was not a barrier to the promotional effort nor was the lack of a common religion or culture, since many of St. Joseph's staff were Roman Catholic, of Spanish descent, and fluent in the language. The multi-colored Spanish language brochures which were de-

> veloped to promote the hospital's services were distributed through institutions in Mexico and Central America which catered to tourists visiting the United States.[11]

As this example illustrates, geographic descriptors alone usually do not give the detail necessary for planning a marketing strategy. Further descriptors are generally required to define useful segments. In this case, income was used together with geography to describe the target market.

Fortunately, in urban areas especially, people with similar lifestyles, demographics, and needs frequently cluster together geographically, so using additional descriptors within geographic areas is likely to help define a segment.

Sociodemographic Descriptors

Sociodemographic descriptors probably are used more frequently than geographic or behavioral descriptors for segmenting a clientele into smaller, relatively homogeneous groups. Their popularity is mainly attributable to the ease with which they can be identified and measured. A second reason for their widespread use in some fields is that sociodemographics are obviously related to service preferences and needs. Consider the case of health care services:

> Demographics are probably the most commonly used set of segmentation descriptors for health care marketing. Age and sex are obviously related to health care needs. Some ethnic groups are more prone to certain problems than others. For example, there is a high incidence of sickle cell anemia among blacks. Other implications of ethnicity may include dietary habits and difficulty in understanding English. Some religions have dietary prescriptions, and other religions strongly influence attitudes toward certain health-related practices. Differences in income levels often have implications for nutrition as well as for the ability to pay for medical care. Educational level, sometimes highly correlated with income, is often associated with understanding hygiene, attitude toward medical treatment, and ability to understand the need for specific behavioral changes.[12]

Sociodemographics often reflect social roles or expected behavior patterns. Culturally patterned expectations associated with such descriptors as age, sex, education, and income are changing. The services sought by males and females, for example, are often a function of their respective roles in society. As their roles merge, the usefulness of these descriptors for differentiating subgroups in a population is likely to decrease.

Behavioral Descriptors

We have noted that geographic descriptors usually offer only very broad segments, while sociodemographics are becoming less useful in some fields as social roles change. Furthermore, people who share sociodemographic characteristics do not necessarily behave alike in their encounters with government or social service agencies.[13] For these reasons, increased attention is being focused on behavioral descriptors. The four behavioral descriptors considered in this section are usage rate, stage of readiness, level of skill, and lifestyle.

Usage Rate. This descriptor category segments a clientele by the extent to which a particular service offering is used. Appropriate categories will vary according to the service, but they are likely to include some combination of the following: nonusers, former users, potential users, first-time users, light or irregular users, medium users, and heavy users. Distinguishing such groups enables an agency either (1) to focus its efforts on delivering the benefits sought only by heavy users and, in the interest of economy and efficiency, disregard the other groups, or (2) to attempt to broaden its base of support by encouraging potential users to try the service, former users and first-time users to return, irregular and light users to become regular participants, and medium users to become heavy users.

Novice marketers are often tempted to concentrate efforts on nonusers, who frequently represent the largest market segment. At first glance this segment appears to offer the greatest potential for increasing use of the service offering:

> Unfortunately, these efforts will be largely wasted. The experienced marketer knows that the greatest access will come from those people who are already loyal supporters. There is no question—arts organizations, for example, will be more successful in increasing patronage from three times a month to four or five times a month than they will be in getting somebody who has never attended a performance to attend once a month. Politicians have learned this lesson well. The greatest efforts in any well-managed political campaign will be directed at those elements of the constituency that are already providing the candidate a large base of support.[14]

This approach ignores the issue of whether or not a government or social service agency designed to serve all citizens can legitimately exclude some of its constituents in its marketing efforts. We address this issue in Chapters 7 and 8.

Heavy users generally constitute only a small percentage of the numerical size of a total market, but they account for a major percentage of use. Table 5.1 illustrates this principle. It shows, for example, that 28.1 percent of the sample surveyed went on at least one fishing trip in the past year, but half of all fishing trips were accounted for by just 3.1 percent of the total sample. Designing an optimum marketing mix to facilitate benefit delivery to the heavy user group will usually be a priority task, because this segment is likely to be the cornerstone of constituency support and/or increased revenue production.

Public transportation usage in the San Francisco area offers an example of

TABLE 5.1. Percent of Individuals Accounting for 100% and 50% of Recreational Trips

	Trips	
Activity	100%	50%
Tent Camping	19.3	2.1
Trailer Camping	8.6	.8
Sailing	4.0	.4
Fishing	28.1	3.1
Visiting Historic Sites	30.4	3.4
Picnics–Cookouts	47.7	7.6
Snowmobiling	18.7	1.9
Bicycling	28.3	3.3

Source: Romsa, G.H., and Girling, S., "The Identification of Outdoor Recreation Market Segments on the Basis of Frequency of Participation," *Journal of Leisure Research,* vol. 8, No. 4, (Fourth Quarter) 1976, p. 253.

differences in usage rate. A survey revealed that respondents could be assigned to one of the following categories:

Nonusers, who had never used transit (13.6%)
Ex-users who had used transit in the past (49.5%)
Occasional transit users (30.1%)
Regular transit users (6.9%)

The study also showed that different usage groups had significantly different perceptions of the characteristics of automobiles, buses, and trains.[15] It is likely that a marketing mix differentially developed for each of these four segments would be much more successful in stimulating increased transit use than one marketing mix aimed at everybody.

A study of social service clients at a multiservice center produced the following segments.[16]

Heavy users, referred to as "buffeted" people, who brought multiple problems to the center and came over and over again in search of help.

Medium users, referred to as "problem solvers," who presented a few difficulties with which they wanted assistance and for which they were willing to contact the center more than once or twice but not nearly as often as the first group.

Light users, called "resource seekers," who focused on one or two problems and had only a few contacts with the center.

The center found by experience that, for service delivery to be effective, a unique marketing mix had to be developed for each of these groups.

Stage of Readiness. Research has shown that people move through distinct stages when making a decision to adopt or reject a program or service offering. This so-called consumer adoption process, discussed in more detail in Chapter 11, consists of the following five steps:[17]

1. *Awareness.* The individual becomes aware of an offering but lacks information about it.
2. *Interest.* The individual is stimulated to search for information about the offering.
3. *Evaluation.* The individual considers whether or not to try the service.
4. *Trial.* The individual tries the service on a small scale to test its usefulness.
5. *Adoption.* The individual decides to make use of the service on a regular basis.

The marketing mixes that can best facilitate exchanges with people at each of these stages are often different. Therefore, segmentation on the basis of stage of readiness may be a useful approach.

Consider distinctions between the market segments for contraception, as illustrated in Figure 5.5.[18]

> The major distinction is between couples who currently regulate fertility and those who do not regulate fertility. Few couples regulate their fertility perfectly throughout their lives and few couples conduct their sex lives without giving some thought to the possibility of conception.
>
> Among those who regulate fertility, some use artificial, "modern" methods and some use "folk" methods.
>
> Among those who do not regulate fertility, some would like to and others do not wish to.
>
> Among those who do not wish to regulate fertility, some may readily change their minds if presented with additional information, whereas others are not likely to change their minds no matter what new information is provided.

Clearly, persons in each of these market segments exhibit different levels of readiness to adopt contraceptives. Market research can provide information regarding the sociodemographic characteristics and number of persons in each segment, their attitudes, media habits, and so on. This information may then be used to develop different marketing mixes for each segment of the market.

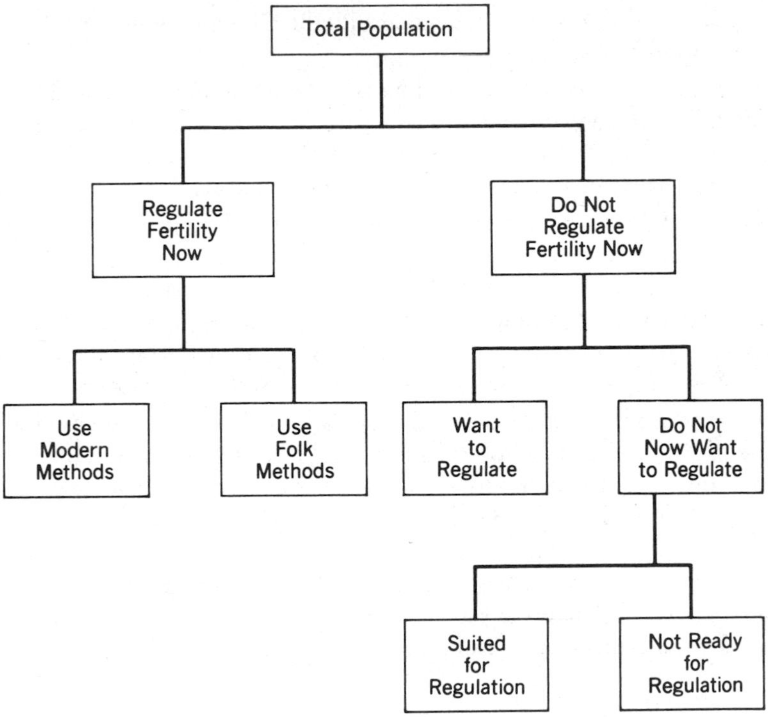

Figure 5.5. An Idealized Operational Scheme of Contraceptive Market Segmentation. (Reprinted with the permission of the Population Council from "Market Segmentation in Promoting Contraception," by Julian L. Simon, Studies in Family Planning 5, no. 3 (March 1974): p. 91.)

Level of Skill. Level of skill or ability is one of the most frequently used segmentation descriptors in many government and social service agencies. One way to maximize participants' satisfaction, learning, or progress is to categorize them with others who are at a similar level.

In developing effective environmental education programs for school children, their different learning capabilities must be recognized. For example, *slow learners* generally respond more readily to learning tasks that are concrete rather than abstract and which consist of a relatively small number of concepts to be absorbed. *Average learners* are better able to perceive partial and whole relationships and to integrate a larger number of concepts than peers with lesser ability. *Gifted children* appear especially able to "understand other situations, other times, and other people, to be less bound by one's own peculiar environmental surroundings."[19]

Each of these segments requires a unique marketing mix. For example:

Slow Learners may visit a nearby woodlot and identify as many varieties of plants and animals as they are able. Differences and similarities would be noted, and ways in which one species might be dependent upon others for survival would be discussed.

Average Learners would identify plants and animals observed (and speculate about those present but unobserved) in a nearby woodlot and then incorporate these into a "pyramid of life." Concepts of ecological niches, natural succession, and consequences of human intervention would be discussed.

After identifying and discussing characteristics of various plants and animals found in a nearby woodlot, *Gifted Learners* would consider their presence in light of man's moral and ethical responsibilities as "custodian" of the planet. How does contemporary man differ in his approach to conservation from other present-day cultures and those existing during other points in time? What implications are suggested for the future of our environment?

A common learning objective is appropriate to all: to enhance the students' knowledge of the concept of environmental interdependence. However, the means through which this is attempted varies with the learning ability of the target group.[20]

Encouraging participants to associate with others of similar abilities is likely to improve the level of clientele satisfaction, as compared with that derived from offering the same product or experience to each group.

Lifestyle. This approach to segmentation seeks to identify potential client groups on the basis of their lifestyle. Its emergence is directly attributable to the increased availability of statistical clustering techniques and advances in data-processing capability. Lifestyle as a ruler for segmentation

> measures people's activities in terms of (1) how they spend their time; (2) their opinions, what they place importance on in their immediate surroundings; and (3) their opinions in terms of their view of themselves and the world around them.[21]

The basic premise of lifestyle descriptors is that the more you know and understand about your potential clientele, the more effectively you can communicate with, and market to, them. Sociodemographics give only limited information about clients' behavior. Lifestyle patterns seek to draw more recognizable "live" human portraits of consumers.

The most widely used approach to lifestyle measurement and segmentation has been Activities, Interests and Opinions (A.I.O.) statements on questionnaires. Typically, respondents are asked to respond to each item on a five-point scale ranging from strongly disagree to strongly agree. Lifestyle items can be divided into two types: *general* items, which relate to general aspects of lifestyle; and *service-specific* lifestyle items, which are concerned only with those dimensions of an individual's lifestyle that may have some bearing on the service

The following statements are about golf. Circle the number which best expresses your agreement or disagreement with each statement. There are no right or wrong answers, so please just give your opinion.

For Example	Strongly Disagree	Disagree	Neither Agree or Disagree	Agree	Strongly Agree
I play golf because I enjoy it	1	2	3	④	5
My ideal vacation would be a tour of the golf courses of Scotland	1	2	3	4	5
I enjoy watching a good golfer hit off the tee	1	2	3	4	5
I prefer playing golf with the opposite sex	1	2	3	4	5
I like playing golf because when you are on the course nobody can help you	1	2	3	4	5
I think golf keeps me humble	1	2	3	4	5
I think you find the best people on a golf course	1	2	3	4	5
I prefer to play on golf courses which are not too difficult	1	2	3	4	5
Most golf tips I get from other golfers are useless	1	2	3	4	5
I think a friendly wager really improves a game	1	2	3	4	5
I enjoy a game of golf because it requires a lot of skill	1	2	3	4	5
Golf has helped me to become a better person	1	2	3	4	5
Golf is an important part of my business life	1	2	3	4	5
I would play golf even if it took 8 hours to complete a round	1	2	3	4	5
I prefer greens that have a lot of break	1	2	3	4	5
I think that generally the standard of golf etiquette is poor	1	2	3	4	5

Figure 5.6. A Sample of Lifestyle Items Used to Identify Potential Target Markets Among Golfers Who Play on Public Courses.

Devoted Golfer

Golf has helped me to become a better person
Golf is an important part of my business life
I think golf is a way of life
Golf has a high priority in my life

Practice Range Golfer

When I am in a slump I ask for help
It is important for my game to hit some balls on the practice range
I would take lessons from a golf pro to improve my game

Chauvinistic Golfer

I think that members of the opposite sex are a nuisance on the golf course
I think that members of the opposite sex make too much noise on the golf course
I do not prefer playing golf with the opposite sex
I think duffers are a nuisance on a golf course

Easy Course Golfer

I prefer to play on golf courses which are not too difficult
To me a good course does not have too many hazards
I prefer golf courses where the rough is cut short

Figure 5.7. A Sample of Lifestyle Segments Among Public Course Golfers.

offering. Experience has suggested that *service-specific* items are much more useful for identifying potential client groups.[22]

Service-specific lifestyle items were used by one researcher to delineate market segments of the golfing population in a community who played on public or quasi-public golf courses. Some of the 50 A.I.O. items used on the questionnaire are shown in Figure 5.6. Statistical clustering techniques were used to segment golfers. Typical segments that emerged were devoted golfer, practice-range golfer, chauvinistic golfer, and easy course golfer. The items that characterize each of these segments are shown in Figure 5.7.[23]

Although the level of sophistication needed to use lifestyle descriptors is considerable, this perspective often provides fresh insights into a clientele. This approach is particularly useful if an agency is going to engage in extensive promotion, especially paid advertising, since it offers guidance for developing messages to which targeted segments are most likely to be responsive.

SUMMARY

A target market is a relatively homogeneous group of people or organizations that have relatively similar service preferences with which the agency seeks to exchange. The identification and selection of target market groups influences and often directly determines all of the ensuing decisions that must be made regarding types of services, their distribution, pricing, and communication.

Once target markets have been identified, everything the agency does must be tailored to the wants of people in these groups.

Traditionally, government and social service agencies have operated under a lowest common denominator principle, seeking to satisfy the maximum number of people at some minimum level by providing an average offering. However, populations are typically characterized by their plurality. Different groups within a total market have different needs. Market segmentation divides a total clientele into subgroups consisting of people who have relatively similar service needs.

The three major criteria for effective segmentation are that a segment should be (1) sufficiently large or important to justify developing a unique marketing mix to service it, (2) of a quantifiable size, and (3) accessible to distribution and communication efforts.

Two alternative approaches to segmentation can be pursued, but both attempt to identify the principal benefits potential clients seek. The first approach starts by delineating market segments in terms of the benefits potential clients seek and then defining the distinctive characteristics of the people who seek each set of benefits by appropriate geographic, sociodemographic, or behavioral descriptors. The second approach to segmentation, which is used more frequently, reverses the sequence. It attempts to delineate market segments by using appropriate geographic, sociodemographic, or behavioral descriptors first, and then to identify the benefits that each of these market segments seek. Potential clients are often interested in combinations of benefits rather than a single benefit. This means an agency may have to divide and classify its clientele in terms of configurations of benefits rather than by individual benefits.

Although a large number of descriptors can be used to segment a heterogeneous market into relatively homogeneous subgroups, nearly all of these descriptors can be assigned into one of three categories: geographic, sociodemographic, or behavioral. Geographic descriptors are frequently necessary but not sufficient conditions for defining target markets, since further sociodemographic or behavioral details are needed for implementing an effective marketing strategy. Sociodemographic descriptors probably are the most frequently used. Their popularity is mainly attributable to the ease with which they can be identified and measured. However, people who share sociodemographic characteristics do not necessarily behave alike in their encounters with government or social service agency offerings. For this reason, increased attention is being given to behavioral descriptors for segmenting markets. The four most commonly used behavioral descriptors are usage rate, stage of readiness, level of skill, and lifestyle.

Many times effective identification of potential target markets requires a combination of descriptors rather than one alone. Determining which descriptors are most appropriate for identifying potential client groups in a particular situation depends on management experience and judgment.

NOTES

1. Adapted from Pride, W.M., and Ferrell, O.C., *Marketing: Basic Concepts and Decisions*. Boston: Houghton Mifflin, 1983, p. 40.
2. McCarthy, E.J., and Perreault, Jr., W.D., *Basic Marketing*. Homewood, IL: Irwin, 1984, p. 251.
3. Rados, D.L. *Marketing for Non-Profit Organizations*. Boston: Auburn House, 1981, p. 93.
4. Cunningham, W.H., and Cunningham, I.C.M., *Marketing: A Managerial Approach*. Cincinnati, OH: South Western, 1981, p. 184.
5. Rados, *Marketing for Non-Profit Organizations*, p. 92.
6. Kotler, P., *Marketing Management* (5th ed.). Englewood Cliffs, NJ: Prentice-Hall, 1984, pp. 264–265.
7. Haley, R.I., "Benefit Segmentation: A Decision Oriented Research Tool," *Journal of Marketing*, vol. 32 No. 3, July 1968, p. 34.
8. Graefe, A.R., "Elements of Motivation and Satisfaction in the Float Trip Experience in Big Bend National Park." Unpublished M.S. Thesis, Texas A&M University, May 1977, p. 45.
9. Nevin, J.R., and Cavusgil, S.T., "Audience Segments for the Performing Arts." In J.H. Donnelly and W.R. George (eds.), *Marketing of Services*. Chicago: A.M.A., 1981, pp. 126–128.
10. MacStravic, R.E., *Marketing Health Care*. Georgetown, MD: Aspen Systems, 1977, p. 117.
11. McConalty, M., "Some Aspects of Health Marketing—An International Perspective." Unpublished paper, Texas A&M University, May 1982, pp. 16–18.
12. Adapted from Lovelock, C.H., "Concepts and Strategies for Health Marketers," *Hospital & Health Services Administration*, Fall 1977, pp. 50–62.
13. Perlman, R., *Consumers and Social Services*. New York: Wiley, 1975, p. 23.
14. Searles, P.D., "Marketing Principles and the Arts." In M.E. Mokwa, W.M. Dawson, and E.A. Prieve (eds.), *Marketing the Arts*. New York: Praeger, 1980, pp. 67–68.
15. Lovelock, C.H. "A Market Segmentation Approach to Transit Planning, Modeling, and Management," *Proceedings of the Sixteenth Annual Meeting of the Transportation Research Forum*, 1975, pp. 247–258.
16. Perlman, *Consumers*, p. 33.
17. Rogers, E.M. *Diffusion of Innovations*. New York: Free Press of Glencoe, 1962, pp. 81ff.
18. Simon, J.L. "Market Segmentation in Promoting Contraception," *Studies in Family Planning*, March 1976, p. 93.
19. Gallagher, J.J., *Teaching the Gifted Child* (2nd ed.). Boston: Allyn & Bacon, 1975, p. 77.
20. This example was contributed by Edward J. Kesgen (private communication, 1981).
21. Plummer, J.T., "The Concept and Application of Lifestyle Segmentation," *Journal of Marketing*. vol. 38 No. 1 January 1974, p. 33.
22. Dhalla, N.K., and Mahatoo, W.H., "Expanding the Scope of Segmentation Research," *Journal of Marketing*. vol. 40 No. 2 April 1976, p. 37.
23. Gray, P., "A Benefit Segmentation Study of Golfers." M.S. Thesis, Texas A&M University, Department of Recreation and Parks.

SIX

Selecting Target Markets and Identifying Sources of Unresponsiveness

Chapter 5 focused on *identifying* potential client groups with relatively homogeneous needs and preferences. This chapter is concerned with *selecting* the group(s) for which the agency intends to develop service offerings. The client groups that are selected become the agency's target markets. In the private sector, organizations identify the most responsive segments—that is, those who are most willing and able to pay for an offering—as their target markets. In the public sector the criteria for selecting target markets are much more complex.

The challenge is to service those potential client groups to whom the most aggregate benefits can be delivered with the scarce resources that are available. This decision regarding how an agency's resources are to be allocated among the segments will be greatly influenced by the political environment and especially by decision makers' interpretation of what is equitable. The equity issue is complex and, for this reason, deferred for detailed discussion until Chapter 7.

This chapter addresses alternate strategies for selecting target markets, market grid analysis, the concept of market positioning, problems in prioritizing target markets, and major constraints that contribute to some members of selected target markets being relatively unresponsive to particular service offerings.

As noted in Chapter 5, selecting target markets is a major decision that influences and often directly determines all of the ensuing decisions regarding types of services or programs, location, scheduling, pricing, and communications. Once target markets have been selected, everything the agency does must be tailored to the wants of people in these groups.

THREE STRATEGIES FOR SELECTING TARGET MARKETS

Any of three strategies may be adopted for selecting target markets. These three strategies, called undifferentiated, differentiated, and concentrated, are illustrated in Figure 6.1.

Undifferentiated Strategy

Providing different services for the various client groups that an agency chooses to serve may not always be the best approach. There may be occasions when a single marketing mix can effectively service everyone. With an undifferentiated strategy a single marketing mix is developed and offered to all of the identified client groups. Such a policy emerges after a review of differences among potential target markets, during which managers conclude that the common needs of the groups are greater than the variations.

The undifferentiated approach can only be effective when a large proportion of the total market has common service needs. Such community services as police, fire, sanitation, and public works may come reasonably close to satisfying the conditions necessary for an undifferentiated approach to be effective. However, even within these areas, it sometimes may be desirable to develop different marketing mixes for different segments of the market. For example, residential users, commercial users, and industrial users may have different service needs, which may also be priced and distributed differently.

Too often, an undifferentiated approach toward service delivery emerges by default, reflecting a failure to consider the advantages of target marketing rather than an analytical, judicious response to a market. The approach is frequently used because of apparent cost economies, but it ignores the benefits side of the equation. Operating under the lowest common denominator principle (see Chapter 5) often results in sterile, unimaginative service offerings that have little appeal to anyone.

Differentiated Strategy

An agency that adopts a differentiated strategy develops a range of marketing mixes, each tailored to a particular target market. This strategy enables an agency to adapt its services to the wants of each selected client group. A differentiated strategy is likely to be particularly appropriate for those service areas that are relatively discretionary, since wants and desires in these areas may be diverse.

In many respects it is easier to develop services for specific target markets than for a clientele as a whole. By definition, individuals within a single client group are more homogeneous. Hence their wants are relatively uniform and

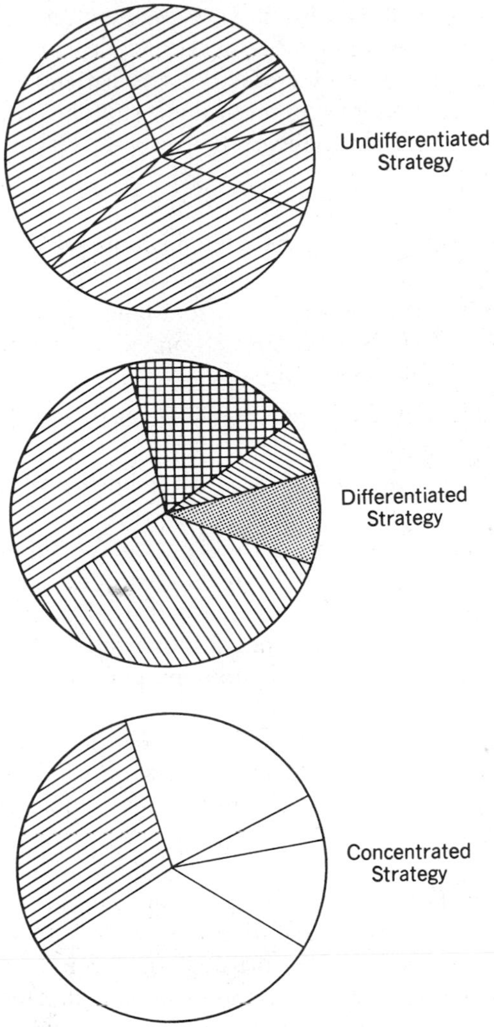

Figure 6.1. Three Strategies Available for Selecting Target Markets.

more easily identifiable. By following a differentiated strategy an agency hopes to attain greater impact on each target market. Such an approach tends to elicit greater support and loyalty because offerings are tailored to each client group's desires.

A differentiated strategy is likely to involve higher costs. For example, if a leisure services agency initially offers a tumbling program, it might adopt an undifferentiated approach, anticipating that most participants will be beginners. However, if the program is subsequently offered again, those who participated in the initial program possess a higher level of skill than those just entering. Trying to provide a satisfactory experience for both groups at the same time is likely to be frustrating to all concerned. In subsequent years, as more people enter the program, an even wider range of skill levels will emerge. To accommodate these varied abilities and increase the satisfaction level of all tumbling groups, the agency could adopt a differentiated strategy. Offering a program uniquely designed for each ability level, however, entails such additional expenses as the following:

Increased salary costs caused by the need for more advanced or specialized instructors and/or for lower instructor-student ratios in advanced groups.

Higher equipment costs. No longer are tumbling mats sufficient. Trampolines, uneven bars, high bars, balance beams, vaulting horses, and other large equipment are now required.

Because more difficult and advanced skills are involved, liability insurance costs may increase.

Additional space is required to store the large equipment.

Although costs are increased, the agency will pursue the differentiated strategy if total clientele satisfaction and/or the revenues produced exceed the extra costs. Otherwise, a differentiated strategy would not be appropriate.

Sometimes different promotional appeals, rather than different services, may be used as the basis for a differentiated strategy. For example, different target markets are likely to be attracted to physical fitness programs called "Keep Fit," "Conditioning," "Fitness Training," "Slimnastics," "Aerobics," "Aerobic Dance," "Health Club," "Figure Control," "Jazzercise," or "Revitalize." The names evoke particular connotations for each program. Basic program content may be undifferentiated, but the different names are designed to meet different perceived wants. This differentiation may be reinforced by other ingredients in the marketing mix. For example, the programs may be located in different facilities at different times and charge different prices.

A public agency, in contrast to a private organization, is required to be equitable in its service delivery efforts (see Chapter 2). This does not imply that it should adopt an undifferentiated strategy. Rather, it supports a differentiated approach. Consider governmental efforts to convert to the metric system, which has now been successfully achieved in Canada. It is highly desirable that everyone adapt to the metric system at the same time:

> But it is still possible, and more efficient, to work harder with some groups than with others and to work on some segments earlier than others. Age might well be a factor in that the young will adopt metrification in a trice, while many of the elderly, those over 40, will lack the will to change. Certain manufacturers and certain industries may be willing, and interested, in beginning metrification of their products now, while others will not change before they have to, and the cooperation of tool makers should be enlisted early. And because reading and viewing habits of citizens differ, it will prove virtually impossible to put together a communications effort that reaches all citizens equally well.[1]

Often it appears that an undifferentiated, mass marketing approach is being used when in fact a differentiated strategy is in place. For example, imagine that a community education agency offers and widely publicizes 200 diverse programs for all possible client groups, and that it announces a requirement of at least 10 people signing up for a program before it will be implemented. That is, in essence, a differentiated strategy. Instead of selecting the strategy and pinpointing target markets in advance, the agency has allowed the marketplace to be the decisive factor. Interested potential clients identify themselves and are reached with the programs that they desire. This multiclient group approach, while appearing product-oriented (since it does not seek to identify client group wants ahead of time), is in fact market-oriented, because the range of services is sufficiently exhaustive to cover many potential client groups.

Concentrated Strategy

If an agency lacks the resources to service segments with a differentiated strategy, then it may elect to pursue a concentrated strategy. This means that efforts are focused on only one or two client groups, which are deemed the most important or the most responsive. For example, a pop music dance is likely to meet the needs of only one particular segment of the total market. Hence an attempt to promote a pop dance to all citizens would probably be less successful than a promotional and pricing strategy directed specifically at that target market. Similarly, if a particular program is targeted at senior citizens, it may best be communicated to them by a personalized letter or brochure, rather than through a general publicity release in the local press. Access to appropriate mailing lists may be secured from welfare, church, transportation, or club organizations that already have a senior citizen clientele. This focused approach is more likely to lead to a successful program.

Examples of a concentrated marketing strategy are particularly abundant among governmental programs offered at the federal level. The wide range of antipoverty programs, manpower, Model Cities, and infant care projects all require resources to be concentrated on specifically delineated market targets.

A frequent pitfall of adopting a concentrated strategy is the temptation to select the largest, most responsive segment. For example, single individuals may be the heaviest users of a particular service. The majority fallacy suggests that they should also be the target market at which efforts are concentrated. That group, however, may be better provided for by commercial, private, and voluntary organizations, with the agency's efforts needed by some other group. As we shall see in Chapter 7, success in the public sector cannot be measured only by counting the *number* of satisfied participants. *Which* constituents are, and are not, receiving benefits from a particular service is equally important.

It is essential that the concentrated strategy not be exclusionary. The courts are unequivocal in recognizing that once a municipality or other political subdivision undertakes to provide a service, that service must be made available to all residents who are eligible for it. For this reason, and the belief that government should serve everybody, an agency will be pressured to adopt a undifferentiated strategy aimed at the lowest common denominator rather than a concentrated strategy that directs resources at one or two specific segments:

> The notion of treating certain groups differently or with special attention while perhaps ignoring other groups completely is not consistent with the egalitarian and antidiscriminatory philosophies that pervade many (governmental) organizations. The marketer is, therefore, frequently asked to avoid segmenting or to try and reach an unreasonably large number of segments. If a marketing plan has to be made to add to the list of targets until—with the limited funds that are usually available—only a very broad and very shallow marketing effort is authorized, this will produce a "shotgun" effect; the opposite of the "rifle" approach a marketer normally attempts to bring to bear.[2]

SELECTING A TARGET MARKETING STRATEGY

Selecting an undifferentiated, differentiated, or concentrated strategy may be decided on the basis of whether the dominant criterion is effectiveness, efficiency, or equity.[3] Efficiency in this sense is a measure of the per capita cost of service delivery while effectiveness is a measure of how well the offering meets a clientele's needs (see Chapter 7 for a discussion of equity). Generally, a *concentrated* strategy is likely to emphasize effectiveness as opposed to efficiency. It relies on customizing the service and marketing strategy to the needs of a particular target market. A concentrated strategy seeks the potential benefits of specialization by meeting client needs as closely as possible.

In contrast, an *undifferentiated* strategy emphasizes efficiency as opposed to effectiveness. It relies on standardizing the service and marketing strategy across client groups. The advantage of such an approach is the potential large numbers who are perceived (often fallaciously) as likely to use the service, thus offering some economies of scale and low per capita cost.

A *differentiated* strategy seeks the best of both worlds. Efficiency is achieved via broad scope, and effectiveness is achieved via differentiation. The more differentiated the approach across segments, the more effectiveness will be achieved at the expense of efficiency. Conversely, the less differentiated the approach, the more efficiency will be achieved at the expense of effectiveness.

MARKET GRID ANALYSIS

One method that is frequently used to select potential target markets to be served by a differentiated or concentrated strategy is called the market grid approach. Target markets are selected by going through a sequential process using several different descriptors as the basis for delineating groups. The approach analyzes a clientele by a series of grids that resemble checkerboards. A different market description is used on the horizontal and vertical axis of each grid.

The continuing education division of a major state university that specializes in facilitating community development throughout the state used the market grid approach to select target markets. The first segment descriptors used (Figure 6.2) were political subdivisions of the state and a set of different types of entities likely to be involved with community development. Discussion and analysis of the groups described by each cell led the decision maker to conclude that the most important and/or responsive groups in the community development process were likely to be associations operating at the county level.

In Figure 6.3, county associations were subdivided and described in terms

Community Unit / Political Subdivision	Political Elements	Associations	Business Firms	Individual Citizens	Other
City					
County					
Multicounty					
State					
Other					

Figure 6.2. Market Grid for Statewide Community Development.

Basis of Belonging / Size of Organization	Voluntary	Membership	Other
Small (1–50)			
Medium (51–150)			
Large (151 and above)			

Figure 6.3. Market Grid for Statewide Community Development for County Associations.

of their size and whether or not they made extensive use of volunteers. Discussion and analysis of the characteristics of groups in each of these six cells caused the division to focus on medium-sized associations who made use of volunteers. Because substantial differences were perceived in the mission and operating procedures of such groups, an offering developed to meet their needs would have to be somewhat generalized. It was thought likely that such a generalized offering might elicit only a 10 percent response from voluntary associations of medium size.

For this reason, a further grid was developed. In Figure 6.4 the total market is narrowed down still further by looking at the particular needs of each type of medium-sized county voluntary association. After examining each of these cells, the division decided to select heart associations as its primary target market and to develop a program offering that would provide training for heart association officers, which appeared to be their greatest priority need. The extension division is here taking aim at a very particular group of voluntary associations rather than soliciting participants from all voluntary associations. As a result, the division may realistically expect a very high positive response (say, over 75 percent) from this target group, since the offering is uniquely tailored to their needs.[4]

Market grid analysis may reorient the perspective of the administrator. Instead of focusing on particular offerings, the administrator starts out by analyzing characteristics of the market. Clearly, the more data there are available for the market grid analysis, the more accurate it is likely to be. However, even if an agency has to rely entirely on judgment, the market grid approach provides a way of systematically assessing the types of wants and preferences that different client groups possess.

Type of Organization / Organization Needs	Heart Association	American Cancer Society	American Red Cross	March of Dimes	Other
Membership Drives					
Officer Training	\				
Financial Campaigns					
Project Development					
Other					

Figure 6.4. Market Grid for Statewide Community Development for County Medium-Size Voluntary Associations.

CONCEPT OF MARKET POSITIONING

The primary role of most government and social service agencies is to provide services, within the scope of the resources that they have available, to those individuals or groups who are *not* adequately serviced by other organizations. Concern is with complementing rather than with offering competition to others' efforts. This means that it is necessary to look at what similar services are being provided by other public and private organizations and to whom they are being offered so that an agency can identify its own distinctive contribution. This process is known as *positioning*.

Positioning assumes that market offerings are arrayed in people's minds along various dimensions that are relevant to the decision-making process of choosing a service. The term *position* refers to how an agency and/or its programs are perceived by targeted clientele. Understanding a service's market position helps in developing strategies aimed at positioning a new service or repositioning an existing offering so that it is complementary to the efforts of others.

Effective market positioning requires (1) assessing the current positions occupied by other suppliers of similar services, (2) determining the important dimensions underlying these positions, and (3) selecting a position in the market where the agency's marketing efforts will generate maximum benefit.[5] Although managers can subjectively develop positioning maps like the one shown in Figure 6.5, they can also develop them empirically from surveys by applying the statistical technique of multidimensional scaling.

A review of existing counseling opportunities offered by organizations in the public and private sectors may show the pattern illustrated in Figure 6.5. Several organizations offer counseling services in Segment *W*, which is characterized by above-average income and early life cycle stages. Each age range seems to be adequately serviced in this segment. In Segment *X*, the four existing suppliers seem to specialize in clients who are in the mid-life crisis phase around 40 or who are senior citizens. There are no agencies specifically offering counseling services directed at the preretirement, "empty nest" (the children have left home) group. A similar niche appears in Segment *Y*, which consists of low-income empty nesters. Finally, in Segment Z, teenagers up through high school are serviced, but no agency is successfully meeting the needs of post–high school groups of low-income people in the 25-to-35 age range.

Hence it appears that there are three potential target markets on which the agency might focus in its marketing efforts (Figure 6.5). However, before deciding to develop counseling services for those groups, the agency must assess whether or not there is a demand for such services. For example, the fact that no other organization is offering services to potential target markets 1 and 2 may indicate that there is very little need for counseling services among the jurisdiction's empty nesters. If this is the case, potential target market 3 may be where the agency should focus its efforts.

The positioning approach helps agencies overcome the urge to rush in and service those groups whose demand for a service appears to be greatest. The French have a marketing expression that sums up this strategy rather neatly:

cherchez le creneau, or look for the hole. To find a creneau, you must think in reverse, go against the grain. If everyone else is going east, see if you can find your creneau by going west.[6] For example, even though the greatest demand for counseling may be among low-income teenagers, agencies *L* and *M* are already serving this market and a decision to target efforts at that group would likely duplicate existing efforts. The creneau here is low- to middle-income persons in the 25-to-35 age range.

Higher education provides a useful example of the importance of positioning. Many public colleges and universities are well aware of the problems associated with declining numbers of high school graduates and rising costs. Most, however, have fallen into the "everybody trap," trying to be all things to all people. An appeal to everyone often turns out to be an appeal to no one. If a college has no unique position, who will want to enroll? Each school must find its creneau or face declining enrollments.

Three things are involved in positioning a service in the marketplace.[7] The first is *consistency*. More than anything else, successful positioning requires consistency. If an agency constantly tries to change position, no one will know who it is trying to serve or for what it stands. Consider the following questions:

> What does your university want its prospects to think about it? That its program is the most well-rounded? That its campus is the most beautiful? That its residence facilities are the most comfortable? That the social life is the most extensive? That its alumni have attained the greatest success in their fields? That the student can develop his or her own curriculum? The fact is that virtually every institution would like every prospect to think all of these things and more, and this desire is reflected in their communications. Is it any wonder that prospects are confused? Or that they tune out your message because it looks and sounds like everyone else's?[8]

Many times agencies forget what made them successful and attempt to reposition themselves. The frequent result is that they confuse their clientele, with disastrous results.

The failure of some colleges illustrates the danger of neglecting to establish—or losing—a unique position in the market by broadening efforts to meet everyone's needs. Religious schools that become nondenominational and all-male or all-female colleges that go coeducational blur their niche in the market. Success does not lie in serving everyone indifferently; rather it lies in carefully positioning a service so that it serves selected target markets extremely well.[9]

A second requirement for successful positioning is *research*. Research provides information regarding positions that are not currently filled. The first agency to establish itself in a position has an enormous advantage. Consider the following questions:[10]

> Who was the first person to fly solo across the North Atlantic? And don't think it couldn't be Charles Lindbergh because it was. Now, ask, yourself, who was the second person to fly solo across the North Atlantic? Not so easy to answer.

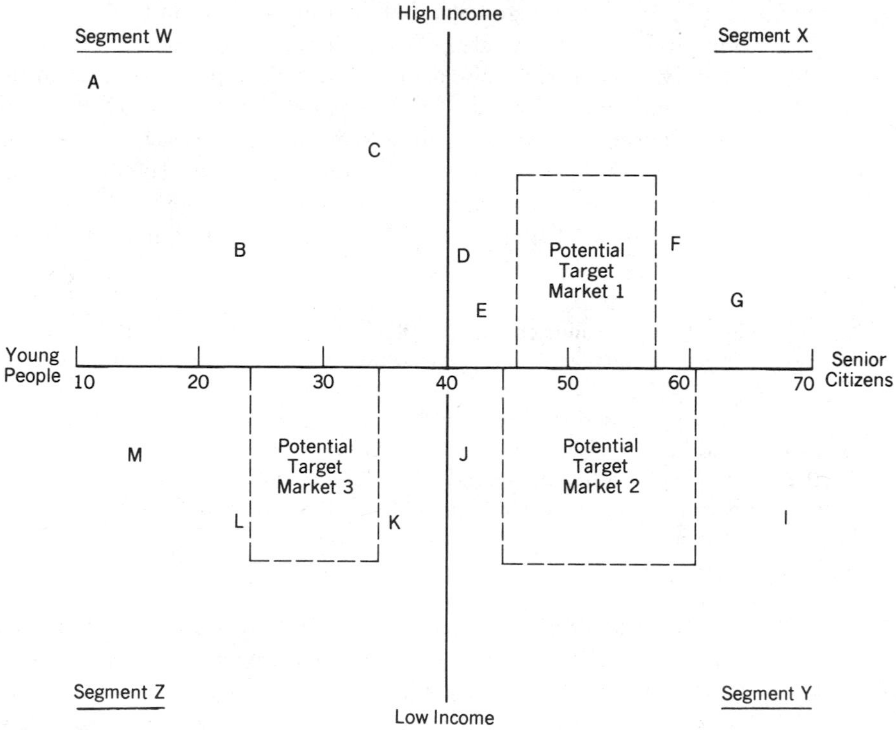

Figure 6.5. Market Positioning: A Method of Determining Priorities Among Potential Target Markets.

> What is the name of the highest mountain in the world? Mount Everest in the Himalayas, right? What is the name of the second highest mountain?

The third requirement for successful positioning is *developing the best strategy based on research*. Consider the following two questions:[11]

1. What position, if any, does an agency already own in the prospect's mind? Before starting any program, it is important to prepare a positioning map such as that shown in Figure 6.5 that outlines in detail who the prospect is and what he or she thinks about the service and about those of other suppliers.
2. What position does the agency want to own? Choose the best position from a long-term point of view.

PRIORITIZING TARGET MARKETS

Private sector organizations usually give priority to developing those target markets that are most likely to be responsive to particular offerings. However, government and social service agencies that seek to service multiple constituencies by using a differentiated strategy face a dilemma. Which target markets should be given service priority? Is the agency to act like a private organization and ignore those segments likely to be least responsive to service offerings? If the role of the public sector is to facilitate delivery of a particular service to as many constituents as possible and to complement the private sector, then in many cases public sector agencies may be required to focus their efforts on the least responsive segments, leaving the more responsive segments to other agencies:

> Consider a hypothetical manufacturing company whose product is bought by, say, 20 percent of its potential consumer population. If a sales campaign succeeded in increasing this volume by another five percent in one year, the company would probably be highly pleased. But if a health program that tried to get all women at risk of cervical cancer to have a yearly Pap smear attracted only 20 or even 30 or 40 percent to begin with, and succeeded only to add another five or ten percent to this number, the program would be regarded as a failure. Indeed, what would be proudly proclaimed as victory in the commercial arena, will often be bemoaned as defeat in the health arena.[12]

The development of marketing mixes aimed at relatively unresponsive target markets is a problem unique to marketing in government and social service agencies. Indeed, the most critical question facing such agencies often is not how to develop marketing mixes to optimally service relatively responsive target markets, but rather what strategies may be most useful for attracting those who are apathetic, disinterested, or reluctant to use a service.

In some situations the dilemma regarding which potential target markets should receive priority in service delivery is not applicable. For example, if a vaccination program is to be successful, all those likely to be exposed to the disease may have to be inoculated. Such a market is probably easily segmented in terms of stage of readiness. At one extreme are those who will be anxious to cooperate, while at the other extreme are those likely to be apathetic or reluctant. Different marketing mixes designed for the various stages of readiness will aid in improving responsiveness. Clearly, it is not appropriate for unresponsive segments to be ignored, for the whole program is in jeopardy if these segments do not participate.

A vaccination program initiated to avert a serious health crisis is likely to receive sufficient funding to ensure that all segments are reached and the task is completed. However, in most situations government and social service agencies have limited financial resources, which means that they must address the dilemma of whom should be given priority in service delivery. Broadly, the alternatives they have can be termed the strategy of least resistance and the strategy of most resistance. The implications of each are well illustrated by the dilemma involved in designing family planning programs:[13]

> *The strategy of least resistance* in marketing family planning is to focus on the most motivated segments. Arguments can be made that this is

The more empirically sound approach because it is based on "the results of fertility surveys carried out in a variety of countries"[14]

The more practical approach because recruiting efforts play on an already existing want rather than on creating one

The more economical approach because results come in faster as a consequence of going after the sector that is fastest to respond

The case for pursuing *the strategy of greatest resistance*, which concentrates on the less motivated segments while giving only minimal recruiting efforts to the motivated, rests on two major points.

It exerts a greater impact on population control. People in these target markets are typically younger with a smaller number of children. Thus, in many countries, they constitute a larger segment of the population with a greater reproductive potential than those who are more likely to accept family planning readily. Because of these characteristics, concentrated efforts on this group can make a bigger impact on controlling population than would be achieved by the strategy of least resistance.

It is a more economical and meaningful strategy. Many members of the target populations selected by a strategy of least resistance will adopt contraception on their own regardless of any official program efforts. Hence it is argued that a strategy of least resistance only appears to be the more economical approach. In fact, it often directs resources to areas where they are not needed.

Managers may disagree on which of these two prioritizing approaches is most appropriate in a particular context. It is clear, though, that on at least some occasions agencies seek to develop relatively unresponsive target markets. In order to develop marketing mixes that will expedite exchanges with such target markets, managers first must understand the causes of the unresponsiveness.

MAJOR CONSTRAINTS CONTRIBUTING TO UNRESPONSIVENESS

Despite the considerable resources expended by government and social service agencies in delivering services, there has been a general reluctance to invest in research on nonuser populations. The relatively few attempts to address underutilization have confined their investigations to identifying which market descriptors are most useful for distinguishing between those segments of a population that do, and do not, use a service. This is a necessary step, but it is not sufficient.

People within target markets vary in their predisposition to use service offerings. That is, people will react differently to the same constraints. An old aphorism among research chemists, "Those who understand the barriers will make the breakthrough," is equally applicable to government and social service managers. When the question is asked, "How can we get more people in a target market to use a service?" the answer has to be, "We don't know until we have found out why underutilizers are not responsive to the service offering." An understanding of how various subgroups in a target population are impacted by constraints should make it possible to plan to better meet their needs and desires.

The taxonomy illustrated in Figure 6.6 suggests that responsiveness is constrained by five types of barriers: product failings; pricing, distribution, or promotion failings caused by weaknesses in an agency's marketing mix; social constraints involving relations with other people; constraints that are a function of individual circumstances; and external physical constraints, particularly climate and physical topography. Evaluation of these potential barriers is personal and subjective. They may be more perceived than actual in some cases, but that does not reduce their constraining influence. Furthermore, an individual's perception of them may change over time.

Once constraints have been identified, appropriate marketing mixes can be developed with the specific objective of reducing their impact. It is unrealistic for an agency to expect to be able to remove all of the constraints that contribute to unresponsiveness in a target market. Thus when the relative impact of each group of constraints is known, a decision has to be made as to whether primary efforts should be directed toward attacking (1) the barriers that impact the most people, which would lead to the largest increase in new clientele; (2) the easiest barriers, which will yield the fastest results; or (3) the blockages impacting the most needy subgroups in the target market.

Figure 6.6 provides a conceptual framework, but this taxonomy should not be viewed as a final definitive categorization. It is intended rather as a guide or checklist to help an agency identify all pertinent barriers and to provide a point of departure for the development of nonuser constraint surveys. The listings under each heading in the figure are not arrayed in any order of priority. Clearly, many of the constraints shown here are expressed in fairly broad terms. For example, a facility has many dimensions. If it is deemed to be of poor quality by underutilizers, the agency needs to know which dimensions are poor and which are acceptable. Thus this item may be usefully split into a number of smaller components.

More than one barrier probably contributes to an individual in a target market being unresponsive to an offering. Several barriers are likely to be interactive. For example, a person may be reluctant to go to a health clinic because it is difficult to get there (distribution constraint); the facility has a poor reputation and discourteous staff (product constraint); the weather is very cold with snow and ice on the ground (external physical constraint); and poor health increases the personal effort required (individual circumstance constraint).

Research so far has been mainly confined to identifying individual, social, and external environmental constraints. Typically, little attention has been

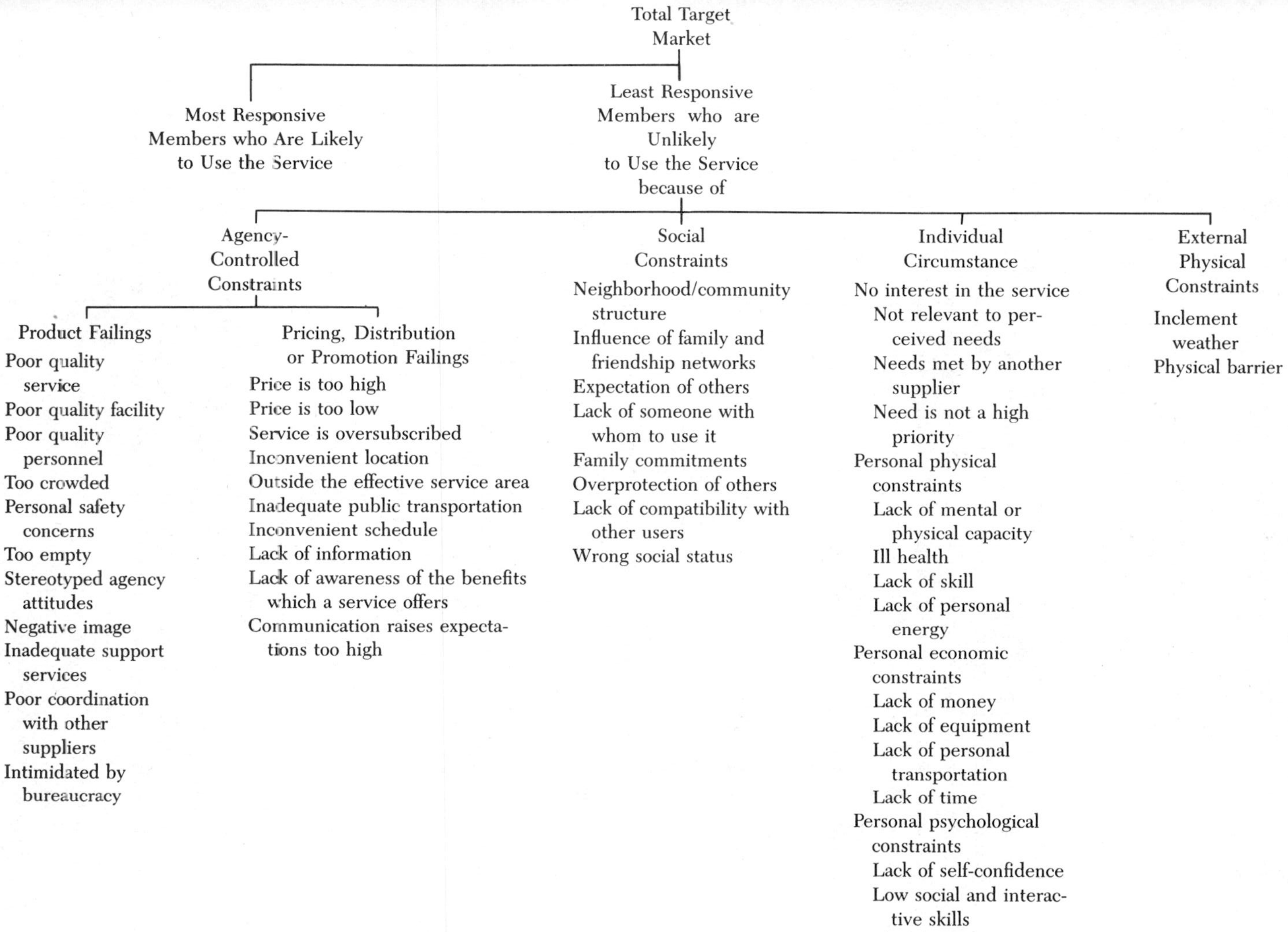

Figure 6.6. Major Constraints Contributing to Target Markets Being Unresponsive.

given to agency-created constraints, since the core of the problem, and hence its primary resolution, has been defined as outside the agency. This approach reveals

> The traditional preoccupation of the planners and administrators of services (and perhaps of society in general) with the personal pathologies of underutilizers and showing very little concern with the organizational characteristics of the services that people underutilize.[15]

Different services and different target markets are likely to be affected by different constraints. The blockages are both service- and market-specific. It is not possible to identify constraints in one situation and assume that their influence is the same for other target markets using the same service, or for the same target markets with a different offering. Because constraints are likely to have limited generalizability, each agency, or even each facility or service operated by an agency, has to investigate which constraints most inhibit its target markets from using offerings.

SUMMARY

Three strategies may be adopted in selecting target markets. An undifferentiated strategy develops a single marketing mix to be offered to all identified client groups. With a differentiated strategy, an agency develops a range of marketing mixes, each tailored to a particular target market. This choice will probably be more costly, but it is likely to yield substantially greater clientele satisfaction. A concentrated strategy focuses efforts on only one or two client groups, which are deemed the most important or most responsive.

A market grid approach may be useful for selecting the potential target markets to be served by a differentiated or concentrated strategy. The approach analyzes a clientele by using a series of grids that resemble checkerboards. Different market descriptors are used on the horizontal and vertical axis of each grid. Market grid analysis may reorient the perspective of an administrator. Instead of focusing on particular offerings, the administrator starts out by analyzing characteristics of the market.

Market positioning involves looking at what similar offerings are being provided by others so that the agency can choose a distinctive contribution for itself. Effective market positioning requires (1) an assessment of current positions occupied by other suppliers of similar services, (2) a determination of the important dimensions underlying these positions, and (3) selection of a position in the market where the agency's marketing efforts will generate maximum benefit. This research, and the development of an effective strategy based on it, has to be complemented by a consistent position so that potential clients are not confused.

Private sector organizations usually give priority to developing those target markets that are most likely to be responsive to an offering. The public sector faces a unique problem in its mandate to also develop marketing mixes aimed at relatively unresponsive target markets. Given limited financial resources, the dilemma confronting public agencies is whether they should give priority in service delivery to the least resistive or the most resistive target markets.

On at least some occasions all agencies seek to develop relatively unresponsive target markets. The key to expediting an exchange with these groups is to learn why underutilizers are not responsive to the service offering. Constraint studies increase the information available to managers. Only after constraints have been identified can appropriate marketing mixes be developed with the specific objective of reducing constraint impact.

Responsiveness is constrained by five types of barriers: product failings; pricing, distribution, or promotion failings that indicate weaknesses in an agency's marketing mix; social constraints involving relations with other people; constraints that are a function of individual circumstances; and external physical constraints, particularly climate and physical topography.

When the relative impact of constraints is known, managers have three alternatives for proceeding. First, they can attack the barriers that impact the most people, which will lead to the largest increase in new clientele. Second, they can attempt to remove the easiest barriers, which will yield the fastest results. Third, they can address the blockages that impact the most needy subgroups in the target market. Different services and different target markets are likely to be affected by different constraints.

NOTES

1. Rados, D.L., *Marketing for Non-Profit Organizations*, Boston: Auburn House, 1981, p. 93.
2. Bloom, P.N., and Novelli, W.D., "Problems Applying Conventional Wisdom to Social Marketing Programs." In M.P. Mokwa and S.E. Permut (eds.), *Government Marketing Theory and Practice*. New York: Praeger, 1981, p. 72.
3. Adapted from Abell, D.F., *Defining the Business: The Starting Point of Strategic Planning*. Englewood Cliffs, NJ: Prentice-Hall, 1980, pp. 178–179.
4. Adapted from Phillips, M., *The Marketing Process: A Handbook to Guide the Continuing Higher Education Administrator*. Memphis State University, 1977, pp. 20–27.
5. Leister, D.V., "Identifying Institutional Clientele," *Journal of Higher Education*, Vol. 46 No. 4, July/August 1975, p. 388.
6. Ries, A., and Trout, J., *Positioning: The Battle for Your Mind*. New York: McGraw-Hill, 1981, pp. 66–67.
7. Geltzer, H., and Ries, A., "The Positioning Era: A Marketing Strategy for College Admissions in the 1980s." In *A Role for Marketing College Admissions*. New York: College Entrance Examination Board, 1976, pp. 73–85.
8. Ibid., p. 81.
9. Weinberg, C.B., "Marketing Planning for the Arts Organization." In M.P. Mokwa, W.M. Dawson, and E.A. Prieve (eds.), *Marketing the Arts*. New York: Praeger, 1980, p. 107.

10. Geltzer and Ries, "Positioning Era," p. 124.

11. Ibid., pp. 126–197.

12. Hochbaum, G.M., "Selling Health to the Public," In I.M. Newman (ed.), *Consumer Behavior in the Health Marketplace*. Lincoln: Nebraska Center for Health Education, University of Nebraska, 1976, pp. 5–14.

13. Adapted from Roberto, E.L., "Social Marketing Strategies for Diffusing the Adoption of Family Planning," *Social Science Quarterly*, vol. 53 No. 2, June 1972, pp. 33–51.

14. Ibid., p. 39.

15. McKinlay, J.B., "Some Approaches and Problems in the Study of the Use of Services—An Overview," *Journal of Health and Social Behavior*, June 13, 1972, p. 132.

SEVEN

Allocation Decisions: The Equity Issue

"Virtually all of the rawest nerves of urban political life are touched by the distribution of urban service burdens and benefits."[1] The delivery of services is the primary function of local governments and a major responsibility of other governmental levels. This task absorbs far more resources than any of the other marketing tasks (gathering information, identifying target markets, program development and management, pricing, communicating, or evaluating). The magnitude of resources now under federal, state, and local government control allows agencies to bestow increasingly significant benefits or penalties on their citizenry. These benefits or penalties arise primarily from the governments' allocation of services.[2]

Two related sets of decisions are involved in the delivery of public services. They revolve around the issues of allocation and distribution. Allocation decisions address the question "Who gets what?" or, in normative terms, "Who ought to get what?" This chapter focuses on allocation decisions that determine which target markets are (or should be) allocated how much of the resources available for a particular service. After "Who gets what?" has been answered, the subsequent distribution questions "When?, where?, and how?" can be addressed. These distribution decisions are discussed in Chapter 8.

When public officials are evaluated by special interest groups, influential citizens, and voters in general, judgments are frequently based on the extent to which existing service delivery is perceived to be satisfactory. A fairly small number of experiences may determine the answer. This point was vividly illustrated in Chicago's Democratic mayoral primary in 1979, when Jane Byrne won a stunning victory over incumbent Mayor Michael Bilandic. Byrne capitalized on public dissatisfaction with the way Bilandic had handled a 40-inch blizzard. A month later many streets were still blocked, garbage was accumulating in alleys, and buses and trains were off schedule. The weather crisis was on voters' minds when they went to the polls.

Despite the extensive commitment of resources to delivering public services, the pervasive role of service delivery in citizens' lives, and the political implications of public service delivery, the public service allocation function has remained "the hidden function of government."[3] It has received relatively little attention in the popular press, in the professional literature, or by empirical researchers. A primary reason for this neglect may be its lack of glamor. Most decisions about public service allocations are mundane and routine. It is difficult for most citizens to get excited about how new library books are allocated among branch libraries, how police manpower is assigned, or how the garbage is collected.[4] Further, differences in service levels between areas within the same governmental jurisdiction are rarely debated by citizens because they are frequently perceived by citizens as being relatively small. They don't realize that the cumulative impact of even small differences can be substantial:

> If a particular neighborhood gets fewer scheduled garbage pick-ups per week than other neighborhoods, if it receives one or two fewer parks and playgrounds, if it is assigned fewer police patrolmen and has a higher crime rate, if the books in the local branch library are not responsive to reader preferences, if police responsiveness to requests for assistance is slower, if neighborhood streets are rougher and requests for maintenance and repair are ignored, if teachers in the schools are poorly trained and motivated, if teacher/pupil ratios are higher and the condition of the physical plant is inferior, if sewer and drainage systems are less effective, if water pressure is lower, and if it receives fewer fire hydrants, the cumulative impact in dollar terms and in terms of the difference it makes in the safety, convenience, and well-being of the residents becomes significant.[5]

RELATIONSHIP BETWEEN TARGET MARKET AND ALLOCATION DECISIONS

Clearly there is a relationship between target market selection decisions and allocation decisions. Both are concerned with who should be served and what proportion of a service's available resources should be devoted to particular subgroups. Once again we face the fundamental distinction between marketing in the public and private sectors. Public agencies are required to distribute services equitably whereas private sector organizations direct resources only at the most responsive market segments.

Marketing efforts begin with a needs assessment, which identifies the differing needs of particular subgroups. Recognizing these needs, elected officials make appropriate legislative and budgetary decisions, and administrators adopt decision rules for implementing those decisions. In this way the population to be served is defined. Members of the population possessing the specified qualifying features (e.g., living in a particular geographical area, in a selected income group or age cohort, owning a home, or whatever) constitute the total set of potential market segments. Equity requires that all of these market segments be considered for service.

When parameters of the population have been established, target market decisions follow. The role of target marketing is, "Given this is the population to be served, how can the exchange process with them best be facilitated?" Since different subgroups within the qualifying population are likely to be viewed as being of different priority, exhibiting different levels of responsiveness to the service, and seeking different benefits from the service, the answer to this question results from dividing the population into subgroups and developing a unique marketing mix for each subgroup. The appropriateness of this relationship is suggested by the following observation:

> Providing services to clients to insure they will receive public benefits entitled to them by law requires: first, a delineation of the characteristics of citizens making them eligible for these benefits; second, an identification of those specific persons who meet the eligibility criteria; and, third, an evaluation of what services will have to be provided to each eligible person to insure he (or she) will receive his (or her) benefits if he (or she) wants them.[6]

Delineation establishes the allocative criteria of who gets the service. Identifying who gets the service means the population has to be defined in terms that are measurable and accessible—key criteria for effective segmentation. The third stage stresses the importance of tailoring a unique marketing mix for each target market in order to best facilitate the exchange.

EMERGING CONCERN WITH ALLOCATION DECISIONS

The once prevailing indifference of citizens, their political representatives, and agency personnel toward allocation decisions is beginning to change. This transition has been stimulated primarily by a scarcity of resources and by the influence of the courts.

Scarcity of Resources

In the 1960s and early 1970s rapid expansion of government and social services often made it possible for governments to respond to vociferous or obviously legitimate claims of inequitable treatment in service allocations by increasing the total budget and providing additional resources. Problems could be resolved with magnamity:

> Are poor people deprived of equal access to the courts? Provide them with lawyers. Equal access to health care? Establish neighborhood clinics. Educational opportunity? Develop preschool enrichment programs.[7]

This approach enabled decision makers to avoid having to make hard trade-off judgments as to who should get what. Now retrenchment is taking place, and the total pie in most jurisdictions can no longer be made bigger. Today the allocation of a greater proportion of resources to one group will usually lead to a reduced allocation of resources to other groups. Consequently, those who expect to benefit from redistribution intensify pressure for change, and those who would be worse off stiffen resistance.[8] In this changed environment, the definitional question of service allocation, "Who gets what?" may need to be rephrased to "Who gets to keep what and who loses what?"[9]

When a service is offered, a constituency is nurtured and a level of expectation and dependence among members of that constituency is established. Reduction of an accustomed service level may be expected to generate dissent and invite closer scrutiny of the fairness of the service's allocation, because the reduced service offering exerts a direct and visible adverse impact on the quality of the lives of individuals who comprise the constituency. This dissent is likely to be particularly acute in urban areas where heterogeneous groups coexist in close proximity.

The increased attention of citizens to allocation questions that occur when services are withdrawn was demonstrated in Detroit when the sanitation district changed procedures for collecting garbage:

> Traditional garbage trucks run by three-person sanitation crews were replaced with one-person loader-packers on a limited number of routes. The change was experimental; but if the new procedures yielded the expected increases in service efficiency, the change would be implemented throughout the city. On these routes alley pick-up was no longer provided, so citizens were required to bring their garbage to the front of their lots.
>
> Because the change applied only to certain areas within the city, the associated change in the allocation of costs and benefits was clearly perceived by citizens and led to protracted, rancorous conflict. The acrimonious citizen reaction to the change caught city officials by surprise. In an effort to stave off bankruptcy, the city had made considerable service cuts with relatively little adverse citizen reaction. One official commented, "They said nothing while the police force was cut by a quarter and the neighborhood firehouses were decimated, and they raise the roof over this!" Heated debates occurred in meetings of neighborhood associations among property owners who had not attended such meetings in years. In response to the outcry the city stopped curbside pick-up and restored alley services in the areas of fiercest resistance.
>
> The vociferous reaction to what city officials thought was a relatively trivial change in the distribution of benefits occurred for two reasons. First, the change was very visible. If police patrols or building inspectors or fire personnel are reduced, the consequences can be severe, but may not be visible to the majority of residents. Second, a minority of citizens felt they were being discriminated against unfairly. They perceived themselves as being forced to give up valuable service benefits they had traditionally enjoyed, while others were not required to do so, and they reacted strongly.[10]

Influence of the Courts

The second, but less dominant, factor stimulating interest in allocation has been the interventionist role of the courts. The legal foundation for challenges to service allocation patterns has usually been the equal protection clause of the Fourteenth Amendment to the U.S. Constitution, which provides that "no state shall make or enforce any laws which shall abridge the privileges or immunities of citizens in the United States . . . nor deny to any person within its jurisdiction the equal protection of the laws."

The most significant court decision in this area was *Hawkins v. Shaw* (1971), in which the U.S. Court of Appeals for the Fifth Circuit ruled that the town of Shaw, Mississippi had violated the equal protection clause by denying services to black residents that were equal to those made available to whites. "The evidence established that nearly 98 percent of homes on unpaved streets were black-occupied; 97 percent of homes not served by sanitary sewers were in black neighborhoods; and all the city's new mercury vapor street lights were in white neighborhoods."[11] The court in the *Shaw* case stated:

> In order to prevail in a case of this type, it is not necessary to prove intent, motive, or purpose to discriminate on the part of city officials. . . . We now firmly recognize that the arbitrary quality of thoughtlessness can be as disastrous and unfair to private rights and to public interest as the perversity of a willful scheme.[12]

An important feature of this ruling was the notion that discrimination need not be proven. The only requirement was demonstration that existing service allocations were unequal, a ruling that had dramatic implications:

> The promise of sweeping change held forth by Hawkins v. Shaw rested on the ease with which evidence establishing racial disparities could be amassed. All the plaintiff had to do to claim racial discrimination was to demonstrate to the court that the government action mentioned in the complaint resulted in disproportionate racial consequences, e.g., that white neighborhoods had more paved streets, larger water mains, or better police protection than black neighborhoods. The plaintiff was not required to show proof of racially discriminatory intent or purpose—only of racially discriminatory impact. The disadvantage at which this doctrine placed municipal authorities is immediately apparent. The burden of proof fell on the city and, unless it could persuade the trial court that a compelling state interest required these differing levels of service—an all but impossible task—the judge had no choice but to condemn its actions as an unconstitutional violation of the Equal Protection Clause.[13]

Given this precedent, it was anticipated that the judiciary would sharply curtail the discretion which local government officials have in the allocation of public services. Two developments, however, have eroded this power of the courts. First, a series of Supreme Court decisions subsequent to *Shaw* made the test of discrimination to be employed by the courts much more rigorous. The Court ruled that official government action will not be declared unconstitutional simply because it results in a discriminatory impact. Rather, such action must have an "invidious discriminatory purpose." This change shifts the onus onto the plaintiff to prove the service disparities at issue would not have existed "but for" an "invidious discriminatory intent" on the part of the city's officials.[14]

Second, the judiciary has realized that it does not have the requisite institutional competence to deal intelligently with the kinds of problems equalization litigation raises.[15] Many of these problems revolve around the difficulties and problems associated with trying to measure equity in quantitative terms (see Chapter 8).

At this time, it appears that the role of the courts is likely to remain much less prominent in allocation decisions than had been anticipated after the *Shaw* case. Indeed, one legal authority has concluded:

> The effort to insure equitable service delivery through an appeal to the constitutional principle of equal protection of the law has not produced a judicial tradition which promises effective remedies for victims of discrimination.[16]

WHO ARE THE WINNERS AND LOSERS?

Allocation decisions resolve who receives what quantity of the services that are to be provided:

> There are only a limited number of building inspectors, police, and capital funds for library branches available. Since the services provided by local governments are generally divisible, consumption by one neighborhood means denial to some other neighborhood. Further, geographic placement of resources implies social distribution of those resources, since individuals with similar social characteristics are not distributed randomly across a city's landscape but are spatially concentrated.[17]

Hence the allocation of every new facility or service favors or disfavors particular segments of the community and thus redistributes well-being or ill-being. In short, in every allocation decision there are winners and losers.

The conventional wisdom about allocation has been that the rich get richer and the poor get poorer:

> The slum is the catch-all for losers . . . the slum areas are the losers in terms of schools, jobs, garbage collection, street lighting, libraries, social services, and whatever else is communally available but always in short supply.[18]

Another dimension of this adage suggests that allocation decisions reflect political power. Hence the first streets to be cleaned in a snowfall are those on which the most powerful politicians reside. In this vein it has been suggested that convenient clean parks are the booty of the winner of political conflicts, while garbage strewn alleys are the badge of the loser.[19]

Reviewers of the studies addressing resource allocation are unanimous in concluding that the evidence refutes this adage. Examples of politically motivated service allocations are exceptions to the general pattern. "Overall service patterns do not seem to be systematically related to measures of power resources."[20] The process of resource allocation appears to be relatively devoid of political content because, on the basis of empirical evidence, the poor do not generally receive fewer or poorer-quality public services. "Surprisingly there is little evidence to indicate that blacks and other low income groups are systematically deprived in the allocations of resources in large metropolitan areas."[21]

Robert Lineberry, for example, found that the allocation of service benefits in San Antonio, Texas, depended on the nature of the services studied, but the benefits tended to be allocated in a fashion that might be characterized as "unpatterned inequalities."[22] While services were unequally allocated, the inequalities were not cumulative; service benefits did not disproportionately and consistently accrue to any class or race.

Generalizations about winners and losers are hazardous because of the relatively few empirical investigations of the allocation of public services yet available. Further, most of the studies that have been completed have examined only one service area rather than a range of areas within the same city. It is likely, however, that the answer to the question "Who are the winners and the losers?" differs among communities and even among services.[23] In other words, "the weight of evidence compels the conclusion that overt, measurable discrimination in the distribution of conventional city services has been overstated by anecdotal commentary and conventional wisdom."[24]

CONCEPT OF EQUITY

The term *allocation* implies that different amounts of a service are assigned to selected groups on the basis of some principle or standard. The generally accepted standard for allocating public services is equity. Equity is a complex concept with no single or accepted definition. However, "the difficulties of specifying equity neither obviate the need for equity decisions nor stop such decisions from being made."[25]

Equity does not necessarily mean equality, which is a related but different idea. Both terms derive from the same Latin word, but in the English language each conveys something different. Equality has to do with sameness in quantity and quality, while equity has to do with fairness and justice. As we shall see later, inequality of resource allocation can be used to promote equity in service distribution. Equity addresses the question "Is the allocation of services in this jurisdiction fair?" To define equity in the context of government and social service delivery efforts, a manager can apply a simple test: What diffe- does a particular allocation decision make in the relative conditi- Are they worse off, better off, or just the same as a resu-

Every service distribution pattern reflects a model of equity. Daily choices are made about who gets what, who benefits, and who pays. Even though not frequently articulated, an equity standard is implied whenever decisions are made concerning services: "Every time a tax is levied or repealed, every time public expenditures are expanded or contracted, every time regulations are extended or abolished an equity decision has to be made."[27]

Alternative Models of Equity

In this section we contend that a selected model of equity has to be justified on the grounds of how public services and their benefits are ultimately apportioned among a jurisdiction's populace. It should be recognized, however, that another approach can be used to judge equity of service allocation. The alternate approach stresses the process of determining allocations rather than the allocation pattern. When equity is a function of process, any allocation by the legitimate public decision-making process (i.e., elected representation) is deemed equitable. In this view, whatever allocations of services emerge from the legal processes of governments are by definition equitable.[28] This approach may be appealing to an elected official because it is expedient and self-serving, but it offers no consistent policy guidance for service delivery decisions.

Trade-offs are involved in adopting any particular concept of equity, and a sound case can be made for the allocation of public services governed by any of the standards developed in this section. This discussion of alternate models of equity is stimulated by a belief that these trade-offs are better confronted and made consciously rather than unconsciously, as decisions rather than non-decisions. Instead, articulation of an appropriate equity standard is often avoided:

> Since professionals might disagree about social goals, internal conflict is mitigated by focusing on how activities are to be carried out or on the quality of service to be made available. Precisely who gets how much of these products is not normally a professional concern.[29]

Despite this reluctance to confront the issue, awareness of alternate equity criteria is still essential. They should govern and guide all subsequent distribution decisions. An equity model may be selected from three fundamentally different alternatives, equal opportunity, compensatory equity, and market equity.

Equal Opportunity. The wide acceptance of this standard of equity is [illegible]bably a reflection of traditional values, which recognize equal protection [illegible] law. *Equal opportunity entails allocating equal amounts of services* [illegible] *regardless of need or the amount of taxes paid.* An equal [illegible]ld support assignment of police protection on a per acre, per household, or per person basis. A district with 500 residents, for example, might be allocated one police officer, while a district with 1500 residents might be allocated three police officers.

In so far as America has had an egalitarian tradition, it has been one of equality of opportunity: the right of every person to get ahead. However, equality of opportunity has little to do with equality if it simply enables people with more income and better education to win out over the less fortunate, even when the allocation of resources itself is equal.[30] All citizens do not arrive at the starting line with equal characteristics and attributes:

> At Oxford there is a rowing race that started only once. Every year boats begin where they left off the year before. The race is never won. Some would argue that this is analogous to adopting an equal opportunity equity model in public service allocation decisions.[31]

In addition, the provision of identical services to two neighborhoods can hardly be considered equal opportunity if the residents of one area deeply desire the service while those of the other feel no need for it.[32] For example, it makes little sense to provide the same amount of day care services in a predominantly senior citizen neighborhood and in a young family neighborhood. Equal opportunity is often selected as the appropriate equity model because, in the face of competition for resources and conflicting pressures from different interest groups, it is the easy way out.

This model may be viewed from the perspective of two different units of analysis.[33] The first unit of analysis is the household. Some services such as solid waste collection and water supply are supplied directly to households. In these cases the meaning of equal opportunity is that households in one neighborhood receive services equal to those in another neighborhood.

Obviously it is impossible, and often undesirable, to distribute certain services equally to all citizens. Fixed facilities such as parks, libraries, and schools can never be equally accessible to all members of a community. Hence the second unit of analysis is the neighborhood or service district. For example, a fire station is located to serve a district within a service radius. Neighborhoods can be compared with each other in terms of the adequacy of these services. Households within each neighborhood, however, will vary in the distance they are located from the fire station.

Compensatory Equity. *Compensatory equity involves allocation of services so that disadvantaged groups, individuals, or areas receive extra increments of resources*. The operational objective of this equity model is to increase the compensatory role of public services in order that opportunities for the underprivileged may be improved. This requires that resources be allocated in proportion to the intensity of the need for them.

Under the terms of this model, for example, equitable allocation of health care services does not imply that everyone should receive the same amount of health services. Instead it implies that illness should be the major determinant of the allocation of resources. Inequity becomes a concern if resources are allocated on the basis of demographic variables such as race, family income, or place of residence, rather than need. Compensatory equity is usually redistributive in nature: It implies that an unequal amount of resources in terms of personnel expenditures, equipment, and facilities will be devoted to those residents who have the greatest need for a service. Frequently these residents are from lower-income groups. However, there will be occasions when compensatory equity may not be redistributive. For example, in order to enjoy the same level of security from risk of loss to fire, a middle-class community of high-rise apartment dwellers may need more elaborate fire services than a poor neighborhood of dispersed single-family dwellings.[34]

Compensatory equity is deemed appropriate by its supporters because of the public benefits that accrue. Three such benefits are usually cited: relief of poverty, greater equality of opportunity, and the fostering of a closer sense of community by erosion of substantial class and wealth barriers. Allocations intended to achieve compensatory results would allocate bigger and better libraries and more parks to poorer neighborhoods whose citizens can afford few books and have less private recreational space; more police officers to high-crime precincts; and more building inspectors to older sections of the city where code violations are concentrated.

Most of the federal aid programs are redistributive in nature and directed at the underprivileged. This principle of compensatory equity was effectively institutionalized at the federal level by the Sixteenth Amendment to the U.S. Constitution, which established a progressive income tax. By that tax the more affluent subsidize the less affluent.

If the disadvantages of selected client groups were fully compensated, then the outcome would be perfect equality of results. This is probably not a realistic goal for the allocation of public services, since the extensive resources needed to achieve it may not be available and it may even be undesirable.[35] For example, it is unrealistic to expect all pupils to score equally on achievement tests at the end of 12 years of schooling, no matter how many additional resources are allocated to the underprivileged. However, it is probably realistic to expect extra increments of resources to exert some compensatory effect by reducing the performance gap.

Market Equity. *Market equity entails allocating services to groups or neighborhoods in proportion to the tax or fee revenues that they produce.* In the case of police protection, for example, each geographic area in a city would be allocated police services in direct proportion to the amount of taxes paid by area merchants and residents. If a particular neighborhood desires a service, they can have as much as they want, provided they pay for it. Special assessment financing and user charges are examples of how this can be accomplished.

In response to demands to cut local taxes, governments can charge a direct price for some public services rather than fully subsidizing them through the tax system. This standard of market equity enhances responsiveness of resource allocation. Citizens do not receive services they do not want, nor are they required to pay through the tax system for what other citizens consume. They can buy as much or as little of a service as they wish.

Market equity draws from the prevalent allocation model used in the private sector. There are likely to be very few government services in which a pure market equity model is appropriate. If users are willing and able to pay a price that covers all capital and operating costs, the service should probably be offered by a private sector organization. A few exceptions to this generalization will be discussed later in this chapter.

Full commitment to this equity model would mean accepting that citizens are not entitled to equal access to outlets, and that citizens' needs are not relevant unless they are backed up by "dollar votes in the market place."[36] This approach offers the most efficient use of resources, but it ignores the social issues associated with equity. Full adoption of this standard would mean that some services would be almost entirely removed from poor neighborhoods and reallocated exclusively to wealthier neighborhoods. As well as being politically infeasible, this probably would violate the public's sense of right. In general, the narrower the clientele and the more removed the service from the necessities of life, the more acceptable market equity is likely to be.[37]

Further, it is possible that the consequences of low service levels in poor areas would spill out of the deprived neighborhood. Too little police and fire protection, inadequate refuse collection, and too few recreation and transportation services would, in the long run, have a significant and detrimental impact on adjoining, and even distant, neighborhoods.[38]

The goals of public agencies differ from those of private firms. One of the distinguishing characteristics of public service provision is its potential for ameliorating the extreme inequities produced by the operation of the private sector. If market equity was completely adopted then individuals and groups deprived by the operation of the private sector would be disadvantaged by the public sector as well. Hence, full commitment to a market equity model is probably inappropriate. It is more likely that a "towards market equity" model will be adopted recognizing different abilities to pay for services, but still recognizing that those who cannot afford to pay full costs should not be denied the service.

Demand: An Inadequate Surrogate. Demand is *not* an equity model, but it is used extensively as a surrogate for a real equity model. *The demand approach allocates resources on the basis of consumption and/or vociferous advocacy or complaints*. It cannot serve to guide the allocation of services in a predetermined direction. Rather it is a complicating factor—a pragmatic, reactive approach to which agency personnel and elected officials frequently resort because it is administratively convenient. Its use is likely to result in an unpredictable and inconsistent set of winners and losers. Demand may lead to adoption of a pattern of services reflecting any of the three equity alternatives discussed previously or it may deviate inconsistently among them.

Demand is different from market equity. Recipients of services under the market equity model pay for the extra increments of services that they receive directly through fees or indirectly through higher taxes. There is a direct relationship between payments and services. The demand surrogate does not require payment for services received.

Demand is manifested in two ways: requests and complaints or use of a service. For example, high book circulation may be interpreted as a demand for libraries to provide more books and other resources. In Houston and Oakland, library expenditures, staff personnel, and new acquisitions are allotted to branch libraries on the basis of circulation rates. The higher its circulation rates, the greater the share of available resources a branch library receives. Since residents of middle- and upper-income neighborhoods read more, branches located in these neighborhoods receive more resources.[39]

On the surface, demand sounds reasonable and defensible. The neighborhood organization movement and the perceived desirability of citizen participation in decisions may have led to the belief that responsiveness to requests and complaints demonstrates accountability to constituents and is an appropriate basis for decision making.[40] However, demand often harbors a hidden allocation bias: If demand varies by, for example, race or class, services also vary by race or class. In situations where demand is used as a basis for allocation, "if better educated people read more library books, or drive their cars more often or call the police more frequently, they receive more services."[41]

Because of its administrative convenience and apparent fairness, demand has been widely adopted as an operational surrogate for equity. It is particularly characteristic of passive agencies. For example, Detroit's Environmental Enforcement Agency, described as "a passive bureaucracy in the extreme," has been geared primarily to respond to citizen complaints concerning problems of litter, overgrowth, and rodents, with few initiatives of its own.[42]

The limited empirical evidence that is available suggests that demand is more likely to contribute to market equity than compensatory equity. That is, when demand is used as a surrogate equity model, wealthier citizens tend to be more active and assertive and hence receive more of the services that they seek than poorer citizens.[43] The findings in Detroit are reasonably typical. Most service demand there did not come from the poor city center neighborhoods where the need for most public services was greatest; rather it occurred in middle-income neighborhoods. The project researchers concluded:

> This implies that agencies relying solely on citizen demand to determine which targets to attack will likely underserve the poorest, most socially disorganized neighborhoods. These neighborhoods contact government at lower rates than their needs for public services would suggest.[44]

Horizontal Equity

The three models of equity already presented represent alternate approaches to what might be termed *vertical equity*. This term connotes the effort to devise a rationale for allocating services among individuals who possess different (greater and lesser) degrees of various personal attributes or characteristics.[45] In the economist's terms, vertical equity thus requires "that unequals be treated unequally."

However, accompanying vertical equity is the notion of *horizontal equity*. Horizontal equity means that two families of the same size with similar preferences and similar earnings should receive goods and services from government and social service agencies worth approximately the same amount, as well as pay the same amount in taxes.

> A study by the U.S. General Accounting Office dramatized the horizontal inequities of the present welfare system. Numerous recipients who shared a similar dependency status often received quite varied dollar value benefits from several federal programs. While these individuals were basically similar in their degree of need, the qualification standards for different programs might summarily bestow benefits on one person but not another.[46]

Assessments of equity in providing government and social services therefore should include an examination of horizontal equity as well as vertical equity.

WHICH EQUITY MODEL SHOULD BE SELECTED?

Each model of equity so far described leads to a different pattern of public service allocation. Table 7.1 illustrates the differences that emerge in school, library, and street services using each of the three equity models (the equal results criterion is the extreme outcome of the compensatory equity model).

It is probably unrealistic and oversimplistic to believe that one model of equity will be considered superior to the others for all public services, not only because individuals have different values but also because different agencies with different personnel do different things in different contexts. Consequently, the same model may not be appropriate for all of them.[47] Many people believe that offerings needed by most of the service area population probably should be guided by equal opportunity or compensatory equity, whereas more specialized services benefiting only small segments can use the market equity model.[48] Thus the market equity model may be deemed most appropriate for discretionary services such as cultural arts, recreation, and library services; but in the same jurisdiction for essential services such as police and fire, the compensatory equity model may be selected, while garbage collection might f... red an equal opportunity approach. ...ociety

Individual opinions as to what is fair and equitable are likely t... opinion of by background and social position. In a heterogeneous, conf... involved, a there is unlikely to be any prolonged consensus or ev... ent. However, what is equitable. Because subjective, normativ... concept of equity cannot be labelled right or...

TABLE 7.1. The Operational Implications of Allocating Resources to Three Public Services, Using Three Alternative Equity Models

	Market Equity	Equal Opportunity	Equal Results[a]
Schools	The per child expenditure in each school should be proportional to the taxes paid by the neighborhood	Each child should receive equal dollar expenditure	Each child should receive enough expenditure so that all children read at the same level[b]
Libraries	The per resident expenditure in each branch should be proportional to the taxes paid by the neighborhood	Each branch should receive equal per capita expenditure	Each branch should receive enough expenditure so that circulation per capita is equal in all branches
Streets	The per resident expenditure on streets in each neighborhood should be proportional to the taxes paid by that neighborhood	Each neighborhood should receive an equal per capita (or per mile) expenditure	Each neighborhood should receive enough expenditure so that the condition of all neighborhood streets in the city is equal

[a]This equal results criterion is the extreme outcome of the compensatory equity model.
[b]If not exactly the same level, at least an equal mean level for racial and income groups.
Source: Levy, F., Meltsner, A.J., and Wildavsky, A., *Urban Outcomes*. Berkeley: University of California Press, 1974. p. 244.

if self-interest is the primary determinant of preference, it seems reasonable to expect wealthy citizens to favor market equity, middle-income citizens to favor equal opportunity, and poor citizens to favor compensatory equity. Ideologically, market equity is a function of conservative thought, while liberals tend to support compensatory equity.

recent years, perhaps, no other work has stimulated as much inquiry and nto the equity dilemma as Rawls' *The Theory of Justice*. The guidelines Rawls suggest that determination of the appropriate model of equity service should evolve through consideration of three basic re illustrated in Figure 7.1: (1) equal opportunity should be t of departure; (2) deviations from this point should be

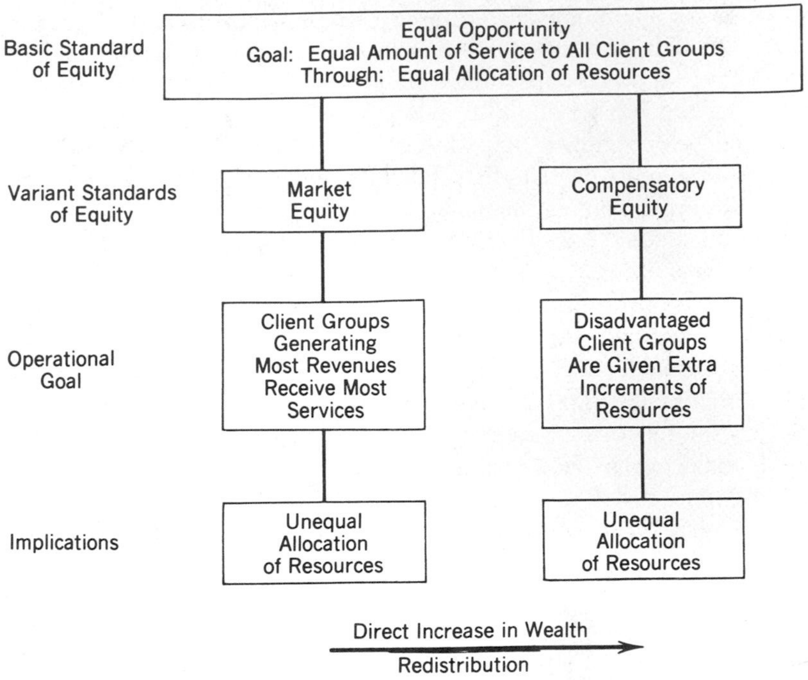

Figure 7.1. Alternate Equity Models.

encouraged if they benefit the least advantaged; (3) there should be, in all cases, a stated minimum level or floor for each service below which quantity and quality should not fall.[49]

This framework enables (1) persons with special needs or deficiencies to be allocated more resources consistent with a compensatory equity model or (2) some reconciliation of the amount individuals pay for services with the amount of benefits they receive, as is consistent with a market equity model. What can be termed specific justification, however, should be gathered to demonstrate that the least advantaged benefit as a result of any deviations from the equal opportunity model. If police patrol forces are allocated equally per capita or per household, they probably will not be allocated equally per crime reported or per call for service. There may be more calls for service from people in poorer neighborhoods.[50] This is an example of a specific justification for deviation from the norm of equal opportunity toward compensatory equity.

Each public agency should provide a minimum floor of service. For exa- ... of
in Rochester, New York, police officers are assigned to districts on th... ever,
calls for service and crime rates (compensatory equity). Each di... base).
also receives a minimum number of patrol officers (equ... uld qualify
This number exceeds the manpower level for which so... cation.[51] Sim-
if crime rates and calls for service alone determi... circulation totals
ilarly, in the Atlanta library system, branch l...

receive a larger share of available resources. Branches located in poor neighborhoods, though, receive more resources than their circulation totals alone would justify. An equal opportunity base level of service is established, but a deviation toward market equity is incorporated.

It should be recognized that whichever equity model is selected, full implementation is unlikely. The first difficulty lies in securing commitment and consistent interpretation of the model by all the political and agency personnel involved. This issue is complicated further by the continued turnover of elected representatives.

Second, even if facilities and services are consistently allocated over time in accordance with a selected equity model, the desired goal is unlikely to be attained because of changes in the community profile. The needs, preferences, and perceptions of residents change as people move in and out of neighborhoods and facilities deteriorate or are created. Thus a pattern of allocation considered equitable today may be viewed as inequitable tomorrow because of the dynamic environment around it. For example, in 1940 less than 5 percent of Oakland's population were racial minorities. By 1970, the percentage had risen to 41 percent.[52] This changing constituency is likely to lead either to a change in the pattern of facility and service distribution under the existing equity model, or a change in opinion about what is the appropriate model of equity.

WHO DETERMINES WHAT IS EQUITABLE?

Apparently, since equity involves individual value judgments, the appropriate model should be determined by citizens' elected representatives. The traditional government model suggests that the allocation of public services is implemented by a policy process that operates in the following way: (1) community priorities and values are articulated by citizens or citizen groups who, (2) influence elected representatives who, (3) convert the various demands into formal policies that, (4) agency personnel endeavor to carry out.[53]

Some argue, however, that the traditional government model does not explain the selection and implementation of equity criteria:

> Our conception of what constitutes proportionality and relative equality tends to be heavily determined by history and culture. Distributions of the past are fair until proven unfair. Great social shocks, such as wars and economic depressions, seem necessary to change specifications of relative deprivation.[54]

eq [illegible] suggests that inertia is a powerful ingredient in determining what is dep[illegible] "The best prediction about the behavior of the bureaucrats in each slight [illegible] year."[55] [illegible]at they will do this year about what they did last year, making [illegible]llow for current conditions and the experiences of the past [illegible] is following a particular equity model that disproportionately rewards one group, it is very difficult for other groups to change that model except in times of crisis.

Often those who discount the traditional government model contend that the prevailing pattern of service allocation is a result of inputs from three sets of actors: elected officials, administrators, and street-level bureaucrats. The degree of influence exerted by each varies from service to service and from community to community.

Factors Limiting the Influence of Elected Officials

Considerable decision-making discretion resides with agency personnel because these public managers are not subject to direct control by the elected officials for whom they work.[56] Elected officials are unlikely to have the time or energy resources to supervise the everyday operationalization of their policy. The budget, which is usually the effective limit to policy makers' equity decisions,

> May have a lot to say about how many inspectors are employed in the Department of Building Inspection, but very little to say about how many buildings are inspected, the order in which they are inspected, and how strictly building costs are enforced. Budgeted dollar amounts provide many constraints on the quality of resources available to governmental units, but few constraints on how these resources are utilized.[57]

One researcher found that intervention by elected officials in the affairs of public departments was limited and "usually concerns selection of a new chief."

> The more general questions . . . how the police allocate their resources, which laws they choose to enforce vigorously and which they choose to slight . . . are rarely raised even in racial issues.[58]

This researcher concluded that the police largely operate in a "zone of indifference" and that control over police policies is left "in many cases to the police themselves." Hence elected officials may nominally establish an equity model, but administrators and street-level bureaucrats decide how to operationalize it.

The elected official is likely to have most influence on achievement of a given equity standard through the budgetary process, which may mandate the type of service or facility to be offered, its capacity, scope, or range, and its location. The relative influence of administrators and street-level bureaucr... on subsequent decisions will depend on the amount of discretion that is ...d in in the service and the degree of control the administrator has. ...

In some instances elected officials may not want to b... resolving an equity issue, because of its potential for ge... conflict. Explicit support for any one model may invite ... from those who support the other two models. The e... equity models and the failure to adopt one of them as the agency's guideline may allow elected officials much more discretion to finesse potential conflict situations.

Role of Administrators

Recent research has revealed that, at least in large cities, resource allocation decisions are made primarily by senior administrators and are influenced relatively little by election outcomes.[59] The administrator exerts this key influence in determining an equity model through the use of the decision rules that he or she formulates in response to, or in the absence of, policy directives from elected representatives. Decision rules are used to make the task of allocating services more manageable. The need for such decision rules is illustrated by the following statistics:

> In San Antonio, during one year . . . among the 26,500 accidents, the 800 vagrancies, the 6,600 prowlers, the 13,700 family disturbances, the 400 assaults, and the rest of the offenses, some allocation of police resources has to be made. Bureaucracies cannot do everything at once. . . . For the 42,000 tons of asphalt allocated to the gravel and asphalt maintenance division of the public works department, someone must decide which potholes get patched. Of the 125,000 new books and materials purchased by the public library, somewhere a decision must be made about the location of those materials by library.[60]

The rules by which police patrols are assigned, streets are repaired, new books are distributed to branch libraries, street lights are installed, and fire stations are built are all decisions affecting the allocation of public services.

The role of administrative rules is particularly obvious at the federal level, where procedure is most formalized. Congress enacts legislation and determines the funding levels appropriate for implementing the legislation. However, administrators interpret and operationalize the legislation through rules and regulations published in the *Federal Register*.

The various potential impacts on citizens of different decision rules can be gauged from Figure 7.2, which illustrates alternate rules developed by police administrators.

These decisional rules are often decisive in determining the winners and losers. Nevertheless, their impact on equity is frequently an unanticipated byproduct of their purpose, which may primarily be to facilitate bureaucratic convenience. At other times these decisions reflect other types of motives, as illustrated by the Oakland street department:

> ...butional decisions in the Oakland street department were dominated by pr...ions of traffic volume, efficiency of traffic flow, and accident rate. These ...iteria of speed, efficiency and safety insured that those streets ... freeways or serving as crosstown arterials would be constructed ... neighborhood streets. Similarly, expenditures for the re... surfaci... were allocated on the basis of traffic volume, citizen

Compensatory Equity

Patrol officers and investigators are assigned on the basis of total reported crime rates. If a district accounts for 10 percent of the total reported crimes in the city, it receives approximately 10 percent of the available manpower.

Equal Opportunity

Patrol officers and investigators are assigned on the basis of population. Each district has *X* patrol officers and investigators per 1000 residents.

Demand

Manpower is at least partially assigned on the basis of total calls for service. The higher the number of calls for service in a district, the more manpower it receives.

Figure 7.2. Results of Decision Rules for Allocating Police Resources That Reflect Different Equity Models.

> complaints and an agreement with the utility company to defer improvements if work was anticipated on underground lines within five years. . . . As a result of these bureaucratic rules, black and other low-income neighborhoods received poorer streets in Oakland.[61]

Role of Street-Level Bureaucrats

Street-level bureaucrats are public employees who interact directly with citizens in the course of their jobs and have substantial discretion in the execution of their work.[62] Such personnel include officers on the beat, sanitation workers, classroom teachers, welfare case workers, lower court judges, p[illegible] officers, prison guards, park maintenance employees, and housing i[illegible]rs. Indeed, a majority of governmental and social services offer co[illegible]ble discretion to personnel interacting directly with citizens.

Even after decision rules have been est[illegible] administrators, street-level bureaucrats are still likely to hav[illegible]le discretion in determining an equity model. Those decision[illegible]ance, are likely to be relatively general, in order to embra[illegible]ge of contingencies. They are more likely to provide guid[illegible]ate behavior. Hence low-level personnel retain flexi[illegible]own procedures, modify goals, ration services, [illegible] control clientele.[63] Their potential influence on [illegible]gest when they work outside the confines of a facility [illegible] such as building code enforcement, housing inspection, and [illegible]on. In other contexts, such as libraries, parks or recreation services, location of the facility itself is likely to be the dominant influence in allocation decisions. In addition, even if an administrator's decision rules are relatively specific, discretion often remains with a low-echelon bureaucrat to define a situation and hence categorize it by appropriate decision rule.

The decisions of street-level bureaucrats clearly have a profound influence on who gets what. The ways in which they deliver benefits and sanctions effectively delimit people's lives and determine their opportunities.[64] The actual model of equity that is implemented may be largely the result of their cumulative actions. Indeed, it has been argued that "in a significant sense, street-level bureaucrats *are the policy makers* in their respective work arenas."[65]

The discretion granted to lower-level functionaries increases the difficulty upper-level administrators encounter in enforcing standards of service delivery. As a result, citizens may find it difficult to alter allocation of the services they receive by complaints or requests to "responsible authorities." Even when elected officials or senior administrators are sympathetic to citizen demands, they will often be unable to respond effectively because of the limited control they can exercise over low-level personnel.[66]

This role of street-level bureaucrats in determining an equity model emphasizes the importance of gaining a commitment to a common standard by all agency employees. A consensus on decisional rules and procedures is essential; otherwise the pattern of services an agency delivers will bear little resemblance to what elected representatives or senior administrators expect it to deliver. Motivation to behave in accordance with an agreed equity model is a function of incentives, which are the written objectives that operationalize equity and by which personnel performance can be evaluated (see Chapter 8).

HOW DOES EQUITY RELATE TO OTHER MARKETING TASKS?

The performance of a government or social service agency is measured against
three [illegible]teria: equity, effectiveness, and efficiency. The U.S. Constitution is
based on [illegible] equal rights of individuals, and there is an emerging recognition
that public [illegible] should be evaluated first on the grounds of equity. That
is, is every indiv[illegible] being treated fairly? Regarding the other two measures,
effectiveness is mo[illegible]tant than efficiency (see Chapter 4). Thus *in prior-*
itizing performance in[illegible] primary concern should be given to equity, then
to effectiveness, and finally [illegible]cy.

This prioritization is the op[illegible]
many public services are justified [illegible] Although
of their compensatory contribution—[illegible] grounds [illegible] succe[illegible] in terms [illegible]
has been evaluated not in equity terms, but [illegible]
to a lesser extent the effectiveness of its services. [illegible] prioritization. First, [illegible]

Two forces have contributed to this inappropriate
cause efficiency measures are generally more readily available than equity
measures, it is expedient to measure public service delivery only in terms of
efficiency. Second, budgetary constraints have forced government and social
service agency managers to increasingly focus on efficiency. Times of financial
scarcity make it relatively easy to increase the cost efficiency of public services
by reducing compensatory equity efforts.

Evaluating services only in terms of efficiency may result in an equity model that is deemed entirely inappropriate. For example, in many jurisdictions an additional dollar, if spent in one neighborhood, may increase book circulation and hence efficiency (maximum use of available books); but that same dollar could produce *greater* equality of opportunity or greater compensatory results for disadvantaged groups if it were spent in a different neighborhood.

Figure 7.3 suggests that segmentation may be particularly useful in situations where market equity or compensatory equity models have been adopted, but less useful with an equal opportunity model. The equal opportunity standard presumes all citizens have relatively similar service needs. Hence an undifferentiated strategy, offering a universally consistent service, may be appropriate. This combination provides economies of scale and resultant cost efficiencies. Such community services as police and fire protection, sanitation, and public works are common examples of the equal opportunity model being implemented with an undifferentiated strategy.

However, as Rawls[67] observes, equal opportunity has few virtues and all citizens do not have similar service needs. It is unrealistic to expect all members of a potential market to respond similarly to a service offering. Typically, populations are characterized by their diversity and plurality. Some client groups will always have different product and distribution needs, exhibit different levels of sensitivity to price, be more exposed and responsive to communication efforts, and be more likely and able to make use of particular services than are other client groups. A government agency may attempt to treat all of its potential market as homogeneous, but in its daily operations it will inevitably (albeit unintentionally) favor some groups over others.

The market equity model is most commonly used where services are perceived to be discretionary, offering benefits to a relatively small group of citizens rather than benefiting the entire community. Differentiated and concentrated strategies enable an agency to adapt its services to the particular needs of those segments of the population willing to pay.

The compensatory equity model also uses differentiated or concentrated strategies. It identifies underprivileged groups and provides them with specially developed marketing mixes. The type and intensity level of service may differ among these targeted groups.

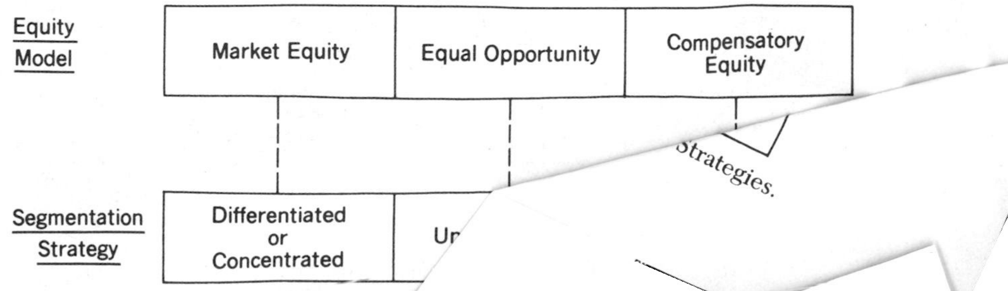

Figure 7.3. Relationship Between E

Selection of an appropriate equity model is almost synonymous with the issue of differentiating between public and private types of services (see Chapter 13), which is the key to formulating rational pricing policies for government services. The relationship between equity models and types of service is illustrated in Figure 7.4. Public and private services constitute opposite poles on a continuum. Much of the debate about pricing public services revolves around whether a particular service exhibits the characteristics of a private or a public service.

If a service exhibits the characteristics of a *private* service, its benefits are received exclusively by participating individuals rather than by the rest of the community. Public agencies provide a substantial number of what are essentially private types of services, but which, because of historical accident, the failure of the private sector to enter the field, or the need for quality controls, now are provided by government. Water and sewerage, public transport, parking spaces, refuse collection, electricity, public marinas, and golf courses are examples of services and facilities that frequently exhibit private service characteristics. The market equity model is likely to be deemed most appropriate in such situations, since it requires those who benefit to pay a price covering the full costs associated with delivering those benefits.

At the other end of the continuum, a *public* service benefits all citizens in the community. Air pollution controls and national defense are frequently cited

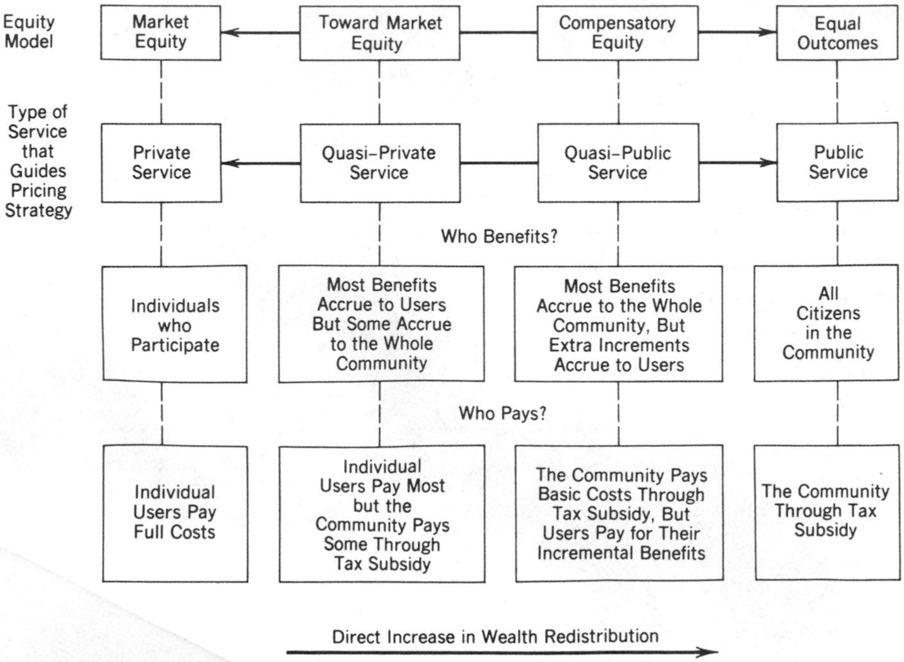

...nship Between Equity Models and Pricing Strategy.

as exhibiting public service characteristics. Since all citizens are perceived to benefit from such public services, these services are paid for by a system of compulsory payments through the taxation system and offered to beneficiaries at zero price. Pure public services such as these take the compensatory equity model to the extreme of equal results or equal outcomes: All citizens receive equal benefit outputs regardless of the amount they pay through the tax system.

The model of equity selected also has implications for promotional strategies. Market equity models are most likely to be directed to better educated groups or areas, since these markets are able and willing to pay for extra increments of service. Communicating to such groups is usually easy: They are more likely to be active information searchers and responsive to desired communication messages.[68]

An equal opportunity model implies that an agency must not only provide a service but also ensure that all have equal knowledge of the service's want-satisfying potential. Only then can all citizens be said to have an equal opportunity to take advantage of the service. In the case of compensatory equity, the communication of a service's availability and its potential for meeting the target market's needs become even more important. Yet these markets in which communication is most necessary are those for whom it is most difficult to design effective communications. When either of these two equity models are adopted, considerable effort will be required to develop effective promotional strategies.

Different equity models will be preferred by different communities and subcultures because society is not a homogeneous mass with uniform tastes and values. Each individual's notions of what is equitable are tempered by his or her background and social position. It would be futile and arrogant for a particular individual to assert that the model he or she prefe... ubject to society. In the final analysis, models are a question of ... discussion of an increasingly vigorous debate. As Fred Hirs... conflicts between who should get what is only beginni... of looking at equity. the desires of various groups ... their concepts and tech-

Nevertheless, mar... ..., address, and investigate the niques in the ... fundamental differentiating factor impli... services. Consideration of equity in ...requisite to the effective marketing of public ... impact on allocation and distribution decisions, ...elationship to evaluation, segmentation, pricing, and

...MARY

Decisions about the allocation of public services touch the lives of all citizens. An inextricable link exists between target market selection decisions and allocation decisions: Both are concerned with who should be served and what proportion of available resources should be devoted to particular subgroups.

The emerging concern with allocation decisions has been stimulated primarily by a scarcity of resources and to a lesser extent by the potential influence of the courts. Declining agency budgets and the accompanying withdrawal of services is likely to invite closer scrutiny of the allocative fairness of those services.

No generalized pattern of consistent winners and losers has emerged from empirical studies. Rather, service allocation has been characterized as having "unpatterned inequities." The winners and losers appear to differ from community to community and even from service to service.

The guiding principle of all allocation decisions is the concept of equity. Three alternate equity models are recognized, each offering different guidelines for implementation. *Equal opportunity* entails distributing equal resources and amounts of services to all citizens regardless of need or the amount of taxes or fees paid. *Compensatory equity* entails allocation of services so that disadvantaged groups or areas receive extra increments of resources. *Market equity* entails allocating services to citizens or neighborhoods in proportion to the tax or fee revenues that they produce. Demand is not an equity model but administrators use it extensively as a surrogate for one because of its pragmatic convenience. *Demand* entails allocating resources on the basis of consumption and/or vociferous advocacy or complaints. The allocating characteristics of demand are arbitrary, inconsistent, and unpredictable.

The three models of equity represent alternate approaches to vertical equity. Accompanying vertical equity is the principle of horizontal equity, which states that citizens who are members of the same subgroups (for example, same family size ... in tax/income levels) should receive similar benefits and pay the same amount

It is li...
even within
those services. ...rnate models of equity will be applied to different services
should evolve thro... ...diction, because of the differing characteristics of
tunity should be reco... ...ropriate equity model for a particular service
point of departure should ... three basic principles: (1) equal oppor-
and (3) there should ... all ca... ...departure; (2) deviations from this
below which quantity and quality ... benefit the least advantaged;
The prevailing pattern of service ... floor for each service
elected officials, administrators, and str...
exercise influence through the budgetary p... ...actions of
fluence through their formulation of decision ru...
and policy directives of elected representatives; wh... ...officials
influence the effective equity model through their in...
rules in their direct interaction with citizens.

The equity issue has only recently been addressed by ac...
scholars. Resolution of the inherent conflicts of various mode...

improbable, or at best far off, because of the complexity and normative nature of equity. Nevertheless, allocation issues should be confronted, since making no choice or leaving things as they are amounts to tacit acceptance of the prevailing equity model. In the context of marketing government and social services, the equity issue is pervasive. It intrudes into every marketing mix decision, and it is an important ingredient in differentiating marketing in the public and private sectors.

NOTES

1. Lineberry, R.L., *Equity and Urban Policy*. Beverly Hills, CA: Sage Publications, 1977, p. 13.
2. Chitwood, S.R., "Social Equity and Social Service Productivity," *Public Administration Review*. vol. 34 No. 1, January/February 1974, p. 30.
3. Jones, B.D., Greenberg, S., and Drew, J., *Service Delivery in the City*. New York: Longman, 1980, p. 2.
4. Lucy, W.H., and Mladenka, K.R., *Equity and Urban Service Distribution*. Report prepared for U.S. Department of Housing and Urban Development. Washington, DC: National Technical Information Service, 1977, p. 18.
5. Ibid., p. 4.
6. Chitwood, "Social Equity," p. 33.
7. Lipsky, M., *Street Level Bureaucracy*. New York: Russell Sage Foundation, 1980, p. 2.
8. Hirsch, F., *Social Limits to Growth*. Cambridge, MA: Harvard University Press, 1976, p. 18.
9. Masotti, L.H., and Lineberry, R.L., *The New Urban Politics*. Cambridge, MA: Ballinger Publishers, 1976, p. 11.
10. Adapted from Hawkins, L., "A Grassroots Movement to Stop a Change in Service Delivery Rules." Unpublished paper, Wayne State University, 1977. Discussed in Jones et al., *Service Delivery*, pp. 243–245.
11. *Hawkins v. Town of Shaw, Mississippi*, 437 F.2d 1286 (5th Cir. 1971).
12. Ibid.
13. Rossum, R.A., "The Rise and Fall of Equalization Litigation," *The Urban Interest*, vol. 2 No. 2, Spring 1980, p. 3.
14. Ibid., p. 5.
15. Ibid., p. 2.
16. Schumacher, M.D. "Equal Protection: The Right to Equal Municipal Services," *Brooklyn Law Review*. vol. 37 No. 2, Spring 1971, pp. 568–587.
17. Jones et al., *Service Delivery*, p. 13.
18. Sharrard, T., *Social Welfare and Urban Problems*. New York: Columbia University Press, 1968, p. 10.
19. Jacob, H. *Urban Justice: Law and Order in American Cities*. Englewood Cliffs, NJ: Prentice-Hall, 1973, p. 1.
20. Jones et al., *Service Delivery*, p. 20.
21. Antunes, G., and Mladenka, K., "The Politics of Local Services and Service Distribution." In Masotti and Lineberry (eds.), *Urban Politics*, p. 159.
22. Lineberry, *Equity*, p. 183.

23. See, for example, the findings reported by Levy, F.S., Meltsner, A.J., and Wildavsky, A., *Urban Outcomes: Schools, Streets, and Libraries*. Berkeley, CA: University of California Press, 1974.

24. Lineberry, *Equity*, p. 186.

25. Thurow, L.C., *The Zero-Sum Society*. New York: Penguin Books, 1980, p. 17.

26. Merget, A.E., "Achieving Equity in an Era of Fiscal Constraints." In R.W. Burchell and D. Listokin (eds.), *Cities Under Stress*. Piscatataway, NJ: Center for Urban Policy Research, State University of New Jersey, 1981, p. 406.

27. Thurow, *Zero-Sum*, p. 406.

28. Chitwood, "Social Equity," p. 13.

29. Levy et al., *Urban Outcomes*, pp. 227–228.

30. Rawls, J., *A Theory of Justice*. Cambridge, MA: The Belknap Press, 1971, p. 507.

31. Thurow, *Zero-Sum*, p. 195.

32. Rich, R.C., "Equity and Institutional Design in Urban Service Delivery." In R.L. Lineberry (ed.), *The Politics and Economics of Urban Services*. Beverly Hills, CA: Sage Publications, 1978, p. 123.

33. Lucy and Mladenka, *Equity*, p. 39.

34. Rich, R.C., "Neglected Issues in the Study of Urban Service Distributions: A Research Agenda," *Urban Studies*, vol. 16, No. 2, June 1979, p. 152.

35. Gans, H.J., *More Equality*. New York: Random House, 1973, p. 67; Rawls, *Theory*, pp. 78, 151; Vernez, G.S., "Notes on Alternative Conceptions of Equity." Unpublished paper prepared for presentation in the lecture series "Equity in the City," Columbia University, Continuing Educational Program, 1976, p. 11.

36. Jones et al., *Service Delivery*, p. 89.

37. Lucy, W.H., "Equity and Planning for Local Services," *American Planning Association Journal*, October 1981, p. 449.

38. Lucy and Mladenka, *Equity*, p. 26.

39. Ibid., p. 39.

40. Lucy, "Equity and Planning," p. 449.

41. Lineberry, *Equity*, p. 157.

42. Jones et al., *Service Delivery*, p. 117.

43. Jones, B.D., and Kaufman, C., "The Distribution of Urban Public Services: A Preliminary Model," *Administration and Society*, vol. 6, No. 3, November 1974, p. 345.

44. Jones et al., *Service Delivery*, p. 227.

45. Chitwood, "Social Equity," p. 34.

46. Porter D.O., and Porter, T.W., "Social Equity and Fiscal Federalism," *Public Administration Review*, Vol. 34 No. 1, January/February 1974, p. 36.

47. Chitwood, "Social Equity," p. 34.

48. Lucy and Mladenka, *Equity*, p. 30.

49. Lucy, W.H., Gilbert, D., and Birkhead, G.S., "Equity in Local Service Distribution," *Public Administration Review*, vol. 37 No. 6, November/December 1977, pp. 687–697.

50. Ibid., p. 688.

51. Lucy and Mladenka, *Equity*, p. 37.

52. Levy et al., *Urban Outcomes*, p. 246.

53. Adapted from Nivola, P.S., *The Urban Service Problem*. Lexington, MA: Heath, 1979, p. 151.

54. Thurow, *Zero-Sum*, p. 199.

as exhibiting public service characteristics. Since all citizens are perceived to benefit from such public services, these services are paid for by a system of compulsory payments through the taxation system and offered to beneficiaries at zero price. Pure public services such as these take the compensatory equity model to the extreme of equal results or equal outcomes: All citizens receive equal benefit outputs regardless of the amount they pay through the tax system.

The model of equity selected also has implications for promotional strategies. Market equity models are most likely to be directed to better educated groups or areas, since these markets are able and willing to pay for extra increments of service. Communicating to such groups is usually easy: They are more likely to be active information searchers and responsive to desired communication messages.[68]

An equal opportunity model implies that an agency must not only provide a service but also ensure that all have equal knowledge of the service's want-satisfying potential. Only then can all citizens be said to have an equal opportunity to take advantage of the service. In the case of compensatory equity, the communication of a service's availability and its potential for meeting the target market's needs become even more important. Yet these markets in which communication is most necessary are those for whom it is most difficult to design effective communications. When either of these two equity models are adopted, considerable effort will be required to develop effective promotional strategies.

Different equity models will be preferred by different communities and subcultures because society is not a homogeneous mass with uniform tastes and values. Each individual's notions of what is equitable are tempered by his or her background and social position. It would be futile and arrogant for a particular individual to assert that the model he or she prefers is "best" for society. In the final analysis, models are a question of values[69] and subject to an increasingly vigorous debate. As Fred Hirsch[70] has noted, this discussion of who should get what is only beginning to grapple with the conflicts between the desires of various groups and between various ways of looking at equity.

Nevertheless, marketers interested in applying their concepts and techniques in the public sector need to understand, address, and investigate the implications of the equity issue, since it is a fundamental differentiating factor between marketing public and private services. Consideration of equity in public service delivery is a prerequisite to the effective marketing of public services, not only because of its impact on allocation and distribution decisions, but also because of its relationship to evaluation, segmentation, pricing, and promotion decisions.

SUMMARY

Decisions about the allocation of public services touch the lives of all citizens. An inextricable link exists between target market selection decisions and allocation decisions: Both are concerned with who should be served and what proportion of available resources should be devoted to particular subgroups.

The emerging concern with allocation decisions has been stimulated primarily by a scarcity of resources and to a lesser extent by the potential influence of the courts. Declining agency budgets and the accompanying withdrawal of services is likely to invite closer scrutiny of the allocative fairness of those services.

No generalized pattern of consistent winners and losers has emerged from empirical studies. Rather, service allocation has been characterized as having "unpatterned inequities." The winners and losers appear to differ from community to community and even from service to service.

The guiding principle of all allocation decisions is the concept of equity. Three alternate equity models are recognized, each offering different guidelines for implementation. *Equal opportunity* entails distributing equal resources and amounts of services to all citizens regardless of need or the amount of taxes or fees paid. *Compensatory equity* entails allocation of services so that disadvantaged groups or areas receive extra increments of resources. *Market equity* entails allocating services to citizens or neighborhoods in proportion to the tax or fee revenues that they produce. Demand is not an equity model but administrators use it extensively as a surrogate for one because of its pragmatic convenience. *Demand* entails allocating resources on the basis of consumption and/or vociferous advocacy or complaints. The allocating characteristics of demand are arbitrary, inconsistent, and unpredictable.

The three models of equity represent alternate approaches to vertical equity. Accompanying vertical equity is the principle of horizontal equity, which states that citizens who are members of the same subgroups (for example, same family size and income levels) should receive similar benefits and pay the same amount in taxes.

It is likely that alternate models of equity will be applied to different services even within the same jurisdiction, because of the differing characteristics of those services. Choosing the appropriate equity model for a particular service should evolve through consideration of three basic principles: (1) equal opportunity should be recognized as the point of departure; (2) deviations from this point of departure should be encouraged if they benefit the least advantaged; and (3) there should in all cases be a stated minimum floor for each service below which quantity and quality will not fall.

The prevailing pattern of service allocation results from the interactions of elected officials, administrators, and street-level bureaucrats. Elected officials exercise influence through the budgetary process; administrators exercise influence through their formulation of decision rules in response to the budgetary and policy directives of elected representatives; while street-level bureaucrats influence the effective equity model through their interpretation of decision rules in their direct interaction with citizens.

The equity issue has only recently been addressed by administrators and scholars. Resolution of the inherent conflicts of various models of equity is

55. Antunes, G., and Mladenka, K., "The Politics of Local Services and Service Distribution." In Masotti and Lineberry (eds.), *Urban Politics*, p. 154.

56. Lipsky, *Street Level*, p. xi.

57. Crecine, J., *Governmental Problem Solving*. Chicago: Rand McNally, 1969, p. 5.

58. Wilson, J.Q., *Varieties of Police Behavior*. Cambridge, MA: Harvard University Press, 1969, p. 231.

59. Mladenka, K.R. "The Urban Bureaucracy and the Chicago Political Machine: Who Gets What and the Limits to Political Control," *The American Political Science Review*, vol. 74 No. 4, December 1980, pp. 991–998.

60. Lineberry, *Equity*, p. 154.

61. Adapted from a summary of the findings of Levy et al., *Urban Outcomes*, discussed by Antunes and Mladenka, "Politics of Local Services," p. 161.

62. Lipsky, M., "Street Level Bureaucracy and the Analysis of Urban Reform." In G. Frederickson (ed.), *Neighborhood Control in the 1970's*. New York: Chandler, 1973, pp. 103–115.

63. Weatherley, R., and Lipsky, M., "Street Level Bureaucrats and Institutional Innovation: Implementing Special-Education Reform," *Harvard Educational Review*, vol. 47, No. 2, May 1977, p. 172.

64. Lipsky, "Street Level Bureaucracy," 1980, p. 4.

65. Weatherley and Lipsky, "Street Level Bureaucrats," p. 172.

66. Rich, R.C., "Equity and Institutional Design in Urban Service Delivery," *Urban Affairs Quarterly*, vol. 12, No. 3, March 1977, p. 129.

67. Rawls, *Theory*, p. 507.

68. Engel, J.F., and Blackwell, R.D., *Consumer Behavior* (4th ed.). Hinsdale, IL: Dryden Press, 1973, p. 382.

69. Falkenberg, A.W., and Wish, J.R., "Efficiency Equity and Freedom of Choice as Evaluative Criteria for Normative Marketing Management." In C.W. Lamb, Jr. and P.M. Dunne (eds.), *Theoretical Developments in Marketing*. Chicago: American Marketing Association, 1980, p. 138.

70. Hirsch, *Social Limits*, p. 152.

EIGHT

Strategic Distribution of Services

The previous chapter addressed the equity question "Who gets what?" The discussion in this chapter focuses on the subsequent distribution questions "How?", "Where?", and "When?". Here we attempt to develop a framework for analyzing service distribution that allows the models of equity discussed in Chapter 7 to be operationalized.

An agency's capacity for distributing its service offerings to potential client groups where and when they want them is typically a key variable in determining the success of those service offerings. The determining influence of distribution has been vividly illustrated by findings from public transit studies. In San Francisco the mass transit system's share of the travel market was found to be a function of the accessibility of origins and destinations from stopping points on the transit route.[1] Similarly, a Toronto transit study revealed that its market share of potential riders was directly related to the time required to walk and/or drive to the suburban station and from the downtown station to potential riders' destinations.[2]

Distribution decisions usually involve relatively long-term commitments. Once a decision has been made to distribute the service through a particular channel and outlet, consumer expectations, political realities, and inertia make it difficult to change that decision. Product pricing, and promotion strategies frequently can be changed more easily than distribution decisions.

IMPLICATIONS OF DEPENDENCE ON FACILITIES[3]

The extent to which a service is dependent on, or independent of, fixed facilities has important implications for distribution decisions. Facility-dependent services such as libraries and parks are immobile, capital-intensive, and sited at discrete points around the community. In contrast, facility-independent services are "deliverable." That is, they can be separated from the facility.

The distribution pattern of facility-independent services can be changed relatively easily, but dependent services are characterized by *distributional uncontrollability*. Once in place their distribution pattern cannot be adjusted easily by subsequent policy makers. Change is likely to be glacial because the basic distribution pattern can be altered only incrementally, as more facilities are added to the present supply. The existing pattern will always be more a function of past than present decisions.

Facility-dependent services confer allocational spillover benefits to a much greater degree than do independent services. In addition to the benefits accruing to users, secondary benefits or costs accrue indirectly to those individuals who live or own property near the facilities, regardless of their own use patterns. These *external* effects can be primarily negative (a sanitation dump) or positive (parks or libraries), depending on the perceptions of the individuals affected, and they may impact the value of property.

Because of these two features (uncontrollability and externality), the distribution of facility-dependent services is usually perceived to be a more important decision than a decision concerning the distribution of facility-independent services. Facility location decisions are particularly significant because they are essentially irrevocable. For this reason such decisions are more likely to lead to organized citizen activity and to more careful justification by policy makers than decisions related to facility-independent services.

In an agency in which services are separable from physical facilities, personnel can overcome a clientele's travel constraints by delivering services at locations that are convenient to them. Counseling, for example, need not take place in agency offices. It may take place at any location where counselors and clients can meet. Probation services, outreach youth programs, and educational courses taught on commuter trains are other examples of deliverable services. This flexibility often provides street-level bureaucrats with more discretion, and hence they play a more substantial role in distribution decisions. The essential differences between facility-dependent and facility-independent services are summarized in Table 8.1.

OVERVIEW OF THE DISTRIBUTION DECISION PROCESS MODEL

Any service distribution pattern emerges from completing a series of related tasks. These tasks may usefully be viewed as comprising a system, which was defined in Chapter 1 as a set of interacting elements.[4] The planning and operational tasks of this system are illustrated in Figure 8.1. This model is the focus of the remaining discussion in this Chapter.

In Chapter 7 we emphasized that equity can be interpreted in a variety of ways. In Figure 8.1 its definition is shown as the essential starting point in any

TABLE 8.1. Differences Between Facility-Dependent and Facility-Independent Services

	Facility Dependent	Facility Independent
Distributional uncontrollability	High	Low
External effects	High	Low
Incremental change	Yes	No
Street-level bureaucratic influence	Low	High

Source: Adapted from Jones, B.D., Greenberg, S., and Drew, J., *Service Delivery in the City*. New York, Longman, 1980, pp. 186–193.

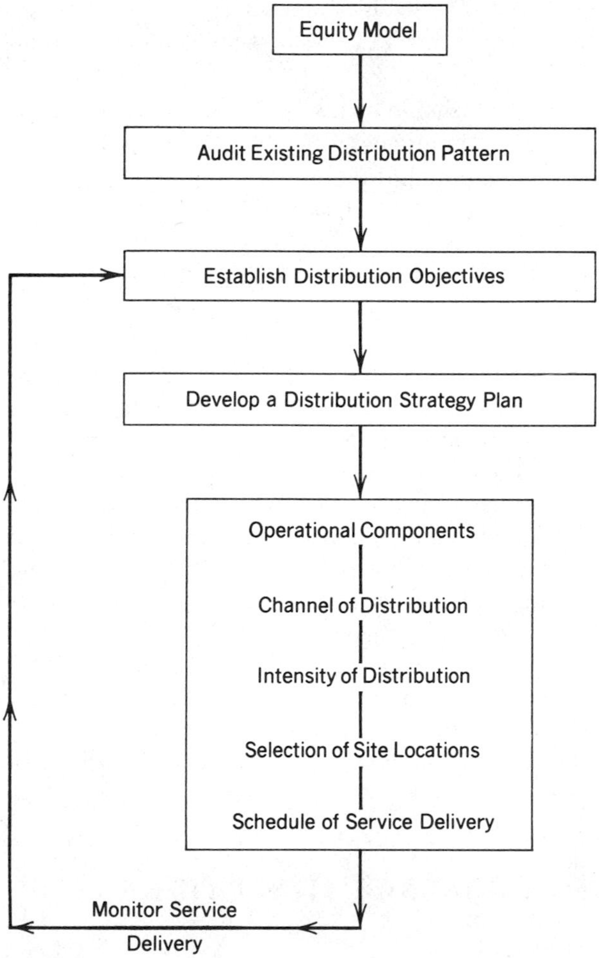

Figure 8.1. A Model of the Distribution Decision Process for Government and Social Service Agencies.

discussion of service distribution: Alternate equity models will lead to different distribution patterns.

The first task in distributing services is developing a plan that will guide the delivery pattern of any particular service in a manner as consistent as possible with the desired equity model. The approach is similar to that suggested in Chapter 3 for developing a total marketing plan. The starting point is an audit to identify who is getting how much of the service at the present time. When the existing allocation pattern is known, then objectives are set to amend or perpetuate this pattern in accordance with the agency's prevailing concept of equity. At that point a distribution strategy plan that establishes how the service will be made available and accessible to citizens is developed and implemented.

The distribution plan addresses four questions:

1. Which agency/division will be responsible for delivering the service to target markets? This involves identifying, and in some cases selecting, alternative vertical and horizontal channels of distribution and types of outlets.
2. How many outlets should be used? Concern here is with the appropriate level of distribution intensity.
3. Where specifically should the outlets be located?
4. When will the service be offered?

Together these four sets of decisions—channel of distribution, intensity of distribution, selection of site locations, and schedule of service delivery—constitute the operational components of a public agency's distribution system.

It is usually much more difficult to modify the earlier than the later operational decisions. Hence, channel of distribution commitments tend to be long-term and require a major effort to amend, while scheduling decisions are relatively flexible and easy to amend.

When these interrelated distribution decisions have been made, the service is delivered and its results and impacts are monitored. These are then evaluated against the established distribution objectives. If the results are not satisfactory, appropriate adjustments to one or more of the four operational components in the distribution system can be made.

The implications of services being relatively dependent on, or independent of, facilities should be apparent in the context of this model. Clearly, it is much easier to adjust each of these four operational components to better meet distributional objectives if a service is independent than if it is dependent on facilities.

EVALUATING DISTRIBUTION PATTERNS

Both auditing and monitoring require the use of similar evaluation techniques. They differ only in that auditing is periodic and long-term, whereas monitoring is ongoing and short-term. By identifying winners and losers, auditing provides the information base necessary for developing objectives to redress any inconsistencies with the prevailing equity model. Ongoing monitoring evaluation efforts measure progress toward achieving established objectives. Every evaluation effort is confronted with three major difficulties: (1) determining the appropriate units of analysis, (2) determining what types of indicators are most appropriate for measuring equity, and (3) comparing services. Each of these issues is discussed in the following paragraphs.

Units of Analysis

Evaluation of the equity of service distribution involves geographic comparisons. The problem lies in selecting which sociospatial or geographic units are appropriate since different neighborhood definitions are likely to produce different analytical results. Three criteria should guide the unit-of-analysis decision:[5]

1. It should be feasible to gather data for each unit. For example, are the data already available or is it possible to gather information on amount of solid waste collected per household or on weekly number of public transit rides made per household?

2. Population data and physical characteristics data (such as housing) should be available for the geographic region of interest in order that it can be related to the service data which are gathered. For example, it may be desirable to relate the service data to the income or race of residents in each geographical unit.

3. The geographical unit should be relevant to decisions that may be made about the service.

The most useful unit of analysis is probably the service district, for reallocation of resources can then be made between districts if inequitable distribution patterns are revealed. Different agencies, however, frequently divide service districts differently. For example, each firehouse is intended to serve a particular area, which is likely to be different from the public schools' service area, and different from refuse collection routes. Thus, it is difficult to make a systematic comparison of the cumulative level of service that various parts of the jurisdiction receive.[6]

Types of Equity Evaluation Indicators[7]

The relative success of service distribution efforts in achieving equity objectives can only be meaningfully evaluated if appropriate indicators are developed for measuring equity. Three types of possible indicators are resources, activities, and results. Resources are used to engage in activities, which achieve results.

Resources are quantitative inputs to the service distribution system that may include money, personnel, facilities, and equipment.

Activities are the way in which the resources are used. Examples include the speed with which fire fighters respond to fire alarms and suppress fires, the number or frequency of police officers who patrol streets and the number of arrests they make, or the frequency with which sanitation workers collect refuse.

Results are the qualitative outputs that measure what happens as a direct consequence of the service delivery. This indicator is the one that the average citizen is most likely to use to evaluate services. How much stolen property has been recovered? How much refuse has been collected? What is the water pressure at the tap?

Examples of indicators for measuring equity in service distribution are shown in Figure 8.2.

Resources

Expenditures ($ per 10,000 population; $ per phenomenon, such as $ per serious crime)

Personnel (number per 10,000 population; number per phenomenon, such as number per serious crime)

Equipment (playground swings per 100 children aged 12 and under)

Facilities (neighborhood park acres per 1000 population)

Activities

Frequency (refuse pick-ups per week; hours branch library open per week)

Duration (response time for police or fire from receipt of call for service to arrival on scene)

Results

Intended consequences (arrests per 100 serious crimes reported; street cleanliness rating after refuse collection; water pressure at the tap)

Unintended consequences (number of missed refuse collections per week per 100 households; complaints about unnecessary use of force by police per 100 arrests for serious crimes)

Use of services by amount (number of branch library books circulated per year; number of swimmers per day; number of park users per week)

Use of services by rate (number of branch library books circulated per year per population in service area; number of mass transit riders per day per population in service area)

Use of services by reasons (percentage of persons not using a park because of anxiety about their personal safety when using the park; percentage of persons not using mass transit for the journey to work because the relationship between transit and work schedules requires waits of 15 minutes or more)

Figure 8.2. Examples of Service Indicators. (*Source:* Lucy, W.H., and Mladenka, K.R., *Equity and Urban Service Distribution*. Report prepared for U.S. Department of Housing and Urban Development, Washington, DC: National Technical Information Service, 1977, p. 60.)

The differences among these three types of indicators can be illustrated with police services. One might analyze police distribution in terms of: (1) dollars spent or the number of police patrol officers per 1000 neighborhood residents (resource indicators); (2) miles covered patrolling, arrests made, or the average response time from receipt of a call for service until a police officer's arrival at the scene for each neighborhood (activity indicators); or (3) the clearance rate for each neighborhood, that is, the percentage of crimes cleared by the arrest of someone suspected of committing those crimes (a results indicator).

Resource indicators are probably the easiest to use because they are most readily available and most easily quantified. However, used on their own they may be misleading. Analyzing resources, such as the expenditures, personnel, and facilities that go into a neighborhood, is of little value without considering how these resources were employed or with what results.[8] Thus resource indicators should be supplemented with activity and results measures.

Unfortunately, from the analyst's viewpoint, different types of indicators may suggest different conclusions. For example, the *resources* invested in police patrols might be unequally distributed per capita, with high crime areas receiving more services. This may enable the *activities* of patrol officers, as measured by response time, to be distributed rather equally. Would that mean that results as measured by percentage of stolen property recovered would be distributed equally? Not necessarily. What about the rate at which property is stolen, in terms of robberies, burglaries, and larcenies per 1000 people? It is quite possible that the high crime area with a disproportionate number of police patrol officers would still remain a high crime area.[9]

Even if resources are allocated according to the prevailing equity model, measures may still not show that equity has actually been achieved. Equal resource inputs can lead to different service levels and different results. The relationship between resource inputs and the actual activities offered or results achieved depends on a variety of factors that may be neighborhood-specific. This was vividly illustrated in the *Beal v. Lindsay* case.[10] Puerto Rican residents living in the neighborhood of Crotona Park alleged that New York City unconstitutionally discriminated against them by failing to maintain the park in a condition equivalent to that of other multicommunity parks in the Bronx. The city showed successfully that it had made a disproportionate effort in providing maintenance and operating *inputs* in favor of Crotona Park. The failure to provide *equal results* was attributed to the high degree of vandalism at Crotona Park. The court ruled that the city could not be held responsible for these external factors that nullified its input efforts.

Other examples showing inconsistencies among different indicators are common. In fact, it has been suggested that "there may not be symmetrical relationships for indicators of resources, activities, and results for any local service."[11]

Even within each of the three indicator categories, inconsistencies between indicators are likely. For example, if *resource* indicators are to be used, which indicators will be selected? Consider the case of fire protection. Resource indicators could include: (1) capital expenditures; (2) total operational expenditures; (3) operational expenditures for one specific aspect of fire protection services, such as fire fighting; (4) number of fire fighters; and (5) operational equipment. Is money or in-kind inputs the most appropriate indicator?

> In-kind inputs raise problems of quality differentials both in manpower and equipment. Is a young fireman on the ladder truck worth less or more than an older fireman? Is a new fire truck better than a similar five-year-old fire truck? On the other hand, total operational expenditures in any service category may be expected to legitimately vary according to age of the structure and other environmental factors.[12]

A similar list of alternative indices could be developed for activities or results measurement. Indeed, if results measures are used, the different *interpretations* of any particular selected indicator make the issue even more complex. For example, a substandard street may slow traffic for some citizens, but for others, it may enhance the rustic character of the neighborhood.[13]

The different conclusions suggested by different types of indicators emphasize the desirability of using multiple measures to assess equity, rather than relying solely on resource measures. Activity measures, such as the time taken to respond to requests for service, the down time of swimming pools, or the frequency of collecting trash, add substantially to an administrator's grasp of a service issue. Results measures, which look at the results achieved by a service, are of even greater use.[14] The trade-off, of course, is that more indicators involve greater cost, and the feasibility of using more indicators is likely to vary considerably among services and jurisdictions.

The selection of appropriate indicators is more art than science. It will be a function of:[15]

1. What data are routinely available
2. How many purposes will be served by gathering additional data
3. What possibility there is that knowledge of the distribution of a particular service indicator might lead to action that otherwise would not occur
4. What the budget is for the data-gathering and analysis process

One city's experience at selecting and operationalizing a broad range of service indicators is provided in the Appendix A to this chapter.

Before leaving this section on measuring equity, it is worth pointing out the close relationship of equity with efficiency and effectiveness. Resource and activity indicators are measures of efficiency. For example, the extent to which dollars per head or response times are equitable is an efficiency measure. In contrast, result indicators are measures of effectiveness. For example, the extent to which serious crime arrests in each neighborhood are equitable is an effectiveness measure. Thus equity evaluations essentially are concerned with the relative efficiency and effectiveness of selected services across different service areas in a jurisdiction.

Comparison of Equity Distribution of Different Services

In some situations, particularly in the discretionary services such as recreation, libraries, parks, and cultural arts, measurement of equity involves trying to assess the benefits offered by very different services. For example, if concern is with the equitable distribution of recreation and park resources, how can the resources in Neighborhood *A*, comprised of four small parks, one large swimming pool, three ball parks, and a golf course, be compared with those of Neighborhood *B*, which consist of two large parks, three small swimming pools, and one recreation center? These are very different combinations of amenities and yet they all seek to provide recreational benefits. Clearly, this problem is compounded in a comparison between different types of services.

Four approaches to making these comparisons have been used. First is the visual approach. By inventorying and mapping the existing outlets for each service, and by developing transparent overlays for each service, relatively deprived and relatively well-endowed areas in terms of the quantity and quality of services can be visually identified. This information also can be computerized, using a code for each street and block. In this way comparisons among services for each block in a jurisdiction would be possible.[16] This visual pattern is then interpreted by decision makers and action taken on the basis of their subjective reaction to the existing pattern. The main strength of the visual approach is also its major weakness. It is relatively simple to do because subjective, normative judgment avoids the difficulty of objectively weighting the value of a recreation center against the value of a park or a swimming pool.

A second approach is to standardize provisions so each neighborhood has the same number of parks, fire houses, libraries, and so on. Decisions could be expressed in such terms as the number and percent of people in a specific geographic area living within a selected travel time or distance from specified facilities or services. Such standardization however, ignores the different need priorities in different neighborhoods. The question of what these priorities are comes logically prior to any question of distributional equity. It is necessary to know what benefits and services communities value most highly before the effectiveness of actual service delivery or the degree to which it is equitable can be assessed and evaluated.[17]

Third, an activity indicator such as participation or visitation could be used to facilitate equity comparisons. Lower total use of a set of neighborhood facilities (unequal results) may be interpreted to indicate unequal opportunity. However, low use of facilities may follow from less interest or demand for the services offered, as well as from fewer opportunities to use the service.

In addition, use rates fail to consider the externalities that may impact nonusers. For example, passive park areas may add to the property values of adjoining homes, while intensively used ball fields may decrease property values if they have glaring lights for late evening games and attract noisy participants and spectators who park their cars in front of homes. Clearly, these externalities provide an extra equity dimension to that of direct use.

A fourth approach is to undertake an investment inventory that measures the current appraised value of all facilities. Thus, for example, dollars invested in libraries, parks, recreation, and cultural facilities could be aggregated to identify current investment value in "quality of life" facilities in each neighborhood. In this way neighborhood inequities could be identified.

The process is simplified because consistent standardized investment values for each type of facility rather than real investment values have to be used in each neighborhood. This is important since investment value in itself serves no service purpose; it is the amount and quality of service opportunity that is relevant. Equity in investment value (resource inputs) may lead to very inequitable opportunity or results if, for example, land is much more expensive in one area of town than another. Hence a set of average values for each facility is needed. These average values may then be adjusted at each facility in order to incorporate an allowance for differences in quality between facilities (otherwise the measurement may be misleading).

This investment inventory approach facilitates better budgetary decisions for the allocation of services among different neighborhoods. At the same time, it enables the more detailed decisions of which particular types of services should receive priority in each neighborhood to be made flexibly in accordance with the wishes of individual neighborhoods.

ESTABLISHING DISTRIBUTION OBJECTIVES

Once an audit of the existing distribution pattern has been completed, it is necessary to establish or revise distribution objectives. As we saw in Chapter 3, objectives are the end results that an agency wants to obtain. These objectives (1) guide the distribution decisions and actions of the agency and (2) provide a basis for subsequent objective measurement and evaluation of progress toward the accomplishment of a desired equity model.

The distribution objectives of government and social service agencies frequently do not lend themselves to measurement because they are too general or vague. This may be unintentional, reflecting a lack of managerial knowledge or control; but adopting nonspecific objectives may also be a deliberate policy action. As discussed in Chapter 7, it is possible to criticize or support almost any equity model on a number of grounds. Hence if distribution objectives are explicitly stated, they are likely to generate controversy that generalized statements of intent may avoid.

The prevailing model of equity in an agency establishes in general terms the extent to which service distribution should shift in either direction away from the equal opportunity starting point (Figure 7.1). Objectives operationalize the equity model. They derive from an assessment of whether variations revealed by an audit in the existing distribution pattern are consistent with the prevailing equity model. Objectives should then be set to amend or perpetuate this existing variance:

> Is a 50 percent variation in arrest rates among police districts acceptable? What should be done to reduce it? Is a 25 percent variation in fire response time acceptable? What changes in fire station location, equipment and manpower are necessary to appropriately amend the existing distribution pattern? Is the variation acceptable to residents in different neighborhoods who are more than half a mile from a neighborhood park?[18]

Distribution objectives may be expressed in terms of resources, activities, and results, which were discussed in the previous section of this chapter. The Austin Parks and Recreation Department adopted the following resource-based distribution objectives for swimming pool provision in the city:

1. To provide, within a five-year period, adequate recreational swimming opportunities for all citizens by raising the level of public investment in basic swimming facilities in all ten planning zones into which the city is divided for planning purposes to $46 per capita (current mean investment in constant 1980 dollars), giving priority to those zones that have the lowest current and projected investment. Primary target areas meeting this criterion are Zones 10, 2, 1, 8, and 5.
2. To provide, within a five-year period, accessible swimming facilities for special user groups within a 15-minute automobile trip of their home. Special user groups are those that require particular facility modification and include the following: (1) mobility-impaired persons, (2) competitive swimmers, and (3) year-round swimmers.

Other examples of specific distribution objectives based on an activity or a results approach may be:

> A family counseling department that has a distribution objective of "visiting each client family in their home every month" (an activity objective).
>
> A police department that has a distribution objective of "achieving arrest rates of at least 50 percent in every neighborhood within 3 years" (a results objective).

The use of results-based objectives does sometimes create problems: It may not be clear how such objectives can be fulfilled:

> It is impossible to accomplish objectives if one does not know how. If teachers know what school inputs lead to an improvement in reading, they can calculate

how much it would cost to raise poor readers to a given level. The feasibility of achieving a given results objective could then be assessed, and a feasible objective stated. The fact is, however, that this knowledge does not exist. "At this time no one knows how to improve significantly the performance of low achievers even if high resources were made available."[19]

Distribution objectives have to be designed so they are compatible with the agency's budgetary capacity, in order that what is attempted in a given time-frame is financially feasible. Further, when distribution objectives are being established, other marketing mix decisions such as prices to be charged, programs to be offered, and promotional methods to be used also need to be considered. It was noted in Chapter 1 that the elements of the marketing mix should be viewed as interacting elements that together form a system. Therefore, distribution objectives should be carefully integrated into the overall marketing plan to achieve an integrated, cohesive strategy.

DEVELOPING A DISTRIBUTION STRATEGY PLAN

The audit of existing distribution patterns establishes "where we are now." The objectives project "what we want our distribution pattern to look like in *X* years time." The distribution strategy plan provides a blueprint of how to get from where we are now to where we want to be in *X* years time. Because the planning process is identical to that described for developing an overall marketing plan in Chapter 3, it will not be discussed further at this point. However, the four main operational components in the plan, which constitute the key issues to be resolved and acted upon, are addressed in the following section.

OPERATIONAL COMPONENTS

Four sets of decisions constitute the operational components of a public agency's distribution system (Figure 8.1). They are channel of distribution, intensity of distribution, selection of site locations, and schedule of service delivery. Each of these is discussed in the following pages.

Channel of Distribution

A channel of distribution consists of the set of organizations, agencies, and outlets that share in the responsibilities for making a service available and accessible to target populations. Channel of distribution decisions are concerned with whether an agency should attempt to deliver its offering directly to consumers, or whether it can better deliver selected offerings indirectly through involving other agencies or organizations. The starting point for effective channel decisions is determining which target markets are to be reached by the agency and the needs of these target markets. The first dimension of channel decisions relates to vertical distribution, while the second is concerned with horizontal distribution patterns. In both cases, the decision of whether to use a direct or an indirect approach is determined by assessing which approach offers the most effective, efficient, and equitable distribution of a particular service.

The third dimension is the decision on the type of outlets to be used. An agency is not restricted to using only one particular channel. Indeed, there are instances in which it is likely to be advantageous to deliver a particular offering through several different types of outlets simultaneously in order to reach different target markets.

Vertical Distribution Decisions. Vertical distribution occurs when services are delivered from a higher level of government, through intermediary government levels, to the ultimate target market. This process is somewhat analogous to a manufacturer's decision to sell either directly to customers or indirectly through retailers or wholesalers. The intermediary government levels should only be included if it is advantageous to deliver some services by using them. If any of the intermediary levels do not increase the effectiveness, efficiency, or equity of the distribution system, then they should be omitted from the delivery system and a more direct approach adopted.

Figure 8.3 illustrates three alternative distribution options that the federal government might use to distribute funds to target markets. The first option, direct distribution, entails providing funds directly to those citizens who qualify under the requirements of a program. Social Security payments are an example of this option. Alternatively, the federal government might use one or more indirect distribution alternatives. It might distribute funds to state agencies, for example, and require the state agencies either to allocate the funds to

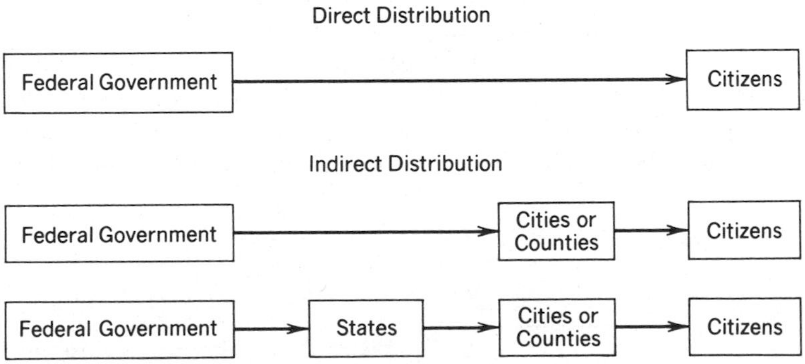

Figure 8.3. Examples of Vertical Distribution Decisions.

qualified jurisdictions in the state or to distribute the funds or services directly to qualified citizens or projects. The Land and Water Conservation Fund, which provides matching grants for acquiring or developing outdoor park and recreation facilities, is an example of this alternative. Alternatively, as in the case of general revenue sharing, the federal government may decide it is more efficient for some programs to by-pass state government and distribute funds directly to local cities or counties.

Agencies within the vertical channel do not always work in harmony. Conflicts may emerge in situations in which the objectives at one level of government can only be achieved if another level cooperates. For example, the welfare program Aid to Families with Dependent Children (AFDC) is regularly and partially funded by the federal government, but it is actually delivered by state governments. Conflicts arise because what one level of government intends is not necessarily what another level wants to do or is capable of doing.

Horizontal Distribution Decisions. Horizontal distribution relates to alternate distribution strategies adopted within a single level of government. Three alternate approaches are illustrated in Figure 8.4. The direct provider role is the model many agencies traditionally have adopted. In this approach, the agency typically assumes exclusive responsibility for planning, organizing, and distributing services and facilities.

Two problems associated with exclusive use of the direct provider model have led many agencies to adopt facilitator and/or outreach roles as additional modes of service delivery. The first problem is that many citizens are unable, or unwilling for a variety of reasons, to go to distribution outlets to use the services offered. This has led some agencies to expand their traditional approach to incorporate an outreach role. The second problem is the high cost associated with direct provider and outreach approaches, which has caused agencies to consider serving as a facilitator and encouraging others to deliver selected services.

Outreach Role. Outreach has been defined as "the effort that takes place when a social service agency reaches out and assists through personal contacts those citizens systematically excluded from, unaware of, or unreceptive to an agency's service or those of related agencies."[20] Traditionally, many public agencies have restricted their distribution efforts to simply administering a facility. They have developed passive facilities to serve the public that showed up and used them. Dependence on facilities prevented them from doing more.

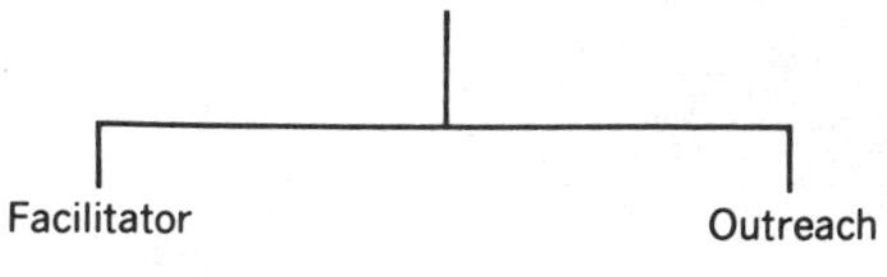

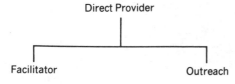

Figure 8.4. Alternative Horizontal Distribution Decions.

Some recognized, however, that their services could be attractively offered to new client groups through outreach efforts. The concept is not new:

> Mobile libraries were first introduced in 1905 when a horse-drawn wagon operating out of Hagerstown, Maryland serviced local rural areas. The motorized variety was widely in use before World War I and grew in popularity until well after World War II. Today there are at least 1,500 mobile libraries in operation in the U.S., although some agencies have replaced them by opening more branch libraries or by using a mail order service approach.[21]

Emphasis is placed on reaching out beyond the confines of a facility or traditional outlets to assist potential client groups. There is no precise model to guide this kind of distribution. Outreach exemplifies a marketing orientation of delivering services that particular groups of people want directly to them instead of expecting those client groups to find their way to the agency's facilities.

Facilitator Role. This broadened approach to distributing services emphasizes the agency's role as a facilitator or enabler of service offerings rather than as an exclusive provider. Implicit in adopting this role is a recognition that the agency alone, relying exclusively on its own resources, cannot meet all the service needs of a community. Adoption of the facilitator role requires the agency to serve as an enabling agent and take on the tasks of coordination, referral, and technical assistance.

The Austin Parks and Recreation Department, for example, facilitates the distribution of some services by financing selected community education programs operated by school districts within the city. Their rationale is that these services can be distributed more efficiently by using this indirect approach since the school systems have conveniently located facilities and qualified staff available. Indirect distribution networks may include private as well as public sector organizations. For example, an indirect distribution system for providing food for the needy includes retail grocers who accept food stamps in lieu of cash. Medicare and Medicaid are also examples of public/private sector collaboration in the distribution of social services.

Increasing the facilitator role means encouraging commercial enterprises to distribute particular services to relieve the agency of the cost of provision. This emerging movement towards "privatization of public services" requires the agency to adopt an open-minded enabling approach. It has been suggested that by the year 2000, police, fire, street maintenance, sewage treatment, and other services in many cities might be performed on a contractual basis by private corporations. Indeed in some jurisdictions, each of these services is currently offered by private companies. For example, private fire protection is being provided to 18 percent of Arizona's population by Rural/Metro Fire Department, headquartered in Scottsdale.[22]

The major concern in encouraging private sector take-over of services is that inequities may occur. For example, if all public recreation facilities were leased to a commercial operator, they could probably be operated profitably. However, those market segments with little profit potential, such as the handicapped, senior citizens, low-income groups and children, may be ignored.

The facilitative function can include the agency assuming the role of a referral agent. In this situation the agency acts as a broker, providing a connection between the service needs of community residents and the supply of opportunities available to satisfy them.

The facilitation of integrative arrangements and provision of services by others is emerging rapidly as an alternative distribution mode in response to diminishing budgets, rising maintenance and operation costs, and greater service demands.

Type of Outlet Decisions. In Chapters 5 and 6 the concept of market segmentation was described and strategies for selecting client groups were discussed. The selection of target markets will directly shape decisions concerned with what type of outlets should be used. If an agency adopts a differentiated target market strategy, it must also consider multiple types of distribution outlets.

There is often a tendency to develop standardized distribution systems designed to accommodate common needs shared by *all* clients. Unfortunately, attempting to accommodate the common needs shared by *all* often results in failure to adequately respond to the particular distribution needs of *any* market segment.

Figure 8.5 provides a simple example of how a library might use different types of outlets to reach various market segments effectively. The *main library* appeals to researchers and others who desire an extensive collection of resources at one location as well as persons who seek specialized sorts of information and/or services. Most people who use *branch libraries* seek either leisure reading materials or limited research information. The main appeal of the *bookmobile* is its convenience to users. *Outreach programs* have improved library services

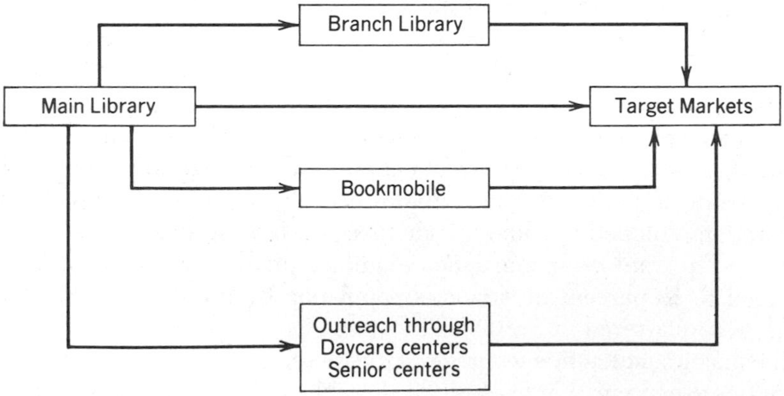

Figure 8.5. Different Types of Outlets for Library Services.

when offered in association with senior citizen centers, churches, day care centers, and headstart programs.

Each of the four target markets have different needs and different distribution preferences. By providing different types of outlets the library is able to reach a larger portion of its total market and provide services consistent with customer needs. All markets that are appropriate for segmentation should also be considered candidates for different types of distribution outlets.

Intensity of Distribution

After determining which channels and types of outlets are to be used for distributing a service, the next decision is to identify how many outlets should be provided. Intensity of distribution refers to the relative availability of a service to the consumer. With reference to Figure 8.5, the question becomes how many main libraries, branch libraries, bookmobiles, and outreach programs will be offered? There are three different courses of action, but they are not really compartmentalized. Instead they form a continuum, or points on a scale, running from *intensive* distribution through *selective* to *exclusive* distribution.

Generally, the intensity of distribution of a service should meet but not exceed the needs and preferences of target markets. Too few outlets may fail to provide the needed level of service and too many outlets may incur unnecessary costs. Although the marketing concept directs us to satisfy client wants, this has to be achieved within some constraints; otherwise, it can be carried to illogical extremes. The term "marketing mania" has been used to describe organizations that become obsessively responsive to the fleeting whims of a clientele without adequate concern for cost considerations.[23] The decision regarding intensity of distribution should be guided by the distribution objectives; but it will also be influenced by such factors as the financial condition of the agency, degree of dependence upon facilities, the availability and extent of complementary or similar services offered by other agencies, type of outlets desired, and volume of demand expected.

A basic factor influencing intensity decisions is the trade-off between costs and accessibility. Intensity of distribution, accessibility, and costs are closely interrelated. The greater the intensity of distribution, the greater the accessibility of a service but the higher the cost.

Intensity of distribution can be viewed in terms of both facilities and services (Figure 8.6). The intensity of distribution of *facilities* refers to the relative number of physical facilities that an agency operates. The intensity of distribution of *services* refers to the relative number of outlets at which a person can receive the service.

Intensive Distribution. Intensive distribution of facilities entails having many physical facilities to service the target market clientele. At an extreme, intensive distribution of *facilities* would entail facilities adjacent to each potential user's residence—for example, roads, street lights, sidewalks, and

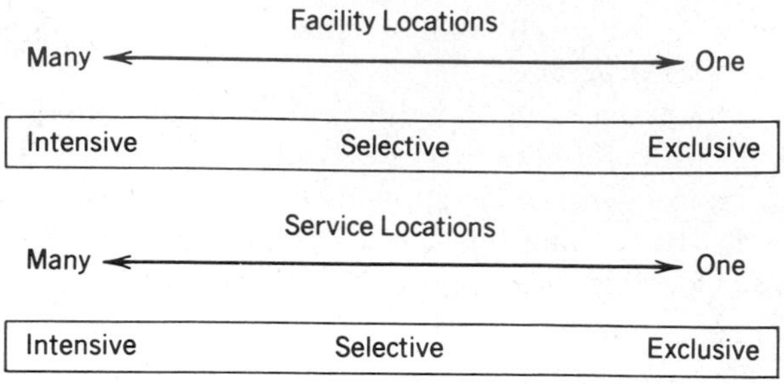

Figure 8.6. Intensity of Distribution Continua.

storm sewers. Alternatively, intensive distribution may mean making facilities available in most neighborhoods. Frequently, totlots are distributed intensively so that they are within walking distance for all children. Accessibility is maximized. Intensive distribution of *services*, on the other hand, entails providing a service directly to clients in their homes (welfare workers), or having it readily available and within easy access (police officers and building inspectors).

Intensive distribution appears to be ideally compatible with the marketing concept since distance and travel time are major deterrents to facility and service use. However, this is not necessarily the case because intensity of distribution is directly related to costs. Since nonusers of services are also taxpayers, the marketing concept requires that attention be paid to their wants as well as to those of users. Frequently nonusers or their political representatives desire that reasonable economies of distribution be achieved at the expense of client convenience.

Selective Distribution. Selective distribution entails having *facilities* and/or *services* available at several outlets. Selective distribution presumes that members of target markets are willing and able to travel some distance to use the facility or receive the service. It also recognizes the inability of agencies to provide some services directly to all users. Selective distribution is a compromise between the economies of scale associated with exclusive distribution and the preference of clients for personalized service delivery. Community centers are typically selectively distributed. Other examples include schools and parks within a community, branch libraries, satellite welfare offices, and family planning clinics. If a selective distribution strategy is adopted, locations should be selected that are most convenient for the target clientele. For example:

Young adult pregnancy counseling clinics should be near where young adults live and work

Welfare offices should be near where clients live

Social Security and legal services should be near senior citizens' homes

Playgrounds should be near where families with young children live[24]

Exclusive Distribution. Exclusive distribution is the provision of *facilities* and/or *services* in only one location within a community or target market area. Immobile facilities offering specialized services, such as hospitals, often use exclusive distribution because their services are used relatively infrequently. Exclusive distribution has the advantage of minimized costs and maximized control. The disadvantage, of course, is inconvenience to a large portion of the target market.

By having one large library in a major city, duplication of books, staff, and building costs can be avoided. The citizen will gain to the extent that he or she will find an extensive collection of books. Restricting the number of locations forces the client to travel, costing him or her more in terms of time, transportation, convenience, and personal energy.

A state university may be an example of exclusive distribution. The cost of running the university is minimized by operating only one campus, but the travel costs to clients of attending classes at that institution are likely to be high. If the university decides to distribute its educational product more intensively throughout the state, it will face all the classic distribution questions faced by large business firms: how many branch locations should be established, how large should they be, where should they be located, and what specialization should take place at each branch?[25]

The advent of more sophisticated communication equipment has enabled some once-exclusive facilities to adopt an intensive or selective service model. College courses taught through the mail or over public TV are examples. In some areas the judicial courts are operating similarly:

> To save time and money, a growing number of judges and attorneys are changing the classic model of litigation in American courts. Instead of relying on in-court appearances, they are conducting legal proceedings by holding conferences on speaker telephones. This expedites the speed with which cases can be dealt and offers clients substantial savings in time and travel costs.
>
> In civil cases, telephone conferences are used to schedule conferences, pretrial conferences, hearings on motions and trial dates. Whenever the matter is reasonably simple it can be settled by phone without bringing attorneys into court. The technique is especially useful in large, sparsely populated areas where court jurisdictions span great distances and attorneys therefore often have to travel long distances.[26]

Thus it appears that an agency may have nine intensity-of-distribution alternatives. Figure 8.7 illustrates these alternative strategies and suggests possible services that might most appropriately fit into the nine cells.

Trends in Distribution Intensity. In the 1960s and 1970s social service delivery tended to move away from exclusive distribution toward decentralization and diffusion of services, which led to more selective or intensive distribution patterns. For example, there was a movement to close problem-ridden and ineffective state prisons and correctional centers in favor of

FACILITIES \ SERVICES	Intensive	Selective	Exclusive
Intensive	Street lights Storm sewers Roads Neighborhood playgrounds	Supervised play at selected neighborhood playgrounds	Performing arts program in the major city park Interpretive nature programs
Selective	Police Fire Welfare workers	Community health care Parks Schools Adult education classes Libraries Community centers	Blood donor drive Public agency day camps
Exclusive	Garbage collection Housing inspectors Health inspectors College courses via mail or public TV	Bookmobiles	Hospitals Universities Judicial courts City hall Zoo Animal shelter

Figure 8.7. Intensity of Distribution Alternatives.

community-oriented places where the number of clients was smaller and the administrative problems more manageable. Similarly, some state and county licensing services began locating branch offices in neighborhood shopping centers for consumer convenience.[27] Many agencies tried to make services more accessible to residents by providing local service centers that were open for extended hours and on weekends, and by coordinating the delivery of a variety of local services at a single location.

The decentralization movement was motivated by the belief that this would help to reach the unserved members of target markets. Physical accessibility was accompanied in some cases by a more open, welcoming atmosphere and improved style of intake and operation.[28] Without decentralization it was argued that certain services were not available near where people lived and experienced most of their service needs. Too many potential clients lacked the time, money, or personal energy to get to a centralized location.

The fiscal constraint movement that gained momentum in the late 1970s may lead to a reversal of the decentralization movement, back toward more exclusive distribution patterns. By closing local facilities and centralizing services, costs to the agency can be reduced. However, these costs are transferred to the potential consumer in terms of time, transportation, and convenience.

Selecting Locations

After channel and intensity decisions have been made the agency is confronted with the task of identifying specific site locations through which a service will be delivered. This decision is more critical for facility-dependent services rather than facility-independent services because of its irrevocability, spillover effect, and long-term impact on distribution.

It has been said that when Conrad Hilton was asked to identify the most important factors in determining the success or failure of a hotel, he responded by saying that there were three important determinants of a hotel's success: location, location, and location. Likewise, leading retail stores will generally not locate in a city unless they are able to secure a site that provides a high degree of visibility and convenient access to their target market(s). They are willing to pay a substantial premium in order to acquire such preferred locations.

If the location and size of a facility are not optimum, then no matter how good its subsequent service offerings, management, promotion or pricing strategies, the facility is unlikely to achieve its full potential. Conversely, a well-located facility may be successful in spite of inadequacies in operating management. A site location is good only if it is accessible and visible to target markets.

Access is primarily a function of geographic proximity to potential users. *The general conclusion about location and utilization is that use tends to vary directly with distance from the facility.* Many studies have illustrated this point. The thinning out of users with distance strongly suggests that consumers do look upon travel with its accompaniments of time, transport fare, and so forth as a cost to be paid for obtaining services. Beyond a certain point they are unwilling to pay the cost.

The *visibility* criterion requires that members of target markets be made aware of a service offering by seeing it. Without awareness that a service exists, it obviously will not be used. The only ways to learn of the existence of any government or social service offering are to hear about it, see it, or see a reference to it. The major promotional tool public agencies possess is locating their facilities and services where they are very visible to target markets.

Reasons for Inappropriate Facility Location. Public agencies often have failed to recognize the crucial importance of location. "The development of our existing pattern of hospitals has been due rather to social attitudes, administrative convenience and economic expediency, than to the medical needs of the community."[29] Although the writer was referring to hospitals in England, the statement is even more appropriate in the United States,[30] and it may be generalized beyond hospitals to embrace most other types of public facilities. Why are public facilities located inequitably or inappropriately?

First, some government and social service agencies have inherited facilities built a long time ago. These facilities may reflect an orientation toward a distribution of population and target markets that has changed considerably since they were built. Facilities established to serve one socioeconomic group may be serving a very different group of people today. The first group may have left the area and been supplanted by people with different social, racial, or economic characteristics and hence different lifestyles and wants. For example, the distribution of firehouses over time is likely to become inappropriate. Neighborhoods once filled with old wooden buildings may be replaced by high-rise office buildings, or a district of once-fine apartment buildings may become overcrowded and run down. Travel and response times to fire calls may then be beyond acceptable limits.[31] However, the costs of abandoning an existing facility for a new one in a superior location may be prohibitive. Because of the expense of large facility and land development, past decisions will heavily influence who gets what publicly provided facilities.

Second, the land and/or building may have been donated. This is a particularly dominant factor in explaining the distribution of parks since many cities have acquired over half their park land from donations. In such cases, the site of a park is dictated by the donor, regardless of equity considerations or the desires of the consuming public. In some instances, the source of the "donation" may have been the federal government. Facilities or services may be offered at a particular location because only that location qualified under the terms of a particular federal grant program.

Third, local, county, state, or federal offices often are centralized in one building or complex because it is administratively convenient for the agencies to be located in close juxtaposition. This expedites bureaucratic procedures, but these offices may not be in the most desirable location from the consumers' perspective.

Fourth, facilities are located in a particular place because a site was available. There are, for example, many areas where parks should be located and where decision makers would like to site them, but no space is available. This problem is particularly acute in central urban areas.

Finally, locations are selected because the land is relatively inexpensive. This is perhaps the most popular criterion currently in use for site selection. This short-sighted reasoning fails to consider the potentially increased benefits of revenues and/or greater utilization that may accrue to an agency if a facility were located on a more expensive, but more visible and accessible site. Proper site selection entails an analysis not only of cost considerations but also of revenue and benefit considerations, including accessibility of the location for the target markets it is intended to serve.

Sometimes public jurisdictions rationalize that they cannot afford to purchase prime locations because the cost of acquisition is too high or because the opportunity cost of removing valuable property from the tax rolls would adversely affect the jurisdiction's tax base. For these reasons public facilities are often sited at less visible and less accessible locations that are not sought by commercial interests. This short-run decrease in costs may actually increase long-run costs and inhibit the agency from achieving its marketing goals.

Adopting a Marketing Approach to Facility Location. Recently a more conscientious effort has seemingly been made to adopt a marketing approach to location selection. This increased consumer orientation is illustrated by the following decision rules for prioritizing new branch library locations. Some combination of the following four decision rules appears to be frequently used by major cities:[32]

1. Priority is given to a maximum distance rule. Libraries are located so that a significant proportion of residents do not live further than an acceptable maximum distance from a branch library. In Rochester, New York, for example, this acceptable distance is two and a half miles. However, in some cities, for example Richmond, Virginia, this acceptable maximum distance to the nearest library is adjusted to take account of the race and wealth of each neighborhood. Because low-income residents have limited mobility, libraries are located so that residents of poor neighborhoods have to travel a shorter distance to reach the nearest branch library. It is felt that greater accessibility will increase use on the part of low-income citizens.
2. The size of existing branches is sometimes related to the *density* of neighborhoods. Standards are used for the number of square feet of library space needed per 1000 residents. If a neighborhood is deficient in branch library space based on this density standard, then it is given extra consideration when the location of a new branch is decided.
3. In Charlotte, North Carolina, in addition to the above two decision rules, circulation levels and citizen requests are also considered. Neighborhoods that heavily use available library services, as well as neighborhoods that have been particularly outspoken in seeking additional library service, are given extra consideration when locational choices are made.

The specific location decision rules for particular services are likely to vary, but a consumer orientation should focus all distribution decisions. Marketing-oriented public managers should first analyze the characteristics of the target market and then locate facilities to provide the desired services at acceptable costs. The starting point should be to identify the location that would provide best access and visibility to the target clientele and then to compromise from that optimum location as little as possible in selecting a specific site for the facility. The site selection process *should not* start by identifying a convenient or inexpensive site, which is then justified and rationalized as adequate to meet the needs of a target population.

Scheduling Services

Scheduling is the final operational component to be considered (Figure 8.1). It addresses the questions "When is the best time to offer a service, for how long, and how often?" No rule is generalizable here, but clearly if a service is not offered at the "right" time then an exchange is less likely to be consummated. The only firm rule for scheduling is that it should be governed by the needs of target markets. Sometimes there is a tendency to schedule services at times that are more convenient for the administrators of those services than for target markets.

The most flexible of the operational components, scheduling can be adjusted relatively easily. However, it is possible that confusion, loss of support, and loss of good will will be incurred by changing well-established schedules. This, together with the expense incurred in communicating changes to target markets, suggests that scheduling changes should be made only after careful deliberation.

The extent to which good scheduling can impact demand for services is frequently demonstrated in education. Many universities now schedule beyond the traditional 8 A.M.–5 P.M. timeframe in order to attract clientele. Through such client-oriented scheduling and through outreach efforts that reflect a realization that the task of effective distribution is to get services to citizens rather than to get citizens to services, some universities have been able to reach entirely new target markets:

> The "Weekend College" concept was originally developed at Wayne State University. It was designed as a liberal arts general studies major which enables full-time working adults to be simultaneously full-time students. "Weekend College" established a course delivery system which would make it convenient for working students to take 12 credit hours per semester, i.e. 3 courses of 4 credit hours each. The Wayne State concept employs a weekly seminar-workshop meeting for 4 hours off-campus, generally at a union hall, community center, or worksite; a television course of 5 half-hour segments per week; and a weekend conference/workshop course which meets 3 full weekends during the semester. By means of this curriculum, working adults can earn a bachelor's degree in 5 years.[33]

SUMMARY

The chapter offers a framework for analyzing the service distribution that enables equity models to be operationalized. Distribution decisions frequently involve relatively long-term commitments. Because of their distributional uncontrollability, decisions regarding distribution of facility-dependent services are usually perceived as more significant than those concerning facility-independent services.

A service distribution pattern emerges as the result of completing a series of interrelated tasks that may usefully be viewed as comprising a system. All elements of the system are governed and directed by the prevailing interpretation of equity.

The first task is to audit and evaluate the existing distribution system to identify who at this time is getting how much of the service. Evaluating the equity of service distribution involves geographic comparisons. Service districts are usually selected as the unit of analysis. Three types of indicators are used for measuring equity: resources, activities, and results. Because these generally support different conclusions, using multiple measures rather than only the readily available resource indicators provides more reliable data.

Four approaches are available for comparing the distribution of different services. They are the visual approach, comparison of the number and percent of people living within a selected travel time from specified facilities, comparison of participation or visitation data, and the investment inventory approach. Each approach has limitations, but the investment inventory approach appears to be the most useful for reducing inequities between different areas.

By identifying winners and losers an audit evaluation provides the information base necessary for developing objectives that seek to redress any equity imbalances. Distribution objectives operationalize the equity model adopted by the agency. These objectives guide the distribution decisions and actions of the agency, and they also provide a basis for subsequent objective measurement and evaluation of progress.

When objectives have been established, a distribution strategy plan is developed that provides a blueprint of how to meet the objectives. It contains four operational components: channel of distribution, intensity of distribution, selection of site locations, and schedule of service delivery.

Channel of distribution decisions are concerned with whether an agency should attempt to deliver its offerings directly to consumers, or whether it can better deliver selected offerings indirectly through involving other agencies or organizations. There are three dimensions to channel decisions. The first relates to vertical distribution, which occurs when services are delivered from a higher level of government, through intermediary government levels, to the ultimate target market. In contrast, horizontal distribution decisions relate to the alternate distribution strategies that may be adopted within a single level of government. These include the traditional direct provider role, outreach efforts, and a facilitator approach. The final channel decision concerning the type of outlet to be used is directly influenced by the selection of target markets. If an agency adopts a differentiated target market strategy it must also consider multiple types of distribution outlets.

Intensity of distribution is concerned with the relative number of locations where a person can receive the service. Intensive distribution entails delivering services close to the client's home. Selective distribution offers fewer outlets or service points and presumes that members of target markets are willing and able to travel some distance to use the facility or receive the service. Exclusive distribution is the provision of facilities or services in only one location within a community or target market area.

After channel and intensity decisions comes the task of identifying specific site locations for outlets through which a service will be delivered. If the location and size of a facility are not optimum, then no matter how good its subsequent service offerings, management, promotion, or pricing strategies, the facility is unlikely to achieve its full potential. Conversely, a well-located facility may be successful in spite of inadequacies in operating management. The two main criteria for good site location are accessibility and visibility to target markets.

For at least five reasons public facilities frequently are located inequitably or inappropriately. They are (1) inheritance of facilities that were located on the basis of outdated decisions; (2) donation of the facility, with a location determined by the donor; (3) centralization of facilities, which expedites bureaucratic procedures; (4) unavailability of other sites in the area; and (5) relatively low cost of the land.

The marketing approach to selecting a location is to identify the ideal site from the target market's perspective, and to compromise from that location as little as possible in selecting a specific site for the facility. The site selection process should not start by identifying a convenient or inexpensive site, which is then justified and rationalized as being adequate to service the population.

Scheduling is the final operational component of a distribution plan. It addresses the questions "When is the best time to offer a service, for how long, and how often?" It is the most flexible of the operational components because it can be adjusted relatively easily.

NOTES

1. Lovelock, C.H. "A Market Segmentation Approach to Transit Planning, Modeling, and Management," *Proceedings of the Sixteenth Annual Meeting of the Transportation Research Forum*. 1975, pp. 247–258.
2. Metropolitan Toronto and Region Transportation Survey (MTARTS). *Go Transit Commuter Rail Project*. Toronto: Special Report No. 9. Second Household Survey, 1968.
3. Jones, B.D., Greenberg, S., and Drew, J., *Service Delivery in the City*. New York: Longman, 1980, pp. 186–193.
4. Von Bertallanffy, L. *General Systems Theory*. New York: Braziller, 1968, p. 55.
5. Lucy, W.H., and Mladenka, K.R., *Equity and Urban Service Distribution*. Report prepared for the U.S. Department of Housing and Urban Development. Washington, DC: National Technical Information Service, 1977, p. 89.
6. Ibid.
7. Much of this discussion of types of equity indicators is adapted from Lucy and Mladenka, *Equity*.

8. Lucy, W.H., Gilbert, D., and Birkhead, G.S., "Equity in Local Service Distribution," *Public Administration Review*, November/December 1977, p. 695.

9. Lucy and Mladenka, *Equity*, p. 65.

10. *Beal v. Lindsay*, 468F. 2d 287 (2nd cir. 1972).

11. Lucy, W., "Equity and Planning for Local Services," *American Planning Association Journal*, October 1981, p. 452.

12. Vernoz, G.S., "Notes on Alternative Conception of Equity." Unpublished paper prepared for presentation in the lecture series "Equity in the City," Columbia University, Continuing Education Program, 1976, p. 13.

13. Levy, F.S., Meltsner, A.J., and Wildavsky, A., *Urban Outcomes: Schools, Streets and Libraries*. Berkley, CA: University of California Press, 1974, p. 259.

14. Lucy et al., "Equity in Local Service," p. 695.

15. Lucy and Mladenka, *Equity*, p. 92.

16. Ibid., p. 89.

17. Rich, R.C., "Neglected Issues in the Study of Urban Service Distributions: A Research Agenda," *Urban Studies*, vol. 16, No. 2 June 1979, p. 147.

18. Lucy and Mladenka, *Equity*, p. 123.

19. Levy et al., *Urban Outcomes*, p. 248.

20. Bannon, J.J., *Outreach—Extending Community Service in Urban Areas*. Springfield, IL: Thomas, 1973, p. xiii.

21. Tippett, F., "In Indiana, Here Comes the Bookmobile," *Time*, September 8, 1980, p. 12.

22. Poole, Jr., R., "Looking Back: How City Hall Withered," *The Futurist*, December 1978, pp. 369–373.

23. Leavitt, T., "Retrospective Commentary on Marketing Myopia," *Harvard Business Review*, September/October 1975, p. 180.

24. Herron, D.B., *Marketing Management for Social Service Agencies*. Columbus, OH: The Association of Professional YMCA Directors, 1978, p. 80.

25. Kotler, P., *Marketing for Non-Profit Organizations*. Englewood Cliffs, NJ: Prentice-Hall, 1982, p. 324.

26. Gottschalk, Jr., E.C., "Courts Calling on Telephones to Economize," *Wall Street Journal*, June 1, 1981, p. 27.

27. Herron, *Marketing Management*, p. 20.

28. Perlman, R., *Consumers and Social Services*. New York: Wiley, 1975, p. 5.

29. Cowan, P. "Hospitals in Towns: Location and Siting," *Architectural Review*, Vol. 137 No. 820, June 1965, pp. 417–421.

30. For example, it has been observed that "in contrast to the British system where there is a relatively homogeneous pattern of health care, the American system exhibits far greater locational inefficiency." Rigby, J.P., *Access to Hospitals: A Literature Review*. Crawthorne, England: Transport and Road Research Lab., 1978, p. 32.

31. Lucy and Mladenka, *Equity*, p. 123.

32. Ibid., p. 40.

33. "T.U.F. Attacks College Enrollment Problems." *Texas Faculty*, vol. 2, No. 1, Fall 1981, p. 1.

APPENDIX: OPERATIONALIZATION OF A COMPENSATORY EQUITY MODEL

The city of Savannah, Georgia developed its Responsive Public Services Program (RPSP) because of a belief that a responsive service delivery program should address the *differences* among neighborhoods. Its objective was to reduce deficiencies in the quality of livability through giving priority attention to the needs of neighborhoods with the most serious conditions that could be improved by city services.

The city officials were committed to a compensatory model of equity. The ultimate goal of their service delivery efforts was to achieve equal results in each neighborhood. The city manager stated:

> From our study of effectiveness measures, we have determined that the level of services being provided uniformly throughout the community is not adequate for some neighborhoods. This is a significant finding, for it means that we must discard the idea that it is enough to provide each neighborhood with the same service levels. Instead, we must plan our service programs to achieve a pre-defined quality within each neighborhood. This will mean that some neighborhoods will have to be supplied with a higher level of service than others if we are to achieve and maintain an acceptable quality of life in these neighborhoods.

The city believed that a primary concern should be the determination of the impact of the services they provide. For example, the sanitation department is responsible for garbage collection. The end product is not the amount of garbage collected; rather it is the resulting cleanliness of the neighborhood. The impact of services is an important element of the RPSP, and it is emphasized throughout the program.

The RPSP employed an analytical approach combined with mapping and urban planning techniques. Savannah's 33 square miles were divided into 21 geographic areas called planning units. These areas incorporated census tracts and respected neighborhood socioeconomic and natural boundaries where possible. Land area, housing units, and the population of 118,000 were not equally distributed among the planning units. This process gave the city a means of systematically approaching the evaluation of service delivery in service areas that are geographically defined, economically and physically homogeneous, and to a degree, heterogeneous in relation to other neighborhoods.

This case study is adapted from Wise, Jr., F. "Toward Equity of Results Achieved: One Approach," *Public Management*, August 1976, pp. 9-12; KMA: Chicago: ICMA Municipal Innovation Report No. 10, June 1976. (Adapted from *Public Management* magazine, August 1976, by special permission © 1976, the International City Management Association, Washington, D.C.)

SERVICES EVALUATED AND INDICATORS USED

Eleven services were included and their effectiveness in each planning unit was assessed using quantified criteria. The services evaluated and the criteria used were:

1. *Litter Conditions*. The litter survey measured the extent to which the streets, lanes (alleys), and lots within each neighborhood were littered with trash, debris, and junk vehicles.
2. *Crime Conditions*. The crime survey measured the number of crimes per 1000 people in each neighborhood for selected serious crimes and for all crimes.
3. *Stray Dogs*. The stray dog survey measured the extent to which loose dogs were present in each neighborhood.
4. *Incidence of Structural Fires*. The structural fire survey measured the number of structural fires per 1000 structures in each neighborhood.
5. *Flooding Conditions*. The flooding incidence survey measured the extent to which dwellings were susceptible to flooding, the degree to which access to properties was hindered by flooding, and the degree to which traffic on heavily traveled streets was impeded by flooding.
6. *Housing Conditions*. The housing conditions survey measured the extent to which substandard housing existed in each neighborhood.
7. *Land Use Compatibility*. The land use compatibility survey measured the extent to which an appropriate mix of land use was found in each neighborhood.
8. *Recreational Services*. The recreational services survey measured citizens' satisfaction with the availability and accessibility of recreational services and facilities.
9. *Street Conditions*. The street conditions survey evaluated the surface condition of paved streets and measured the number of miles of unpaved streets.
10. *Street Signs*. The street signs survey measured the deficiency in street name signs and traffic control signs.
11. *Water/Sewer Services*. The water and sewer service survey measured the extent to which improved properties within each neighborhood were not adequately served by water and sewer facilities.

Basically, four techniques were used to collect data.

Field inspections using a trained observer. These were employed for the surveys of litter, dog control, housing condition, street condition, and street signs. Standardized visual inspection methods were used and a random sample of blocks was surveyed in each planning unit.

Citizen surveys, which were employed for recreational services. The survey polled 5 percent of the households in each planning unit.

Special studies. Geographic, geological, zoning, and public utility maps and studies were used to access flood hazards, land use compatibility, and water and sewer adequacy for each neighborhood. These surveys consisted primarily of research and analysis with field work limited to verifying data or investigating problems. Also flooding and sewer stoppages were monitored for deficiencies.

Operational information. For public safety, the number of crimes per capita and the number of fires per thousand structures were calculated for each planning unit, using departmental records. Every crime and fire incident was plotted by geographic location. This analysis was performed without field research.

DERIVING CONCLUSIONS FROM THE DATA

Planning units were compared using a statistical method applying the concept of the normal curve. The citywide average was used as an indicator of the minimum acceptable service level. In other words, the average became the established standard. Neighborhoods were rated by their relative deviation from the norm to identify problem conditions occurring in particular areas. The severity of the deficiency was ranked according to the magnitude of the score. With these rankings, the city was able to distinguish the high-need areas objectively (as well as those needing the least assistance).

The net result of this process was an information resource that provided, on a neighborhood-by-neighborhood basis, measurements of deficiency in established quality needs or minimum levels of service, a comparison of each neighborhood's position relative to the city norm, its relative standing compared to other areas, and a cost factor for eliminating the deficiency.

RESOURCES AND ORGANIZATION

Responsibility for measuring each of the conditions in neighborhoods was assigned to the departments that provide the subject service. Thus the fire department measures the structural fire rates, the police department measures crime rates, the water and sewer department measures these service deficiencies, and so on. In theory, at least, each department should already have the information on hand; unfortunately this is not always true. Nevertheless, most have the resources available within their normal operating budgets to obtain the required information. As a result, much of the data collection for the RPSP was achieved without special appropriations.

HOW WERE THESE DATA ON NEIGHBORHOOD DEFICIENCIES USED?

In several ways, RPSP information was helpful:

1. As a logical method for establishing city service priorities on the basis of objective criteria.
2. As a way to strengthen service programs in substandard neighborhoods.
3. As guidance for the allocation of community development block grant funds.
4. As a valuable community relations device. Citizen communication was strengthened. The RPSP pointed out to citizens in all neighborhoods that elected officials were aware of the problems of their neighborhood, and it clearly depicted for them, through the budgetary process, what priorities were set and the timetable for eradicating these deficiencies.
5. As an excellent planning tool, with measured deficiencies, set objectives, and assigned costs. The only remaining task was to determine how much of a given year's resources would go into one service deficiency versus another. With the RPSP, the question is no longer which neighborhood will get its streets paved; but rather, should limited resources be allocated to paving streets, correcting drainage problems, providing more recreation, or extending sewer lines? The RPSP does not attempt to answer those questions.

NINE

Program Management

We begin this chapter by identifying the main tangible and intangible dimensions of a service. The major portion of the chapter is then devoted to a discussion of the nature, scope, importance, and implications of the program life cycle, a key concept in marketing management.

A service may be defined as a bundle of want-satisfying attributes. This includes everything, both favorable and unfavorable, that clients receive in an exchange. The prime reason for an agency's existence is to provide want-satisfying programs and services to targeted individuals and groups. Hence services define the fundamental nature of an agency and are the most visible answer to the question "What business are we in?"

In the past, many agencies perceived that the most effective way to attract a large number of clients was to charge a low, or zero, price. Relatively little attention was given to providing a high-quality service. In the last decade citizens have learned to expect, and have received, high-quality services from businesses in the private sector. As a result there has been a substantial rise in the level of service quality that clients expect from the public sector.

A well-known marketing aphorism says, "The bitterness of poor quality remains long after the sweetness of low price is forgotten." Today's potential clients demand high quality. Yesterday's standards are no longer adequate. If quality is compromised the agency will acquire a negative image and suffer from the repercussions.

DIMENSIONS OF A SERVICE

A service offering has both tangible and intangible dimensions. Tangible dimensions include the program itself, the facility in which the service is offered, and the personnel who administer the program. Equally important components of any service offering are relatively intangible attributes such as the image of the agency and the name of the program. It is the combination of these tangible and intangible attributes that deliver functional, social, and psychological benefits to clients.

The Program

The program refers to the actual service offered to the client, including all ancillary components of the offering. A client, for example, may enroll in a continuing education class. The program would include lectures by the instructor, readings from one or more textbooks, homework assignments, and examinations. However, there is more to the program offering than these basic components. Everything associated with attending the class is actually an attribute of the program offering. Transportation to and from the facility, parking arrangements, the availability of restroom and child care facilities, and social interaction before and after class are all components of the program. In sum, a program is everything, both positives and negatives, that the client receives in the exchange.

The ancillary components augment the central program and are likely to be critical to a potential client's perception of the offering. Thus, when considering whether or not to play on a public golf course, the golfer considers not only the quality of the golf course, but also such things as the quality of the golf carts, pro shop, lessons, food/beverage services, locker rentals, club house, putting green, and driving range.

The importance of these ancillary components is frequently overlooked by agencies that tend to regard expenditures on items outside of the narrow focus of their core mission as nonessential investments:

> If the hospital is to meet the expectations of the patient's hospital-of-choice, it is a legitimate management priority to provide facilities and services that meet the patient's need for the amenities of care. As a result of this emphasis, persuasive arguments can be made for the necessity of expending scarce capital resources on patient accommodations within the physical plant. This has been a particularly difficult task for the manager because of the strong arguments for the expenditure of capital funds on technological equipment to deliver direct technical medical care in the institution that has little or no effect on the hospital's appearance or the patient's reaction to the hotel aspects of the hospital stay.[1]

Facilities

Creation of the right environment and atmosphere at facilities that clients visit, or from which services are delivered, is a critical component of the total service offering. These mood setters should be deliberately designed to complement and enhance the program itself by fostering feelings of well-being, safety, intimacy, or awe:

> Physicians' offices provide an interesting example of intuitive environmental management. Although the quality of medical service may be identical, an office furnished in teak and leather creates a totally different "reality" in the consumer's mind from one with plastic slipcovers and inexpensive prints.[2]

Messages about the professionalism of an agency are communicated to clients through such elements as the decor of the offices, the clutter or neatness of desks, the manner in which the telephone is answered, staff manners and dress. An agency can choose to communicate indifference or a responsive sensitivity to clients. Little things can have a major impact on the atmosphere created, such as comfortable waiting stations, coffee, and staff smiles. People use visual and audio cues to generalize about the entire agency. Overflowing waste baskets, filled ash trays, temporary signs, and outdated posters may lead a client to infer that (1) this is "just a job" for the staff and they do not take any pride in their agency, (2) the manager is ineffective, or (3) the agency is not concerned about its clientele.[3]

If an environment is perceived as desirable, relaxing, comfortable, nonhostile and hence rewarding, it is likely that the activities that take place in that environment will also be perceived as desirable and rewarding.[4] A facility's atmosphere is a critical ingredient in a client's participation decision. For example, when a restaurant is selected for an evening out, frequently it is not selected only because of its food quality since there are probably a number of others of similar standard. Rather, selection is made at least partially on the basis of "atmosphere." According to one restauranteur: "Customers seek a dining experience totally different from home, and the atmosphere probably does more to attract them than the food itself."[5]

The atmosphere created is a function of the following three primary factors: (1) physical design, (2) interior design if it is a building or structure, and (3) personnel. The physical design reflects quality of imagination and the ability to create something interesting and aesthetically attractive. Interior design appeals to four senses. The principal visual dimensions of atmosphere are color, brightness, size, and shapes. The main aural dimensions are volume and pitch, while the sense of smell responds to scent and freshness. The chief tactile dimensions are softness, smoothness, and temperature.[6]

Too often the aesthetics of agency facilities are dismal, dowdy, and unattractive, which causes users to feel uncomfortable and unwelcome. One of the most dramatic changes in atmosphere has occurred in abortion clinics.

> When abortions were performed illegally, women would enter a depressing office with a single table on which the abortion would be performed. The sight of the office contributed to the patient's feeling of risk and sense of guilt and shame. Today's abortion clinics resemble normal doctor's offices with a comfortable wait-

> ing room and a competent receptionist who shows great understanding in dealing with the patient's needs and fears. The patient feels that she is being professionally supported in this difficult moment in her life.[7]

When discussing facility development or renovation, government and social service agencies frequently think only in terms of functional considerations and minimum costs. Economies are made on such items as carpeting, drapes, furnishings, lighting and landscaping because they are considered peripheral items that can be cut from the budget without adversely impacting the basic service. In fact, however, these are often the most critical ingredients in a new facility: They are the very things that create the welcoming atmosphere necessary to encourage potential clients to use the service.

Sometimes these atmosphere-enhancing elements are omitted from a capital development program as a cost-saving device on the rationalization that they can be added later. In subsequent years, however, they are frequently not given the priority necessary in the allocation of operating funds. Even if they are added later, the initial image of the facility has been established in the minds of its potential clientele. Unfortunately, this initial image is very difficult to change. Indeed, upgrading a facility's image in the minds of its potential clientele is one of the most difficult tasks in marketing.

Personnel

Someone once remarked that you never get a second chance to make a first impression. The first impression that an individual has of an agency and its services is normally contact with an agency employee. It may be an exaggeration to say that "the people are the program," but there is no doubt that clients' perceptions of agencies and programs are substantially influenced by the personnel with whom they interact. For this reason, personnel hiring, training, motivation, and supervision should be undertaken with as much vigor and enthusiasm as program development.

Compare the philosophy and practice of the Walt Disney organization with that of any government or social service agency.

> We love to entertain kings and queens, but the vital thing to remember is this: Every guest receives the V.I.P. treatment . . . . It's not just important to be friendly and courteous to the public, it is essential . . . . At Disneyland we get tired, but never bored, and even if it is a rough day, we appear happy. You've got to have an honest smile. It's got to come from within. And to accomplish this you've got to develop a sense of humor and a genuine interest in people. If nothing else helps, remember that you get paid for smiling.[8]

At Disneyland and Walt Disney World the entire operation is based on three components: the set (facility), the cast (personnel), and the audience. Guests (not customers) are served by hosts and hostesses (not employees) at attractions and shops (not rides and stores). *Guests* and *hosts* are not just names. They reflect an effort to treat visitors as they would be treated if they were friends invited into a private home. Disney's proud boast is, "We are people experts." They seek to exceed guests' expectations by going beyond what is required and expected: "Our applause is guests who return and our reward is the guest's smile." The direct applicability of these approaches to government and social service personnel is obvious. But there are more lessons to be learned from the Disney model.[9]

When cast members are hired they are given written information about the training they will receive, when and where to report, what to wear, and a variety of other information. The first day on the job is spent at "Disney University," learning about the Disney philosophy, management style, history, and how all parts of the organization work together to provide the highest possible level of guest satisfaction. Every member of the cast is important whether they work "onstage" or "backstage." Disney treats the employees as they expect the employees to treat the guests. They emphasize, "It's nice to be important, but it is more important to be nice. Make people smile with the smile you are wearing."

Four days are spent in prejob training on how to better serve guests in designated cast roles. Peer group members conduct orientations because new hosts can better identify with them. Experienced hosts who are familiar with and proud of the Disney standards effectively watch over the behavior of the new hosts. Only after a full week of training does a host or hostess meet a guest. And then they are carefully supervised until they have demonstrated competence in their role.

In the Magic Kingdom the cast is just as important as the set. In public and social service agencies the program managers, counselors, staff members, receptionists, and all other members of the "cast" are as much a part of the total experience as are programs and facilities.

Image

Image is the sum of beliefs, ideas, and impressions that a person has of an agency or of its programs, facility, or personnel. It may be formally defined as the mental construct developed by an individual on the basis of a few selected impressions among the flood of total impressions. It comes into being through a creative process in which these selected impressions are elaborated, embellished, and ordered. Images are ordered wholes built from scraps of information, much of which may be inferred rather than directly observed or experienced, and these inferences may have only a tenuous and indirect relationship to fact.

Thus image refers to something that is not "real" but that is visualized in the mind's eye. It is a mental map representing some real phenomenon, but it is not the phenomenon itself. The image may be derived from cognitive or sensory stimuli. For example, an image of a city's police department may be the result of that agency's mode of operation, relative authority, or values, or of sensory stimuli such as the visual impact of the police building, vehicles, or the officers' appearance. Many kinds of sensory stimuli may be assimilated, including the visual sensations of color, shape, motion, or polarization of light, as well as other responses to smell, sound, touch, and kinesthesia. Cognitive and sensory types of images are similar in that they only emulate some actual thing.

Each individual creates his or her own image of the environment:

> Images are the result of a two-way process between the observer and his (or her) environment. The environment suggests distinctions and relations, and the observer—with great adaptability and in the light of his (or her) own purposes—selects, organizes, and endows with meaning what he (or she) sees. The image so developed now limits and emphasizes what is seen, while the image itself is being tested against the filtered perceptual input in a constant interacting process. Thus the image of a given reality may vary greatly among different observers.[10]

Substantial agreement, however, has been found in the way members of homogeneous market segments based on such descriptors as age, sex, ethnicity, occupation, temperament, and familiarity perceive an agency.[11] These group images that symbolize significant consensus are useful to marketers who work to align image with the other dimensions of a service.

A program may be excellent, but if the image of the agency, its facilities, or personnel is negative, the program is unlikely to be successful.

> A hospital that projects an old fashioned, rundown visual appearance can hardly be expected to inspire confidence among physicians or patients that it really does offer the latest in medical treatment. Such an institution will have more difficulty than its more contemporary-looking competitors in recruiting capable medical professionals. Certainly it will encounter problems in trying to attract grants and public spending.[12]

All government and social service agencies have an image or collection of images that are held by their various publics. For example, a continuing education agency may be viewed as the place where they give belly-dancing lessons, or as a place to meet interesting people, or as a place to obtain upgrading for a better job. In each case, the image helps to determine the response pattern of the individual holding it.

Decisions are made on the basis of image, since this represents the totality of what is known about particular services. Agencies, such as educational institutions seeking gifts from individuals and foundations, are aware that resources are tied to image. Potential patrons see some universities as great, several as good, many others as average, and still many others as poor. Their image may not be currently accurate; nevertheless, it is on the basis of these images that resources are allocated.[13]

Publics holding a negative image of an agency will avoid or disparage its services, while those holding a positive image will be attracted to it. A positive image affects more than just potential client use decisions. Internally, an improved image can bring such benefits as improved morale, lower employee turnover, and greater employee awareness and loyalty to the agency. In addition, it impacts exchanges with other external publics with whom an agency does business. Consider the case of a hospital:

> A good image can have a positive impact on civic pride—"our hospital is second to none for its size"; appeals for financial support; and calls for volunteers. A high-quality image also directly affects the recruitment of professional and support staff—everyone wants to be on a winning team. Finally, an institution that projects professionalism and excellence is bound to enjoy a better relationship with state and federal oversight bodies than is one that provides care that is perceived as being less than first-class quality.[14]

Image is not static. It is amended by information received from the environment. However, it is unlikely to change easily; in some cases people are remarkably stubborn and tenacious in holding on to an image. Once people develop a set of beliefs and impressions about a service or agency, it is difficult to change them.

> Image persistence is explained by the fact that once people have a certain image of an object, they tend to be selective perceivers of further data. Their perceptions are oriented toward seeing what they expect to see. It will take highly disconfirming stimuli to raise doubts and open them to new information. Thus an image enjoys a life of its own for a while, especially when people are not likely to have new first-hand experiences with the changed object.[15]

Many factors preclude the success of any endeavor to change the existing images perceived by target audiences. These include the likelihood of an audience to reject information that is contrary to existing predispositions, the anchorage of already-existing images in group affiliations, the ineffectiveness of communications stemming from low-credibility sources, and audience resistance to perceived manipulation attempts.[16] Thus, if an agency decides that it wants to modify its existing image, it must have great patience. The change will take time.

The agency first has to decide where it wants to shift its image. Its image is a function of its deeds and its communications. "Good deeds without good words, or good words without good deeds, are not enough."[17] The agency must decide what real changes to make in its policies and behavior. After changing its real behavior, it must disseminate information to its publics who may not have experienced the changes firsthand.

A marketing communications program designed to improve an agency's image is likely to succeed only if it brings information to people about attributes of which they are not aware or of which they have a distorted view. To the extent that a citizen lacks awareness of certain attributes of an agency and is not likely to experience them directly, he or she will add them to an image of the agency as long as they are not contradicted by other beliefs. Information must be disseminated to the uninformed with some regularity. Demonstration of a new behavioral reality for the agency, with frequent dissemination of convincing information, is likely to bring about the desired image change eventually.

Various techniques have been used for measuring image, with the most common being semantic differential scales and multidimensional scaling analysis. If use is made of these techniques at regular intervals, then a manager can easily construct a "moving picture" of the shifting position of an agency or of one of its component parts for each of the attributes measured.

Program Name

The name given to a program contributes to its image and is a key dimension of the overall service offering. The importance of a brand name selected for a commercial product has been expressed in the following terms.

> The name is the hook that hangs the brand on the product ladder in the prospect's mind . . . the single most important marketing decision you can make is what to name the product. Shakespeare was wrong. A rose by any other name would not smell as sweet. Not only do you see what you want to see, you also smell what you want to smell . . . . And Hog Island in the Caribbean was going nowhere until they changed its name to Paradise Island.[18]

The Ford Mustang is one of the great success stories in the automobile field. Would it have been equally successful if it had been called the Ford Donkey instead of the Ford Mustang? The answer is probably no. Government and social service agencies tend to give only cursory attention to naming their programs, but names can substantially impact a service's overall image and both the number and type of clientele attracted to it. For example, to many people the terms "mental health" and "birth control" have a stigma attached to them. Because of this, some agencies have chosen new names. Thus "family planning" has become a synonym for birth control.

Recall from Chapter 6 our example of different names for physical fitness programs. "Keep Fit," "Slimnastics," "Aerobics," "Health Club," and "Jazzercise" all have different connotations regardless of whether the program content varies. The name of the program will influence and may even determine whether it will be a success or failure.

Names can be used to implement geographically different prices when political constraints prohibit this from being achieved explicitly. For example, it may not be politically feasible for an agency to charge lower prices for a class in a poor part of town that it charges in a wealthy area. Indeed, most jurisdictions insist on standardized pricing policies. However, in the poor part of town *tumbling* classes could be offered for $1 an hour, while in the affluent part of town *gymnastics* may be priced at $2 an hour. In reality, the classes may be exactly the same, but the naming device enables price to be differentiated to reflect the differing ability of the two target markets to pay.

Agencies should avoid the no-name trap. Two common forms of the no-name trap are meaningless names and initial names. The selection of generic, innocuous names such as Family or Human Services and Community Services fails to provide prospective clients with any idea of the nature or scope of the offerings. Umbrella agencies that provide a variety of services often fall into this trap.

The federal government and the military are notorious for using initials shorthand, which conveys no meaning to most people. What do HUD, EPA, FCC, and FTC mean to the average person? Municipalities and other government agencies also fall into this trap. There are at least ten DP&Ls in the United States. Each is a municipal power and light company.

Besides lacking meaning, acronyms are quite difficult to find in the telephone directory. For example, there are seven pages of listings in the Manhattan phone directory that begin with the letters U.S.[19] To further complicate matters, most people do not realize that acronyms are not integrated with word names in the telephone directory. The initial names appear first.

There are exceptions to every rule and one exception to the initial name trap is YMCA. The Y has been around for a long time, and many people know that the letters stand for Young Mens Christian Association. The organization's name has not made it famous. Its deeds have overcome its name limitation.

Choosing the right names for agencies and programs is more art than science. There are, however, some general guidelines. Names should:

Be easy to pronounce
Be easy to spell
Be easy to recall
Describe the agency or program so the client knows what to expect
Communicate the benefits that the service offers
Distinguish the agency or program from all other organizations and programs

PROGRAM LIFE CYCLE

The product life cycle concept is one of the most familiar concepts in marketing. Few, if any, other general concepts of clientele behavior have been so widely discussed or so generally accepted. Its potential contribution to public agency management is considerable.

The concept is derived from an analogy with human biological development, which may be described as a period of ascending, a period of maturing, and a period of decline (see Figure 9.1).[20]

This physiological life cycle is fixed, with one stage remorselessly following another in an immutable and irreversible sequence that medical progress has been unable to change substantially. However, it has been suggested that human psychological development does not follow such an unequivocal pattern; it does not necessarily parallel biological development. A decrease in psychological performance does not occur automatically after the age of 40 or 45, as is the case with biological performance. Some people at this stage in their life cycle rise to a new level of creativity based on prior experience and a wider horizon. The creativity can last for a long period of time before it finally succumbs to the onslaught of old age or actual physical infirmity. This additional dimension of renewed growth has been incorporated into the product life cycle model.[21]

The life cycle concept has been adopted as a way to trace the stages of a program's acceptance from its introduction to its demise. Like the human life cycle, the course of program life cycles can be modified by careful management, but the inevitability of finite end cannot be changed. The services offered by public agencies should change constantly in response to clientele demand and hence exhibit distinctive life cycle forms.

The life cycle through which programs are likely to pass consists of five stages (see Figure 9.2). In application, the vertical axis can be measured in terms of the number of program participants. The horizontal axis represents the passage of time. The first stage is *introduction,* in which clientele acceptance is slow; second is the *take-off* stage, which is a period of rapid growth; third is *maturity,* during which the growth rate slows down; fourth is *saturation,* in which no further growth takes place and clientele acceptance begins to wane; and finally, *decline,* resulting either in *death,* which means removal from the marketplace, or *petrification,* which is a substantially reduced level of market acceptance remaining constant over a period of time. At the point of onset of decline, some modification to the program may be made to enable it to renew its growth rather than to decline; and hence it may extend its useful life.

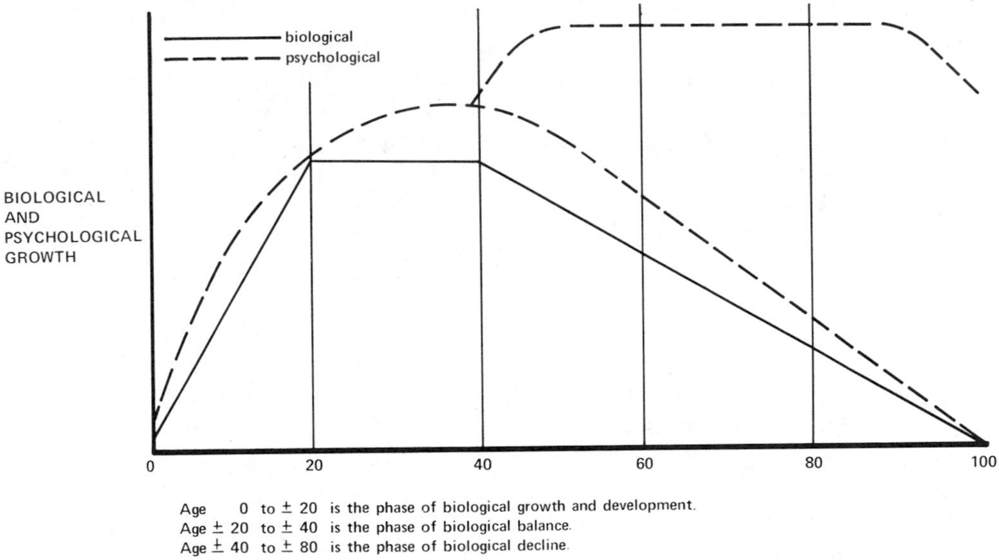

Age ± 20 to ± 40 is the phase of biological balance.

Figure 9.1. Human Cycle of Biological and Psychological Development. (*Source:* Lievegoed, B.D.J. *The Developing Organization*, Tavistock Publications, London, 1973.)

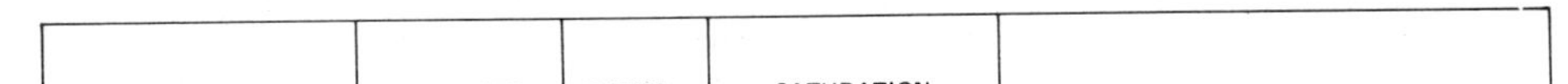

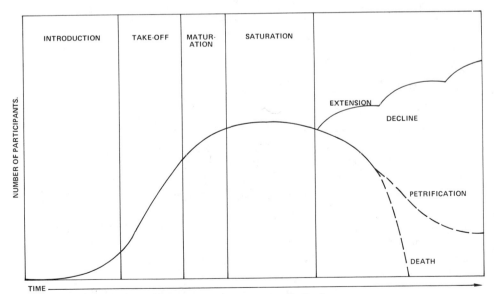

Figure 9.2. Program Life Cycle.

Characteristics of the Stages

In the *introduction* stage, considerable effort is needed to generate support and acceptance for a new program. Targeted client groups need to be made aware of the want satisfaction potential of the program. A management effort and commitment of resources disproportionate to the number of program participants is often necessary. Such substantial promotional effort is required because there are few people in the program who can "spread the word." Much of the promotional effort will be in the form of personal selling, with agency personnel seeking to persuade the leading participants or opinion leaders in the community to join the program or to solicit the participation of others.

Most new programs require modification during the introduction stage of their life cycle. It is important to solicit feedback from early users so that any initial sources of irritation are quickly removed. Considerable effort must be made to ensure a high-quality program. The newer the program the more important it is that the user has a good first impression of it, because others will be awaiting initial users' reactions and will be greatly influenced by them. Early participants are the key to success. Their trial and approval is a necessary condition to acceptance from others who are not willing to take a blind risk:

> If their first experience is unfavorable in some crucial way, this may have repercussions far out of proportion to the actual extent of the underfulfillment of the customer's expectation. But a favorable first experience or application will, for the same reason, get a lot of disproportionately favorable publicity.[22]

Take-off is the market acceptance stage at which the number of participants in the program grows rapidly. This may be partially the result of introducing the program to additional target markets. Less management effort is required during this stage, for all the problems of starting the program have been resolved. Participants in the program begin promoting it through their social contacts and new participants quickly enroll. The end of this stage is reached when the rate at which participation increases begins to slow down.

The length of the introduction and take-off stages will vary according to (1) the newness of the program, (2) its complexity in terms of the level of skill required to use it, (3) the cost of any required equipment, (4) the presence of other suppliers offering substitute programs such as private groups or commercial organizations, (5) the ease with which it is possible to participate in it, (6) the degree of promotion undertaken and the visibility the program has achieved in the community, and (7) the extent to which it is compatible with other programs offered.

During the *maturity* stage the number of participants will continue to increase, but typically the rate of increase declines. No program can expect to gain an ever-increasing number of new participants. All members of the target client group(s) are aware of the program and, by the end of this stage, have made a decision as to whether or not they wish to participate in it.

At the end of the maturity stage there is a tendency for managers to believe "that's the way it's always going to be." Often this causes agencies to assume its clientele will always use a service and they shift focus from the clientele to concentrate on efficient delivery of the service. This shift from a marketing to a product orientation is likely to contribute to demand for a service leveling off or beginning to decline.

The most important characteristic of the *saturation* stage is the program's reliance on repeat usage. No new participants seek out the service except newcomers to the community. Hence, if existing participants drop out, few others take their place. At this stage, the program is highly vulnerable to new opportunities offered elsewhere that may attract existing users. These participants are unlikely to be replaced. Typically, this stage lasts much longer than the previous stages.

It is at this point that management should consider strategies for extending or stretching the program life cycle. Four strategies are available and these are shown in Figure 9.3. *Market penetration* seeks to increase usage from the existing target market without modifying the program. This is likely to be the least useful. By the time the saturation stage has been reached, all members of a target market who are interested in the program are likely to have made a final evaluation of its usefulness.

Market development involves offering an existing program to a different target market. *Program development* consists of making calculated modifications to the program or its marketing mix to increase usage by existing client groups. This may involve new leadership or equipment, an alternate facility, a reduction in user price, or changes in location, scheduling, or communication efforts. *Diversification* entails some major form of program modification to adapt it to

	Present Programs	Modified Programs
Present Target Market	Increased market penetration (lowest risk strategy)	Program development
New Target Market	Market development	Diversification (within existing resources of the department) (highest risk strategy)

Figure 9.3. Strategies for Stretching the Life Cycle.

the particular benefits sought by new and different target markets. Figure 9.4 shows how a YMCA could successfully stretch the life cycles of its services through market penetration, market development, and program development.

The lowest risk of these market-stretching strategies is increased market penetration, because the agency has experience with both the service and the target markets (Figure 9.4). It is more difficult and risky to offer existing services to a new target market, and it is also more difficult to offer new services to an

1. *Market Penetration*—Increase the use of present services.
   a. Increase the present consumers' rate of service usage.
      i. Give fee incentives or rewards for increased use.
      ii. Promote other uses of the service.
      iii. Offer more service for the same price. Longer swim lessons, longer day care period, counseling for the entire family, more gym time.
   b. Attract some competitors' consumers to your service.
      i. Increase promotional effort.
      ii. Establish sharper differences between the values of your services and those of your competitors.
   c. Attract non-users.
      i. Induce trial uses, sampling.
      ii. Offer fee inducements.
      iii. Advertise new uses.
2. *Market Development*
   a. Open new geographical markets.
   b. Develop different versions of the same service to appeal to other market segments.
      i. Counseling: easy in and out, when one just wants to talk things over, nothing heavy.
      ii. Swimming pool for those who just want to relax during their noon hours.
   c. Advertise in other media than those you have been using.
      i. College newspapers, rock radio stations, national magazines, grocery stores.
3. *Program Development*—Develop modified or new services for the markets you are already serving.
   a. Develop new program service features.
      i. Front door pick-up and delivery.
      ii. Check cashing and mini-legal services.
      iii. Temporary babysitting service.
      iv. Free meals.
      v. Photocopying, laundry, or similar service while they are here.
   b. Develop quality variations.
      i. Medium, high, and low.
   c. Develop additional modules and time segments. This is known as product proliferation.
      i. One-day day camp. All summer day camp. Rainy-day-only day camp. Once-in-a-while day camp.
      ii. Night day camp. Week-end camping.
      iii. The 60 minute refreshing lunch break, complete with jogging one mile, 4 laps of swimming, shower, sun lamp for 5 minutes, a bowl of soup and back to work in 60 minutes.
      iv. The marathon couples' communication program, complete in 24 hours.

Figure 9.4. How a YMCA Might Implement Market Stretching. (*Source:* Herron, D.B., *Marketing Management for Social Service Agencies*. Columbus, OH: The Association of Professional YMCA Directors, 1978, pp. 17–18.)

existing market. The highest risk of failure comes when a new service is offered to a new market.

Not all programs can be revitalized. Some will have become redundant because of basic changes in client group wants or the emergence of a superior program by other providers. In such cases, it is important to acknowledge the telltale signs and to reduce the time and money invested in the program.

In the *decline* stage other programs or activities have become more attractive to users and the number using the service declines. Decline may be due either to (1) the introduction of new services by the agency or others that better deliver sought benefits, or (2) a growing disinterest with the familiar and a search for new experiences by targeted clientele. This latter response may be referred to as "psychological obsolescence."

During the decline stage the program is no longer a subject of social conversation and participants are no longer exercising a positive influence on others. If an attempt is made to arrest the decline, a primary promotional effort aimed directly at potential client group members has to be initiated. Management and promotional efforts typically become disproportionate to the number of participants in the program. A decision has to be made regarding when the service should be terminated. An alternative may be to offer the program intermittently or less frequently. The decline may arrest itself and participation remain at the petrification level rather than disappear altogether. This level is characterized by a relatively small number of enthusiastic participants remaining in the program who may take over responsibility for running it.

Core and Fringe Participants

In all programs clients can be categorized as either "core" or "fringe" users. The core members of a clientele consist of enthusiasts committed to supporting the program whatever may happen. However, they are likely to be a relatively small proportion of the total number of potential users. The majority of participants are fringe members.

It is unlikely that a program will be deemed successful if it attracts only core users; the fringe participants are usually also required for program success. It is the fringe clientele who constitute the greatest challenge to the manager because their involvement is more difficult to retain. Fringe participants are relatively fickle and are not really committed; if a substitute or alternative opportunity for use of their time and energy emerges, they may take advantage of it. Those out at the extreme fringe margin may exist in a "zone of indifference." A slight change in circumstances will cause them to foresake Program *A* and drift into Program *B* or vice-versa. Hence, the farther out toward the fringe the participants are located, the more difficult they are to retain in a program (Figure 9.5).

This core-fringe concept is reflected in the nature of market acceptance traced by a program's life cycle (see Figure 9.5). The early users are typically

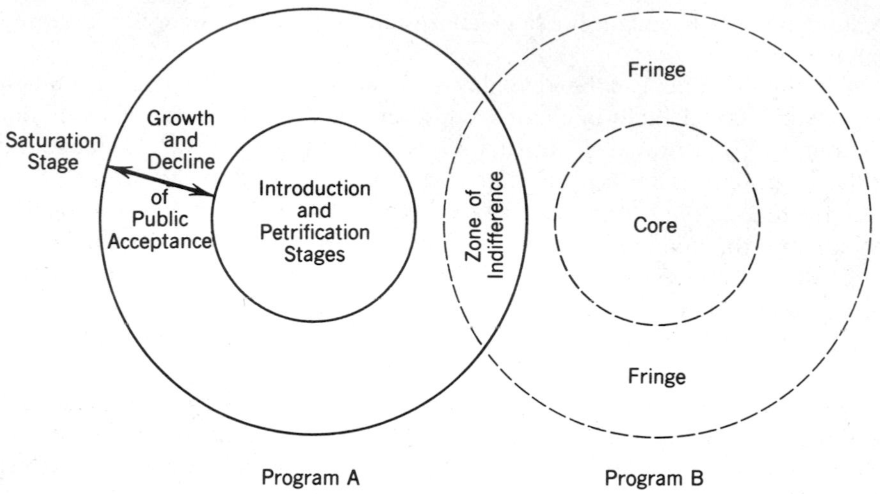

Figure 9.5. Movement of Core and Fringe Participants over Time During a Program's Life Cycle.

core enthusiasts. As momentum grows there is a movement out toward the fringe. The maximum number of participants is reached at the Saturation stage. It has been found that later adopters of a service are more likely to discontinue using it than are earlier adopters.[23] Thus, decline reflects a movement back toward the core, with fringe participants departing from the program. The petrification level is reached when all of the fringe market has disappeared and only the core market of dedicated enthusiasts remains.

Implications for Managing Programs

Many managers may intuitively be aware of the life cycle concept. Our discussion has perhaps served to define the process and place it in a formal framework. Unfortunately, few have recognized the usefulness of the life cycle as a management tool. Analysis of program life cycles can be very useful in shaping management and marketing strategy.

Most fundamentally, the life cycle concept encourages preplanning so that managers can take the initiative instead of having to react to events that have already happened. Program development can be systematically planned in advance, rather than thrown together as a stop gap response to an immediate situation. This is possible because the program life cycle identifies in advance the characteristic pattern that client group acceptance of a new program is likely to follow.

A significant value of the program life cycle is its usefulness as a predictive or forecasting tool. Since programs pass through distinctive stages, then a framework for prediction is available. Prediction of the profile of a proposed program's cycle is hazardous, but nevertheless necessary; and it makes possible the formulation of underlying plans and strategies in response to the projected situation. When a new program is inaugurated an attempt should be made at the outset to plan a series of actions for the various stages in the program's life.

Each stage of a program's life cycle requires a different marketing strategy and different emphasis on the allocation of resources. For example, any decision as to how much to spend on promotion and the appropriate type of promotion for a particular program should include consideration of its life cycle stage. Clearly, considerable promotional effort is needed at the introduction stage, while relatively little value is likely to accrue from promotional expenditures in the saturation stage. Further, in the introduction stage promotional efforts are concerned with creating new demand, while in the saturation stage promotion should be directed toward reminding the existing participants of the value of their choice.

Life Cycle Audits. Another use of the program life cycle is the development of a program life cycle audit. Life cycle management should consider not only individual program life cycles but also the total mix of program life cycles. This is done by prudent introduction of new programs, pruning of old programs, and careful allocation of money and manpower among existing programs according to their potential for attracting users. The following steps can form the basis of a program life cycle audit.[24]

1. Use historical data of attendance at each program, going back to the beginning of the program if possible, to fix its present position on its life cycle curve. In order to identify a true life cycle pattern, data have to be adjusted to allow for population changes. Thus a ratio such as attendance per thousand population may be most appropriate. Similarly, the data should be adjusted to remove the impact that any major changes in the cost of admission to the program may have exerted.
2. Check recent trends in the number and nature of competitors offering a similar or substitute program. These competitors may be other public agencies or the commercial sector. Consider the relative advantages enjoyed by competitive programs.
3. Project program participation over the next three years based on all of the information gathered.

Once the life cycle position of each program has been identified and projected forward three years, the agency has a profile indicating where its programs will be located at that time. With these steps completed, priorities can be assigned to such functions as development of new programs, termination of old programs,

Program Life Cycle Analysis

Program Number ________ Program ______________________ Activity ________

Program Manager ______________________________ Date ________

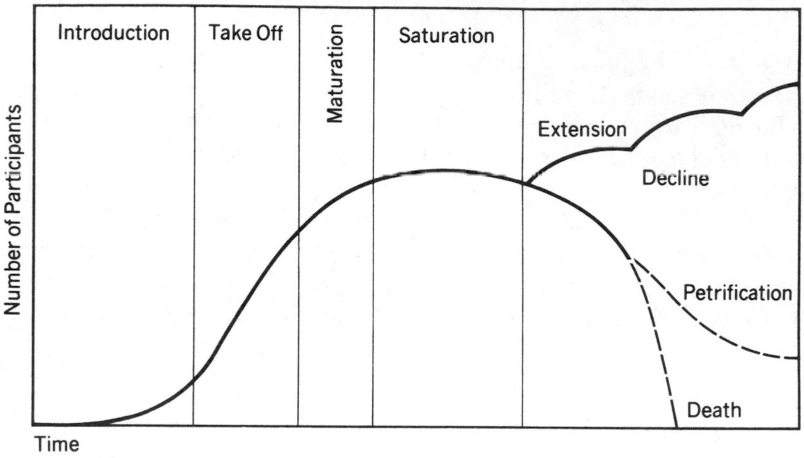

Mark an "X" on the above curve where you think this program currently is, according to the Stage Indicators listed below.

Program Data

	Actual 81/82	*Actual* 82/83	*Actual* 83/84	*Project* 84/85	*Project* 85/86
Annual Productivity (i.e., participant hours)	____	____	____	____	____
Productivity Growth Rate (use 81/82 as the base year)	____	± %	± %	± %	± %
W/H Growth Rate (use 81/82 as the base year)	____	± %	± %	± %	± %

New Marketing Strategy

List new marketing techniques you will use, utilizing the "Marketing Mix" of program, distribution, price, and promotion.

1. ______________________________

____

2. ______________________________

____

Figure 9.6. Anaheim Parks, Recreation and Community Services Department Use of a Program Audit.

3. ____

____

4. ____

____

5. ____

____

Program Life Cycle Stage Indicators

Introduction Stage
1. Program costs of money and time are high.
2. Revenue production is slow as public is introduced to program.
3. Program is at half participant capacity.
4. Productivity units are minimal to moderate.

Take-Off Stage
1. Less time is needed for start-up publicity and other activities by supervisor.
2. Amount of revenue increases dramatically as popularity increases.
3. Program is at ¾ or maximum participant capacity.
4. Productivity increases dramatically as the word gets around regarding the program.

Maturity Stage
1. Supervision time and costs are cut back as program begins to "run itself."
2. Amount of revenue still increases, but at a slower rate.
3. Program is at maximum participant capacity, but beginning to drop.
4. Productivity begins to level out but maintains consistent numbers.

Saturation Stage
1. Amount of time and costs going out are minimal except for efforts toward extending the program.
2. Revenues level off and begin to drop.
3. No new participants are entering the program.
4. Productivity units begin to drop off.

Decline Stage
1. Amount of supervision time increases. Time to decide future status of program. Program is costing more time and money than it's worth.
2. Amount of revenue takes a nose dive.
3. Program is at minimum capacity and dwindling.
4. Productivity is low and on the decline as the public lacks interest in the program.

Figure 9.6. (Continued)

and allocation of resources. Figure 9.6 illustrates how the Parks, Recreation, and Community Services Department in Anaheim, California, has used program life cycle analysis.

In nearly all agencies there is a need to develop methods for allocating the limited resources of the agency in an optimum manner. The program life cycle audit provides a useful framework if the current and future position of each program is carefully scrutinized and related to the position of all other programs and the objectives of the agency. Clearly, if the audit reveals that all programs are likely to be located in the saturation or decline stages in three years' time, the agency has to make a major effort to develop new programs or else risk becoming obsolete itself. The program life cycle provides a guiding framework within which some assessment of both the current status and future potential of particular programs may be made. Theodore Levitt states:

> The significance of (executive) decisions is that they inescapably deal with the future, with what is to be done, rather than with what has been done. To know where the present is in the continuum of competitive time and events is more important and useful than to know it for itself alone. It therefore often makes more sense to try to know what the future will bring, and when it will bring it, than to know in exhaustive detail what the present itself actually contains.[25]

Implications for Assigning Management Resources[26]

The life cycle concept indicates that the different stages through which a program, service, or agency passes should influence the assignment of management resources to the program. Manpower planning that seeks to link managers' skills with program life cycle stage has emerged as a key component in strategic planning. It has been recognized that some managers are better equipped and more successful at initiating development, while others are more effective at managing an existing operation, and still others are more effective at rescuing or retrenching a service or agency. These three types of managers have been termed *growers*, *caretakers* and *undertakers*, respectively.[27] Jackson Martindell describes them as follows:

> The man (or woman) best fitted to organize a company is not necessarily, or even usually, the man (or woman) best fitted to run it in the days of its maturity. The initial stage of creation of a company usually requires domination by an individualist who, when the problem changes to that of coordination of the activities of a team of men (and/or women), is found to lack the requisite qualities for continued leadership. This is no criticism of such men (or women). On the contrary, it defines their area of greatest usefulness and warns that the stage of evolution of a corporation (or agency) must be examined carefully before we can decide whether the chief executive is actually the type of man (or woman) to lead and oversee the operation.[28]

The problem has been expressed in another way: "Too often it's like trying to put your best guard into the quarterback's slot—it just can't work."[29] Once an agency moves into a new stage, the most critical part of the transition is the adjustment of the management behavior of its senior executives. The selection of key personnel requires an understanding of the shift in problems that occurs as the organization moves from one stage of development to another.

In the introduction stage, the size of the organization is probably small, but it is likely to increase in accordance with the growth of clientele acceptance of its services. Changes of emphasis occur as a department moves through its different stages of development. The early stages require organization, motivation, risk taking, and personal selling skills as well as a thorough understanding of the program.

As the program grows in size and reaches maturity, administrative skills, particularly those associated with budget controls, cost cutting, and improved productivity, become of paramount importance. However, at this stage the manager's preoccupation with administrative tasks may preclude concern for innovation and change. As the organization begins to decline there is often renewed awareness of the importance of continual program innovation and renewed emphasis on technology. At each stage, different types and levels of management capabilities, styles, and methods are required if the program is to prosper. If the requisite management functions are not performed to at least a minimum level of competency, the life cycle curve of the department will accelerate prematurely toward the decline stage, thus failing to achieve its optimum potential. Figure 9.7 describes the typical evolution of an agency life cycle together with the characteristics of personnel frequently associated with each stage.

Larry Greiner has observed:

> Every organization and its component parts are at different stages of development. The task of top management is to be aware of these stages, otherwise it may not recognize when the time for change has come, or it may act to impose the wrong solution.[30]

The continued broadening of the program range offered by many government and social service agencies means that more programs are in different phases of the life cycle at any given time. Each has different problems and opportunities and requires a distinct managerial response.

Can one person do it all or are the managerial skills needed at various stages sufficiently different that different people are required? One school of thought claims that "the man (or woman) most effective in getting an organization off to a fast start is the man (or woman) who is least effective in other phases of organizational development."[31] While this may be overly dogmatic, there are sufficient differences in the management skills required so that a conscious effort should be made to secure the best fit between an individual's managerial skills and the life cycle stages of a program.[32] Too often an agency manager tends to hire people who are similar to his or her self-image, instead of hiring people who are complementary. A manager is like an orchestra leader who needs a wide array of talents in order to most effectively produce the right service. The task is to know the skills required at a particular life cycle stage and to put together the orchestra by hiring people who have those complementary skills.

Of the four predictable stages in the life cycle of organizations, whether public or private, the first is entrepreneurship. An energetic individual has a new idea and quickly gets something going. Morale is high and people enjoy what they are doing, which is one reason why government so often creates a new agency for a floundering program instead of trying to breathe new vigor into an old one. The entrepreneur has a certain kind of personality: high-strung, self-confident, imaginative, bulldozing, and contemptuous of obstacles. Scientists and all true innovators have the same bundle of traits. But often the innovator is a poor manager, once the initial enthusiasm has passed. He often lacks patience and attention to detail. A true inventor will go on to something else as soon as he has got all the satisfaction he is going to get out of his latest invention.

The second stage is the administrative one. The executive who takes over from the entrepreneur is as orderly as his predecessor was temperamental. The peak stage in the enterprise often occurs at this point because it still enjoys the energy of innovation that is now joined by the logic of orderly procedure. Leadership here requires a personality that blends dynamism and steadiness, initiative and order. Most government programs, until they begin to slow down, are on this kind of course.

In the third stage the program's goals are obscured, subordinated to a concentration on means as ends in themselves. This is appropriately called the triumph of technique over purpose. Nonhuman factors such as organization, procedures, and especially rigid rules are elevated to a kind of pedestal and dominate the undertaking. The morale of employees and customers alike, once high, becomes progressively lower, to the point of inertia. Innovativeness comes to a virtual halt and is outdistanced by more vigorous competitors. In many cases the social need still exists, but the service is not forthcoming.

The final stage is renewal, if renewal is to occur, for it takes a deliberate effort of will to bring it about. Again, there is an infusion of entrepreneurship, usually accompanied by the firing of the old leadership, while a new one is brought in. Bureaucratic pathologies are rooted out to be replaced with larger draughts of inventiveness and humanness. Taking risks and breaking with obsolete habits are rewarded. Some individuals have a genius for this kind of assignment, much as others have a genius for initially starting something. The creaking organization begins to shake itself and look up, to regain the energetic personality it had lost. In a word, entrepreneurship is personal and human, while pathological bureaucracy is automatic and colorless. In a struggle between the two in isolation, it is not difficult to predict which would win.

But even in this renewal stage it is necessary to work through others. The entrepreneur usually does three things: picks the key men (or women) with innovative ability he (or she) can work with harmoniously, develops a team of managers from all levels to update the goals and targets of the enterprise in terms of products and services as well as methods of operation, and then develops a first-rate re-training program for the enterprise as a whole in which the field managers (ultimate incidence of service) are given the main responsibility for training and indoctrination. In other words, the thing is turned upside down in more respects than one. This system has worked over and over again!

Figure 9.7. Typical Personnel Characteristics at Different Stages of an Agency's Life Cycle. (*Source:* Dimock, M., "Revitalized Program Management," *Public Administration Review*, May/June 1978, pp. 201–202. Reprinted with permission from *Public Administration Review* © 1978 by The American Society for Public Administration, 1225 Connecticut Avenue, N.W., Washington, D.C., All rights reserved.)

Limitations of the Life Cycle Concept

Like most useful concepts, the life cycle model has its limitations. First, it cannot be assumed that the pattern of market acceptance that the program life cycle reflects should always determine market strategy. An alternative position suggests that, rather than the life cycle determining marketing strategy, the marketing strategy variables of program, price, distribution and promotion determine the program life cycle curve. However, the nature of the causal relationship between the program life cycle and the marketing mix variables is probably not critical. It is more important to recognize that program life cycle stages require some adjustment in marketing strategy, which in turn controls those cycle stages themselves.

A second limitation is that the life cycle concept is essentially a demand model, whereas program usage rate depends on both demand and supply. Hence the model assumes an adequate supply base that never constrains demand. For example, if participation was restricted because of the limited carrying capacity of a facility, then the life cycle is essentially a function of that condition and not a reflection of the pattern of client group acceptance.

Third is the timeframe of program life cycles. Unfortunately, the length of a program's life is not known in advance. Checking back on the life cycles of similar or related programs that have been terminated may give some insight. Perhaps the single generalization that can be made is that with rapid societal and technological change, an increasing range of opportunities, and new sources of competition for individuals' time and money, the useful life cycle of services is probably becoming shorter.

Although life cycle timeframes are not known in advance, it is known that their length does increase at each higher level of aggregation in a field. Thus life cycles of particular local library programs such as writer workshops or story hours may be less than one year in duration, while those of city library systems may already have endured for many decades. Six meaningful levels of aggregation can be distinguished, as illustrated in the library field (Figure 9.8).

The *library services field* is that group of service enterprises whose primary aim is to serve consumers' informational needs.

Program categories are the different macrocomponents that, when aggregated, comprise the market structure of the library services field. *Public* refers to government-supplied information. *Nonpublic* refers to information suppliers of commerce, institutions, private research organizations, or homes. Both categories provide opportunities for meeting information needs. Their distinctive characteristics arise from the nature of the restrictions on their use as well as the nature of their individual service collections.

Agencies are the individual units of government that provide public information services at all levels of government.

Program lines are clusters of like products.

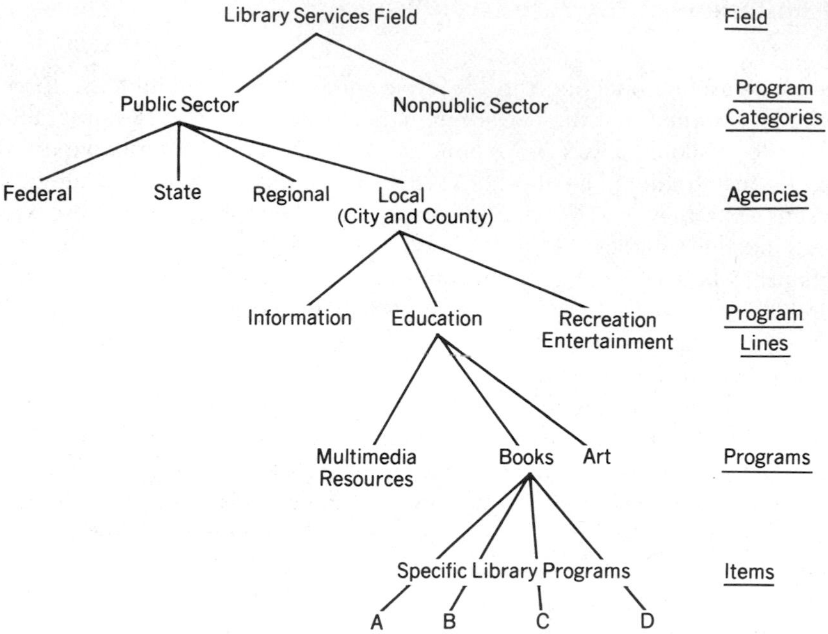

Figure 9.8. Structure of the Library Field.

Programs are related items within a program line, such as books, films, projection equipment, works of art, records, or tapes.

Items are distinctive units of a program identified through some unique characteristic such as location, timeframe, personnel, or content of a particular library program.

The final limitation of the program life cycle concept is that it is not only the total life span of the program that is unknown, but also the timeframe of each stage. Like all useful concepts, the generalized program life cycle model exposes the underlying pattern but ignores the complex variations that actually arise. With a particular program, some stages may be very short and others very long. For example, some programs may have a minimal introduction stage, going directly into take-off. This would suggest that the program had no substantial learning requirement, that a large latent demand was just waiting for the program to be offered, or that it represented a desirable substitute for a similar program offered elsewhere. Alternatively, a new program may be introduced whose curve does not have any resemblance to a classical life cycle. Indeed, it may fail to gain support and show an irreversible descending curve soon after its introduction.

Careful judgment, in other words, must be used in the analysis and application of program life cycles. The various characteristics of the stages described earlier will assist in identifying the stage a particular program occupies at any particular time, but hindsight will always be more accurate than present understanding. The assignment of particular programs to appropriate stages is still more art than science.

Clearly these limitations restrict the precision of the program life cycle concept. However, it remains a valuable tool. Perhaps the usefulness of the program life cycle concept was best summarized by Chester Wasson, who stated:

> The (Program) Life Cycle alone does not furnish an easily-read road map of an automatically unfolding highway to successful strategy. Rather it provides a framework of expectations—a set of patterns of the kinds of developments to which we need to be on the alert and for which we need to plan in advance.[33]

SUMMARY

A service is defined as a bundle of want-satisfying attributes. It has three tangible dimensions. First is the program itself, which includes all the ancillary components that augment the central program. Second comes the facility in which a service is offered. Creation of an environment and atmosphere at the facility that complement and enhance the program itself is a critical ingredient in a client's participation decision. Third, personnel substantially influence the extent to which benefits are delivered to clients.

In addition to the tangible dimensions of a program, the total offering includes a number of intangible dimensions, the chief of which are image and the name given to an agency or service. Image is the sum of beliefs, ideas, and impressions that a person has of an agency or of one of its services. Even though an image is not "real," it is a basis for decision making since it represents the totality of what clients know about a particular service. The name given to a program contributes to its image, and selecting a name is a critical marketing decision to which substantial thought and effort should be given.

The program life cycle concept provides a conceptual framework of the probable course of client acceptance of programs. The life cycle through which programs are likely to pass consists of five stages. The first stage is introduction, in which clientele acceptance is slow; second is the take-off stage, which is a period of rapid growth; third is maturity, during which the growth rate slows down; fourth is saturation, in which no further growth takes place and clientele acceptance begins to wane; and finally, decline, resulting either in death, which means removal from the market place, or petrification, which is a substantially reduced level of market acceptance remaining constant over a period of time. At the point of onset of decline, some modification to the program may be made to enable it to renew its growth rather than to decline; and hence it may extend its useful life.

The life cycle concept makes it possible to preplan, so managers can take the initiative instead of having to react to past events. When a new program is inaugurated, a series of strategic actions can be planned for implementation at various stages in the program's life. The model may apply not only to services and agencies but also to social causes and movements to which agencies are required to respond. A program audit provides an agency with a profile of its programs' current and future status. This makes it possible to assign priorities to such functions as developing new programs, terminating old programs, and allocating resources.

The life cycle stage should influence the assignment of management resources to a program. It has been recognized that some managers are better equipped and more successful at initiating development, while others are more effective at managing an existing operation, and still others are more effective at rescuing or retrenching a service or agency. These three types of managers have been termed growers, caretakers, and undertakers.

The life cycle model has four limitations. First, it cannot always be assumed that the program life cycle stage should determine market strategy, since market strategy may have been responsible for determining a program's life cycle stage. Second, the model is a demand model and thus assumes an adequate supply base that never constrains demand. Third, the length of a program's life cycle is not known in advance. Fourth, the timeframe of each stage is not known in advance.

NOTES

1. Tucker, S.L., "Introducing Marketing as a Planning and Management Tool," *Hospital and Health Services Administration,* Winter 1977, p. 39.
2. Shostack, G.L., "Breaking Free from Product Marketing," *Journal of Marketing*, Vol. 41 No. 2, April 1977, p. 78.
3. Herron, D.B., *Marketing Management for Social Service Agencies*. Columbus, OH: Association of Professional YMCA Directors, 1978, p. 82.
4. Kotler, P., "Atmospherics as a Marketing Tool," *Journal of Retailing*, vol. 49, No. 1 Winter 1973, p. 50.
5. "More Restaurants Sell an Exotic Atmosphere as Vigorously as Food," *The Wall Street Journal*, August 4, 1965, p. 1.
6. Kotler, "Atmospherics," p. 62.
7. Kotler, P., *Marketing for Non-Profit Organizations* (2nd ed.). Englewood Cliffs, NJ: Prentice-Hall, 1982, p. 325.
8. Schickel, R., *The Disney Version*. New York: Simon & Schuster, 1968, p. 318.
9. Some of the material in this section is based on Pope, N.W., "Mickey Mouse Marketing," *American Banker*, July 25, 1979.
10. Lynch, K., *The Image of the City*. Cambridge, MA: MIT Press, p. 5.
11. Ibid, p. 6.
12. Delano, F., "A New Identity Can Create a New Image," *Hospitals*, September 16, 1979, p. 197.
13. Kotler, P., and Dubois, B., "Education Problems and Marketing." In J.N. Sheth and P.L. Wright (eds.), *Marketing Analysis for Societal Problems*. Champaign, IL: University of Illinois Press, 1974, p. 194.

14. Delano, "New Identity," p. 197.

15. Kotler, "Non-Profit Organizations," p. 62.

16. Smith, D.C., "Mass Communication and International Image Change," *Journal of Conflict Resolution*, 17, 1973, p. 116.

17. Kotler, "Non-Profit Organizations," p. 56.

18. Ries, A., and Trout, J., *Positioning: The Battle for Your Mind*. New York: McGraw-Hill, 1981, p. 66.

19. Ibid., p. 118.

20. Lievegoed, B.C.J. *The Developing Organization*. London: Tavistock Publications, 1973, pp. 146–148.

21. Levitt, T., "Exploit the Product Life Cycle," *Harvard Business Review*, November/December 1965, pp. 81–94.

22. Levitt, T. *Marketing for Business Growth*. New York: McGraw-Hill, 1974, p. 157.

23. Rogers, E.H.M., and Shoemaker, F.F., *Communication of Innovations: A Cross-Cultural Approach* (2nd ed.). New York: Free Press, 1971, p. 116.

24. Clifford, D.K., "Managing the Product Life Cycle." In R. Mann (ed.), *The Art of Top Management: A McKinsey Anthology*. New York: McGraw-Hill, 1971, p. 225.

25. Levitt. *Marketing*, p. 161.

26. For a more detailed discussion of this implication see Crompton, J.L., and Hensarling, D.M., "Some Suggested Implications of the Product Life Cycle for Public Recreation and Park Managers," *Leisure Sciences*, vol. 1, No. 3, 1978, pp. 295–307.

27. "Wanted: A Manager to Fit Each Strategy," *Business Week*, February 25, 1980, pp. 166–173.

28. Martindell, J., *The Scientific Appraisal of Management*. New York: Harper and Row, 1950, pp. 268–269.

29. *Business Week*, "Wanted," p. 166.

30. Greiner, L.E., "Evolution and Revolution as Organizations Grow," *Harvard Business Review*, July/August 1972, p. 44.

31. Swayne, C., and Tucker, W., *The Effective Entrepreneur*. Morristown, NJ: General Learning Press, 1973, p. 18.

32. *Business Week*, "Wanted," pp. 166–173.

33. Wasson, C.R., *Product Management: Product Life Cycles and Competitive Marketing Strategy*. St. Charles, IL: Challenge Books, 1971, p. 12.

TEN

New Program Development

Government and social service agencies are frequently depicted as archaic and outmoded in their technologies and approaches to service delivery.[1] Managers are often perceived to be reluctant to embrace new approaches. Criticism of local governments has been particularly severe. Some observers have pictured them as hostile to new ideas with little capacity to accept new programs.[2]

Three reasons for this attitude have been suggested.[3] First, as monopolistic suppliers of services, many agencies are not required to compete intensely for clientele or resources, which, some argue, leads to inefficient and possibly noninnovative behavior. Their secure environment enables agencies to continue to operate in traditional ways. Second, managers are not rewarded for using their resources to better service citizens. Finally, many services are intangible, making it difficult to apply performance criteria and measurement. In such cases, it is difficult to assess whether or not a new service is superior to an existing offering.

Even among those personnel and agencies who are interested in developing new programs, there is a real temptation to become so preoccupied with the day-to-day task of managing existing programs and services that little attention is given to their development. Every government and social service agency emerged to meet particular societal wants in the environment. But all environments change, and agencies must, therefore, change to permit adaptation to new environments. New programs are necessary for an agency to remain relevant.

The term "new" has different meanings for different people. Some see a new program as an invention, something that has never been offered before by anyone. Others feel a program is new if the agency's clientele view it as being new. In this chapter *we use the term "new" to refer to a program that is offered by an agency to a client group for the first time, even though it may have previously been offered to that client group by other private or public*

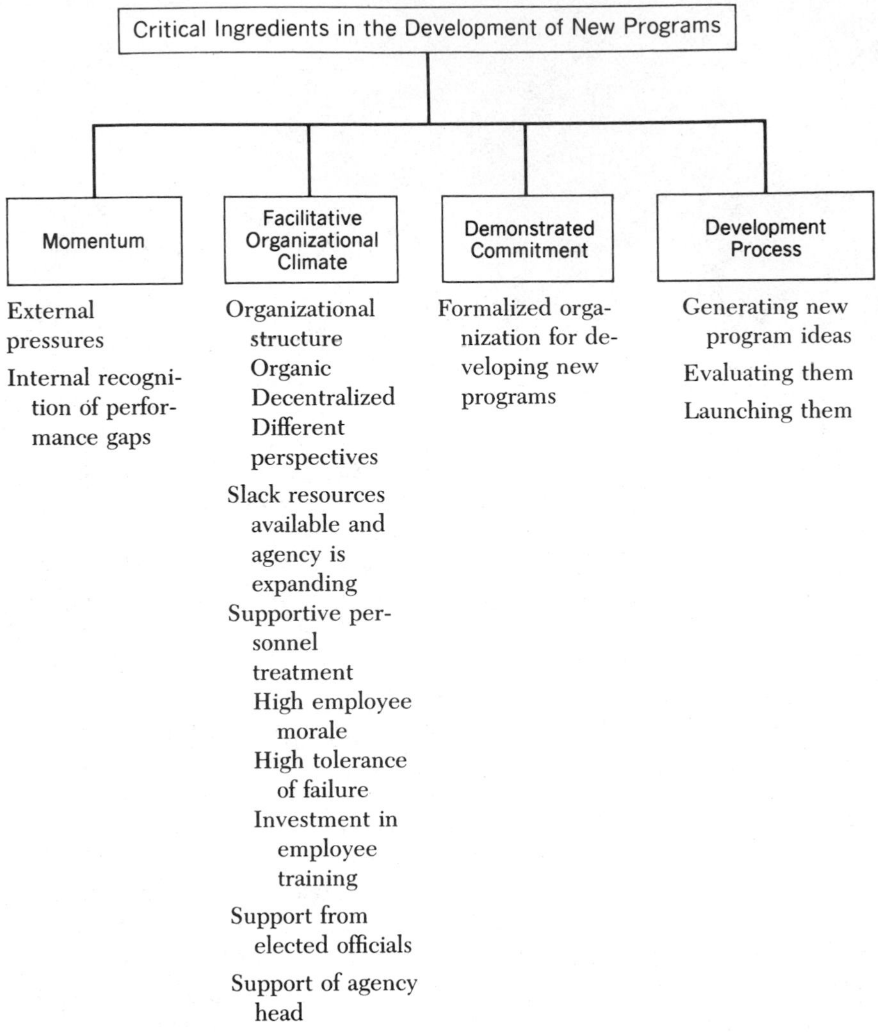

Figure 10.1. Critical Ingredients in the Development of New Programs.

sector organizations. This classification includes completely new programs, modifications of existing programs offered to present client groups, and existing programs offered to new clienteles, regardless of whether or not these programs are similar to those offered by other private or public organizations. It also includes internal program changes that improve cost efficiency or service effectiveness even though these changes may not be visible to clientele.[4]

If, for example, computerization is introduced to register program participants or to schedule maintenance tasks, cost efficiency and/or service effectiveness may improve, yet agency clientele may not be aware of this change. It does, nevertheless, represent a new program for the agency. We have adopted this broad view of the term "new" because any time a program is modified, offered to a new client group, or is new to the agency, the problems inherent in its development and management may be unique. That is, it may present problems and opportunities different from those previously encountered by the agency or others elsewhere.

The development of new programs should be separated from the decision to implement them. An agency may identify a need and arrive at an appropriate marketing mix to meet the need; but it does not necessarily follow that the agency should be the program supplier.[5] For example, if it was determined that a selected target market needed an increase in child care facilities and programs, the agency's role might be to convene a meeting of other agencies, private organizations, and citizen groups to determine what agency or organization was best suited to provide the service.

The organization of this chapter is shown diagrammatically in Figure 10.1. First we examine sources of momentum, which are the stimuli primarily responsible for the emergence of new offerings. Momentum sources can be found both outside the agency and within.

Internal momentum for new programs is generated by agency personnel, who must feel encouraged by the environment within the organization to innovate. Thus without a facilitative environment only new program ideas that are mandated by external forces are likely to come to fruition. Even in these cases, if they have not been embraced by agency personnel their delivery may be inferior.

Given a facilitative environment, the agency's commitment to new programs should be made visible by a formally organized committee that is responsible for new program development. This committee's charge should be to generate new program ideas, evaluate them, and see that the best of them are implemented.

SOURCES OF STIMULI FOR DEVELOPING NEW PROGRAMS

Reaction to External Pressure

External pressures may be exerted by client groups, professional peers, higher levels of government, or elected officials. Client groups who lobby vigorously may be successful in persuading even a reluctant agency to implement a particular program. For example, consider the introduction of computer instructional programs in early school grades:

> It has been suggested that a lot of money is going for computerized educational materials that research has shown can be taught just as well with pencil and paper. However, parents, who may know very little about computers, tend to fear their children will be unemployable if they haven't mastered computer technology. Consequently, they urge schools to offer computing in the early grades. A spokes-

> man for the Educational Products Information Exchange Institute stated, "Many schools are yielding to parental impatience and are purchasing hardware without sound educational planning, so they can say "O.K. we've moved into the computer age." The dilemma was expressed by a high school principal who observed, "We found ourselves caught in the middle of the problem—between parental pressure and wise educational decisions.[6]

Many managers place considerable importance on having their reputation and expertise recognized by professional peers. The development of new programs may aid in establishing a manager's reputation as being progressive, someone who searches for innovative ways to effect cost reductions or to improve service delivery. One criminologist has implied that this phenomenon accounts for the rapid diffusion of SWAT teams in police departments:

> Police departments are adopting this policy before any evaluative research can be done on it. It is the kind of thing that quickly catches on in police departments because of the pressure to be up-to-date without any knowledge of exactly what they are getting into.[7]

Sometimes local or state agencies are mandated by the federal government to develop a new program. For example, it has been reported that patient advisory committees in community public health agencies would not have been accepted by many of these agencies if the U.S. Office of Economic Opportunity had not required them as a condition for granting federal support.[8] Examples of federal government mandates requiring local governments to respond with new programs abound, and they include such well-known mandates as the Clean Air Act and the 55 mph speed limit. Similar outside pressure may also be exerted by the judiciary. The busing requirements imposed by courts on many school districts to facilitate integration are well-known examples. Sometimes these new program mandates are encouraged and welcomed by members of an agency because they provide a means of overcoming resistance by other members in the organization.

Higher levels of government can exert external pressure to innovate by the judicious use of incentives. The availability of grants or free technical expertise, for example, can be persuasive in enticing local agencies to initiate new programs.

The final external source of pressure is elected officials who feel that a particular new program will convince a voting constituency of their progressiveness, sensitivity to client needs, or advocacy for efficiency or better service delivery, then they will exercise their influence on the agency to offer the new program.

Internal Recognition of Performance Gaps

Internal momentum for developing new programs is stimulated by voluntary recognition of performance gaps and an agency's efforts to close them. *A per-*

formance gap is the difference between what an agency is currently achieving and what its managers believe it could and should achieve.

The most frequent reason for the existence of performance gaps is probably changes in environmental conditions, especially citizen priorities. It has been found that the greater the degree of environmental uncertainty, the more conscious an agency becomes of performance gaps, and the more likely it is to introduce new programs.[9] A safe and predictable environment creates little incentive to introduce new programs. But when the environment is turbulent, agencies must be willing to experiment with new programs. They must respond to change with change; otherwise they become irrelevant and obsolete.

Demographic changes in the community may create performance gaps that require agencies to modify existing programs for new target markets. For example, nationwide enrollment projections for postsecondary education show traditional student enrollment declining at least until 1995. In order to offset the impact of these trends, postsecondary institutions are developing new programs that attract entirely new clientele.[10]

Frequently, new programs emerge from agencies that recognize changes in the lifestyles of client groups. Interest in youth soccer programs in the 1970s; increased interest in home crafts and do-it-yourself programs; and the influx of women and older people into aerobics, jogging, bicycling, and physical fitness in general have all presented opportunities for leisure agencies to provide new programs for existing clientele and modified programs for new client groups.

New technology and inventions capable of producing new want satisfactions or of substantially improving the satisfaction of wants now only partially appeased may facilitate the development of new programs. The kidney dialysis machine, improvements in communication technology, interactive computers, and even the introduction of skateboards with polyurethane wheels created opportunities for the successful introduction of new government and social service programs.

The more stringent financial climate of the 1980s has encouraged some agencies to invest in new services that offer potential for revenue production in order to reduce tax support. For example, a county board of supervisors requested its parks director to develop a series of new programs that would cut the county's tax support for parks each year, until after seven years it would fall to zero. They provided a 10 cent property tax for this seven-year period, which was used to acquire, develop, and promote the additional revenue producing facilities needed to offset the losses incurred by conventional park services.[11]

The availability of underutilized resources is sometimes the stimulus for developing new programs. One source of such resources may be substantial fluctuations in demand. Public schools are an example. They are used for seven hours per day, five days per week, and nine months per year. In many cases, these facilities are idle for the remaining seventeen hours per day, weekends, and summers. This has served as a stimulus for some school districts to offer new programs in recreation, adult education, and other community services, to ensure better use of these resources.

Finally, performance gaps may be dramatically exposed by a critical environmental event. For example, one community experienced two accidents: a furnace explosion that killed nine people and another accident that killed two young high school coaches. Many felt that more lives would have been saved if onsite medical attention had been available. This prompted the community to introduce a mobile intensive care unit program, which required the purchase of an emergency vehicle and the training of seventeen firefighters to serve as paramedics.[12]

CHARACTERISTICS OF A FACILITATIVE AGENCY CLIMATE

Traditionally, discussions of new program development have focused exclusively on the technical development and appropriateness of new programs for selected target markets, rather than on the organizational environment needed to nurture them. This is unfortunate because the stimuli for developing new programs require a supportive agency climate.

For an agency to have a facilitative organizational climate, its personnel must be predisposed toward implementing new programs. There appears to be considerable agreement among experts regarding the agency characteristics that are associated with an inclination to develop new programs. Unfortunately, many of these appear to be the opposite of those most frequently found in government and social service agencies.

In this section, we briefly discuss the facilitative characteristics that have been identified. They are summarized in Figure 10.2 and presented under five headings: organizational structure, availability of organizational slack, peronnel treatment, support from elected officials, and support of the agency head.

Organizational Structure

Positive environments for new program development tend to exist when agencies are organic, decentralized, and staffed by people from diverse backgrounds.

Organic agencies are loosely structured, encourage openness, frequent interaction between colleagues, and participation in the decision process. They are characterized by a maximum of individual discretion and a minimum of subjection to higher authority. In contrast, a mechanistic agency is multitiered with senior management, remote from contact with the community, making all decisions. It tends to be depersonalized, rigid, and centralized with emphasis placed on following specified rules and procedures, which are set down for performing tasks in the organization.

Organic organizations have been found to be more responsive to new program stimuli than those that are mechanistic.[13] However, most government

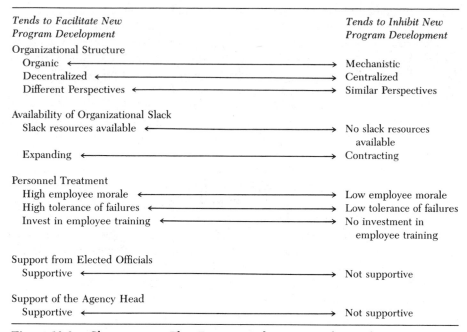

Tends to Facilitate New Program Development	*Tends to Inhibit New Program Development*
Organizational Structure	
Organic	Mechanistic
Decentralized	Centralized
Different Perspectives	Similar Perspectives
Availability of Organizational Slack	
Slack resources available	No slack resources available
Expanding	Contracting
Personnel Treatment	
High employee morale	Low employee morale
High tolerance of failures	Low tolerance of failures
Invest in employee training	No investment in employee training
Support from Elected Officials	
Supportive	Not supportive
Support of the Agency Head	
Supportive	Not supportive

Figure 10.2. Characteristics That Determine the Agency Climate for New Program Development.

and social services agencies tend to be mechanistic, which inhibits their development of new programs.

Centralization of authority stifles new program development because it incorporates too many checks and balance points that have to be surmounted. Clearly, the more time and effort needed to gain permission from those in positions of higher authority, the less incentive there is to invest in the procedure. Decentralization offers greater autonomy and local responsibility, which in turn provides fewer obstacles and more incentives for developing new programs.

An organization's size and whether or not it is growing have frequently been associated with a proclivity to introduce new programs.[14] However, this may be misleading. Researchers who have reported this relationship tend to agree that size and growth are most likely to be proxies for other factors, particularly the availability of slack resources, which is discussed in the following section.

Greater size may ensure availability of the "critical mass" of personnel necessary to stimulate and foster new programs. Increased size permits more specialization. If an agency is large and/or growing, it is better able to add new occupational specialities and new functions, which tend to lead to more new programs being introduced. Conversely, if an agency is contracting it tends to increase centralization and not focus on new programs. Further, if no new people are being hired, then fewer new ideas from the outside are likely to enter the agency.

In many instances, the assets of size and slack resources are nullified because an agency is bureaucratic and mechanistic. Smaller agencies often have the advantage of being organic with less red tape and fewer levels of management. In the private sector, the ability of small organizations to develop new products has been repeatedly reported: "To an amazing extent, major new products incorporating new technology have been brought to market by new (and therefore presumably small) companies, rather than by those (presumably large) companies with large investments in fundamental research."[15]

In a large, mechanistic agency ideas may have to be approved by several levels of superiors before they are fully developed. Since it is often difficult to adequately defend ideas in the early stages of development, they tend to be rejected. Further, as we shall see in Chapter 12, developing a new program may imply that resources have to be taken from an existing program. In large organizations this is more likely to lead to resistance because there are more people who are in danger of losing resources.

An agency that has a diversity of backgrounds among its personnel is more likely to generate new program ideas. Personnel with similar backgrounds can suffer from what psychologists call "functional myopia"—a tendency to view the agency, its opportunities, and problems from the same set of reference points. Differences in background stimulate constructive conflict between individuals and a consequent cross-fertilization of ideas.[16]

Availability of Organizational Slack

Organizational slack is the difference between the resources necessary for an agency to carry out its basic functions and the total resources it has available.[17] It is difficult for an agency to develop new programs if it is fully extended, applying all of its resources to carrying out existing commitments and solving today's problems. Without slack, in terms of uncommitted staff time, expertise, or money, new programs will not consistently emerge.

Organizational slack influences whether or not an agency can afford the resource costs associated with developing new programs.

> The existence of slack means that the organization can afford to (1) purchase costly innovations, (2) absorb failures, (3) bear the costs of implementing the innovation, and (4) explore new ideas in advance of an actual need.[18]

Slack may be created by retrenchment efforts that release resources from existing programs. In the past, resources from federal and state governments, whether provided annually or on a one-time basis, have provided some slack for local agencies. These resources were directly applied to a host of new programs developed in public housing, police departments, and public schools.[19] It is unfortunate that some elected officials have failed to distinguish between "fat" and "slack." They feel a mandate to remove the fat, but removing the slack along with the fat in the long term can only serve to reduce an agency's efficiency.

Personnel Treatment

It has been argued that an agency can only successfully implement a new activity if there is high employee morale.[20] Several studies have related high staff morale to organizational innovativeness.[21] People who are satisfied with their jobs are more committed to the organization; consequently, they are more receptive to new ideas for improving the agency's services.

An agency's treatment of its personnel with regard to new programs may foster or inhibit their development. Although reliable data are not available for the public sector, estimates of the proportion of new products and services that fail in the private sector range from about 35 to over 90 percent.[22] The wide variation results from surveys that address diverse industries at different times and use different definitions of failure. This high failure rate occurs despite the substantial investment in research that typically is made before products and services are launched. It would be surprising if many new programs offered by government and social service agencies did not fail as well.

Mistakes and failures must be anticipated, accepted, and not unreasonably penalized if a sympathetic agency climate is to be fostered. This does not mean that sloppy work, poor planning and implementation, or incompetence should be excused. It simply means that risk is inherent in new program development and some failures are inevitable.

Many public sector managers are averse to taking large risks because they judge the personal cost of failure as greater than the gains possible from success. Their feelings have often been borne out in the past:

> Where there is only limited external pressure for improved performance, there may also be real negative incentives to undertaking innovations which may improve performance but which also involve some risk. For example, a police chief who uses standard procedures is unlikely to be criticized for not innovating; if he does undertake nonstandard procedures to improve performance, there may be little reward. Furthermore, if something goes wrong with a nonstandard procedure, the police or fire chief may find himself without a job. The inability to appropriate gains from improving efficiency, combined with the high risk of mistakes, does not provide top officials with incentives to try to improve public sector performance.[23]

Consistent investment in employee training is a key ingredient in creating a sympathetic agency climate for new program development. The availability of appropriate expertise is likely to influence the enthusiasm personnel have for new program suggestions. If expertise is not currently available, the agency must be prepared to invest in the training necessary to enable personnel to confidently operate the program. Consider the case of a computer-assisted instructional program (CAI) introduced into a school district:

> The CAI program was introduced by the district's mathematics supervisor. It received consistent financial support. Initially many teachers were enthusiastic about CAI, but only one round of in-service training was formally offered. Most

teachers, particularly those in subjects other than mathematics, remained largely unaware of the ways in which CAI could be integrated into their classroom activities.

There was no formal training program for teachers and practitioner certification to teach in the school district did not include any requirement to have a computer background or CAI training. As a result, there have been no adoptions of CAI-oriented textbooks and most students and teachers have no contact with CAI.[24]

Support from Elected Officials

The requirement that elected officials be reelected after a short period in office is likely to influence the fate of relatively large new program proposals. The program life cycle concept suggests that a lead time may exist before a new program realizes its full potential. This may deter some officials from supporting major new programs since they will incur the adverse political impacts associated with the high start-up costs of a program, while the benefits are reaped by their successors. Others may see that investment in plant and equipment can stimulate the local economy during their term of office.[25] Political gain may be the greatest during the construction phase of a project, when construction activity provides visible signs of "progress" and officials receive the benefits associated with being "doers."

The conclusions of a study of new programs introduced in a major city are informative:

> The lesson is clear from the cases: innovation usually costs money. In the long run, it may save money or produce such user benefits worth the added operating costs. However, since local politicians react primarily to immediate pressures, administrative entrepreneurs are advised to find ways to shift costs upward, forward—or "under the rug."[26]

Some elected officials may abide by the old aphorism, "If you do nothing you'll be elected forever, because you won't make mistakes." Generally, there is likely to be less political risk associated with rejecting a new program proposal than with accepting it, for the risk associated with failure may be high while the gains associated with success may be low.

Support of the Agency Head

In mechanistic agencies, implementation of new programs is highly dependent on the role played by the agency head. If the head of an agency favors new program development and spends time supporting innovative projects, he or she can bring about their implementation rather easily. On the other hand, a noninnovative agency head can stymie nearly all new program development. Empirical studies repeatedly suggest that strong, visible support by top leadership is the most important factor in fostering a climate to facilitate innovative endeavors.[27]

ORGANIZING FOR NEW PROGRAM DEVELOPMENT

Since (1) the life cycles of many programs are becoming shorter because consumer priorities are changing rapidly, (2) the rate of new program failure is fairly high, and (3) the lead time from initial suggestion of an idea to its implementation may be fairly substantial, it is desirable to have a steady stream of new programs in order to keep an agency's offerings relevant. Fostering a continual stream of new programs requires minimum dependence on the accidental and maximum attention to the purposeful cultivation of new program ideas.

In many agencies, personnel tend to be passive receivers rather than active solicitors of new program ideas. Moreover, the ideas that are received frequently are so poorly processed that it is a matter of chance as to whether or not they receive full consideration. The infant mortality rate of ideas must be reduced. An agency cannot hope to be consistently successful in nurturing new programs by employing a sporadic hit-or-miss approach. An organized structure is essential for purposeful new program cultivation.

A commitment to new program development implies a commitment to be proactive rather than reactive. An agency is proactive if it explicitly allocates resources to search for unmet clientele needs and designs new programs to meet them.[28]

The preferred approach to organizing for new product development is to appoint a committee to be responsible for this function in every division of the agency. In large agencies, subcommittees may be formed at various levels within the divisions. The basic mission of each of these organized entities should include generating new ideas, evaluating them, and nurturing the best of them to implementation.

It is essential that accountability be built into the structure. Otherwise efforts toward new program development are likely to be dissipated by the pressure of day-to-day events. Each division-level entity should be required to report to the agency director every four months detailing the progress of its new program efforts. This accountability and consciousness about new program development throughout the agency might be further enhanced by setting agencywide goals. For example, "At least 15 percent of our patronage should come from services which we did not offer 5 years ago." (This is the average percent in the private sector of current sales volume attributable to new products first introduced in the past five years.)[29]

Establishing a New Program Committee

New program committees should be established with proper authority to oversee the new program development process and to review key decisions at interim points in time. While five to seven members may be an optimal size, committee size and composition will obviously vary in accordance with the size of the agency and the complexity of its services.

Committee members should be highly motivated, enthusiastic individuals, who preferably have already demonstrated ability to introduce new programs. They should be a microcosm of the divisions the committee oversees. In this way, the ideas and wisdom of managers with diverse perspectives can be pooled. However, the thinking and skills of people within an agency are honed to what is presently done in that agency. They are experts on what has been done in the past but may be myopic or less expert on new programs with which they have had no experience. For this reason, individuals from outside the agency, such as advisory committee members and community representatives, should be part of new program committees.

These committees have the responsibility to "move" the planning process and keep senior management involved and informed. Effective coordination and control procedures need to be established because a lack of clear responsibility may result in "buckpassing." One person should be specifically charged with overseeing the development of each program idea.

These new program development committees should also be responsible for identifying programs that could be retrenched. Ideally, as we shall see in Chapter 12, the two tasks should be complementary. If some existing offerings are retrenched, it may be easier for personnel to be enthusiastic about accepting new program responsibilities. Retrenchment provides the response to the question "Why should I take on any more? I've got enough to do."

NEW PROGRAM DEVELOPMENT PROCESS

Most managers will agree at least in most part with the process for developing new programs that is presented in this section. However, there are many cases in which substantial resources are committed to a new program idea with little or no systematic evaluation of its feasibility. The service is implemented at great expense and then it is found that no viable market exists for it. An organized procedure should preclude hasty and random decisions and ensure that new programs have potential to be relevant for the clientele, accepted in the community, and financially feasible.

Chance has played, and will continue to play, an important role in successful new program introduction. However, in the long run, the "luckiest" agencies will be those whose new programs are rooted in a thoughtful and soundly conceived framework. Even when a systematic new program development process is pursued, there will be opinions, personalities, and political factors that influence it. A procedure will not remove that aspect of an agency's operation, but it will set the tone and provide the framework within which decisions must be made.

Effective new program planning involves generating new ideas, evaluating them, and then implementing a procedure for bringing the program from a germ of an idea to a successful launching. Although the number of steps in the new program development process may vary among agencies, a distinctive sequential pattern can be discerned. In some cases, there will be an ample length of time and adequate data to utilize the total approach thoroughly. In other cases, time constraints may dictate a shortening of the process and a combining of certain steps. For every program, the same type of thought process and decision-making rationale should take place. The sequential pattern of the six major stages are discussed in this section and are illustrated in Figure 10.3. They are:

Generating new program ideas
Screening
Concept development
Feasibility analysis
Testing
Launching the new program

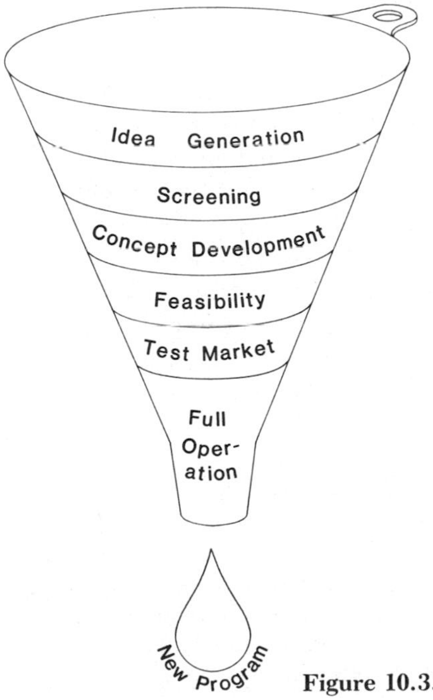

Figure 10.3. New Program Development Process.

Figure 10.3 shows that at each stage in the process, some program ideas are discarded. Each stage becomes progressively more expensive in dollars and scarce manpower. Although the later stages are most costly, equal evaluative effort should be spent in the earlier stages: Most programs fail because either the idea or the timing was wrong, not because the agency lacked the ability to implement them satisfactorily.[30]

Generating New Program Ideas

Some new program development procedures place emphasis on the evaluation and implementation of ideas that already exist. In other words, there is no formal mechanism for generating new ideas. Most agencies do not give enough organized thought, or develop disciplined procedures, to ensure that truly innovative ideas are available for the evaluation phases of the new program development process.

A great deal of evidence suggests that many efforts to produce new programs to meet client needs are "incestuous."[31] That is, there is a tendency to reach for prior experience, prior approaches, or modest distortions of old answers, as opposed to really searching for new ideas. We become victimized by habit. The challenge is to transcend the habit of restricting new program ideas to the limits of past experience. All else being equal, the greater the number of ideas generated and the more diverse their points of origin, the better the best ideas are likely to be. The major sources of new program ideas are citizens, other suppliers, and agency personnel.

Ideas from Citizens. The marketing concept suggests that citizens should be the starting point for developing new programs. Too often this source of ideas has been restricted to existing clients, if it is used at all. Asking citizens who do not use an agency's services about their needs and the benefits they seek may be equally fruitful for suggesting new directions.

The historical need for data to justify predetermined service planning decisions has been replaced with a need for data that will clearly define citizen wants and help to identify the most effective new programs to resolve them.[32] Increasing recognition of this need will help to rectify the discouraging situation of the past when few agencies systematically sought new program ideas by focusing on citizen wants.

> There is a great variety in the degree to which formal needs assessment data are used by human service agencies as a basis for the development of new human services. *Few* agencies have an overall needs assessment strategy that develops a composite review of the potential population actually served by the agency and particular service recipients. *Few* have ongoing observers in the community who constantly monitor the human environment. *Few* perform statistical analyses of population data and agency statistics. *Few* provide the opportunity for clients to

address and discuss need issues in individual or group sessions. *Few* go to the public through town meetings and open forums.

> *Most* agencies collect and display statistics rather than analyze and utilize them. *Most* agencies use only the observations of their own personnel to monitor the human environment rather than seeking out other observers. *Most* agencies use public hearings and open forums only when required to do so. *Most* agencies make an effort to review their own client data but "never quite get around to it." *Many* agencies rely upon mandates or funding availability to determine their new program activity. *Many* agencies regard needs assessment as a luxury to be pursued when "extra time is available."[33]

Periodic interviews with influential citizens representing various clientele groups are a particularly useful source of programming ideas. For example, a community institution of higher education might interview influential representatives of business, industry, trade unions, special groups, professional societies, social agencies, government, civic groups, and hospitals.

> Such leaders are frequently in an excellent position to know the educational needs of their constituencies and what resources can be made available to support programs to meet their needs. Meetings with them should be held on a regular basis; good programming ideas generally emerge after an influential has been cultivated for some time and has a clear idea of the services the institution can provide to his clientele group.[34]

As noted earlier in this chapter, there are occasions when client groups exercise external pressure to persuade agencies to offer a new program. However, there are many other occasions when potential clients make requests without attempting to pressure. If an agency is receptive and imaginative, these unsolicited program requests can emerge as major new offerings:

> In 1979, Johnson County Park and Recreation District in Kansas was asked for assistance by Bendix Corporation. Bendix provided recreation opportunities for employees, but had difficulty securing adequate facilities to accommodate all of their employees' demands. This initial approach prompted recognition by the district that corporations were a potential target market in need of recreation services which was not being served. Three years later over 15,000 employees from 84 corporations were enrolled as members of the district's corporate program and this had become its largest and fastest growing target market.[35]

Ideas from Other Suppliers. An agency's personnel should be aware of new programs that have been introduced by other suppliers of similar services elsewhere. It is more expensive to engage in trial and error learning about the potential effectiveness of a new program than to share experiences. Government and social service managers can take advantage of national networks of similar professionals. Through each professional association's conventions, personal contacts, journals, and other publications managers are exposed to a steady flow of information, which can be a useful source of new program ideas. For example, "a change in local refuse collection practices is more likely to occur because of the diffusion of information by the National Solid Waste Management Association than because of a decision by local elected officials."[36]

The telephone often is an underused resource for soliciting new program ideas from other suppliers. Within seconds contact can be made with professionals elsewhere in similar positions who can share their experiences. Many managers do not call others who are outside of their own, well-established professional network. However, more fresh ideas are likely to emerge by calling professionals with whom there has been no previous contact.

Leads will multiply as a professional taps other suppliers' networks. The result is often the identification of new key resource people who are able to share ideas. The sifting and winnowing of external sources of information in this way has been shown to be a more important source of new ideas than the conventional literature search.[37] Indeed, the literature often becomes meaningful only after personal conversations have provided necessary background information.

Ideas from Agency Personnel. The training and experience of people within an agency are prime sources of information for successful new program ideas. Personnel dealing face-to-face with client groups are likely to be the first to learn about changes in client group wants and to be the most responsive to them. Hence it is important that all levels of the organization be involved in developing new programs.

Several techniques have been developed over the years to help individuals and groups develop better ideas, but the most successful method probably has been brainstorming. The basic principles of brainstorming were developed by Alex Osborn.[38] Generally between five and seven people are invited to participate in sessions lasting for about an hour. This group could include people from outside the agency, both experts and nonexperts, since agency personnel may be stereotypical in their view of a problem. The same group should not repeatedly be asked to brainstorm together over a long period of time. This develops a rigid pattern of thinking, in which one member can almost anticipate the reactions of another. The group should consist of people who are substantially at the same rank in their respective organizations. If superiors are involved, their presence may serve to inhibit freewheeling on the part of their subordinates.

Group members should be acquainted with the topic area in advance of the session and have some opportunity to think about it. A key to successful brainstorming is adherence to the deferment-of-judgment principle. When the meeting takes place, the convener states at the outset, "Remember now, we want as many ideas as possible—the wilder the better, and remember, no evaluation." Wild ideas are encouraged so that chains of habit are broken and ideas flow freely without being condemned by previous experience. The goal is to create an environment in which participants feel psychologically safe and nonthreatened.

As the ideas emerge, one idea sparks another. One member of the group should be designated to write down the ideas where they are clearly visible to all participants. For a brainstorming session to yield maximum dividends, Osborn states that the following four rules must be observed.[39]

> *Criticism is not permitted.* Adverse judgment of ideas must be withheld until later. The following type of reactions are prohibited:
>
> "We tried that before and it didn't work"
> "We've never done it that way"
> "It's too radical"
> "It's against policy"
> "The boss won't like it"
> "That's ridiculous"
> "No one will accept it"
> "You'll be laughed out of town"
>
> Creativity is so delicate a flower that praise tends to make it bloom, while discouragement often nips it in the bud. Any of us will put out more and better ideas if our efforts are appreciated. Unfriendliness can make us stop trying. Wisecracks can be poison . . . . Every idea should elicit receptivity, if not praise.[40]
>
> *Freewheeling is welcomed.* The wilder the idea, the better; it is easier to tame down than to think up.
>
> *Quantity is wanted.* The greater the number of ideas, the more likelihood of useful proposals.
>
> *Combinations and improvement are sought.* In addition to contributing ideas of their own, participants should suggest how ideas of others can be turned into better ideas; or how two or more ideas can be joined into still another idea. Brainstorming takes advantage of the power of association. "This" suggests "that" and "that" leads to something else.

Frequently, a brainstorming session starts with a flood of ideas followed by a sudden slackening off (see Figure 10.4). There is a tendency to give up too easily or too early. If the group perseveres through this first lull, the flow will often increase after participants have had time to think beyond their initial ideas. Indeed, early ideas are not usually the best because they tend to be the most obvious and superficial. It has been observed that "quantity of ideas breeds

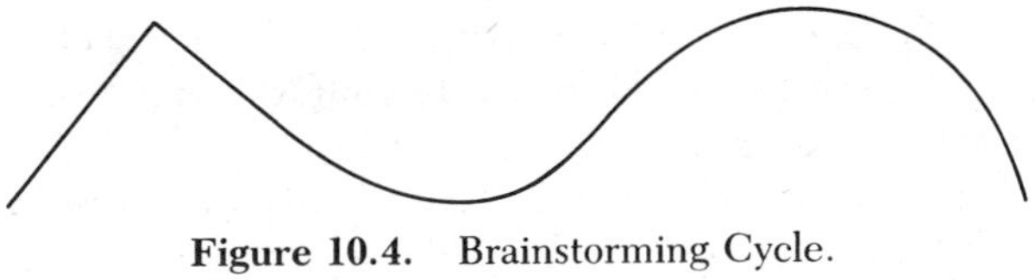

Figure 10.4. Brainstorming Cycle.

quality. In case after case, the last 50 ideas produced at a brainstorm session have averaged higher in quality than the first 50."[41]

When the brainstorming session is completed the new program ideas should be classified into logical categories—usually between five and ten such categories emerge. The typed list is then circulated to all participants within 24 hours of the session, with plenty of blank spaces for additional ideas to be inserted. After this short incubation period more ideas may have occurred to the group members, supplementing their original efforts.

Personnel at all levels of the organization can use brainstorming effectively. Better results are not necessarily related to high levels of education or seniority in the agency. Indeed, some evidence suggests that new program ideas tend to contract as knowledge and judgment expand:

> Probably the most difficult panel members are executives who have been over-trained in the usual kind of non-creative conference . . . . Executives traditionally rate each other on the basis of judgment . . . . "We are far more apt to look up to the other fellow if he makes no mistakes than if he suggests lots of ideas."[42]

As education and experience increase, individuals may develop inhibitions that rigidize thinking and make it more difficult to engage in freewheeling thinking.

It is sometimes valuable to engage in reverse brainstorming as a prelude to a brainstorming session because of the critical comment that can be stimulated. After listing all the things wrong with an agency's existing services, the group then reverts to brainstorming and seeks a solution for each negative feature.

Evaluating New Program Ideas

When all of the fragile original ideas have been allowed to live for a brief period (because nobody was permitted to critique or eliminate them), an agency must decide which to discard and which to investigate further. The usefulness of the tentative ideas depends on what is done with them—how effectively they are evaluated and how creatively they are developed. As ideas are developed, the viable number can be expected to decrease substantially.

Opinion is mixed over whether evaluation of the initial ideas should be done by the same group or whether another group should take over. Morale-wise, it seems important that those who suggested new program ideas should have the satisfaction of guiding them through to fruition. Further, it may be difficult for others to fully understand the raw ideas until they have been through at least the concept development stage. At the feasibility stage, however, it may be advantageous for another group to take over, so that more objective decisions can be made. "Otherwise it's like a beauty contest judged by the mothers of the would-be Miss Americas."[43]

Before evaluation can start, criteria for what makes a successful new program have to be established. The criteria may be given importance weightings. For each idea the group asks, "Does it have the potential to measure up to the criteria?" or "Can it meet at least the most important of them?"

> To what degree is the idea compatible with the agency's mission and its objectives?
> Is the need served by the new program a high priority for the agency?
> What is the size of the potential target market?
> Are existing opportunities provided by other suppliers?
> Is it technically feasible; for example, are the necessary facilities available?
> What present and potential personnel knowledge and skills are needed?
> Are monetary and personnel resources available?

Each idea passes through a sequential process comparable to a series of filters, each succeeding filter having a finer mesh than its predecessor (Figure 10.3). There are four steps in this process: screening, concept development, feasibility analysis, and testing. At each stage management must decide whether to (1) move on to the next stage, (2) abandon the program, or (3) seek additional information.

Screening. This initial filter serves to eliminate unrealistic alternatives. It is a review undertaken by the new program development committee to assess which ideas merit further study, given the established criteria. For example, if the mission of a park and recreation agency is primarily to serve client groups with resource-based facilities, it may decide to remove nontraditional, social-type programs from the set of possibilities, even though they might have appeal to defined target markets. To adopt such ideas may mean alienating client groups the agency currently serves, who may resent resources being allocated in this new direction. It may also mean having to hire several new people with the skills to operate social programs as well as acquire the facilities to house them. The agency may be put under undue financial strain by these needs.

Just because ideas have been unsuccessfully tried in the past should not necessarily exclude their being introduced again.

> Younger executives come to me with what they think are good ideas. Out of my experience I could tell them why their ideas will not succeed. Instead of talking them out of their ideas, I have suggested that they be tried out in test areas in order to minimize losses. The joke of it is that half the time these youthful ideas, which I might have nipped in the bud, turn out either to be successful or lead to other ideas that are successful. The point I overlooked was that while the idea was not new, the conditions under which the idea was to be carved out were materially different.[44]

In the screening process, each program idea should be rated against each of the criteria as "very good," "good," "fair," or "poor." This rating should first be done independently to enable each member of the committee to record his or her opinion without being influenced by the views of other members. Then it is the leader's responsibility to negotiate a consensus about the best ideas through committee discussion. The ideas should be ranked and those with the greatest potential selected for concept development.

Concept Development. During this stage the ideas are developed further, from a rough idea to a more elaborate description of a specific program. Alternative marketing mixes should be formulated and input solicited from potential users to identify the best of those formulations. Those programs that still appear likely to be successful are taken to the next stage.

Soliciting input from the potential clientele will improve the chances of developing a relevant service and create an environment that may later enhance acceptance of the service idea when it is finally launched. This is also likely, however, to raise a clientele's expectations, which may create a problem if the idea is dropped in a subsequent evaluation stage. By the end of this stage a fairly detailed picture of the proposed program should have emerged so that its feasibility can be meaningfully assessed.

Feasibility Analysis. Feasibility analysis submits the proposed program to a more rigorous examination of the costs and benefits that are likely to be associated with it. The extent and depth of the analysis will vary according to the amount of resources the program is likely to require. If these are substantial, obviously it will be important to study the implications of introducing the program more fully. If the idea is relatively inexpensive, this stage will be completed more quickly.

Before initiating the feasibility analysis, it is important to establish criteria regarding feasibility. Must the program be financially self-supporting? If a subsidy is acceptable, then what is the maximum level of subsidy beyond which the program is considered nonfeasible? Without such criteria no judgment can be made on a program's feasibility. Further, there is a real danger of a creeping commitment to a program by all associated with it, as they become more involved in its development. The result may be a loss of impartial, objective perspective.

Assessment of the probable demand for a program and the need for new capital investment if any, together with its estimated operational costs and the income likely to accrue from users, is an essential feature of the feasibility analysis. This is a critical stage, because if the program survives feasibility analysis a pilot program will be developed and tested, committing the agency to investment of money, people, and perhaps equipment and facilities.

The final task at this stage is to establish a timetable for testing and implementing the program and to assign operating responsibility for these next stages. Every potential new program needs to be nurtured by someone. Major new programs may otherwise be stalled, because they call for disruption of accustomed procedures. New program development can easily be avoided, postponed, even blocked, unless every aspect of the program's development from this point is made the primary responsibility of a designated manager or unit.[45]

Testing. "Whatever you do, do it on a grand scale at the first try. Otherwise, God forbid, you might learn how to do it differently."[46] This attitude has been deemed one of an administrator's deadly sins.[47] The final evaluation step in the new program development process is testing or demonstration. This involves exposing the program to a small number of intended clients. It is important that the test groups are genuinely representative.

> A number of "laboratory schools" were established in the United States in the 1960s. The intent was that they should be used for the introduction and trial of new teaching methods. They were usually affiliated with a College of Education and located on a university campus. The typical lab school had almost unlimited funds, and its student body was composed of bright faculty children. Supposedly, the lab school was an attempt to demonstrate educational innovations which would then spread to other schools. But the lab schools, with their enriched environments and talented students, were perceived as too unique and different from the average school. Visiting teachers and administrators would come to the lab schools compelled by a curiosity motive, but would go away unconvinced of the applicability of the ideas they had observed in their own schools. Most of these schools have been terminated in recent years.[48]

The decision to pilot test a program will be influenced by the magnitude of the resources involved, based on the feasibility analysis. In cases in which only small amounts of resources are to be committed and a general consensus supports the program in the agency, there may be some justification for omitting the testing phase and going to a full-scale launch. However, omitting the testing phase should be an exceptional decision: "In the entrepreneurial fervor of belief in the innovation, it is easy for the advocate group to generalize their convictions that their program innovation will meet enthusiastic embrace throughout the delivery system."[49]

A testing against reality before total commitment should always be required. Any new program, no matter how well conceived, will run into the unexpected.[50] Testing enables the agency, for a relatively small amount of money, to avert the expense and embarrassment of a program that is given a full-scale launch and fails.

Introducing a program on a small scale provides two important advantages.[51] First, it furnishes an opportunity to obtain a measure of its actual demand by a potential client group. Second, offering the program in a restricted way allows identification of weaknesses in its structure or in the overall marketing plan. As a result of the pilot program, some aspects may be adjusted before a wide-scale launch. A program weakness that is not discovered until after a full-scale introduction can irreparably damage the program's credibility and image. If a new program acquires a negative image among a target clientele, it will be extremely difficult to change. Once users have tried the offering and have had a bad experience, subsequent resolution of the failings and persuasive promotion is unlikely to entice them to try it again.

Launching

In this final stage, the program is implemented and the agency fully commits its resources and its reputation. The launching stage is equivalent to the introduction phase of the program life cycle, which we described in Chapter 9. The relationship of the development of new programs to the program life cycle is shown in Figure 10.5.

At this point, it is appropriate to reiterate that the hopes of even the most optimistic managers for the success of new offerings should be tempered by an awareness of the substantial possibility of failure. There are many factors which are outside of an agency's control that influence a program's success or failure. Four conditions within an agency's control, however, also appear to account for many new program failures:

Hurried conception and implementation, with inadequate market analysis and initial evaluation. These problems lead to optimistic assumptions of demand and the launching of programs that either do not meet any real clientele need or that do not meet a need better than other suppliers.

Failure to release and reallocate sufficient personnel resources to effectively evaluate and launch a new program.

Disillusionment with the initial quality of a program so that anticipated benefits are not matched by performance. Once a program has been launched, it is difficult to change fundamental decisions. If a service has been underpriced, it is extremely difficult to raise the price later. If the program develops technical bugs, goodwill is lost, which will be hard to retrieve later on. Minor problems, and resulting irritations, have given many programs a bad reputation before they have had a chance to acquire a good one.

Inadequate promotional efforts accompanying the launch of a new program. Funding for these is often kept to an unrealistically low level because an agency merely allocates what can be spared from other operations. This expenditure should be viewed as an integral part of the cost of offering the program and included in the feasibility analysis. It should not be regarded as an optional extra. If promotional resources are not available, then the decision to proceed with the program idea should be reviewed.

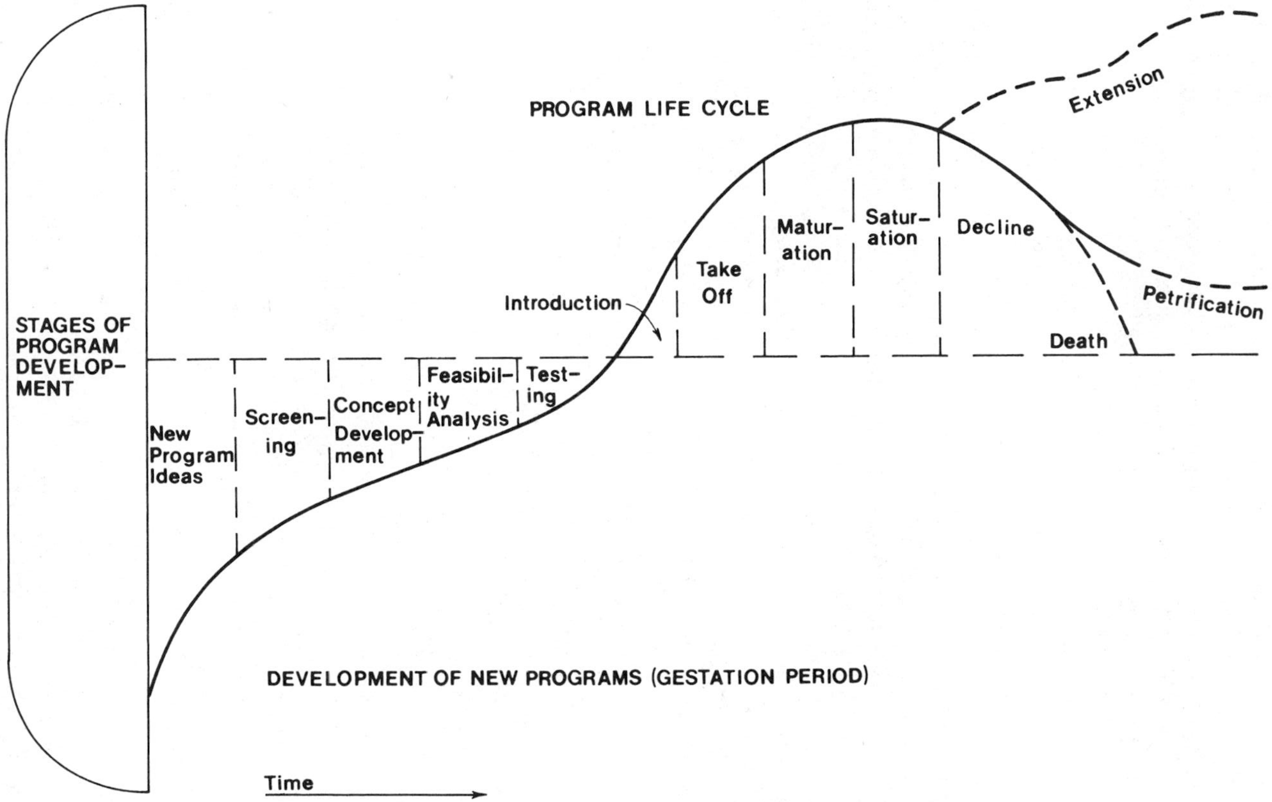

Figure 10.5. Relationship of the Development of New Program to the Program Life Cycle.

SUMMARY

A new program refers to one that is offered by an agency to a client group for the first time, even though it may have been previously offered to the client group or another group by other private or public sector organizations. The term implies either improved cost efficiency or improved service effectiveness or efficiency. Traditionally, government and social service agencies have been perceived as reticent to adopt new programs.

Momentum for the development of new programs may be stimulated from two sources. First, external pressures may be exerted by client groups, professional peers, higher levels of government, or elected officials. A second source is the internal voluntary recognition of performance gaps between what the agency is currently achieving and what its managers believe it could achieve. Such gaps emerge from changes in citizen priorities or lifestyles, a shifting of target markets, new technology, a changed financial environment, availability of underutilized resources, or a sudden critical environmental event.

The stimuli for developing new programs need a supportive agency climate if such programs are to emerge consistently. Unfortunately, many of the characteristics that tend to be associated with a supportive climate appear to be the opposite of those frequently found in government and social service agencies. The primary organizational features characteristic of a sympathetic environment for new program development are an organic, decentralized agency staffed by people from diverse backgrounds. The availability of slack resources, typically found in expanding rather than contracting agencies, determines whether or not an agency can afford the resource costs associated with developing new programs. Organizational slack is the difference between the resources required to enable an agency to carry out its basic functions and the total resources it has available.

The failure of some new programs must be accepted and not penalized if innovation is to be encouraged. Other key personnel ingredients are a willingness to invest consistently in employee training and high employee morale. Finally, the most important factors in the success of any new program efforts are support from elected officials and senior management.

A commitment to new program development requires a commitment to the proactive allocation of resources to search for unmet clientele needs and to design new programs to meet them. This involves establishing new program committees to be responsible for generating ideas, evaluating them, and seeing that the best of them are implemented.

A sequential pattern of six major stages is suggested for developing new programs: generating new programs ideas, screening, concept development, feasibility analysis, testing, and launching the new program.

In the past, preoccupation with short-term operating problems has often reduced the attention that many managers have devoted to new program planning. Most agencies could greatly improve the effectiveness of their mix of offerings by adopting a formal approach to new program planning. This requires only that managers commit some serious efforts to the new program planning process.

NOTES

1 Feller, E., "Public-Sector Innovation as 'Conspicuous Production,'" *Policy Analysis*, vol. 7, No. 1, Winter 1981, pp. 1–20.

2. Crawford, R., "The Application of Science and Technology in Local Governments in the United States," *Studies in Comparative Local Government*, No. 7, Winter 1973, p. 12.

3. Adapted from Roessner, J.D., "Incentives to Innovate in Public and Private Organizations," *Administration and Society*. vol. 9 No. 3, November 1977, pp. 341–365.

4. Feller, "Public-Sector Innovation," p. 7.

5. Schoenberger, E., and Williamson, J., "Deciding on Priorities and Specific Programs." In W.F. Anderson, B.J. Frieden, and M.J. Murphy (eds.), *Managing Human Services*. Washington, DC: International City Managers Association, 1977, p. 165.

6. Williams, D.A. and McDonald, D.H., "The Great Computer Frenzy," *Newsweek*, December 27, 1982, p. 68.

7. Dr. Marvin Wolfgang, as quoted in the *New York Times*, July 14, 1975, 1 : 1.

8. Bradshaw, B.R., and Mapp, C.B., "Consumer Participation in a Family Planning Program," *American Journal of Public Health*, vol. 62 No. 7, July 1972, pp. 969–972.

9. Brightman, H.J., "Constraints to Effective Problem Solving," *Business*, vol. 31 No. 2, March/April 1981, p. 31.

10. Lee, W.A., and Gilmour, J.E. "A Procedure for the Development of New Programs in Postsecondary Education," *Journal of Higher Education*, vol. 48, No. 3, May/June 1977, p. 305.

11. Howard, D.R., and Crompton, J.L., *Financing, Managing, and Marketing Recreation and Park Resources*. William C. Brown, Dubuque, Iowa: 1980, p. 46.

12. Yin, R.K. *Changing Urban Bureaucracies*. Lexington, MA: Lexington Books, 1976, p. 6.

13. Burns, T., and Stalker, G.M. *The Management of Innovation*, London: Tavistock, 1961, p. 121.

14. Walker, W.E., and Chaiken, J.M., "The Effects of Fiscal Contraction on Innovation in the Public Sector." Paper presented at a conference entitled Prospects for Local Government: Coping With the New Fiscal Environment, Rand Corporation, April 1981.

15. Riggs, H.E. "The Case for Technology Entrepreneurs," *The Stanford Engineer*, Spring/Summer 1980, pp. 11–19.

16. Brightman. "Constraints," p. 31.

17. Walker and Chaiken, "Fiscal Contraction," p. 20.

18. Rosner, M.M., "Economic Determinants of Organizational Innovation," *Administrative Science Quarterly*, vol. 12 No. 2, March 1968, pp. 614–625.

19. Bingham, R.D., *The Adoption of Innovations By Local Government*, Lexington, Mass: Lexington Books, D.C. Heath and Co., 1976, pp. 39, 88, 154.

20. Hage, J. and Aiken, M. "Program Change and Organization Properties: A Comparative Analysis," *The American Journal of Sociology*, vol. 72, No. 5, March 1967, pp. 503–519.

21. Walker and Chaiken, "Fiscal Contraction," p. 28.

22. Crawford, M.C., "New Product Failure Rates—Facts and Fallacies," *Research Management*, September 1979, p. 9.

23. Bish, R.L. and Nourse, H.O., *Urban Economics and Policy Analysis*. New York: McGraw-Hill, 1975, p. 184.

24. Yin, *Urban Bureaucracies, p. 7.*

25. Feller, "Public-Sector Innovation," p. 13.

26. Lambright, W.H., Teich, A., and Carroll, J.D., *Adoption and Utilization of Urban Technology: A Decision-Making Study*. Syracuse, NY: Syracuse Research Corporation, p. 208.

27. Walker and Chaiken, "Fiscal Contraction," p. 24.

28. Urban, G.R., and Hauser, J.R. *Design and Marketing of New Products*. Englewood Cliffs, NJ: Prentice-Hall, 1980, p. 572.

29. Hopkins, D.S. *New-Product Winners and Losers*. New York: The Conference Board Report #773, 1980, p. 1.

30. Stanton, W.J., *Fundamentals of Marketing*. New York: McGraw-Hill, 1975, p. 180.

31. Delbecq, A.L., "The Social Political Process of Introducing Innovation in Human Services." In R.C. Sarui and Y. Hasenfeld (eds.), *The Management of Human Services*. New York: Columbia University Press, 1978, p. 320.

32. Moroney, R.M. "Needs Assessments for Human Services." In W.F. Anderson, B.J. Frieden, and M.J. Murphy (eds)., *Managing Human Services*. Washington, DC: International City Managers Association, 1977, p. 131.

33. Association of Minnesota Counties Process for the Development of New Human Service Programs: A Guide for Human Service Agencies, Association of Minnesota Counties, St. Paul, MI, June 1977, n.p.

34. Lee and Gilmour, Jr., "Programs in Postsecondary Education," p. 308.

35. Crompton, J.L., and Younger, L.E., "What Are You Doing for Your Corporate Constituency?" *Parks and Recreation*, May 1983, pp. 42–46.

36. Antunes, G., and Mladenka, K., "The Politics of Local Services and Service Distribution." In L.H. Massotti and R.L. Lineberry (eds.), *The New Urban Politics*. Cambridge, MA: Ballinger, 1976, p. 155.

37. Delbecq, "Social Political Process," p. 321.

38. Osborn, A.F., *Applied Imagination* (3rd ed.). New York: Scribner's, 1963.

39. Ibid., p. 156.

40. Ibid., p. 50.

41. Ibid., p. 167.

42. Ibid., p. 159–160.

43. Ibid., p. 199.

44. Ibid., p. 378.

45. Wasson, C.R., *Product Management: Product Life Cycles and Comparative Marketing Strategy*. St. Charles, IL: Challenge Books, 1971, p. 12.

46. Drucker, P.F., "The Deadly Sins in Public Administration," *Public Administration Review*, March/April 1980, p. 104.

47. Ibid., p. 104.

48. Rogers, E.M., and Shoemaker, F.F., *Communication of Innovations: A Cross-Cultural Approach* (2nd ed.). New York: Free Press, 1971, p. 221.

49. Delbecq, "Social Political Process," p. 324.

50. Ibid., p. 104.

51. Pride, W.M., and Ferrell, O.C., *Marketing: Basic Concepts and Decisions*. Boston, MA: Houghton Mifflin, 1983, p. 187.

ELEVEN

Diffusion of New Services

> Have you ever watched a stone fall into a pool of water? From the initial splash, concentric circles move out through the rest of the pool. At first the small waves reach only the area immediately surrounding the splash, but with time the widening ripples reach across the expanse of water into nearly every area of the pool.[1]

The ripples in the pool are analogous to the way in which members of a targeted client group respond to a new service. Some people are likely to start using it sooner than others. In this chapter we explain how and why this ripple effect occurs.

Marketing communication, often referred to as promotion, is one of the four elements of the marketing mix. It is discussed in detail in the last four chapters of this book. Diffusion is one aspect of communication, but it is addressed at this point because it relates specifically to new programs. *The diffusion process is an aspect of communication that is differentiated by (1) its exclusive concern with the communication of services perceived as new by a potential target market and (2) its heavy emphasis on the development—or use of existing—strong networks of interpersonal relationships within a target group.*

Better understanding of diffusion will aid managers in stimulating more potential users to take advantage of appropriate service offerings. Familiarity with the concept will also enable managers to reduce the amount of time between the initial offering of a service and the point at which all potential users have made a decision to use or reject it.

Diffusion has a rich heritage. The concept has been used extensively by sociologists, concerned with the spread of lifestyles and values within societies; anthropologists, whose traditional interest is the spread of cultural mores and artifacts in earlier societies, but who have recently turned to evaluating planned changes in underdeveloped countries; rural sociologists, whose studies have focused on acceptance of new farm practices; educators, who have tried to understand the rate of acceptance of innovations by school systems; public health agencies, interested in the acceptance of new products and practices; and political scientists, concerned with the spread of ideas and services within and between communities.

Although much of the research into diffusion has been pursued independently within disciplines, a remarkably consistent and well-developed conceptual framework has emerged that is generally applicable to the communication of new services, ideas, and products in all fields.

GENERAL MODEL

In this section, a number of generalizations are identified that have been drawn from over three thousand studies of the diffusion process. The general form of the diffusion curve is shown in Figure 1.1. The sygmoid (S-shaped) curve in Figure 11.2 depicts the same process but is a cumulative graph.

These figures show that the first people to adopt a new service represent a small proportion of the potential client group. These people are called innovators. After some innovators have adopted the service other categories of users follow. The curves in Figures 11.1 and 11.2 suggest that the first users of a new service enthusiastically advocate it to other members of the target group, who in turn pass endorsements of the service on to their peers. The resulting distribution explains the S-shaped curve in Figure 11.2.

Classification of the "adopter categories" from innovators (first to adopt) to laggards (last to adopt) is well tested and has been shown to apply in many areas of social research, regardless of cultural and structural differences between communities. The categories' sizes were derived by drawing vertical lines marking off the standard deviations on either side of the mean.* The result is a standardized percentage of respondents in each category. This approach was derived from research in rural sociology and it is unlikely that these percentages would be exactly replicated in the government and social services field. Indeed, the actual percentage of a client group classified in each category is likely to vary both from service to service and from one target market to another. The percentages, therefore, are best seen as approximations. "Innovativeness is a continuous variable, and partitioning it into discrete categories is only a conceptual device, much like dividing the continuum of social status into upper, middle, and lower classes."[2]

Relationship of the Diffusion Model to the Program Life Cycle Concept

Figure 11.3 illustrates the relationship between the program life cycle concept that was discussed in Chapter 9 and the diffusion process. It suggests that the

*The standard deviation is a convenient statistical device that explains the average amount of variance on either side of the mean for a sample.

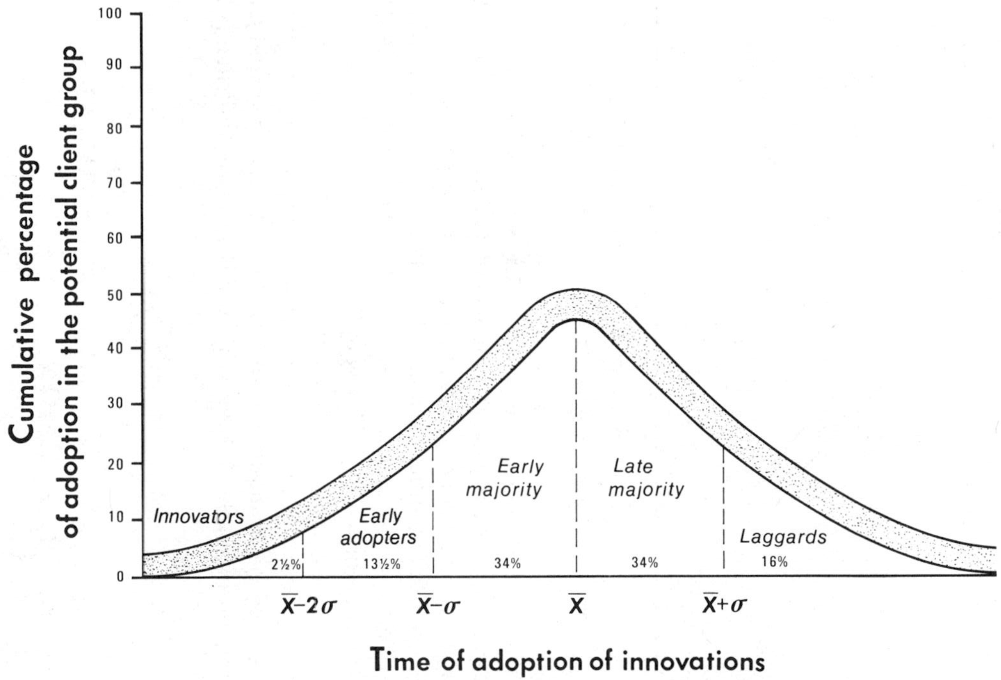

Figure 11.1. Adopter Categorization on the Basis of Relative Time of Adoption of Innovations. (*Source:* Reprinted with permission of The Free Press, a division of Macmillan, Inc. from *Diffusion of Innovation* by Everett H.M. Rogers. Copyright © 1962 by The Free Press.)

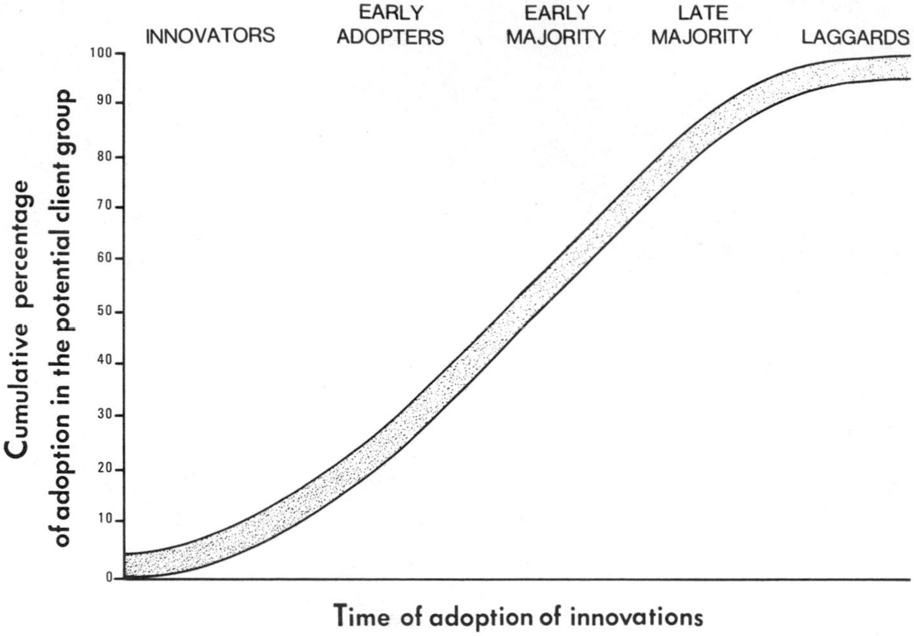

Figure 11.2. The Cumulative Pattern of Adoption.

introduction stage of the program life cycle consists primarily of innovators; the take-off stage consists of early adopters and early majority; and the maturity stage is comprised of late majority and laggards. By the end of the maturity stage of the life cycle, all members of a target market who are going to use the service will have done so. Saturation is a leveling off stage characterized by no new participants while decline is when people leave a program.

Figure 11.3 emphasizes the key role played by opinion leaders, who are referred to as early adopters in this model. Their disproportionate influence and peer respect may be primarily responsible for initiating the rapid take-off stage of the program life cycle. If their response is positive, diffusion is likely to be successful.

FACTORS INFLUENCING THE EFFECTIVENESS AND SPEED OF DIFFUSION

At one time the rate of diffusion was relatively slow:

> In 1953, Mort, a leading early diffusion researcher in the education field, concluded, "Fifteen years typically elapse before a new technique is found in 3 percent of the school systems. . . . Additionally twenty years usually suffices for an almost complete diffusion in an area of an average state.[3]

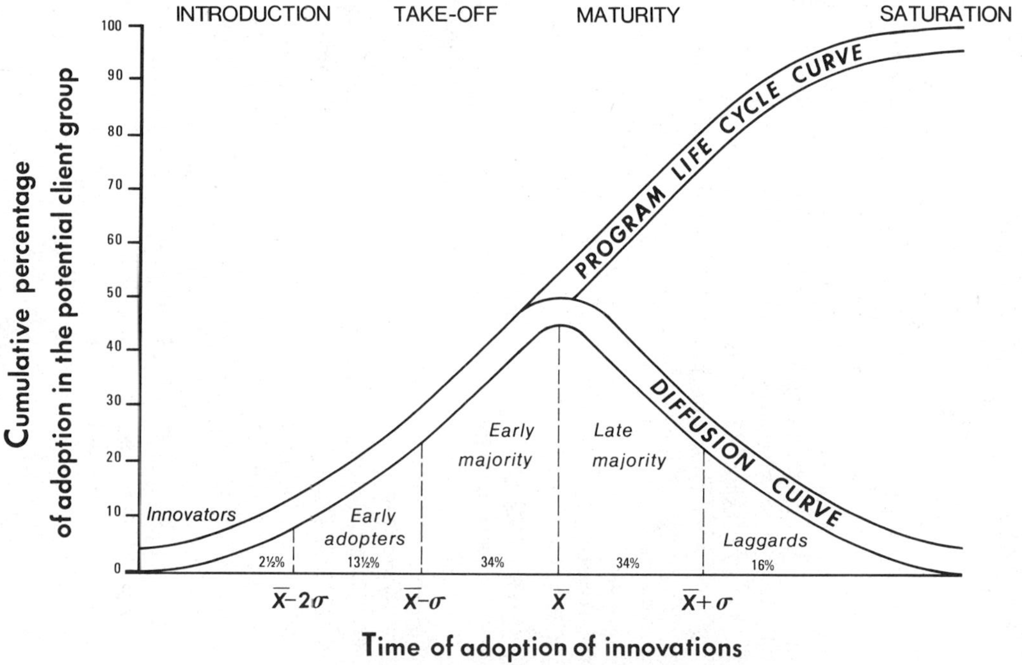

Figure 11.3. Relationship of the Diffusion Process to the Product Life Cycle.

Since that time diffusion has speeded up considerably. In the same context of school systems, two examples illustrate that change.

> In 1963, 2/10 of 1 percent of the total number of secondary schools had language laboratories. Five years later 17 percent of the total had such installations.[4]
>
> More recently, only 5 years were required for modern math to reach nearly 100 percent adoption in U.S. schools.[5]

All new services do not diffuse to the same extent and at the same rate through a given target market. Further, the extensity and speed differences cannot be attributed to a single influence. Clearly, the way in which the promotional tools of personal selling, advertising, incentives, and publicity are implemented and integrated with the other marketing mix components of product, price, and distribution will be a factor. However, at least two other interacting forces play an important role in diffusion. They are (1) the perceived attributes of a new service, and (2) the use made of interpersonal communication pathways. Each of these is discussed in the following sections.

Perceived Attributes of a New Program

Undoubtedly the characteristics of a new program, as perceived by its potential users, contribute directly to the extent and speed of its spread in a target market. *It is the potential users' perceptions of the attributes of new services, not the attributes as classified by agency personnel, that affect their rate of diffusion*.

The primary attributes influencing diffusion are complexity, compatibility, relative advantage, communicability, and trialability. After reviewing a number of research studies, Everett Rogers and Floyd Shoemaker concluded that from 49 to 87 percent of the variance in the rate of diffusion could be explained by these five attributes.[6] Although discussed separately in the following paragraphs, these five attributes are frequently interrelated.

Complexity refers to the degree of difficulty involved in using a new service. Generally, the more complex and confusing a new service is to use, the slower its acceptance and diffusion will be. Similarly, those services that require large investments of money, time, and energy will spread more slowly than those requiring modest investments.

The more complex a new service, the more important it is to undertake educational and/or informational efforts both before and after it is introduced. For example, periodic orientation programs and user training in library resource use are conducted by university libraries, particularly for disadvantaged persons who may perceive them as complex systems because they lack experience in using libraries.[7]

Compatibility refers to the degree to which a new service is consistent with the existing values, past experiences, and current needs of its potential users. Compatibility helps ensure greater security and less risk to the receiver and makes the new service more meaningful. A new program with an image inconsistent with existing cultural norms will diffuse less rapidly than one that is consistent. An example of such an incompatible new service is the introduction of the IUD (intrauterine contraceptive device) in countries where religious beliefs discourage use of birth control techniques.[8]

Relative advantage is the degree to which a new service is perceived to be superior to the one that it supercedes or with which it competes. If benefits are not perceived to be greater than those from other services, potential users will lack incentive to voluntarily use the service. Relative advantage may be viewed in terms of money or time costs, social approval, lower perceived risk, decrease in discomfort, or immediacy of reward. It doesn't matter whether the service has a great deal of "objective" advantage. What does matter is whether the target clientele perceives it as being advantageous.

In government and social services difficulties arise because the relative advantage of a new service is often hard for potential users to assess. Often public managers assume that a program's virtues are obvious. They fail to make the informational and educational effort necessary to point out the superior benefits offered by the new service to a clientele group.

Communicability refers to the degree to which information regarding a new service may be easily communicated to other people. In some government and social services, communicability is difficult to attain because the services have no physical product to display. This can lead to material innovations being diffused and adopted more readily than nonmaterial ideas.[9]

Trialability is the degree to which a new program may be tried on a limited basis. New programs that can be tried out without substantial commitment will generally diffuse more rapidly than programs that are less trialable. The amount of risk, in terms of time, money, or prestige, is minimal for a short trial and allows potential users to evaluate the service. Thus, for example, a community education program may offer the first session of any series of classes free—a particularly useful policy if the classes are expensive or the subject matter unfamiliar. Inhibitions arising from risk or uncertainty may be removed through trial.

Interpersonal Communication Pathways

The diffusion process is dependent on the communication of information to potential users. Traditionally, communication was regarded as a one-step process, flowing from a source to a receiver via a media channel. This communication model has been termed the "hypodermic needle" model[10] because of the postulated direct and immediate effect of the source on receivers.

Such a pathway however, has not been found to be an accurate representation of the communication process in many cases. Influence is instead filtered and mediated through a web of interpersonal networks. These findings have led to recognition of a two-step communication pathway.

Two-Step Communication Pathway. The two-step approach has become an important technique for effectively communicating with a community. For example, it has been used to solicit representative public involvement and input.

> The two-step model is based on the simple empirical finding that interest in community issues is not distributed randomly within a population. Certain people, who may be termed opinion leaders, will take an interest in a great many issues and will be willing to become active in disseminating information about particular subjects, while most people will tend to depend on the opinion of others. If a network of communication is established between opinion leaders and people who want to distribute information as well as assess the opinions of the general population, it is possible to have an effective two-way flow of communication in even the largest and most complex population area.[11]

Although opinion leaders sometimes may not have the technical knowledge needed to make relevant input, they can be provided with this knowledge if they can be identified. *Opinion leaders may be defined as persons within a group to whom others turn for information and advice.*

The two-step process is illustrated in Figure 11.4. Communications about new services spread from an agency by either its personnel or a media channel to opinion leaders, and from them by way of personal communication to their followers. The opinion leaders will not always initiate conversation with their followers. Often communications will flow as a result of nonleaders approaching opinion leaders and requesting information or an opinion.

Opinion leaders may be viewed as gatekeepers. They can open a gate and provide access to many others. Thus community health agencies, for example, may identify physicians who dispense primary care as gatekeepers who could aid in communicating the agencies' programs.

The two-step flow may occur either through a "trickle down" from an elite subgroup to other members, or by a "trickle across" within relatively homogeneous groups. Both approaches should be considered as part of a diffusion strategy.

Trickle-Down Approach. The trickle-down approach assumes that recognized formal leaders—for example, elected officials, wealthy citizens, or business leaders—are opinion leaders in a community and that other citizens will follow their lead. Thus securing the support of these leaders should be a primary objective when launching a new service. This communication pathway is particularly dominant in closed autocratic social systems such as military organizations. The personal preferences and priorities of a military base commander frequently diffuse rapidly, resulting in others on the base adjusting their own preferences and priorities accordingly.

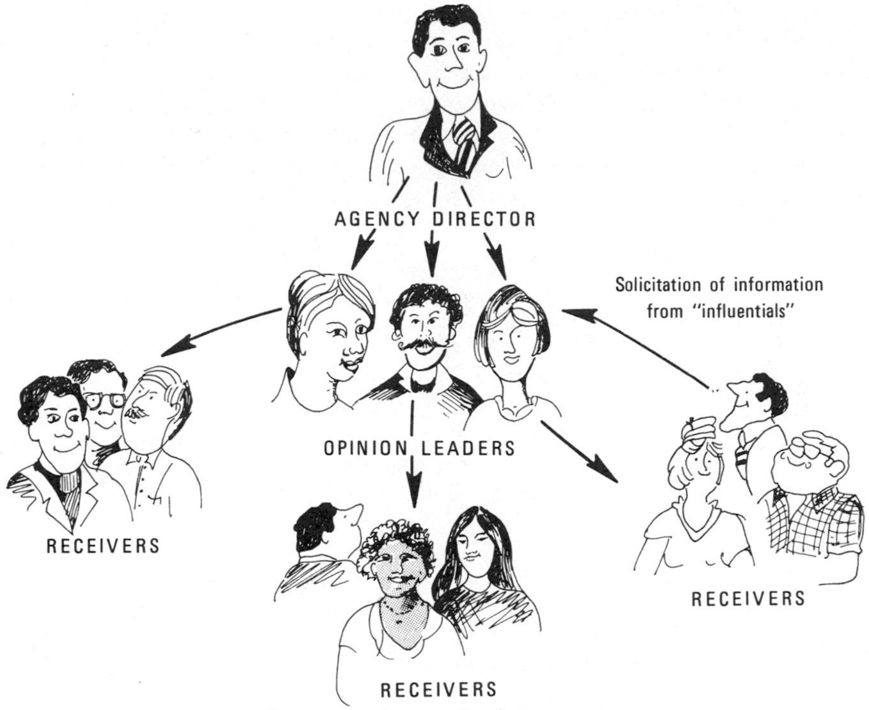

Figure 11.4. Two-Step Flow Communication Pathway. (*Source:* Harold W. Berkman and Christopher G. Gilson, *Consumer Behavior: Concepts and Strategies* (Boston: Kent Publishing Company, 1978), p. 388. © by Woodsworth, Inc. Reprinted with permission of Kent Publishing Company, a division of Woodsworth, Inc.)

Insights into how the trickle-down process may operate in a community are provided by the example in Figure 11.5. Typically there are various levels of opinion leadership in the trickle-down process. The three levels most frequently identified are influentials, lieutenants, and doers.[12] In general, *influentials* address themselves to major policy matters concerning new services, projects, or issues in a particular area. They are in positions in which they either own or control considerable resources, including jobs. They may initiate policy; undertake the initiation, direction, or supervision of major new services or projects; and veto ideas or suggestions made by others.

Individuals in the second echelon of opinion leadership are the *lieutenants*. Their primary function is usually to disseminate information regarding new projects or services approved by the influentials. Because of the higher social visibility of lieutenants, the less knowledgeable persons in a clientele often identify them as influentials. Occupationally, lieutenants frequently are elected officials, middle management personnel, and younger professionals in the community.

The third level of opinion leadership, the *doers*, are often referred to as leg people because they play a major role in implementing policy decisions. Persons in this category tend to be from salaried, white collar occupations such as

A study of opinion leaders in Dallas identified and described those opinion leaders who had a determining influence on community decisions. A distinctive trickle-down communication network was apparent. Opinion leaders were separated into three recognizable layers that were named by the leaders themselves: key leaders, the top level, and the second echelon. The distribution of these leaders into the three layers is shown in the figure.

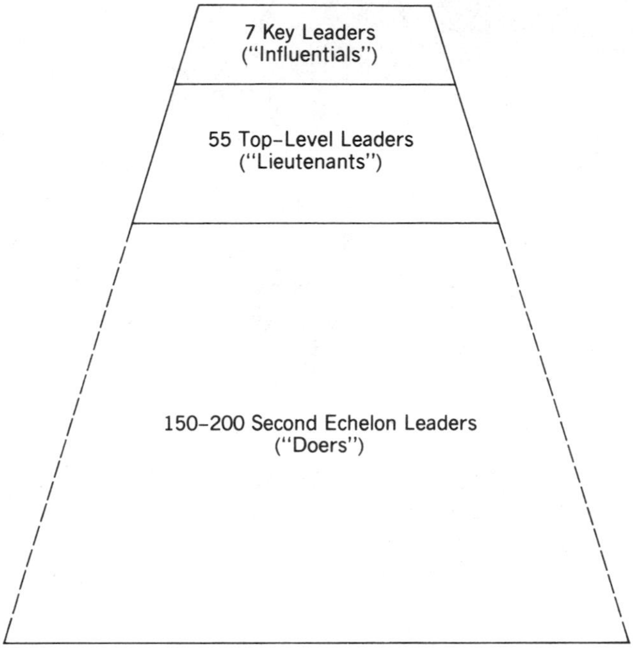

At the very top were seven key leaders who performed more continuously and occupied positions of greater leadership prominence than the top-level leaders. Below the key leaders were 55 top-level leaders. The second echelon consisted of a broad base of 150 to 200 leaders. Many in the second echelon were young people "on the way up."

Community decisions on all kinds of issues were reached in the same general manner with more or less the same people contributing to the decisions. A rather uniform pattern of opinion leadership in Dallas emerged.

The process began when one or more of the key leaders got an idea or recognized that some problem existed. The initiative may have been his or her own. More often, however, the matter was brought to the key leader's attention by someone lower in the opinion leadership hierarchy or by a business, civic, or social associate. The contact may have been casual, even unplanned, or in

Figure 11.5. An Example of the Trickle-Down Communication Flow. (This case study is adapted from Thometz, C.E., *The Decision-Makers: The Power Structure of Dallas*. Dallas: Southern Methodist University Press, 1963.)

the form of a written statement or formal appointment. If the key leader was impressed, he or she discussed the problem informally with one or two other key leaders. If they agreed that the problem needed attention, they arranged a luncheon and invited several other influential leaders.

The first leaders consulted were the other key people and perhaps a few of the most influential top-level leaders. Essentially the same people were involved every time.

Simultaneously with the formal discussions of the problem, the key leaders presented the problem to the board of the Civic Committee, whose purpose was to promote projects for the welfare of the community. The board members of the Civic Committee were "well recognized influential leaders" in the city. At the time of the study, four of the seven key leaders were on this board, as were fifteen of the fifty-five top-level leaders. If these people thought the proposed idea deserved more definite consideration, they appointed a committee to investigate it formally.

Thus, the key and top-level leaders determined the fate of propositions and ideas brought to their attention. Theirs was the power of selection—selection of those proposals that would be considered further or brought to the attention of other leaders. Therefore, the values of these people determined which ideas would move forward and which would not.

When an idea did develop through discussion, informally and in the board of the Civic Committee, a careful assessment was made of its feasibility by an investigative committee under the direction of key and top-level leaders. Only then, often after years of planning, was there active involvement of a broad base of second echelon leaders. The first solicitation of their interest and help was often through luncheons given by one of the highest-ranking leaders. It was then that the carefully thought-out plans of the decision makers were formally and publicly presented for the first time.

Such luncheon meetings, designed to build enthusiasm, represented only the beginning of a preconceived campaign to induce cooperation of the whole community in implementing the proposed solution. Once the leaders decided to do something, they used a variety of community resources to promote their projects.

Figure 11.5. (Continued)

teaching, social work, ministry, or from government agencies. Doers perform the many tasks associated with the successful execution of a project as it moves through the various stages of completion. They serve on working committees, collect funds, carry petitions, and take care of details.[13]

Trickle-Across Approach. Research evidence suggests that the dominant communication flows are horizontal rather than vertical.[14] Trickle-across flow recognizes that most people in a target market gain information through casual conversations with people of similar social status.[15] *Opinion leaders are found at all levels of society in all groups,* and the transmission of information, personal influence, and acceptance of new services is communicated horizontally within social strata as well as vertically between strata. Individuals in a target market tend to discuss a new service most frequently with friends and acquaintances who are very similar to themselves.

OPINION LEADERS AND THEIR IDENTIFICATION

Opinion leadership is the ability of certain individuals in a social system to influence other individuals' attitudes or overt behavior in a desired way with relative frequency.[16] The leadership is often informal, rather than necessarily being a function of an individual's formal position or status in a group. "Opinion leadership is often casually exercised in a group, sometimes unwitting and unbeknown. . . . It is an almost invisible, certainly inconspicious form of leadership at the person to person level of ordinary, intimate, informal every day contact."[17]

Opinion leadership resides to some extent in all group members. Even the most uninfluential member of a group is likely to have some influence. Informal discussions within a group may serve as a learning experience for a number of people, each of whom give and receive information and in the process influence and are influenced.

It is unclear how generalizable opinion leader influence is across different government and social services. However, it appears likely that leadership is service specific. That is, a group member may be an opinion leader on some matters but not on others. For example, Robert Dahl in his classic study of community opinion leaders in New Haven concluded, "A leader in one issue area is not likely to be influential in another. If he is, he is probably a public official and most likely the mayor."[18] Nevertheless, it is likely that if similar services are offered by the same agency and targeted at the same client group, the same people within that client group will be opinion leaders for these services.

Techniques for Identifying Opinion Leaders

Identifying opinion leaders represents a major challenge for government and social service managers. Opinion leaders are not easily and readily distinguished from their followers because they do not deviate from group norms but rather "are in a certain sense the most conformist members of their groups—upholding whatever norms and values are central to the group."[19] The task is further complicated because leaders and followers may exchange roles in different spheres of influence.

Four techniques however, have been recognized by which managers can identify people in a target group who are influential in determining whether or not a new service will be used or even offered. These are the positional approach, the reputational approach, the event analysis approach, and the social participation approach (see Table 11.1).

Positional Approach. This technique identifies formal leaders—those persons who occupy key positions in "important" organizations within a target clientele. The meaning of the words "key" and "important" depend largely on the personal judgment of the manager who determines which positions are influential or indicative of leadership. Persons are usually rated or ranked as influential in terms of the number and kinds of positions they hold in leading economic, political, and/or civic organizations.

The major advantages of the positional approach are that (1) these opinion leaders are visible and relatively easily identified and (2) little cost is involved in using this technique.

Offices are recognized as indicators of opinion leadership. However, the assumption that individuals who occupy positions of formal authority and prestige exert the most influence on service decisions may be false. In some cases, office holders may only announce or administer decisions that are made by others. As we noted in the previous section, opinion leadership is often less formal than this approach implies. Hence the positional approach may be too restrictive if opinion leaders within a target clientele do not hold formal leadership positions.

Reputational Approach. This technique assumes that there is "power behind the scenes"; that there are people who persuade, advise, or strongly influence the positional leaders; that there are opinion leaders who have no formal relationship with officeholders; and that these people can be identified by asking informed people the question, "Who do you think is influential?" or "With whom do you check before you act?"

The reputational approach may be implemented in one of three different ways.[20] First, a random sample of a target clientele's members may be selected, each of whom is asked to identify and, in some cases, to rank the opinion leaders in their group. The votes are tabulated and those leaders receiving the largest number are designated as being the primary opinion leaders. Criticism of this method questions whether ordinary citizens with little interest in a particular service area have adequate knowledge to be considered reliable sources of information.

Second, an agency may establish a panel of experts, each knowledgeable about the service area, who also may occupy positions of formal leadership themselves. Each member of the panel is asked to name and/or rank the opinion leaders in the target clientele. This method, to some extent, overcomes the limitation of questioning average citizens in the reputational survey. Those people in the group who are more knowledgeable of activities and interactions

TABLE 11.1. Four Methods of Identifying Opinion Leaders

Method	Assumptions	Type of Leader Identified	Advantages	Limitations
Positional	Opinion leadership rests in important positions of formal organizations. Position holders make decisions and control resources.	Higher civil servants, corporation executives, elected and appointed formal office holders, voluntary association officers.	Leaders are visible, thus easily identified. Less costly. Insight into potential role. Good cross-section of leaders.	Positional opinion leaders may not exercise their potential. Fails to identify informal leaders. Difficult to determine which positions do or do not have opinion leadership potential.
Reputational	Opinion leadership is reflected in reputation. Knowledgeables know opinion leaders by reputation. Some opinion leaders are concealed.	General leaders that are concealed as well as those visible to the public.	Identifies visible and concealed leaders. Determines leaders in several issue areas. Relative ease in carrying out technique.	Determining who is or is not knowledgeable. Reputed opinion leadership may not be exercised opinion leadership. Fails to identify specialized opinion leaders.

Event analysis	Opinion leadership is acquired through participation in decision-making processes.	Instrumental leaders in the resolution of community issues.	Determines actual behavior rather than reputation. Reveals overlap of opinion leadership in issue areas. Identifies specialized opinion leaders. Identifies roles of opinion leaders.	Time-consuming and costly. Fails to identify leaders who are "behind the scenes" or in "non decisions."
Social participation	Opinion leadership is acquired through participation in activities and offices in voluntary associations.	Visible participants in activities of voluntary associations.	Identifies active community leaders and those likely to be active in action programs.	Time-consuming and costly. Fails to identify concealed leaders or specific areas of participation.

Adapted from Tait, J.L., Bokemeier, J., and Bohlen, J.M., *Identifying the Community Power Actors: A Guide for Change Agents*, Ames: Iowa State University, North Central Regional Extension Publication Number 59, 1978.

among key citizens in this service area should be able to identify the most influential opinion leaders.

The third method of implementing the reputational approach is often called the snowball method. Beginning with some base group of informants, those people receiving mentions as opinion leaders are themselves asked to name the leaders in the target clientele. These newly named opinion leaders are, in turn, also asked to name opinion leaders in the target clientele. As the interviewing process snowballs, certain names are likely to be mentioned by numerous respondents, others are likely to be mentioned by fewer respondents, and a large number may be mentioned by only one or two respondents.

This method is time-consuming and requires administrators to decide where to set the limits and when to assume that the snowball has reached its most productive proportions. If conducted properly, however, it probably provides a high degree of accuracy because a wider spectrum of the local population is interviewed than only a panel of experts. At the same time, though, the interviewing is confined to people with a potentially greater knowledge of opinion leaders than a purely random sample of respondents would have.

Three primary criticisms have been directed against using the reputational method to identify opinion leaders. First, it reports a static distribution of opinion leadership whereas in reality a continuous shift is likely. Such studies should be frequently repeated in order to monitor any changes in opinion leaders.

Second, critics assert that the reputational method falsely assumes that opinion leadership is exerted to the same extent by the same people for different services. As noted previously in this chapter, opinion leaders may possess specialized influence not applicable in all major new service areas. Finally, it is argued that the reputational approach directs attention to intentions rather than to outcome and that *potential* for effective opinion leadership is not necessarily the same as actual effective opinion leadership.

Event-Analysis Approach. Event analysis involves tracing the history of particular public decisions about some government or social service issue. It consists of selecting a number of representative events and historically reconstructing them with data obtained from records or by interviews with active participants in the decisions. As in the reputational method, the agency should select past services or issues that are very similar to the new services to be offered. This technique assumes that opinion leaders can best be identified by analyzing which people have been influential in past key decisions. The presumption is that they will continue to exercise influence in similar decisions in the future.

Supporters of this approach argue that it is more reliable than the opinions of informants. They believe that opinion leaders can be identified only by examining instances in which they have participated: "I do not see how anyone can suppose he has established the dominance of a specific group in a community or a nation without basing his analysis on the careful examination of a series of concrete decisions."[21] Event analysis focuses on a particular service or issue. Since the composition of opinion leaders may vary among services, event analysis offers the additional advantage of identifying opinion leaders who are influential in specific service or issue areas.

The major criticism of this technique is that it may overlook those opinion leaders who play a quiet role in decisions, often operating through other people. Further, it is historic and static, assuming that leadership roles are preserved and that new leaders do not emerge. For example, in the early 1970s Richard Nixon and Spiro Agnew were opinion leaders, but by the middle 1970s their opinions were no longer influential.

Social Participation Approach. This technique involves identifying individuals who are associated with a variety of different organizations. Diffusion studies have established significant relationships between opinion leadership and the level of individuals' social involvement. It has been found that the most influential opinion leaders are usually more gregarious than the general population and have more social contacts, which provide more opportunity for discussing and passing on information and opinions to others. Opinion leaders must be accessible. They must have the opportunity as well as the ability to influence others. Members of this group are frequently involved in a range of community activities.

The social participation approach has several limitations. It is time consuming and costly to implement. It also identifies only the active, visible participants in community organizations and not the power actors who operate behind the scenes. Finally, it fails to identify the specific issues in which these individuals are likely to be decision makers or active participants.[22]

Integrating Identification Techniques

Each of the approaches for identifying opinion leaders has advantages and limitations (see Table 11.1). Not surprisingly, used independently they have often yielded different results. This does not show inconsistency; rather it demonstrates the complementary nature of the four methods, each of which is likely to identify some opinion leaders that the other methods overlook. *Thus identifying opinion leaders in a client group requires the use of a combination of approaches*. An example of this integrated approach, demonstrating how each of the three major identification methods may be integrated, is shown in Figure 11.6.

It has been suggested that in smaller, relatively independent and relatively homogeneous target clienteles, the different techniques will tend to converge and identify the same group of opinion leaders. However, in larger, more heterogeneous groups, some combination of all four measures is likely to yield

The event analysis, reputation, and positional techniques for measuring leadership were employed to see whether different leaders were identified through the three approaches.

For *event analysis*, leaders on major community issues during a five-year period were identified. A list of local issues was obtained from reviewing newspapers and other documents, as well as from formal interviews with community residents. The leaders were selected by using a four-step process. First, individuals identified from the above sources for each issue were interviewed. Second, through the interview schedule, information was obtained on the nature and extent of each respondent's involvement in an issue, and the names of other persons most active in the issue. By gaining detailed information on the nature and extent of each respondent's role in each issue, the researchers were able to differentiate between the actual decision makers and those active participants who were essentially implementers of those decisions.

A third step was the interviewing of all persons named as participants until no additional participants or relevant information were obtained. Finally, the specific operational measure used to identify decision leaders was the number of major issues in which an individual participated.

Interviewers using the *reputation approach* first contacted the manager of the Chamber of Commerce as the initial respondent. People mentioned as being leaders were then contacted and interviewed in the same manner. The chain-referral technique was continued until the list produced far more duplications than new names.

The *position approach* was based on the occupants of key authority positions in the community. These were used in the following manner. Selected public and civic officials included the mayor, chairman of the county board of supervisors, chancery court clerk, publisher and editor of the newspaper, president and secretary-manager of the Chamber of Commerce, superintendent of schools, chairman of the school board, chairman of the hospital board, and the administrator of the county hospital. Business leaders included the local bank presidents and the chief executives of the largest industries in each community.

Figure 11.6. An Example of an Integrated Approach to Identifying Opinion Leaders. (Adapted from Preston, J.D., and Guseman, P.B., "A Comparison of the Findings of Different Methods for Identifying Community Leaders," *Journal of the Community Development Society*, vol. 10, No. 2, 1979, pp. 51–62.)

a much broader and more representative set of opinion leaders.[23] Ultimately the choice of which technique(s) to use must be made by each agency on the basis of expertise, time, and resources available.

Implications of Opinion Leaders' Influence

The respect that opinion leaders typically command among their peers makes them a very important determinant of the success or failure of a new service.

Their trial and approval of a service is a necessary condition to its acceptance by others who rely on them to validate the claims made by an agency. Thus they are people who should be carefully courted by government and social service managers.

The time and energy of government and social service managers are scarce resources and opinion leaders offer a way to effectively expand those resources:

> Economy of effort is achieved because the time and resources involved in meeting with opinion leaders is far less than if each member of the client system were to be consulted. Essentially the leader approach magnifies the manager's efforts. He or she can communicate the innovation to a few opinion leaders and then let word-of-mouth communication channels spread the new idea from there.[24]

In addition, working through opinion leaders improves the credibility of a new service offering, thereby increasing the probability of it being used. People trust opinion leaders in their social network much more than any communication emanating directly from agency sources who are outside of that network.

SUMMARY

The way in which a new service diffuses through a community is likely to follow a predictable pattern. This diffusion model provides the public service administrator with a structure for visualizing how new services are adopted in a community and the background necessary for developing adoption strategies.

Members of a target group may be divided into five categories, which are differentiated by the immediacy with which they begin to use the service. These five categories are innovators, early adopters, early majority, late majority, and laggards. The most important people for influencing the success of a new service are opinion leaders, who typically are found within the early adopter category.

The extensity and speed with which services diffuse varies widely. In addition to marketing mix and promotional mix decisions, there are two other important forces that influence the extent and rate of diffusion. First is the characteristics of a new program as perceived by its potential users. The five program attributes that explain most of the variance in the rate of diffusion are complexity, compatibility, relative advantage, communicability, and trialability.

The second influence on diffusion extensity and speed is the effectiveness of interpersonal communication pathways. It has been demonstrated that direct communications from media have much less influence than previously thought. Communications spread from an agency via either its personnel or a media channel to opinion leaders, and from them by way of personal communication to their followers. The two-step flow may occur either through a trickle down from an elite subgroup to other members or by a trickle across process within relatively homogeneous groups.

Opinion leadership is the ability of certain individuals in a social system to influence other individuals' attitudes or overt behavior in a desired way with relative frequency. Identifying opinion leaders represents a major challenge because their acceptance of a new service is critical to its widespread adoption. Four approaches may be used for identifying opinion leaders. They are complementary, with each of the four approaches likely to identify some opinion leaders that the other methods overlook.

The positional approach focuses on those individuals who occupy key positions in important organizations. The reputational approach seeks out those who do not hold any visible position of influence, but who have the reputation of being influential. The event-analysis approach identifies people who were influential in past issues or service diffusion. The social participation approach searches for individuals who are associated with a variety of different organizations.

NOTES

1. Engel, J.F., and Blackwell, R.D., *Consumer Behavior*. Hinsdale, IL: Dryden Press, 1982, p. 379.
2. Rogers, E.M., and Shoemaker, F.F., *Communication of Innovations: A Cross-Cultural Approach* (2nd ed.). New York: Free Press, 1971, p. 181.
3. Mort, P.R., *Educational Adaptability*. New York: Metropolitan School Study Council, 1953, p. 17.
4. Miles, M.B., "Innovation in Education: Some Generalizations." In M.B. Miles (ed.), *Innovation in Education*. Columbia University, New York: Teachers College Press, 1964, p. 6.
5. Rogers and Shoemaker, *Innovations*, p. 157.
6. Ibid.
7. Zaltman, G., Florio, D.H., and Sikorski, L.A., *Dynamic Educational Change*. New York: Free Press, 1977, p. 226.
8. Rogers and Shoemaker, Innovations, p. 22.
9. Ogburn, W.F., *Social Change*, New York: Huebsch, 1922.
10. Robertson, T.S., *Innovative Behavior and Communication*, New York: Holt, Rinehart & Winston, 1971, p. 122.
11. National Park Service, *Draft Environmental Statement, Gateway National Recreation Area*, Denver Service Station, National Park Service, April 1978, p. 173.
12. Mitchell, J.B. and Lowry, S.G., *Power Structures, Community Leadership and Social Action*, North Central Extension Sociology Task Force Leadership Series No. 5, Ohio State University, September 1973, p. 8.
13. Ibid.
14. Berkman, H.W., and Gilson, C.C., *Consumer Behavior: Concepts and Strategies*, Encino, CA: Dickenson Publishing, 1978, p. 388.
15. Van der Ban, A.W., "The Role of Interpersonal Communication and Opinion Leadership in the Diffusion of Agricultural Innovations." Paper presented at the Second World Congress of Rural Sociology, Ensched, Netherlands: 1968.
16. Rogers and Shoemaker, *Innovations*, p. 199.

17. Katz, E., and Lazerfield, P.F., *Personal Influence: The Part Played by People in the Flow of Mass Communications,* Glencoe, IL: Free Press, 1955.

18. Dahl, R.A., *Who Governs? Democracy and Power in an American City*. New Haven, CN: Yale University Press, 1961, p. 183.

19. Scheuing, E.E., *New Product Management*. Hinsdale, IL: Dryden Press, 1974, p. 251.

20. Ruesink, D.C., Pelham, J.T., and Mallett, J., "Identifying and Working with Decision Makers for Community Development." Paper presented at the Rural Sociology Society Annual Meeting, College Park, MD, August 1973.

21. Dahl, R.A., A Critique of the Ruling Elite Model," *The American Political Science Review,* vol. 52, No. 2, June 1958, pp. 463–469.

22. Tait, J.L., Bokemier, J., and Bohlen, J.M., *Identifying the Community Power Actors: A Guide for Change Agents,* Ames: Iowa State University, North Central Regional Extension Publication Number 59, 1978, p. 16.

23. Preston, J.D., and Guseman, P.B., "A Comparison of the Findings of Different Methods for Identifying Community Leaders," *Journal of the Community Development Society,* vol. 10, No. 2, Fall 1979, pp. 51–62.

24. Rogers and Shoemaker, Innovations, p. 224.

TWELVE

Program Retrenchment

Until the middle 1970s, most government and social service managers operated in a growth climate characterized by growing financial resources and an expanding role for government. Service delivery strategies frequently were based on assumptions of perpetual enlargement of resources and expenditures. However, many public service managers today have a different responsibility—that of determining which services should be reduced or terminated. Whereas the challenge of public sector management for most of the 1970s was creative use of expanding resources, the contrasting challenge of the 1980s is managing with reduced resources.

The quality of an agency's services to its clientele is, and will continue to be, dramatically affected by its ability to make effective retrenchment decisions. Retrenchment occurs when fewer resources are allocated by an agency to an existing service. This may lead either to a reduction in the quantity or quality of service provided, or to termination when all resources allocated to a service are withdrawn.

The inability of public agency administrators to abandon programs may be their "most damning and most common failing. It alone guarantees nonperformance and within a fairly short time."[1] It is much easier to add new services than to remove existing ones. Creation of new programs traditionally has been viewed as a positive response to change, while the deletion of existing programs frequently has been perceived as a depressing negative task associated with failure. Historically, therefore, the range of services offered has tended to mushroom unless a definitive management effort was made at pruning.[2] Many university curricula offer good examples of this mushrooming result. If a subject has become obsolete, the university faculty may make a required course out of it, which "solves the problem" for the time being. Every university adds courses to its curricula, but very few ever consider dropping any of the old ones.[3]

Instead of recognizing retrenchment as a positive strategy that could release resources for new or high-priority projects, the response in the past was often to throw more resources at an ailing program. This is the automatic, unthinking response that sometimes emerges from a program's supporters. A more appropriate response is to conduct a rational diagnosis of the program's status and problems:

> The greatest self-delusion is the belief that the outlook for a (program) improves with the more resources one pours into it. Few popular maxims are as wide of the mark as, "If at first you don't succeed, try, try, try again." "If at first you don't succeed, try once more—and then try something else" is more realistic. Success in repetitive attempts becomes less rather than more probable with each repetition.[4]

Such self-delusion is no longer possible in most agencies. Public agency managers are being required to terminate some offerings, to lower the service level of others, and to confront trade-offs between new demands and old programs.

The life cycle concept suggests that no service can be expected to deliver high levels of satisfaction to a large proportion of its targeted clientele forever. Demand for a particular service will decrease over time as lifestyles and interests change. Termination or reduction is not exceptional; rather it is inevitable. Every "right" product sooner or later becomes the "wrong" product.[5] Every program ages and eventually becomes obsolete. Therefore procedures to facilitate retrenchment should be an essential part of every service delivery effort.

A MODEL OF THE RETRENCHMENT PROCESS

The framework of this chapter is illustrated by the model in Figure 12.1. Momentum for retrenchment of a service is derived either from a recognition of the advantages of initiating an ongoing procedure for systematically identifying and evaluating opportunities for withdrawing resources from services, or from external conditions that require an agency to enforce retrenchment involuntarily.

Resistance to this momentum is likely to emerge and may discourage managers from retrenchment actions. Resistance may come from personnel within the agency or it may emanate from external sources beyond their control. If momentum for retrenchment is sufficient to surmount these barriers, then a retrenchment procedure will be implemented. The prevailing tendency is to adopt a product-oriented approach to retrenchment, which appeals to superficial commonsense ideals of justice, avoiding conflict, and minimizing morale problems within an agency; but it does not represent a sensitive response to citizen priorities. A marketing approach that allocates resources to services based on citizen needs and wants is suggested as a preferred alternative.

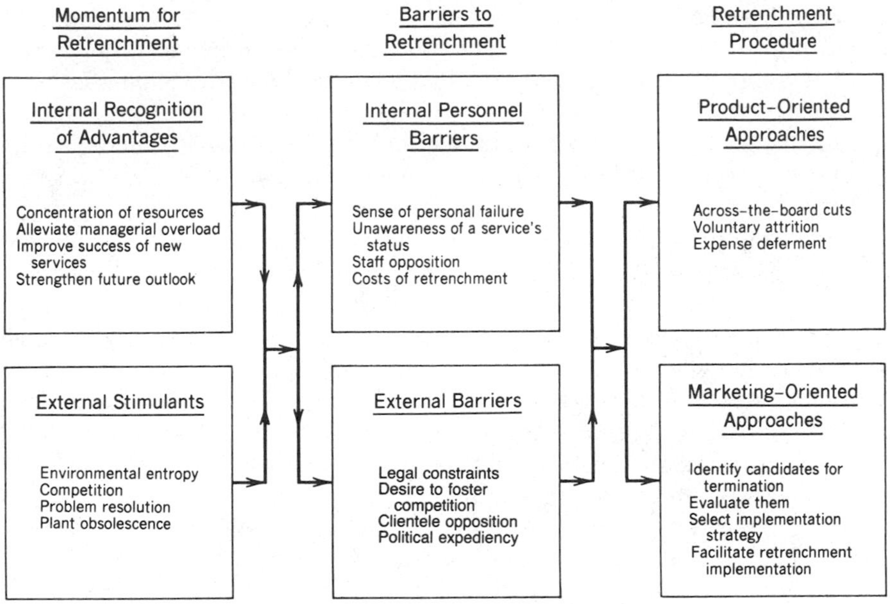

Figure 12.1. A Model of the Retrenchment Process.

INTERNAL RECOGNITION OF RETRENCHMENT ADVANTAGES

Four major benefits are likely when an agency voluntarily implements a formal procedure aimed at reducing or terminating relatively unproductive services: (1) resources become concentrated on the most important offerings, (2) managerial overload is alleviated, (3) new services have a greater probability of being successful, and (4) the agency is in a stronger position to face the future.

Concentration of Resources on the Most Important Offerings

An agency's success ultimately depends not on anybody within the organization, but upon the client groups it serves and the political representatives who reflect the satisfaction or dissatisfaction of those client groups. Achieving clientele satisfaction often requires concentration of resources on a relatively small number of services aimed at specified client groups.

> No other principle of effectiveness is violated as constantly today as the basic principle of concentration. Governments try to do a little of everything. The problem with the motto "Let's do a little bit of everything" is that enormous staffs are built up, and yet do not concentrate enough effort in any one area.[6]

In order to enhance an agency's overall effectiveness, resources appropriated to low-priority services should sometimes be diverted to higher-priority services. This approach may be resisted by people who feel that if an offering is retrenched, total benefits delivered will be reduced. This thinking equates quantity of services with total consumer benefits. A reduction in the quantity of service offerings that leads to an increase in the quality of some services may actually stimulate a net increase in total consumer benefits.

The Pareto principle, sometimes termed the *20/80 law*, explains why concentrating resource allocations on high-priority services is so important to effective service delivery. According to the principle, a small proportion of an agency's services are likely to account for a large proportion of the overall satisfaction and clientele served. Interpreted literally, this means that 20 percent of an agency's offerings are likely to account for 80 percent of the total clientele satisfaction that its programs generate. That ratio, however, should be viewed as an approximation; it is the principle rather than the precision of the ratio that is important. It may be possible, in other words, to withdraw resources from many services without having much adverse effect on total clientele satisfaction.

Alleviation of Managerial Overload

Since the major cost to most public agencies is personnel, time is the major resource to be allocated. It has been observed that "as the (number of offerings) increase numerically, the range of management problems seems to grow geometrically."[7] Adding service responsibilities without curtailing other responsibilities causes managers to feel overwhelmed: "It's like someone just handed me a bucket and told me to go bail out the Mississippi River."

An overabundance of services spreads an agency's managerial resources too thin. Some programs with undeveloped potential are likely to be ignored, problems with mature offerings may go undetected, and new programs may fail to receive the close attention that they require. Assigning a little of a manager's time to a wide range of services means that he or she is not able to commit a great deal of time to anything.

The principle of assigning the highest-caliber people to the highest-priority services in the agency, and not overloading them, is of fundamental importance. The temptation to diffuse the best managerial resources across all programs or, even worse, to assign such resources to marginal offerings in an effort to upgrade them should be resisted. Retrenchment of marginal services permits the reallocation of management time. The managerial effort required to sustain weak programs is frequently disproportionate to the benefits that those programs yield.[8]

Improvement of the Success Rate of New Services

Additional resources are often not available for developing new programs. Hence, if new programs are to emerge, resources have to be taken from existing programs. *Abandonment is an opportunity. It is the key to innovation because it frees necessary resources.*[9]

The question frequently arises: Did we give the new program a reasonable chance to succeed? Often the answer depends on whether or not an agency has a functioning retrenchment procedure. A new offering is unlikely to receive a fair chance in circumstances in which services that should be deleted are retained.

> New efforts over the last 20 years have produced fewer and fewer results. The new programs may well have been necessary and even well-planned, but their execution had to be entrusted to whoever was available rather than to the many experienced people stuck administering unproductive and obsolete programs.[10]

Strengthening an Agency's Future

If weak services are permitted to continue, they weaken an agency's foothold on the future by reducing its ability to adapt to a changing environment. By freeing resources through retrenchment an agency is better able to avail itself of opportunities and is more likely to initiate an active search for replacement programs. By seizing the initiative, an agency becomes proactive rather than reactive. This will ensure that it does not have a lopsided range of programs long on yesterday's and short on tomorrow's bread winners.[11] Retrenchment creates "space" out of which recycled resources become available for new uses. Without retrenchment, all resources would become committed to services that were established with reference to a prior time period's set of problems.[12]

> Unless steps are taken to generate new resources for new needs, typically by some systematic "taxation" of old resources, there is a major risk that no innovation can be tolerated, a very risky strategy if needs are in fact changing.[13]

EXTERNAL CONDITIONS THAT STIMULATE RETRENCHMENT

Even if an agency does not voluntarily implement retrenchment, it is likely that external circumstances will force it to confront the issue. The external events most likely to stimulate retrenchment are environmental entropy, competition, problem depletion, and plant obsolescence.

Environmental Entropy

The erosion of tax bases by population movements to suburbs and the tax revolt have led to crisis-inspired house cleaning, forcing agencies to retrench some services. This situation has been labeled *environmental entropy*. Environmental entropy occurs where the capacity of the environment to support a government or social service agency at previous levels of activity erodes.[14] It refers primarily to financial cutbacks that leave managers with the choice of either trying to acquire replacement resources or retrenching services.

Although they receive fewer funds, some agencies still may be pressured to substantially broaden their range of services. For example, many communities are requiring their leisure service agencies to take over a much broader range of social programs, including food programs for children and senior citizens, general counseling services, delinquency and drug abuse programs, leisure counseling, and so on. In order to accommodate these demands, priorities must be re-examined to determine which existing services should be deleted.

This problem is sometimes aggravated by what has been termed the "mandate without money" dilemma.[15] This refers to the practice of legislative bodies and courts passing laws and issuing court orders without providing funds to offset the additional expenses incurred by compliance:

> These mandates without accompanying financial assistance, ranging from occupational health and safety standards in public works to minimum education and social service requirements in correctional facilities, have had the effect of committing absolute levels of local resources to programs that sometimes have low local priority or are already overfunded relative to other programs.[16]

Competition

Retrenchment may be initiated when client participation in a previously successful program falls to such a low level that its continuance is a conspicuous embarrassment to the agency.[17] Continuance of such programs may contribute to a poor image for the agency, communicating to some citizens that the agency is unable to develop offerings that serve people's wants and needs.

Low levels of participation may arise from changing tastes or lifestyles. More frequently they occur because competition has emerged from other suppliers. Thus, for example, a public recreation center may be adversely impacted by a private leisure complex opening nearby. A program at one time perceived by a client group as worthwhile and satisfying may suffer in comparison with newer competitive offerings.

Problem Resolution

Problem resolution represents the ideal final stage in a program's life cycle. For example, sometimes a jurisdiction identifies a problem and commits substantial resources to resolve it. After the problem has been resolved or alleviated, resources are withdrawn and the program is retrenched or terminated.[18] In this category fall government involvement in short-term crises like national disasters (floods and earthquakes); medium-length government intervention (immunization programs, war mobilization, and countercyclical employment programs); and longer-term public programs (tuberculosis facilities, polio research or treatment, smallpox eradication, and space exploration).

Problems sometimes dissipate rather than become resolved. A school closing because of a neighborhood aging or a hospital closing because it no longer relates to its community illustrates this process. A study of hospital closures concluded:

> One of the most common characteristics of the hospitals studied was their irrelevance to their communities at the time they closed or merged with other corporate entities. The loss of mission, either medical or social, by these institutions was the most common underlying cause of closure.[19]

Sometimes retrenchment occurs not because the original problem has been resolved, but rather because it has been redefined. For example, many types of illness that once required hospitalization may now be treated on an ambulatory basis or can even be prevented, leading to retrenchment of some types of hospital facilities. Similarly, the movement to deinstitutionalize the mentally ill has led to retrenchment of some agencies responsible for treating clientele in institutions.[20]

Plant Obsolescence

The obsolescence of an existing physical plant may cause a facility to close and hence involve some retrenchment of services to clientele in the impacted geographic area. This has contributed to the closure of many schools and hospitals. A survey of 130 general care hospitals in New York City reported that 47 warranted complete replacement, 24 required extensive modernization, and 59 needed some renovation.[21] Obsolescence may involve not only plant deficiencies but also failure to adopt current techniques or equipment.

BARRIERS TO RETRENCHMENT

Although retrenchment efforts may be voluntarily initiated or involuntarily enforced, obsolete services often demonstrate a remarkable ability to survive:

> Certain things are inherently difficult for government and one of these is the elimination of services. It cannot really abandon anything. The moment government undertakes anything, it becomes entrenched and permanent.[22]

This is an overly pessimistic view, but it draws attention to the need for a focused effort to overcome the inherent tendency for services to be delivered forever.

In this section the major sources of resistance to retrenchment are discussed. Some understanding of these barriers is essential if strategies to surmount them are to be developed. Barriers may emerge from the active resistance or passive failings of personnel within the agency, or from external sources beyond the control of agency personnel.

Internal Personnel Barriers

Nobody likes to take unpleasant actions such as cutting back a service. The temptation is to procrastinate and avoid such actions. Four internal sources of resistance to retrenchment are a sense of personal failure, unawareness of a service's status, staff opposition, and inadequate cost savings.

Sense of Personal Failure. A sense of guilt or personal failure sometimes permeates retrenchment discussions. Traditionally managers have been conditioned to equate growth with success and contraction with failure. They are often reluctant to admit that the need for a service has declined because they fear that a service's demise will be interpreted as their personal failure.

Managers sometimes become committed to particular services and refuse to accept that "their" programs are no longer needed, do not produce results, or no longer represent the best use of resources. In such cases sentiment may become a powerful influence in the decision-making process and lead to the retention of weak programs. As has been noted, "putting (programs) to death—or letting them die—is a drab business, and often engenders much of the sadness of a final parting with old and tried friends."[23] This reluctance is intensified if managers have overpromised in their initial efforts to secure support for a program.

A new manager's review of services is frequently based on a more objective evaluation, which encourages a pruning of existing programs. The new manager is less likely to be personally committed to these programs. Indeed he or she may actually seek to de-emphasize past programs that are associated with immediate predecessors.

Unawareness of a Service's Status. In Chapter 4 we discussed the importance of program evaluation. Too often this is not implemented, with the result that managers may be unaware that a service is ailing. Management often thinks of evaluation as something that should be done but that can wait until tomorrow. In some instances, even if performance criteria are developed, the data required to assess the service against these criteria may not be available.

Staff Opposition. A major difficulty facing agencies that seek to reduce services is opposition within the agency. Most internal opposition is likely to be motivated by concern for self-preservation:

> The issue of how, where, and when cuts are to be made is directly important to all members of the organization. Much of the time, most of the issues confronting an organization are of low salience to most of its members. Whatever decision is made, they will hardly be affected. Thus, they do not become involved. Not so for retrenchment. Everyone is threatened; so the decisions to be made are of immediate, personal interest to everyone.[24]

There is no doubt that some resistance to retrenchment will occur when individuals' livelihoods are affected adversely or their social standing within an agency is threatened. If a particular service is dropped and not replaced by another, a loss of jobs, status, prestige, or influence may follow. If a replacement service is to be offered, some people will still resist the change because they know or fear that they will not be able to develop the new skills and behaviors it requires. The natural reaction of those adversely affected by retrenchment is to try to influence the decision process in their favor. That is, they press for continuance of the service.

If the total number or extent of services offered is to be reduced, fewer promotions and rewards will be available to motivate and retain successful and loyal managers. Hence the quality of management responsible for the delivery of the remaining services may suffer. The most talented personnel are likely to be the first to leave an agency in search of what they feel are better promotion opportunities and resources.

Costs of Retrenchment. Intuitively it seems obvious that reducing or terminating services or facilities will lead to resource savings. Indeed, that is the point of such actions. Savings may not be as substantial as anticipated, however, and may be realized only in the long term. For example, it has been estimated that the most any community can expect to save by closing a school is half of what it cost to operate it.[25] That is because fixed costs are associated with maintaining a building and because most teachers are transferred to other schools in the district.

In the short term there are likely to be substantial financial and political costs. If retrenchment involves reductions in the workforce through layoffs, then labor agreements requiring high severance pay for discharged employees may multiply costs. Additional costs may be incurred in transferring and retraining personnel, transferring equipment, and closing facilities. Thus in the short term it is possible that the costs of continuing to operate a service may be less than the costs of terminating it:

> "City Defense Office Costs More to Shut Than Run For Year," announced a headline in the *Washington Post*. The story reported that it would cost the District of Columbia \$134,000 to operate the mayor's civil defense office in 1977, but \$313,000 to close it.[26]

Unfortunately, some managers are concerned exclusively with short-term costs and benefits and reject retrenchment actions that offer only long-term benefits. The temptation to take this course is even stronger if the people who appointed them must stand for re-election every two or four years or if they expect to move into a new position after a short period of time. For example:

> A series of National Park Service superintendents ignored the problems created by the agency's beach erosion-control program at the Cape Hatteras National Seashore. In part, they may well have been motivated by the unconscious recognition that the inevitable turmoil resulting from any termination attempt would reflect badly upon their managerial competence. Yet, since they would be superintendents of the park for only two or three years, the benefits of eliminating the expensive and, many argued, harmful program would appear only during the terms of their successors.[27]

Finally, it should be noted that the overall context or perspective of an agency can be critical to retrenchment efforts. The savings that accrue from terminating a specific service or facility may be perceived as being so small as to be "insignificant" when compared with the total agency budget.

External Barriers

This section discusses four types of resistance to retrenchment which may emanate from sources external to the agency. They are clientele opposition, legal constraints, a political desire to foster competition, and political expediency.

Clientele Opposition. Every beneficiary of a government program immediately becomes a constituent.[28] Ironically, the more successful and satisfying a service has been, the more clientele opposition its retrenchment is likely to arouse. An agency's constituent groups can bring pressure on decision makers to reverse termination or reduction decisions. The problem has been expressed by U.S. Senator Phil Gramm in the following terms:

> The average spending bill we voted on in the last Congress cost about $50 million. The average beneficiary got between $500 and $700. There are 100 million taxpayers, so the average taxpayer paid 50 cents. You don't need a lot of economics to understand that somebody getting $700 is willing to do a lot more than somebody who is paying 50 cents. So, every time you vote on every issue, all the people who want the program are looking over your right shoulder and nobody's looking over your left shoulder.[29]

Elsewhere he described citizen reaction to his proposal to cut funding for 72 federal programs in an effort to balance the federal budget:

> In response to our proposal, I received literally hundreds of letters from people as diverse as governors and junk dealers. With very few exceptions, the writer

> always agreed with the goal of balancing the budget, agreed that hundreds of federal programs could and should be cut and commended me for my efforts. But in virtually every letter, the writer said that I was making one tragic mistake which revealed both my ignorance and my prejudice; proposing to cut a program that provided some benefit to the writer.[30]

Impacted client groups base their arguments on *particular* benefits that will be foregone by identified users. In contrast, those in favor of retrenchment are often able to base their case only on the less convincing grounds that *general* benefits will accrue to others when the resources are reallocated. For example:

> When New York City was in the process of closing Francis Delafield Hospital, those who opposed the termination pointed to specific individuals who were dependent upon the hospital. "If the city closes Delafield," said one doctor on the hospital's staff, "Gloria Flanagan's life will be shortened." Such arguments are potent, for even if those who advocate the closing can point to the greater opportunity cost in terms of lives lost from not closing the hospital, they are talking about statistical lives, not identified ones. The general benefits from saving a statistical life simply do not appear to be as great as the particular benefits from saving an identified life.[31]

In some cases client groups may be actively encouraged to resist retrenchment by agency personnel:

> The U.S. Navy, when threatened with the closure of a naval yard, quickly enlists the aid of local labor unions, industrial concerns, and members of Congress. Whatever arguments for economic and operational efficiency underlie the suggested closing of a naval base, they can rarely withstand the internal and external opposition that a large organization like the Navy can muster.[32]

Legal Constraints. Two types of legal constraints may create barriers to retrenchment. The first is the legislative authority required to terminate a program. In most cases the issue of rescinding authorization is not addressed because a legislative body simply ceases to appropriate funds for a service that it wants to terminate.

The second constraint is civil service procedures, which may be involved if the intent is to lay off, terminate, or regrade personnel. These procedures are typically cumbersome and time-consuming. The key to successfully terminating personnel using civil service procedures is the conscientious use of existing evaluation devices for employee performance:

> Most evaluation systems become pro forma and must be continually revised and promoted to ensure use by line managers. Evaluations become increasingly important as courts provide added protection of employment rights, and pressures to reduce the size of government continue to mount. The highest priority must be given to this area by anyone facing meaningful retrenchment. The most productive concentration of effort is at the end of the probationary period. Statistics

show that this period is not being adequately utilized to evaluate employees. Few employment rights are vested during the initial probationary period and removal is relatively easy.[33]

Desire to Foster Competition. A service may be retained in order to provide competition and incentive for other suppliers to retain a high standard. Some have argued that competitive market forces can be used to improve government services. In Minneapolis, for example, refuse collection was undertaken by both the city and a private corporation. The city administration assiduously cultivated a constructively competitive environment and exploited that powerful tool to the advantage of the citizens:

> The corporation, acutely conscious of its work performance relative to that of the city agency, has added more services at no extra costs, and agreed to a four percent price reduction.[34]

In this situation, terminating the competitive element that the city service provided may lead to a reduction in the quality of service delivered to citizens.

Political Expediency. The prevailing attitude among elected officials toward sunk costs often inhibits retrenchment.[35] In the private sector sunk costs are ignored because, although the decision that committed them may now be regrettable, it is too late to do anything about it. Thus they are not considered in retrenchment decisions. The long-term viability of the enterprise is likely to be more important to a decision maker's reputation than any specific project decision, making it more palatable to terminate offerings in which a substantial investment has been made.

In contrast, elected officials and managers of government and social service agencies frequently seek to justify sunk costs. Sunk costs represent a commitment that has to be justified to salvage a reputation. There is reluctance to admit to what may appear to be mistakes because these offer leverage to political opponents.

Taking no retrenchment is a tempting political expedient because it avoids confrontation and alienation. Thus prudent politicians have tended to shy away from retrenchment decisions. However, this is changing. Citizen reluctance to sanction new government financing has served as leverage that encourages elected representatives to actively retrench obsolete services.

PRODUCT-ORIENTED APPROACHES TO RETRENCHMENT

The resistance from both internal and external sources encourages the use of a product-oriented rather than a marketing-oriented approach toward retrenchment. Most momentum for retrenchment is stimulated by external circumstances rather than by internal recognition of its advantages. Thus strategies are adopted because they are expedient rather than because they reflect an effort to prioritize citizens' needs and wants.

Typically retrenchment is implemented by (1) cutting resources equally across-the-board to all services, (2) relying on voluntary attrition accompanied by a hiring freeze, or (3) deferring necessary expenditures. These approaches may appeal to commonsense ideals of justice, avoiding conflict, and minimizing morale problems within an agency; but, as shown in the following paragraphs, they do not represent a sensitive response to citizen priorities.

Across-the-Board Cuts

Services do not contribute equally to satisfying citizen wants, and reduced resource allocations should reflect the different priorities citizens assign to services. Across-the-board cuts, instead of achieving this goal, tend to penalize past and current efficiencies. When cuts are made in this way, efficient organizations are likely to be penalized more than their poorly performing peers because the easy and obvious improvement strategies have probably already been implemented. For poorly performing organizations the task is much simpler: To achieve higher performance, all they have to do is borrow the management practices and productivity ideas already employed by high-performing agencies.[36]

Voluntary Attrition

Voluntary attrition, with an associated hiring freeze, results in arbitrary outcomes that cannot be anticipated. Employees do not retire or otherwise voluntarily leave their jobs in response to citizens' service priorities. Thus the services that are most impacted may or may not be those which are the lowest priority to citizens. It is most likely that resignations will come from those employees with the best skills because they will have more opportunities for employment elsewhere.

Expenditure Deferment

Deferring necessary expenditures is another prevailing short-term strategy that involves retrenching service areas in which the withdrawal of resources has no immediate negative impact. For example, maintenance of infrastructure and plant, or investment in staff training and new equipment needed to improve or maintain productivity, may be deferred. In the short term, this policy enables an agency to continue offering a wide range of services. However, it will eventually result in either substantially inferior services or the need for a large infusion of resources that can be obtained only by withdrawing resources from other service areas.

A MARKETING APPROACH TO RETRENCHMENT

Every new program's demise, whether in the near or distant future, is inevitable. Hence the retrenchment process should be an ongoing part of the managerial process rather than a reaction to an external crisis. In contrast to the prevailing product-oriented strategies for retrenchment, the primary objective of a marketing approach is to allocate resources to services so that they reflect citizens' needs and wants. The procedure developed in this section offers a framework to achieve this objective.

Since retrenchment decisions are normally unpopular, service reduction or termination is unlikely to occur unless specific responsibility and formal accountability for the process is assigned. One approach that has been proven effective is to appoint a retrenchment committee responsible for making recommendations to top management twice each year. If this group is also charged with developing new programs (see Chapter 10), then coordination between the two procedures can be facilitated. Formalizing the retrenchment process helps institutionalize it as a routine strategy for matching agency offerings with citizen priorities and provides the initiative for subjecting all services to periodic review.

As Figure 12.2 illustrates, retrenchment is a four-stage process including (1) identifying those services that should be considered as possible candidates for retrenchment, (2) evaluating each program to determine if retrenchment is appropriate, (3) retrenchment implementation, and (4) facilitating the implementation decision.

Identifying Candidates for Retrenchment

A marketing approach to retrenchment requires comparative data on the costs and positive impacts of services. Without such data retrenchment decisions have to be based on little more than visceral impressions. With the data, five tools for identifying retrenchment candidates are available: the sunset concept, zero-base budgeting, program life cycle audits, citizen surveys, and cross-priority analysis. This stage of the retrenchment procedure seeks only to identify programs for which retrenchment is a possibility; it does not make retrenchment inevitable.

The *sunset concept* was the brainchild of the Colorado chapter of Common Cause. Its sponsors recognized that programs and agencies tend to proliferate

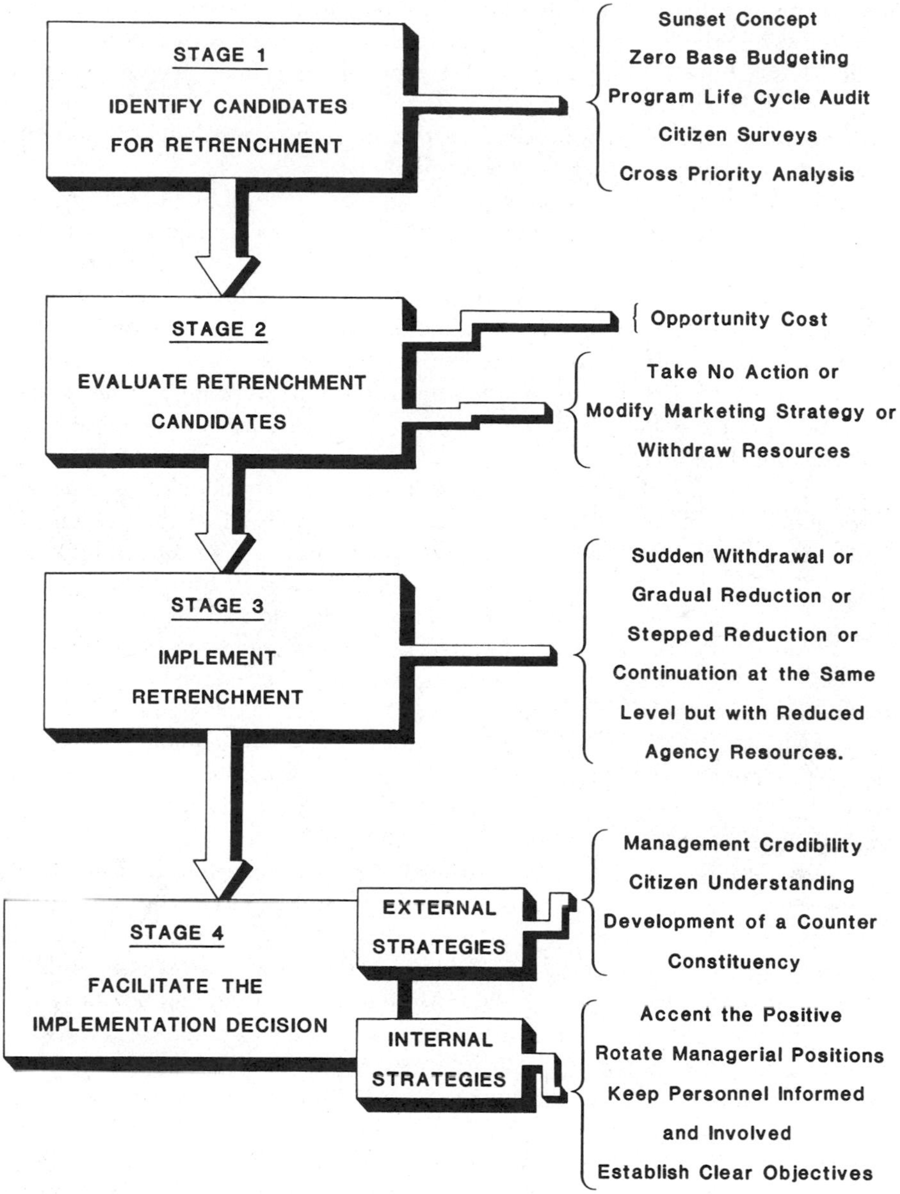

Figure 12.2. The Retrenchment Process.

and perpetuate because termination is difficult, controversial, and time consuming. While the concept has many possible applications, a typical sunset law establishes a timetable for review of a program or agency. These programs automatically terminate on a specified date unless their existence is positively reaffirmed after the review process. In the absence of affirmative action, the status quo is changed rather than continued.

Zero-base budgeting is an attempt to provide an alternative to the conventional incremental approach to budgeting. Rather than using current budget allocation levels as the customary starting point when budgeting for the next year, the zero-base approach requires participants to start from the ground up. This means that because an item was included in the last year's budget does not mean that it will appear in the budget for the next year. Each year an agency must look at its entire budget and project, if warranted, a new set of allocation priorities for the upcoming year. Both existing and proposed new activities must be analyzed.

The program life cycle audit is based on the concept that all programs pass through a life cycle (see Figure 9.2). The audit requires that the present life cycle stage of each of the agency's programs be identified.[37] To do this, historical usage data for each program is needed, going back to the beginning of the program if possible to fix its present position on its life cycle curve.

In order to identify the true life cycle pattern, data have to be adjusted to allow for population changes. Thus a ratio such as attendance per thousand population may be most appropriate. Similarly, the data should be adjusted to remove the impact of any major changes in the cost of admission to participants in the program (see Chapter 9). Clearly, those programs that are shown to be located in the saturation or decline stages of their life cycle should be subject to evaluation as possible candidates for retrenchment.

Citizens are the ultimate beneficiaries of services. Direct input from *citizen surveys* provides opportunities for individuals and groups to indicate which programs are most and least important to them. If a service is rated as being a lower priority by its targeted clientele than other new services that could be offered with the same resources, then it qualifies as a candidate for retrenchment. For example, when Proposition 13 was passed in California, the City of Walnut Creek hired a consulting firm to survey 1,500 citizens regarding which services should be cut. The results were used in budget proceedings to develop overall service priorities.

Cross-priority analysis is a round robin technique that permits an agency to compare a service with every other offering by using a matrix approach of priority ranking. Two programs are compared at a time, with the higher-rated program being assigned one point and the lower-rated offering zero points. After each service has been compared with every other one, the points are added up. Those programs receiving the most points become the highest-priority programs, while those with the least become lowest priority. Thus, in the example shown in Figure 12.3, the highest-priority project was softball field lighting while the lowest-priority project was greens renovation.

ITEM LISTING

		Raquetball courts	Softball field lighting	Boat dock	Youth center	Filter system	Renovate greens	
		1	2	3	4	5	6	RANKING
New raquetball courts	1	■		x	x	x	x	2
Softball field lighting	2	x	■	x	x	x	x	1
Repair boat dock	3			■	x	x	x	3
Alterations to youth center	4				■		x	5
Install filter system	5				x	■	x	4
Renovate golf course greens	6						■	6
RANKING		2	1	3	5	4	6	

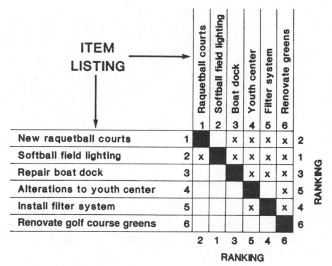

Figure 12.3. A Cross-Priority Analysis Matrix.

Deciding which service is higher priority in each comparison is dependent on the criteria used. Appropriate criteria may include (1) self-sufficiency potential, (2) net cost, (3) number served, (4) whether future costs associated with the services are likely to remain stable, increase, or decrease, (5) the availability of other providers of the service, and (6) cost per participant, which is a combination of criteria 2 and 3.

Evaluating Retrenchment Candidates

The evaluation has to be measured against agreed-upon criteria. Appropriate criteria will vary among services and situations. Figure 12.4 shows the criteria used by the Madison Public Schools system during the process of closing three elementary schools. Using these detailed criteria, a rank order list of over 30 elementary schools was developed and used as the basis for selecting the schools to be closed.

A critical question in evaluating each service is, "If we did not already deliver this service, would we now start, knowing what we know now?" If the answer is no then it is time to ask, "How can we get out of this?" or at least "How can we stop pouring more resources into this?"[38]

Two concerns are involved in evaluating retrenchment candidates. First, a crucial criterion in the evaluation decision is opportunity cost. That is, can resources freed by withdrawing them from an offering provide more benefits if assigned to another service? Second, after opportunity costs have been clarified, a decision has to be made as to whether or not a service should be retrenched.

1. *Neighborhood factors,* including a child proximity count (density of student population near each school); child proximity overlap (student population density of surrounding area); and percent of student overlap (closeness of other attendance area).
2. *Building factors,* including school building area in square feet; school building capacity; building age; classrooms in use; classrooms not in use; area divided by enrollment, current year; area divided by capacity; area divided by enrollment, previous year; capacity divided by proximity; proximity divided by capacity; maintenance cost; and percent of classrooms for instructions.
3. *Energy factors,* including fuel consumption (BTU); electricity consumption (KWH); building heat ($); electricity consumption ($); fuel divided by area; electricity (KWH) divided by area; heat divided by area; electricity ($) divided by area; fuel (BTU) divided by capacity; fuel ($) divided by capacity; total energy consumption; and total energy consumption divided by area.
4. *Enrollment factors,* including enrollment, current year; enrollment, previous year; current enrollment divided by classrooms; enrollment difference; and enrollment ratio.
5. *Minority factors,* including minority enrollment, current year; percent minority enrollment; and minority population to capacity.
6. *Dollar factors,* including total expenditures; salaries, current year; and total expenditures divided by area.

Figure 12.4. Criteria Used for the Retrenchment of Elementary Schools in Madison, Wisconsin. (*Source:* Stefoner, T., *Effective Management in Contracting Public Organizations*. Division for Management, Planning, and Federal Services, Wisconsin Department of Public Instruction, Information Series, Vol. 7, No. 3, August 1979.)

Opportunity Cost. The opportunity cost of a service is the clientele satisfaction and/or revenues that other existing programs or new programs could produce if the effort and resources currently allocated to the existing program were redirected.[39] A program may be well received by a relatively large number of clients but it must still be exposed to the question, "Could the resources allocated to this program generate greater total satisfaction to the community if they were reallocated?"

The concept of opportunity cost rarely enters into any discussion of service offerings and yet there are always alternate client groups to be served or alternate services to be offered. A decision to continue to offer a particular service implies a willingness to forego all other opportunities for which the resources could be used.

Costs of initiating a new service or the cost savings from retrenching an existing program usually are expressed only in dollars, not in terms of alternative program opportunities foregone or made available through retrenchment. In many instances it is not obvious that "free" public services incur opportunity costs and foreclose other alternatives. If a teacher or police officer had to be discharged every time another public boat dock or tennis court was built, the real cost of these public services would be apparent.[40] In the past, it was not necessary to make so many of these difficult choices because budgets were simply expanded to accommodate the hiring of another teacher or police officer. Now, with more severe economic constraints, identifying opportunity costs and program evaluation are critical because of the need for implementing retrenchment.

Evaluation Options. Three options are available when evaluating retrenchment candidates:[41] leaving the program alone, modifying its marketing strategy, or withdrawing resources from it. The first option should be implemented if no better alternative use for the resources currently allocated to the service has been identified. On some occasions resources will not be withdrawn even when superior opportunities for their use have been identified. To continue offering a program that serves very few, has to be heavily subsidized, or provides minimum clientele satisfaction is not necessarily a managerial crime. It is reprehensible only when management does not know the extent of its use, subsidy, or satisfaction benefits or, knowing the facts, retains it without sound reasons for doing so.[42] Consider the hospital that is torn between maintaining or closing its underutilized maternity ward:

> A cost-benefit analysis of the advantages of keeping or closing the maternity ward would more than likely result in a consideration of closing the ward. The space and resources allocated to the maternity ward might be better used for other purposes.
>
> However, almost every community thinks it should have a full service hospital; having a full complement of community services plays a significant part in community pride and image. It also plays a role in the spirited competition between some neighboring towns; no town wants to place its real estate agents in the position of having to say to a prospective buyer, "We have a good hospital here, but you'll have to go to the neighboring town to have your baby." The desires of the community may thus dictate keeping an underutilized maternity ward open.[43]

A second evaluative option is to modify a service's marketing program rather than withdraw resources from it. This may involve assigning new leadership to the service or using a different facility. Alternatively, increasing the promotional effort, promoting the service differently in terms of theme and media, or retargeting it to a different clientele may be needed. The price may be too high, thereby discouraging some users. Or the price may be too low which will make some potential clientele think the program is inferior. Adjustment of any of these ingredients may revitalize a service and make retrenchment inappropriate.

The third option is to retrench. Once this decision has been made, considerable thought needs to be given to the choice of implementation strategy and how it should best be brought to bear on the service.

Retrenchment Implementation Strategies

Figure 12.5 shows four alternate strategies for service reduction or termination. Option (a), the sudden change strategy implemented without appreciable warning, has the advantage of surprise to groups that see themselves adversely affected by retrenchment. This strategy reduces the time available to these

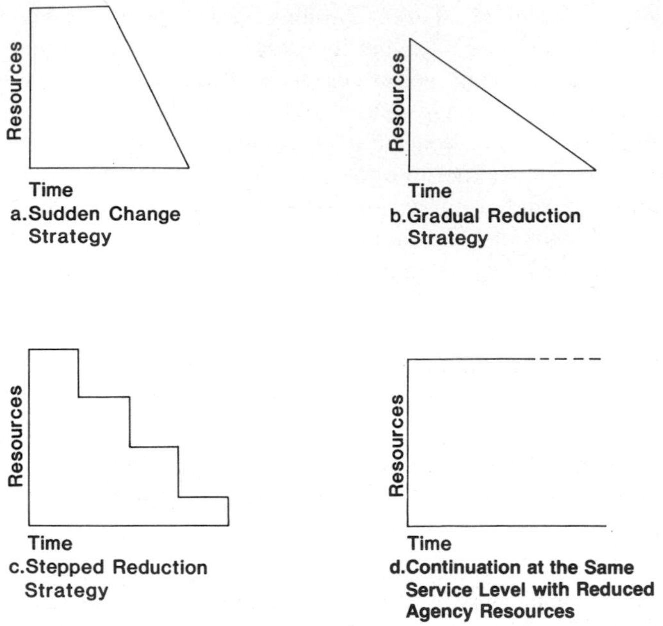

Figure 12.5. Alternative Strategies for Program Retrenchment.

groups to develop organized resistance. If effective opposition emerges, retrenchment may be expensive in terms of time delays and opportunities foregone, and the retrenchment decision may even be reversed. To avoid conflict, some public sector managers may prefer to take swift, sudden action. In that way they confine the conflict to as short a period of time as possible. However, such action may be perceived by citizens as high handed or arrogant and as failing to meet a moral obligation to assist those adversely affected by the service cuts.

Many perceive agencies as having an obligation to help those directly and adversely affected by service reductions and not to discontinue support abruptly. These client groups may have come to depend on a service that represents—or at least they perceive it to represent—a commitment to a clientele.[44] It is perfectly reasonable for that clientele to assume indefinite provision of the service. Indeed they may even come to believe that they are entitled to the service and to the benefits that flow from it.

For this reason government and social service managers may seek to inform participating clientele of the intent to retrench far enough in advance to permit transition to alternate programs if they are available. These managers might adopt one of the gradual decremental strategies (b) or (c). In these instances the program continues to be operated over a given time period, but with continually lowering levels of support. These strategies have the advantage of providing time for reexamining the impact of various levels of retrenchment and for adjustments, if necessary. Further, the decremental approaches allow affected clientele to adjust to the change and to seek alternatives elsewhere.

If personnel are to be phased out with a service's retrenchment, then a decremental strategy also allows them time to find alternate positions. For example, Congress mandated the gradual phasing out of the Civil Aeronautics Board, the federal regulator of aviation fares and routes, over a seven-year period between 1978 and 1985. This leeway provided both employees and the aviation industry time to adjust to the agency's termination.

Strategy (d) calls for a service to continue at the same level of support, but without the agency's resources. There are two ways that this may be accomplished. First, instead of being a direct provider, the agency's role can change to that of a facilitator or broker, providing a link between the needs of its clientele and the supply of private services available to satisfy them.

Many times it is particularly difficult to terminate a service when capital-intensive facilities are associated with it. However, it may be possible to eliminate the service from an agency's budget by leasing the facilities out to private groups or consolidating them with duplicate or similar services provided by other departments.

The second way to implement strategy (d) is to increase user contributions, which will enable the agency to save resources. This choice may be particularly appropriate in the case of discretionary services. Increasing price might be a sound strategy even if a program appears to be relatively poorly supported by the targeted clientele. Those clients who do use it may have a strong desire for the benefits it offers, thus creating an inelastic demand curve. In such instances an increase in user price may result in higher revenues that make agency resources unnecessary.

Facilitating the Implementation Decision

A major advantage of assigning responsibility for the formal retrenchment procedure to the same committee charged with new program development is the likelihood of increased awareness that every new offering will become a future retrenchment candidate. Indeed, one of the criteria for new program selection may be the ease with which a service can be terminated when the necessity arises. The most effective retrenchment occurs when a long-term perspective is adopted at the time new programs are introduced. For example, the Dallas Park and Recreation Department, instead of purchasing vest-pocket parks, enters into permission-to-use agreements with landowners to provide these parks. Removable play equipment and plant materials are placed on these small areas, which often are unused building sites. Either party may cancel the simple lease agreement with 30 days' notice. Purchase of these small areas would require the department to maintain and equip them indefinitely with resources that may yield more benefits in the future if used elsewhere. Leasing provides flexibility to respond to demographic shifts and makes subsequent retrenchment much easier.

Strategies for External Publics. Successful retrenchment requires that opposition from affected citizen groups be eliminated or at least neutralized. Three ingredients are critical in this task. The first is management's personal credibility. Before client groups accept that they are being treated fairly and provided with accurate information, they have to be convinced that "incompetence and corruption are not so widespread that the problem can be simply solved by eliminating those two evils."[45] Client groups must believe that recommendations for service retrenchments are based on a genuinely impartial professional determination of the appropriate levels of services, made without bias toward any one group.

A second critical ingredient in alleviating clientele opposition is for impacted citizens to have an understanding of the agency's financial constraints and of its decision-making processes. Even impartial professional evaluations are likely to be resisted unless there is a general supportive belief among citizens that their conclusions are reasonable. Many clients are not likely to be aware of either the source and magnitude of budget restraints or the wide range of services that a typical agency is committed to delivering. For client groups to accept the need for service reduction and not to believe that an arbitrary decision has been made to retrench "their" particular services, it is essential that they gain an understanding of a program's restraints and full responsibilities. As experienced by one city manager in dealing with groups representing the elderly:

> Many programs were developed which expanded the services to the elderly, including meals and more medical services. These programs were good. When, however, deficiencies of resources demanded some consideration of cutbacks, it was necessary to objectively evaluate the impact of more traditional services on the elderly citizens. We had to include their advocates in this process to allow an understanding of the manner in which the police service, fire service, city health services, and other traditional municipal services affected elderly citizens. Only then could they evaluate the traditional services in contrast to new services and concur with decisions on which must be reduced. Clearly this situation was reached by the involvement of those concerned citizens in a process which enabled them to understand the full scope of services provided by the municipality.[46]

The third element in successfully dealing with external publics is to develop counterconstituencies. Even if management credibility is strong and there is an understanding of the parameters and criteria that have led to the retrenchment decision, the natural inclination is to resist such action. In these instances, it becomes imperative to enlarge the political arena in which a service's fate is debated by developing a counterconstituency.

As noted earlier in this chapter, vigorous opposition to termination is to be expected while active support of the change is unlikely. Unless those advocating retrenchment are able to attract a counterconstituency, those resisting retrenchment will control the debate:

> To close the Massachusetts public training schools, the Department of Youth Services' Commissioner recruited a number of liberal interest groups that were upset with the treatment of juveniles at the institutions. This new constituency broadened the scope of the conflict and was able to defeat the coalition of state legislators, county office holders, and employees of the institutions that had quietly controlled the training schools in the past.[47]

An obvious counterconstituency is another client group who would benefit from the resources released from the retrenched program. Its credibility, however, is likely to be limited because of its ulterior motive.

If retrenchment is extensive then the media may become an effective counterconstituency by claiming that the service reduction is in the best interest of the whole community. It is always important to assist the media in grasping the real constraints and parameters within which the agency operates as well as why the proposed retrenchment is in the best interests of the community.

Strategies for Internal Personnel. Four strategies can be used to ease acceptance of retrenchment among affected agency personnel. First, it is important to *accent the positive* and stress the advantages of retrenchment. Whenever possible, improvement should be advocated rather than retrenchment: "We are going to put increased resources into improving the quality of the most popular flower beds in the city. In order to achieve this we will be eliminating some of the less appreciated, inferior-quality flower beds." Incentives may be an important part of this strategy. For example, if personnel in the affected service area are unable to retain the resources saved by retrenchment and to reallocate them according to what they perceive to be higher priorities, then they have little incentive to support curtailment of programs.

A second strategy is to *rotate managerial positions* within the agency. A new manager will be more divorced from past decisions and less compelled to justify an agency's past priorities. By rotating managers, interpersonal loyalties and sentimental attachments to programs will not interfere with retrenchment decisions. New managers may be better able to make hard, unpopular decisions, take the flak, and move to another position in the agency.

A third strategy is to keep *personnel informed and involved,* particularly in major retrenchments. Retrenchment will engender feelings of insecurity and fear among employees. Their full awareness and involvement is essential in minimizing resistance and in prioritizing retrenchment candidates. For example, throughout retrenchment of the Civil Aeronautics Board, the board conducted what it called "sunset in the sunshine" sessions with employees to keep them informed of the agency's close-down policies and their own job prospects.[48]

The final strategy is to ensure that *clear objectives are established* that provide a context and planned direction for retrenchment decisions so they do not seem arbitrary. If efforts to introduce retrenchment are not carefully presented in the context of an overall plan and accompanied by a personnel informational program, then they will almost always meet resistance. Retrenchment should be explained as part of a larger purpose so all concerned personnel know why it is taking place and are aware of its implications.

SUMMARY

The viability of an agency and the mix of its programs is as much a function of paring as it is of proliferating new programs.[49] Retrenchment requires innovation because it is a relatively new phenomenon. It has been stated that the concepts, indicators, and methods of retrenching public services remain to be invented.[50] Clearly, it is time to invent them.

Momentum for retrenchment is derived either from recognition within an agency of advantages that accrue or from external conditions that require an agency to enforce retrenchment involuntarily. Four major advantages are likely to follow from retrenching services. First, it enables an agency to concentrate resources on services identified as being most important. It is possible to withdraw resources from many services without having much adverse impact on total clientele satisfaction. Second, retrenchment alleviates managerial overload. Assigning a little of a manager's time to a wide range of services makes him or her less able to concentrate on the important priorities with the highest pay-offs. Third, retrenchment is often a prerequisite for successful introduction of new services because it releases resources. Fourth, by not retrenching programs at the appropriate time, aggressive search for replacement programs is delayed. This may lead an agency to have a mix of programs that is long on old successes and short on new ones.

Often only the substantial impact of external circumstances will provoke a serious effort to retrench programs. Environmental entropy, usually in the form of financial cut-backs, is the most frequent of these events. Competition from other suppliers may lead to a substantial reduction in the number of clients served by a program and, hence, encourage withdrawal of resources. Problem resolution represents the final stage of a program's life cycle when the problem the program addressed has been resolved or alleviated. At that point resources should be withdrawn. The obsolescence of existing physical plant may also cause a facility to close and retrenchment of the services provided in that facility.

Although retrenchment efforts may be voluntarily initiated or involuntarily enforced, barriers are likely to emerge from the active resistance or passive failings of personnel within the agency, or from external sources beyond the control of agency personnel. Within the agency, resistance to retrenchment may be encountered if personnel believe that a service's demise will be interpreted as a personal failure. The personal bias of managers toward particular services may lead to retention despite strong evidence supporting demise. Sometimes obsolete programs are retained because of the lack of performance criteria or evaluation efforts in the agency. Managers may simply be unaware that particular services should be retrenched. Personnel opposition is likely if retrenchment is seen as causing loss of jobs, status, promotional opportunities, or influence. Finally, retrenchments may offer long-term benefits but incur substantial short-term costs, which serve to deter managers from taking any action.

Resistance to retrenchment may also come from sources external to the agency. Legal constraints include not having appropriate legislative authority for retrenchment, but more commonly involve civil service procedures if the intent is to lay off or regrade personnel. An inefficient service may be retained in order to provide competition and incentive for other suppliers. The major external resistance is likely to be encountered from a service's beneficiaries. The more successful and satisfying a service has been, the more clientele opposition its retrenchment is likely to arouse. Finally, politicians tend to avoid retrenchment because of its potential for confrontation and alienation.

The prevailing strategies adopted by government and social service agencies toward retrenchment enforced by the external environment include across-the-board cuts, reliance on voluntary attrition accompanied by a hiring freeze, and deference of necessary expenditures. These are product-oriented strategies. A marketing approach to retrenchment requires that resources be allocated to services so that they reflect citizens' needs and wants. A committee responsible for making retrenchment recommendations should be established.

The first stage in the retrenchment procedure is to identify programs that should be considered for retrenchment. Five evaluative tools might be used to aid this process: the sunset concept, zero-base budgeting, program life cycle audits, citizen surveys, and cross-priority analysis.

Once potential candidates for retrenchment have been identified, the second step is to determine if withdrawal of resources is the best course of action. A crucial criterion in the evaluation decision is opportunity cost. The opportunity cost of a service is the clientele satisfaction and/or revenues that an existing or new program could produce if effort and resources were redirected to it from the retrenchment candidate service. Three options are available when evaluating retrenchment candidates: leaving the program alone, modifying its marketing strategy, or withdrawing resources from it.

There are four alternative strategies for implementing retrenchment. The preferred strategy is continuation at the same service level with reduced agency resources. If this is not possible then stepped or gradual reduction strategies should be implemented in preference to a sudden change strategy.

The final stage of retrenchment is to expedite its acceptance. A long-term perspective is needed here: No new program should be introduced without considering the ease with which it can be terminated when the necessity arises. Specific facilitation actions have to be taken that anticipate the major internal and external sources of resistance. Key factors for successfully dealing with external resistance are the personal credibility and perceived integrity of management, an understanding by affected client groups of the parameters and criteria that led to the retrenchment decision, and the development of a counterconstituency that supports retrenchment.

To gain the support of agency personnel, it is important to accent the positive by stressing the advantages of retrenchment to them and focusing on the benefits it will yield. Rotating managerial positions and keeping personnel informed and involved are helpful, particularly in major retrenchments. Finally, clear objectives should be established that provide agency personnel with evidence that the retrenchments are not arbitrary, but rather planned and purposeful.

NOTES

1. Drucker, P.F., "The Deadly Sins in Public Administration," *Public Administration Review,* Vol. 40 No. 2, March/April 1980, p. 105.
2. Kotler, P., "Phasing Out Weak Products," *Harvard Business Review,* March/April 1965, p. 107.
3. Drucker, P.F., *The Age of Discontinuity*. New York: Harper and Row, 1969, p. 194.
4. Drucker, P.F., *Managing for Results*. New York: Harper and Row, 1964, p. 62.
5. Drucker, P.F., *Managing in Turbulent Times*. London: Pan Books, 1981, p. 67.
6. Drucker, *Managing for Results,* p. 12.
7. Kotler, "Phasing Out," p. 107.
8. Ibid., p. 109.
9. Drucker, *The Age of Discontinuity,* p. 143.
10. Drucker, P.F., "Meaningful Reorganization," *Wall Street Journal,* February 4, 1977, p. 12.
11. Drucker, P.F., "Managing for Business Effectiveness," *Harvard Business Review,* May/June 1963, p. 53.
12. Biller, R.P., "On Tolerating Policy and Organizational Terminations: Some Design Considerations," *Policy Sciences,* No. 7, 1976, p. 137.
13. Biller, R.P., "Leadership Tactics for Retrenchment," *Public Administration Review,* November/December 1980, p. 606.
14. Levine, C.H., "Organizational Decline and Cutback Management." In C.H. Levine (ed.), *Managing Fiscal Crisis: The Crisis in the Public Sector*. Chatham, NJ: Chatham House, 1980, pp. 13–30.
15. Levine, C.H., "More on Cutback Management: Hard Questions for Hard Times." In C.H. Levine (ed.), *Managing Crisis,* pp. 305–312.
16. Ibid., p. 308.
17. Kotler, "Phasing Out," p. 111.
18. Levine, "Cutback Management," pp. 13–30.
19. Pleines, K.M., and Williams, H., "Planning With the Community in Mind Can Prevent

Hospital Closings," *Hospitals: Journal of the American Hospital Association*, Vol. 52 (December 1, 1958), p. 89.

20. Levine, "Cutback Management," p. 17.
21. Pleines and Williams, *Planning with the Community*, p. 88.
22. Drucker, *Discontinuity*, p. 226.
23. Alexander, R.S., "The Death and Burial of 'Sick' Products," *Journal of Marketing*, vol. 28, April 1964, p. 1.
24. Behn, R.D., "Leadership for Cut-Back Management: The Use of Corporate Strategy," *Public Administration Review*, November/December 1980, p. 618.
25. Gumpert, D., "School Closings Bring an Emotional Debate to Nation's Suburbs," *Wall Street Journal*, June 14, 1977, p. 16.
26. Valentine, P.W., "City Defense Office Costs More to Shut Than Run For Year," *Washington Post*, March 5, 1976, p. 1.
27. Behn, R.D., "Can Public Policy Termination Be Increased by Making Government More Businesslike?" In C.H. Levine and I. Rubin (ed.), *Fiscal Stress and Public Policy*. Beverly Hills, CA: Sage Publications, 1980, p. 264.
28. Drucker, *Discontinuity*, p. 226.
29. Congressman Phil Gramm, as cited in Freeman, M., "Tax Camouflage," *Newsweek*, November 23, 1981, p. 98.
30. Gramm, P., *The Washington Report: Annual Constituent Questionnaire*. January 1981, p. 2.
31. Behn, R.D., "Closing a Government Facility," *Public Administration Review*, July/August 1978, p. 334.
32. DeLeon, P., "Public Policy Terminology: An End and a Beginning," *Policy Analysis*, vol. 4, No. 3, Summer 1978, pp. 369–392.
33. Wilburn, R.C., and Worman, M.A., "Overcoming the Limits to Personnel Cut-Backs: Lessons Learned in Pennsylvania," *Public Administration Review*, November/December 1980, p. 610.
34. Savas, E.S., "An Empirical Study of Competition in Municipal Service Delivery," *Public Administration Review*, November/December 1977, p. 717.
35. Behn, R.D., "Public Policy Termination," p. 268.
36. Levine, "Cutback Management," p. 309.
37. This notion of a program life cycle audit is adapted from Clifford, D.K., "Managing the Product Life Cycle." In R. Mann (ed.), *The Arts of Top Management: A McKinsey Anthology*. New York: McGraw-Hill, 1971.
38. Drucker, "Deadly Sins," p. 45.
39. Bell, M.L., *Marketing: Concepts and Strategy*. Boston: Houghton Mifflin, 1972, p. 684.
40. Thompson, W., "The City as a Distorted Price System, 2," *Psychology Today*, No. 28, August 1968, p. 130.
41. Kotler, P., *Marketing Management: Analysis, Planning, and Control*, Englewood Cliffs, NJ: Prentice Hall, 1984, p. 372.
42. Alexander, "Sick Products," p. 5.
43. Clarke, R.N., "Health Care Marketing: Problems in Implementation," *Health Care Management Review*, vol. 3 No. 1, Winter 1978, pp. 206–207.
44. Behn, "Closing a Facility," p. 333.
45. Behn, R.D., "Leadership in an Era of Retrenchment," *Public Administration Review*, November/December 1980, p. 603.
46. Wilson, A.J., "It is Easier to Give Than to Take Away," *Public Management*, vol. 59 No. 3, March 1977, p. 4.

47. Behn, R.D., "How to Terminate a Public Policy: A Dozen Hints for the Would-be Terminator," *Policy Analysis*, vol. 4 No. 3, Summer 1978, p. 397.

48. Karr, A.R. "CAB Sheds Workers As It Prepares to Fly Slowly Into Sunset," *Wall Street Journal*, November 11, 1980, p. 1.

49. Sturdivant, F.D., et al. *Managerial Analysis in Marketing*. Glenview, IL: Scott Foresman, 1970, p. 363.

50. Hans, H.J., "Planning for Declining and Poor Cities," *American Institute of Planners Journal*, September 1975, p. 307.

THIRTEEN

Objectives of Pricing

There are two pricing questions that the government and social service manager must answer. The first is "What are my objectives in pricing this program?" The objectives will serve as guidelines in determining a specific price. After briefly exploring the nature of price and the extent to which direct pricing is used in government, the remainder of this chapter discusses the primary objectives that an agency must prioritize in all pricing decisions. The second question managers must address is "How do I establish a specific price for a service in accordance with the prioritized objectives?" Chapter 14 presents a logical method for translating the pricing objectives into the charged price.

Pricing is one of the most technically difficult and politically sensitive areas in which public service managers have to make decisions. Pricing decisions are influenced by a myriad of ideological, political, economic, and professional arguments. The debate that accompanies this diversity of perspectives, however, should be focused on some sound principles. The intent of these two pricing chapters is to explore those principles and their implications.

The main failure of most user price policies is that they have been designed solely or primarily to raise revenue. The prevailing approach is to raise all prices by some arbitrary or percentage amount each year. Little effort is made to discover who is benefiting, who is paying, and the level of benefits and payments involved for each service. Even if incremental price increases are based on some acceptable criterion, they assume that the original price was appropriate. If the initial price was arbitrarily derived, then subsequent incremental increases are also likely to lead to an arbitrary price that does not accurately reflect the agency's objectives or its clientele's best interest.

An important goal of these pricing chapters is to increase understanding of the rationale and desirability of charging appropriate prices for many government services currently provided free or below cost. In the past, agencies have tended to be reactive, often being forced into higher user pricing as a last resort for increasing revenues. A proactive, more studied approach to the design and implementation of prices is needed to ensure that the *right* prices are charged for services.

POLITICAL CONSIDERATIONS

We are aware that politics and values sometimes exert a determining influence on government and social service agency pricing decisions. Decision makers often oppose user pricing even though it is appropriate from an equity or efficiency perspective. As Arnold Meltsner has noted:

> The "perfect" local user charge is not one where the payer gets the benefit, or where resources are properly rationed, or where service levels are determined, or where there are no income distribution effects. For the local official, the perfect user charge may have these features but of overriding importance to him or her is whether the public will resist paying for the service.[1]

The political costs involved in raising prices and the resistance of many agencies to change often prevent the modification of established prices that is necessary to cope with changing conditions. Those seeking to gain or retain political office can often identify the winners and losers from price changes, and they fear the advocacy of those people who would be damaged. Politicians may believe that changes toward greater employment of user pricing may make large numbers of service users, including politically powerful people, feel that they are among the losers.[2] Further, campaign promises to deliver more and better public services lose much of their appeal if user prices are imposed. If services are offered virtually at market prices, the public is not likely to think the politician is delivering any special benefits.

The reasoned approach discussed in these two chapters will not always be convincing to decision makers. In our view, the political and rational approaches to pricing are not mutually exclusive. Incompatibility between political position and pricing can often be reconciled if there is an understanding of the income distribution, equity, and efficiency implications of the pricing decision as well as its revenue effects. This understanding must be fostered not only among elected officials, but also among the various publics to whom the elected officials are responsive and responsible. Failure to communicate *all* the reasons for, and implications of, a pricing decision is one of the greatest causes of conflicts in developing and implementing new prices.

The introduction of better information is not likely to lead to a diminishment of the elected official's role—indeed, it should strengthen it. If a rational approach is not presented to elected officials, they will be encouraged to continue irrational pricing and it will imply recognition of their policy to determine those who pay and those who benefit according to whatever personal or arbitrary criteria they care to adopt.

NATURE OF PRICE

In Chapter I we saw that voluntary exchange is the central process that underlies marketing. An agency offers facilities and/or services. In exchange citizens support the agency through providing tax dollars, and users of the service pay both monetary and nonmonetary prices to use it.

Price is normally viewed as the amount of money that is paid to acquire a unit of service. Actually it should be defined more broadly, for a direct user price is only one way in which people pay for government and social services. The full range of resources that users may pay in exchange for a service is shown in Figure 13.1. In some situations a direct trade-off may lie between monetary and nonmonetary investments. For example, a library user has a choice of performing a time-consuming manual search at no direct charge or a faster computer-based search for a fee. The user's decision will depend on urgency of need and the value of his or her time.[3]

Direct monetary prices come in a variety of guises: *tuition* is the user price charged for the purchase of educational courses; *admission prices* are charged by recreational facilities; *recommended donations* are suggested for admission to art galleries; a *fee* is paid for a building inspection; *tolls* are levied on bridges, tunnels, and highways; a *rate* is charged by water and electricity enterprises operated by local government; and a *fine* is imposed on late books by public libraries.

In addition to paying a direct price, a service user's monetary investment may include travel costs. Travel costs are the actual costs of transportation necessary to consume the service. The magnitude of these costs is a function of the distance between a user's home and the site at which the service is offered, as well as the cost of the relevant means of transportation.

The importance of costs other than a direct user price is illustrated by the large number of eligible citizens who do not take advantage of valuable social services that are offered to them free. Examples include public assistance, food stamps, Head Start, publicly assisted housing, and publicly supported health care. Although available figures are somewhat inconsistent, nonparticipation rates in such programs appear to hover around 50 percent.[4] Nonmonetary costs consist of the opportunity costs of time, embarrassment costs, and effort costs (Figure 13.1).

Opportunity Cost of Time

Opportunity cost was defined in Chapter 12 in the discussion of reducing and terminating services. In that context it refers to the opportunities for alternative services that are foregone by an agency when it allocates resources to a service. Here it refers to the resources that clients forego because their time (and their dollars, when a direct price is paid) is invested in using a service. Using a service may mean time lost from work and wages foregone or the need to hire a babysitter, as well as the opportunity to use an alternate service.

In addition to the time taken to use a service (consumption time), citizens may incur two other types of time costs: travel time and waiting time (Figure 13.1). The amount of travel time that makes a barrier to service use obviously varies according to the individual and the service, but apparently even small

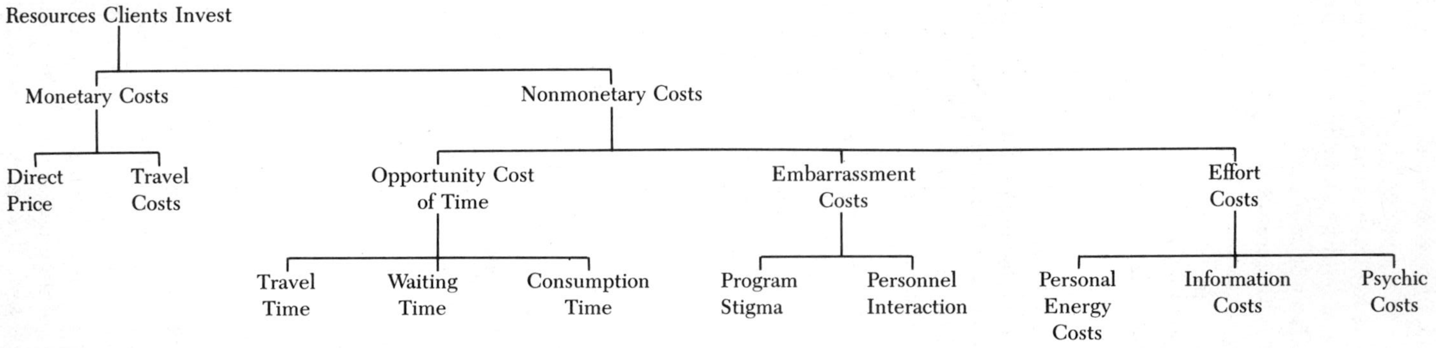

Figure 13.1 The Different Types of Price That Clients May Pay to Use a Service.

travel times will inhibit users. Substantial effects have been reported for travel times of 30 minutes and less.[5] Studies of health care programs and public assistance have found that the elderly, disabled, and poor are more strongly dissuaded from participation by travel distance than others.[6] Thus changes in location may mean a change in the time price clients are asked to pay.

The cost of waiting time—for example, in medical emergency rooms or in completing the process of applying for food stamps—may be substantial. Application processes can be greatly prolonged by their complexity. If several different agencies must be consulted, if documents must be presented, and if other agencies must approve parts of the application, then waiting time and its costs are increased. Waiting time costs are not imposed on clients equally. Long lines processed on a first-come, first-served basis benefit people who can afford to wait, people whose time is not particularly valuable to them, or people who do not have other obligations.[7]

Embarrassment Costs

Embarrassment costs are imposed when there is a stigma associated with being an eligible client, such as for programs in public welfare, housing, and health care. Any initial embarrassment may be compounded by the application process itself and by the attitude of agency personnel who administer the program.

Proving eligibility for a program is often unpleasant. A citizen may be required to answer questions about his or her income, family, and living conditions that, in any other context, would be considered socially inappropriate.[8] All of these intrusive questions are asked by a stranger (often an unsympathetic one) in a very public setting. It has been suggested that the application process contains many of the elements of a public degradation ritual:

> Most programs require that applicants come to an office to make their application. Once there, their status in the eyes of the organization is suggested by the conditions under which they are forced to wait. Overcrowding is common and the physical condition of waiting areas is generally poor. Treatment is, at best, impersonal and disinterested; at worst rude and humiliating. The wait is often hours long and the length is without explanation other than that everyone is busy. The message of being made to wait is clear: your time is not valued, your convenience is not important. As perceived by the applicants, this message becomes translated into: poor and not important.[9]

In this type of situation many eligible potential clients do not complete the application process because they prefer not to suffer these pressures and indignities. Since agency personnel control access to resources, they may be tempted to be indifferent or condescending toward their clients. By varying stance, attitude, and tone of voice, agency personnel can vitally affect the client's emotional costs of obtaining service.

Effort Costs

The personal energy effort needed to withstand the wear and tear of traveling may be substantial. In addition, there may be emotional upset resulting from an awareness of the other uses to which the travel and waiting time could have been put. Any confusion or uncertainty about the service or processes associated with it may exacerbate the emotional anxiety.

RECENT TRENDS

Table 13.1 shows that the ratio of user charges to general revenues at the federal and state levels has not substantially changed in recent years. However, at the local level the ratio has consistently grown. Charges provided 16.5 percent of general revenues collected by local governments in 1966–1967 and 21.4 percent in 1981–1982.

Many public service decision makers previously opposed to user pricing have been persuaded to charge realistic prices. This change in attitude has occurred because user pricing has emerged in recent years as an increasingly critical source of revenue. The pressure has grown, particularly on local agencies, to expand their expenditures on services while reducing their reliance on the property tax as the main source of locally raised revenues.

Restrictions on new programs as a result of financial constraints are often removed if the new offerings are shown to be self-financed through user price income. Furthermore, capital expenditures may be more palatable to taxpayers and their elected representatives if facilities can generate sufficient revenues to pay their operating expenses.

The change in attitude was summarized by the sign prominently displayed at the front desk of one city's leisure services department: "We do not render service to collect money—however, it is now necessary for us to collect money to render service." There has been a transition during which the question, "Should a charge be levied for a particular service?" has changed to "How much should users of the service be charged?"

User pricing brings the individual citizen into a much closer and more personal relationship with government than does taxation. This situation should generally be considered desirable in a democracy. As Milton Kafoglis has noted, "Generalized discussions concerning whose ox is being gored tend to become emotional and ideological; user pricing provides a firm and specific basis for rational debate."[10]

Enterprise Funds

In some cases a reluctance to increase user prices results from a fear that any increase in revenues could result in reduction of the agency's support from

TABLE 13.1. Ratio of Federal, State, and Local User Charges[a] to General Revenue from Own Sources[b]

	Federal			State			Local		
Year	General Revenue from own Sources	User Charges	Ratio	General Revenue from own Sources	User Charges	Ratio	General Revenue from own Sources	User Charges	Ratio
1966-67	130,896	10,602	8.1%	37,782	4,197	11.1%	38,340	6,318	16.5%
1967-68	133,240	10,397	7.8	43,197	4,891	11.3	40,886	6,894	16.9
1968-69	162,845	11,479	7.0	49,537	5,460	11.0	45,861	7,845	17.1
1969-70	163,582	11,401	7.0	47,507	6,102	10.6	51,392	8,770	17.1
1970-71	156,887	12,444	7.9	61,290	7,066	11.5	57,491	9,819	17.1
1971-72	172,122	12,481	7.2	70,651	7,820	11.1	64,449	10,904	16.9
1972-73	187,613	14,455	7.7	80,432	8,609	10.7	70,489	12,285	17.4
1973-74	217,932	18,278	8.4	89,157	9,597	10.8	76,742	13,571	17.7
1974-75	222,067	19,680	8.9	96,784	10,437	10.7	84,357	15,152	18.0
1975-76	237,713	22,532	9.4	107,401	11,652	10.8	93,186	17,668	19.0
1976-77	283,641	25,083	8.8	121,191	12,768	10.5	102,031	18,977	18.6
1977-78	319,215	27,135	8.5	135,638	13,554	10.0	110,730	21,146	19.1
1978-79	372,428	30,957	8.3	150,906	14,859	9.8	117,209	24,610	21.0
1979-80	417,336	35,759	8.6	169,266	16,545	9.8	130,027	27,828	21.4
1980-81	487,705	40,296	8.3	187,373	18,775	10.0	145,736	31,463	21.6
1981-82	496,021	46,283	9.3	205,996	21,043	10.2	163,240	34,998	21.4

[a] *User Charges* (termed by the census "current charges"—comprise amounts received from the public for performance of specific services benefiting the person charged and from sales of commodities and services except those by liquor store systems and local utilities. Includes fees, toll charges, tuition, and other reimbursements for current services, rents, sales incidental to the performance of particular governmental functions, and gross income of commercial-type activities (parking lots, school lunch programs and the like). These amounts are reported on a gross basis without offset for costs of operations or purchases. It excludes charges related to regulatory activities and privileges granted by the government in connection with such regulations. Thus license charges and fees in connection with filing for licenses are excluded.

[b] *General Revenues*—All revenue of a government except utility revenue, liquor stores revenue, and insurance trust revenue.

Source: U.S. Bureau of Census, *Governmental Finances* annual issues for the given years.

Numbers are millions of dollars.

taxes by an equivalent amount. Replacing tax-generated funding with user pricing may be an appropriate strategy if it benefits the taxpayer. However, it serves as a major disincentive to the agency which finds that, instead of additional revenues to improve the delivery of its services, its only reward is the equivalent loss of financial support from taxes, which may be difficult to regain in the future. In addition, the agency may lose political support from user groups angered by the new pricing policy.

Some cities have recognized the effect of this disincentive and have tried to remove it by setting up *enterprise funds*. Essentially, an enterprise fund is a governmental accounting tool developed for recording transactions in much the same way as a private enterprise does. It allows tracking of services through a separate fund that records all transactions. All revenues and expenses, as well as assets and current liabilities, are accounted for. Any revenues earned in excess of expenses are carried over or used for capital improvements.

Revenues collected do *not* get deposited in the General Fund to be used for other public services. Instead they are used to expand or improve the service to the user. Use of enterprise funds also creates an incentive for agency personnel to be more cost efficient.

OBJECTIVES OF PRICING

The opportunities and problems that a government or social service agency faces in establishing a price are contingent on its pricing objectives. That is, what results does the agency expect to occur as a result of the prices it charges? All too often service providers have failed to realize that pricing is not only a means of accruing revenue, but also leads to a number of other outcomes. User pricing is not a simple concept. In the wide spectrum of services and related user prices, some user charges will be equitable, lead to efficient allocation of resources, and produce revenue, and some will not.

It is essential to decide on objectives before determining the price itself. These objectives must be explicitly prioritized to guide the pricing decision. Unfortunately, very few agencies consciously establish pricing objectives or clearly state their specific pricing policies. Even fewer have written statements of their pricing goals. There are four pricing objectives to consider: income redistribution, equity, efficiency, and revenue production.

Pricing may be used to facilitate *income redistribution*. One of the rationales for taxation is that it is a means of redistributing wealth from higher-income to lower-income groups. If a service is financed by tax revenues but used primarily by the wealthy, then revenues from lower-income groups are contributing to the support of higher-income groups and the redistribution goal is not being realized. If such a service is financed by revenues from user charges, then the redistribution intent of taxation is not abused.

Equity is concerned with the allocation of benefits and payments—that is, with ensuring that those who benefit from a service bear the cost of that service.

User pricing promotes *efficiency* in the use of services by serving as a demand priority indicator, alleviating congestion, increasing accountability, providing incentive for responsible behavior, and encouraging the private sector to deliver services.

Revenue production recognizes that most public service agencies do not have sufficient funds to deliver all of the services that their client groups desire. User pricing generates funds that may be used to supplement other revenue resources. We noted earlier in this chapter that the recent trend toward increased use of direct pricing was stimulated by the need to find sources of revenue other than taxation. Most elected officials tend to consider only the revenue-generating function of pricing and do not consider the other three objectives. *In the commercial sector revenue production is the primary objective of pricing, but in government and social service agencies the other three objectives are at least equally as important as revenue production*. User prices should not be seen as a quick way of balancing budgets in the coming year. If they are, then the revenue-raising objective will predominate and poorly designed pricing systems are likely to result.

One overall pricing objective may not be applicable to all the services that an agency offers. Multiple, and sometimes conflicting, objectives are often pursued. For example, if the major concern is with income redistribution, that is, to encourage lower-income citizens to use a service, then a relatively low, or even zero, price should be charged. However, this may stimulate a higher demand than the agency can accommodate. Hence a low price may be inefficient because it does not perform a rationing function.

There can never be an unqualified "right" price for a public service. The principles presented here provide the basis for rational thinking, but they can never offer more than a guide toward establishing a price. The final pricing decision will depend on which objectives are highest priority and should represent the best compromise among conflicting objectives. Pricing decisions are more art than science because politics, ideology, and judgment all have roles to play.

Income Redistribution

Income redistribution occurs in the provision of every government-supplied service—unless everyone pays for it and receives benefits exactly proportionate to his or her tax share. It is important to determine whether the redistribution is in congruence or in conflict with generally held social and ethical values.

Some services, such as medical care, police and fire protection, and education, are perceived to meet needs that are common to all citizens. Thus it is argued that children should have equal opportunity for an education, regardless of their parents' ability to pay school fees, and that the poor should not be denied hospitalization and other health care simply because they cannot afford to pay. These services are therefore subsidized by the taxation system so that higher-income groups help pay for basic services that lower-income groups may not otherwise be able to afford.

It is this heritage of concern for the poor that underlies the frequent anti-pricing argument that direct user prices impose hardships on poor people. However, providing subsidized services as opposed to charging direct user prices may not achieve the anticipated redistributional results. Indeed, *in some cases low-income groups are better off when user prices are charged.*

The primary reason for this paradox is that property and sales taxes, which are the main sources of tax revenues for most local governmental agencies, are regressive. That is, they tend to bear much more heavily on low-income groups than on higher-income groups. Property taxes generally represent a larger proportion of a poor person's total income than of a wealthier person's income. In some instances, the burden on low-income groups would be lighter if a charge were imposed for a service and taxes lowered.[11] In other words, user prices give low-income groups the option to not use the offered services. Hence they would avoid paying for those services that they did not want or use rather than being forced to pay for them through the tax system.

Indeed, some services may actually redistribute income from the poor to the wealthy. If low-income groups are nonusers, then subsidized services impose hardship on them because they are required to pay through the tax system for a service that they do not use. For example, one might reasonably suspect that people who visit libraries, museums, zoos, or aquariums, or who use boat marinas, have above-average incomes. Many times low-income groups do not drive cars to work in the central business district, nor do they have large lawns to water; they tend not to be users of golf courses and they are not the predominant consumers of higher education.[12]

Even if some of the users of a service are the poor, the relatively wealthy receive the same dollar subsidy from the service as do the poor. When such services are subsidized from taxes they represent a distorted price system. In such a system the richer elements in society are subsidized by workers at the lower end of the income scale. Such a system results in a perverse income or benefit redistribution.[13] The essence of this argument is provided in the following descriptions of public parks and libraries:

> By and large, the supply of free public parks in the United States is less adequate in crowded city areas where people are poor, than it is in suburban and higher income residential areas where the people concerned are more nearly able to pay for their own outdoor recreation. On a state or national basis, the discrepancy is even worse: the really poor people do not own the private automobiles which are necessary to get to most state parks and to all national parks and national forests, nor can they in most areas afford the travel costs of such visits. The argument that free public parks help the poor is almost wholly myth.[14]
>
> User data for public libraries show that low income groups use them very little, and subsidized service appears to redistribute income from lower to higher income groups.[15]

Sometimes programs are subsidized because decision makers believe they will be of particular benefit to low-income groups. Wilbur Thompson has suggested that the provision of such services is often "a case of the majority playing God and 'coercing' the minority by the use of bribes to change their behavior."[16] This may be an overstatement, but it must be recognized that subsidized services may reflect impositions of the preferences and values of decision makers rather than those of the target population. These cases represent a product rather than a marketing orientation. Services are provided that decision makers think low-income client groups need or should have, rather than those that the client groups themselves indicate they want.

It is important to recognize that agency resources are finite, not infinite, and that there is an opportunity cost associated with all revenues that are foregone. In some cases, failure to price will effectively penalize poor people because there is no revenue available to offer other services that they may desire:

> If we have a goal of providing free recreation to all citizens, then we will be destined for failure and frustrating careers. The statement, "If we charge fees, only those who can afford it will have recreation and those who can't won't" offers a conclusion contrary to what we hope to accomplish by assessing fees. Charging those who can afford to pay for recreation allows subsidization of a greater number of people who cannot. Striving to subsidize everyone hinders the opportunities for people who are poor.[17]

If low-income client groups of a service need subsidization, then the price should be waived or reduced for them rather than offering the service to all at a reduced price regardless of income. Such a strategy may be implemented by waiving or reducing prices on an individual basis or at particular times of the day or week; having local citizens, businesses, or service clubs provide scholarships or subsidize programs; adjusting prices according to the income of the neighborhood; allowing extended payment schedules; or providing subsidies to all those with an appropriate identification card. Alternatively, a uniform price may be charged to all users and a rebate given to those with low incomes. Rent supplement programs are a good example of this approach. Arrangements for administering price concessions should confer anonymity on the client. If a stigma is placed on them, then the embarrassment costs incurred may be a greater disincentive to use the service than is the direct user price.

Equity

Equity means that a price should be fair. Unfortunately decision makers seldom consider the relationship between who pays for and who benefits from public services. Tradition and emotion have often been more powerful influences on pricing decisions than rational economic thinking. Too often, "the squeaky wheel gets the grease." That is, those who are most vociferous and persistent succeed in persuading decision makers to subsidize the services from which they receive a disproportionate amount of benefits. However, financial constraints are forcing reexamination of traditional irrational approaches, greater criticism of emotional rhetoric, and more emphasis on justification of taxation subsidies and the level of user prices adopted.

Public, Merit, and Private Services What services should government provide and subsidize? If the answer is "public" services, then what are they? This section defines features of services that determine their classification as public or private. Economists classify services into three categories: private, merit, and public services. Much of the debate about whether or not user prices should be levied, and if so at what level, revolves around the classification of the service. The differences among these categories are summarized in Figure 13.2. The classification provides the underlying equity basis on which decisions about user pricing should be made.

This system assumes an objective of pricing each service at a level that is

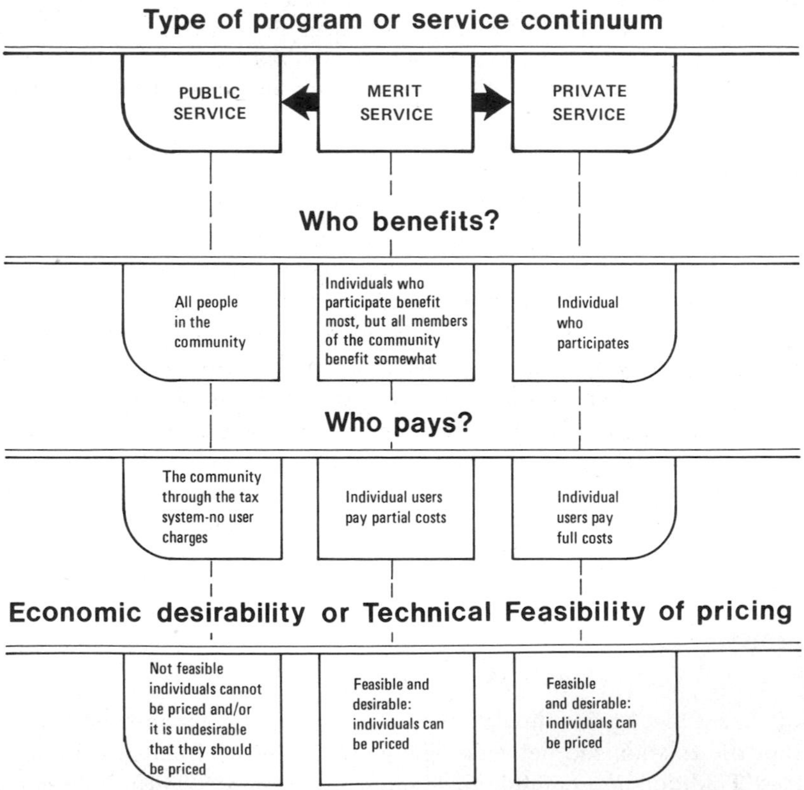

Figure 13.2. Differences Between Services with Public, Merit, and Private Characteristics.

fair and equitable to both users and nonusers. It helps the manager to determine which services lend themselves to monetary pricing, on what basis, at what level, and with what effects.

If a program exhibits the characteristics of a *private* service, its benefits are received exclusively by participating individuals rather than by the rest of the community. It is usually possible to exclude persons who are not willing to pay for the service. The essential differences between public and private services are listed in Table 13.2, but *exclusion* is the key differentiating factor. A fence around a drive-in theater or park may be all that is required to convert a public service into a private one.

Government and social service agencies provide a substantial number of essentially private services that, because of historical accident, failure of the private sector to offer a service, the need for quality controls, or where monopolies are necessary to achieve sufficient economics of scale (for example, the Postal Service and water and electricity supplies) are provided by government. Water and sewerage, public transport, parking spaces, refuse collection, electricity, public marinas, and golf courses are examples of services and facilities that usually exhibit private service characteristics.

Activities that require public regulation or supervision to prevent individual users from adversely affecting the general population are usually considered to be private services. For example, the revenue from dog license fees is generally used to pay for animal regulation activity, for which there would be no need if no one kept animals. In such instances the rationale for financing the service through direct charges to the user is apparent. When someone receives a direct benefit from government it seems only fair and logical that he or she should

TABLE 13.2. The Essential Differences Between Public and Private Types of Services

Private Services	Public Services
Easy to exclude someone who doesn't pay	Difficult to exclude someone who doesn't pay
Individual generally has a choice of consuming or not	Individual generally has no choice as to consuming or not
Individual generally has a choice as to kind and quality of services	Individual generally has little or no choice as to kind and quality of services
Payment for services is closely related to demand and consumption	Payment for services is not closely related to demand or consumption
Allocation decisions are made primarily by market mechanism	Allocation decisions are made primarily by political process

Adapted from Ostrom, V., and Ostrom, E., "Public Goods and Public Choices." In E.S. Savas (ed.), *Alternatives for Delivering Public Services*. Boulder, CO, Diebold Institute for Public Policy Studies, Inc., Westwood Press, 1977, p. 16.

pay for it. If the benefits from such a service do not apply to other citizens in the community, then it is reasonable to expect the users to pay all of the costs:

> The main beneficiaries of municipally supplied electricity are those who use the electricity, and these users enjoy the benefits in relation to their consumption. Nonusers are relatively unconcerned; hence, commonly accepted ideas of simple justice dictate that the costs of municipally supplied power should be directly billed to users in relation to the amount they consume.[18]

At the other end of the continuum (see Figure 13.2), a *public* service, in its pure form, is equally available to all citizens in a community. Often this is because there are no feasible ways of excluding any individuals from enjoying the benefits of the service. Because individuals cannot be excluded, it is not possible to implement a user pricing system unless such a system relies on voluntary payment. Unfortunately, when payment is voluntary, some individuals will take a free ride without paying. To prevent this abuse public services are financed by compulsory payment through the taxation system. Air pollution abatement, police protection, flood control, mosquito extermination, and urban parks are frequently recognized as services that exhibit public service characteristics.

There are some services from which it is possible to exclude people and levy a user price, but which, nevertheless, are offered as public services. Obviously these services are perceived by the community as contributing to the physical health, mental health, cultural knowledge, or welfare of all citizens in the community. Indeed much of the growth of government has resulted from decisions to provide private services at public expense. The rationale has been, implicitly more often than explicitly, that everyone benefits when no one is starving, when anyone can get medical attention, and when everyone receives at least a minimal amount of education. Such contributions may be viewed as an investment in human capital from which everyone in society profits. This benefit may be particularly applicable to those citizens with lower incomes who do not have the means for satisfying even their most essential needs. Hence it is sometimes argued that imposing user charges is undesirable even when it is technically possible to do so, if by such action certain people will be excluded. For example:

> Low income housing may confer indirect benefits on high-income people in surrounding areas. Subsidized housing projects may replace unsightly slums, arrest urban blight which threatens to encroach on better neighborhoods, and reduce fire and police protection costs. To this extent taxes on high income people to subsidize low cost housing may in large part be a payment for the indirect benefits they receive.[19]
>
> While the American humanitarian tradition plays some part in demanding that the medical establishment provide public health care, a deeper and more compelling social force dictates the need for some "charity" health

> care. Rampant epidemics among the poor create both health and social hazards. Disease in modern urban society crosses class lines and presents serious health problems for all. The daily unavoidable contacts in mass transportation, public education, retail and industrial plants imply that the entire society has a strong self-interest in reducing contagious illness.
>
> Further, social discontent among the poor could be easily escalated to social disruption if there were not some resources for treatment of self and loved ones. "Charity" health care, while not immediately profitable to the individual fee-for-service practitioner, becomes a social necessity.

Viewing public and private types of services as opposite poles of a continuum is helpful in understanding the essential differences between them, but most services lie somewhere between the two poles. Such services are called *merit* services. Merit services have been defined in several ways, but fundamentally they are private services that have been endowed with the public interest. In the case of merit services, the individual receives more of a private service than he or she would have purchased on his or her own.

The initial attitude toward merit goods was to see them as imposed on the population by a group of moralists, or the intellectual elite, or a pressure group with power, but with a recognition that the imposition might be a legitimate activity in a democratic society. Now a merit service is more usually considered a private service that has some public service characteristics. That is, part of the benefit is received by the individual consumer and part is received by the public in general. Although it is possibly to levy user prices for merit services, it is not reasonable to expect users to cover all costs because the spill-over benefits are received by the whole community. Users should be subsidized only to the extent that benefits to the whole community are perceived to occur.

> Higher education is a good example of a merit service. A state university's doors could be closed to those who do not pay the full cost, but society chooses to open those doors and to subsidize the service to ensure that few will turn away because of its cost. Once it is established that a college education is important, not just to the individual and his or her family, but to society as well, then it becomes legitimate to use taxation to augment direct user charges to pay for the individual's education. Public subsidy of higher education is justified by the benefits which are perceived to accrue from it to all members of society.
>
> Most urban mass transit systems charge relatively low fees which do *not* cover the full costs of transit operations. Urban transit is thus recognized as a merit service. The requirement that the users pay some price recognizes that they receive extra increments of benefit that do not accrue to nonusers. However, nonusers subsidize the service since they derive the benefit of reduced traffic congestion. If fares were raised and were successful in recovering full-costs, many riders would opt to use automobiles and traffic congestion would be increased, causing a loss of benefits to nonusers.

Most government and social services for which a user price is charged are not totally self-supporting. Most are partially supported by tax funds, which suggests that such services are perceived as merit rather than private services. Tax subsidy can only be justified if collective benefits accrue to the majority of the community that subsidizes the program.

Locating a Service on the Public-Private Continuum. An important point in understanding this public-merit-private classification is that the decisions as to where a service should be located along the continuum shown in Figure 13.2 are defined through political processes. Hence this position may ebb and flow with changes in the values of a community and it is likely that some services will be defined differently in different communities depending on a community's prevailing concept of equity. For example, in a market equity milieu a service may be perceived as being private, whereas in a compensatory equity milieu the same service may be regarded as a merit or public service. A tennis facility in a high-income neighborhood may be perceived as a private service from which only participants benefit. Hence all costs incurred should be covered by user prices. The identical tennis facility located in a low-income neighborhood may be perceived as a pure public facility, or at least as a merit facility. In this case the whole community is seen to benefit from the provision of wholesome activity for its citizens; from improvement of the living environment, which increases the value of all property; or from the psychological satisfaction of knowing that the less wealthy are provided with recreational opportunities that they could not otherwise afford.

Figure 13.3 shows that user groups in a community typically seek to shift perceptions of their activity of interest as far as possible toward the public end of the continuum, in order to persuade the agency and the community to pay more of the costs through taxation revenues and to reduce user prices. These user groups are likely to be vociferous and politically active in their efforts to

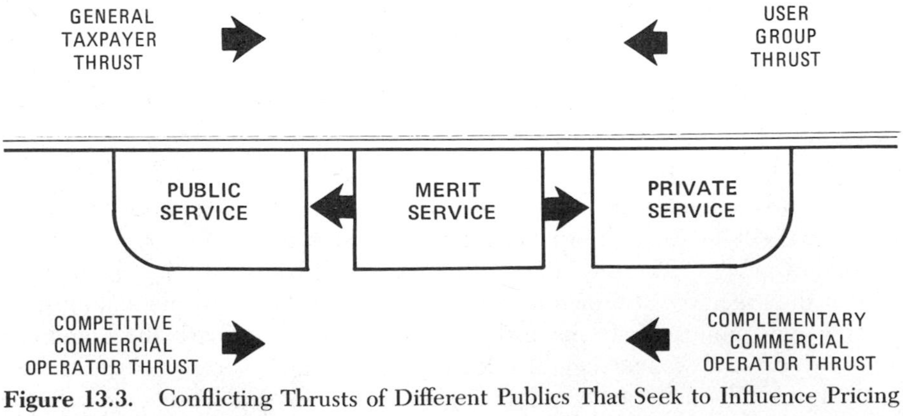

Figure 13.3. Conflicting Thrusts of Different Publics That Seek to Influence Pricing Decisions.

preserve their benefits. In the past, reductions in taxes brought about by specific user price revenues were so small that the average benefiting citizen was disinterested. Hence user groups frequently succeeded in retaining the status quo. Now, however, the public appears to recognize that adoption of user prices can contribute significantly to a reduction of general tax burdens. More efforts are being directed to shifting services toward the private end of the spectrum in order to make participants pay for the benefits they derive. The actual point on the continuum at which a particular service is located will depend on the relative size and political strength of various interested groups.

Some people belong to both groups. That is, they are in favor of tax reductions, but are not in favor of the subsequent lower-quality offering, price increases, or termination of services that result from such reductions!

The role in this conflict of the commercial business that delivers similar services varies according to the situation. When entrepreneurs are in competition with a public agency, they will support the taxpayer who is seeking user fees. Higher prices provide more opportunities for the entrepreneur to compete. However, when demand for the entrepreneurial service is complementary rather than competitive, commercial interests will support the user interest groups. Lower prices may mean a larger number of participants who require particular commercial services. For example, a concessionaire in a public park would probably oppose increases in the park's admission price because fewer visitors may then use the concession.

Efficiency

The efficiency objective of price is concerned with getting the most out of a given set of resources, so that society derives the maximum possible benefit from the services offered and from the scarce resources used to finance those services. An appropriate price should encourage more efficient delivery and use of government and social services. Indeed, its contribution to allocative efficiency is probably the strongest single reason for advocating expansion of user pricing in the public sector.

Efficient allocation of scarce resources involves rationing them in some way. Typically rationing involves increasing the costs of services to clients. Although discussion here is limited to direct monetary price, the other forms of price discussed at the start of this chapter (see Figure 13.1) may offer alternative ways of rationing services. Organizations that cannot charge money for their services must develop nonmonetary costs to impose on their clients as a means of rationing their outputs "because requests for free services always rise to meet the capacity of the producing agency."[20] Indeed, it is likely that they will rise to exceed the capacity of the agency if no rationing procedure is imposed.

In this section we discuss five different dimensions of using price to improve efficiency. First, it may serve as a demand priority indicator. Without price, there is no readily available means of assessing which government services should be given priority. Second, using differential pricing alleviates congestion. Third, pricing requires agencies to be more accountable for the quality of services delivered. Fourth, it may lead to a more responsible use of services and facilities by client groups. Fifth, if reasonable prices are charged the private sector may be encouraged to deliver competitive services. The agency is in turn stimulated by the competition to optimize its performance. It may choose to withdraw partially from a particular program if it cannot effectively compete with the private sector and reallocate its resources to another service or return them to the taxpayers.

Demand Priority Indicator. Because there is always competition for government services by various beneficiary groups, some demand priority indicator for efficiently allocating the limited available resources between services is essential. Demand is defined as desire for a service *and* an ability and willingness to pay for it. User pricing serves as a demand priority indicator by excluding those potential users of a service who are not both willing and able to pay the designated price. In this way, the limited resources at the disposal of an agency are allocated to those individuals who are prepared to make the most sacrifices for them.

If services are financed exclusively from taxes, then the act of paying for a service occurs at a time and place far removed from the act of consuming the service. Individual costs are widely separated from individual benefits, with some far-reaching implications:

> The principle of fiscal equivalence—that those receiving the benefits from a service pay the costs for that service—must apply in the public economy just as it applies in a market economy. Costs must be associated with benefits if people are to have any sense of economic reality. Otherwise beneficiaries may assume that public goods are free goods, that money in the public treasury is "the government's money," and that no opportunities are foregone in spending that money. When this happens the foundations of a democratic society are threatened.[21]

If a service is offered without the user having to pay a direct price at the time of use, there is likely to be a perceived shortage of the service. Without price, people may demand an unreasonably high level of the service because those who benefit from it correctly think that increased supply occurs at no cost to themselves. While the marketing concept directs agencies to satisfy client wants, some constraints will prevent demand from being carried to illogical extremes.

Theodore Levitt describes an unbridled, runaway consumer orientation as marketing mania.[22] An organization that tries to fully meet all clients' wants without adequate concern for cost and price considerations suffers from this illness. The two following hypothetical analogies show the results of marketing mania.

> Suppose that a city decides to finance all steak consumption through general taxes rather than to allow butcher shops or supermarkets to operate in the private market. Individuals would consider steaks to be "free"; they would try to secure as many as possible. The result would be the immediate appearance of a serious "shortage." If the government tries to respond to this "shortage" by supplying more steaks, far too many resources will be drawn into this line of investment relative to its alternatives.[23]
>
> If individuals were to be allowed to mail letters and parcels free of charge, this would obviously place formidable demands on the postal facilities. If the postal service tried to build additional facilities to accommodate the "free" demand, far too many resources would be devoted to the postal system.[24]

Providing services "free" out of general tax revenues is likely to result in one or both of two conditions. Either there will be a serious shortage of the service combined with congestion, or too many resources will be allocated in order to alleviate the perceived shortage.[25] Price helps to ration and allocate scarce resources efficiently. It assists public decision makers in determining target levels of both quality and quantity of a service and in deciding when increased investment is justified.

User pricing contributes to curbing the demand for expansion of public services by making their real costs apparent to those who benefit from them. This is achieved by the price correctly reflecting both opportunity costs and demand for a service (i.e., users' desire *and* their willingness and ability to pay for it). If they are not willing to pay for expansion of a service, then it should not be expanded; if they are, it should be—and the financing will be available out of the revenues from the prices charged.

The subsidy or provision of free government services leads to increases in the supply of such services. The absence of appropriate user prices ultimately results in increased political pressure from benefiting groups for expansion of the services. The natural desire to obtain more free or subsidized services traditionally has united with the equally natural desire of politicians to be popular (and re-elected), and of bureaucrats to be part of a growing organization. These forces form a powerful upward pressure on the level of government spending. It has been argued that the most important role of pricing for public services is to restrict demand rather than simply to expand supply.[26]

In addition to providing a check against excessive claims of beneficiaries, pricing provides valuable information to decision makers about the demand for a public service. When consumers pay directly for public services their individual purchase decisions can signal shifts in demand more quickly and accurately than can the inherently cumbersome political mechanism. This should lead to a more rapid adjustment in service delivery priorities than would otherwise occur. Public services can easily be overfinanced or underfinanced if they are not directly priced because decision makers may have higher or lower preferences for particular services than do the citizens they serve. Thus they may allocate more tax monies to these services than their constituents desire, or vice versa. Price gives users an effective way to voice their needs.

By serving as a clear indicator of demand, pricing helps an agency better satisfy its clientele. User prices allow the agency to rank the demand for its services more accurately, thus encouraging it to be more responsive to its clients' needs.

Alleviation of Congestion. User pricing may be used to reduce congestion at peak times. Excessive demand occurs for many reasons, but among the most common is that the service or facility is inexpensive (perhaps free). In the face of continued inflation it becomes progressively cheaper. While the cost of other purchased goods goes up, zero price remains zero price, unaffected by inflation. Further, normal population growth also increases use and contributes to overcrowding.

Many facilities are used intensively during a relatively brief period of time, and moderately or even lightly at other times. Consider the pattern of higher education facilities:

> Traditionally, colleges and universities have reacted to increases in student enrollments by building additional classrooms, laboratories, and support facilities, and by incurring the associated furniture, equipment, and maintenance costs which accompany such construction. Little attention appears to have been given to the possibility of accommodating increasing enrollments without additional construction through using differential tuition rates.
>
> Empirical studies have consistently verified the frequent casual observation that educational plant is not fully utilized. One of the sources of underutilization is empty classrooms. Typically, classrooms are at a premium during the mid-morning hours. Beyond this popular period the rate of classroom utilization decreases and after 2 or 3 P.M. it falls substantially. In this situation, a peak load lasting for a period of three or four hours determines the size of a plant that is underutilized during the longer off-peak period.
>
> It has been calculated that the rate of classroom utilization on the basis of a schedule running from 8 A.M. to 6:30 P.M. is likely to amount to almost 40 percent. This suggests that if the morning peak time use could be diverted to the afternoon, additional facilities giving increased capacity would not be needed. To encourage this shift a student demanding the service during the popular hours would pay a relatively high tuition rate, but a student willing to use the service during the less popular hours would pay a lower rate.[27]

A price structure could serve to ration use at peak times. For instance, prices could be charged on days or in seasons of heaviest use, but not at other times, as one inducement to secure a more nearly even pattern of use; or they could be charged at heavily used facilities but not at lightly used ones as a means of distributing use more evenly to available facilities. The function of pricing in this way is to bring about better use of the resources by influencing users to choose certain times, locations, and/or facilities. Such charges could not be effective unless they were high enough to represent a meaningful cost to the user who paid them and a real saving to the one who avoided them.

Using price to persuade people to use services at off-peak times is likely to be preferable to engaging in a costly expansion needed to meet peak demand. For example, projections of water supply needs frequently ignore the influence of price on demand. Invariably such projections conclude, "Our forecasts indicate that we will face a critical water shortage in ten years time, as our water needs will then exceed our supplies. We therefore must expand our current water system." Differential pricing could be used to ration water supply and serve as an alternative to expansion. In this way, nonpeak users would not be required to support and pay for expansion of facilities for peak users.

At the beginning of this chapter we noted that time, rather than money, may be the resource that participants give up (in other words, the price they pay) in exchange for the benefits derived from a program. Thus many public services offered at no charge, or only nominally priced, are nevertheless rationed. The length of waiting lines rather than monetary price may provide a manager with indications of the demand pressure on existing services. The cost to the user is the time spent waiting to use the service. For example, the motorist who is not willing to spend time circling the block looking for a place to park, and who drives away, forfeits the scarce space to the one who undertakes the challenge. Waiting time may thus serve as an alternative to or substitute for a monetary price in reducing congestion. Client groups could even be offered a choice between rationing devices.[28]

Accountability. User pricing induces efficiency by requiring agencies to be more accountable to citizens for the quality of services delivered. An aphorism in the private sector says, "A poor salesperson sells on price whereas a good salesperson sells on the quality of the product." Too often clients use agency services either because they have no alternative or because they are inexpensive, rather than because they are satisfied with the services' quality.

Price is perhaps the most potent tool available for fostering increased accountability among elected officials and agency personnel for the quality of service offerings. Funding from tax sources often makes agencies less sensitive to their clients' needs than when they are directly dependent on client revenues for their continued survival.

If users pay a direct monetary price at the point of service they are more likely to assume responsibility for delivery standards and insist on a high standard. In contrast, when services are funded indirectly from taxation, users often regard them as free, assume that responsibility for their quality lies with "the city," and thus accept lower delivery standards. It is not easy for users to assess what the level of service quality should be if they are not aware of a service's costs. A price that closely reflects the cost of delivering a service enables consumers to better judge if the quality of the service is appropriate.

User pricing may also encourage elected officials to maintain or increase service quality. When a direct price is paid, the expectations of users are likely to be higher and there is more pressure on elected officials to allocate the resources necessary to ensure these expectations are met.

Direct pricing also makes accurate usage records more likely. These data are important in evaluating the relative success of a service and the per capita cost of delivering it. Without user pricing the integrity of usage records is open to challenge. Agency personnel may have incentives to inflate them artificially in order to justify the resources allocated for the service.

Incentive for Responsible Behavior. Charging a direct price may lead to a more responsible use of public services and facilities by client groups. Such price incentives may discourage activities that make inefficient use of scarce resources and thus are considered undesirable to society. Consider the following examples:

River pollution may be reduced if a substantial price is charged for the right to dump wastes into national water systems. If there is a substantial charge for disposing of wastes in rivers, then alternative and less damaging ways will be found to dispose of them.

Public libraries charge fines for overdue books to encourage readers to return them.

Hospital emergency rooms charge a high price to discourage use for non-emergency conditions.

The Golden Gate Authority of San Francisco charged motorists tolls according to how many passengers were in the car, with the highest price charged to cars which carried only the driver. This led to the formation of more driving car pools.[29]

One explanation for abuses such as graffiti, littering, and vandalism is that participants pay nothing for the privilege of using the facilities. Provision of *anything* at zero price, the argument goes, tends to diminish both its psychological and its economic value.[30] Some sense of personal contribution may enhance a user's feelings of responsibility toward, and esteem of, the service or facility.

In some cases—for example, community education classes or subsidized theater, music, or art performances—the price for a service may be paid by a client group before the service is actually delivered. Besides helping the agency make an efficient decision concerning allocation of resources to the program (staffing, equipment, and facilities), this approach also provides increased incentive to commit to the program. The clientele will feel a pressure to use a service fully after they have voluntarily paid for it. If a price is not charged to encourage this commitment, then classes or performances may draw participants who do not make the effort to attend all the classes or performances. Others who would have made the effort may have been turned away if full capacity had been reached. A user price can help resolve these problems of commitment.

Encouraging Private Sector Delivery. User pricing is essential if the private sector is to be encouraged to deliver services. If user prices are heavily subsidized, then the agency is in effect excluding the private sector from offering a similar public service. In other words, "we cannot give away cake and expect people to rush into the bakery business at the same time."[31]

There are two reasons why agencies should encourage private sector delivery. First, in some circumstances private sector service delivery may offer competition to an agency's service. This may stimulate the agency to optimum performance both in responsiveness to user demands and minimization of costs. Traditionally public sector delivery has implied agency monopoly. Private enterprise may substantially improve the efficiency of the agency if agencies raise prices sufficiently so that private enterprise can realize a normal return on capital invested.

> The City of Minneapolis assiduously cultivated a competitive environment for refuse removal services. A corporation, Minneapolis Refuse Inc., comprised of several dozen private firms, was formed. This consortium of private firms serviced parts of Minneapolis, under contract to the city, while the remaining sections of the city were serviced by the Municipal Sanitation Division. The city was divided into districts that were assigned at random to the city agency and the corporation. There were no significant differences between the city's territory and the corporation's territory. Analysis of the results over a five year period indicated that since the corporation was formed the productivity of the city agency had substantially increased. It was stated that, "competition, the presence of a yardstick systematically used for comparison of alternative delivery systems, was primarily responsible for the large observed increase in productivity."[37]

In this case, the powerful tool of competition was exploited to the advantage of the citizens, with due regard to the welfare of the city's workers and its local business firms.

The second reason why agencies should encourage private sector delivery is that most agencies are unable to fully satisfy all the demands expected of them. If some of these can be met by the private sector, agency resources can be stretched further and redirected to meet other needs. Unfortunately, agencies sometimes allocate resources by initiating a new service directed at a target market that is already being served by the private sector and charging a lower price than the private sector can for that service. An editorial in the *Wall Street Journal* illustrates the inefficiency that results from this move:

> Gore Mountain Ski Center, a public facility operated by New York State, received an annual tax subsidy of $50,000 and was constructed with tax-free bonds. It applied for $246,000 in federal grants to aid in funding a $2.87 million capital extension involving the installation of snowmaking machinery

and other equipment. The balance of the capital was raised by issuing tax-free bonds. After implementing the improvements Gore Mountain charged $400 for a family season pass. Commercial resorts in the area charged an average of $1,125, since they had to pay commercial prices for investment capital and did not recieve any assistance from federal grants. They also desired to show a reasonable return on their investment. Thus, the publicly operated project gradually forced the commercial operation out of business. The editorial comments: "By a sort of Gresham's law of competition, we have noticed that state enterprises in the mixed economy tend to drive out private enterprise."[33]

Revenue Production

Although we have noted that revenue production is only one of four objectives in a pricing policy, there is no doubt that interest in raising revenue has been the main reason for the increased attention given to pricing by agency decision makers. User pricing can ease financial pressures in two ways. Not only can it serve to increase revenue but, more indirectly, it can reduce the level of costs. The costs of operating a particular service may be reduced as the number of users declines in response to higher user prices.

Even when the political climate is favorable and using price to raise revenue is consistent with the other three pricing objectives, three constraints can inhibit managers from levying a charge. First, in some instances a price is not imposed because it is administratively too difficult. For example, it is difficult to charge admission to a public park to which access is not easily controlled. This problem could be surmounted by building a fence around the park, but such modifications could cost more than the revenues collected.

Second, collection methods may cause substantial inconvenience to users. If tolls were collected for the use of all streets, roads, and highways, the inconvenience would be considerable. Hence it has generally been decided that the cost of this inconvenience outweighs the advantage of raising revenue.

A third constraint on instituting user pricing for a tax-supported service is the protest that clients must pay both taxes and direct charges for the service. A counterargument to this double-taxation complaint is that taxes would be even higher in the absence of the service charge.

When attention is focused on revenue production, the primary concern of managers is likely to be the reaction of users to increases in price. The key questions are, "If a proposed price increase or decrease is implemented, by how many will the number of users go down or up?" and "Will the total revenue produced increase or decrease?" This relationship between price and use is known as the *price elasticity of demand*.

Price Elasticity of Demand. Elasticity of demand is the relative sensitivity of user participation to changes in price. A synonym for price elasticity of demand would be user sensitivity to price change. The concepts of elastic and inelastic demand may be defined in the following way:

> If demand is *elastic*, a change in price causes an opposite change in total revenue; an increase in price will decrease total revenue, and a decrease in price will increase total revenue. An *inelastic* demand results in a parallel change in total revenue; an increase in price will increase total revenue, and a decrease in price will decrease total revenue.[34]

If the purpose of a price increase is to raise total revenue, then prices can only be raised in those services for which demand is relatively inelastic.

When a change in price is being considered, three main factors should be reviewed; together they are likely to determine the magnitude of any change in revenue. The first factor is the availability and relative price of substitute services. If a similar service of comparable quality is offered by another supplier, then a substantial change in the agency's price relative to the alternative supplier's price is likely to lead to a substantial change in the demand for the agency's service.

The second factor is the proportion of total costs that the direct use price of a service represents. If substantial nonmonetary costs or monetary travel costs (see Figure 13.1) are involved, then a small change in the direct user price is not likely to lead to a meaningful change in demand. The third factor is the affluence of the target market: The greater the level of affluence, the less likely a price adjustment will cause a change in use.

These principles are illustrated in the hypothetical example shown in Figure 13.4. The admission price at a national park, such as the Grand Canyon, is likely to be relatively inelastic. This means that if the entrance price to a national park is increased from $1 to $2, the annual number of visitors to the park is likely to decrease only slightly, say from 250,000 to 230,000. In terms of the three factors discussed, no direct substitutes exist for the Grand Canyon; the cost in time, effort, and money of getting there is high compared to the admission charge; and surveys show visitors to the Grand Canyon are affluent.

In contrast, demand at an urban recreation center may be very elastic. Thus if the entrance price is increased from $1 to $2 the number of users may decline substantially, say from 250,000 to 80,000. In this case there may be several substitute opportunities available at a lower price, the entrance price is more likely to represent a high proportion of the total costs, and the target population is assumed to be relatively poor.

It should be noted that price elasticity of demand depends on the magnitude of the proposed price change. For an urban recreation center, a raise of 10¢ instead of $1 may cause only a small reduction in annual attendance. Thus demand may be inelastic at the 10¢ level of price increase, whereas it is elastic at the $1 level.

At times decision makers will not raise prices even when they are confident of increasing revenue because they do not want to lose political or public

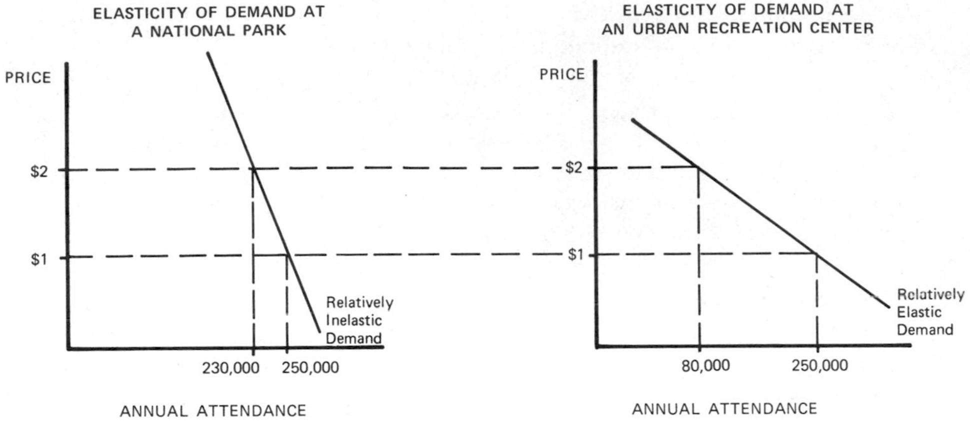

Figure 13.4. Elasticity of Demand.

support. If fewer people use an agency's services, then the agency's public support base is eroded. The manager has to evaluate whether increased revenues are worth the cost of reduced participant support. If a price increase is projected to lower the number of participants at the urban recreation center from 250,000 to 150,000, then total revenue would increase from $250,000 to $300,000. The agency then has to decide, "Is an increase in revenue of $50,000 worth the loss of support that is likely to occur if annual use decreases by 100,000?"

Organizations with fixed capacities may set their prices at a level that will produce a capacity audience. For example, a symphony orchestra experiencing low attendance might lower its price in order to fill more of the seats in the auditorium.[35] Concern in this instance may not be with maximizing revenue, but rather with creating the right atmosphere. A full auditorium creates a more stimulating atmosphere for the orchestra players and is more likely to inspire them to a better performance than if the auditorium has many empty seats.

When revenue production is a primary pricing objective, it is necessary to consider the impact of pricing decisions on legal liability. Experience in each state with court decisions regarding governmental immunity varies greatly. In some jurisdictions, governmental services are still protected from tort liability by the doctrine of governmental immunity, which protects agencies in the exercise of a "governmental function." No clear definition of a governmental function exists, and court decisions are made on a case-by-case basis. However, the more revenue a service generates, the more likely it will be considered a proprietary rather than a governmental function. At that point an agency loses its governmental immunity and can be sued for tort negligence.

SUMMARY

Price is normally viewed as the amount of money paid to acquire a unit of service. It should actually be defined more broadly to include the monetary costs associated with traveling to use a service and the nonmonetary issues of the opportunity cost of time, embarrassment costs, and effort costs.

Although the ratio of user charges to general revenues has not substantially changed at the federal and state levels in recent years, it has grown consistently at the local level. A growing scarcity of alternative sources of funds, particularly at the local level, has led to an increased interest in user pricing.

Pricing decisions have often been determined by political considerations rather than by rational analysis. Managers have contributed to the problem by not helping politicians understand the other objectives of price besides revenue production. Failure to communicate *all* the reasons for, and implications of, a pricing decision is one of the greatest causes of conflicts in developing and implementing new prices.

The opportunities and problems which an agency faces in establishing a price are contingent on its pricing objectives in terms of income redistribution, equity, and efficiency as well as revenue production. Different pricing objectives are likely to be appropriate for the various kinds of services that an agency offers. Usually the price adopted for any particular program will reflect a compromise of several conflicting pricing objectives.

The purpose of income redistribution is to redistribute wealth by requiring higher-income groups to subsidize with taxes the basic services used by lower-income groups. Some services, however, may actually redistribute income from the poor to the wealthy. If low-income groups are nonusers, then subsidized services impose hardship on them because they are required to pay through the tax system for a service they do not use. In these situations, the burden on low-income groups would be lighter if a direct price were charged for the service instead of a tax subsidy being used. They could then avoid paying for those services that they do not want or use.

Equity addresses the relationship between who benefits and who pays for services. Tax subsidy for a service can only be justified if some collective benefits accrue to the majority of the community that subsidizes the program. Hence it is important for decision makers to determine whether a particular service displays public, merit, or private characteristics. If a program exhibits the characteristics of a private service, its benefits are received exclusively by users rather than by the rest of the community. A public service, in its pure form, is equally available to all citizens in a community. Most services lie between these poles and are called merit services. These are private services that have been endowed with the public interest, so users receive more of the service than they would have purchased on their own. Decisions as to where a service should be located along the continuum are made through political processes; therefore, the point at which a particular service is located will depend on the relative political strength of various interested groups.

The efficiency objective of pricing is concerned with the use of a given set of resources so that society derives the maximum possible benefit from them. There are five different ways in which price may contribute to improved efficiency. First, it may serve as a demand priority indicator. Without price, there is no readily available means of assessing which services should be given priority. Second, it can be used to reduce inefficiencies caused by congestion and overcrowding at particular times or in particular areas. Third, pricing requires agencies to be more accountable for the quality of services delivered. Fourth, it may lead to a more responsible use of services and facilities by client groups. Fifth, if reasonable prices are charged the private sector may be encouraged to deliver competitive services. This contributes to efficiency if the agency is stimulated by competition to optimize its performance or if it is able to partially withdraw and reallocate its resources to another service or return them to the taxpayer.

The revenue production objective has received the most attention as user pricing has emerged as a critical source of revenue. Not only can user prices serve to increase revenue, but they can also reduce costs if the number of users declines in response to the price increases. Three constraints may inhibit agencies from levying a charge: an administrative difficulty in implementing the price, any substantial inconvenience caused to users, and the protest against double taxation.

The relationship between changes in price and level of use is known as the price elasticity of demand. Three primary factors determine the magnitude of any change in usage resulting from a price change. They are the availability and relative price of substitute services, the proportion that the direct use price of a service represents of the total costs users incur in using the service, and the affluence of the target market.

The main failure of existing user prices in government and social services is that they have been designed solely or primarily to raise revenue. They should not be viewed as a quick way of balancing budgets in the coming year. Seen in that light, the revenue objective will predominate and poorly designed pricing structures will result.

NOTES

1. Meltsner, A.J., *The Politics of City Revenue*. Berkeley, CA: University of California Press, 1971, p. 271.
2. Hirsch, W.Z., *The Economics of State and Local Government*. New York: McGraw-Hill, 1970, p. 45.
3. Drake, M.A., *User Fees: A Practical Perspective*. Littleton, CO: Libraries Unlimited, 1981, p. 9.
4. Prottas, J.M., "The Cost of Free Services: Organizational Impediments to Access to Public Services," *Public Administration Review*, September/October 1981, p. 526.
5. Ibid., p. 529; Perlman, R., *Consumers and Social Services*. New York: Wiley, 1975, pp. 55–56.
6. Prottas, "Free Services," p. 529.

7. Lipsky, M., *Street Level Bureaucracy*. New York: Russell Sage Foundation, 1980, p. 95.
8. Ibid., p. 528.
9. Ibid.
10. Kafoglis, M.Z., "The Potential of Local Service Charges." In P.B. Downing (ed.), *Local Service Pricing and Their Effect on Urban Spatial Structure*. Vancouver, Canada: University of British Columbia Press, 1977, p. 19.
11. Mushkin, S.J., "An Agenda for Research." In S.J. Mushkin (ed.), *Public Prices for Public Products*. Washington, DC: The Urban Institute, 1972, p. 441.
12. Netzer, D., *Economics and Urban Problems*. New York: Basic Books, 1970, p. 188.
13. Chappelle, D.E., "The 'Need' for Outdoor Recreation: An Economic Conumdrum," *Journal of Leisure Research*, vol. 5, Fall 1973, p. 50.
14. Clawson, M., and Knetsch, J.L., *Economics of Outdoor Recreation*. Washington, DC: Resources for the Future, 1966, p. 270.
15. Pfister, R.L., "The Allocation of Resources: An Economists View On Libraries." In M.A. Drake (ed.), *User Fees: A Practical Perspective*. Littleton, CO: Libraries Unlimited, 1981, p. 37.
16. Thompson, W., "The City as a Distorted Price System," *Psychology Today*, vol. 2 No. 3, August 1968, p. 30.
17. Ellerbrock, M., "Some Straight Talk on User Fees," *Parks and Recreation*, January 1982, p. 59.
18. Buchanan, J.M., *The Public Finances*. Homewood, IL: Irwin, 1970, p. 432.
19. Heller, W.W., "Reflections on Public Expenditure Theory." In E.S. Phelps (ed.), *Private Wants and Public Needs*. New York: Norton, 1965, p. 158.
20. Downs, A. *Inside Bureaucracy*. Boston: Little, Brown, 1976, p. 188.
21. Ostrom, V., and Ostrom, E., "Public Goods and Public Choices." In E.S. Savas (ed.), *Alternatives for Delivering Public Services*. Boulder, CO: Westview Press, 1977, p. 31.
22. Levitt, T., "Retrospective Commentary on Marketing Myopia," *Harvard Business Review*, September-October 1975, p. 180.
23. Buchanan, *Public Finances*, p. 453.
24. Ibid.
25. Ibid.
26. Bird, R.A., *A New Look at an Old Idea*. Toronto, Canada: Canadian Tax Foundation, 1976, p. 233.
27. Adapted from Avila, M., "Peak Load Pricing in Higher Education," *The Journal of Experimental Education*, vol. 40 No. 3, Spring 1972, pp. 6–11.
28. Mushkin, "Agenda," p. 443.
29. Kotler, P., *Marketing For NonProfit Organizations* (2nd ed.). Englewood Cliffs, NJ: Prentice-Hall, 1982, p. 309.
30. Becker, B.W., "The Pricing of Educational-Recreational Facilities: An Administrative Dilemma," *Journal of Leisure Research*, vol. 7 No. 2, 1975, p. 89.
31. Diamond, H.L., "The Private Role in the Provision of Large Scale Outdoor Recreation." in B.L. Driver (ed.) *Elements of Outdoor Recreation Planning*. Ann Arbor: University of Michigan, 1970, p. 172.
32. Savas, E.S., "An Empirical Study of Competition in Municipal Service Delivery," *Public Administration Review*, November/December 1977, pp. 717–724.
33. "Mike Brandt's Competitors," *Wall Street Journal*, September 12, 1975, p. 4.
34. Pride, W.M., and Ferrell, O.C., *Marketing: Basic Concepts and Decisions*. Boston: Houghton Mifflin, 1983, p. 422.
35. Kotler, *Non-Profit Organizations*, p. 271.

FOURTEEN

Establishing a Price

In Chapter 13 we discussed the objectives of pricing. In this chapter we consider how to establish an actual price. The logical approach to this task consists of four stages, which are illustrated in Figure 14.1. Stage 1 requires an agency to determine what proportion of the costs incurred in delivering a service should be recovered from direct pricing. In other words, each service must be positioned on the public-private continuum discussed in Chapter 13. However, deriving a price only from the costs of service delivery is a product-oriented approach that ignores market considerations and client groups.

Stage 2 recognizes that a service's price has to be perceived as reasonable by potential client groups or they will either refuse to pay (in the case of discretionary services) or vigorously protest through the political process (in the case of nondiscretionary services). Using surveys to find out the going rate charged for similar services by other agencies and/or the commercial sector may lead to the cost-based price being adjusted downwards to ensure that it is perceived as reasonable.

In stage 3 the appropriateness of varying price for some user groups or in specified contexts is considered. Finally, stage 4 recognizes that potential client groups often react emotionally, even to logical price changes. Consideration of psychological dimensions of price may lead to its further adjustment or to other marketing actions taken to support the proposed price decision.

STAGE 1: DETERMINING THE PROPORTION OF COSTS THAT THE PRICE SHOULD RECOVER

Critical Role of Cost Accounting

Accurately deciding the proportion of costs that a price should recover requires knowing the cost of delivering the service. Unfortunately, current accounting

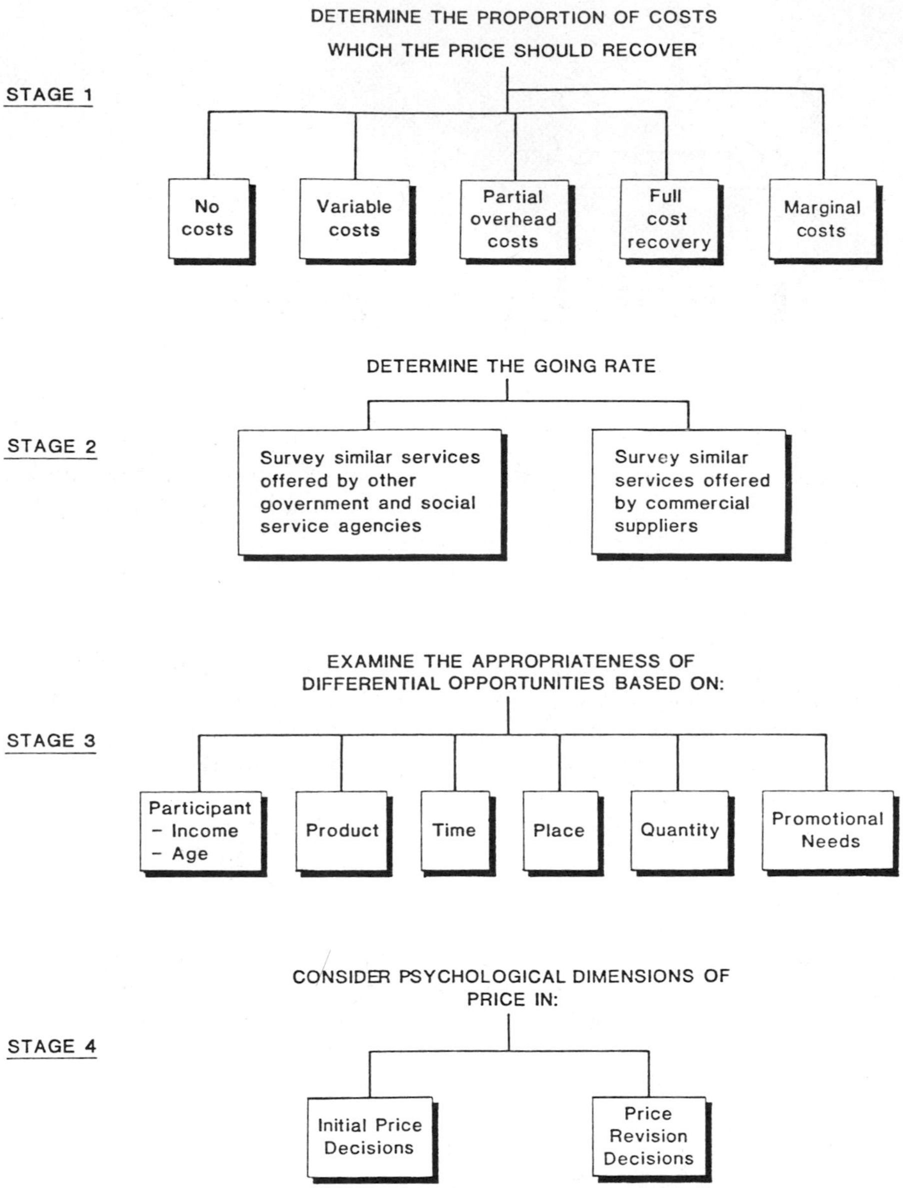
DETERMINE THE PROPORTION OF COSTS WHICH THE PRICE SHOULD RECOVER
STAGE 1
No costs
Variable costs
Partial overhead costs
Full cost recovery
Marginal costs
DETERMINE THE GOING RATE
STAGE 2
Survey similar services offered by other government and social service agencies
Survey similar services offered by commercial suppliers
EXAMINE THE APPROPRIATENESS OF DIFFERENTIAL OPPORTUNITIES BASED ON:
STAGE 3
Participant – Income – Age
Product
Time
Place
Quantity
Promotional Needs
CONSIDER PSYCHOLOGICAL DIMENSIONS OF PRICE IN:
STAGE 4
Initial Price Decisions
Price Revision Decisions

Figure 14.1. A Logical Approach to Establishing a Price.

systems in many government and social service agencies are not structured to capture and report cost data for each specific service delivered. Instead they are designed to provide expenditure information and appropriation control, by which an agency can demonstrate compliance.

Historically agencies have gathered cost data for services such as water, sewer, power and light, and hospitals because of the businesslike nature of these services. Often these services are treated as separate enterprises for accounting purposes. Determining the cost of services financed out of the General Fund has not been required in the past. Budgeting systems typically do not group expenditures related to a single service in one place—often not even in budgets labeled "program budgets."[1]

Cost accounting, which is sometimes referred to as managerial accounting, is defined as

> that method of accounting which provides for assembling and recording of all the elements of cost incurred to accomplish a purpose, to carry on an activity or operation, or to complete a unit of work or a specific job.[2]

Typically, the cost of providing a service consists of three tasks which can be viewed as a series of 3 layers.[3] Each layer represents a type of cost that must be allocated to the levels beneath and adjacent that benefit from the service. Figure 14.2 illustrates this typical cost-flow pattern.

The first task in determining a program's cost is identifying and allocating a jurisdiction's central service costs. Typical central service functions are executive administration, purchasing, accounting, personnel, data processing, mo-

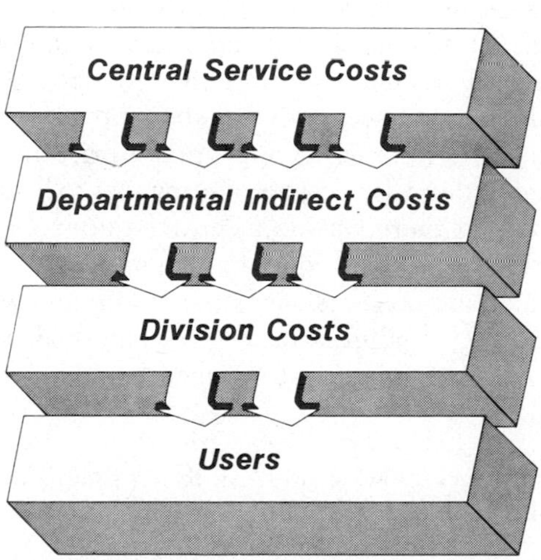

Figure 14.2. A Typical Cost Flow Pattern. (*Source:* Adapted from Robert D. McRae, "The Cost Burden Study: A Method for Recovering Costs from Non-Residents," *Governmental Finance*, March 1982, p. 10.)

tor pool, and budget. Since support departments constitute the central service cost pool, it is necessary to equitably allocate these costs to each benefitting department.

After all central service costs have been allocated to the direct service departments, a second task is to develop a framework for allocating departmental indirect costs to each of the agency's operating divisions. Departmental indirect costs generally will be a combination of central service costs allocated to the department and the department's administrative support activities costs. The third task in determining a program's cost requires that each division's costs (including the share of central and departmental costs that it has been assigned), be allocated to the users of each of its services. This method of cost accounting involves layering costs and then allocating them to successively lower echelons of the agency until a true service cost is developed. Cost information permits public officials to present the citizenry with a clear outline of the diverse and perhaps substantial financial resources necessary to support each service delivered.

If there is resistance to a formal cost accounting system, then the less rigorous approach of cost finding may be adopted. Cost finding is defined as

> a less formal method of cost determination or estimation on an irregular basis. There may be no formal accounting entries during the year to record costs incurred in delivering specific services. Instead, cost finding usually involves taking available fund financial data and recasting and adjusting it to derive the cost data or estimate needed.[4]

In other words, cost finding is the process of using available financial data or finding costs from budget details, the budgetary accounting system, analysis of detailed transactions (such as payroll records, invoices, and contracts) and interviews with staff. These data are collected, assembled on worksheets, and analyzed to determine individual service delivery costs.[5]

It is rare that an agency's accounting system provides the complete cost information essential to determine an appropriate price intelligently. In most instances cost finding, rather than cost accounting, has to be used. This situation exists because in the past there was no incentive to develop an elaborate cost accounting system. Prices were infrequent and nominal, tax-supported budgets were expanding so no trade-off decisions between services were necessary, and the relative cost efficiency of alternative delivery methods such as contracting out was not a concern. The movement toward cost accounting is well illustrated in the hospital field:

> The nation's hospitals face growing pressure to cut treatment costs. But many still don't know what their costs are, much less how to reduce them.
>
> That didn't matter so much when Medicare, Blue Cross and other health insurers generally reimbursed hospitals on the basis of total costs. But since October 1, Medicare has been phasing in a payment system based on what it thinks specific treatments should cost; hospitals can't get more for the treatment, but if they keep costs below Medicare's level, they get to keep the difference as profit.

> Other health insurers are starting to adopt the same system. So not surprisingly, many hospitals and their accountants are scrambling to develop cost-tracking methods related to the 467 Medicare treatment categories.[6]

A cost accounting system is likely to be increasingly recognized as an essential management tool. No logical pricing decisions that consider equity, income redistribution, or efficiency can be made until the cost of service delivery is known. Without such data opponents of pricing decisions can justifiably argue that they are arbitrary.

Which Costs Should Be Included? Before establishing a cost accounting system, an agency must determine which costs are to be included. Even if an agency intends to recover something less than full costs, it needs to know the full price of delivering a service:

> Overlooking indirect or other costs leads policy makers to an inaccurate cost assessment that may result in under pricing and consequently subsidizing the service. While a service may be priced at less than full cost, such a decision should be a policy decision by the elected officials and not the results of data non-availability during the policy making process.[7]

Some agencies adopt such decision rules as "aim for 30 percent cost recovery" or "aim to cover operating costs," but incorrect definitions of costs invalidate the measure of achievement.

Figure 14.2 shows a series of cost layers. These layers include all administrative costs, but a policy decision also has to be made concerning depreciation of capital equipment costs, debt charges on facilities, and the costs of pensions and other employee fringe benefits. Should the cost accounting system attempt to allocate all of these costs to each service delivered?

Depreciation of assets and employee fringe benefits probably should be included. However, debt charges probably should be excluded unless the facilities were financed through revenue bonds or similar self-financing mechanisms. In most instances, citizens agreed to pay the debt charges on capital facilities with their tax dollars when they voted to develop the facilities in a referendum. Further, debt charges associated with facilities represent sunk costs—that is, expenses already incurred that cannot be revoked or changed. Expecting today's clients to carry the cost of past decisions in which they may have had no part is often viewed as unreasonable. Debt charges may also be ignored if capital facilities were financed by intergovernmental transfers or other grants, since such financing is not a direct burden on local taxpayers.

Positioning Services on the Cost Recovery Continuum

In our discussion of the essential differences among services that exhibit public, merit, and private characteristics (see Figure 13.2), we concluded that users should pay a price if a service was defined as merit or private, but no price if it was a public type of service. In Figure 14.3 merit-type services are referred to as quasi-public and quasi-private to more fully reflect the range between public and private services.

This section discusses four methods for recovering some predetermined proportion of costs. They are: full cost recovery, partial overhead cost recovery, variable cost recovery, and marginal cost pricing. Three of these methods relate to the private-public services continuum shown in Figure 14.3. The relationship between positioning on the cost recovery continuum and these three methods is shown in Figure 14.3. The fourth method, recovery of marginal costs, is a conceptually different approach and is not shown in the figure.

Full-Cost Recovery. Full-cost recovery is also termed *average cost pricing*. The price of a service is intended to produce sufficient revenue to cover all the fixed and variable costs associated with the service (however, these have been defined in the cost accounting system) and enable the breakeven point to be reached. Because the total costs of a service are divided among those who receive it, full-cost recovery is sometimes called the "fair price." For example, in the case of a hospital, if patients in need of care pay the full unit costs, the hospital breaks even. This is considered fair because no one has been "taken advantage of." Figure 14.4 shows how to determine a price that is intended to recover full costs.

Full-cost recovery is an appropriate strategy for those services perceived as private that benefit only users and offer no external benefits to the general community. Many social service agencies charge commercial users of their facilities at the full-cost recovery level. Examples include the use of parks by circuses, group picnics, or for filming commercial advertisements; and the use of convention centers or halls for dances, pop concerts, or fundraising dinners. However, full-cost recovery pricing is most commonly used by government agencies in the pricing of tolls for highways, airports, and bridges, sanitation services, hospital services, and utilities. These are perceived to be private services operating on a self-financing basis.

Rates for public utilities typically are set not only to recover full costs but also to permit a profit margin. This ensures the availability of capital for reinvestment and pays for the cost of capital invested. Even government agencies that operate their own utilities frequently include a profit margin and assign this surplus to the General Fund to keep property taxes down. This kind of pricing has given rise to what students of utility pricing call the Averch-Johnson effect:

> When cost determines price, and profit is a percentage of price, then the greater the costs, the greater the absolute profits, even though the rate of profits remains fixed. So long as the cost of capital funds is lower than the allowable rate of return, public utilities have a powerful incentive to invest like crazy in capital projects which create fixed costs, which in turn create profits. The more non-productive the capital, the more attractive it is, since non-productive capital adds to the rate

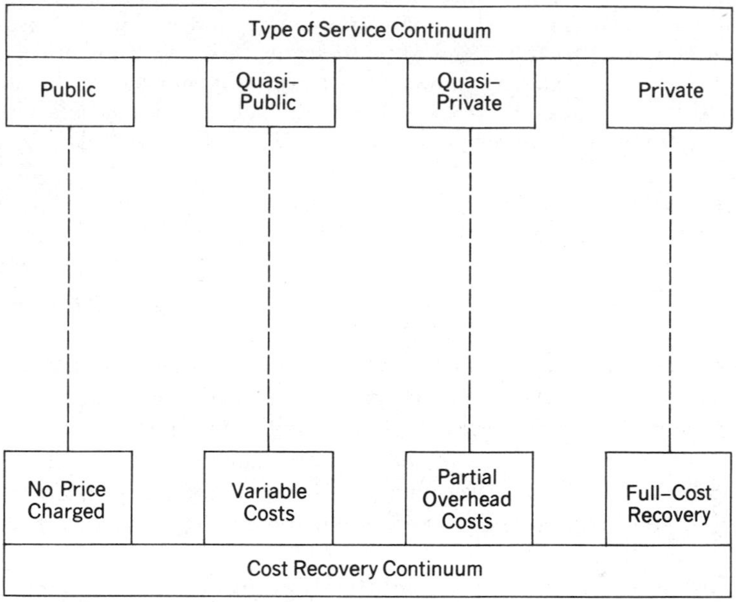

Figure 14.3. Relationship Between Type of Service and Cost Recovery Strategy.

A price that is intended to recover full costs is determined by using the following formula:

Average cost price = Average fixed cost + Average variable cost

$$\text{Where: Average fixed cost} = \frac{\text{Total fixed costs}}{\text{Number of users}}$$

$$\text{Average variable cost} = \frac{\text{Total variable costs}}{\text{Number of users}}$$

If: Total fixed costs = \$1000

Total variable costs = \$500

Projected number of users = 100

$$\text{Then: Price} = \frac{1000}{100} + \frac{500}{100}$$

Thus: Price = \$15.

Figure 14.4 Pricing to Recover Full Costs.

base without increasing day-to-day operating expenses, and thus does wonders for cash flow. The "Averch-Johnson effect" explains why the terminals that airlines own themselves (as at Kennedy Airport) tend to be so lavish while the ones that they rent (as at La Guardia) tend to be so spartan; why New York Telephone seems to have a new building on every corner; and why, in many smaller cities, the handful of extravagant skyscrapers almost invariable includes the local electric utility and the local phone company.[8]

Efforts to implement a pricing policy that is intended to recover all or some predetermined proportion of costs have to contend with five major problems. First, as we discussed earlier in this chapter, it is difficult to systematically identify, classify, and equitably allocate the costs associated with each service.

Second, the charged price will only recover the costs anticipated *if* the projected number of service users is accurate. This number may be relatively easy to estimate if historical records show a consistent pattern of participation in a particular program over a period of years. However, a new service may be established with considerable error in the participation projection. If the projection is too high, then the agency will receive less revenue than it had anticipated.

The third problem also relates to accurately projecting the number of service users. Prices based on recovery of a proportion of costs are determined not by market considerations but by the costs of providing the service (this does not apply when the agency has a monopoly position in the market). Thus the prices charged by suppliers of similar services are ignored even though their lower price is likely to adversely impact the number of users of the agency's service. Cost-based pricing assumes that client groups are willing and able to pay the proposed price. Particularly in situations in which the price is intended to fully recover the costs of delivering a relatively discretionary service, it is likely that client groups may resist. A minimal use of service and consequent erosion of the agency's political support base may then result.

In many social services, the very high fixed costs involved in equipment and facilities make full-cost recovery an inappropriate pricing strategy. Indeed, it has been shown that the need to cover these overheads has been a primary cause of driving private nonprofit social service organizations, especially those in the arts, health, and education, into bankruptcy.[9] Federal or philanthropic grants have provided the facilities and equipment, but the organizations cannot persuade their users to pay the price necessary to support their upkeep.

The fourth problem in using cost-based pricing is that it may encourage inefficiency. There is a danger that little concern will be given to controlling costs or requiring efficient management since the costs can be directly passed on to client groups in the form of higher prices. Consider the following example:

The highest annual tuition ever charged by an institution of higher education will be the $12,500 that entering students will have to pay at the medical school of Georgetown University in Washington.

Another medical school in Washington, the one affiliated with George Washington University, will charge incoming students $9,000 a year tuition.

Both institutions were forced to adopt steep tuition increases because of the expiration this year of the District of Columbia Medical and Dental Manpower Act under which Congress had provided assistance.[10]

Can it really be that the costs of medical education at George Washington are so much lower than at Georgetown as to permit George Washington's tuition to be 28 percent below Georgetown's? Dare we entertain the possibility that Georgetown is wasteful?[11]

Perhaps Georgetown charged $3,500 more than George Washington because it offered a superior or different program, but questions of efficiency at the two schools should at least be raised.

The fifth weakness of cost-based pricing is encouragement of an irrational price structure. Consider the implications of the following pricing strategy, which was adopted by a church camp.

The camp sought to recover all of its costs. Most of the costs were fixed so the cost of operating the camp was about the same all year round. The prices charged were $80 per three-day weekend in the winter months and $40 per three-day weekend in the summer months. These prices reflected the much higher occupancy rate at the camp in the summer months, which enabled the costs to be spread over more users. However, the price structure had the effect of persuading more people to come in the summer than in the winter. Hence there were long waiting lists for the summer, but the camp had very low winter occupancy rates.

Full-cost recovery pricing is only appropriate for some services. Many services do not exhibit the characteristics of a pure private service because, frequently, people other than the individuals using the service receive *some* benefits from it. In these situations an agency should seek to recover only partial overhead costs or variable costs.

Partial Overhead Cost Recovery. In order to recover partial overhead costs, a price is established that meets all direct operation and maintenance costs and some proportion of fixed costs. The remaining proportion of the fixed costs that it is not intended to recover represents the tax subsidy given to the particular service. Figure 14.5 shows how to determine a price that is intended to recover partial overhead costs.

The proportion of fixed costs that should be subsidized is dependent on the extent to which nonusers benefit from a client using a service. As the benefits that accrue to nonusers increase, the proportion of fixed costs met by the subsidy should increase (Figure 14.3).

It is important to note that the anticipated per-person subsidy is built into the formula. This is a very different approach to the frequent practice of assigning, say, a 20 percent overhead figure to direct operations and maintenance

A price that is intended to recover partial overhead costs is determined by the following formula:

Partial overhead recovery price = Average fixed cost + Average variable cost − Average subsidy

where:

Average subsidy represents the amount to which each user is subsidized out of tax funds.

If: Average fixed cost = $8
Average variable cost = $4
Average subsidy = $3

Then: Partial overhead recovery price = $8 + $4 − $3

Thus: Service price = $9.

Figure 14.5. Pricing to Recover Partial Overhead Costs.

costs. This latter approach does not indicate the extent to which individuals are subsidized:

> If it is decided that a service should be subsidized then the subsidy should be made explicit in the budget and built into the authority's financial control system. This is important because managers responsible for services should set performance targets based on costs, subsidies and targets.[12]

Lack of attention to subsidies expressed on a per-unit or per-capita basis is likely to lead to substantial inefficiency in the allocation of resources and inequities in service delivery. Users of Service A may be receiving much larger subsidies per capita than users of Service B even though the price they pay is the same, because the costs of operating the two services are substantially different.

Variable Cost Recovery. If variable cost recovery pricing is used, the established price is equal to the average variable cost of providing a service. In this context, variable costs are direct operating and maintenance expenses. No attempt is made to contribute toward meeting fixed costs. Figure 14.6 shows how to determine a price that is intended to recover variable costs.

Because direct operating and maintenance expenses can be easily documented, basing price decisions on them is tempting. This is a popular approach with many agency personnel because when fixed costs are omitted, a relatively low price can be charged and a larger client support constituency is likely to emerge. Others argue, however, that the facilities and amenities offered by social service agencies add to the quality of life or to the "liveability" of a community. Some nonusers receive benefits from knowing that facilities exist

A price that is intended to recover total variable costs is determined by the following formula:

$$\text{Variable cost recovery price} = \frac{\text{Total variable costs}}{\text{Number of participants}}$$

If: Total variable cost = $500

Projected number of participants = 100

Then: Variable cost recovery price = $5

Figure 14.6. Pricing to Recover Variable Costs.

(this "opportunity to acquire" is sometimes called *option demand*), and nonusers should therefore pay the indirect fixed costs required to make these amenities and facilities available.

Marginal Cost Pricing. Marginal cost is defined as the addition to total cost resulting from the last unit of output. If it is intended to recover marginal costs, then a service is provided at a price equal to the cost of providing an additional unit of service, or the cost of serving the incremental user. Each user pays the additional cost caused by his or her own use of the service. For example:

> If a medical school is considering increasing the number of students it accepts each year by one, what is the marginal cost of the extra student? In principle, the process is straightforward. Estimate all costs of running the school without the extra student; then estimate all costs of running the school with the student. The differences between the two total cost figures is the marginal cost of adding the one student, and that is the price which the student should be charged for admission to the program.[13]

Marginal cost pricing is the price-setting principle most widely accepted by economists because it maximizes economic efficiency, which is attained when there is no unsatisfied demand and when price equals marginal cost. While the practicing manager is likely to concur that in principle marginal cost pricing is conceptually superior, he or she may feel it is too difficult to implement. Three major obstacles stand in the way.

First, the data necessary to calculate marginal costs are more difficult to obtain than those needed to implement other cost recovery pricing strategies. The costs involved in collecting such data are frequently perceived to outweigh the extra benefits marginal cost pricing offers. Second, marginal cost pricing disregards objectives other than efficiency. Managers also have to be concerned with the income distribution and equity effects of a price. Finally, a price based on marginal costs may not allow recovery of full costs. For example, on a golf course one additional golfer adds practically nothing to the cost of maintenance and upkeep. Thus a price set equal to marginal cost often will not raise sufficient revenue to cover all costs of service delivery.

Despite these difficulties, in some situations marginal cost pricing can be advantageously implemented, particularly in the pricing of utilities. The marginal cost of utility distribution is sometimes included in the calculation of utility prices. Part of the service cost is based on the cost of transporting, for example, water from the source of supply or central distribution site (treatment plant) to the user:

> It is sometimes suggested that failure to equitably allocate distribution costs provides an incentive to develop urban sprawl, because more distant developments are more expensive to serve than more proximate developments. A full cost recovery user price undercharges outlying areas and overcharges interior areas, so central city residents subsidize outlying residents. The result of the subsidy is to give general encouragement for development to leapfrog outward. If each location is charged the full marginal costs of providing services to that location then this subsidy is eliminated and more concentrated development is likely to follow. It is probably not practical to calculate the marginal cost of service attributable to each individual. However, marginal distribution costs could be allocated on the basis of distance zones.

STAGE 2: DETERMINING THE GOING RATE PRICE

At the end of stage 1, a provisional price should be determined based on the proportion of costs that it is expected to recover. However, pricing based on costs is not market-oriented because it assumes that service users will pay the suggested price. This may be a false assumption. Cost-based pricing also ignores the impact that this price may have on other suppliers of the service. Stage 2 of the process for establishing a price is intended to ensure that the provisional cost-based price is adjusted, if necessary, so it is responsive to the willingness and ability of users to pay and does not have an unintended impact on other suppliers (Figure 14.1).

Determining the going rate requires a survey of prices charged by other suppliers of the service. Usually this survey will be confined to other government or social service agencies, but in situations in which a service is also offered by commercial suppliers they should be included in the price survey. For example, if a jurisdiction offers day care services it should include private day care suppliers in its going rate survey. The agency may then adjust its cost-based price in order to ensure that the public day care opportunity does not impede the success of private day care suppliers or reduce the range of day care opportunities available. A charge substantially less than that of private suppliers may harm them and lead to congestion of the agency's own facilities.

Adjusting a price to be consistent with the going rate has two major advantages. First, the going rate price range can be said to represent the collective wisdom of professionals in the field and elected officials in other jurisdictions. For this reason a price within the range will probably avoid controversy and be regarded by most publics as fair. For example, if the survey reveals that an agency's prices are lower than those charged by others for a similar service, then the agency can justify an increase in price to both user publics and elected representatives.

Some may argue that instead of reflecting the conventional wisdom of the field in price decisions, a survey of prices charged by others serves only to pool the field's collective ignorance! That is, few of the other jurisdictions have any rationale for the price they charge, so using their prices in a price decision process only compounds irrationality.

However, a major advantage of comparing existing prices with those charged for similar services elsewhere is establishing the *range* of prices that are likely to be acceptable to users of a particular service. It is possible that services may not be exactly of the same quality or serve identical types of client groups, but in most cases they are substantially similar.

Determining the going rate forces an agency to address what potential client groups are willing to pay for a particular service. It is a misconception to believe that costs should necessarily determine price, for often the prices that an agency charges may be used to determine costs. For instance, if a craft program was being priced, an agency might first try to find out what prices it could reasonably expect its potential client groups to pay. When it has this information the agency works backwards from this figure to determine the nature of the materials, equipment, and facilities that are suited to such a price.

The going-rate price is not "the manager's impression" of what others are charging. It is found by formally surveying what is being charged elsewhere. It is tempting to omit stage 1 if the provisional price set there will have to be substantially adjusted by the going rate. This would be a mistake. The going rate often bears little relation to the cost of provision. As a result, if stage 1 was omitted, sound financial management would not be possible and substantial inequities between services might emerge (some would be more heavily subsidized than others). Without stage 1 a jurisdiction would not be able to purposely trade off the opportunity cost of one service compared to another; nor would it know whether it should price a service at the high or low end of the range of going-rate prices.

STAGE 3: EXAMINING THE APPROPRIATENESS OF DIFFERENTIAL PRICING

At the end of stage 2 the adjusted price is accepted as the average price that service users should be charged. However, stage 3 recognizes that there are occasions when offering variations of this price to particular groups may achieve more equitable and efficient service delivery (see Figure 14.1).

Examining the appropriateness of differential opportunities means that an agency considers charging a different price to different groups for the same service, even though there is no directly corresponding difference in the costs of providing the service to each of those groups. Such market-oriented price adjustments assume that the market is segmentable and the segments show different price elasticities of demand. A fundamental requirement for an agency to be able to offer the same service at two or more prices is to avoid arousing resentment from a majority of clients, which will create antipathy and loss of goodwill.

In some situations agencies have adopted the Robin Hood principle. That is, some users are charged a high price, which is used to subsidize other users. This principle was expressed by a hospital administrator in the following terms:

> I don't feel that we are robbing the rich because we charge them more when we know they can well afford it; the sliding scale is just as democratic as the income tax. We operated today upon two people for the same surgical condition—one a widow whom we charged $100, the other a banker whom we charged $500. We let the widow set her own fee. We charged the banker an amount which he probably carries around in his wallet to entertain his business friends.[14]

It may be argued that this strategy is inequitable. Why should the wealthy who are sick be singled out to subsidize the service of others? In nonprofit organizations in which the price charged is the only source of income, then enforcement of the Robin Hood principle through sliding scales is probably essential for the institution's survival. When services are delivered by governmental agencies, however, there appears to be no rationale for such inequities. If some users of a service should be subsidized then the cost of the subsidy should be shared by the whole community. It is unfair to select some citizens to carry this compensatory burden solely because they happen to be users of the service.

This section discusses the following six criteria for dividing a clientele into distinct groups that offer differential pricing opportunities: participant category, product, place, time, quantity of use, and incentives to try.

Participant Price Differentials

Price differentiation on the basis of participant category is usually related to a perception that some groups may find it difficult to pay a recommended price. Three groups are frequently identified as less able to pay: children, senior citizens, and the economically disadvantaged.

Children. Children represent society's investment in its future. Hence subsidy of many children's educational, health, and recreational services is widely recognized as appropriate. This does not imply, however, that all children's services should be fully subsidized. In many instances it is not unreasonable to suggest that the ability of children to pay for a service is no different from that of adults, because parents frequently pay for their children. Thus a child's use of a service may not be contingent on his or her ability to pay. Further, children are likely to require more careful supervision and inflict more damage on a facility than adults, so the costs associated with servicing them may be greater than the costs of servicing adults.

Senior Citizens. The rationale for offering services to senior citizens at reduced prices rests on the assumption that senior citizens are a low-income sector of the population who cannot afford to pay regular prices. The image of an elderly person struggling to survive on a fixed pension perhaps supplemented by a meager interest income from modest savings is a disturbing one. Although such an image reflected reality for a large proportion of the elderly 20 years ago, it is misleading today. Poverty is still a problem in the United States but the aged—those over 65 years of age—are now on average no more likely to be poor than any other age group.

The data in Figure 14.7 trace the remarkable change that has occurred since 1959 in the economic status of people aged 65 and over. The proportion of elderly below the poverty level dropped from 35.2 percent in 1959 to 25.3

Year	All Persons	65 Years and Over
1959	22.4	35.2
1966	14.7	28.5
1967	14.2	29.5
1968	12.8	25.0
1969	12.1	25.3
1970	12.6	24.5
1971	12.5	21.6
1972	11.9	18.6
1973	11.1	16.3
1974	11.2	14.7
1975	12.3	15.3
1976	11.8	15.0
1977	11.6	14.1
1978	11.4	14.0
1979	11.7	15.2
1980	13.0	15.7
1981	14.0	15.3
1982	15.0	14.6

Figure 14.7. Poverty Rate (%). (*Source:* U.S. Department of Commerce, Bureau of the Census; Series P-60, *Characteristics of the Population Below the Poverty Level: 1982*. Superintendent of Documents, U.S. Government Printing Office, Washington, DC, 1983.)

percent in 1969, an average of one percentage point per year. In the next five years the impact of antipoverty programs was most forcefully felt, as the poverty rate for the elderly declined two percentage points per year to 14 percent in 1974. Since then it has fluctuated between 14 and 16 percent. In 1982, however, the proportion of the population over 65 that was below the poverty level was less than the proportion under 65 years of age with poverty-level incomes. In 1980 the national average household income per person after taxes was $5,964, but for households headed by people over 65 the average was $6,299.

The elderly's improved economic status can be attributed to legislated increases in Social Security benefits in the late 1960s and the indexing of benefits in 1974, as well as the introduction in 1974 of Supplementary Security Income, an inflation-indexed negative income tax for the aged. The data shown in Figure 14.7 are national averages and the situation in particular jurisdictions may be different. However, the data suggest that in many instances no rationale exists for charging senior citizens a lower price than other users of public services.

Economically Disadvantaged. Most agencies attempt to lower prices for the economically disadvantaged to overcome their poverty or unequal opportunity and ensure that they are not excluded from receiving services. This is not an easy policy to implement in such a way that no stigma is perceived by persons receiving the low-price privileges. One common method is to give eligible clients a card to be presented at the time of using the particular service. Such cards might be good for a certain period of time or for a certain number of uses before renewal is required.

Generally, not enough thought and effort has been given to the problem of how to implement low-price privileges for the economically disadvantaged. Agencies should be expected to be proactive in finding disadvantaged people and giving them the necessary card. Instead agencies most often adopt a reactive stance, which lets disadvantaged people receive a reduced price if they apply for it. For example, many agencies offer a scholarship program whereby low-income individuals apply for funds to pay for the services that have been provided by sponsors. This approach inevitably stigmatizes the applicants.

Product Price Differentials

Differential pricing can be used to offer client groups extra levels of service—for example, in trash collection, street cleaning, street parking, park maintenance, police patrols, or foreign language instruction. The agency would provide a basic level of service, but those clients who wanted a higher level could receive it by paying a higher price, just as those extra services in some instances are now purchased from private sources. The prices for these added services would be set to cover the incremental costs of providing them.

Differential pricing could also serve as a market test of the public's preferred level of service. It offers

> A method for trying out and responding to the public's desire for quality changes in public services. The consumer who desires a quality differential could pay for that option—a choice now frequently denied him or her when quality changes must be financed from general revenue.[15]

Presumably, if a large proportion of a clientele opted for a higher level of service, then it would become the new norm.

Place Price Differentials

Pricing that differentiates on a place basis is commonly practiced at spectator events. At a concert, theater, or sports event a higher price is charged for front-row than for back-row seats. The most common use of price differentials based on place is higher prices charged to nonresidents. Such differentials are relatively easy to impose since nonresidents are likely to have relatively little political influence outside of their own jurisdiction. For example, state universities charge out-of-state residents a higher price for tuition than residents. The rationale for such pricing is that residents frequently pay at least some of the costs associated with a service through their property taxes, while nonresidents make no such payments. That argument is less persuasive if services are paid for from other tax sources such as a sales tax. In this case people living outside the community may legitimately argue that since they purchase a variety of goods from within the community, they have contributed their fair share of sales tax. Hence there is no rationale for charging them more than residents for use of these services.

At the municipal level, the authority of agencies to impose differential prices based on residence varies among states. As a result, such agencies must be aware of relevant statutes and court decisions in their particular jurisdictions to determine their authority to impose a different price for nonresidents. Generally, if a municipality can demonstrate a reasonable relationship between the differential price and legitimate governmental goals, the price will be upheld in the courts.[16] In a typical case the court stated that a city had the sovereign duty of maintaining the health of its residents.

> It owes no duty to non-residents. Residents are entitled to preference over non-residents and such action is not in contravention of the rights of non-residents. The primary purpose of a municipality corporation is to contribute toward the welfare, health, happiness, and interest of its inhabitants . . . not to further the interests of those residing outside its limits.[17]

If a service is being used to capacity, then a high differential price may be an effective method of discouraging nonresident use. However, if a service has spare capacity, then an agency may want to attract as many outside residents as possible who are willing to pay a price that is higher than the variable cost of servicing them. The revenue from this source will contribute to fixed costs, so the service will need less subsidy from taxpayers.

The major problem in establishing differential prices for nonresidents is implementation. In those situations in which a client has to show proof of residence each time a service is used, then the irritation cost to local residents may offset any financial gain. This problem does not exist when proof of residence must only be established periodically. Most states, for example, charge substantially higher annual hunting and/or fishing license fees to nonresidents than to residents. Proof of residence, in the form of a driver's license or similar document, must only be provided once each year.

Time Price Differentials

With differential prices set on a time basis, lower prices are charged for services that are identical except with respect to time of use. This strategy encourages fuller and more balanced use of capacity (see Chapter 13). The intent is to encourage use of services at off-peak times and to ration use during peak times. Public utilities, computing centers, and parking lots or meters have used this approach, varying their prices according to the time of week (weekend versus weekday) or time of day (charging higher rates for peak periods). These price differentials, however, have so far been underutilized. Consider the obvious example of residential water supply:

> A number of studies have shown clearly that, apart from industrial uses, lawn sprinkling is the principal determinant of the peak loads on the water system and that, as a result, the capacity of water systems has to be much larger than would be otherwise necessary. Seasonal pricing would therefore help to regulate water use and hence the apparent need for investment in water systems.
>
> Water should, as one writer has noted, cost more in July than in December, just as Friday night theatre tickets cost more than Wednesday night tickets: "These are sound pricing practices which businessmen understand, but which somehow seem beyond the comprehension of some municipal authorities."[18]

Price Differentials Based on Quantity of Use

Quantity discounts are deductions from the regular price that reflect economies of purchasing in large quantities. They are intended to stimulate additional demand and to reduce the costs of meeting that level of demand. When commercial businesses give quantity discounts, these discounts provide specific benefits to both the seller and the buyer of the service or good. The benefits accruing to a business might include the following:

Saving in production costs. Larger orders may result in lower-cost production runs.

Improved cash flow, because a relatively large cash payment is made.

Reduced costs associated with transportation. That is, there may be fewer orders to process, ship, and invoice.

Reduced inventory and storage costs. The costs of storage, financing inventory, and carrying stock are transferred from seller to buyer.

Reduced selling expenses. Many expenses such as billing, order filling, and the salaries of salespeople are about the same whether the seller receives an order totalling $10 or $500. Thus the seller shares such expense savings with the purchaser of large quantities.

Incentive to a buyer to purchase only from a given seller rather than buying from multiple sources.

Inducement for clients to purchase more of a good or service than they would otherwise have done.

In contrast to the use of quantity discounts by a commercial enterprise, there are many government and social services in which benefits from this policy accrue predominantly to the clients rather than to the agency. In such cases direct users gain at the expense of all other citizens.

Two primary types of quantity discounts are used by agencies. The first is declining block rates, which often are used in water and utility pricing. Because water delivery involves high fixed costs and low variable costs, the cost of delivering the last gallon of water is less than that required to deliver the first gallon of water. Water pressure has to be kept high, leaks occur at the same rate, and administration costs remain the same, regardless of whether or not people use the water. The output of water (i.e., obtaining it from a source and treating it for human consumption) is subject to decreasing costs over the relevant market size once the plant is in place. For these reasons, as the quantity of water used by a client increases, the price per 1,000 gallons decreases. This approach is short term and inappropriate. It encourages careless use of water by large-volume users. For best conservation of a scarce resource, the price should increase rather than decrease with the quantity used.

The second type of quantity discount is the season or multiuse discount pass employed by many recreation facilities such as swimming pools, golf courses, and arts complexes. Before such passes are issued an agency, as the steward of resources entrusted to it by the citizenry, must identify the benefits that it or the general citizenry receives from such an arrangement in addition to the benefits that clients receive. There appear to be four situations in which such benefits may arise:

1. Where there are competitive services, the quantity discount ticket provides incentive for a client to purchase the service exclusively from the agency. This choice is particularly important if the purchase of other agency services is involved. For example, at a golf course the discount ticket holder is likely to rent golf carts and make purchases in the golf shop, concessions, and food areas.

2. Clients may be induced to purchase more of a service than they would otherwise have done. For example, in the arts a primary reason for buying a season ticket is to provide incentive to attend each performance.[19]
3. If a service is operated through an enterprise fund, then a guaranteed cash flow at the start of a season allows an agency to plan ahead and develop strategies for resolving budget short-falls over the rest of the season. This reduces the risk associated with not achieving necessary revenue goals.
4. Positive promotional impact. Committed multiusers of a service are likely to be effective word-of-mouth promoters in the community.

In some instances multiuse discounts may not be appropriate. The first requirement of any agency's pricing policy is that it should be equitable for every citizen. Offering quantity discounts may lead to inequities. Consider the case of a public swimming pool in a small community, which operates at a loss of $50,000. Two questions arise:

1. Why should the taxpayers who swim only occasionally be required to pay more for each swim (that is, the full admission price) than the taxpayer who swims frequently and takes advantage of the multiuse discount?
2. The major beneficiary of the $50,000 subsidy is the frequent swimmer because he or she makes most use of the pool. Every visit to the pool is subsidized by the taxpayers by $1.50. Is it fair that frequent swimmers should receive a discounted admission price *and* receive the greatest benefit from the subsidy?

The only reason a multiuser purchases a discount pass is because he or she perceives a financial advantage. That advantage may not be appropriate—as, for example when an agency operates the only swimming pool in the community. The most equitable and efficient price system may be one in which all users pay the same per-use price.

One argument in favor of these discounts is that some users do not take full advantage of their passes, so the agency gains income it would otherwise not receive. The issue then becomes, is it fair that people should pay for visits they don't use?

Price Differentials as Incentives

Price discounts can be used as an incentive to persuade people to try a service. New clients may be offered prices lower than those paid by established clients in the hope of encouraging them to become regular users. It is important that such discounts be selective. Those receiving the discounts should recognize their limited duration or restriction to a particular set of circumstances. More detailed discussion of this promotional pricing is deferred until Chapter 18.

STAGE 4: CONSIDERING PSYCHOLOGICAL DIMENSIONS OF PRICE

This final stage of the process for establishing a price recognizes that the logical derivation of a price has to be tempered with a realization that elected officials and potential client groups do not always respond positively to rational pricing decisions. In addition to being influenced by the political considerations discussed in Chapter 13, a logically derived price may also have to be adjusted to accommodate the emotional reactions of targeted client groups.

The reactions of client groups to price changes are often irrational, stemming from historical perspectives, analogous experiences, self-interest, or emotion. Hence, in addition to economic principles, establishing a price that will be accepted by client groups requires a consideration of psychological dimensions of pricing.

There are 10 of these psychological concerns. Five of them are likely to be of primary importance in determining an initial price for a new service, while the other five are of greatest concern when the prices of existing services are being revised.

Psychological Considerations in Initial Price Decisions

The five psychological dimensions to be considered with new services are protection of self-esteem, establishing the reference price, price-quality relationship, consistency of image, and odd pricing (Figure 14.8). Although each of these may also be a concern in subsequent price revisions, their impact is likely to be less substantial than in the initial planning decision.

Protection of Self-Esteem. Many government and social services are directed at the physically and economically disadvantaged. These client groups are in need of subsidized services, but they may be too proud to accept handouts. It is frequently argued that recipients of subsidized services are less likely to feel a sense of stigma or indignity if they make some payment in exchange for a service. This is a particular concern, for example, when dealing with the physically handicapped.[20] If the handicapped person pays the same as any able-bodied person, then he or she has no feeling of being a charity recipient. Also, `by paying the same amount as others for services, the handicapped individual moves away from the area of special consideration and toward normalization. Many handicapped people who want to be accepted as

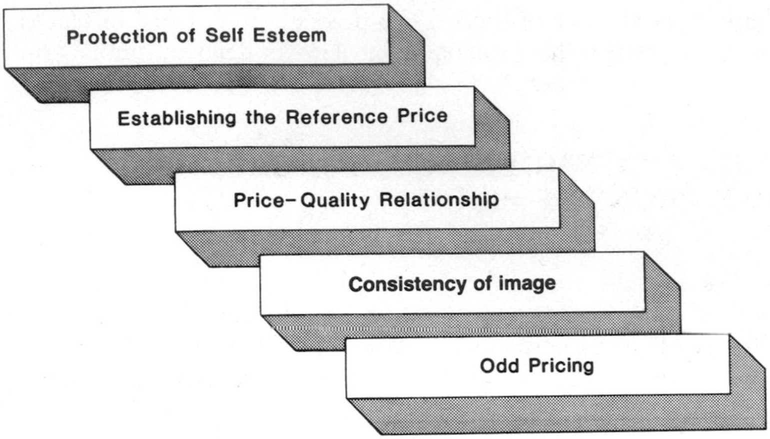

Figure 14.8. Psychological Considerations in Initial Price Decisions.

ordinary members of the community may feel a need to pay the same price for services as others in the community. A payment may only be a small proportion of the total cost of a service, but the act of contributing enhances an individual's sense of self-esteem or social responsibility.

Establishing the Reference Price. The most important pricing decision is the initial price that is charged for a service. This first price firmly establishes in a client's mind the fair price for the service. Hence it becomes the reference price against which subsequent price revisions are compared. An agency is likely to have more flexibility in the first pricing decision than in any subsequent decisions, which will always be constrained by client groups' relating their appropriateness and fairness back to the former price. The first pricing decision, therefore, usually has a strong determining impact on the level of price that can be charged for that service throughout its life. Further, it may impact subsequent initial pricing decisions of other services.

The role of the first pricing decision in formulating a reference point emphasizes the dangers involved in pricing a service low when it is first offered so that potential users will try it. As we saw earlier in this chapter, this objective can best be achieved by offering a promotional price that is recognized by all potential users as being temporary. A fixed, relatively short time period during which the special low promotional price will apply should be established. This should be communicated *together with* the regular price that will be charged for the service at the end of this time period.

The constraining influence of existing prices on subsequent price revisions is illustrated by the data presented in Tables 14.1 and 14.2. These data were collected from a representative probability sample of respondents in the City of Austin, Texas, as part of a household personal interview survey. Respondents consisted of both users and nonusers of city recreational offerings. They were

TABLE 14.1. Appropriate Prices for Existing City Leisure Services

Service Area	Current Average Price	Most Appropriate Price	Price (%)	Per Visit Cost of Provision
Parks, playgrounds, greenbelts	No Charge	0	83	$1.50
Tennis	$1.25	$1.25	66	2.25
Swimming	.50	.50	72	2.25
Golf	2.75	2.75	53	6.25
Recreation centers	.75	.75	68	2.50
Organized athletics	.95	.95	62	1.50
Outdoor nature programs	.50	.50	67	2.25
Senior citizen programs	.25	.25	68	1.50
Arts facilities or programs	.50	.50	62	1.50
Community education programs	.50	.50	62	3.00
Programs for handicapped	No Charge	0	90	2.75

TABLE 14.2. Appropriate Prices for Two Proposed New Services

Fishing Piers		Squash/Handball/Racquetball	
Price	%	Price	%
No charge	16	No charge	5
.75	20	$1.00	19
1.25	28	2.00	33
1.75	14	3.00	25
2.25	7	4.00	4
3.00[a]	15	5.00[a]	14

[a] = Estimated per visit cost to Austin Park and Recreation Department of providing the service.

asked to check which of six alternative prices they considered to be the most appropriate for each of the 11 types of recreational services listed in Table 14.1. The alternative prices differed for each service.

In each case, respondents were provided with two pieces of information. First, they were informed of the current average price charged for the service (Table 14.1, column 1). Second, they were informed of the per-visit cost to the agency of servicing each user (column 4). In all 11 service areas a substantial majority of the sample (column 3) indicated that the most appropriate price (column 2) was the price currently being charged.

The same sample was also asked to identify the appropriate price, from six alternatives, for two services not yet offered but likely to be made available in the future. In these two instances, the sample was only given the estimated per-visit cost to the agency of servicing each user since there was no existing price. Table 14.2 shows that without an existing price to serve as a guide, no consensus was reached among respondents as to what was the most appropriate price. Clearly, an agency has much more flexibility in pricing an initial service that has no clearly defined reference price.

The amount of flexibility available in pricing a service for the first time is at least partially influenced by a clientele's perception of prices of comparable services in either the public or private sector. These services delineate the upper and lower reference boundaries within which the first price usually must fall. One of the reasons that going-rate surveys are an important step in establishing a first price is that they ensure that the new service price falls within a potential client group's expected range. Nothing will move an intended client group away from a program faster than a price structure that the group perceives as being too high or too low. In cases where there are no comparable services and consequently no point of reference from which a clientele can draw price comparisons, then an agency has greater flexibility in the first price decision.

Price-Quality Relationship. Prices are often perceived as indicators of a service's likely quality. Marketing research studies have consistently shown that consumers' perceptions of product quality vary directly with price. Thus it is often assumed that the higher the price, the better the quality—not an irrational assumption, because higher quality does invoke higher costs and thus a higher price. The importance of price as an index of quality is suggested by the change in meaning associated with the word "cheap." It has almost entirely lost its original meaning of "not expensive," and become a synonym for "flimsy" or "shoddy." Similarly, the word "expensive" has come to stand as much for high quality as for high cost.

This relationship suggests that if a list of prices charged, for example, for lessons by different agencies in a community (YMCA, private club, recreation and park department, community education) was shown to a number of citizens, they would probably assume that the highest-priced lessons were the best. The rejection of lower-priced services is a form of risk avoidance, the risk being that inexpensive services may be less likely to give appropriate satisfaction. Given the investment in the opportunity cost of their time, the personal energy involved, and the travel incurred, many potential consumers may feel it unreasonable to risk using a low-priced service for the relatively small monetary saving that may accrue. Consider the following example of the price-quality relationship:

> A summer youth day camp program was offered and priced at $5 for the week. Too few signed up for the program to be offered. The following year the same agency offered the same program at $20 per week and it was fully enrolled. This suggests that the potential client group took price to be an indicator of the quality of the day camp program.

In some situations a higher price might add prestige to a service and the image of the providing agency. For example, if much of the proposed clientele for a particular community service is middle class, it is possible to argue that the use of low prices may imply an inferior program, which may dissuade them from participating. Price is a cue to targeted client groups that a service is designed for them. If a service is targeted at a middle-income group and is priced too low, it is possible the group may not recognize it as being intended for them. Greater involvement in some services may follow from increasing price rather than from reducing it.

Consistency of Image. Retail stores establish an image and use pricing to reflect that image. For example, K-Mart goods are low-priced, goods at Sears are medium-priced, and those at Neiman Marcus are high-priced. K-Mart does not offer a product at a high price because that would be inconsistent with what their clientele expect. Prices must be consistent with customers' perceptions of an agency and its offerings. Consider the following example:

> A solarium was located at a public swimming pool. The price for using the solarium was set at $8 per 30-minute session, which was the going rate for solarium use at commercial installations in the city. The intent was to use the solarium to generate funds that could be used to offset the substantial losses incurred by operating the pool, without undercutting the private sector.
>
> The installation and the services associated with the solarium were high quality, but the venture was a failure. It appears that the public could not reconcile paying $8 for a session in the solarium when admission to the swimming pool was only $1.25. The solarium's price was incompatible with the public's image of prices appropriate for services offered at a public pool. In this situation, if the solarium experience was to be offered, it should have been priced at around $2. Alternatively, a $5 or $6 price might have been acceptable if the pool admission price was $5 or $6 (as it is at some of the new leisure and wave pools), since this would have been more consistent with the pool's overall image.

Odd Pricing. This is a very common form of psychological pricing in the commercial market place. A product is said to carry an odd price if it costs 19¢ instead of 20¢, $4.95 instead of $5, or $9.99 instead of $10. Odd prices are thought to create the illusion of low prices, but there is little concrete evidence to support this contention. Indeed it is entirely possible that odd prices repel some consumers, just as they attract others. Odd pricing can be considered in price revision decisions as well as in initial price decisions. This practice does not appear to have been widely adopted by government and social service agencies.

Psychological Considerations in Price Revision Decisions

Prices are periodically revised. In most cases "revised" is synonymous with "increased." When prices are being revised five psychological dimensions should be considered (Figure 14.9): tolerance zone, client adjustment period, changing the perceived value of a service, anchor pricing, and customary pricing.

Tolerance Zone. The concept of a tolerance zone suggests that if price increases are within a sufficiently small range or zone they will not adversely impact use of the service (Figure 14.10). For example, an increase in the admission charge to a museum from $1.20 to $1.30 may be noticed by the clientele, but it is likely to be sufficiently small that it will not alter their pattern of using the facilities. Perception of price increases and decreases are relative to the original price. An increase in price of a service from 25¢ to 50¢ may arouse vigorous protest, while an increase in the price of a different service from $2 to $2.25 may raise no comment. Even though the increase in each case is 25¢, the first is a 100 percent change while the second is only a 12.5 percent increase.

A series of small incremental increases in price over a period of time—all of which fall within the tolerance zone—are less likely to meet client group resistance than a single major increase (Figure 14.10). Agencies should thus consider increasing their prices regularly rather than holding back increases until a large relative change in price is required. Given the frequency with which costs change, a systematic review of prices should be conducted at least on an annual basis; otherwise prices will not keep pace with the cost of providing a service. The best time to review service prices is probably during the annual budget review process. The strategy of frequent small incremental increases may be difficult to enforce in jurisdictions in which an agency has to seek authority from its elected representatives to implement each price increase. Elected representatives may be reluctant to engage in the political controversy with interest groups that frequently emerges when price increases are debated publicly.

To avoid this situation and to facilitate frequent small price increases, some governing bodies have authorized agencies to implement price increases without seeking their prior approval. In such cases, an agency is required only to provide details of the new prices, with full supporting documentation, to its controlling body for their information. This enables elected representatives to avoid controversy by deflecting any criticism of new prices away from them-

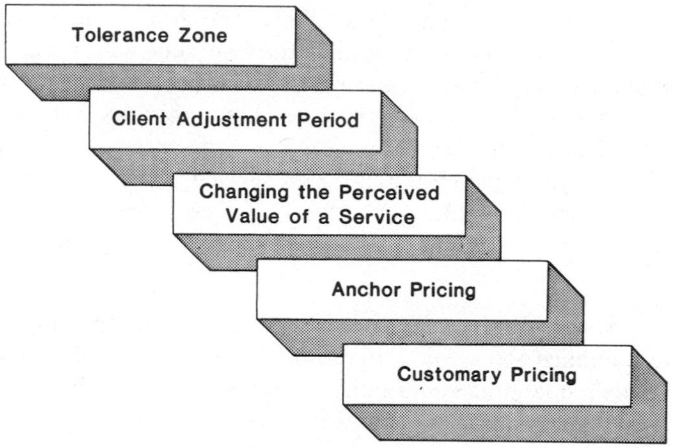

Figure 14.9. Psychological Considerations in Price Revision Decisions.

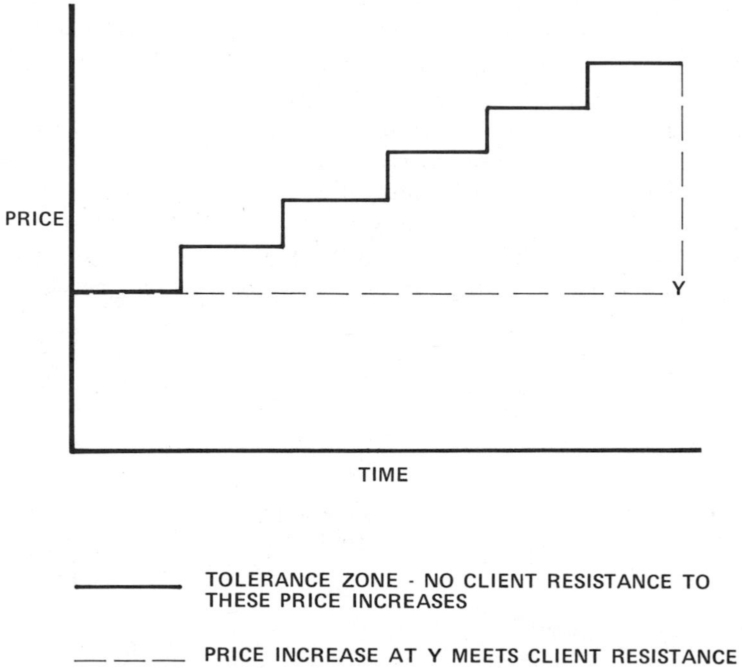

Figure 14.10. Concept of Tolerance Zones.

selves to the agency head. It does not remove pricing decisions from the political arena because elected representatives retain the authority to intercede. This low-key approach, however, usually leads to intercession only in exceptional cases. It avoids extensive public debate of all proposed price increases and thus facilitates frequent small increases within the tolerance zone.

Consideration should be given to raising prices proportionately whenever a client group is aware of substantial increases in an agency's costs of delivering a service. For example, immediately after a well-publicized labor contract has been signed, the additional costs placed on service delivery can be passed on to users. Clients are likely to accept these extra costs as within the tolerance zone because they are aware of their legitimacy.

Client Adjustment Period. On occasion it may be necessary to raise prices beyond the tolerance zone. Such quantum increases may reflect changes in a governing body's operating philosophy, changes in an agency's environment, or conscious efforts to make prices of like services more compatible.

Immediate clientele resistance will probably follow such price increases. This response will be particularly marked if the price goes from zero to some monetary value for the first time. After an initial period, however, client groups will usually adjust, accept the new price as the reference price, and regard it as fair. This process is illustrated in Figure 14.11.

The length of adjustment period will vary according to (1) the availability of substitute service suppliers, (2) the income level of the client group, (3) the type of service offered, and (4) the magnitude of the increase. However, only with very substantial price increases is it likely to endure for longer than three months. If use of a service does not return to its former level within that time, then the problem may lie in the quality of the service. The new price may be reasonable compared to that of substitute services, but client groups may feel the service is inferior to that offered by others. Here the best solution may be to increase the service's quality rather than to reduce its price back to the former level.

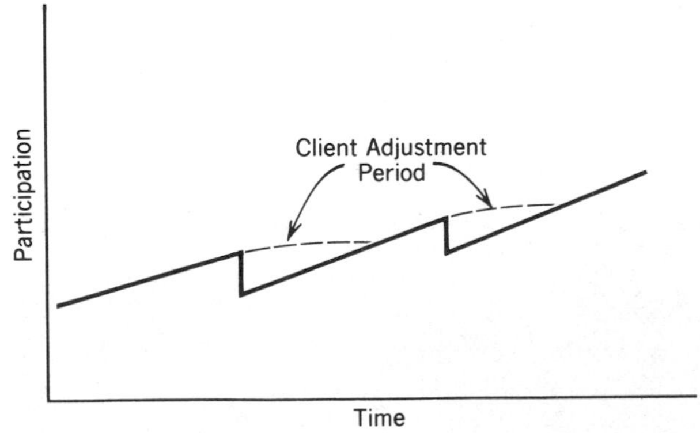

Figure 14.11. Concept of Client Adjustment Period.

The most effective way to minimize length of the client adjustment period is to provide client groups with as much warning as possible of a forthcoming price increase. If awareness of such an increase is established in clients' minds some time before actual implementation, then at least some client adjustment is likely to have taken place by the time the price change occurs.

Changing the Perceived Value of a Service. If a price is to be charged for the first time or if a relatively large price increase beyond the tolerance zone is to be made, clientele resistance may be reduced if their perceived value of the service is raised. If client groups think that the value of the service they are purchasing is commensurate with the new price being charged, then they are less likely to react adversely to the price increase.

The reference or expected price that clients have in their minds for a service is associated with an anticipated level of quality for the service. Increases in quality needed to justify increase in price do not require substantial investment. For example, if a charge is imposed for the first time at a museum or the price of admission is increased, an additional feature such as a conducted tour, special lecture series, or a new exhibit may increase users' perceptions of the value of the service and thus foster acceptance of the price increase.

Alternatively, increasing client groups' perceptions of value may be achieved without any tangible improvement in the service being offered. The perceived improvement may be established in clients' minds by more effective communication of what already exists. There are four ways in which this might be achieved.

First, if an agency receives outside recognition or awards, this can serve to raise the value of its services in users' minds. For example, the City of St. Petersburg won a prestigious White House Award for its Nature Center and Trails while the city's golf course was selected as one of the best 50 municipal courses in the United States. These awards served to point out to citizens the superior quality of the services being offered and made it easier for users to accept price increases.

Second, a detailed description of all a service's attributes and the benefits it offers may assist in raising its perceived value. One recreation agency decided to charge a price of $2 for family uses of a beach at which there had previously been no charge. For the first time the agency stressed all the 20 amenities available at the beach and pointed out that they cost only 10¢ each for a family's use for a whole day. These amenities, which included such things as professional life guards, picnic tables, barbecue pits, and so on, had been available in previous years when there was no admission price. However, no attempt had been made to make users conscious of them. By stressing the range of services available, the agency was seeking to raise its clients' perception of the value of the beach and to reassure them that the $2 admission charge was a reasonable price to pay in exchange for what they received.

Third, changes in perceived value may be obtained by using price comparisons with other substitute services or with nonsubstitute services. Comparison with other suppliers offering similar services may help to emphasize that, although an increase in price has occurred, the new price is still very reasonable. "A round of golf on this course costs $8, which is lower than that of any other course of comparable quality in the area." Comparisons with nonsubstitute services may provide users with a point of reference with which to favorably compare a service's price, "For 75¢ you can swim all afternoon *or* have one large Coke at a fastfood outlet."

Finally, comparing a proposed price with the cost of delivering a service can facilitate its acceptance. One agency that offered a meals-on-wheels service every mid-day to senior citizens in the city requested they give a $1 donation toward the cost of providing the meal. Over a one-year period, 54 percent of their clients donated a dollar. The agency then included a rider on its standard donation request slip that stated that the cost of providing each meal was $2.50. In the subsequent one-year period the proportion of clients offering a donation increased to 73 percent. The cost information provided a reference point enabling clients to quickly identify the magnitude of the subsidy and made them more willing to contribute toward the meal.

Anchor Pricing. The marketing literature suggests that the lowest and highest prices charged for various agency services are likely to be the most noticeable.[21] Thus they serve to anchor potential clients' judgments about the quality of services offered by an agency. In addition, these end prices, together with the reference price, may accentuate the perceived value for a given service (as a bargain) or may diminish the perceived value (as too expensive), depending on where a service's price lies along the continuum of prices. Because swimming prices are very low, a golfer may perceive the price charged for using a public golf course to be too high. Finally, because these anchor prices are more visible than in-between prices, changing them is likely to arouse more clientele resistance than changing any of the intervening prices.

Customary Pricing. Some programs and services have traditional or customary prices. People expect libraries to be free and national parks to have nominal admission charges of $1 to $3. Customary prices are difficult for a manager to ignore. In a sense the existence of customary or traditional prices simplifies the pricing task. These prices have been determined by historical precedent or custom, and it is up to the agency to produce programs or services that may be offered economically at those prices. Clearly the emphasis has to be on cost control.

Customary prices become troublesome during periods of rising costs because of the increasing difficulty of keeping costs low enough to offer a service profitably. In these circumstances it may become necessary to reduce the quantity or quality of the service offered in order to maintain a customary price. For example, street median mowing may be done every four weeks instead of every two; the number of receptionists at a city hall may be reduced from two to one; continuing education classes may be reduced from 90 minutes to 75 minutes; the number of classes in an education program may be reduced from eight to seven; and middle-grade rather than high-grade materials may be used in an arts class. In each case the level of service offered is reduced as an alternative to increasing price.

Whenever possible, cost savings should lead to a reduction in the quantity of an offering rather than a reduction in its quality. The long-term viability of an agency depends on the effectiveness of its services. If this is compromised, then its reputation and image suffer and the confidence and support of users together with their elected representation diminishes.

SUMMARY

A four-stage process is suggested for establishing a price. Stage 1 requires an agency to determine what proportion of the costs incurred in delivering a service should be recovered from direct pricing. Ideally this stage involves a cost accounting system so that an agency can assess the costs attributable to each service delivered. In agencies without a cost accounting system the less accurate method of cost finding can be used. Available financial data are adjusted by some agreed-upon decision rules followed by allocation of costs to derive the needed cost estimates. Before using cost data, the agency has to establish which costs are to be included and attributed to services.

Four methods for recovering some predetermined proportion of costs are available. The full cost recovery, partial overhead cost recovery, and variable cost recovery methods may be viewed as on a continuum. The fourth method, recovery of marginal costs, is a conceptually different approach.

At the end of stage 1, a provisional price is determined based on the proportion of costs that price is designed to recover. Stage 2, in which the going-rate price is determined, is intended to ensure that the provisional cost–based price is adjusted, if necessary, so it is responsive to the willingness or ability of users to pay.

The price at the end of stage 2 is accepted as the average price that service users should be charged. Stage 3 examines the appropriateness of differential pricing, recognizing that there are occasions when offering variations of the average price to particular groups may achieve more equitable and efficient service delivery.

Six criteria are available for dividing a clientele into distinct user groups with differential pricing opportunities. Three groups of participants, children, senior citizens, and the economically disadvantaged, are frequently identified as less able to pay. Product price differentials can be used to offer client groups extra levels of service beyond that usually provided. The most common use of price differentials based on place is charging higher prices to nonresidents. Differential prices on a time basis are intended to encourage use of services at off-peak times and to ration use during peak times. The purpose of a price discount based on quantity is to stimulate additional demand. Finally, price discounts may be used as an incentive for people to try a service.

Stage 4 of establishing a price is a consideration of the psychological dimensions of price. This final stage recognizes that the logical derivation of a price has to be tempered with a realization that client group reactions to pricing decisions are not always logical.

When the price of a new service is being determined, five psychological dimensions should be considered. Contributing to the cost of a service by direct payment of a price may *protect self-esteem,* enhance social responsibility, and remove any sense of stigma or indignity. The first publicized price firmly establishes in the clients' minds what is a fair price for a service. That amount becomes established as the *reference price* to which subsequent price revisions are related.

Sometimes price is used as an *indicator of quality* by intended target markets. In such cases the higher the price, the better the quality is perceived to be. Lower-priced services may be rejected by middle- and upper-income groups who are not prepared to risk the investment of their time, energy, and resources to use a service that the price suggests may be inferior. Prices must be *consistent* with client groups' perceptions and image of an agency and its offerings. *Odd pricing* is frequently used in the commercial sector but appears to have little utility in the public sector.

When existing prices are being revised another five psychological dimensions should be considered. Users have *tolerance zones* for price and if increases are sufficiently small, client usage will not be adversely impacted. Thus increases in price should be frequent and incremental rather than infrequent and substantial. When price is raised beyond the tolerance zone, clients will resist. However, after a *client adjustment period,* client groups will usually adjust, accept the new price as the reference price, and regard it as fair. Client resistance to price changes outside the tolerance zone may be reduced if the *perceived value of a service is raised*. Increases in the *anchor prices,* that is the highest and lowest prices charged for various agency services, are likely to arouse most clientele resistance. Where historical precedent has established a *customary price* which cannot be increased without meeting substantial resistance, then it may be necessary to reduce the quantity or quality of a service in response to increases in costs.

In the past most user prices have been set arbitrarily and intuitively. They have relied heavily on tradition. It cannot be denied that pricing is at least as much an art as a science, and that judgment must play a key role in pricing. Services can be priced purely on the basis of intuition or "feel of the situation" without any attempt to employ a systematic logical approach to price or any examination of the psychological dimensions of consumer reactions to price. An agency that prices by intuition does not necessarily have a poor pricing strategy. However, the chances are good that the agency does not have the best possible pricing strategy. Judgment is required, but it should be informed judgment and not merely a hunch.

NOTES

1. Logalbo, A.T., "Responding to Tax Limitation: Finding Alternative Revenues," *Governmental Finance,* March 1982, p. 19.
2. *Governmental Accounting, Auditing, and Financial Reporting,* Municipal Finance Officers Association of the United States and Canada, Chicago, IL, 1980. Appendix B, p. 59.
3. McRae, R.D., "The Cost-Burden Study: A Method for Recovering Costs from Non-Residents, *Governmental Finance,* March 1982, p. 9.
4. Holder, W.W., Freeman, R.J., and Hensold, Jr., H.H., "Cost Accounting and Analysis." In *State and Local Governments Cost and Managerial Accountants Handbook*. New York: Dow Jones–Irwin 1979, p. 797.
5. Kory, R.C., and Rosenberg, P., "Costing Municipal Services," *Governmental Finance,* March 1982, p. 22.
6. Schoor, B., "Hospitals Scramble to Track Costs as Insurers Limit Reimbursements," *Wall Street Journal,* December 2, 1983, p. 25.
7. Glisson, P.C., and Holley, S.H., "Developing Local Government User Charges: Technical and Policy Considerations," *Govermental Finance,* March 1982, p. 5.
8. Vladeck, B.C., "Why Non-Profits Go Broke," *The Public Interest,* vol. 42, Winter 1976, pp. 86–101.
9. Ibid., p. 89.
10. *New York Times,* March 3, 1977, p. 20. Cited in Rados, D.L., *Marketing For Non-Profit Organizations*. Boston, MA: Auburn House Publishing, 1981, p. 463.
11. Ibid.
12. Coopers and Lybrand Associates Limited, *Service Provision and Pricing in Local Government: Studies in Local Environmental Services*. London: Her Majesty's Stationery Office, 1981, p. 47.
13. Rados, *Non-Profit Organizations,* p. 52.
14. Adapted from Kessel, R.A., "Price Discrimination in Medicine," *The Journal of Law and Economies,* vol. 1, October 1958, pp. 20–53.
15. Mushkin, S.J., and Bird, R.M., "Public Prices: An Overview." In S.J. Mushkin (ed.), *Public Prices for Public Products*. Washington, DC: The Urban Institute, 1972, pp. 22–23.
16. Kozowski, J.C., "Validity of Non-resident and Other Discriminatory Regulations in Municipal Recreation," *Parks and Recreation,* March 1982, pp. 28–34.
17. *McClain v. City of South Pasadena,* 155 Cal. App. 2d 423, 318 P.2d 199 (1957).
18. Kafoglis, M., "Local Service Charges: Theory and Practice." In H.L. Johnson (ed.), *State and Local Tax Problems*. Knoxville: University of Tennessee Press, 1970, p. 183.
19. Weinberg, C.B., "Marketing Planning for the Arts Organization." In M.P. Mokwa, W.M. Dawson, and E.A. Prieve (ed.), *Marketing the Arts*. New York: Praeger, 1980, p. 109.
20. Baron, C., "Recreation Costs and Disabled People," *Recreation Australia,* vol. 1 No. 1, September 1981, p. 26.
21. Monroe, K.B., *Pricing: Making Profitable Decisions*. New York: McGraw-Hill, 1979, p. 45.

FIFTEEN

Promotion: An Overview

Promotion is basically an exercise in communication. Its role is to facilitate exchanges with present and potential clients by informing, educating, persuading, and reminding them regarding the benefits offered by an agency, its programs, or services. To illustrate the importance of these activities, consider the communication tasks facing a performing arts organization:[1]

1. *Informing*. In order to make their decision on whether or not to attend, patrons need basic information on the event itself (what it is, who will be performing) as well as the date, location, time, cost of tickets, and how tickets may be obtained. Promotion is necessary to inform target audiences about the event.
2. *Educating*. For most people, an appreciation of the performing arts is learned or acquired over time. This means that expansion of the audience for the arts requires the development of a level of understanding sufficient to arouse the desire to attend an arts event. This objective is distinguished from informing and persuading because only through education can a patron recognize the value of a particular motivation (a featured performer is of little interest to someone who has no way of evaluating the quality of the performer's work). Thus agencies must educate prospective clients regarding the value of programs and services.
3. *Persuading*. In addition to information, prospective patrons may need to be persuaded to attend events. There are a wide variety of possible "persuaders" including the quality of the performance, the presence of a recognized star, the unique nature of the event (e.g., premiere), special price offers on tickets, convenience of location, pleasant atmosphere, opportunity for personal enrichment, social satisfaction, and the like. The importance of these will vary according to the type of event and the target audience. Promotion communicates this benefit information in an effort to persuade target audiences to attend.
4. *Reminding*. Individuals have many alternatives on which to expend their

time and money. It is necessary to reassure existing supporters and patrons that support of the arts is a wise use of their resources. Reminding them of the personal and community benefits that accrue from their support, as well as demonstrating appreciation for their patronage, is important for confirming and reinforcing future purchase decisions.

The need to educate before attempting persuasion is vividly illustrated by media campaigns encouraging people in developing countries to improve their diets. These campaigns often miss the point that many people lack knowledge of which foods are more healthful.[2]

Effective communication with target audiences is critical to the success of an agency's marketing strategy. Even a well-designed program or service that is capable of satisfying an important need is not likely to be successful unless prospective clients are made aware that it exists, have some understanding of the benefits that it offers them, and know when, where, and how they can obtain these benefits.[3] The City of New Rochelle, New York, for example, relies heavily on promotion to stimulate participation in its CITY-FIT program. Examples of some of their promotional efforts include[4]

A morning CITY-FIT program on a local radio station, giving one specific exercise per week

A daily cartoon in the local newspaper showing the same exercise

Tennis-on-the-streets demonstrations by CITY-FIT staff and recreation leaders

Presentations in junior high school assemblies and grade school classes by CITY-FIT staff

Guest appearances by staff members on local radio and cable television stations

Inserts on fitness and nutrition and other programs in local school newspapers and church bulletins

This chapter provides an overview of the various dimensions of promotion. It begins with a brief discussion of the role of promotion in the marketing process. The second part of the chapter describes the program adoption process and the communication process. This is followed by an introduction to the four main promotional tools available to public agencies: advertising, personal selling, incentives, and publicity. These are explored in detail in Chapters 16, 17, and 18. The chapter concludes with a section regarding budgeting for promotional activities.

ROLE OF PROMOTION

Promotion is frequently viewed from one of two extreme positions, both of which reflect a misunderstanding. In one the terms "marketing" and "promotion" are synonymous, which limits the entire field of marketing to promotional activities. In the other, promotion is seen as wasting taxpayers' money and as misleading.

Marketing: Synonymous with Promotion?

Although all agency activities that are visible to potential client groups are part of the total message that an agency communicates, the term *promotion* refers only to *communication that seeks to inform, persuade, educate, or remind members of a potential client group of an agency's programs and services*. It aids both agencies and clients by (1) establishing exchange contacts, (2) maintaining flows of information that enable an exchange to occur, (3) creating aware and informed clients and agencies who are more likely to negotiate a satisfactory exchange, and (4) improving decision making so that the whole exchange process is made more effective and efficient.[5]

It is important to emphasize that promotion is only one of four basic elements of the marketing mix. Just as a well-designed program or service is not likely to be successful without effective promotion, a first-rate promotional effort cannot overcome deficiencies that result from poor program, pricing, or distribution decisions. As we have stated previously, effective marketing results from careful blending and proper coordination and balancing of *all* of the components of the marketing mix:

> Faced with the problems of getting people to lower their thermostats in winter, those in an energy agency whose view of marketing is limited to promotion would see the problem largely as one of exhorting people to lower their thermostats using patriotic or fuel-cost saving appeals. In contrast, the marketer will in addition seek to encourage the development of products that make it easier for people to adopt the desired behavior, such as devices that automatically lower home heat during the middle of the night or that compute fuel cost savings at various temperature settings. He or she will also be concerned with establishing the right price for these products and ensuring their easy availability.[6]

Effective Promotion: Wasteful or Misleading?

Some people believe that promotion is wasteful—an opinion expressed in a passage often attributed to Ralph Waldo Emerson:

> If a man can write a better book, preach a better sermon, or make a better mousetrap than his neighbors, though he builds his house in the woods, the world will make a beaten path to his door.[7]

Better books, sermons, and mousetraps have all been produced. Many have remained unread, unheard, and unused. Unless the world knows that agencies, programs, and services exist, as well as believing that they offer want-satisfying benefits, these offerings will remain unsuccessful. Without promotion a program literally does not exist in the public eye.

Others who contend that promotion is wasteful cite specific television advertisements as evidence in support of their position. There are, no doubt, television commercials that offend many viewers. However, both public and private sector organizations advertise on television because it is an effective and efficient means of communicating with target audiences. That is the reason why the U.S. government has been one of the 25 largest national advertisers for several years, spending over $100 million annually on advertising.

Although private sector organizations consider promotion as an investment, many public agencies and their constituents view it as a (perhaps unnecessary) cost. In both sectors the ultimate purpose is to stimulate demand. For example, when the U.S. Congress passed the Food Stamp Act of 1977, many members expressed concern that low-income families should be informed about how it would work. Accordingly, the law required the states to inform low-income people, including those receiving public assistance, unemployment compensation, and Supplementary Security Income, about the availability of food stamps and eligibility requirements. In this type of situation, promotion increases the total costs associated with offering a program, not only by its direct costs but also by the increased costs incurred by stimulating demand for the program from additional clientele. This increased cost is a positive outcome because it enables the program to better achieve its objective.

In other situations, if an agency's promotional efforts are successful, it may be able to reduce the net cost associated with the program or service since increased participation may result in increased revenue from user fees or indirect payments.

Effective promotion increases the net benefits provided by the agency. That is, if promotion increases the number of people who take advantage of a public service, the benefit of the service to the community increases. If promotion decreases net costs or increases community benefits, it should be viewed as an investment. If there is no promotion or if the promotion is ineffective in informing, persuading, educating, or reminding potential clients, then net costs are likely to increase and community benefits are likely to decline. Further, if an agency fails to invest adequately in promotion activities, then it is failing in its obligation to communicate to taxpayers, Clearly it is inequitable and unethical for those who are paying for programs or services through the tax system not to be made aware of their existence.

The argument that promotion (particularly advertising) is sometimes misleading has some merit. For example, a chairman of the Federal Trade Commission sent the following memorandum to the heads of federal government agencies that advertise.

> In recent months, the FTC has received complaints that government advertising is inaccurate, misleading, or even occasionally deceptive. Although these complaints are not verified, I am concerned that they may ultimately undermine public confidence in the integrity of communications between the public and the

> government. I therefore want to alert you personally to this potential problem, and offer the services of our advertising review staff should you wish to consult with them regarding any of your advertising campaigns.
>
> Many public and private organizations routinely implement their own internal review procedures to ensure that their advertising is true. FTC staff members also routinely review commercial advertising for truthfulness and accuracy. If you wish to enlist our staff's assistance, either to help review your own advertisements or establish your own internal review procedures, FTC staff members would be happy to assist you in any way.
>
> I am taking the liberty of raising this issue because I strongly believe that we in government have an obligation to monitor our own advertising as scrupulously as we review the advertising in the private sector. There is a special reason for this. In the commercial marketplace we can count on consumers to maintain a healthy skepticism toward product claims because they understand that the purpose of advertising is to encourage sales for a profit. But citizens expect that their government will deal honestly with them, without expectations of gain or profit. To merit their trust, we must hold our own advertising to standards of integrity which are at least as stringent as those to which we hold private advertisers. Indeed, government may ultimately be held to an even higher standard of "fiduciary" responsibility toward the public, and must thus aspire to standards of absolute accuracy and fair dealing in its advertising.[8]

Dishonesty in government is a very sensitive issue, particularly since the so-called Watergate era. Concern about this matter is not restricted to promotion or even to marketing. However, since promotion is highly visible, administrators should take particular care to assure that it is not inaccurate, misleading, or deceptive. An agency seeking the lasting patronage of its clientele will succeed only if it provides accurate and honest information about its programs and services. If the agency promises more from a program than it is able to deliver, its credibility will be damaged. In the long run this is likely to reduce support for the agency and its programs.

Temptation to Overpromise. Sometimes agencies create future problems for themselves by unintentionally misleading client groups through overenthusiastic promotion. This leads to overpromising and exaggeration of the benefits that a program can deliver. Client groups formulate expectations on the basis of messages sent out by the agency and other information sources. If the message claims are exaggerated, clients who use the service will experience dissatisfaction because of the gap between expectations and performance.

Consider the case of the Houston Metropolitan Transit Authority (MTA). When the MTA was established as a regional metropolitan agency it took over existing transit systems that had poor reputations and poor track records. At the outset MTA established unrealistic goals for itself:

> Inheriting extremely poor maintenance facilities, a fleet of Grumman buses with severe structural flaws, and possibly one of the worst traffic situations in the

country, the public's and MTA's, expectations were much too high. The first mistake of MTA was failing to conduct an extensive investigation of where it stood at the outset. Had it done so, the true situation could have been ascertained, and steps taken to ameliorate the situation.

The initial marketing plan devised by Metro illustrates an all-too-familiar scenario. Although the public was told to be patient, the timeframe given was only one year. And *then*, the public was told to expect great things—construction of railways, elevated expressways, etc. The story is similar to that faced by losing sports teams: the season starts with the fans excited about the prospects for the "new" team; by the time the end of the season nears, most fans have gone home, and those who stay are generally disgruntled.[9]

PROGRAM ADOPTION PROCESS

Potential clients pass through a series of stages from first becoming aware of a service to finally using it on a regular basis—stages generally known as the program adoption process. The particular stage in the process that characterizes most potential users directs whether the intent of the promotional effort should be to inform, educate, persuade, or remind.

The five stages that comprise the adoption process are shown in Figure 15.1. They are awareness, interest, evaluation and maybe trial, decision, and confirmation. These five stages evolve over varying time spans. They may take years to come about or they may occur within short periods of time.

Awareness is the stage in which an individual becomes aware of the existence of a particular service but has no detailed knowledge about its content, quality, price, location, or scheduling. The knowledge is vague and generalized. If this stage is characteristic of most potential users then the primary intent of the promotional efforts should be to inform.

At the *interest* stage there is an active search for more detailed information about the service. The potential client believes a new service may provide certain benefits that he or she is seeking and is stimulated to seek information. In this situation, the promotional focus should be to persuade or to educate the clientele by stressing benefits the service offers.

The *evaluative* stage involves an appraisal of the merits of the service and maybe a decision to try it on a small scale. In essence, there is either a mental or an actual trial of the program, with its pros and cons weighed against each other.

If an actual *trial* is impractical, the individual may gain knowledge and insight into the new service through friends, neighbors, or acquaintances. Certainly information and advice from other people may reinforce or assist the evaluation process. If a major equipment, travel, facility, or instruction cost must be incurred, or if a major time commitment is required, many potential clients will be reluctant to participate without first using the service on a small scale.

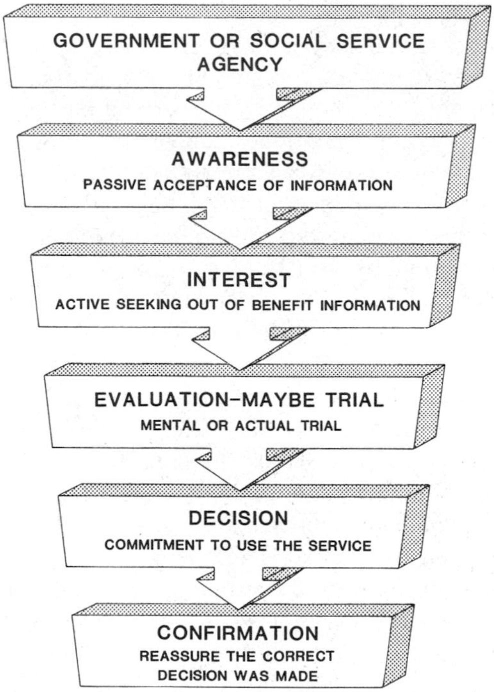

Figure 15.1. The Program Adoption Process.

At this stage the promotional challenge is to persuade potential users to try the service.

At the *decision* stage the service is either accepted or rejected. Here is the culmination of all that has gone before. Initial trial is the result of the decision made at the evaluation stage.

In the *confirmation* stage a client continues to seek assurance that the right decision was made. After experiencing the program, an individual may have second thoughts about continued participation. These subsequent doubts may lead to dissonance, which is a form of tension arising out of uncertainty about the rightness of a decision. Dissonance is likely to be an important factor when a substantial commitment of money or time resources is made. The individual is likely to compare the benefits received from a service with the benefits that might have been received if those resources had been used in some alternative way.

As we observed in the previous section of this chapter, negative feelings may arise through using a service and finding that it fails to create the anticipated benefits. If an agency raises expectations too high, then it increases the risk of clientele disappointment and dissonance.

Dissonance may cause a client to search for additional information from friends or printed material to confirm the wisdom of the initial decision to participate. The role of promotion at this stage is to remind a service's users of the positive benefits that they have received as a result of their decision to participate. If clients cannot be adequately reassured of the correctness of their decision to participate, then they may discontinue participation.

The program adoption process model encourages managers to focus on the decision process rather than only on the actual decision to use or not to use a service. It emphasizes that a decision to participate is usually the culmination of a process that may have started long before the actual participation takes place and may continue long after the first experience with a program.

The promotional challenge is to design communication efforts so they move individuals from their present stage in the adoption process on to the next stage toward a confirmed decision. When a new service is launched the promotional objective should be to inform and generate widespread awareness of the program. Once a target market is aware of an offering, the next stage is to persuade or educate them to become interested in using it.

The toughest promotional challenge often is to move people from the interest stage to trial. There are likely to be many services in which we have an interest, but that we have never tried. Trial is a prerequisite to regular use. Incentives are likely to be a particularly useful promotional tool for inducing trial among those whose interest has been aroused. Finally, an agency should recognize the necessity to remind, reinforce, and reassure its clients that the program in which they are engaged is the most beneficial way of using the resources that they have committed to it.

COMMUNICATION PROCESS

Figure 15.2 shows how the communication process works. The agency has information it wants to share with a potential client group. This information is coded into a transmittable form by putting it into written copy, audio-visual, or verbal forms. The coded message is then transmitted by personal contact, by print or broadcast media, or informally by agency personnel to people they believe will be interested. Members of the potential client group decode (interpret) the message in light of their individual experiences or frames of reference.

The reactions of potential clients provide the agency with feedback on the extent to which the communication was shared. Hence communication is not a one-way, one-time process from an agency to its potential clients. Rather it is an ongoing, endless, two-way process. If the feedback is not satisfactory, the information, the way it is coded, or the way it is disseminated can be amended. This feedback mechanism gives the agency some measure of evaluation and, hence, control in the communication process.

It is also noteworthy that a message from an agency to its targeted client group(s) is subject to the influence of extraneous and distracting stimuli that

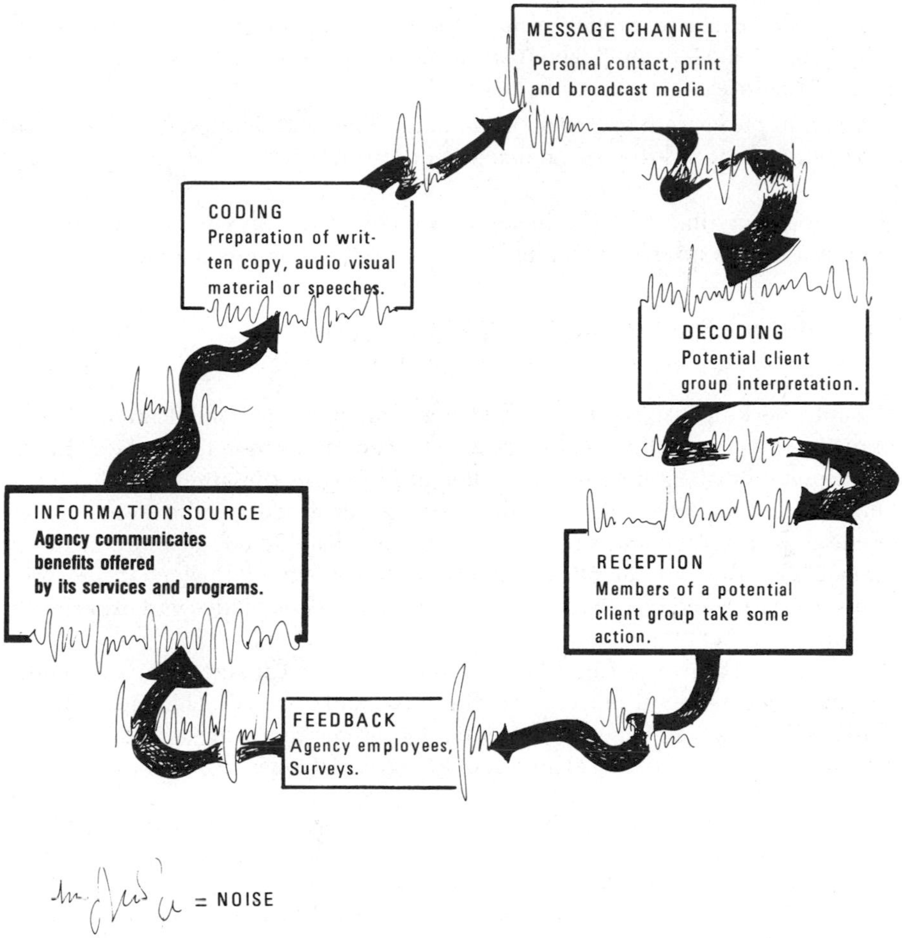

Figure 15.2. Communication Process.

interfere with communication of the message. This interference is referred to as noise. As Figure 15.2 illustrates, noise may distract the transmission or reception of a message at any stage in the process. This noise may prevent the message from being received by members of the potential client groups or lead them to interpret it differently from the way the agency intended:

> When a story about the agency appears near the bottom of an inside page of the newspaper without an eye-catching headline, the competition from other stories and messages on the page may overwhelm it and cause it to be ignored.
>
> Some potential clients of a community education "slimnastics" exercise program may not enroll because they think the program is intended only for "fat people."

A health clinic's promotion of its "stop smoking" program may be ignored by people who feel guilty about smoking but are afraid to try to stop because of past failures.

A poison prevention sticker on a container filled with toxic material may not be heeded by children unfamiliar with the symbol.

Noise exists anytime that the meaning a receiver decodes is not exactly the same as a source intends when he or she codes the communication.

Conditions for Successful Communication

It should be emphasized that contact does not mean communication. Three conditions must be fulfilled before successful communication takes place. First, the message must be designed and delivered to gain the attention of the intended target audience. Second, the message must address the wants of the potential client group and suggest a means for satisfying one or more of those wants. Third, the message must be appropriately positioned, which means that it must relate to, and be consistent with, the existing knowledge and experience of a target market.

It should be apparent from these requirements that if an agency is to communicate successfully it must "start where the audience is." This means identifying, selecting, and analyzing potential target markets as discussed in Chapters 5 and 6. It also implies a commitment to undertaking research. For example

> When immunization levels in Missouri dropped to ominous levels, a promotional plan was designed on the basis of a statewide study of the social-psychological factors affecting the problem. The market was segmented and promotional material was directed to parents and expectant parents. The campaign spokesman, "Marcus Rabbit, M.D.," was created to link the program to children, but to appeal to adults.[10]

The following is a more detailed look at the requirements for successful communications.

Gaining Attention. *The message must be designed and delivered to gain the attention of members of the intended target audience*. This is not as easy as it sounds. Earlier we discussed the difficulties created by noise in the communication system. Each of us has available far more communication than we can possibly accept or decode. We therefore scan our environment in much the same way as we scan newspaper headlines or read a table of contents. We choose messages according to our impression of their general characteristics—whether they fit our needs and interests. We choose usually on the basis of an impression we get from one cue in the story, a picture, a patch of color, or a sound. If that cue does not appeal to us, we may never open our senses to the message. To illustrate, consider the route that you follow to and from work each day. You have probably traveled this path nearly five hundred times during the past year. Yet there are many commercial messages along the way that you do not recall; you have not perceived them.

Perception is the process by which an individual selects, organizes, and interprets information. Three perceptual factors—selective exposure, selective distortion, and selective retention—influence the extent to which an agency's promotional messages reach potential clients with the intended meaning and are remembered.

As the previous example illustrated, we only become aware of a small portion of the numerous pieces of information that are available to us. We engage in a process called *selective exposure*. That is, we select the available inputs of which we want to become aware and ignore the rest. Several conditions facilitate awareness of information:[11]

Addresses a currently felt need. People who have children in school are more likely to read newspaper articles about school activities than those who do not have school-age children.

Relating to an event that is anticipated. A radio advertisement about a forthcoming community theater performance is more likely to reach a regular patron than a person who never attends community theater performances.

Referring to a significant change. The announcement of a small increase or decrease in the price of garbage collection may go unnoticed. A major increase or decrease, however, is more likely to stimulate awareness.

Selective exposure means that agencies have to work especially hard to gain the attention of prospective clients. People who do not recognize a current need for a particular service or program will not select information about the service or program and will not become aware of it. Even interested potential clients may not notice information about a program or service if it does not stand out from competing sources of information.

Selective distortion results when information that reaches awareness is twisted or changed. This condition may occur when information is inconsistent with a person's feelings or beliefs. If, for example, a person has recently been given a speeding ticket by a police officer and is resentful of that action, he or she may distort any positive information received about the police department to make it more consistent with his or her prevailing feelings. This substantially lessens the impact of promotional messages on the individual.

Selective retention means that people remember information that is consistent with their feelings and beliefs and forget information that is not. After hearing a presentation advocating the passage of a bond issue, a person in favor of the issue is likely to remember many of the positive points raised, whereas a person who does not support the measure is likely to quickly forget them.

Addressing Clientele Wants. *The message must address the wants sought by members of the potential client groups and suggest some ways to meet those wants*. In Chapter 1 we discussed two important concepts to which we return at this point. The first concept is that agencies are in the business of facilitating client benefits as opposed to selling programs. The second concept is the importance of asking the question "What is in it for them?" These two concepts provide important guidelines for developing communications with potential client groups. The successful agency must not only offer its potential clientele more than the program itself, but must also communicate and relate these benefits to the aspirations of potential clients.

The literature that public agencies produce to communicate the programs and services they offer is frequently limited to documents that read like telephone directories. They inform but do not persuade or educate. Usually, they list factual information such as the title of the program, its location, and the time it will be offered. Such reference guides are necessary and important, but they should represent only one small part of an agency's overall promotional effort. Reference guides should be complemented by promotional activities and materials that communicate to target audiences the potential benefits of each of the agency's programs. *Typically agency messages do not attempt to communicate the sizzle as well as the steak, but it is the sizzle with which many potential clients are primarily concerned:*

> The Paul Taylor Dance Company took full-page advertisements in the *New York Times* promising that for the $21 price of a ticket, "you will understand sex, power, gravity, music, fear, humor and joy better than ever before." The dance company's subscriptions tripled, and advance sales doubled. Though this frankly commercial pitch ruffled the oh-so-tasteful feathers of the dance community, the company continued to use this approach.

Figure 15.3 shows an extract from a brochure produced on a no-cost, voluntary basis for the Houston YMCA by a commercial advertising agency in Houston. The brochure directly addresses the question "What's in it for you?" It explains benefits that individuals may derive from participating in the services offered by the YMCA. The YMCA uses this brochure as part of their campaign to solicit donations to support their operations. Hence the brochure also addresses the question "What's in it for everyone?" That section seeks to explain to corporate donors and other supporters the benefits to the community of YMCA programs and why their donations should support the YMCA.

Positioning. In Chapter 6 we discussed the concept of positioning. Positioning, which is also important to communication efforts, starts with a program or service. It is what resides in the mind of a client, however, not the physical attributes of the product, that is important. This is the promotional challenge.

To be successful in communicating, it is essential to touch base with the images that already exist in a client's mind. If a communication is transmitted

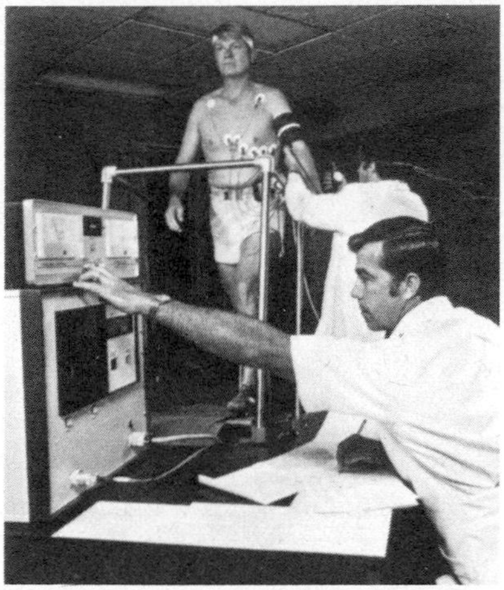

The Downtown Y. What's in it for you?

Fitness Testing Laboratory

The first step before embarking on any program of exercise or strenuous activity should be to find out just where you stand. You need to know how fit you really are so you can decide the kind and amount of exercise you need — and the kind and amount of exercise you should take on. Then, once you get going, you should be re-evaluated periodically to find out how you are doing.

At the Downtown Y, fitness testing is a battery of sophisticated tests conducted by skilled technicians and evaluated by medical personnel. They're carefully planned to evaluate your fitness. Then, essentially, we write an exercise prescription for you. A program that will be suited to your needs and objectives, your interests, your timetable.

The staff makes a detailed analysis of your test results, then sits down with you to work out an exercise program that includes the activities you enjoy and that you have time to participate in. If you request it, we will also forward these test results to your own doctor.

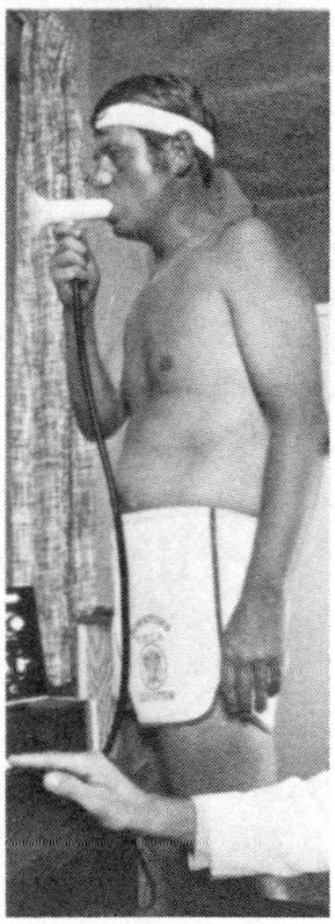

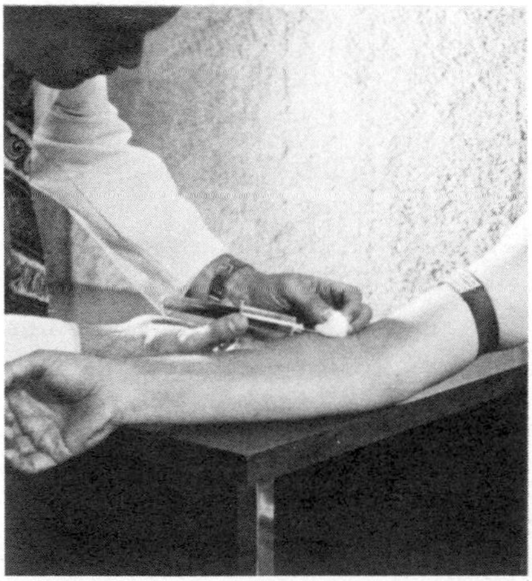

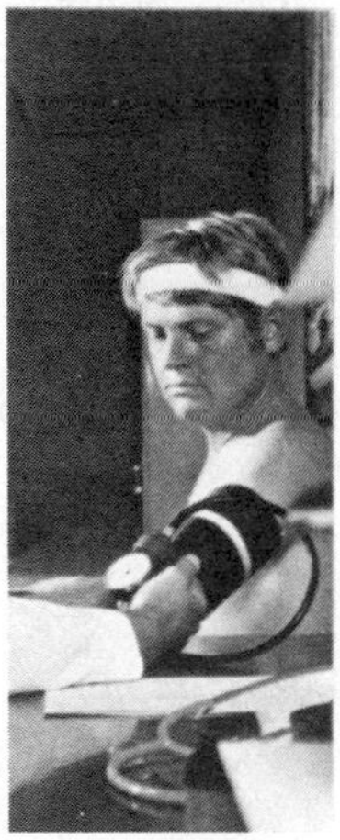

Figure 15.3. Promotional Material Stressing What's in It for You. (*Source:* Houston YMCA).

in a vacuum, its message is unlikely to be received. *An agency must start by relating to the target group's existing experience and knowledge so there is something with which clients can identify and build upon. The communication task is to take a target market from here to there: "Don't wish they'd get there—take them there."*[12]

The use of superlatives suggesting that a program is the "best," "greatest," "highest," "most," or whatever is not likely to communicate effectively. Comparatives that start with where the target market is now and move to where the information source wants the service to be positioned are likely to be much more effective:

> You thought we did that, but in fact we do this.
>
> Our response time was bad, but look at what we have achieved in the past month.
>
> You thought the arts were for the rich, but look who comes.
>
> The $2 million park budget is not an indication of "fat" in government. Rather, it represents an investment of only $10 by every citizen, who for that investment receives free use of all parks in the city for a whole year. That is less than the cost of a single meal in a good restaurant.

Comparative communications such as these are more likely to survive noise and to be received, because they relate to a target market's existing set of beliefs. One final implication should be noted: Don't try to change minds. Accept what is already there and build incrementally upon it. Don't try to wipe it out—people don't change attitudes; they reject messages or information that doesn't fit what they already "know."[13]

PROMOTION MIX

The promotion mix includes those communication tools that an agency uses to inform, educate, persuade, and/or remind members of a potential client group of an agency's programs and services or the agency in general. As noted previously, all agency activities that are visible to potential client groups may be considered parts of the agency's promotion mix. However, the four major activities that we normally consider as components of the promotion mix are (1) advertising, (2) personal selling, (3) incentives, and (4) publicity. These four promotional activities are shown in Figure 15.4.

The following is a brief description of these activities. A more detailed discussion is presented in Chapter 16, 17, and 18.

Advertising is a paid form of nonpersonal communication about an agency and/or its programs and services. It is sponsored by the agency and transmitted to a target audience through a mass medium such as television, radio, news-

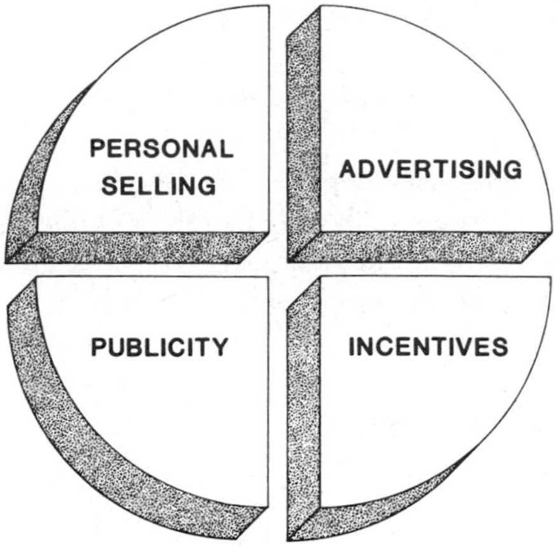

Figure 15.4. Promotion Mix.

paper, magazines, direct mail, mass transit vehicles, outdoor displays, handbills, and directories. Public Service Announcements (PSAs) are a unique form of advertising that are not paid for by the agency. The radio and television air time or print space are donated by a network, local station, or print media vehicle rather than paid for by the agency. However, the agency is often identified as the sponsor of the communication. Advertising and PSAs are discussed in detail in Chapter 16.

Personal selling is direct, personal communication between agency representatives and one or more prospective clients for the purpose of facilitating and expediting an exchange. Personal selling is probably the promotional form most used by public agencies. Every time personnel interact in a professional capacity with present or prospective clientele, they are directly or indirectly communicating something about the agency and/or its services. Thus they are engaging in personal selling. This subject is explored further in Chapter 17.

Incentives are temporary promotions such as price reductions, prizes and special events used by an agency to stimulate trial or increase usage by a client group. Incentives are especially useful when launching new programs and services or when introducing old programs and services to new client groups. Incentives add value to the program or service and therefore reduce the trial costs to clientele. Chapter 18 addresses the nature, scope, and uses of incentives in detail.

Publicity is any unpaid form of news or editorial comment about an agency or its programs that is transmitted through a mass medium at no charge to the agency. It differs from advertising in that it is not paid for and is not sponsored by the agency. Common examples of publicity are news stories, human interest feature stories, and other items in newspapers, radio, television, and magazines. Chapter 18 addresses publicity in detail.

Like the marketing mix, the promotion mix is a set of activities that must be properly coordinated and balanced to achieve optimum results. Decisions regarding one element of the promotion mix influence decisions about each of the other three. No one promotion tool is better, *per se*, than any other. All are equally important. Some situations lend themselves to primary use of one or two ingredients, while in other situations a completely different mix may be appropriate.

Many agencies use personal selling and publicity in preference to incentives and advertising because they perceive the former as free. This may not always be the best strategy. It must be recognized that very real costs are frequently associated with personal contact and publicity. An agency must bear the costs of making up publicity and having it circulated. Similarly the time a manager requires to prepare and deliver a speech to a potential client group or to prepare a publicity release may represent a substantial cost. Indeed if the monetary value of the personnel time committed to these activities was calculated, more effective communication would often be achieved by spending the same amount of money on incentives and/or advertising.

COORDINATING THE PROMOTION MIX

In most instances the ideal promotion mix includes some combination of all four components. In this section we briefly review five factors that influence, and often constrain, promotion mix decisions. These factors are (1) promotion objectives, (2) characteristics of the target market, (3) stage in the program life cycle, (4) financial resources available for promotion, and (5) prohibitions.

Promotion Objectives

The overall goal of promotion programs is to encourage the public to derive full benefit from the services that the agency provides. However, as we discussed in Chapter 3, useful objectives must be specific, operational, measurable, and specify a timeframe for achievement. The objectives should clearly establish whether the promotional effort is intended to inform, educate, persuade, or remind.

If an agency's objective is to inform, then it may attempt to create mass awareness of a new program or service by emphasizing advertising and publicity. In Seattle, Washington, for example, a promotion campaign to create awareness of a special bus service running through the major parks of the city included[14]

Publicity in daily and community newspapers

PSAs on local radio stations

Wide distribution of the bus schedule through community centers, public agencies, and tourist accommodations

Posters in libraries, restaurants, community centers, and other public locations

Advertising in a local news magazine

Extensive use of freelance writers and photographers, resulting in a feature article appearing in *Sunset Magazine*, which has a Seattle circulation of almost 150,000.

If the objective is to stimulate trial usage or participation, incentives may be emphasized.

> Some colleges in recent years have passed out frisbees with their names on them on the beaches of Fort Lauderdale; sent up scholarship balloons; offered finder's fees; sponsored all-expense-paid college weekends for high school counselors and prospective students; and so on. Some hospitals have sponsored filet mignon candlelight dinners for new mothers; televised bingo games for patients; and provided country club memberships for new doctors joining their staff. And family planners in many parts of the world have offered incentives—transistor radios, cookware, costume jewelry, free bank accounts, and so on—to potential adopters of birth control measures.[15]

If the objective is to gain a commitment from individuals to participate, personal selling is often emphasized. Social service organizations whose mission is to reduce personally destructive or antisocial behavior (alcohol, drug, spouse, or child abuse, juvenile delinquency or truancy, suicidal tendencies, rape) must rely heavily on personal selling to gain and maintain commitments from clients to participate in therapeutic programs. Regular personal contact and reinforcement is needed to maintain commitment to, and participation in, corrective programs.

Characteristics of the Target Market

The size, geographic distribution, existing level of awareness, and socioeconomic characteristics of an agency's target market influence the selection of promotion mix variables.[16] If the size of the target market is small, personal contact is usually the most effective means for reaching a limited number of persons. Larger target markets normally require a blending of all four elements of the promotion mix, often with an emphasis on advertising. Likewise, if prospective clients are concentrated in a relatively small geographic area, personal contact may be the most efficient promotional tool to use. If, however, the clientele is dispersed over a wide geographic area, advertising and publicity may be the most efficient promotional tools because of their relatively low cost per client contacted.

Socioeconomic characteristics of targeted clientele such as age, education, and income influence promotional mix decisions in several ways. For example, less educated people are difficult to reach through the print media because they do not tend to read extensively. Thus pamphlets and other printed materials employed in fields such as nutrition and birth control typically reach higher socioeconomic, more literate target markets and neglect the less literate, poorer groups who may have a more compelling need for such information. Similarly adult populations are more likely to read newspapers than are youth populations and lower-income clients may be more influenced by incentives than higher-income groups.

Stage in the Program Life Cycle

In Chapter 9 we observed that programs go through a life cycle beginning with introduction and ending with decline. In the introduction stage, the promotional objective is normally to inform and educate prospective clients. Normally personal contact and publicity are emphasized in this stage. Incentives may also be used to stimulate trial.

In the middle stages of the program life cycle, advertising is often used to persuade and remind clients of the availability of the program or service. During the final stage of the program life cycle, promotional activities are normally reduced and phased out as fewer and fewer clients remain interested in the offering.

Financial Resources Available

In times of tight government budgets it is unlikely that an agency or department will have sufficient funds available to develop what management considers to be an ideal promotion program. Clearly, the amount of money that an agency has available for promotional activities has a substantial influence on the number of promotional tools that can be used and the intensity or frequency with which they can be used. Agencies with extremely limited promotional funds tend to use mainly personal contact and publicity because these activities are considered to be free. Agencies with larger amounts of money available for promotion tend to use the full range of promotion mix techniques.

Prohibitions

Prohibitions often inhibit the range of promotional tools available to the agency. For example, most federal agencies are prohibited from purchasing time or space for advertising purposes.[17] Hence many agencies must rely on publicity and public service announcements to reach prospective clientele through the mass media. At the local and state level, budgets are often allocated for specific purposes. While advertising and/or incentives may not be explicitly prohibited, money simply may not be budgeted for these purposes. This results in implicit prohibitions against such activities. Clearly explicit and implicit prohibitions on the use of some elements of the promotion mix influence strategy alternatives and subsequent decisions.

ESTABLISHING A PROMOTION BUDGET

The promotion budget is the total amount of money allocated for promotional activities for a specific time period. Agencies generally lack reliable guidelines for determining how much to spend on promotion in total, by promotion mix element, and/or by program. Establishing such guidelines is not easy for it is usually impossible to determine the precise impact of promotional activities even after the budget period is over.

Various methods are used to determine promotional budgets. Some of the more common methods are the (1) arbitrary approach, (2) percentage approach, (3) service participation or use approach, and (4) the objective and task approach. These techniques are commonly used to determine promotion appropriations in total as well as the appropriation for individual promotion mix activities.

Arbitrary Approach

The arbitrary approach, sometimes referred to as the *executive judgment* approach, relies solely on the judgment and experience of top management in deciding how much money will be spent on promotion. This approach often results in underspending or overspending because of its arbitrary nature and lack of direct relationship to the agency's communication objectives. However, over time, through trial and error, a "feel" for the appropriate amount may emerge. This occurred, for example, at the Johnson County Recreation Department in Kansas, which offers a wide range of recreational classes. The user registration fee for each class includes $1.60 for the agency's promotional efforts. This amount yields sufficient funds to adequately support a comprehensive promotional effort by the department.

A related approach is called the *all-available-funds* method. Agencies with limited resources may decide to plow back as many dollars as are available into the promotional program. Agencies that adopt this approach usually recognize that their promotional expenditures will be less than desirable but hope to do the best they can with available funds. Typically the all-available-funds approach results in an underbudgeted promotional program that does not produce the desired results. It does, however, challenge the creativity of an agency's staff to get the most "bang for their bucks."

Percentage Approach

This approach entails allocating a percentage of an agency's (or program's) total budget, or revenue from users, to promotion. In using this approach an agency simply multiplies its present or projected total budget or revenues from user fees by a predetermined percentage to arrive at its promotion budget.

The advantages of this method are that it is fairly easy to apply, easy to understand, and appears objective and rational. Furthermore, it seems reasonable to allocate the most money for promotion to those programs that receive the largest budget allocation and/or produce the greatest amount of revenues. These programs or services often reach the largest number of people, frequently have the lowest cost per participant, and usually are deemed the most important.

These advantages, however, are offset by several serious limitations inherent in the percentage approach. First, promotion allocations may be the result (rather than a cause) of success. Almost any program can be made to generate participation given enough promotional resources. Following the same line of reasoning, a program that is not producing adequate participation or revenues from user fees may be considered relatively unsuccessful because it has never had the level of promotional funding necessary to make it successful. If the program continues to have minimal promotional support, it may remain unsuccessful for the same reason.

The percentage approach typically allocates either too little or too much money to specific programs by increasing the promotional allocation for programs that do not need more promotional money and underfunding promotional activities for those programs that need these resources the most. Several other disadvantages that this method shares with the service participation or use approach will be discussed in the following section.

Service Participation or Use Approach[18]

The service participation or use approach to determining promotional allocations has been a popular approach especially with agencies that do not make direct charges to program participants. This method advocates allocating promotional resources in direct proportion to service usage. In other words, those programs that have had the largest use in the past receive the most substantial promotion allocations in the coming time period. Alternatively, those programs that have not demonstrated their success in terms of participation or use (including new programs) receive relatively small promotion allocations.

The popular use of participation or use figures as the criterion for allocating promotional resources among programs and services can be attributed to a number of factors. First, the method is intuitively appealing. Given a limited amount of funds to allocate among various programs or services, it seems reasonable to allocate the most money to those programs or services that are in greatest demand. Not only do these programs or services reach the largest number of people, but frequently they also have the lowest cost per participant.

A second reason for using attendance to allocate promotional resources is that it is ostensibly politically appealing. It appears to adhere to the maxim of the greatest good for the greatest number of people, thereby becoming noncontroversial. An important corollary to this strategy is the belief that more participants means more supporting votes for the program from both legislators and their constituents.

Another justification for using "numbers through the door" is the simplicity and apparent objectivity of the approach. Often instead of using absolute attendance figures for establishing promotion allocations, a ratio of attendance to costs is derived. This ratio gives the cost per client served and may be used to determine which programs and services are most cost-efficient. This approach seemingly eliminates any bias for or against particular individuals, groups, or programs.

A fourth often-stated reason for basing promotion budget allocations on service participation or use is the absence of alternative decision-making criteria. Level-of-use data are readily available, inexpensive to collect, and hence expedient. Although some managers recognize that use is not an ideal criterion for allocation, they are unaware of any better way to allocate resources. Many also use participation or use figures because they believe that this is the only basis for justifying promotion budget requests that will be acceptable to their superiors.

An obvious pragmatic limitation of using participation or use to establish promotion allocations concerns the difficulty of securing accurate data. If one knows that next year's promotion allocation will be based on this year's participation or use, a strong incentive exists to produce large participation figures any way possible. For example, if turnstiles are used to monitor the number of persons entering an art gallery or museum, it is a relatively simple task for employees to inflate attendance data by spinning the turnstile. This possibility also exists when traffic counters are used. Employees may inflate attendance figures by running their vehicles over the traffic counters as often as they like.

Even when electronic or mechanical devices are not used to monitor attendance, program managers or other employees have considerable discretion in determining attendance. A playground supervisor may count casual walkers through the playground as facility users if he or she thinks this will aid promotion allocation prospects. Securing accurate use data is particularly difficult at programs or facilities for which no admission price is charged. If a price is charged, then receipts can be used to cross-check attendance records and the data are likely to be more accurate.

And what about new programs? If promotion resources are allocated based on past participation levels, how is the funding level for a new program to be determined? It is possible that established programs no longer need the same level of promotional support. These resources might be better used to launch new programs or to resuscitate programs that have previously received only modest promotional support. Some new programs or services may require relatively more promotional resources in order to become established, and some older programs may require relatively fewer resources. It takes time for new programs or services to become established and build up demand. They also usually require a substantial allocation of promotional resources if they are to be successfully launched. Attendance may simply be an indicator of a program's stage in its life cycle. Higher attendance figures for one program over another may not indicate the superiority of the former. They may simply be a reflection of the length of time that the program has been offered.

Objective and Task Approach

The method of determining promotional allocations most often recommended by marketing educators and private sector promotion managers is the objective and task approach. This method entails setting promotion objectives, identifying the tasks necessary to achieve the stated objectives, and then determining how much it will cost to achieve the objectives. The objective and task approach is generally considered to be the most desirable method for determining promotional appropriations because it:

- Forces management to focus their attention on setting objectives and the role of promotion in achieving these objectives
- Is based on a philosophy of what is needed as opposed to the availability of funds
- Entails comparing possible outcomes with the cost of achieving them
- Is consistent with the Management by Objectives (MBO) philosophy that many agencies have adopted.

The objective and task approach has two principal drawbacks. First, the approach is difficult and requires specialized skills and judgment that many agencies do not possess because they lack personnel with the necessary training and experience. Second, it often produces promotional allocation requests that exceed available resources, which means the promotion plan will have to be revised. Such a shortage of promotional resources, however, is likely to be encountered whichever allocation approach is adopted.

SUMMARY

Promotion is primarily communication that seeks to inform, educate, persuade, or remind members of a potential client group of an agency's programs and services. Promotion has been criticized as being wasteful, unethical, and manipulative. Abuses of these sorts do occur; however, they are shortsighted and show a failure to understand the real purposes of promotion. An agency must provide accurate and honest information to gain support for its programs. Particular care should be given not to overpromise or exaggerate the benefits a program can deliver because the subsequent gap between client expectations and program performance may lead to client dissatisfaction.

Potential clients pass through a series of five stages from first becoming aware of a service to finally using it on a regular basis. They are awareness, interest, evaluation/trial, decision, and confirmation. Together these stages comprise the program adoption process. The promotional challenge is to design communication efforts so they move participants from their present stage in the adoption process on to the next step toward a confirmed decision. The communication process used in promotion can be broken down into six steps. First, an agency has information it wants to share. Next, this information is coded into a transmittable form by putting it into written copy, audio-visual, or verbal forms. Then the coded message is transmitted. After transmission, members of the potential client group decode (interpret) the message. The last step is feedback; the reactions of the potential clientele provide feedback to agency personnel. Any of these steps can be interrupted by noise. Noise is extraneous and distracting stimuli that interferes with communication of the message.

Three conditions must be satisfied for successful communication to occur. The message must gain attention, address clientele wants, and be appropriately positioned. Individuals' perceptions through the operation of selective exposure, selective distortion, and selective retention influence the extent to which an agency's promotional messages reach intended clients with an accurate, remembered message.

The promotion mix is the set of four communication tools available for an agency's use. These tools are advertising, personal selling, incentives, and publicity. To coordinate the promotion mix, an agency must consider five factors. These factors are the promotional objectives of the agency, characteristics of the target market, stage in the program life cycle, financial resources available for promotion, and prohibitions.

An agency can select from four methods to determine promotional appropriations. These methods are the arbitrary approach, the percent of revenues approach, program attendance approach, and the objective and task approach.

NOTES

1. Adapted from Strang, R.A., and Gutman, J., "Promotion Policy Making in the Arts: A Conceptual Framework." In M.P. Mokwa, W.M. Dawson, and E.A. Prieve (eds.), *Marketing the Arts*. New York: Praeger, 1980, p. 227.
2. Fox, K.A., and Kotler, P., "The Marketing of Social Causes: The First 10 Years," *Journal of Marketing*. vol. 44, Fall 1980, p. 25.
3. Lovelock, C.H., "Concepts and Strategies for Health Marketers," *Hospitals & Health Services Administration*, Fall 1977, p. 52.
4. National Park Service, Marketing Parks and Recreation. State College, Pennsylvania: Venture, 1983, p. 115.
5. Adopted from Nickels, W.G., *Marketing Principles: A Broadened Concept of Marketing*. Engelwood Cliffs, NJ: Prentice-Hall, 1978, p. 301.
6. Fox and Kotler, "Social Causes," p. 26.
7. Fern, Donna. "A Better Mousetrap," *Inc*., March 1985, p. 69.

8. Martin, A.J., "Marketing and Manning the Military," In M.P. Mokwa and S.E. Permut (eds.), *Government Marketing: Theory and Practice*. New York: Praeger, 1981, pp. 90–91.

9. McCoy, M., "Houston Mass Transit Authority." Unpublished paper, Texas A&M University, College Station, Texas. n.d.

10. Fox and Kotler. "Social Causes," p. 29.

11. Berelson, B., and Steiner, G.A., *Human Behavior: An Inventory of Scientific Findings*. New York: Harcourt, Brace, Jovanovich, 1964, pp. 100–102.

12. Ries, A. and Trout, J., *Positioning: The Battle for Your Mind*. New York: McGraw-Hill, 1981, p. 43.

13. Ibid., p. 26.

14. National Park Service, op. cit. p. 116.

15. Kotler, P., *Marketing for Nonprofit Organizations* (2nd ed.). Englewood Cliffs, NJ: Prentice-Hall, 1982, p. 372.

16. Pride, W.M. and O.C. Ferrell. *Marketing: Basic Concepts and Decisions* (3rd ed.). Boston: Houghton Mifflin Co., 1983, p. 40.

17. Weber, S.J., "Government Marketing Through Public Service Advertising." In M.P. Mokwa and S.E. Permut (eds.), *Government Marketing*. New York: Praeger, 1981, pp. 90–91.

18. Based on Lamb, Jr., C.W. and Crompton, J.L. "Qualitative Measures of Program Success." In T.L. Goodale and Witt, P.A. (eds.), *Recreation and Leisure: Issues in An Era of Change*. State College, Pennsylvania: Venture, 1980, pp. 326–338.

SIXTEEN

Advertising and Public Service Announcements

ADVERTISING

In Chapter 15 we defined advertising as *any form of nonpersonal communication about an agency or its programs, which is paid for by an identified sponsor*. The following examples of communication efforts initiated by public agencies are illustrative of the activities embraced by this definition of advertising:

- Brochures, fliers, and other literature describing programs or services
- Annual reports
- Agency newspapers, distributed either quarterly or seasonally, directly by the agency or as a supplement in the community newspaper
- Listings in the Yellow Pages
- Posters
- Direct mailing of information and materials to users and/or nonusers of services
- Billboards
- Newspaper, radio, television, or magazine presentations paid for by the agency
- Signs and posters inside and outside of buses, or on maintenance vehicles

The federal government is consistently listed as one of the 25 biggest sources of paid advertising. Each year the Defense Department spends over $100 million on military recruiting advertising; the U.S. Postal Service engages in extensive advertising; the Peace Corps advertises for volunteers; Amtrak advertises to sell seats on its passenger trains; and the Energy Department advertises to try to boost fuel conservation. State and local government agencies are also actively involved in advertising. Consider the following expenditures in one year by the City of Seattle:[1]

$30,000 for research and $270,000 for production and media placement of advertisements for Metro Transit

$235,000 for a television, radio, and newspaper advertising campaign by Seattle City Light to sell the idea of energy conservation and to promote its own image

$2,500 on six television spots to promote the advantages of living in the city

$2,500 on four television spots promoting the concept of car pooling

This chapter begins with a brief description of the common uses of advertising. The extent to which an agency uses advertising is primarily dependent on its marketing and promotion objectives and the resources that are available. The second section of this chapter is devoted to the subject of developing advertising campaigns. This section describes a seven-step approach to campaign development beginning with identifying and analyzing the advertising target and concluding with evaluating campaign effectiveness. One particular type of advertising on which government and social service agencies rely heavily is public service announcements (PSAs) or advertisements. The third major section of the chapter focuses on the subject of PSAs.

Common Uses of Advertising

There are a number of reasons why an agency may elect to incorporate advertising into its promotional mix. This section briefly reviews several of the more common uses of advertising by public and social service agencies.

Promoting Programs and Agencies. The most general uses of advertising are to promote either specific programs or the agency in general. These goals are often achieved simultaneously. Because a wider audience than the agency's potential client group may be exposed to advertising communications, *agency-sponsored materials have the potential for enhancing not only the image of particular services and programs, but also the image of the agency itself.* Advertisement materials can create awareness and build the image of an agency in a community. This assists the agency in advancing beyond being "another faceless government agency."

Brokaw Hospital's Poison Control Center in Bloomington-Normal, Illinois, developed an educational program to teach children to avoid poisons and instruct teachers and parents in the basics of poison prevention. This program was widely promoted on television, radio, and local newspapers. Terry Trudeau, Director of the Center, has noted that "we have certainly achieved our goals of decreasing the number and severity of childhood poisonings in our area. The Brokaw Poison Center has become a visible entity in the community."[2]

As the Brokaw Poison Center example illustrates, advertising can assist agencies in achieving both specific program goals and enhancing their image. A good image is a valuable asset likely to enhance the acceptance of the agency's programs. Alternatively, if the agency has a negative image or even a neutral, faceless image, it will be difficult to persuade people to try programs. Figure 16.1 is a popular private sector cartoon that illustrates this point clearly.

Adding Value to the Program or Service. *Advertising materials can sometimes add value and meaning to a program or service. "People buy things not only for what they do, but also for what they mean."*[3] Agency-sponsored materials may suggest to potential clients what a program means. Such materials may add value by providing not only factual service information, but also by pointing out hidden meanings and benefits that may be facilitated by the program. Potential clients may be unaware of some of these benefits, particularly if they have had little previous experience with that type of program. Hence the communication may change some potential clients' perception of a program. For example, in Chapter 5 we discussed the results of Graefe's study of people who took float trips on rafts through Big Bend National Park on the Rio Grande River. A wide range of potential benefits one might receive from this experience were identified. Many people seeking adventure, autonomy, or learning about nature do not even think about a float trip as offering these benefits. If the National Park Service desires to stimulate demand for this service, an advertising campaign stressing these benefits might be undertaken.

Making Personal Contact More Efficient. The cost per person exposed to an advertisement is relatively low. For example, the cost of a black-and-white, one-page advertisement in *Time* magazine is approximately $49,335. Since the magazine reaches 4.4 million subscribers, the cost of reaching 1,000 subscribers is only $11.21.[4] Similar cost-per-person-reached figures can easily be derived for any particular media vehicle. The point is that advertising is an economical way to inform prospective clients about available programs and services, and, at the same time, encourage them to contact the agency for additional information. People who seek out additional information about programs and services are more likely to become participants than those who do not. Inquiries provide agency personnel with the names and addresses of likely prospects.

Reminding and Reinforcing Clients. Advertising is often used to remind clients that an established agency, its programs, and/or services still exist and

Figure 16.1. Customer Meets the Salesperson. (Reproduced with permission from McGraw-Hill Publications Company.)

provide certain benefits. Figure 16.2 illustrates this type of advertising. Reinforcement advertising is intended to assure present clients that their participation in programs or use of services is a wise decision. A campaign of the National High Blood Pressure Education Program to encourage hypertensives to maintain their treatment regimen is an example of a program to reinforce existing health behavior.

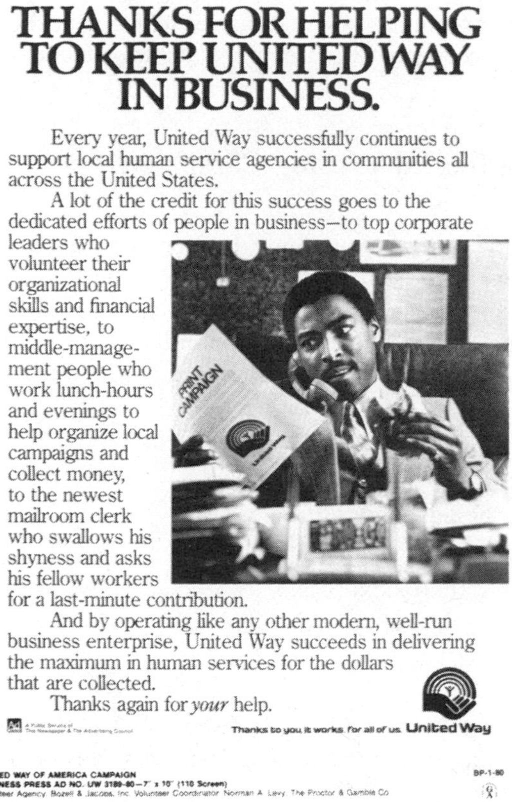
THANKS FOR HELPING
TO KEEP UNITED WAY
IN BUSINESS.
Every year, United Way successfully continues to support local human service agencies in communities all across the United States.
A lot of the credit for this success goes to the dedicated efforts of people in business—to top corporate leaders who volunteer their organizational skills and financial expertise, to middle-management people who work lunch-hours and evenings to help organize local campaigns and collect money, to the newest mailroom clerk who swallows his shyness and asks his fellow workers for a last-minute contribution.
And by operating like any other modern, well-run business enterprise, United Way succeeds in delivering the maximum in human services for the dollars that are collected.
Thanks again for *your* help.
PRINT CAMPAIGN
Thanks to you, it works. For all of us. United Way
UNITED WAY OF AMERICA CAMPAIGN
BUSINESS PRESS AD NO. UW 3189-80—7" x 10" (110 Screen)
Volunteer Agency: Bozell & Jacobs, Inc. Volunteer Coordinator: Norman A. Levy, The Proctor & Gamble Co.
BP-1-80

Figure 16.2. Thanks for Helping to Keep United Way in Business. (Courtesy of The Advertising Council, Inc.)

Reducing Fluctuations in Participation Patterns. Many programs face fluctuations in the number of persons participating in them. Advertising is sometimes an effective means for stimulating demand during those periods when participation is low. Likewise, an agency may refrain from advertising during periods when participation levels are high.

The Miami Beach Chamber of Commerce uses advertising to stimulate vacationing in the area during the summer months, which is its off-season.

Several municipal transit authorities have combined reduced fares during nonpeak hours with widespread advertising of these discount fares to stimulate shoppers to ride between morning and evening rush hours.

A museum that is undervisited on weekdays and overvisited on weekends could (1) shift its special events to weekdays instead of weekends, (2) advertise only its weekday program, and/or (3) charge a higher admission price during the weekends.[5]

A hospital that has an abundance of unoccupied beds on weekends may use advertising in conjunction with incentives to even out the workload between weekdays and weekends. Figure 16.3 is an advertisement designed for this purpose.

Developing the Advertising Campaign[6]

Advertising campaigns are sometimes developed by agency personnel, sometimes by volunteer experts, and occasionally by advertising agencies. Regardless of whether agency personnel play a primary or secondary role in the development of campaigns, it is useful to be familiar with this process. The steps involved in developing an advertising campaign are

1. Identifying and analyzing the advertising target
2. Defining the advertising objectives
3. Creating the advertising theme
4. Determining the advertising budget
5. Developing the media plan
6. Creating the advertising message
7. Measuring effectiveness

In the following sections we will briefly discuss each of these steps and illustrate them using an advertising campaign that was developed by Kent State University.[7]

> In the summer of 1978 Kent State was facing a projected 30 to 40 percent decline in the 1978 entering class following a decline in enrollment of 1,000 students the previous year. The university was already in serious financial trouble. Enrollment had followed an erratic downward trend since 1970 when four students were killed and nine wounded by Ohio national guardsmen during a Vietnam War protest. Throughout the 1970s Kent State suffered an image problem and a variety of incidents widely publicized by the news media reinforced this problem. In 1977, for example, a massive demonstration resulted in the County Sheriff's deputies using tear gas to disperse the crowd and several persons were arrested. Dr. Bruce Allen, a marketing professor at KSU, and the Dix & Eaton advertising agency were assigned the task of halting the decline in enrollment as soon as possible.

Identifying and Analyzing the Advertising Target. The advertising target is the group to whom a specific advertising campaign is directed. It may include the entire target clientele for a program or service or only a portion of the target clientele. Libraries, for example, often direct different campaigns toward specific age groups rather than one campaign toward their total clientele.

Once an advertising target has been identified in terms of age groups, sex, geographic location, and/or other segmentation descriptor, the agency must

Introducing the Sunrise Cruise.

Win a once-in-a-lifetime cruise simply by entering Sunrise Hospital on any Friday or Saturday

RECUPERATIVE MEDITERRANEAN CRUISE FOR TWO

That's all there is to it! Just schedule your admittance into Sunrise Hospital for **any** Friday or Saturday. You'll be eligible to win a free recuperative vacation cruise for two. There's nothing to do. No obligation.

Why this offer?

On weekends Sunrise Hospital has an abundance of unoccupied beds. Yet our facilities and staff must operate around the clock on a 7-day schedule. This costs money!

To reduce operating costs we must even out this workload — make greater use of our facilities on weekends. By shifting weekday admissions to Friday and Saturday we can actually reduce per patient expenses. This will help hold down our rates.

Who is eligible to win?

Every patient who checks into Sunrise Hospital on a Friday or Saturday is eligible to win this free luxury cruise for two. There will be a new drawing every Monday.

You can't always select the day to enter the hospital obviously. But in many cases you can. So suggest to your doctor to arrange your admittance on a Friday or a Saturday. You may check out with an expense-paid "recuperative cruise" for two!

What do you have to do?

Just enter Sunrise Hospital **any** Friday or Saturday. One of the patients who checks in on either of these two days will win the cruise in the Monday drawing.

This is an expense-paid luxury cruise for two. And you'll have your choice of several cruises to be taken within the year. All first class passage!

Most important — there will be a drawing every week, 52 weeks a year! Come aboard.

Sunrise Hospital Medical Center

3186 MARYLAND PARKWAY • LAS VEGAS, NEVADA 89109 • TELEPHONE 731-8000

Figure 16.3. Introducing the Sunrise Cruise. (Courtesy of Sunrise Hospital Medical Center.)

carefully analyze the relationship between its offering and the needs or problems of the advertising target. The advertising target wants to know "What's in it for me?" Identifying salient needs and/or problems of the advertising target is an important step in developing the overall campaign.

As we have noted at other places in this book, the importance of this first step cannot be overemphasized. The identification and selection of advertising targets influences, and often directly determines, all of the ensuing decisions that must be made regarding the advertising campaign as well as the likelihood of its success. Since the process of identifying and selecting advertising targets is analogous to the process of identifying and selecting target markets, which was discussed in Chapters 5 and 6, we will not discuss this matter in detail here.

> The advertising targets for the Kent State campaign were (1) recent high school graduates who might be undecided about attending college and could be "last-minute" full-time enrollees, and (2) older adult part-time students who typically made college attendance decisions near the time of registration. Research on reasons why students choose to attend Kent State and on the permanent home residences of the current student body suggested that the northeastern Ohio corridor encompassing the metropolitan areas of Cleveland, Akron, Canton, and Youngstown would be targeted. The composite market area comprised a population of almost 3 million people.

Defining the Advertising Objectives. After identifying and analyzing the advertising target, the agency should consider what it wants to accomplish with the campaign. This entails specifying advertising objectives. Objectives are normally stated in terms of number of clients reached or serviced. Although the long-run purpose of most campaigns is to increase the number of clients served, not all campaigns are aimed at producing immediate increases in participation. Some campaigns are intended to increase public awareness or knowledge about an agency or program or to influence prospective clients' attitudes, beliefs, or opinions.

Properly stated advertising objectives should possess the same characteristics as other marketing objectives (see Chapter 3). That is, they should be appropriate, unambiguous, prioritized, specific, and attainable, as well as specifying timing.

> The objective of the Kent State campaign was divided into two phases. Phase one was to be focused on an intensive campaign to achieve the maximum enrollment for fall registration in early September. Phase two was to carry forward phase one and begin focusing on student recruiting for the fall term in 1979. In terms of the characteristics of properly stated objectives, Kent State's objectives were clearly appropriate, unambiguous, prioritized, perhaps attainable, and combined with specified timing. However, they were not specific enough because they did not state enrollment goals for each advertising target. We will return to this issue later.

Creating the Advertising Theme. An advertising theme is a statement of the main issues or selling points that the agency wishes to address in its advertisements. A theme should focus on the features, advantages, and benefits that a program offers to prospective clients. In other words, it addresses the question "What do we want to communicate?"

A theme should consist of dimensions of the program that are important to prospective clientele. The best way to identify these dimensions is usually through surveys of members of the advertising target. For example, staff at Children's Memorial Hospital in Chicago solicited theme ideas from their patients. They asked children to tell in their own words what they thought about the hospital and their experiences in it. The children were encouraged to talk about anything they wanted and their comments were recorded on a tape recorder. Their words were the inspiration for a number of themes providing a creativity and spontaneity beyond the capability of professional writers.[8] An alternative approach is for agencies to develop their themes on the basis of past experience, brainstorming, and/or the judgment of their personnel.

The Kent State group generated the following potential themes at a brainstorming session:

We are different and we'll show you the difference is better
Your future is our business
Plan for tomorrow at KSU
KSU road to everywhere
Find yourself
A ticket to where you want to go
Passport to the future
Progression to passport
A different direction
Kent can
Kent State is growing great
The time, the place, the people (your future)
Because we're different, we're better
Kent State makes a difference . . .
. . . Makes all the difference
It can make a difference for you

The "Kent State Makes a Difference" theme was selected unanimously by the planning group and the KSU administration. Time did not permit testing this and other possible themes. As is often the case, a decision had to be made immediately.

Determining the Advertising Budget. The advertising budget is the amount of money that the agency allocates for a campaign over a specified period of time. If the budget is too small the campaign will not be able to achieve its full potential. If it is set too high scarce resources may be wasted. The principal methods used to establish advertising budgets are the four approaches discussed in Chapter 15.

> The advertising budget for the Kent State campaign was $100,000 for one year. This appropriation was arbitrarily set by top administration officials. Their rationale for selecting this figure is not known. Of the available $100,000, campaign planners allocated $60,000 to phase I activities—arresting the enrollment decline for the school year beginning in September 1978.

Developing the Media Plan. Media planning is a three-step process with an overall goal of reaching as many people in the advertising target as possible for each dollar spent. *The first step is to identify the type or types of media that could be used in the campaign.* The most common options include newspapers, magazines, direct mail, brochures, flyers, annual reports, radio, television, transit, and outdoor advertising.

Newspapers. More than 1,800 daily newspapers and over 650 Sunday newspapers provide local, national, and international news to the citizens of the United States. Most of these media vehicles serve local audiences and achieve extensive penetration in their communities. For example, more than 75 percent of the U.S. population are regular newspaper readers. Because of this extensive local penetration, newspapers provide excellent geographic but poor socioeconomic selectivity.

Newspapers normally sell advertising space on the basis of agate lines. An agate line is one newspaper column wide and 1/14 inch deep. Sometimes rates are quoted on the basis of column inches, which are one newspaper column wide and one inch deep.

Magazines. Many magazines provide excellent socioeconomic but poor geographic selectivity. In other words, magazines tend to be targeted at specific age, sex, race, income, vocational, and/or interest groups as opposed to specific communities. Some magazines, however, are targeted at specific geographic *and* socioeconomic groups. *Southern Living, Arizona Highways,* and *Los Angeles* are examples of magazines that focus on regional, state, and local audiences respectively. Other national magazines have regional editions that enable advertisers to focus on regional audiences.

Magazines usually sell space on a full-page or fraction-of-a-page basis. Rates are generally based on circulation. Two common sources of information regarding advertising space charges are rate cards provided by individual media vehicles and the Standard Rate and Data Service (SRDS). The SRDS is the most popular reference source for media planners who want to find out circulation and audience figures, rate information, and production requirements. Since most libraries subscribe to SRDS, this media buying guide is easily accessible.

Direct Mail. Direct mail advertising includes all advertising sent by mail. The use of direct mail as an advertising medium is increasing rapidly among government and social service institutions. Cities and school districts mail out monthly newsletters informing taxpayers of recent events and decisions. Continuing education and recreation agencies inform citizens of upcoming classes in this way. Direct mail's most aggressive use, however, has probably been by institutions of tertiary education.

Successful direct mail advertising is dependent on the availability of good lists of prospects and on the selective use of those lists. For example, colleges and universities obtain lists giving the names and addresses of high-quality high school students from the National Merit Scholarship Corporation. Other lists of students are derived from their registration for the Scholastic Aptitude Test (SAT). With this information universities communicate with qualified potential applicants on a personalized basis by direct mail. Typically they report a response rate of 5 to 10 percent to the direct mail efforts, with 1.5 to 2 percent actually applying to the school for admission.

The main advantages of direct mail are selectivity and timeliness. Direct mail can be targeted as selectively as an agency chooses and can be sent out as quickly as it can be prepared. Lists can be subdivided by geographic area, curricula interest, age, sex, and other relevant descriptors, thus enabling an agency to communicate with its selected target markets. Lists can be obtained that break down the population of a city by small, economic units based on census data supplied by the federal government. Subdividing lists on the basis of census tracts lets an agency reach units of approximately 1,000 individuals who are likely to have similar socioeconomic characteristics.

Because relevant lists are so important for direct mail success, a continual search is made to uncover new prospect lists. For example, in membership renewal mailings, cultural institutions may include a slip that asks for the names of three friends who might be interested in membership. Such institutions may also exchange membership lists with other noncompeting types of cultural institutions.

The average person will spend about five seconds glancing at a piece of third-class mail. If his or her interest is not stimulated in that time, the message will be lost. One axiom in the direct mail business states, "Let a brochure do the telling, but let a letter do the selling." The same sentiments can be expressed a little differently: "A letter is the salesperson; the brochure is his or her sample case."

The classic composition of a direct mail advertising message includes a letter, brochure or folder, return envelope, and a response mechanism. The letter should include an invitation to act by dialing a local or 800 number, returning a postcard, or whatever. The more personalized the approach, the more likely it is that the message will be received. Computerized letter writing has made such personalization feasible.

The major disadvantage of direct mail is that its per-person cost is often much higher than the cost of reaching a similar number of persons through other media. This cost can be reduced if the direct mail piece is included with utility bills or other mail that is regularly sent out to selected individuals or households, or if the direct mail recipients are carefully selected.

Brochures and Fliers. Brochures and fliers are similar to direct mail advertising. The distinguishing feature is that they are not distributed through the mail. Instead they are hand delivered to residences; sent home with school children; made available at agency facilities and/or other locations such as physicians' offices, YMCAs, or commercial establishments; or distributed by hand at meetings, events, shopping centers, and so on. Brochures and fliers share the advantages of selectivity and timeliness with direct mail advertising. They can be targeted as selectively as the agency chooses and can often be distributed as quickly as they can be prepared.

Brochures and fliers can be used to inform, persuade, educate, remind, or reinforce targeted clientele. Simple one-page fliers are commonly used to inform and remind people of the dates, times, and locations of specific events or programs. This is a cost-effective means of achieving widespread dissemination of information.

Persuasion, education, and reinforcement are more difficult communication objectives and often require higher-quality, more sophisticated brochures. An eye-catching headline, stimulating artwork, convincing copy, and a skillful layout enhance the chances of clientele actually reading the brochure. If the communication objective is to convince readers to take action such as immunization, registration, or examination, a local telephone number where prospective clients can acquire additional information should be prominently displayed.

A key to preparing successful brochures and fliers is deciding precisely *who* is the advertising target, *what* is the communication objective, *why* prospective clientele should take the proposed action, *when* action should be taken, and *where* additional information can be gained and action can be taken. These decisions substantially influence the layout and information contained in the advertisement.

Annual Reports. Many government and social service agencies are required by law to prepare and distribute annual reports. Others voluntarily provide this information to their constituents. Many agencies, following the lead of private sector corporations, have recognized the advantages of combining advertising with reporting. Full-color annual reports combined with calendars of scheduled events, important telephone numbers, and information about the agency and its services are often kept in accessible locations throughout the year. They serve as a daily reminder that services are available and the agency is "ready to serve." Figure 16.4 illustrates consecutive pages of an annual report designed to combine advertising with reporting.

The major drawback of professionally prepared annual reports is their cost, often $1 or more per copy excluding mailing charges. Many agencies and even municipalities are unable to bear this expense. One way to reduce the expenses is to sell advertising space in the annual report to commercial enterprises in the jurisdiction. This practice is becoming increasingly popular:

> The Foothills Metropolitan Recreation and Park District near Denver, Colorado, for example, recovers the full cost of publishing its quarterly brochure by selling advertising space in the center section and on the back cover of the brochure.

Another cost reduction method is for multiple agencies to share the cost of preparing and distributing reports. For example,

> The City of Walnut Creek, California combined forces with the Department of Civic Arts and the Department of Leisure Services to prepare and distribute 48,000 copies of a high-quality report. The $12,000 cost was shared by the three agencies on the basis of space used by each.

Radio. There are more than 7,000 radio stations in the United States. Like newspapers, radio is primarily a local medium that is available at a relatively low price. Radio also offers both geographic and socioeconomic selectivity. Geographic selectivity is a result of the relatively short range (about 25 miles) of most radio stations. Socioeconomic selectivity results from programming formats ranging from news/talk to classical, easy listening, rock, soul, and country.

Radio costs vary from station to station and by time of day for each station. The most popular and expensive time is the so-called drive time when people are commuting back and forth between home and work. Advertising rates for most radio stations are published in the *Standard Rate and Data Service*. This publication, available in most libraries, quotes charges for various length spots at different times of the day.

Television. The more than 700 commercial television stations in the United States reach 97 percent of the population. Like radio, television provides the opportunity to be selective on the basis of geographic area and, to a lesser extent, socioeconomic variables.

Spot TV time is normally sold in 10-, 20-, 30-, and 60-second increments. Advertising rates are based primarily on audience size. A principal advantage of television compared to other media is the ability to employ sight, sound, and movement simultaneously.

Transit. Transit advertising consists of posters inside or outside of buses, trains, or other vehicles and around public transportation facilities. Transit is

Patients Served

New	8,506		
Continuing	14,923		
Total	23,429		

Age	%	Race	%
Under 15	2%	White	63%
15-17	15%	Black	21%
18-19	19%	Asian	1%
20-24	38%	Hispanic	14%
25-29	18%	Other	1%
30-34	6%		
35 and over	2%		100%

Clinic Locations

Arlington
Henderson
Northeast
Northside
Southeast
Westridge

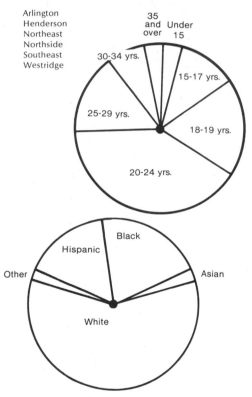

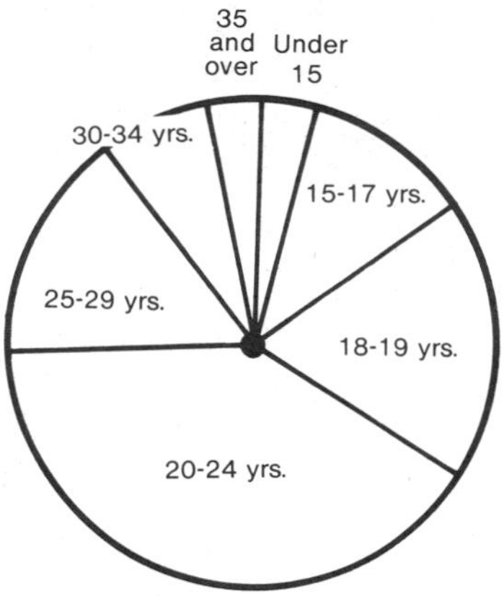

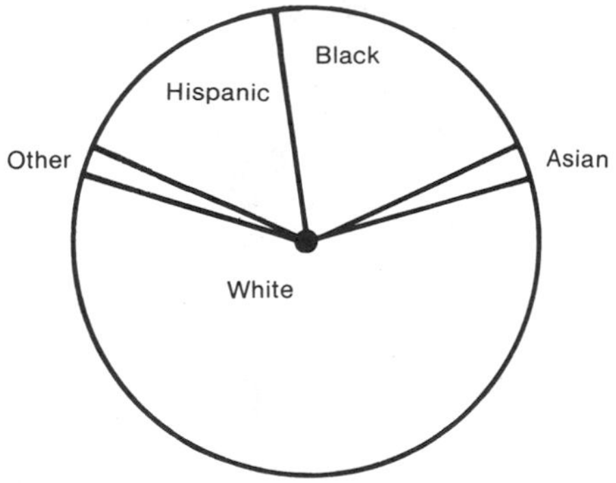

COMMUNITY SERVICES

Goal: To encourage the importance of sexuality education as a lifelong process by making appropriate educational opportunities available in the places where people work and live, and to be an advocate to create and maintain a positive community climate for sexuality education and family planning.

The Community Services Department quadrupled in size during 1983 with the addition of two full-time Community Educators, one part-time Community Educator, and a full-time Information and Communications Assistant. This increase in personnel brought a new diversity to the department; the people hired have skills in communication, counseling, nursing, teaching, media relations, graphic design, program development and presentation.

With this wealth of experience and talent, the Community Services Department sought to improve the quality and increase the availability of sexuality education to the community. Rather than targeting only teenagers and women in their childbearing years, the department began to include people of all ages and stages of life with topics like self-esteem, decision making, family roles and social lifestyles, etc.

Led by Marilyn Farris, Ph.D., Director of Community Services, the Community Services Department served a wide variety of people in diversified settings, as shown by the chart on the following page.

Figure 16.4. Annual Report: Planned Parenthood of North Texas.

a relatively inexpensive medium that offers many advantages including geographic selectivity, repetition, and broad reach. Since transit messages must be short, their primary purpose is to remind prospective clientele that a program or service is available. In some instances, however, transit posters also have pockets for small brochures with more detailed information.

Outdoor. The main purpose of outdoor advertisements is to catch the attention of motorists and repeat a short, clear message to them regularly at a low cost per exposure. Outdoor advertising space is normally rented by the month from so-called plant operators or through advertising agencies. It is sometimes possible for government and social service agencies to "piggy-back" on other people's outdoor posters. For example, a local bank may be prepared to donate the lower third of one of its posters for a message such as "Inoculate your child, public health center next left."

Phone Lines. Some institutions have installed phones lines with recorded messages that provide general information, such as the agenda for a future city council meeting, or that are designed for specific purposes. For example, many recreation departments have installed a "leisure line" that informs citizens about the opportunities available that day or during the coming week. These phone numbers should be listed on all promotional messages and prominently displayed in the telephone directory.

Special promotional efforts may be initiated to make citizens aware of this mechanism. In some instances, incentives are offered to encourage use. For example, a leisure line recording may occasionally say, "If you call the tennis center between 10 and 11 this morning to make a reservation you will receive a 20 percent discount."

Table 16.1 summarizes a number of factors to consider in choosing among alternative media.

The Kent State planning group recommended a campaign combining radio and newspapers. Television was ruled out because of the relatively high cost per message and the necessity of covering a large number of media markets while targeting on specific segments of the viewing audience. Television was considered to be an inefficient luxury that the budget simply would not permit. Other possible media were rejected because of the timeframe for phase I. The campaign had to begin within one month and would only last for approximately five weeks.

The second step in the media planning process is selecting the media vehicle or vehicles. A media vehicle is a specific newspaper, radio or television station, magazine, and so on. Selecting it entails considering not only its cost-effectiveness in reaching the target market, but also the contribution it will make to the agency's image. For example, a private educational institution may reach its 18 to 22 age cohort prime target market most cost-effectively through radio advertisements on a rock music station. Association with a rock music station, however, may hurt the institution's image as a legitimate, serious educational institution.

TABLE 16.1. Characteristics, Advantages, and Disadvantages of Major Advertising Media

Medium	Types	Unit of Sale	Factors Affecting Rates	Cost Comparison Indicator	Advantages	Disadvantages
Newspaper	Morning Evening Sunday Sunday supplement Weekly Special	Agate lines Column inches Counted words Printed lines	Volume and frequency discounts Number of colors Position charges for preferred and guaranteed positions Circulation level	Milline rate = cost per agate line × 1,000,000 divided by circulation	Almost everyone reads a daily newspaper; total circulation is increasing; purchased to be read; read by entire family; nationwide geographic flexibility; short lead time; frequent publication; favorable for cooperative advertising, merchandising services	Not selective regarding socioeconomic groups; short life; limited reproduction capabilities; large volume prevents extensive exposure for any one advertisement
Magazine	Consumer Farm Business	Pages Partial pages Column inches	Circulation level Cost of publishing Type of audience Volume discounts Frequency discounts Size of advertisement Position of advertisement (covers) Number of colors Regional issues	Cost per thousand (CPM) = cost per page × 1000 divided by circulation	Socioeconomic selectivity; good reproduction; long life; prestige; geographic selectivity when regional issues are available; read in leisurely manner	High absolute dollar cost; long lead time

Direct mail	Letters Catalogs Price lists Calendars Brochures Coupons Circulars Newsletters Postcards Booklets Broadsides Samplers	Not applicable	Cost of mailing lists Postage Production costs	Cost per contact	Little wasted circulation; highly selective; circulation controlled by advertiser; few distractions; personal; stimulates actions; use of novelty; relatively easy to measure performance; hidden from competitors	Expensive; no editorial matter to attract readers; considered junk mail by many; criticized as invasion of privacy
Radio	AM FM	Programs: sole sponsor, cosponsor, participative sponsor Spots: 5, 10, 20, 30, 60 seconds	Time of day Audience size Length of spot or program Volume and frequency discounts	Cost per thousand (CPM) = cost per minute × 1000 divided by audience size	Highly mobile; low-cost broadcast medium; message can be quickly changed; can reach a large audience; geographic selectivity; socioeconomic selectivity	Provides only audio message; has lost prestige; short life of message; listeners' attention limited because of other activities while listening
Television	Network Local CATV	Programs sole sponsor, cosponsor, participative sponsor Spots: 5, 10, 15, 30, 60 seconds	Time of day Length of program Length of spot Volume and frequency discounts Audience size	Cost per thousand (CPM) = cost per minute × 1000 divided by audience size	Reaches extremely large audience; low cost per exposure; utilizes sight and sound; highly visible; high prestige; geographic and socioeconomic selectivity	High-dollar costs highly perishable message; audience may enjoy commercial but ignore message; size of audience not guaranteed; amount of prime time limited

(Continued).

TABLE 16.1. (Continued)

Medium	Types	Unit of Sale	Factors Affecting Rates	Cost Comparison Indicator	Advantages	Disadvantages
Inside transit	Buses Subways	Full, half, and quarter showings are sold on a monthly basis	Number of riders Multiple month discounts Production costs Position	Cost per thousand riders	Low cost; "captive" audience; geographic selectivity	Does not reach business and professional persons; does not secure quick or direct results; limited growth
Outside transit	Buses Taxicabs	Full, half, and quarter showings; space also rented on per-unit basis	Number of ads Position Size	Cost per thousand exposures	Low cost; geographic selectivity; reaches broad, diverse audience	Lacks socioeconomic selectivity; does not have high impact on readers
Outdoor	Papered posters Painted displays Spectaculars	Papered posters: sold on monthly basis in multiples called "showings" Painted displays and spectaculars: sold on per-unit basis	Length of time purchased Land rental Cost of production Intensity of traffic Frequency and continuity discounts Location	No standard indicator	Allows for repetition; low cost; message can be placed close to the point of sale; geographic selectivity; operable 24 hours a day	Message must be short and simple; no socioeconomic selectivity; seldom attracts readers' full attention; criticized for being traffic hazard and blight on countryside.

Source: MARKETING: Basic Concepts and Decisions, Fourth Edition, by William M. Pride and O. C. Ferrell, pp. 364–367. Copyright © 1985 by Houghton Mifflin Company. Used by permission.

The third step is determining the dates and times that the advertising will appear. These decisions are based on a number of factors, some of the most important of which are:

- The location and media habits of the advertising target
- The size and type of audiences reached by specific media and media vehicles
- The cost of alternative media
- The amount of the advertising appropriation
- The desired *frequency* or number of times the agency wishes to reach the advertising target
- The advantages and disadvantages of alternative media given the objectives of the advertising campaign.

Sources such as the *Standard Rate and Data Service* and media representatives can provide useful information regarding advertising rates, production requirements, closing dates for advertisements, and the demographic characteristics of specific media vehicle audiences.

> The Kent State planning group identified seven radio stations and 14 newspapers that would be used in the campaign. Newspaper advertisements were to appear in the entertainment section of each newspaper on Thursday, Friday, or Saturday for the duration of the phase I campaign. Radio spots were to run during morning and evening drive time and late evening time slots.

Creating the Advertising Message. The advertising message is influenced substantially by several factors, including the program's features and benefits, characteristics of persons in the advertising target, the campaign's objectives and theme, and types of media selected. The basic components of a print advertising message are copy and art work. Copy is the verbal portion of an advertisement—the headline, subheadline, body copy, and signature. These components are shown in Figure 16.5.

One major commercial advertising agency pointed out the importance of the *headline* to its personnel with this reminder: "Research shows that 90 percent of the people who see your advertisement read *only the headline*."[9] It is the headline that causes a person to decide whether or not to read further. The headline's job is to make contact with members of the potential client group and to persuade them to read the body of the text.

Most effective headlines offer advice or communicate benefits to potential clients and suggest a solution to their problems. Often the headline is in the form of a question designed to gain attention by arousing interest and encouraging potential clients to look for the answer, which should appear in some part of the copy. The *subheadline*, if an advertisement contains one, links the headline to the body copy and/or provides an explanation of the headline.

Headline

Copy

Art Work

Subheadline

Signature

Figure 16.5. Advertisement with the Five Basic Components. (*Source:* The Advertising Council, Inc.)

Body copy seeks to provide potential clients with important facts about the program. Hence the brochure or literature should amplify and support the claims of the headline with more details. It should also address any doubts that individuals may have about the program. Body copy may also provide potential clients with supporting evidence that the program will in fact facilitate the benefits claimed. Endorsements from opinion leaders in the community or previous participants in the program are examples of appropriate evidence. Obviously all claims made for the program must be supportable.

The final objective of body copy is concerned with *action*. Advertising materials are intended to strengthen the determination of potential clients to try the service. Hence the body copy should finish with some suggestion that may spur the reader to take the next step of trying the service.

The *signature* identifies the sponsor of the advertisement. It usually includes the name of the agency, its mailing address, telephone number, and any logos commonly used to identify the agency.

The *art work* is any photograph, drawing, or other form of illustration used in an advertisement. Art work is used to attract attention, to encourage the audience to read the copy, to communicate an idea quickly, or to communicate an idea that is difficult to put into words.[10]

Some useful generalizations concern ways in which the technical or physical attributes of communication materials can best capture the attention of potential client groups.[11]

Movement or the illusion of movement attracts greater attention than static material

Material that is unusual or novel attracts attention

Larger materials attract more attention than smaller ones

The use of contrast in material attracts attention

Color material attracts more attention than black-and-white material

The shape of literature affects attention; taller-than-wide material attracts more attention than wider-than-tall literature

Features or items that appear in isolation in material attract attention

Communications that stimulate more than one physical sense are effective in gaining attention (for example, combined use of sight and sound)

The challenge in advertising is to be selective. The sharper and simpler the message, the more chance it has of being received by a target population. In advertising, more is often less.

Testimonials are often effective in advertising. Intended recipients of a message are more likely to believe a well-known public figure with a reputation for integrity or fellow citizens who have experienced an agency's services than they are claims made by the agency itself. Testimonials are perceived as impartial and objective assessments.

Figure 16.6 is extracted from a brochure advertising a professional training

I thoroughly enjoyed the Southwest Professional Training Institute and found it to be a great learning experience. This was an excellent opportunity to be brought up to date on the latest techniques and methodology being used in the field. I found the instructors to be very knowledgeable in making their presentations.

Rudy Otero
Community Center Supervisor
Albuquerque, New Mexico

All Park & Recreation professionals want to keep up with current trends and developments in their field. The Southwest Professional Training Institute offers an opportunity to do this by providing excellent instruction in a good learning environment. Administrators, Supervisors and all Park and Recreation employees can gain good knowledge to take back to use in their own communities.

Jay E. Ellington
Director of Parks & Recreation
Shreveport, Louisiana

The Southwest Regional Professional Training Institute provided me with an immediate learning experience in determining energy efficiency in facilities, and consequently saved the city an untold number of dollars.

Larry L. Staggers
Community Recreation Supervisor
Little Rock, Arkansas

The new format for the Regional Institute offers an outstanding opportunity for professional growth and development for all therapeutic personnel at all levels.

Larry Mildren
Recreation Program Supervisor
Oklahoma Dept. of Human Services

It has often been said that we must never stop learning, and in our profession one of the best ways to continue learning about our field is by attending the Southwest Region Professional Training Institute, which I wholeheartedly recommend to professionals of all levels and disciplines.

Jack O. Ashworth
Assistant Director of Parks & Recreation
Fort Worth, Texas

Figure 16.6. Opinions of Professionals in the Field. (*Source:* Extracted from National Recreation and Park Association promotional flier advertising their Southwest Regional Professional Training Institute, 1984.)

program for recreation and park professionals in the southwest. Testimonials were obtained from individuals in different states who had previously participated in the program and who were well-known and respected among their peers. Such testimonials are intended to enhance a program's credibility and to encourage the target market to think, "If people of their caliber found it beneficial, then it will probably be beneficial for me." Consider Kent State's use of testimonials in its advertising campaign:

> The Kent State planning group decided to use satisfied customers—present students, alumni, and parents—to convey the "Kent State Difference" theme to the advertising targets. They also decided that a cross-section of spokespersons—by age, ethnicity, program major, and perceived benefits—would be chosen for the campaign. One spokesperson was to be featured per week, or biweekly, in newspapers and on radio in each major market. Each person would be interviewed concerning their Kent State experiences and excerpts of the interviews would be used in the ads. Figures 16.7 and 16.8 illustrate the newspaper and radio spots using former all-pro football player Paul Warfield as a spokesperson. Figure 16.9 shows the media plan for this particular advertisement.

Evaluation. The final step in developing and implementing an advertising campaign is evaluating its effectiveness. This step is necessary to

Determine the extent to which the campaign achieved its stated objective(s)

Evaluate the relative effectiveness of different copy, artwork, layouts, media, and media vehicles

Evaluation may take place before, during, or after a campaign has been completed. *Before tests,* also called pretests, are usually aimed at comparing two or more themes, messages, illustrations, or layouts to identify their relative strengths and weaknesses. Techniques commonly used in pretesting ads include direct ratings and portfolio tests.

Direct ratings use agency personnel and/or panels of target market clientele to evaluate alternative advertisements. Direct rating may be very simple (in other words, "Which advertisement do you think is best?") or may involve several rating scales to evaluate headlines, copy, illustrations, meaning, conviction, and intention to respond.

Portfolio tests entail exposing a group to a "portfolio" that includes both test and control advertisements and perhaps even articles or programming. After subjects are exposed to the entire portfolio they are asked to recall everything that they can remember about it. Recall scores of alternative ads are used to assess their power in gaining and holding attention.

During tests usually assess the efficacy of alternative ads in terms of direct responses:

> One option that was not exercised in the Kent State campaign was to include in newspaper ads coupons or forms for prospective students to send in for additional

Kent State made the difference for Paul Warfield

Paul Warfield won't have any trouble making the transition from an All-Pro player in the National Football League to a member of the Hall of Fame in Canton, Ohio. It's only a matter of time.

A greater challenge for Warfield—as well as other former athletes—is making the successful transition from one career to another.

In his own words, here's how Kent State University helped Warfield prepare to move from the playing field to broadcasting.

"While I attended Kent State University during the off-season for three years, I was especially impressed by the quality of instruction in the telecommunications program.

"I feel very proud that I was able to go to Kent State. The University's academic program, whether in telecommunications or whatever, is excellent. Depending on what students want, they can find it at Kent State. There are strong academic programs, social life, fraternities and sororities, intercollegiate athletics. It is all at Kent State University.

"Kent State does make a difference."

When you register for pre-college tests—either ACT or SAT—make sure Kent State gets your test results. We'll do the rest. For more information, call the Admissions Office collect at (216) 672-2001.

Kent State

makes a difference

Figure 16.7. Kent State Made the Difference for Paul Warfield. (*Source:* Kent State University.)

Testimonial: Paul Warfield *KSU spot 6*
Air: 10/22-10/29
Running time: 60 seconds

Music up and under

Ancr. 1: Paul Warfield talks about Kent State University.

P.W.: Well, I feel very proud that I was able to go here to school and rightfully so, because here in Northeastern Ohio, in television work, there are a lot of Kent State alumni who are doing quite well. There are many others who are working not only on camera but behind camera in Cleveland. . . .

Ancr. 2: Kent State makes a difference.

P.W.: The academic program here, regardless of whether it is in Telecommunications or whatever, is excellent. Depending on what a student wants. I think he can find it here at Kent State. You know, he can certainly find social life, interfraternity life, academics, intercollegiate athletics . . . it is all here at Kent State University. . . .

Ancr. 2: Kent State makes all the difference.

Ancr. 1: Put the Kent State difference to work for you. When taking the ACT or SAT, make sure Kent State gets your test results. To get in touch, call us collect at 672-2001 . . . that's 672-2001.

Ancr. 2: Kent State makes all the difference.

P.W.: It does make a difference.

Music up and out.

Figure 16.8. Script for Paul Warfield. (*Source:* Kent State University.)

Radio Station		*Gross*	*Net*
WGAR	12 spots at $54 =	$648.00	$ 550.80
WWWE	12 spots at 66 =	792.00	673.20
WABQ	15 spots at 12 =	180.00	153.00
WAKR	10 spots at 47 =	470.00	399.50
WKNT	24 spots at 8 =	192.00	192.00(net only)
WKBN-AM	12 spots at 22 =	264.00	264.00(net only)
WDOK	12 spots at 56 =	624.00	530.40
		$3,170.00	$2,762.90

Newspaper		
Plain Dealer (1½)	3 col. × $10 =	$543.90
Beacon Journal (2⅛)	3 col. × 10 =	367.50
Record Courier (1⅜)	4 col. × 10 =	120.40
Canton Repository (1½)	3 col. × 7 =	152.88
Vindicator (1⅝)	3 col. × 7 =	137.55
Reporter (1¾)	3 col. × 7 =	84.00
Call & Post (1⅝)	3 col. × 7 =	73.50
Hub (1 9/16)	5 col. × 10 =	84.37
Parma Post	3 col. × 7 =	132.30
South Euclid	3 col. × 7 =	107.10
Shaker	3 col. × 7 =	132.30
Garfield	3 col. × 7 =	111.30
Chagrin/Solom	3 col. × 7 =	68.25
Metro Student News (1¾)	3 col. × 7 =	176.40
		$2,291.75

Figure 16.9. Media Buys for Paul Warfield Spot 6.

information. Forms could have been coded to identify the specific ad and media vehicle that produced the response.

After tests, also called posttests, involve evaluating the advertising campaign after it has been completed. The two most common posttest methods are recognition and recall tests. In recognition tests, members of the advertising target are shown the advertisement and asked whether they have seen it before. If they respond that they have, then additional questions may be asked. The most widely used recognition test is conducted by Daniel Starch & Staff, an independent research service. The Starch survey measures the following three levels of recognition:

Noted. The percent of readers of a specific magazine who say that they have previously seen the advertisement in the particular magazine.

Seen/Associated. The percent of readers who say they have seen or read any part of the advertisement identifying the sponsor or program/service.

Read Most. The percentage of readers who not only looked at the advertisement but say that they read half or more of the copy.

Recall tests involve asking respondents to recall advertisements that they have seen lately without showing them the actual advertisements. Two types of recall tests are commonly used. In an unaided recall test respondents are asked to identify advertisements that they have recently seen or heard with no clues to aid their memory. Aided recall tests provide respondents clues such as slogans, lists of advertisers, and so on to help them recall specific advertisements.

What effectiveness measures did Kent State use? None! This omission is an obvious flaw in their overall campaign. However, since their objectives were not very specific, it would be difficult to measure the campaign's success. Enrollment did not decline as much as projected before the campaign. The entering enrollment decreased 18.2 percent from 1977 to 1978 and overall enrollment declined 5.3 percent. The administration was quite pleased by these results.

Epilogue: The KSU administration continued the "Difference" theme on a much reduced scale through the spring of 1979. During the summer of 1979 another last-minute recruiting drive was initiated featuring humorous advertisements. Since the initial campaign in the summer of 1978 the trend in enrollment has been reversed and advertising has been continued but with much lower budgets.

Who Develops an Advertising Campaign?

Advertising campaigns may be developed by persons within the agency, specialists within the same government body (city, state, and so on), advertising agencies, or volunteer specialists from outside the agency. In most small agencies advertising materials are developed in-house by personnel. Sometimes these people have the necessary expertise, but generally not. These people often work with representatives from local media vehicles in developing copy, art work, and media schedules. In the development of in-house advertising materials, agency personnel often rely only on their instincts and creativity.

Some agencies, such as municipal departments, can look to other departments within the jurisdiction to assist them in the development of advertising materials. Many cities, for example, have public information offices that employ personnel with previous media experience.

When a government or social service agency retains an advertising agency, the advertising campaign is usually a joint effort developed by representatives of both agencies. The government or social service agency usually assumes responsibility for establishing policies, objectives, and budgets. The advertising agency normally performs the creative tasks of writing copy and preparing artwork. They also develop the media plan, purchase media time and space, and assume the major burden in all aspects of campaign development. The responsibility for overall strategy development, campaign supervision, and evaluation is shared.

Many agencies do not have the resources to retain advertising agencies or specialist promotional personnel on their staff. In some cities members of the commercial advertising community might be an available resource. These specialists are often willing to volunteer their services to a public agency. The benefits to a specialist of volunteering in this way are important even if nonmonetary:

> You won't get paid. In money, that is. But remember how bored you were? You may be getting unbored just thinking about the possibilities. And once you jump in, watch for fringe benefits. Like unshackled creativity. Nothing pumps creative juices like doing something you don't *have* to do. It could be the pure writing pleasure you've been craving. And don't be surprised when these creative juices start spilling over into your nine-to-five work. Public service work is recreation because it breaks your routine. It not only makes you feel good, it gives you a fresh perspective.[12]

In some instances an advertising agency may be prepared to donate its services for some potential long-term benefits. For example, one advertising agency donates it services to a major symphony orchestra because the orchestra has a blue ribbon board of directors. Donated services create goodwill, personal contacts, and general awareness of the advertising agency's competency, which may assist in securing future business accounts from the executives on the orchestra's board.

Professional associations are another possible source of assistance. The Houston Chapter of the Business/Professional Advertising Association (B/PAA), for example, initiated a program in 1982 to provide professional assistance to one public service project annually that is dedicated to the betterment of Houston and its citizens. B/PAA assistance consists of volunteering the time and expertise of members to assist in writing, designing, and producing promotional material for selected nonprofit agencies at no charge.

PUBLIC SERVICE ADVERTISING

An advertisement that appears in space and time donated by the media for the public good is called a public service advertisement (PSA) or announcement. A PSA is defined as

> An announcement for which no charge is made and which promotes programs, activities, or services of Federal, State, or local governments or the programs, activities, or services of nonprofit organizations and other announcements regarded as serving community interests, excluding time signals, routine weather announcements, and promotional announcements.[13]

A PSA differs from a usual advertisement in that the agency does not pay for the allocated time or space. Because the time or space allocated for PSAs is donated, a sponsoring agency does not have any control over when, where, how often, or even whether its message will appear. This is the practical difference between sponsor-paid advertisements and PSAs. In this section we discuss the background of PSAs, characteristics of both broadcast and print PSAs, and how agencies can enhance their PSA exposure in the media.

Background of PSAs

In 1941 the Advertising Council (initially called the War Advertising Council) was formed to inspire public support for conservation of materials, armed services enlistment, and war bonds. After the war, the Council voted to continue its efforts on behalf of philanthropic organizations and government agencies.[14] Since that time the Advertising Council has become the largest single advertiser in the United States. In 1978, for example, the media contributed over $570 million worth of traceable advertising time and space to the council's major public service advertising campaigns.[15] Figure 16.10 shows the extent to which the media used PSAs developed by the Advertising Council to elicit citizen support and cooperation in the 1980 census.

Vitt Media International, an independent media research firm based in New York, has completed an evaluation study of media advertising for the 1980 census. The study estimates that the 1980 census promotion campaign received without charge, approximately $38 million in broadcast time and print space in the nation's media. The campaign, which was placed through the Advertising Council, was one of the main thrusts of the 1980 Census Promotion Program and ran between January and June 1980. Ogilvy and Mather, one of New York's largest advertising agencies, contributed the creative work, and the bureau's only cost was for staff salaries and certain production expenses. The evaluation indicated the dollar values for the free time and space received by the 1980 census campaign to be as follows:

Network TV	$ 8,095,000
Local TV	6,100,000
Network radio	160,000,000
Local radio	15,700,000
Consumer magazines	1,055,000
Trade magazines	100,000
Daily newspapers	520,000
Weekly newspapers	410,000
Outdoor billboards	550,000
Public transit advertising	1,100,000
All black media	500,000
All Spanish language media	3,700,000
Total value	$37,990,000

For the six-month period evaluated, it is estimated that the advertising resulted in an average exposure of 100 census advertising messages for every person in the country.

To demonstrate the relative magnitude of this public service advertising campaign, the $37,990,000 value received in six months can be compared to the following average six months paid advertising media expenditures reported by industry sources for the ten largest U.S. brand advertisers:

Expenditure Rank	Brand	1979 Average 6 Months Gross Advertising Expenditure (millions)
1	McDonalds	$71.0
2	Ford	44.2
	Census Bureau's We're Counting on You Campaign	38.0
3	Purina	36.4
4	Kelloggs	33.5
5	Chevrolet	32.9
6	Bell Telephone	29.4
7	Miller Beer	28.7
8	Toyota	25.9
9	Kodak	25.5
10	Burger King	22.1

Thus the dollar value of the census advertising campaign placed between the second and third largest commercial advertisers in the nation.

In addition to the value of the free advertising reported above, a large but unmeasurable media exposure came from newscasts, interviews, and special programs on radio and television; news stories, articles, and features in newspapers and magazines; support in company, union, and national organization publications; corporate bulletin boards; employee publications; and paycheck and bill inserts. Also, advertising, promotional, and public information materials for print and broadcast media were produced by the bureau and the media for special events and markets. While there is no acceptable audit method for measuring the value of media space and time devoted to this public information (nonadvertising) effort, early reports from studies now underway show that the exposure was very extensive.

Figure 16.10. Evaluation of 1980 Census Promotion. (*Source:* Vitt Media International, New York.)

Figure 16.11 is an example of an Advertising Council message that was seen in newspapers, magazines, the business press, company and college publications, on television, billboards and transit boards, and heard on radio throughout the country.

While the Advertising Council has its critics, it does an outstanding job at achieving its objectives and performs a valuable public service. Although the services of the council are not available to local, state, or even regional agencies, its unique role in the history of PSAs is noteworthy. The process that the council uses to analyze, select, and develop approximately 30 public service advertising campaigns each year from among the 400 or more requests that it receives annually is shown in Figure 16.12.

Broadcast PSAs

In order to use the public air waves a broadcaster (radio or television station) must hold a valid license from the Federal Communications Commission (FCC). When applying for a license applicants have to make specific pledges regarding what percentage of air time will be devoted to commercial uses and what percentage to noncommercial uses such as civic, educational, and other public service programming. When the broadcaster's license expires (normally after a three-year period), the FCC compares the record with pledges made at the time of application. If the FCC decides that the broadcaster has served the "public convenience, interest, or necessity," the license is renewed for another three-year period. If not, the broadcaster's license is subject to revocation. While no formulas are specified, the FCC does consider the number of PSAs aired in its assessment of a station's commitment to public service programming.

The PSA should be regarded by agencies as a product to be marketed. Thus it must be designed with the wants and needs of the media vehicle in mind. In the case of broadcast PSAs, their length should be consistent with the station's practices. Some stations run only 15-second PSA spots. Others use various combinations of 10-, 15-, 20-, 30-, 40-, 50-, or 60-second spots. Different stations accept different combinations of slides, cassette tapes, video tapes, or written scripts. Others write all of their own PSA spots. This information should be elicited before designing the PSA.

Print PSAs

A fundamental difference between broadcast and print PSAs is that broadcasters are committed to providing a specified number of PSAs each year whereas the print media are not. Newspapers and magazines usually regard PSAs as filler. That is, they are used to fill blank spaces that appear while the publication is being prepared.

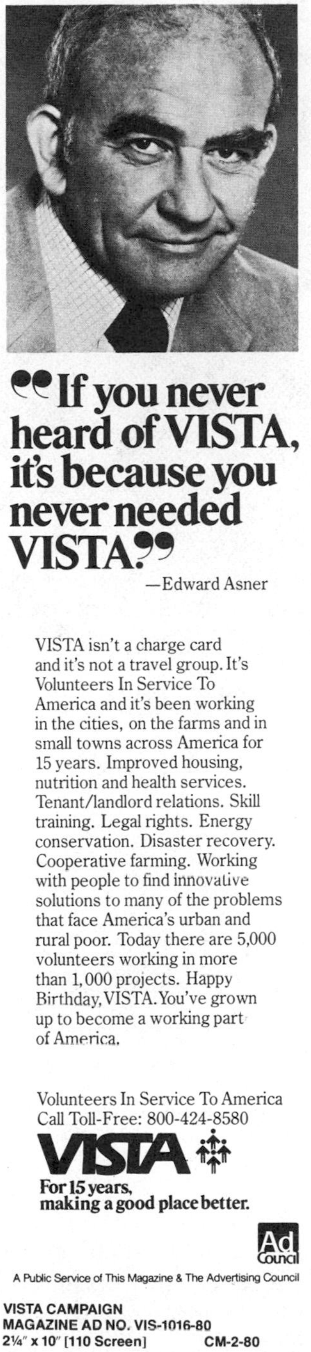
"If you never heard of VISTA, it's because you never needed VISTA."
—Edward Asner
VISTA isn't a charge card and it's not a travel group. It's Volunteers In Service To America and it's been working in the cities, on the farms and in small towns across America for 15 years. Improved housing, nutrition and health services. Tenant/landlord relations. Skill training. Legal rights. Energy conservation. Disaster recovery. Cooperative farming. Working with people to find innovative solutions to many of the problems that face America's urban and rural poor. Today there are 5,000 volunteers working in more than 1,000 projects. Happy Birthday, VISTA. You've grown up to become a working part of America.
Volunteers In Service To America
Call Toll-Free: 800-424-8580
VISTA
For 15 years, making a good place better.
Ad Council
A Public Service of This Magazine & The Advertising Council
VISTA CAMPAIGN
MAGAZINE AD NO. VIS-1016-80
2¼" x 10" [110 Screen] CM-2-80

Figure 16.11. VISTA. (*Source:* The Advertising Council, Inc.)

How the Ad Council Works

A. Approximately 400 requests from private organizations and government agencies are received annually by the Advertising Council requesting campaign support.

B. These requests are analyzed and reviewed by the Council's Director of Campaigns Analysis and other staff executives. The Director gets any needed clarifications from the requesting organizations and forwards the information to the —

C. Campaigns Review Committee — a committee of the Advertising Council Board of Directors which considers the requests in detail and makes recommendations to —

D. The Board of Directors of the Advertising Council which, after discussing and acting on the committee's recommendations, votes on whether to accept the proposal as a major campaign or not.

E. The Public Policy Committee, an independent committee comprising leaders from many walks of life, recommends areas of concern and advises the Board of Directors about their importance to the public, acting as the Council's conscience, and reviewing ongoing campaigns and new proposals.

F. The Industries Advisory Committee, composed of leading business executives, assists the Ad Council and the board in financial, development and other supportive areas.

G. Through the Media Committees of the Board and outside consultants the Council maintains liaison with all the media to help insure maximum usage of the Ad Council's public service advertising campaigns.

H. When a campaign is accepted, a Volunteer Advertising Agency is appointed by the American Association of Advertising Agencies to carry out the creative effort of all media, gratis, charging only for out-of-pocket costs.

I. A Volunteer Coordinator — usually an advertising or marketing executive from a major advertiser is appointed by the Association of National Advertisers, to coordinate all aspects of the approved campaign.

J. The Ad Council appoints a campaign manager from its staff to facilitate the progress of the campaign and maintain liaison with client, agency and coordinator. Staff media managers prepare the public service advertisements for mass duplication and distribution to —

K. All major media who each year contribute available time and space worth over a half billion dollars.

Figure 16.12. Blueprint of Advertising Council Campaigns. (*Source: The Advertising Council 1978–1979 Annual Report*, p. 14.)

Print PSAs are screened soon after they are received by the publication's advertising director or similar official. Many are rejected because they are of poor quality, the wrong size, too controversial, compete with advertisements placed by commercial clients, or judged not to be of interest to the publication's audience. The rest are divided into two categories: those that the publication definitely wants to run and those that it will run if and when space permits. Sometimes a priority number is assigned to each acceptable PSA.

In most cases, decisions regarding which specific PSAs to run are made during the final stages of preparing the publication. For example, morning newspapers are made up the evening before. In most cases this is when decisions regarding which PSAs to run are made. Makeup people identify the dimensions of blank spaces, check their priority lists, and select the highest-ranking PSAs that offer the needed dimensions.

Because the dimensions of available space dictate to some extent which PSAs will and will not appear, it is important to prepare several camera-ready versions of a PSA. The width should be tailored to each publication's column width, and various lengths (for instance, 1″, 2″, 3″, and 5″) should be submitted to each publication.

Billboard PSAs

On occasion billboard companies have space available because it has not been sold. If the space remains vacant, the operators will not receive any revenue. However, if the space is donated for a PSA, the operator receives a tax credit for its donation. This incentive makes billboard operators responsive to requests for PSA space:

> The Friends of the Zoo in San Francisco received $30,000 worth of backlit billboard space from a large outdoor advertising firm. As a public service the Friends were given use of dozens of billboards for a one-year program period. The free advertising for the Adopt-an-Animal program resulted in over $100,000 in new memberships. The outdoor advertising firm received a tax write-off and promoted their new backlit billboards, which were subsequently leased for paid advertising.

Marketing PSAs

Marketing PSAs is, fundamentally, no different from marketing anything else. It entails (1) identifying, selecting, and analyzing target markets and (2) creating and maintaining an appropriate marketing program that satisfies the wants of the individuals and organizations comprising these targets. Although there is intense competition for PSA time and space, a skilled marketer should have little trouble in successfully placing PSAs. One reason is that the media support the concept of public service advertising. Most station managers, program directors, public service directors, publishers, managing editors, and advertising directors take their community service responsibilities seriously and feel pride in their public service performance. In addition, most agencies competing for space and air time are not skilled marketers. Even among those that are, many do not approach the marketing of PSAs with the intensity and commitment that they exercise in their development of services.

A key to success in marketing PSAs is selecting the media that will best reach selected target markets. When the preferred media vehicles have been selected, their PSA policies, procedures, and preferences have to be ascertained. The best way to do this is to schedule appointments with those who are responsible for PSA decisions, thereby establishing a rapport with them and gathering information regarding PSAs in their particular media vehicle.

In some cases media vehicles even offer assistance in the development of an agency's PSAs. Certainly their input before the PSA is developed can improve production quality. Such a cooperative effort is likely to increase media officials' enthusiasm for the campaign, which may help improve the PSA's chances of being used.

PSAs should be distributed one week to 10 days before the planned starting date because many media vehicles develop tentative plans for PSA placements on a weekly basis. In all cases the product should be high quality: "An effective campaign does not need a large number of spots, but rather, just frequent exposure of one professionally produced PSA."[16] Scripts should be typed; tapes and photographs must be crisp. The organization's name, address, telephone number, a contact person and telephone number, the number of seconds the announcement will run (for broadcast), and the preferred dates for the announcement to start and stop should be included.

A number of product characteristics attract media vehicle managers who are selecting PSAs.[17] Most, for example, have a preference for local as opposed to national spots. Many avoid PSAs that are primarily fund-raising appeals, address controversial subjects, compete with commercial clients, or are submitted by agencies that advertise in other media vehicles. Since media vehicles generally avoid running the PSAs of organizations that advertise elsewhere, decisions regarding whether or not to advertise influence the PSA decision as well. In some cases, a media vehicle may be prepared to agree to use a fixed number of PSAs if an agency contracts for an agreed amount of paid advertising.

On the other hand, managers give highest priority to spots that they perceive to have high appeal to their target audience. One of their measuring sticks is to periodically conduct "community ascertainments," which entail interviewing community leaders regarding the most pressing problems in the community. The FCC requires broadcasters to conduct ascertainments and keep them on file. This research may be used to aid in the selection of PSAs.

Whenever possible, PSAs should be personally handed to the decision-making official. This is rarely done, is likely to make a good impression, and will enhance the chances of a PSA appearing. It also establishes contact with a person who can be called to find out if and when an announcement will be used.

The agency should then follow up with a personalized letter of thanks, which will improve the chances of a future PSA being used. Broadcasters are required by the FCC to keep a file of letters that they receive from individuals and organizations. Letters of appreciation from government and social service agencies help a station at license renewal time.

PSAs should be pursued, but their usefulness is limited because the media decide when and where they will be used. Thus in the broadcast media, for example, they are most likely to be aired during non–prime time hours when there is a relatively small audience. Similarly in the print media, they are likely to be found at the bottom of an inside page where they receive relatively little reader attention. Prime time and good locations are reserved for paid advertisements and PSAs are fitted in the remaining space.

SUMMARY

Advertising is any paid form of nonpersonal communication about an agency or its programs, which is paid for by an identified sponsor. The common uses of advertising by government and social service agencies include (1) promoting programs and agencies, (2) adding value to the program or service, (3) making personal contact more efficient, (4) reminding and reinforcing clients, and (5) reducing fluctuations in participation patterns.

Seven steps are involved in developing an advertising campaign. The first step is identifying and analyzing the advertising target. The advertising target may be the entire target clientele for a program or service or only a portion of the target clientele. Once the advertising target has been defined the agency must carefully analyze the needs, wants, or problems of that target that might be served by the agency or specific programs or services.

The second step is defining the advertising objectives or what the agency hopes to achieve with the campaign. Objectives range from increasing the number of clients served to increasing public awareness of the existence of the agency or specific programs.

The advertising theme is the main issues or selling points that the agency wishes to address in its advertisements. An advertising theme should focus on the issues or dimensions of a program that are most important to prospective clientele. Marketing research is often necessary to clearly identify these issues or dimensions.

The fourth step is determining the advertising budget, which is the amount of money that will be allocated to a particular campaign over a specified period of time. Several methods are commonly used for determining advertising budgets, including the arbitrary approach, the percentage approach, service participation or use approach, and the objective and task approach. The objective and task approach is the generally preferred method.

Media planning is a three-step process including (1) identifying the type or types of media to use, (2) selecting specific media vehicles, and (3) determining the dates and times that the advertisement will appear. Commonly used media include newspapers, magazines, direct mail, brochures, fliers, annual reports, radio, television, transit, and outdoor. Each has advantages and disadvantages depending on the campaign objectives and the circumstances.

The sixth step is creating the advertising message. The components of an advertisement include the headline, subheadline, body copy, artwork, and signature. These components work together to attract and maintain the attention of target clientele.

The final step in developing and implementing an advertising campaign is evaluating its effectiveness. Evaluation may take place before, during, or after a campaign.

Advertising campaigns may be developed by agency personnel, specialists within the same government body, or external specialists. Creative managers can draw on the expertise of a wide range of people who can provide direct and indirect assistance in preparing ads.

PSAs appear in space and time donated by the media for the public good. They are similar to other advertisements except that the agency does not pay for the allocated time or space. The Advertising Council has had a profound effect on the quantity and quality of PSAs in the United States and around the world.

Public service announcements on radio and television, in newspapers and magazines, and on billboards can help an agency achieve its promotional objectives. The key to gaining air time or print space is marketing. Although there is keen competition for PSA time and space, a skilled marketer can develop messages and relationships with key decision makers that will produce impressive results at a low cost.

NOTES

1. Lewis, L., "Local Government Agencies Try Advertising," *The Seattle Post-Intelligence Northwest,* March 20, 1977.
2. Trudeau, T., "SIOP—A Poison Prevention Program." In P. Kotler, O.C. Ferrell, and C.W. Lamb, Jr., *Cases and Readings for Marketing For Nonprofit Organizations*. Englewood Cliffs, NJ: Prentice-Hall, 1983, p. 44.
3. DeLozier, W.M., *The Marketing Communications Process*. New York: McGraw-Hill, 1976, p. 221.
4. Pride, W.M., and Ferrell, O.C., *Marketing* (3rd ed.). Boston: Houghton Mifflin, 1983, p. 324.
5. Kotler, P., *Marketing Management: Planning, Analysis and Control*. Englewood Cliffs, NJ: Prentice-Hall, 1984, p. 16.
6. This section is based on Pride and Ferrell, *Marketing,* pp. 345–364.
7. This example is based on Allen, B.H., "Kent State University: Coping with An Image Crisis." In Kotler, Ferrell, and Lamb, Jr., *Cases and Readings,* pp. 249–263.
8. Edwards, S.S., "Would You Listen To What They're Saying," *Hospitals: Journal of the American Hospital Association,* March 1, 1979, pp. 82–84.
9. Cohen, D., *Advertising,* New York: Wiley, 1972, p. 427.
10. Dunn, S.W., and Barban, A.M., *Advertising: Its Role in Modern Marketing* (4th ed.). Hinsdale, IL: Dryden Press, 1978, p. 417.

11. Adapted from DeLozier, M.W., *The Marketing Communications Process*. New York: McGraw-Hill, 1976, p. 221.
12. Spinks, M., *Advertising Age,* February 12, 1979, p. 67.
13. 47 Code of Federal Regulations, 73.112 Note 4.
14. "The Advertising Council: In the Public Interest," *AAAA Newsletter,* May, 1979, p. 4.
15. *The Advertising Council, 1978–1979 Annual Report*. New York: The Advertising Council, 1979, p. 11.
16. Moore, T.J., Gombaski, W.R., and Ramirez, A.G., "Use of Television Public Service Messages by Non-profit Health Institutions: Improving Their Effectiveness." In J.H. Donnelly and W.R. George (eds.), *Marketing of Services*. Chicago: American Marketing Association, 1981, p. 120.
17. Rados, D.L., *Marketing For Non-Profit Organizations*. Boston, MA: Auburn House, 1981, pp. 139–180.

SEVENTEEN

Personal Selling

Personal contact plays three important roles in the marketing of government and social services. First, it is used to gather market intelligence. Personal contact with clients and others in the community provides valuable information for identifying client wants and evaluating the performance of existing programs. Personal contact is an agency's "ears" and helps answer the question "How are we doing?"

A second important role of personal contact is its tangible contribution to the overall benefits provided by a program. Although it may be an exaggeration to say that "the people are the program," there is no question that the people are an important dimension of the program. This issue was addressed in Chapter 9. The Disney example clearly illustrated the importance of personal contact as a program component.

The third role of personal contact is communication—that is, to inform, educate, persuade, and/or remind existing and potential clients of the benefit opportunities offered by an agency and its programs. As noted in Chapter 15, personal selling is one of four elements of the promotion mix. We defined personal selling as *direct, personal communication between agency representatives and one or more prospective clients for the purpose of facilitating and expediting an exchange*. These agency representatives may be agency personnel, board members, volunteers, or others representing the agency in efforts to facilitate exchanges on its behalf.

Personal selling is used extensively by government and social service agency personnel. It involves personally communicating with individuals or groups, and it contrasts with the impersonal communication that is characteristic of the other three elements of the promotion mix. The principal limitation of personal selling is its higher cost per person contacted compared to advertising, incentives, and publicity. Because it involves person-to-person interaction, however, personal selling almost always has a greater impact on prospective clients than the other promotional tools.

Personal selling is unique in its ability to facilitate two-way instead of one-way communication. Agency representatives can receive immediate feedback in the form of verbal exchanges and sometimes nonverbal cues such as expressions and gestures. The flexibility of personal selling enables a communicator to use this feedback to adjust his or her presentation to the specific needs of the individual or group being addressed and to answer any questions and deal with any objections as they arise. The ability to respond to objections makes personal selling a particularly critical element in any communication effort that must overcome resistance from prospective clients. No other promotional tool shares this advantage.

COMMON USES OF PERSONAL SELLING

Agencies rely on personal selling to assist them in achieving a broad range of marketing goals. In this section we briefly review three activities that typically rely heavily on personal selling: recruiting and retaining clients, fundraising, and lobbying.

Recruiting and Retaining Clients

Agencies rely heavily on personal selling to recruit and retain clients. In Chapter 6 we noted that the development of marketing mixes aimed at relatively unresponsive target markets is a problem unique to marketing in government and social service agencies. Often those most in need of alcohol, drug, family planning, emotional, or other kind of treatment, counseling, or service are the least responsive to agency assistance offers. These individuals are also the most difficult to keep enrolled in therapy, counseling, or other types of programs. Advertising, incentives, and publicity are rarely effective in attracting and retaining these least responsive market segments. Success is often dependent on interpersonal relationships that are developed and reinforced through personal selling.

Other types of targeted clientele that need to be recruited and retained include *audiences, members,* and *subscribers*. Joe Kobryner, marketing director of the Old Globe Theater in San Diego, has noted that

> Telemarketing will be *the* marketing tool for the arts in the 1980s . . . . It is revolutionizing nonprofit arts subscription sales . . . .We are still active in direct mail promotion. We use the telephone to follow up on brochures, allowing 7–10 working days for optimum response. After that incubation period, we go after the nonrespondents via phone.[1]

Telemarketing substantially reduces the cost of personal selling while retaining the individual attention provided prospective clients and the opportunity to engage in two-way communications. In fact, Kobryner estimates that it costs the Old Globe less than 15 percent of the subscription price to sell by phone compared to 30 percent for direct mail.[2]

Fundraising

Charitable giving in the United States amounts to over $50 billion per year. Approximately 10 percent of this money is given to social welfare organizations.[3] Several methods are commonly used to solicit these funds from individuals, businesses, foundations, and government agencies. These are begging, collecting, campaigning, and development.[4]

Begging is the pleading by needy people and organizations with others to give them money or other items of value. More fortunate people and organizations, as the argument goes, should take pity on their less fortunate neighbors and give them a helping hand.

Collecting is done by organizations that regularly accept donations from individuals and organizations. Churches, Goodwill Industries, the Salvation Army, and various organizations such as the Muscular Dystrophy Association (MDA) and March of Dimes, place donation containers in convenience stores and rely on them to collect donations. Their attitude is that people should support their cause because it is worthy and makes a positive contribution in the community. This is a passive, inward-looking approach to fundraising.

Campaigning occurs when organizations appoint individuals and groups to actively solicit donations from the public. The normal goal is to canvass every possible source of contributions in a systematic manner. Most universities, the United Way, and many other organizations practice this method of fundraising. The prevailing attitude in campaign-oriented organizations is that many people in the community owe them or ought to support them. They view their task as locating these individuals and/or organizations and convincing them to give.

Development is characterized by carefully identifying homogeneous groups or segments within a heterogeneous market, identifying their motivations for giving, and designing marketing programs that will bring about mutually satisfying exchanges over an extended period of time. The prevailing attitude in development-oriented organizations is

> We must analyze our position in the marketplace, concentrate on those donor sources whose interests are best matched to ours, and design our solicitation programs to supply needed satisfaction to each donor group. This approach involves carefully segmenting the donor markets; measuring the giving potential of each donor market; assigning executive responsibility for developing each market through using research and communication approaches; and developing a plan and budget for each market based upon its potential.[5]

Although the four methods of fundraising evolved sequentially, they all exist today. Some organizations believe that they must beg for support. Others subscribe to the better-mousetrap theory and simply assume that support will be forthcoming for a good cause. Still others believe that if they ring enough doorbells, shake enough hands, mail enough appeals, and generally saturate the market that their fundraising goals will eventually be met. The most progressive and most successful fundraising organizations have moved to the development stage. They have adopted a marketing orientation and have implemented sound, proven, contemporary marketing practices. They recognize that potential donors want to know what's in it for them, and personal selling is often assigned a key role in communicating these benefits to prospective donors.

Lobbying

Supporters of government and social service agencies often seek to influence legislative decision making by gaining the support of elected officials. Lobbying, which might be called legislative marketing, is simply the application of marketing to the target market known as legislators.[6] Hence the set of marketing activities identified in Figure 1.7 provides an appropriate guide for developing a lobbying strategy, which begins with gathering marketing intelligence and includes targeting appropriate legislators, setting objectives, developing, implementing, and evaluating a carefully planned marketing program. Marketing programs designed to influence legislators almost always emphasize personal selling by paid lobbyists, organization leaders, constituents, friends, allied interest groups, and/or other legislators.

Other Activities

Personal selling assumes a major role in a variety of other marketing activities such as recruiting and retaining volunteers and employees, securing grants and contracts, and managing retail operations such as hospital and museum gift shops and university bookstores. Because the tasks involved in personal selling are essentially the same regardless of the specific purpose or audience, the remainder of this chapter focuses on the personal selling process. As Figure 17.1 illustrates, this process includes six steps: prospecting and targeting, preparation, presentation, handling objections, closing, and follow-up. In the following sections we will discuss each of these steps and illustrate them by discussing the personal selling technique used to acquire donations from businesses.

PROSPECTING AND TARGETING

The initial stages in the personal selling process address the first part of a well-known sales aphorism: "Plan your work—and then work your plan." Typically too little thought is given to planning a presentation, which is often the difference between success and failure.

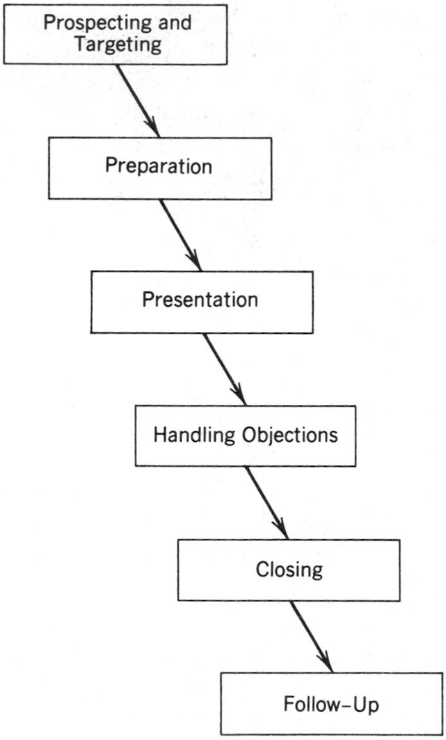

Figure 17.1. Personal Selling Process.

If the first stage is done well and the right prospects are identified, then even if the presentation is difficult some success is likely. On the other hand, an outstanding personal presentation delivered to inappropriate prospects is unlikely to be successful.

The first task involved in prospecting is defining the solicitation target. In our example the target is local business organizations. But all businesses may not be appropriate targets. Some, based on their past donation behavior or other characteristics, are not as likely to respond to the agency's appeal as others. Hence the agency must first obtain a comprehensive list of all local businesses and then classify these prospects based on how likely they are to be responsive to a donation request.

Developing a List of Prospects

A list of businesses in a jurisdiction is likely to be available from the Chamber of Commerce. To limit the list to a manageable length, a minimum size criterion might be established for including a business on the list. The minimum size will vary according to the number of businesses in the community and the magnitude of the donations being sought. For example, in Dallas, Texas, an appropriate minimum size may be businesses that employ over 500 people. Almost 400 businesses in Dallas meet this criterion. In a city of 15,000 people an appropriate criterion may be businesses that employ more than 10 people.

Agencies may consider adopting not only a minimum size but also a maximum size criterion. This enables them to find a niche or market segment in which not as much competition exists for donations. It is likely that the largest business enterprises are prospects of many other agencies in a jurisdiction. Thus, in the case of Dallas, an agency may find more responsive prospects among those businesses that employ 250 to 500 people rather than among larger companies that are always being approached for donations.

Targeting

A campaign-oriented agency targets its efforts at "everybody," while a development-oriented agency aims at "specific somebodies." Once the prospect list has been developed, businesses should be assigned into one of three prospect categories: "hot," "medium," or "cold." Their assignment should be based on four criteria: (1) the size of the business; (2) its image in the community; (3) its past proclivity for working with public agencies; and (4) the extent to which a corporation's interests, products, and target markets match the make-up of the clientele likely to participate in a program.

Larger businesses have greater potential capacity for investing resources in government and social services. In addition, their senior managers are more likely to be "big people" with a broader view of the world and a more sensitive community conscience.

Businesses which have a negative image may be responsive because of their need for good publicity. Government and social service agencies generally have a wholesome, positive image and linkage with them may help a business redeem its public image. However, an agency has to be careful that support from such sources does not tarnish its own image.

If a company has worked with a public agency in the past, then it is likely to be a prime prospect. Such businesses are aware of the benefits to be gained from supporting in the past.

For a company to be "hot" prospect, a program's target markets must match a company's product and target markets. Thus, a key question staff must ask about each program for which corporate support is being solicited is, "What kinds of companies can take advantage of this service, given the target market it is likely to attract, to improve their business?"

PREPARATION

After a list of the most probable prospects has been compiled, the next stage is to prepare an approach tailored to each of these prospects. The preparation commitment is time-consuming but essential. Large donations are more likely to result from good preparation than from good presentation technique, and the larger the donation sought the more detailed and comprehensive the preparation should be. It is often said that failure to prepare is to prepare for failure. Knowledge is power and the more information that can be gathered about a probable prospect, the better an agency is able to develop a presentation that precisely communicates with a prospect and elicits the desired result.

Two questions should be addressed in the preparation stage: (1) what's in it for them? and (2) who in the business enterprise should be contacted and what is their role?

What's in It for Them?

The marketing approach requires an agency to identify what potential donors are likely to want in return for their donation. This information forms the basis for developing a presentation for each prospect. Tailoring the presentation is probably the most important phase in the whole personal selling process. Too often agency personnel spend too much time thinking about their own needs and not enough time considering what their client, the potential donor, wants.

There is no doubt that corporate donations are encouraged by the federal tax laws that permit them to be written off, thus reducing the amount of taxes a company pays on its profits. The tax laws are necessary incentives but they are not sufficient to explain why a company makes a donation. Indeed, although this tax incentive is available to all businesses, only a small proportion of them make donations.

The managers of a business have no mandate to give the company's money away in donations to needy causes. A business makes contributions because it believes that it is in its selfish interest to do so. The president of one of America's largest corporations stated:

> I have heard more than one company say that concern for the arts as such is the guiding force behind its contributions. You won't hear that from us . . . . We do not sponsor . . . . out of the goodness of our hearts. We do it because it's good for the arts, it's good for the millions of people who get pleasure viewing great works of art, and—not least—it's good for our corporation.[7]

If a company's officers make wise donation decisions, then the business will benefit in some way. As Figure 17.2 suggests, the funds at the disposal of a business belong to its stockholders and hence the officers are required to "invest" those funds in projects that will bring a return to stockholders.

Businesses select projects that offer the best return from the large array of donation investment opportunities available to them. A company's "problems" should be the focal point of a personal presentation. The challenge confronting an agency is to suggest how the benefits that a project offers can be translated into investment opportunities by a business so they will contribute to solving or alleviating these problems.

A businessman sees a donation as an "investment" from which some form of benefits will be returned to the business at some future time

Figure 17.2. Businesses Invest; They Do Not Donate.

There are at least four overlapping categories of benefits that business donors seek: (1) financial rewards, (2) enhanced image and visibility, (3) improvements in their community, and (4) higher employee morale.

Financial Rewards. Many firms are now employing the principle of enlightened self-interest in selecting donation recipients. The question "What's in it for me?" is placed at the very top of potential donors' criteria for choosing among alternative appeals for support:

> With deep gratitude, the Statue of Liberty–Ellis Island Foundation recently accepted two special traveler's checks totaling more than $1.7 million from American Express Co.
>
> The gift, along with contributions from others, meant the grande dame of New York Harbor could be restored to past glory, Americans could gaze upon it with renewed pride and the donor could be hailed a corporate patriot.
>
> Moreover, by doing good, American Express managed to do well. It generated the gift money by promising in a national advertising campaign in last year's fourth quarter to donate a penny to the statue for each use of its charge card and a dollar for most new cards issued in the United States. The result: Card usage increased 28 percent during the quarter over the same period in 1982; before the campaign was devised, the company had forecast a card-usage increase of 18 percent for last year's fourth quarter. New card holders rose more than 45 percent during the campaign, and the company's card business had its best fourth quarter ever.
>
> One of the changes in corporate giving involves new meaning for an old term: enlightened self-interest. That has actually been a watchword of corporate phi-

> lanthropy to some degree ever since the nineteenth century, when railroads supported the Young Men's Christian Association, which provided cheap housing for their workers. But now companies have begun applying the principle with greatly heightened sophistication. American Express, for one, is tying charitable outlays to business income far beyond the shore of Liberty Island. In 31 markets around the country, it has supported everything from the Cape Hatteras lighthouse to the San Jose Symphony with the same formula: an advertising blitz pledging a contribution to a local institution for each American Express card use or application. In the case of the San Jose Symphony, the company directly generated $30,000 for the ensemble, raised another $205,000 for it out of the publicity, and raised card usage and new applications in that city by 25 percent. American Express calls it "cause-related marketing."[8]

A less direct example of enlightened self-interest is support for organizations that provide services to the business. Donations may enable the quality or quantity of that service to be extended. For example, some companies view universities as sources of skilled labor for their organization. To ensure that certain skills are taught, they donate money or equipment to specific programs. They may also ensure a steady supply of graduates from these programs by providing students with tuition assistance and assuring jobs for them upon graduation.

Enhanced Image and Visibility. A major goal of many businesses is to establish a positive image and remain visible to their target markets. Agencies can offer companies visibility in several ways besides direct public recognition. Recognition that is of long duration can be achieved by a corporation donating a building, which will always be there for the community to see and use. Alternatively, companies may seek extended recognition beyond the immediate target market through media coverage. One executive, when discussing the donations potential for arts institutions, observed:

> More often than not they take the "hat in hand" approach and ask for charity. Someone in the institution should be assigned to call upon companies to point out that sponsoring an exhibition isn't terribly expensive and that it can play a part in solving communications problems as well as general image building. This is especially true in smaller arts organizations throughout the country. I'm sure there are more than a few business executives who would be interested in this type of constructive approach. A clearly defined return on their investment is something they can easily understand and relate to . . . . In crude terms, the company says "We want to be known as a company that recognizes and pays tribute to excellence. We do so publicly in this exhibition." The institution says, "We will lend our prestige to X company and help it to get the recognition it deserves for bringing this exhibition or concert to the public."[9]

Some managers believe that failure to be visibly responsive to social concerns damages their public image. They view donations as a means to counter criticism that their business is "not a good neighbor," is "profit hungry," or serves no social good. One executive observed:

> It is no longer enough to perform your services well and produce a good product. You have to develop a relationship with your constituency—what I term a psychic bonding. Donations are a means of building empathetic links with constituencies.[10]

Another dimension of using donations to alleviate criticism was expressed by a vice-president of Kaiser Aluminum Company, which is based in Oakland, California. The major financial beneficiaries of Proposition 13 were businesses, and donations were perceived to be one means of averting a backlash against business from the general public:

> Frankly, we wanted to lessen the criticism which we knew would come to the business world and to our corporation if we were not to undertake some sharing of the profits we gained from Proposition 13 in a very visible way.[11]

Community Improvements. A third major benefit that many agencies can offer to businesses is the opportunity to contribute to making their community healthy and attractive. If a community is healthy then its business climate is more likely to be healthy. Urban customer service businesses such as retailers and financial institutions are particularly sensitive to the need for an ordered, attractive environment. If the quality of life in the service area in which they are located deteriorates, the financial health of their business is also likely to deteriorate. Improvement in the health of society will mean, in the long term, improvement in the profits of business.

In addition, an area has to be an attractive place to live and work in order to entice desired employees. Hence businesses may be prepared to invest in projects that contribute to this end. It is increasingly difficult to persuade people to relocate because of the prevailing high interest mortgage rates and the social upheaval that a move inflicts on families. An environment that offers superior amenities and quality of life is likely to be a more effective incentive than money in enticing highly skilled and sought after people to move.

Employee Morale. Donations may be perceived as a means of building employee morale. Matching gifts programs, for example, directly reinforce donation efforts and thus enhance the morale of individual employees. Such a program demonstrates to employees that their company is concerned about the social causes they are concerned about. Shell Oil Company specifies this concern in its donations policy statement:

> Our programs of charitable giving are related to the civic responsibilities of employees of the sponsoring Shell Companies. In a sense, the Company regards itself as their partner in citizenship. For this reason, most charitable support is made on a local basis where Shell people live and work.[12]

These four categories of benefits overlap, representing a broad framework to guide agencies' thinking. An agency has to identify and articulate the specific attributes of a project and relate them to the benefits companies seek. After reviewing the specific benefits a project is able to offer, an agency can winnow a few prime candidates from the probable prospects list. These companies are most likely to be those seeking the primary benefits the project is able to offer *and* access to the target market it is intended to service. At this point the agency concentrates on this small number and asks the remaining preparation question, Who in the business enterprise should be contacted and what is their role?

Who Should Be Contacted?

Most businesses keep donation decision making within the company. Others have established corporate foundations through which donations are channeled. A foundation is intended to "take the heat off" company officers being inundated with requests from impassioned fundraisers and permit a professional staff to make donation decisions. In addition, a foundation is an independent, nonprofit arm of a company: If any negative results should emerge from a donation, the company is better able to disassociate itself from responsibility for the project. The discussion here is limited to decision making within the company.

The coordination of donation investments in a large business may be performed in any one of a variety of different departments. The donation contact person in eight major companies in Houston, Texas, for example, have the following titles:

Community and Employee Relations Manager
Manager of Contributions and Public Relations
Public Relations Director
Director of Civic Affairs
Vice President in Charge of Human Resources
Director of Communications
Director of Donations for the Houston Region
Vice President of Advertising

Sometimes a substantial effort is needed to identify the key contact person with responsibility for donations in major companies. This responsibility is assigned differently by each business. Seldom does a single person spend all of his or her time on donations. It is more common for this responsibility to be one of several that the individual undertakes.

Once the contact person has been identified, that individual's role in the decision-making process has to be ascertained. The corporate actors who play a role in the decision process fall into three categories: gatekeepers, influencers, and decision makers.[13] One person may fill more than one of these roles.

It is likely that the contact person will be a gatekeeper. This person may simply receive the donation request and forward it to others who make the decisions through the company's established channels. Alternatively, the gatekeeper may be assigned the role of a "first screener" who eliminates some requests and forwards a selective list to the decision makers. The manner in which a gatekeeper passes along a request may be critical. If he or she is not personally supportive, the information may be related less accurately and with fairly evident disapproval. Thus the gatekeeper is a key person in determining the success of a request and should be "won over" by the personal selling effort. Agency personnel should try to persuade gatekeepers to permit them to present their case directly to the decision makers. This will ensure that the proposal is presented in its best light and that any questions or objections can be answered.

An influencer's views or advice help shape the attitudes of decision makers, while the latter decide how to respond to the donation request. The decision maker may be either a member of an in-house contributions committee comprised of executives from a variety of divisions who review donation requests, or an individual. If any individual is the sole decision maker, he or she is likely to be limited in the amount of money that can be authorized for individual donations. For example, managers at local and regional levels may be authorized to invest in donations up to say $2,000, and $5,000, respectively, and amounts over these limits may have to be forwarded to corporate headquarters for approval.

Donation requests should be initiated at the highest level to which an agency can gain access. It has been observed that "top level managers are paid to say yes, while middle-managers are paid to say no." Senior managers generally have a broader perspective and a more acute community social conscience than junior managers. For these reasons they are more likely to be responsive to donation requests. Too often agencies make the mistake of confining personal contacts to employees at lower levels because managers feel less intimidated with them and hope that the request will filter up to the key decision makers.

An important adage in soliciting donations is that people give to people first and needy causes or organizations second. This is true of corporate executives. Donation success is more likely to be attributable to positive personal chemistry than to the worthiness of a cause.

An agency must search for linkages between its personnel and the gatekeepers, influencers, and decision makers in a targeted company. The key questions are: "Who on the staff knows any of the key corporate actors?" and "Who can we enlist as an ally?" The best types of linkages are personal acquaintances, but if these links are relatively weak then it becomes important to seek referrals. Are there any mutual contacts who could introduce agency personnel to key company officials? The more intimately an agency's personnel are interwoven into the community structure, the more likely it is that there will be either personal acquaintances or referral opportunities.

The agency's task is to learn as much as possible about the individuals who are gatekeepers, influencers, and decision makers and to match their backgrounds with those of senior agency personnel. A substantial body of empirical research demonstrates that positive interaction between the potential donor and agency representatives is greatly facilitated if their backgrounds, personalities, interests, and lifestyles are compatible.[14] The greater the perceived similarities, the stronger the mutual attraction or affinity between them is likely to be. When personal contact between agency and company officials takes place, any common experiences and interests help create personal chemistry and emotional ties.

PRESENTATION

An effective sales presentation completely and clearly explains all aspects of the agency's proposition as it relates to the benefits sought by each prospective donor or donor group. During the presentation the prospect perceives and reacts to mannerisms and nonverbal communications as well as vocal messages. The nonverbal communication consists of signal language (handshake, posture, personal grooming, facial expression, proxemics, and so on), object language (clothing, briefcase, office decor), and sign language (gestures).[15] During the initial exchange of social formalities the speech volume, speed, pitch, resonance, rhythms, and intonations say as much or more than the words themselves. The sum effect of all the vocal qualities communicates the emotional feelings and intensity behind the message. To quote a popular aphorism, "It is not what you say, but how you say it that counts."[16]

While there are many ways of making a presentation, the three most commonly used methods are presented here. As Figure 17.3 illustrates, these approaches vary from highly structured to semi-structured to unstructured.

Stimulus-Response Approach

The stimulus-response approach is based on the assumption that there are direct links between stimuli and behavioral responses. This technique is based on stimulus-response learning theory, which has its origins in psychology. Pavlov's classic study in which dogs associated the ringing of a bell with being fed is one of the best-known experiments supporting the stimulus-response technique.

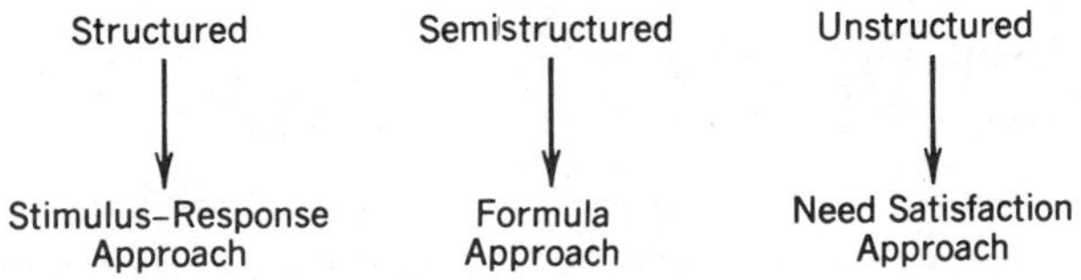

Figure 17.3. Structure of Sales Presentations.

In practice, memorized or "canned" presentations that are used over and over again are examples of the stimulus-response approach. The agency representative presents a series of words or phrases (stimuli) in an orderly manner to elicit a sought response from the prospect. There is a hope that the presentation will "ring the bell" with the client.

The stimulus-response approach has been proven effective in situations in which the desired response requires only simple decision making by the receiver(s). Its major advantage is that it is a comfortable technique for persons who are relatively inexperienced. The speaker is never at a loss for words, never loses his or her place, and never misses an important point that they wish to cover.

The major limitation of the stimulus-response technique is that it assumes that all persons and audiences will respond to the same stimuli in the same way. It fails to recognize differences in the needs and motives of prospects. Furthermore, the person using this technique controls the conversation and does most of the talking. Two-way communication is not developed, the receiver's viewpoint is not revealed, and the speaker often fails to gain any feedback from his or her prospective client or audience.

Formula Approach

The formula approach is similar to the stimulus-response method. It is based on the assumption that similar prospects in similar situations can be approached with similar presentations. The presentation is structured but not memorized or canned. The formula approach is so named because the salesperson uses the attention, interest, desire, action (AIDA) "formula" in developing and making sales presentations.

The advantages of this approach are its simplicity and ease of adaptation to almost any situation. Furthermore, the agency representative does most of the talking in the early stages of the communication. This enables him or her to attract the prospect's attention and interest, as well as establish important persuasive points before the receiver has an opportunity to raise objections. As the communication proceeds, the receiver is brought into the discussion to help clarify the particular needs and benefits that are sought.

The main limitations of this approach are similar to the shortcomings of the stimulus-response approach. The formula technique has a tendency to be agency-oriented as opposed to client-oriented, which is inconsistent with the marketing concept.

Need Satisfaction Approach

The need satisfaction approach is the recommended approach, but it is also the most difficult and challenging of the three presentation techniques. It differs from the stimulus-response and the formula approaches in that it is interactive with the prospect being an active participant in the communication.

This approach begins by exploring the client's needs: "What benefits would you want to see from a donation in which you invested?" The primary task of the agency representative during this stage is to listen and to suppress all premature tendencies to talk about what the agency has to offer. If the representative is unclear about something that is said, he or she should ask the prospect to elaborate on the point. During the listening phase, the agency representative should be considering the features, advantages, and benefits (FAB) of the agency's services, which are relevant to the potential donor's needs.

After the prospect has described his or her needs, the salesperson explains the unique features, advantages, and benefits of the service or project. The advantages portion of the presentation addresses the ways in which the service or project is superior to other donation opportunities available to the potential donor. The benefits section translates features and advantages into benefits and addresses the important question "What's in it for you?" The presentation can be personalized to address and emphasize only the features, advantages, and benefits that are relevant to the articulated needs.

The major limitations of this approach are that it requires a greater amount of skill than the other two techniques and it is not easily adaptable to group presentations. The technique is difficult in a group situation because diversities exist in the particular needs of the audience and there is not enough time available to explore all of these needs.

The major strength of this approach is that it is client-oriented and consistent with the marketing concept. It is essentially a problem-solving approach. Agency representatives explore the nature and scope of a potential donor's needs and propose solutions that the agency can provide. By uncovering and responding to a client's needs, agency personnel ensure the presentation is relevant.

Guidelines for Improving the Effectiveness of a Presentation

Table 17.1 offers some guidelines for improving agency representatives' personal selling performance.

The fundamental maxim of successful personal selling is "sell yourself before selling your product." The more *likeable or attractive* an individual is to an audience, the more positive the audience is likely to respond to the communication. An integral part of selling yourself is generating *enthusiasm*. If it is obvious that the source of a communication is excited by the potential of a service, then the audience is more likely to respond positively to it.

Earlier in this chapter we noted that the greater the perceived similarity between the communicator and audience, the more likely the audience will

TABLE 17.1. Some Guidelines for Improving Agency Personnel's Effectiveness in Personal Interaction and Communication with Potential Clients

The *initial impression* of agency personnel on a potential client group largely determines the success of their future interactions with the members of that group and the degree to which they will like them.

Up to some point, the more *familiar* agency personnel become to members of a potential client group, the more they will like them.

The more *likeable and attractive* agency personnel are to a potential client group, the more positively that group is likely to respond to their communications.

Agency personnel are more persuasive and convincing if they are perceived by members of the potential client group as being *similar* to themselves.

Agency personnel will be more successful in communicating to the potential client group if they are perceived as highly *credible* (that is, trustworthy, prestigious, expert, etc.).

Agency personnel are more persuasive and convincing if they are more *empathetic* toward members of the potential client group.

Enthusiasm is contagious; infect others with it so it spreads! If agency personnel are enthusiastic about the subject material, the communication is more likely to evoke a positive response from the potential client group.

Adapted with permission from DeLozier, M.W., *The Marketing Communications Process*. New York. McGraw-Hill, 1976, p. 252.

respond positively. Hence it is important for an agency to match communicator and audience whenever possible. For example, a middle-class female anglo prospect or group is likely to be most receptive to a middle-class female anglo communicator; while a young black audience is likely to be most responsive to a young black communicator. This relationship has obvious implications for assigning personnel to districts and neighborhoods. If maximum donations or participation in a service are to accrue, an agency should match agency personnel with the type of people characteristic of the target market.

The *credibility* of a communicator strongly influences how his or her message will be received. Hence if an agency, or one of its representatives, loses credibility with a potential donor or client group, or is unable to establish credibility initially, personal communication efforts are likely to be ineffective. Credibility includes the individual's level of respect, prestige, expertise and trustworthiness.

Several other message characteristics influence presentation effectiveness. In general a presentation is more effective if it[17]

Emphasizes benefits to the potential client, not the project or service. It should emphasize ends not means. For example, discussion should not focus on a new hospital wing; rather it should focus on lives saved and health restored.

Appeals to a client's immediate interests or concerns.

Is supportive of a client's presently held attitudes and opinions.

Provides testimonials of similar projects or services for which the agency has been responsible in the past that delivered similar benefits to those sought by this clientele.

Repeats the major benefits of the service during the presentation.

Is unique or unusual.

Associates the service or project with popular ideas.

Arouses a need first, then offers the service as a means of satisfying the need.

Is directed at opinion leaders so that they might, in turn, favorably influence their followers (see Chapter 11).

Uses visual aids such as models, artist sketches, photographs, and so on. It is much more effective to show prospects than to tell them. Not only do visual aids arouse attention and interest but they also reinforce the verbal message.

HANDLING OBJECTIONS

If the presentation is to yield the anticipated result, it is necessary to draw out any objections that prospects may have. Objections should not be dreaded; they should be welcomed. They provide valuable feedback and are the prospect's way of communicating how to make the presentation successful. Answering objections removes barriers and provides clues as to the best approach to take for the remainder of the presentation.

Quiet prospects who hold questions and reservation in their minds and give few clues about their inward resistances are likely to be the least influenced by the presentation. If no objections are raised then either the prospect was prepared to respond positively at the start or the prospect was not sufficiently interested to raise an objection.

Over a period of time agency personnel are likely to hear all of the various objections that can be raised. They should "keep track of flack"—that is, document the objections received and determine the best way to handle them. In soliciting donations from businesses, the following negative arguments are likely to be forthcoming and strategies to refute these objections must be developed if presentations are to be successful.

If it is seen to make a donation, a business opens itself to pressures and demands that it cannot effectively control. It lays itself open to new conflicts, stresses, and strains.

A business does not have the right to give away stockholders' money. After being given all the income, they can make gifts as they see fit.

Business sticking to business will increase individuals' ability to finance philanthropy. Corporations sticking to their job will provide rising real income to permit individuals to enlarge their donations.

The total program may produce results but the particular business could not give enough to make any appreciable difference.

Other companies that are comparable in size are not contributing, so why should we?

Agency personnel should listen carefully to objectives and then repeat them to the prospect to ensure no misunderstanding: "Let me be certain that I understand what you are saying, Mr. Smith. You believe that . . . ." This restatement also provides time to think about a response.

For an objection that is not refutable, an agency spokesperson's best response is to recognize it as a minus and proceed with all the pluses of the project in the hope that they will counterbalance the negative. To refute an objection there has to be an empathetic identification with it: "seeing Jack Jones through Jack Jones' eyes." Hence responses should start with "yes and" rather than "yes but." The little word "but" butts. The little word "and" shakes hands with the objection. The "yes and" approach protects the prospect's feelings by agreeing with him or her and gently permits issue to be taken with the objection in the last part of the response.

CLOSING

The fifth step in the presentation process is called the closing. At this point the agency representative typically summarizes the major benefits on which there has been agreement, addresses anticipated objections or reservations about taking the action sought, and requests that the prospect or members of the group take specific affirmative action. Many people find that closing is the most difficult part of the presentation process. They feel guilty or lack the self-confidence to ask for a commitment, or they have not thought through ahead of time how they will orchestrate the closing to obtain a commitment from the prospect.

There are many approaches to closing, three of which are illustrated in the following.

Obtain agreement on a major benefit and then build on it:

"If I understand you correctly, Mr. Smith, you are most interested in increased visibility from your donation investments."

"Yes."

"An investment of $5,000 would enable us to . . . ."

Ask an open question and pause:

"Mr. Smith, you've seen the benefits this donation investment could provide. What are your reactions?" or "How should we now move ahead?"

Use the "based-on" technique, which defers to a major point that was previously agreed upon and builds on it:

"Based on your desire for maximum visibility, I'd like to suggest a donation of $5,000, which would give you high visibility and make you the leading donor for this project."

On occasions a prospect may not be prepared to invest in a project at the level the agency seeks. He or she may be willing, however, to invest either in a different project at that level or in the same project at a lower level. Thus it is desirable for an agency representative to have more than one project and more than one donation level in mind. If the main investment opportunity is rejected other options can be presented.

FOLLOW-UP

The success of the initial personal selling interaction with a prospect should not be viewed in the immediate context of whether or not a donation was forthcoming. Rather it should be regarded as the beginning of a long-term relationship. People give to people first and causes second, so a period of time may be needed to consolidate the personal relationship before donations accrue. The relationship may follow the life cycle pattern described in Chapter 9. Although the early efforts may yield relatively little, they are invested in the anticipation of increased return in the future as the personal relationship is nurtured.

The way in which the follow-up is handled will determine the size of future donations from the prospect. The follow-up stage should enhance the relationship already established. A key to a successful ongoing solicitation effort is not the securing of new donors but the retention of previous ones. According to an old marketing adage, "Your best customers are your best prospects." If donors are pleased with the results of their investments, then they are likely to be receptive to future requests for donations. They are also likely to be valuable sources of testimonials and referrals to others whom they think may be of assistance.

If a personal selling effort has been successful and a donation is received, an agency has two main responsibilities to the donor. First, the donor should be kept informed and provided periodic progress reports on the status of the project or service. Second, donors should feel appreciated and part of the team, which means thanking and recognizing them in a way they deem appropriate. Some businesses may not seek public recognition and visibility:

> A generous corporation has a natural desire to set the record straight by disclosing facts of corporate contributions to counteract uninformed criticism for its lack of involvement. But, by doing so, and publicizing the nature and amount of financial

> participation, the corporation exposes itself as a prime target for an increased number of financial requests, which it must be careful to handle with delicacy, tact, and fairness.[18]

Most businesses are likely to seek recognition and an agency should have a recognition program that is structured in the shape of a pyramid so there is incentive to donate more in order to receive more recognition. Figure 17.4 illustrates the pyramid principle and shows the types of donor recognition used by the City of Dallas.

Smaller agencies can use the same principle scaled down to their level. For example, the Recreation and Parks Department in Grand Island, Nebraska (population 33,000) used the following recognition program:

> Everyone was recognized no matter how small the gift. Gifts of $15 or more were acknowledged with a certificate of thanks and a paperweight with the Parks and Recreation Department logo. A paperweight was selected because it sits on top of a desk and is a very visible symbol of the donation. People who donate over $100 got a personalized plaque etched in gold. The plaque was presented at a formal ceremony by the mayor if the donation was over $100. Any donations over $1,000 rated a presentation by council, complete with media coverage. If the

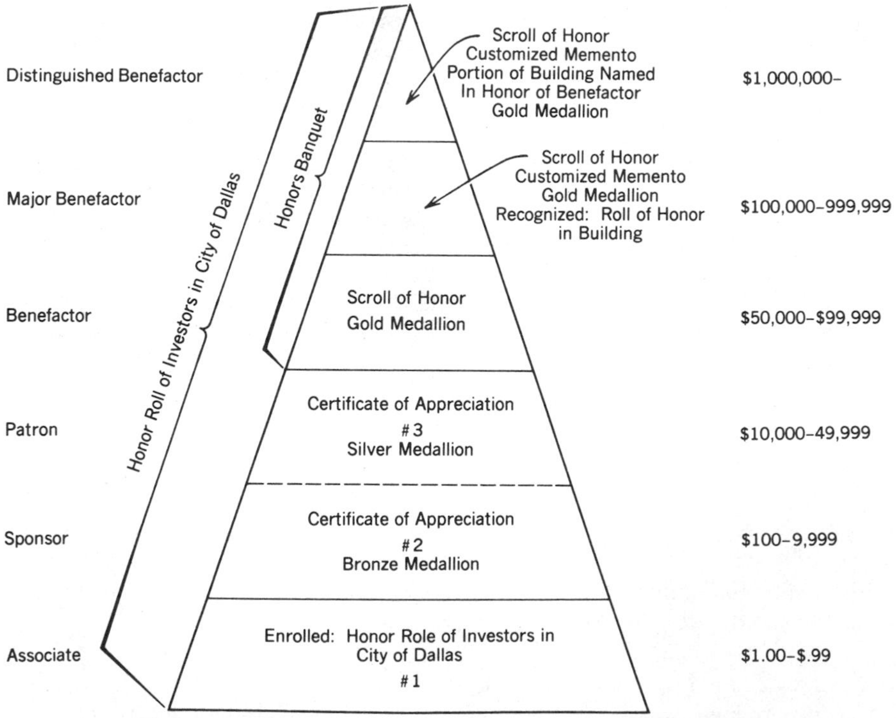

Figure 17.4. City of Dallas Donation Recognition Program.

donor was a member of a local civic or business group, the presentation was made in front of the group by council members to maximize felt importance and to get others in the groups excited about making a contribution. After the presentation ceremony an 8″ × 10″ color photograph of each donor was posted in the "Hall of Fame," located in the lobby of City Hall, where it stayed for a month.[19]

When projects are turned down it is often not because a business cannot benefit from them, but rather because their timing is not right for the company. Polite persistence pays off. Persistence is one of the major differences between the success and failure of personal selling efforts.

Thus immediately after an unsuccessful visit a thank you letter should be sent, telling prospects how much the time they spent with the agency representative was appreciated. The agency representative should keep in touch with these prospects and ensure that they receive any materials the agency distributes.

SUMMARY

Personal selling is an element of the promotion mix that is used extensively by government and social service agencies. Effective personal selling entails a six-stage process: (1) prospecting and targeting, (2) preparation, (3) presentation, (4) handling objections, (5) closing, and (6) follow-up. These stages are appropriate for every personal selling communication effort.

The first stage, prospecting and targeting, is concerned with identifying the solicitation target. A two-phase process is involved: first compiling a list of all potential prospects and then evaluating which of the prospects are most likely to be responsive to a personal selling effort.

In the preparation stage an approach is tailored to each of these prospects. The more information that can be gathered about a prospect, the better an agency representative is able to develop a presentation that precisely communicates with the prospect and elicits the desired result. Two questions should be addressed in this stage: (1) What's in it for them? and (2) Who in the organization should be contacted and what is their role? Tailoring the presentation is probably the most important phase in the whole personal selling process. Too often agency personnel spend too much time thinking about their own needs and not enough time considering what their clients want.

A key ingredient in effective personal selling is a positive personal chemistry between the participants. This makes it imperative that an agency search for linkages between its personnel and the gatekeepers, influencers, and decision makers in a target clientele. The best types of linkages are personal acquaintances, but if these links are relatively weak then it becomes important to seek referrals. Are there any contacts who could introduce agency personnel to key members of the target group? Positive interaction is facilitated if the backgrounds and lifestyles of the parties are compatible. Thus an agency should attempt to match its personnel with the characteristics of the target clientele.

The third stage, the presentation, is the most visible of the personal selling process. The three most commonly used presentation methods are called the stimulus-response, formula, and need satisfaction approaches. The best approach is the need satisfaction approach because it is client-oriented and consistent with the marketing concept. However, it is also the most difficult and challenging of the three presentation techniques. Agency representatives explore the nature and scope of a clientele's needs and propose solutions that the agency can provide. Agency personnel ensure that the presentation is relevant by uncovering and responding to a clientele's needs.

The fourth stage is handling objections. Objections should be encouraged because answering them removes barriers and also because they provide cues that can guide the direction of the presentation. The fifth stage is closing. Here the agency representative requests that the prospect take some specific affirmative action.

Follow-up is the final stage of the personal selling process, in which the relationships that have been established are fostered. Initial contacts should be regarded as the beginning of a long-term relationship. Early efforts may yield relatively little but may produce increased return in the future as the personal relationship is nurtured. How the follow-up is handled will determine the likelihood of a future positive response from the target clientele.

NOTES

1. Higgins, K., "Theater Groups Discovering the Power of Telemarketing," *Marketing News*, June 22, 1984, p. 1.
2. Ibid.
3. Lovelock, C.H., and Weinberg, C.B., *Marketing for Public and Nonprofit Managers*. New York: Wiley, 1984, p. 500.
4. Kotler, P., *Marketing for Nonprofit Organizations* (2nd ed.). Englewood Cliffs, NJ: Prentice-Hall, 1982, p. 425.
5. Ibid.
6. Kotler, *Nonprofit Organizations*, p. 451.
7. Elicker, P.H., "Why Corporations Give Money to the Arts," *The Wall Street Journal*, March 31, 1978, p. 22.
8. Wall, W.L., "Companies Change the Ways They Make Charitable Donations," *The Wall Street Journal*, June 21, 1984, pp. 1, 19.
9. Elicker, "Why Corporations Give," p. 22.
10. Spiers, R., Untitled presentation given at the California Parks and Recreation Society Annual Conference, Sacramento, 1980.
11. Ibid.
12. *Pattern for Giving*, Shell Companies Foundation, 1979, p. 5.

13. Zaltman, G., Flonio, D.H., and Sikorski, L.A., *Dynamic Educational Change*. New York: Free Press, 1977, p. 225.

14. Zimmer, R.J., and Taylor, J.W., "Matching Profiles for Your Industrial Salesforce," *Business*, March/April, 1981, pp. 2–13.

15. Ruesch, J., and Kees, W., *Nonverbal Communication*. Berkeley, CA: University of California Press, 1959, p. 15.

16. Zimmer and Taylor, "Matching Profiles," p. 4.

17. Adapted from DeLozier, M.W., *The Marketing Communications Process*. New York: McGraw-Hill, 1976, pp. 253–254.

18. Martin, S.A., *Financing Humanistic Service*. Toronto: McClelland and Steward Ltd., 1975, p. 92.

19. Crompton, J.L., and Duray, N.A., *Developing and Implementing a Gifts Catalog*. College Station, TX: Texas Agricultural Extension Service, 1984, p. 23.

EIGHTEEN

Publicity and Incentives

This chapter addresses the remaining two components of the promotion mix—publicity and incentives. After defining publicity and differentiating it from advertising, the chapter focuses on developing relationships with media personnel, preparing press releases, and conducting a publicity campaign. The publicity section concludes with a discussion of cable television as a publicity tool. The incentives portion of the chapter addresses the purposes, strengths, and limitations of incentives. It concludes with an outline of how to plan and coordinate an incentive program.

PUBLICITY

Many government and social service agencies rely heavily on publicity because of their limited financial resources. *Publicity is any unpaid form of nonpersonal communication, in which the agency is not identified as being the direct sponsor of the communication*. It consists of news and feature coverage about the agency, its people and its programs, communicated to the general public through the mass media at no direct charge to the agency.

Distinguishing Between Publicity and Advertising

Although publicity is transmitted to the general public in the same media as advertising, the two promotional tools differ in four important ways.[1] First and most obvious, advertising is a paid form of marketing communication. It appears in the media because someone has purchased the media time or space. Publicity is free to the agency. Second, advertising has an identified sponsor. Publicity, on the other hand, appears in the media as a significant news item or editorial comment. It has no identified sponsor. Third, advertising messages may be informative, persuasive, or both. Publicity messages are primarily informative. Fourth, advertisements are usually separated from the broadcast or editorial portions of the media, whereas publicity is part of the broadcast or editorial component.

Publicity has at least three advantages over advertising. First, news stories have a higher level of credibility than messages that are sponsored by an agency. The media constitute more than channels of communication: They are also opinion leaders. Agencies seek to take advantage of the two-step communication process by communicating to the media and having them inform their readers or listeners. Most people respect and believe in the integrity of the media. Since the public considers news items as originating from the media instead of from an agency, they normally view this information as an impartial assessment of a situation by thoughtful and expert people. Hence they regard it as being more objective, truthful, and factual than agency-sponsored messages. A second advantage of publicity compared to advertising is that it may reach individuals who would normally ignore the same message in an advertisement. Publicity often catches readers, listeners, or viewers off guard. The third advantage is publicity's low cost per exposure. The cost of preparing and presenting publicity to the media is often only a fraction of the cost of securing comparable space or air time for advertising.

Publicity has two major limitations compared to advertising. First, the media has complete control over its use of publicity items. The agency is dependent on media decision makers who decide whether or not to use specific publicity items, where to use them, and when to use them. This often frustrates agency personnel, who devote considerable effort to developing a publicity item only to find that it is not used, is buried in a back section of a newspaper, or appears too late to be of any use. The second limitation of publicity is that it generally appears only once in the media. At that point it is no longer newsworthy. Advertisements, on the other hand, can be repeated as often as the agency desires to repeat them.

Developing Relationships with Media Personnel

Regular, favorable publicity doesn't just happen. Agencies have to be constantly on the lookout for publicity opportunities. Ideally an individual within each of the agency's organizational units is assigned the task of managing the publicity program. This individual should also be responsible for establishing and maintaining good relationships with media personnel.

The principles of target marketing are directly applicable to effective publicity management. Comprehensive contact lists of key media personnel should be developed, but most publicity efforts should not be directed at the whole list. Rather they should be targeted at segments of the list that represent the most effective gatekeepers for the specific publicity effort. The list may include the following segments:[2]

Local daily and weekly newspapers, including toss-aways and penny savers. The list should specify the division contacts, such as local, city, business, sports, and entertainment within each of these media

Local radio and television news reporters and producers of public affairs programs

Local ethnic newspapers and radio and television shows

Local, regional, and national trade publications and corporate in-house publications

Friendly and related organizations with newsletters, for example, Chambers of Commerce, Homeowner Associations, PTA

Funding agencies, government bureaus and agencies, and legislators.

Contact lists need to be updated regularly—about every six months—because news personnel change positions and organizations frequently.

Development of a contacts list is merely a starting point. It is not sufficient to ship out press releases to these targeted contacts. All publicity efforts must go through a gatekeeper. This gatekeeper is the media editor, reporter, or program manager who decides whether or not an item will be used, and if it will be used, how much of it, in what form, and when. Thus a relationship of mutual trust and understanding with reporters, editors, and producers has to be built and nurtured. Understanding is the goal, not agreement on issues, policies, or precedents. This involves recognizing the gatekeepers' needs and providing them with the types of stories that will appeal to their audiences in a form that they can readily use. Personal follow-up visits or phone calls offering further assistance or information will draw extra attention to a story. Specifically, a media contact must be convinced that:[3]

1. *Your Story Is Newsworthy*. Show that it has enough of the following attributes: it is timely; has consequence either in being directly important to a large number of people or gravely important to a few; is controversial; involves conflict; is new; involves famous people; is novel, weird, different, mysterious, or funny; is going to change the future; has human interest (involves love, hate, tragedy, sex, children, or animals); has suspense or adventure; will help the reader earn more money, enjoy better health, or live longer; and relates to a "hot" news item.
2. *Your Story Would Be Ideal for Their Particular Format*. For example, show that it would be a good story for their 30-second taped interview or for their one-half-hour discussion.
3. *Your Story Would Be Interesting to Their Audience*.
4. *You Will Provide Intelligent, Interesting Spokespersons*. Call well before their deadline and be brief. Expect to complete your conversation in two minutes or less. Identify yourself and your organization, and state why they will be interested in your story. Remind them of any appro-

priate dates, times, or special problems. Offer to provide additional background documents and visual materials, and ask whether you should call back later for a response.

Unless there is evidence of deliberate misrepresentation, criticism of the media's treatment of an item is likely to be counterproductive. Definitions of news abound; most say that news is anything an editor sees as timely, interesting, and significant to readers or viewers. The most important news has the greatest degree of these three qualities for the greatest number.[4] The only constant in most definitions of news is that news is what a particular editor decides is news.

Two events should occur annually in the ongoing effort to foster understanding and goodwill with the media. First, senior agency managers should seek an annual meeting with the editorial boards of the agency's most important media to explain the agency's mission, its constraints, problems, and opportunities. Second, the agency should host key media personnel once a year on a tour of the agency's facilities, explaining its operations and inviting questions. Media representatives attending this tour should be treated as VIPs. It should be carefully planned and all key staff made available to respond to questions.

Press Releases[5]

The term *press release* is used generically to refer to all media, not just the written press. Press releases are short descriptions of news prepared by agency staff in a specialized format that imitates newspaper writing. The lead paragraph is the most important part of the release. It summarizes two or three of "the five Ws" in your story—the who, what, where, why, and when. Editors will often decide on the basis of this lead paragraph whether your release is important enough to consider.

If a newspaper prints only the first paragraph due to space limitations, it is essential that it include all of the most important information about the story. The second paragraph answers any of the five Ws not covered in the lead, and any subsequent paragraphs should include progressively less important information. Provide a headline that briefly summarizes the most important point of the article. The editor may change the headline, but the agency should use the headline to catch the editor's interest.

A press release should be one page or shorter if possible. A second page is acceptable for a very important story. It should be typed on letterhead, preferably with the agency's logo. Some organizations have special stationery printed for press releases saying "News From . . . ." Indicate the date and time that the news is to be released. Either state that the release is effective immediately, or in the case of a story breaking at a preset time (like a news conference), indicate the precise time for its release (such as 10 A.M., July 17). There should always be an agency contact person listed at the top of the release.

Looks are important. Untidy, mimeographed efforts are unlikely to receive much attention. Double spacing and wide margins enable the editor to quickly tailor the release to the media vehicle's needs. Colored paper may help attract attention and a handwritten cover note to the editor or reporter with whom a good rapport has been established will help.

The media are particularly interested in human interest feature stories. They account for about half of the available space in most papers and much of the programming on electronic media. Human interest stories are also generally friendlier and longer than straight news stories.

The likelihood of a press release being used will vary according to its news or human interest value and the number of other stories with which it has to compete. The competition in larger metropolitan areas is likely to be substantial. One study, for example, revealed that: (1) out of 300 releases received in a five-day period by a typical morning newspaper, 242 were rejected; and (2) out of 339 publicity releases received in a five-day period by a typical evening newspaper, 218 were rejected, 42 were rewritten, and 32 were used as received.[6]

Publicity Campaign

The publicity campaign is a periodic, intensive effort to focus public attention on a specific issue. It consists of a series of news events and of human interest stories that are created over a fixed, relatively short time period and are focused around a common theme. Such campaigns often are associated with fundraising or upon issues that are of interest to a large segment of a community. The agency's task is to ensure that a sequential flow of news and human interest stories emerge throughout the campaign. These should be scheduled so that the media regularly have something new and interesting to report on the theme. Figure 18.1 identifies 20 suggestions offered by the National Tuberculosis and Respiratory Disease Association to sustain the media's interest in a stop smoking campaign.

Cable Television[7]

Cable television is emerging as a valuable publicity outlet that is available to many government and social service agencies. It has considerable potential both for improving the distribution of services by delivering them directly to clients (see Chapter 8) and for improving agencies' communication efforts with citizens.

Cable television began in the late 1940s as a means of delivering service to outlying areas, especially those surrounded by mountains that were unable to receive over-the-air television channels. By the late 1960s, 5 percent of the nation's television homes subscribed to cable. By 1982, the number of cable subscribers had increased to 26 percent, and it is expected to reach 50 percent by 1990.[8] By 1985, it was estimated there were more than 35 million cable

1. Make sure the key media people in your community are informed about your campaign in advance of kickoff day.
2. Arrange for some kickoff day news. The mayor can proclaim KICK THE HABIT month. Include in the festivities other newsmakers such as sports figures. Have the newspaper, radio, and TV figures who are supporting your campaign open the gates with news, interviews, commentary, and other mention.
3. At the end of the campaign, a wrap-up story usually is possible. Summarize the good that has been done if you can (how many people said they would quit smoking?)—and recognize the people who volunteered their help.
4. Capitalize on human interest; smoking is loaded with it. People love to talk about their operations, for the same reason they love to talk over their opinions about smoking. Give them a chance. And use their stories—with permission, of course—in your publicity.
5. School will be closed during part of the campaign, but use the drive of youngsters before and during the campaign if you can. A poster contest is an obvious, if sometimes overworked, possibility; prizes could be donated and winners could be displayed in department store windows and other public places. Compositions by fifth graders on why no one should smoke make wonderful reading. More important, get some young people to work with you and dream up their own ideas.
6. Of course, you'll want to go to your clubs and other organizations with speakers, pamphlets, and other activities. Gear up for this in advance of the campaign when there's still room on their programs. And plan the topic for your annual meetings.
7. Try a photography contest of best KICK THE HABIT photos. Get a store to contribute prizes.
8. How about having the celebrity public figure expert of the day make a statement, one each day of the campaign. This probably would best be worked up as an exclusive with an interested newspaper or radio or TV station.
9. Anybody who is anybody should be wearing a KICK THE HABIT sticker during June. It's your job to see that they do when they make a public appearance, especially on TV. And scatter pretty young girls around to "sticker" everyone who passes. Ask that the stickers be worn regularly by doctors, librarians, pharmacists, and so on.
10. Convince a prominent newspaper feature writer who smokes to get in on your KICK THE HABIT campaign and try to give up smoking. Have him/her keep a diary that would be published regularly—a real, honest, personal, hopefully funny, running account of the agonies of giving up smoking.
11. Do the same for TV and radio personalities with daily running accounts of the fight. Incidentally, try to convince TV stations not to have their people smoke on camera. One Boston TV station waged a full-scale war on smoking and publicized their "Stop Smoking" campaign, which involved employees and announcers who tried to quit cigarettes.
12. Men are supposed to give up smoking easier than women. Or vice versa: Have a big contest between a men's group (Rotary, Kiwanis, etc.) and a prominent women's group.
13. Have a local psychologist or psychiatrist focus on the human/emotional/personal trauma of quitting.
14. Do follow up stories on all kinds of groups and interesting persons who are trying. Report new methods, rewards, and so on (no matter how kooky) developed by people in attempts to quit smoking: "I'll bet you can't quit smoking for a week. If you do, I'll climb to the top of the courthouse tower and raise a banner saying 'John Jones Really Did KICK THE HABIT.' "

Figure 18.1. Suggestions for Sustaining Media Interest in a Publicity Campaign to Stop Cigarette Smoking. (*Source:* National Tuberculosis and Respiratory Disease Association, 1740 Broadway, New York, NY 10019.)

15. One of the things sweeping the country is the "call-in" radio programs. People like to hear the sound of their own voice, particularly when they can talk to a "celebrity." Talk the MC into doing a special program of talking with people trying to give up smoking (even those against it); have a doctor present to answer people's medical questions on smoking.

16. Competitive quitting among a large number of organizations is good. And emphasize (a) the ones with large constituencies such as churches and (b) the ones that have a large number of exhibitionists and PR addicts (some luncheon and service clubs.) Try to reach all ethnic and racial groups.

17. Set up a plastic coffin in city square or town green. (Get a permit first, of course.) Have people dump cigarette packs there. Get volunteers to hand cigarette leaflets or stickers to everyone who dumps in a pack. Put KICK THE HABIT and LUNGS ARE FOR LIVING signs on the coffin. . . . Or set up a giant plastic football with a slot on the side so people can slip in their discarded cigarettes.

18. Distribute leaflets to employees in industry and businesses, maybe with their paychecks. Encourage companies to help pick up the tab.

19. Arrange a candlelight parade some night for people who are kicking the habit. (Permit is necessary.) Finish off in some prominent spot with a giant bonfire of people's cigarette packs. Invite a Congressman or public official to the ceremonies. Why not have him or her arrive on a fire engine? Alert all media.

20. Contact the program directors of the radio and TV stations in your area, tell them about the KICK THE HABIT campaign, and suggest ways in which this campaign can fit into their particular programming needs: Talk shows are a "natural" for a doctor-dean of a medical school to discuss the hazards of smoking and how to go about quitting. Be sure the guests you furnish are—above all—articulate.

Mid-day women's shows also welcome guest speakers, especially when the topic has to do with health. And remember, research has shown that smoking may be hazardous to the unborn child.

Contact the Host of a teenage dance show. He or she might be interested in having a member from your association or a doctor talk to the audience about smoking during a break in the record playing and dancing. Or they might prefer to include the message as a spot announcement in their own special patter.

Contact your local rock station. Since these stations have a young audience, they may be willing to work out an entire day, week, or month's worth of programming with you for the KICK THE HABIT campaign. For instance: before a time check the announcer might say: "It's time to kick the habit at 10:25 A.M." Or, its a great day to KICK THE HABIT, the temperature in ________________ is ______ degrees. Aside from these reminders, you might like to supply the disc jockeys with facts about smoking that they could tell their audience about between records.

Figure 18.1. (Continued)

subscribers. Most of the largest 100 cities in the nation have now selected a cable franchise.

Typically a city selects a cable franchise after a competitive bidding process. The city conducts a comprehensive needs assessment to determine the community's communication needs and then issues a request for proposals soliciting bids from prospective cable companies. After analyzing the financial ability, proposed technical design, past record, and community service components of each competitor, a city selects the cable company that can best meet the community's needs.

The city and cable company negotiate a franchise agreement obligating the company to a wide range of services throughout a long-term contract that usually lasts for 15 to 20 years. As part of the negotiation process a city may seek to include such items as channels set aside for public, educational, and governmental access, as well as free installation of cable facilities for the city's use. Community service or public access provisions usually include designated access channels and the provision of facilities, equipment, and staff needed for programming.

Public access programming can be produced under two arrangements. In the first, the programming is produced by the cable company, which is termed *local origination*. In the second arrangement, the cable company serves only as an advisor and facilitator. After being instructed on planning, scripting, and equipment operation, an agency produces the program.

An ideal model for organizing public access programming would be to form a public access organization that is independent of the cable company, which is recognized by city council and is eligible to receive a portion of the franchise fee to facilitate the citizen participation process in community television.[9] There should also be an entity, a policy board consisting of the cable company and public access organization representatives, that has responsibility for the public access channel. The access organization should, over time, assume primary responsibility for programming.

Illustrative Uses of Cable Television. Some communities have required that a cable company provide studio facilities, multicamera production hardware, and editing equipment as part of the franchise agreement. In Norwood, Ohio, the cable franchise recipient committed to construct a local production studio, provide a full-time local programming coordinator to organize and present locally originated community programs, establish a student intern program in conjunction with the Norwood High School Telecommunication Center, construct an independent two-way institutional network connecting all public buildings, provide a 5 percent franchise fee to the city for support of local programming, and dedicate five channels of the 35-channel system for local origination, governmental, educational, and public access programming.

The Norwood cable television commission ensures compliance with the terms of the franchise agreement. The most promising programs developed to date include "Mayor's Forum," a monthly call-in show featuring the mayor and spotlighting selected city departments and services; "Our Town," a weekly magazine highlighting community activities; "Superintendent's Corner," a monthly call-in show featuring the school system superintendent; and "School Scoop," a weekly school news program with in-depth features produced by students.[10]

In East Lansing, Michigan, six cable channels are dedicated for access purposes, one each for city government, public schools, public access, the public library, and two for Michigan State University. City government, in particular, uses its channel to increase community awareness of city services, activities, and policies. One of its most successful programs was an explanation of the average 12 percent boost in homeowner assessed value. A tape was produced and shown three times daily during the assessment period.[11]

Volunteers can play a major role in developing and operating access programming. The community access channel of the Hayward, San Leandro, and San Lorenzo, California cable system enlists the aid of 25 to 30 volunteer program producers with help from another 150 to 200 volunteers. Twenty-five to 75 community organizations use the channel to communicate with local residents by appearing on regularly scheduled programs. Programs are produced by and for the local community. Specific programs are targeted for blacks, Mexican Americans, women, senior citizens, and teens. Other programs include public government shows, religious shows, and community activity shows.[12]

In Dallas, Texas, the franchise was awarded to Warner Amex. As part of the agreement, Warner Amex committed to providing 20 of the 75 cable channels as public access channels administered through its subsidiary QUBE Cable Community Access organization. The organization provides a cable medium for individuals, groups, and institutions to communicate with the Dallas community. Figure 18.2 explains the programming focus of these 20 public access channels. By early 1983, QUBE Cable was airing 1,000 hours per week of access programming.

Equipment, facilities, and channels are available for use by Dallas citizens for the production of noncommercial programs ranging from entertainment to serious concerns and issues. QUBE Cable acts only as a facilitator and advisor, leaving programming under the control of Dallas citizens. All services and facilities are available at no charge to Dallas citizens 18 years of age or older, on a first-come, first-serve basis.

Five community access studios and five centers will be available for access users to produce programs. They are scheduled to open in conjunction with construction of the cable system. Each studio and center has a professional staff of advisors and technicians to assist users. The studios contain both studio facilities and portable video equipment, while the centers contain only portable video equipment. All community access functions, including scheduling channel time, equipment, and facility use, are coordinated by the professional staff at the community access facilities.

Each of the community access studios and centers has two color portapaks and light kits for portable videotaping. Studio time and equipment is available for use to videotape or cablecast live programs. Postproduction editing equipment is also available for scheduled use at the studios. Mobile vans are provided for program applications that cannot be accommodated through other community access facilities and equipment. The mobile vans, supervised by QUBE Cable staff, contain sophisticated television production equipment and require professional operation.

CHANNEL LINE-UP

The Warner Amex Cable System has set aside channels for a wide variety of community uses. Each channel has a focus that may be of interest to a particular viewer. The identifying specialty channel allows viewers to select the kind of programs that match their interests. Access producers, on the other hand, may request to have their programs aired on any of the access channels available in order to reach the desired audience.

GENERAL PUBLIC ACCESS CHANNELS

Channel 7—Black Focus: Programming that focuses on cultural events, political issues, and neighborhood concerns in the black community.

Channel 9–Video Crossroads: This general Community Access channel offers a variety of programs produced by a cross section of Access Producers. CABLE TOWN HALL, ACCESS TRAFFIC, DALLAS SPEAKS, and ARTS EYE are examples of regular programs. A program guide to all access channels can also be seen on this channel.

Channel 10–Neighborhood Access: Programming on neighborhood activities, needs, and events (still in the development stage).

Channel 12–Interfaith: Programming on this channel is scheduled by local church congregations. Special lecture series, midweek services, concerts, mission projects, and choirs are featured.

Channel 18–Older Adults: Older adults often serve as producers for programming by and for this special group of citizens. Their needs and interests are reflected in the programming.

Channel 19–La Voz Del Barrio: Spanish or English language programming that highlights Hispanic life in Dallas. Political issues, self-help features, and consumer tips are just a few of the shows that are offered on this channel.

Channel 21–Special Needs: Programming to serve the needs of individuals with handicaps. (Still in the developmental stage.)

Channel 58–Community Bulletin Board: Continuous information about upcoming events.

Channel 67–Woman to Woman: This channel serves the Dallas woman whatever her age or lifestyle.

EDUCATIONAL ACCESS CHANNELS

Channel 2–Dallas Independent School District: The channel offers a variety of informational programming for and about the Dallas Independent School System. Sports, student and academic programs, and parent/student information are carried on this channel.

Channel 6–Dallas County Community College District: Higher education instructional programming produced by and for local institutions is featured on this channel. Credit courses and information about activities at the seven college campuses are also included.

Channel 22 through 26–Educational Programs: Features for kindergarten through high school are highlighted in programming on these channels. After 4 P.M. these channels run upper-level noncredit college course programming.

MUNICIPAL ACCESS CHANNELS

Channel 17–Municipal: Programming about city council meetings, City of Dallas information and city services will be provided by City Hall on this channel.

Channel 75–Municipal: (For future municipal use).

Figure 18.2. The Programming Focus of Public Access Channels in Dallas.

QUBE Cable conducts a series of workshops to make potential users aware of the production capability of the community access facilities. These workshops are intended to train and certify interested parties in the proper operation of production equipment. A potential user is required to complete a workshop covering rules and equipment operation, as well as pass a standardized performance test.

INCENTIVES

Incentives may be defined as direct inducements that offer extra value to encourage participation in a program or use of a service:

> Incentives are offered to persons or groups who are normally insufficiently motivated, indifferent, or antipathetic to a particular program or service. They alter the perceived price of a program in an effort to overcome the client group's resistance or indifference.[13]

In contrast to the other components of the promotion mix, incentives are generally supplementary activities that are conducted for a limited period of time and are intended to produce immediate, short-run effects.

Purposes of Incentives

Incentives may be used to achieve one of three objectives. First, they may be used to educate or inform prospective clients. This goal is often accomplished by using displays and/or demonstrations. Some community education programs, for example, allow interested persons to attend the first class free of charge. Arts and crafts programs often display selected projects completed by students enrolled in previous classes. These programs also demonstrate the techniques and skills that are covered in particular classes.

Second, they may be used to stimulate trial. Specific goals for incentives used in this way may include:

1. Introducing new programs or services
2. Identifying and attracting new clients to existing programs or services
3. Stimulating more frequent usage of programs or services
4. Stabilizing fluctuations in participation patterns
5. Attracting potential clients to a facility

Free trials, demonstrations, reduced prices, and premiums are commonly used incentives to stimulate trial of new programs. By reducing the cost or increasing the value of a program, the agency may be able to *educate and encourage* potential clients who otherwise would not make the necessary effort to learn about the features, advantages, and benefits of a new program. The same rationale applies to identifying and attracting new clients to existing programs.

Incentives that are intended to stimulate more frequent usage of a program or service often seek to establish participation as a regular part of clients' daily or weekly routine. Many people drop out of programs before they establish participation as part of their routine activities. Once a habitual pattern of participation in a program is established, clients tend to schedule other activities and commitments around the program.

Many facilities such as recreation centers, swimming pools, and parks experience wide fluctuations in participation patterns based on time of day, day of the week, or season of the year. Incentives can contribute to a leveling out of this demand in much the same way as variable pricing. That is, incentives can be used to stimulate usage in periods when demand is low.

Sometimes incentives are not intended to stimulate immediate action, but rather to introduce people to a facility in hopes that they will later enroll in one or more programs. Open house events and contests that require people to pick up entry blanks at a specified location are often used to achieve this objective.

The third alternative objective of incentives is to encourage regular participation. This is somewhat different than stimulating more frequent usage because it entails giving the incentive after the program is completed. A rebate, trophy, or certificate may be offered to all clients who attend every class or meeting. Schools and churches often use this incentive to stimulate children to maintain perfect attendance records.

Strengths and Limitations of Incentives[14]

Incentives have both strengths and limitations in comparison with other promotion mix elements. On the positive side,

Incentives establish the feeling among clients that they are getting something for nothing.

Incentives are provided in addition to other inducements. They are the "extra something" that sometimes attracts insufficiently motivated clients.

Incentives are often direct inducements. They are intended to get action now rather than later, and if they are successful, immediate participation increases take place.

Incentives are extremely flexible. They can be introduced and withdrawn as the need arises.

Some of the commonly cited limitations of incentives are

Incentives are usually temporary in nature and short-lived, generally running less than 90 days. They are not useful for long-term, sustained promotional campaigns.

Incentives are not meant to be used by themselves. They are intended to supplement other promotion efforts and should be used in conjunction with one or more other promotion mix elements.

Too many incentives may hurt a program's image. Prospective clients may view the agency's efforts as attempts to "whip a dead horse."

Incentives cannot build a loyal clientele. They can only stimulate trial.

Planning and Coordinating Incentive Programs

Seven steps are needed to build an incentive program. These are[15]

1. Specifying the *objective* of the incentive program
2. Determining the *inclusiveness* of the incentive(s)
3. Specifying the *recipient* of the incentive(s)
4. Determining the *direction* of the incentive(s)
5. Selecting the *type* of the incentive(s)
6. Establishing the *amount* of incentive
7. Selecting the *time of payment* of the incentive(s)

As noted earlier, incentives may be used to achieve three different types of objectives. A clear statement of the objectives of an incentive program is important because it is the point of reference for each of the succeeding steps in the planning process.

The second step identifies the incentive target and specifies who is eligible for the incentive. Most incentives are offered to individuals but this is not always the case. When individuals are the target of an incentive program, the basic decision in this step is to resolve whether the incentive will be offered to everyone or only to those who meet certain criteria specified by age, sex, income, and so on. When groups are the target of an incentive program, the agency must specify the criteria for eligibility, such as group size and the nature of qualifying groups (in other words, church groups, civic groups, adolescent groups, school groups).

In most incentive programs the potential client is selected as the recipient of the incentive. However, some incentive programs are directed toward employees and present clients. In these cases the employee or client receives an incentive for enrolling new clients or bringing guests.

Incentives may be either positive or negative. In most instances the direction of an incentive program is positive—that is, the incentive is rewarding. It is also possible to have negative incentives. A negative incentive is a penalty for not participating regularly in a program. Parole officers and some social workers have the authority to offer negative incentives to clients.

There are four main types of positive incentives (Figure 18.3). First is promotional pricing in which the incentive involves some form of a price discount. Second are free offers that typically entail one free trial during which prospective clients can evaluate a service at no financial risk. Third are prizes that usually serve as rewards for clients who enter or persevere with a program. Fourth are celebrities whose presence is sufficient incentive to persuade potential users to see a program and the media to provide extended coverage of

---

Promotional Pricing
Reduced prices at off-peak times
Discounts for a short time period
2 for 1 offers, "bring a friend free"
Free passes on the Welcome Wagon so newcomers are encouraged to try things
Discounts to existing users for new offerings as "valued customers" to get them to try the new offerings.
Season passes to commit people to your facility rather than a competitive facility
Coupons
Free passes to corporations who pass them out to employees, without the employees realizing the company did not pay for them
Tokens that lead to a reduced price in subsequent attendances
Family passes
Free Offers
Birthday pass granting free admission on birthdays (Few people come alone!)
To identified opinion leaders so they can influence others, e.g., service clubs, ministers
Occasional free "open-houses" at which the range of offerings can be sampled
Free sampling opportunities in shopping malls or other areas in which there is extensive pedestrian traffic
Special event nights or clinics, e.g., free music night to attract music lovers and then can sell them classes or future concert tickets
First session is a free trial to see if you like it
Free passes to children for activities in which adults will also attend, so the adults pay full price
Prizes
Benefit packages with corporations, e.g., for good sales performance, receive a free season pass
Door prizes for every *n*th person attending
Give free passes as prizes instead of just trophies in order to build business
Poster art work contests, brings in parents to see their children's work
T-shirts, caps may serve as a prize for entering. These become "walking advertisements" for the program
Celebrities
To start new programs and give them publicity
When a program is first offered, a well-recognized instructor may draw people
To reintroduce people to a service after they have dropped out
To endorse facilities or services. Upgrading its quality by the association of prestigious people with it

---

Figure 18.3. Examples of Each of the Four Main Types of Positive Incentives.

it. Celebrities may also upgrade the perceived quality of the service because of the association of prestigous people with it.

Determining the amount of the incentive is an important decision. If the incentive is too small, it will not be effective. If it is too large, it will be wasteful. This difficult decision requires a thorough understanding of the incentive target, including its economic circumstances and motivation. This does not imply that well-to-do prospects will not respond to incentives. It does, however, suggest that nonmonetary incentives may be more attractive to these individuals than cash incentives.

Time payment of the incentive refers to whether the incentive will be given immediately or at some later time. Although most incentives are immediate, some are delayed. Examples of delayed incentives include such things as certificates and awards based on successful completion of a program or incentives offered for perfect attendance for a specified period of time.

SUMMARY

Publicity is any unpaid form of nonpersonal communication, where the agency is not identified as being the direct sponsor of the communication. Publicity has a high level of credibility, may reach individuals who would ignore the same message in an advertisement, and has a low cost per exposure. Publicity has two major limitations compared to advertising. The media have complete control over the use of publicity items, which generally appear only once.

Publicity has to be marketed to the media. This involves targeting press releases at specific contacts, understanding their needs, and providing them with the types of stories that will appeal to their audiences in a form that they can readily use. Meetings with editorial boards and hosting tours of the agency's facilities are two events that should occur annually.

While the format of press releases influences whether or not they will be used, their news or human interest value is of greater importance. A publicity campaign consists of a series of news events and/or human interest stories that are created over a fixed, relatively short time period and are focused around a common theme. In recent years, cable television has emerged as a valuable publicity outlet because it offers public access channels to many government and social service agencies.

Incentives are direct inducements that offer extra value or incentive to encourage participation in a program or use of a service. They may be used to inform or educate potential clients, to stimulate trial, or to encourage regular participation. Seven stages of planning an incentive program can be identified. Positive incentives include promotional pricing, free offers, prizes, and celebrities.

NOTES

1. Pride, W.M., and Ferrell, O.C., *Marketing: Basic Concepts and Decisions* (3rd ed.). Boston: Houghton Mifflin, 1980, p. 366.
2. Adapted from National Park Service, *Marketing Parks and Recreation*. State College, PA: Venture Publishing, 1983, p. 127.
3. Ibid, pp. 130–131.
4. An anonymous quotation cited in "Effective Working Relations with The Media—Some Do's and Don'ts." Notes prepared for use at the November 1977 Seminar on Transition and Leadership for Newly Elected Mayors at the Harvard University Institute of Politics. Cambridge Massachusetts: Harvard University.
5. This section is adapted from the National Park Service, *Marketing Parks*, p. 128.
6. Berkman, D., "The Segregated Medium," *Columbia Journalism Review*, vol. 5, Fall 1966, p. 32.
7. The authors acknowledge the assistance of Shannon Sanders in the development of this section on cable television.
8. Williams, J.D., "Using Cable Television for More Effective Non-Profit Marketing." in F.K. Shuptrine and P.H. Reingen (eds.), *Non-profit Marketing: Conceptual and Empirical Research*. Tempe, Arizona: Bureau of Business and Economic Research, College of Business Administration, Arizona State University, 1983, p. 36.
9. Bell, J., "A Different Kind of Television," *Public Management*, Vol. 62 No. 5 June 1980, p. 7.
10. Dettmer, R., "Negotiating the Franchise," *Public Management*, vol. 62 No. 5 June 1980, p. 21.
11. Muirhead, G.B., "Six Access Channels," *Public Management*, vol. 62 No. 5 June 1980, p. 8.
12. Van Dalsen, R., *Access Center Handbook*. Denver, Colorado. United Cable Television Corporation, 1981, p. 25.
13. Adapted form Kotler, P., *Marketing for Nonprofit Organizations*. Englewood Cliffs, NJ: Prentice-Hall, 1975, p. 217.
14. Adapted from Stanley, R.E., *Promotion* (2nd ed.). Englewood Cliffs, NJ: Prentice-Hall, p. 303.
15. Kotler, P., *Marketing for Nonprofit Organizations* (2nd ed.). Englewood Cliffs, NJ: Prentice-Hall, 1982, pp. 372–373.

Index